Limited Classical Reprint Library

THE BIBLICAL DOCTRINE
OF
CREATION AND THE FALL

by

Donald MacDonald, D.D.

Foreword by Dr. Cyril J. Barber

Klock & Klock Christian Publishers, Inc.
2527 Girard Avenue North
Minneapolis, Minnesota 55411

Originally published by
Thomas Constable and Co.
Edinburgh, 1856

ISBN: 0-86524-165-1

Printed by Klock & Klock in the U.S.A.
1984 Reprint

FOREWORD

Were it not for an entry in C. H. Spurgeon's *Commenting and Commentaries*, this work might have passed into oblivion with its worth and value known only to those fortunate enough to possess a copy. Now, however, the assiduous labor and theological acumen of its author may once again challenge and stimulate the thinking of the people of God.

Of Dr. MacDonald, little is known. A note about him is to be found in the *New Schaff-Herzog Encyclopedia of Religious Knowledge*, and from this isolated reference we glean the fact that Donald MacDonald was active in the affairs of the Free Church of Scotland. We also learn that he lived at a time of spiritual decline. Following the Declatory Act passed by the General Assembly in 1892, Dr. MacDonald and certain others found it necessary to withdraw from the Free Church. They formed the Free Presbyterian Church and incorporated into their constitution the infallibility of Holy Scripture, purity of worship, and the whole Confession of Faith. All of this serves to show us Dr. MacDonald's staunch adherence to the truth (as he saw it). These same characteristics are to be found in his treatment of Genesis 1–3.

The importance of a correct understanding of Genesis 1–3 cannot be underestimated. Contemporary theological mores have tended to look upon these chapters as being, at best, mythological. The result, however, is that theologians are then at a loss to explain the dignity of man, his rulership over the earth, the obvious presence of a destructive force within all mankind, and a host of other important truths which find their source in the biblical record of creation and the Fall.

In few works of this kind (Dr. Richard Gilpin's *Demonologia Sacra* being a noted exception), is the treatment of creation, the *imago dei*, temptation, and the Fall as thorough as it is in this volume. In clear, unmistakable terms Dr. MacDonald separates the Creator from the things He created. In doing so, he shows our accountability to Him and the need for us to acknowledge His sovereignty.

To all who seek for answers to the dilemmas of life, we commend this work by Dr. Donald MacDonald. So deft is his treatment that, in reveiwing his work, the *Journal of Sacred Literature* stated emphatically:

> We do not hesitate to designate this volume as the foremost examination of the literature and the exegesis of the creation and fall which has appeared to date.

We are most grateful that it can once more grace the bookshelves of Bible students everywhere.

Dr. Cyril J. Barber
Author, *The Minister's Library*

PREFACE.

REGARDING the object of this volume, and the call which at present exists for an investigation of the subject treated of, enough has been said in the Introduction. Some explanation may, however, be necessary of the presumption which may be supposed to attach to the Author's undertaking a task of such magnitude. At the commencement of his exegetical study of the Hebrew Scriptures, he encountered several of the difficulties which he here attempts to solve, and while seeking information from all available sources, was surprised to find how little satisfaction could be obtained in the productions of the best-accredited writers—some making exceedingly light of such difficulties, or only partially considering them, and others having lived before the more pressing questions of the present day were raised.

In these circumstances, the Author resolved to examine the subject for himself; having at the time, however, no idea of the extent to which his inquiries might reach, and indeed little of the plan eventually followed, which at first was intended to embrace merely a few topics, but from the amount of misapprehension found to prevail on the subject,[1] gradually assumed

---

[1] The subjoined extract from a letter in the " Times " of June 2, 1855, will shew better than any arguments the necessity of the plan adopted in Part I. :—" On Septuagesima Sunday last, (when the proper lesson is Gen. i.,) I happened to be present at a church in the north-west portion of the metropolis, and heard a discourse, of which I shall say no more than that it placed that very material question [the discrepancy between the discoveries of geology and the Mosaic narrative of the creation] in a light in which I believe every enlightened and serious inquirer would rejoice to see it explained, including a recognition of the scientific facts, and *a full admission of their irreconcilable contradiction to the narrative,* coupled with the most earnest assertion of the truth of the New Testament dispensation, and *its entire independence of any such representations belonging to the Old.*"

the form which it now presents. While availing himself of all
the helps at his command, independence of investigation was,
as far as possible, kept in view; and while special benefit has
been derived from the labours of foreign writers, this is in
many cases, it is believed, more in the way of suggestion than
of servile imitation.

The Author cannot flatter himself that he has succeeded in
mastering all the difficulties of his momentous subject,—of his
shortcomings none can be more conscious than himself; but,
at the same time, it would be affectation to deny, that he conceives that his labours may contribute to shed some light on
this important and greatly misunderstood portion of Divine
Truth. On this, however, it would be out of place to enlarge.
Such as it is, the work is submitted to the judgment of those
who take an intelligent interest in whatever tends to illustrate
and confirm the Oracles of the Living God.

EDINKILLIE, *April* 1856.

CONTENTS.

CREATION AND THE FALL.

INTRODUCTION.

THE two terms, " Creation" and the " Fall," though here
placed in close proximity, are suggestive of very opposite
trains of thought,—the one denoting *a formation* or *beginning*
of the universe of dependent being, and by implication indicating it as the product of prescience and design; the other a
falling away from, in a moral point of view, or *change on*, a
previously existing state. Abstractly considered. the ideas
to which they give rise have no real or necessary connexion.
Indeed, from *à priori* reasoning on the character and perfections of the Creator, it might be inferred that the two ideas
are incongruous or incompatible ; and yet they are intimately
related in the experience of everyday life, observation and consciousness unmistakably testifying that man's present dwelling-place is a *fallen creation*, and that he himself is a *fallen
creature.* But another, and for the present purpose,—of which
it forms no part to prove the reality of a Creation or a Fall,—
the chief consideration for placing these two terms in juxtaposition, is the circumstance that they indicate the subjects of
the opening pages of a very ancient record, which, both by
Jews and Christians, is regarded as a part of their Sacred
Scriptures.

The record in question is the first book of the Bible, or *Genesis*, (Γένεσις, *production* or *generation*,) as it is very appropriately named in and after the Greek version, from the subject with which it commences. Apart altogether from its claims to an inspired origin, this record is in various respects most interesting and important. Its great age, traces of which, in its pictures of primitive and patriarchal times, are vividly impressed on every page, forms no insignificant portion of the interest with which it is to be viewed. For it may be said to be all but universally admitted, that the Book of Genesis is the most venerable literary muniment extant, and separated by a wide interval from every non-biblical composition. As such, were its contents a mere collection of poesy or historic romance, it would be invaluable, as affording indications of man's feelings and modes of thought at a very early period of mental culture; but the interest in the subject is vastly enhanced by the consideration, that the book purports to be, in certain particulars, an historical record of the period which it embraces,—a period opening with the *beginning* of the material universe and of the earth, the dwelling-place of man and the theatre of his history.

The value to be assigned to the narrative as a statement of facts—leaving for the present undetermined the origin of the work itself—must be greatly affected by the early date which, as already observed, is assigned to its composition, and by which it is placed in closer connexion with the transactions recorded than any other production. Indeed, it may be remarked that, strictly speaking, there exist no rival documents on the subject, nothing which has any claim to be reckoned a history of the same period, and nothing which could supply its loss were the book itself wanting. From considerations such as these regarding its character and contents, but chiefly, no doubt, because of his belief in its inspired origin, it was that Luther was accustomed to say, " *Nihil pulcrius Genesi, nihil utilius.*"

This estimate of the great Reformer, which is true of the whole book, applies in an especial degree to its opening chapters, containing, as they do, matters not of a limited or even a national character, but relating to truths and teachings of universal concern and enduring application. The early chapters of Genesis are not confined to any individual race or tribe, but constitute chapters in the history of man. It is true they serve as an introduction to the history of the theocracy and the fortunes of the Hebrew nation, to whom " were committed the oracles of God ;" but then the theocracy itself is only a chapter, though a very important one, in the grand history of redemption, and of man's recovery from the Fall, and restoration to the image of his Creator.

The first three chapters of Genesis, of which a Vindication and Exposition are attempted in the following pages, are pre-eminently important from their relation to the great questions involved in man's origin and primeval state. They comprise three distinct, but, as will be seen in the sequel, closely connected narratives, which, in whatever light they are viewed, have a peculiar bearing on the history and happiness of the human race, and on man's existing, as well as his original, relation to his Creator and Moral Governor. These narratives may be thus classified :—*First*, A view of creation in general, the origin of the earth and all things therein, from the lowest organization up to man, constituted by the Sovereign Creator the head of the lower world. *Second*, A more specific and detailed representation of the creation of man than is comprehended in the preceding epitome, with the circumstances, physical, moral, and social, amid which he was placed ; and *Third*, An account of man's *Fall*, as it is called in theological language, or his transition from an original state of innocence and uprightness into sin, with the causes and consequences of this catastrophe. It must also be observed of this last portion of the narrative, that while it distinctly records the direful consequences of that act of disobedience to the law of God which issued in and evidenced the apostasy, it affords before its close a brief but cheering intimation of a Divine purpose of grace respecting the transgressor, and a promised restoration to the Divine favour.

It will in this view of the subject be seen, that these narratives, but especially the last of them, involve the very fundamentals of the Christian religion ; and thus at the opening of the sacred volume we are made acquainted with matters of the highest possible concern ; upon which, it may be safely stated, reason and philosophy have at best been able to cast but a feeble and glimmering light. With regard to creation in particular, the ablest cultivators of physical science with true modesty admit that their pursuits, which of all others might be presumed most conversant with such inquiries, cannot conduct them to the origin of things. " To ascend to the origin of things," says Sir John Herschel,[1] " and speculate on creation, is not the business of the natural philosopher." And yet even with the admission, that the " subject of creation"—and the same might be said with equal truth of the Fall—" in its entire compass and highest meaning, must necessarily be beyond the reach of positive investigation, or even of human comprehension,"[2] there are not wanting at the present day Natural Histories and Philosophies of Creation and the Fall, in which the account of these matters, as furnished in the book of Genesis, is unceremoniously ignored or derided. This, however, if it cannot be remedied, can at least be satisfactorily accounted for.

Questions connected with creation, and with man's origin and character, have, in some shape or other, afforded grounds for speculation, and forced themselves, as by a common necessity, upon the attention of the thoughtful in all ages ; but the almost invariable result attending such investigations, when

---

[1] Preliminary Discourse on the Study of Natural Philosophy, p. 38.

[2] Essays on the Spirit of the Inductive Philosophy, &c. By the Rev. Baden Powell. Lond. 1855, p. 320.

conducted on so-called *independent* grounds, has been insuper-able difficulties and disappointments. And yet amid all the dissatisfaction arising from the investigations of the past, the desire to entertain the subject, and penetrate its mysteries, is as intense now as at any former period. Indeed, the question of creation, on the authority of the eminent writer last quoted, " has at the present day excited an unprecedented degree of general interest ;"[1] and at the same time it has to be remarked with regret, that there has been manifested, in a lamentable degree in several quarters, a disposition to free the subject from what is called " *Semitic influences,*"—in other words, to get rid of the biblical account of it altogether, because of its alleged hampering of free inquiry and independent research. In this, however, there is nothing new, save in the mode of its manifestation, and the peculiar circumstances by which it is at present specially called forth.

Conclusions deducible from the discoveries of Geology, as well as speculations in kindred sciences, have with many minds been deemed sufficient to throw discredit on the account of creation as contained in the Book of Genesis. Indeed, it has been broadly asserted that *irreconcilable* contradictions exist between the teachings of science and the narrative of creation, as unfolded in this portion of God's word, and the statement is perseveringly and pertinaciously reiterated. " The irreconcilable contradiction between the whole view opened to us by Geology, and the narrative of the creation in the Hebrew Scriptures, whether as briefly delivered from Sinai, or as ex-panded in Genesis,"[2] are the terms in which this assertion is most recently advanced. Language of this and of similar import—

---

[1] Essays on the Spirit of the Inductive Philosophy, &c., p. 316.

[2] Ibid., p. 457. On this very subject, the late Dr. Pye Smith wrote long ago in reference to similar sentiments in the author's " Connexion of Natural and Divine Truth," 1838 :—" I fear that Mr. Powell's expressions are in danger of involving some inconsistency with his own sacred professions and obligations ; and that, if followed out, they would lead to consequences deeply injurious to the cause of Christianity."—*Scripture and Geology,* 3d edit. 1843, p. 198.

however qualified it may be, and whether used in the first instance, or simply sanctioned by the authority of men who, in consequence of their attainments in particular departments of science or of literature, are, as regards their own pursuits, in a position which entitles their opinions to respect, but who may nevertheless be ill qualified to pronounce a judgment on the character and contents of the Hebrew Scriptures,—besides tending to confirm the careless and indifferent in their neglect of the Bible,—is felt to exercise a very perplexing influence upon the minds of many a believer in its truths as the infallible testimony of God, and is causing a stumblingblock to many who are imposed upon by such dogmatic assertions.

These alleged contradictions have been also seized on by Rationalistic interpreters, to support theories of their own fully as much opposed to the character of the Bible narrative, as anything propounded as scientific conclusions; while to the sceptic they have afforded occasion for renewed attacks upon the credibility and authenticity of this portion of Holy Writ. This real or apparent collision of the works and word of God, has likewise in too many cases led to attempted reconciliations, inconsistent not only with the demands of science, but with the just requirements of biblical interpretation.

In a word, the hopes and fears of all who take an intelligent view of the bearing of learning and science on the Divine authority of Scripture, may be said to centre, in a great measure, on the early chapters of Genesis, particularly on the portion now under consideration. From the doubts which, more particularly in recent times, have been cast on various questions connected with Creation and the Fall, as commonly apprehended, the assailants of Scripture are emboldened, and its friends and defenders perplexed. The attacks which were, on former occasions, directed against the Bible as a whole, are now seemingly concentrated rather on its opening chapters, as its presumed outworks and most assailable points. And some who in charity must be supposed to be friends of revelation, are found weakly abandoning these positions, after pronouncing them untenable.

But although it may be freely admitted, that it would be too much to affirm that every instance of the assault or surrender in question is a purposed or even a conscious renouncement of the authority of Scripture in general, this does not affect the nature of the act itself, which can be regarded in no other light than as a virtual impeachment of the whole word of God, and the betrayal of a most sacred trust. It no way improves the aspect of the matter to take refuge in the assumption that the portion of Scripture disavowed is part of " a record of older and imperfect dispensations adapted to the ideas and capacities of a peculiar people and a grossly ignorant age." If such a procedure is to be acquitted of the charge of knowingly impugning or renouncing all that is sacred in the inspired volume, it is only by laying itself open to another, of gross ignorance of the character and contents of this particular portion of Scripture, the fundamental character which it sustains, and its essential relation to all revealed truth.

These remarks, though of a somewhat anticipatory character, and more properly belonging to a future stage of investigation, and the section appropriated to the statement of objections, are designed to show the necessity for a work such as is the aim of the present, and at the same time to prepare for the mode in which the subject is here discussed, particularly as explaining why so much attention is given to the apologetic compared with the exegetic department. And yet it is only from a correct exegesis of the text, to the rigid exclusion of any popular but erroneous notions which may have crept into the views entertained regarding its utterances, that a satisfactory explanation of difficulties, and reconciliation of differences, can be expected.

But if there is a call at the present time for an undertaking such as is here proposed, which involves many difficulties, scriptural and scientific, there is at least no small encouragement for engaging in it ; and whatever may be the success of this effort as regards the elucidation of the three first chapters of Genesis, it is consolatory to reflect, that if the present age is profuse in objections against the credibility of this time-honoured Record, no former period has furnished such ample materials for obviating these objections, and elucidating and confirming the contents of the sacred page. For some time past there were good reasons for anticipating that the application of exacter rules of interpretation, together with a more careful examination of the sacred text, but, above all, the progress of science itself, and all human learning, would not have failed to show that the contradictions of the man of science had no real existence, and that the objections of the sceptic were entirely out of place. Such anticipations, it is believed, are in a fair way of being realized, and materials are daily collecting for vindicating the authority of Scripture, and harmonizing it with all truth.

PART FIRST.

THE HISTORICAL AND INSPIRED CHARACTER OF THE FIRST THREE CHAPTERS OF GENESIS VINDICATED.

UNDER this head it is proposed to show that the Biblical narratives of Creation and the Fall are to be interpreted as literal historical statements, in opposition to such as regard them as poetry, allegory, or mythology; moreover, that they constitute an integral, and indeed a fundamental part of the divinely inspired word, and are not the product of human speculation or discovery.

In order to prevent ambiguity, and particularly to obviate a common objection, that all commentators feel in some degree compelled to depart from the literal sense, it will be necessary to settle, at the outset, what is strictly implied by the terms " literal" and " historical," as used in the above or in a similar connexion. This cannot be better done than in the words of Holden, the author of an able " Dissertation on the Fall of Man." " In applying the designation of literal history to the passage in question," says this writer, " it is not meant that every word is to be understood in its proper and grammatical sense; but that AS A WHOLE it does not convey a mystical, hidden, or allegorical meaning. A sentence or paragraph may be interpreted literally, though every single word is not received in its proper and literal acceptation. It is sufficient to establish the literal interpretation, if they are upon the whole *literally* and not *mystically* understood; and with respect to the portion of the Pentateuch under consideration, it is only intended, by asserting it to be a literal history, that it is a narrative of events which really happened in the infancy of the world. If the trees of life, and of the knowledge of good and evil, were designed to convey a mystical and spiritual meaning, it would be no argument against their actual existence. They would still be real trees, though with a symbolical signification, just as the emblems of our Lord's body and blood in the holy sacrament are real bread and wine, though they are made the visible means of an inward and spiritual grace. If the serpent were a metaphorical expression for the evil spirit, and the sentence denounced against that reptile were a figurative declaration that the empire of Satan would be destroyed ; yet, supposing this to be true, it would not militate against the literal exposition. Though some expressions were to be understood in a figurative or tropical sense, it might, as a whole, be a plain narrative of facts."[1]

Farther, in order to the better understanding of the true state of the question, it may be necessary, or at least advantageous, in the first place, to take a brief historical review of the various interpretations of these narratives current at different periods in the history of the Church

SECT. I.—HISTORICAL REVIEW OF THE VARIOUS INTERPRETATIONS OF GENESIS I.-III.

No portion of Scripture, the Song of Solomon perhaps excepted, has been the subject of such varied and conflicting interpretations as these chapters. This may have had its origin, in some degree, no doubt, in the peculiar difficulties here encountered. It is however chiefly owing to a disposition to bring the narrative into harmony with the preconceptions or prejudices, philosophical and theological, of the numerous interpreters. How largely the various systems of philosophy of ancient and modern times have contributed to obscure and complicate the simple utterances of this Scripture, will appear in the course of the following remarks on the history of its interpretation.

[1] A Dissertation on the Fall of Man ; in which the literal sense of the Mosaic account of that event is asserted and vindicated. By the Rev. George Holden. Lond., 1823, pp. 25, 26.

I.—JEWISH INTERPRETATIONS.

Throughout the Canonical Scriptures, the narratives of Creation and the Fall, wherever referred to, are taken in a literal historical sense, and such references are exceedingly numerous.[1] But a departure from this interpretation can be traced back to a period considerably anterior to any of the New Testament writings. How far the puerilities ingrafted by Rabbinic interpreters on the letter of these narratives may have contributed to a revulsion, it is difficult to say : nor is it known when, or on what grounds—if not as containing something deep and mysterious—the first chapters of Genesis were classed, according to a Jewish rule, with the Song of Solomon, and the beginning and end of Ezekiel, the reading of which was forbidden to all who had not attained to the age of thirty.[2] The allegorical interpretation, however, if it did not originate with, was zealously promoted by the philosophizing Jews at Alexandria in Egypt, and this from a desire to harmonize Moses with Plato, whose system exercised great influence over them. Traces of this mode of interpretation may be found in the Jewish Apocryphal Books, especially in that entitled the " Wisdom of Solomon." But the most distinguished representative of the allegorical scheme, and in whose hands it may be said to have reached its culminating point, was Philo of Alexandria, who flourished in the first century of our era. This system of interpretation, according to Neander, pushed " the opposition to the altogether literal mode of interpretation, so far as to deny the reality of the literal and historical facts throughout, recognising only some ideal truth, some universal thought, that presented itself out of the train of speculations created by a fusion of the Platonic philosophy with religious ideas of Judaism."[3] Thus with Philo, paradise is the dominant character of the soul, which is full of innumerable opinions, as this figurative paradise was of trees :—the serpent is the symbol of pleasure, and it is said to have uttered a human voice, because pleasure employs innumerable cham-

[1] See sect. xi., *infra.*

[2] See Carpzovii Introductio ad Libros Canonicos Veteris Testamenti. Lips. 1757, vol. ii. p. 260.

[3] Church History, Torrey's Translation, vol. i. p. 76. Edin. 1847.

pions and defenders to advocate its interests. After pointing out the difficulty of understanding the account of the woman's creation, Philo remarks, the literal statement conveyed in the words is a fabulous one.[1] Josephus, on the other hand, shows the mode of interpretation followed by the Hellenists of Palestine. Being more removed from the influence of the Alexandrian school, there is with him far more respect for the historical contents of Scripture; yet he does not hesitate to affirm that Moses speaks some things wisely, but enigmatically, and other things under a decent allegory. And it would appear that he understood the contents of the *second* and *third* chapters of Genesis in some such allegorical or philosophical sense.[2]

II.—INTERPRETATIONS OF THE EARLY CHRISTIANS.

The early Christians, in earnest simplicity, received the doctrines of Creation and the Fall, as taught in Scripture, without doubt or disputation. But it was not long till speculation and philosophy claimed a hearing, when the allegorical system was introduced into the Christian Church, and that, too, at Alexandria. The restless school of philosophizing Christians which flourished in that city, dissatisfied with the notion of creation having taken place in time, resorted to an allegorical interpretation of the work of the six days, (*Hexaemeron.*) Origen held the doctrine of an *eternal* creation, or of innumerable ideal worlds : Adam he considered to be a true historical existence, but looked upon him in no other light than as the first incarnate soul which had fallen from a heavenly state. Paradise he regarded as the symbol of a higher spiritual world[3] Clement regarded the narrative of the Fall partly as fact, partly as allegory : the transgression, he held, consisted in man's not waiting for the suitable period appointed by God for the gratification of the sexual impulse.[4]

On the other hand, Irenæus and Tertullian maintained, the one in opposition to the Gnostics, the other to Hermogenes—

[1] De Opif. Mundi, §§ 54, 56 ; Legis Allegor. ii. 7. Or Philo's works translated by Yonge. Lond. 1854, vol. i. pp. 46, 48, 85.

[2] Antiqq. Pref., ₴ 4 ; lib. I. i. 2.

[3] Hagenbach, History of Doctrine, vol. i. p. 124, where the authorities are stated.

[4] Neander, Church History, vol. ii. p. 388.

the simple biblical doctrine of the creation in its entire literality.[1] How far Irenæus adhered to the literal interpretation of the Fall is uncertain; but Tertullian unhesitatingly
affirmed its strictly historical character.[2] Origen's notions of
creation were also rejected by Athanasius and Augustine;
while the figurative interpretation of the Fall fell into disrepute with the allegorical system in general, which gradually
came to be denounced as "incerta allegoriæ."[3] Moreover, the
doctrine of the Fall was now made to assume an important position in theological systems, particularly in that of Augustine.

III.—INTERPRETATION OF THE MIDDLE AGES.

Of the views which prevailed during this extended period
little need be said. The study of the Old Testament was diligently cultivated by many distinguished Jewish Rabbis; but
among Christians, the interpretation of Scripture was neither
held in due estimation as a study, nor pursued in the right
way.[4] The exposition was drawn almost exclusively from the
writings of the Fathers, and especially from the works of
Augustine, who, in matters of theology, was the chief authority,
as was Aristotle in all that pertained to philosophy. The
account of the creation, however, was understood literally by
some, and figuratively by others. But even when admitted in
a literal acceptation, many of the Schoolmen detected strange
mysteries in the matter. Thus Hugo St. Victor (✠ 1141)
taught that the mode of creation was selected with the view of
teaching how man is to be transformed from moral deformity
into moral beauty. Friar Berthold traced in the work of the
first three days, faith, hope, and love.[5] But though both the
Schoolmen and Mystics frequently gave an allegorical interpretation to the Fall, yet the former represented the first man
with historical accuracy. John Damascenus connected the
allegorical interpretation with the historical. Peter Lombard
in theory admitted the latter view, but many of his practical
expositions are allegorical. According to him, the serpent

---

[1] Neander, Church History, vol. ii. p. 316.   [2] Hagenbach, vol. i. p. 156.
[3] Jerome on Malachi, I. 16.
[4] Gieseler, Ecclesiastical History, vol. iii. p. 310.
[5] Hagenbach, vol. i. p. 488.

represents that sensuality which still suggests sinful thoughts to man ; the woman is the inferior part of reason, which first persuades, afterwards leads, the man, the higher reason, into temptation. Scotus Erigena considered the narrative as an ideal description of the happiness designed for man on condition of our first parents successfully resisting temptation.[1]

IV.—THE REFORMATION PERIOD TO THE CLOSE OF THE SEVENTEENTH CENTURY.

In this period more correct principles of interpretation were recognised and followed. The character of the Holy Scriptures was better understood. Mysticism and allegory, which held a high place in scriptural interpretation during many previous centuries, were now discountenanced in favour of the letter. Accordingly, the historical character of the narratives of Creation and the Fall was generally recognised. The great questions which occupied the theologians of the Reformation— man's creation, his original state, the consequences resulting to himself and his posterity from the Fall—were all discussed on the assumption of the historical verity of the account given in Genesis. To Luther and Calvin, the leaders of the Reformation, we are indebted for two noble Commentaries on the Book of Genesis.

The only indication of any moment of an opposite tendency was that shewn in the question raised by Isaac Peyrerius, who afterwards went over to Popery, and died in 1676, as one of the priests of the Oratory. This author, in 1655, published a work, in which he broached the opinion, that there had been human beings in existence previous to the creation of Adam, who was to be regarded as the ancestor only of the Jews.[2] This opinion he founded on Gen. i. 26, 27, compared with Gen. ii. The question gave rise to a short controversy in the Reformed Church. It was warmly opposed by Calov, who styles it " monstrosa opinio."

[1] Hagenbach, vol. ii. p. 8.

[2] Systema Theolog. ex Præadamitarum Hypothesi. This was translated into English under the title, Men before Adam, or a Discourse upon Romans v. 12-14, by which are proved that the first men were created before Adam, with a Theological System upon that pre-supposition, Lond. 1656. This wild notion is finding advocates at the present day. See *Journal of Sacred Literature*, Jan. 1855, p 436.

In Britain, the literal interpretation of the early chapters of Genesis was strictly adhered to by theologians and commentators in general, of whom may be specified Bishops Kidder and Patrick, whose works appeared in 1694.[1]

V.—FROM THE BEGINNING OF THE EIGHTEENTH CENTURY TO THE PRESENT TIME.

The state of matters originating in the Reformation, and maintained more or less through the succeeding century, gave way by degrees to other influences. Cold philosophical speculations had to a great extent superseded faith, when, in the beginning of the last century, the philosophy of Leibnitz, as modified by Wolf, extended its influence to theology. This, which was an attempt to form a system of natural religion on the basis of demonstration independently of revelation, and in which a distinction was made between religion which may be proved by demonstration, and religion to be received by faith, prepared a way for the ascendency of the deistic principle of natural over the theistic principle of revealed religion.[2] The Wolfian philosophers in vain endeavoured to reconcile the Mosaic account of Creation and the Fall with the results of their demonstrations, and at length gave up the attempt as hopeless. Indeed, the spirit of the age was such, that even the allegorical interpretation, which had sufficed in former emergencies, must be discarded equally with the literal, and the whole resolved into myths, or the speculations of some ancient sage.

While the authority of Moses was thus openly, or by implication, renounced by the philosophers and theologians of the Continent, and, to some extent, of Britain, another school sprung up which went to the opposite extreme. The founder

---

[1] " We may very well grant that these first chapters of Genesis do insinuate some farther meaning than the bare letter amounts to. We yield that there is couched a mystery under the letter. 'Tis agreeable to the belief of Jews and Christians to allow this. But still the letter is to be preserved, and not questioned by any means."—*Kidder on the Pentateuch*, vol. i. pp. v. vi.

" I hope I have made it appear that there is very good reason to believe every-thing that Moses hath related [in the account of Creation and the Fall] without forsaking the literal sense, and betaking ourselves to, I know not what, allegorical interpretations."—*Patrick, Pref. to Commentary on Genesis.*

[2] Lechler, Geschichte des Deismus, p. 448.

of this school, whose philosophical and exegetical views exerted considerable influence for a time, was John Hutchinson, who, in 1724, published the first part of a work, entitled *Moses' Principia*, in which he held that the writings of Moses contain the principles of all science. Hutchinson accordingly extracted from the first chapters of Genesis a system of philosophy which he flattered himself would entirely refute and supersede the Newtonian system of the world. Much about the same time the allegorical interpretation found zealous exponents in Britain, and views were put forth which, in extravagance, rivalled those of Philo or Origen.[1]

But the writer who may be said to have exercised the greatest influence on the interpretation of these chapters, towards the close of the last century, was Johann Gottfried von Herder. Herder, whose mind was deeply imbued with oriental poetry, represented the account of Creation as a *myth* clothed in a poetic dress; admitting, however, its internal truth.[2] The view of Herder, variously modified, has been adopted by almost all the German, and not a few British theologians and critics, who would designate themselves as *liberal*. It were no easy task to enumerate the variety of forms which the mythical theory has assumed in the hands of these writers. The guiding principle of the literal historical statements once lost sight of, the interpreter is entirely at sea —without sun or stars, and with fancy, not faith, for his pilot. The conflicting *expositions*, if such a term can be applied to them, bear upon their face unmistakable evidence of the truth of this assertion. Thus, to notice first the narrative of

[1] *e.g.*, Notes and Observations upon the three first chapters of Genesis. By John Scott, D.D. Lond. 1753. A work " drawn up," as the author states in his preface, " for the benefit of all ranks and orders of mankind." As a specimen of the exposition, let the following suffice :—" The garden of Eden is the body of man, represented by a garden as a covering for his spirit."—(P. 72.) The trees of the garden " are not to be understood literally, but of the bodily sensations and appetites of man."—(P. 81.)

[2] His views on the subject varied. In his Alteste Urkunde des Menschengeschlechts, 1774, he viewed the account of creation as a *pictorial representation of opening day*. But in his Ideen zur Philosophie der Geschichte der Menschen, 1785, vol. ii. p. 314, he considers it as *the views of an ancient sage on the origin of the world*. Of this latter work of Herder, Bunsen says, " It will continue to live and to be studied, when ninety-nine out of a hundred celebrities of this century and of the last shall have been forgotten."—*Outlines of the Philosophy of Universal History*. Lond. 1854, vol. i. p. 16.

Creation, Eichhorn saw in it a picture,—not a history of creation, every feature betraying the pencil of the painter, not the pen of the historian, and in its arrangement a pious fraud, to give Divine sanction to the law of the Sabbath.[1] Bauer regarded it as a popularly clothed philosopheme, or the reflections of some ancient sage on the origin of things ; and in this view he is followed by Tuch and Winer.[2] The elder Rosenmüller held it to be a translated hieroglyphic.[3] But according to the most recent phase of Rationalism, the description is after the type of day,—its visions and activities emerging from the still, damp night.[4]

The narrative of the Fall was of course subjected to the same pressure as that of the Creation, and underwent, if possible, still greater transformations. In regard to it there were special dogmatic influences at work to get rid of it, if practicable, altogether. The view most current for many years among the learned of Germany, was that which regarded it as an historically clothed philosopheme of a reflecting Israelite, or some other Orientalist, on the origin of physical and moral evil. This view was embraced by Ammon, Bauer, Vater, Gesenius, and others. But Von Bohlen denied that there was in the narrative any intimation of a Fall (*Sündenfall*), —the myth rather describing the exaltation of man to the godhead.

Others, as Werner,[5] stop short of this extreme, and content themselves with what Winer calls *the half-literal* view, (*halbbuchstäbliche,*) which, recognising an historical kernel, endeavours to separate it from the shell. To this class belong some usually regarded among the more orthodox authors of Germany, as Tholuck[6] and Julius Müller.[7]

---

[1] Urgeschichte, herausgegeben von Gabler, 1790, vol. i. pp. 142, 230.

[2] Bauer, Hebr. Mythologie, 1802, vol. i. p. 63. Tuch, Kommentar über die Genesis,1838, p. 2. Winer, Bib. Realwörterbuch, 1847. Art. *Erde*, vol. i. p. 338.

[3] Antiquissima Telluris Historia. Ulm, 1776.

[4] Sörensen, Histor. Krit. Commentar zur Genesis, 1851, p. 32. A work which Delitzsch (die Genesis, p. 99) truly characterizes as *silly.*

[5] Geschichtliche Auffassung der drei ersten Kapitel des ersten Buchs Mose, 1829.

[6] Die Lehre von der Sünde, p. 211. 7te Ausg. 1851.

[7] Müller (Christian Doctrine of Sin, translated, vol. ii. p. 388) says, " If we find ourselves constrained to go beyond the mythical conception to the acknowledgment of an historical fundamental basis of the narrative, it is not thereby meant that

Among British writers these views have not been shared in to a large extent. On the contrary, there have been many able defenders of the literal historical interpretation of the scriptural account of the Creation and the Fall. The defence of the narrative of Creation was very much marred, however, by the inadequate notions which were entertained by all parties on the subject, but which in the circumstances were unavoidable. The literality of the account of the Fall was maintained by Sherlock,[1] Horsley, and others; and more recently, and in a special treatise already referred to, by Holden. The most recent writer on the subject is Topham,[2] who may be said to be *ultra-literal*, even to absurdity. But still there were some Socinian writers, and others who, like the late Dr. Geddes, considered the account of the Fall as "a mere poetical mythos, historically adapted to the senses and intellects of a rude unphilosophical people."[3] And even now expressions are given utterance to, similar to those of Professor Baden Powell, a divine of the Church of England, who thus speaks of the narrative of creation:—" As to the particular form in which the descriptive narrative is conveyed, we merely affirm that it cannot be *history*—it may be poetry."[4]

But it is some satisfaction to observe, in conclusion, that even in Germany, where the lax views adverted to have been most at home, more healthy symptoms are manifesting themselves. Rationalism is on the wane; and, with a reviving Christianity, more reverence is paid to the word of God. Rationalistic works, which have passed first editions, as, for instance, the " Scholia" of the younger Rosenmüller, shew in this respect marked improvement in the subsequent impressions. And although rationalistic voices are still raised, yet within the last few years many able defences have appeared of the historical character of these chapters. Even Winer admits that " many recent theologians and naturalists have come

theology must take upon itself to defend the historic character of every individual feature."

[1] *Dissertation* II., with Appendix annexed to his Discourses on Prophecy, 1749. Also in Works, vol. iv. pp. 155-214. Lond., 1830.

[2] The Philosophy of the Fall. By the Rev. E. C. Topham: Lond. 1855. A production in which there is as little of philosophy as there is of common sense.

[3] Translation of the Bible, vol. i. p. 33. Lond. 1792.

[4] Cyclopædia of Biblical Literature, Art. *Creation*, vol. i. p. 486. Lond. 1845.

back to the historical view."[1] Among the writers of " Intro-
ductions" to the Old Testament, the historical character of
these sections of Genesis has been defended by Jahn and
Hävernich, more particularly the latter : among commentators
mention may be made of Tiele, Baumgarten, Schröder,
Delitzsch, and Richers, to all of whom frequent reference will
be made in the following pages.

SECT. II.—LEADING OBJECTIONS TO THE NARRATIVES OF CREATION
AND THE FALL CHARACTERIZED AND CLASSIFIED—THE CRITI-
CAL, ARCHÆOLOGICAL, AND SCIENTIFIC.

From the brief sketch given in the preceding section, it has
appeared that these narratives have been viewed in a great
variety of lights, and subjected to the most conflicting interpretations. It will, in particular, be observed, that while. in
the simple exercise of faith, the account of man's creation, and
of his subsequent fall into sin, as narrated in Genesis, has been
received by the great body of believers in all ages as of equal
authority with the remaining portion of that book, or with the
entire volume of which it forms a part—the whole being
esteemed as the indubitable word of God—there have not
been wanting men imbued with a very different spirit, who,
though professing respect for the Bible as a whole, have, nevertheless, been indisposed to recognise this portion of it as of
equal authority with the remainder. It has happened, too,
that where assent has been accorded to the early chapters of
Genesis as a part of God's revealed word, certain qualifications
have been attached, which go far to nullify the acknowledgment ; and modes of interpretation have been resorted to, if not
with a view, yet which certainly have had the effect, of neutralizing the plain statements and historical facts which the
narratives embody.

The opposition manifested to this particular portion of Scripture by other than avowed enemies of revelation, is exceedingly
striking, whether it appears in the form of contempt, or of
more active contradiction. It can, it is believed, be traced to
a variety of causes, more or less connected, having its origin,

[1] Biblisches Realwörterbuch, vol. i p. 338.

for the most part, however the feeling may be disguised, if not in hostility to revelation in general, and impatience of its restraints, in ignorance at least of its character, and a criminal indifference to its claims. But along with the principles and passions common to the unsanctified heart, there are, in the instances referred to, certain peculiarities or prepossessions to be taken into account, which affect the reception extended to these chapters. These are partly of a theological, but chiefly of a scientific character ; the one class bearing more particularly on the account of the Fall, the other on that of Creation.

It is well known that there is a class of persons who, while adopting the designation of Christians, have banished from their creed the peculiar and distinguishing doctrines of Christianity, such as hereditary depravity, and the atonement and satisfaction of Christ. These doctrines, in the apprehension of those who receive and maintain them, are clearly traceable to the narrative of the Fall, and are, as it were, firmly rooted in it. Thus the third chapter of Genesis has become the battle-ground of opposing creeds ; and as the letter of the narrative is plainly in favour of the one party, prudence and policy has made it incumbent on the other to decline this test of controversy, by questioning its authority, or explaining away its statements, as figure or allegory.

While there is one class of persons offended with the theology of this portion of the Bible, there is another and a numerous one who stumbles at its science. Many it is believed of this latter description, know so little of the theology of the Bible, that they would deem the volume no less complete were it found that its opening pages contained only poetry or fiction, —and not greatly mutilated, should this portion of it be torn away ; and, of course, they cannot be greatly perplexed at either of the supposed results. The objectors now in view have no quarrel with the Bible as a collection of sublime poetry, or a code of morals, or as containing the annals of the Hebrew nation, but they are impatient at being told that it knows anything of physical science, the system of the universe, or the creation of the world,—studies which they cultivate and claim as peculiarly their own. It is no wonder, then, that misapprehending the purport of the first chapter of Genesis, where, more than in any other portion of Scripture, revelation comes into contact with science, there should be a disposition on the part of such parties to sacrifice the authority of the former to what they conceive to be the indications of the latter.

It may be proper, however, to observe in this place, that there are not wanting many students of science—and the number is continually augmenting—who take a more enlarged view of the character and claims of Scripture, and who, while truly loving and reverencing the Bible, feel themselves in a position of pain and perplexity, being led to this by what, as already adverted to in the Introduction, are considered by certain scientific inquirers as discrepancies between scientific truths and the scriptural statements in regard to the Creation ; as, for instance, the age of the world, and the distribution of the work into six days ; as also the entrance of death into the world, and other conclusions commonly deduced from the account of the Fall. Such persons feel that their path is beset with difficulties which they cannot obviate, and are burdened with doubts which they cannot satisfy or dispel. In these circumstances it is often felt that in order to retain the Bible, and unimpaired faith in it, or to retain Genesis in its integrity, they must give up at least the literal, historical character of its account of the Creation, if not also of the Fall.

But whatever may have been the motives which at various times prompted the attempt to invalidate this portion of sacred writ, ᴄ induced the disposition to renounce its plain statements, the matter has been gone about with earnestness of purpose, judging from the numerous arguments and objections adduced, and the long and laboured reasonings resorted to. Aid has been sought from every quarter which in any way promised to prove the falsity of this record. Objections, first urged, as would appear, by Julian the Apostate, have been again in requisition, and to these have been added many new arguments not dreamt of by that enemy of Christianity.

Little advantage would be derived from specifying in detail these objections ; nor is this the place to enter upon an examination of their weakness or validity. It may, however, be convenient to arrange them for future consideration under the three heads of Critical, Archæological, and Scientific Objections; but at present it will be sufficient to indicate generally their nature and tendency, reserving, for the sections which are to follow, a more extended examination of them.

1. The class of objections peculiarly Critical will comprise the usual and most important arguments on which are founded various attempts to cut up these chapters, as indeed the whole Pentateuch, but particularly Genesis, into shreds or fragments, thereby to establish a diversity of authorship. This *disintegrating* process, as it may be called, proceeds mainly on the striking change in the divine names, Elohim and Jehovah— *God* and *Lord* of the English version—occurring in different sections of Genesis, and with especial distinctness in the first three chapters, and was at first probably no more than an attempt to explain that phenomenon. This leading argument, however, is supposed to gather additional weight from the diversity of style, and also from several *alleged* contradictions between the *first* and *second* chapters ; all which, in the opinion of many continental and a few British critics, can be accounted for only on the supposition that, in the passages in question, documents, of various authors and ages, have been collected by accident or design into a whole. This is what is known in Germany, where it has been for a long time laboriously cultivated, and whence it is being cheaply imported for the benefit of the English reader, by men of Neological views, both British and American, as the " Document," " Fragment," or more recently, the " Complementary Hypothesis," according to its varying forms and phases.

2. Under the Archæological head of objections may be classed the numerous appeals made to the real or fancied historical records and remains of antiquity ; as, for example, to the Indian and Chinese annals, but especially to the hieroglyphic inscriptions and other monuments of Egypt, with the view of shewing that the chronology of Genesis is entitled to no credit, inasmuch as those other records extend to a far higher date than the Bible assigns to the origin of the human race. But the consideration of the many theories on this special point, though for a long time confidently propounded, demands at present little more than a passing remark, as they have been satisfactorily disposed of by the investigations of the geologist, whose science in this, as in other particulars, unequivocally corroborates the Mosaic statements.

What is chiefly deserving of notice in connexion with the present subject, is the comparisons which have been instituted between the biblical account of Creation and the Cosmogonies of heathen antiquity, industriously examined for the purpose of showing that all alike—the biblical and non-biblical theories—have had a common origin in the mythologies and legends of the world's infancy. So, in like manner, with the account of the Fall : to explain away the narrative of man's apostasy from his Maker, with the loss of his pristine righteousness, it is often deemed amply sufficient by many objectors if they can instance parallel traditions in the heathen world, and they accordingly point to the legends of a *golden age*, the garden of the Hesperides, the story of Prometheus and Pandora, without once making the attempt to assign any sufficient cause for the rise and almost universal reception of those remarkable traditions, which must have had some basis of truth, some relation or accordance with human consciousness and experience ; and as if unconscious that this remarkable concord of Scripture and tradition is confirmatory than otherwise of the Sacred Record.

3. More recently, however, the objections directed against these narratives, and especially against that of Creation, have been drawn mainly from Scientific sources. Man's acquaintance with nature, her laws and operations, has of late been wonderfully enlarged. Science has successfully pushed her inquiries into the heights of heaven and into the depths of earth, has spanned the immensity of space and past duration, and when advancing in a right spirit, has extracted thence many clear and cogent proofs of creative wisdom and power. But if in this wide field of investigation any fact, or supposed fact, has presented itself, seemingly at variance with any biblical testimony or interpretation, the enemies of revelation are not slow to avail themselves of its support. Of course, as might have been expected,—looking to the extended boundaries of nature, and at the same time to the brief but comprehensive narrative which records God's mighty acts and operations—a narrative which is co-extensive in its statements with creation itself, and so presenting points of contact to all human science,—such facts are not wanting. Accordingly, it is often triumphantly proclaimed that Astronomy, Geology, Physiology,

or Ethnology, as the case may be, refutes Moses, and demonstrates that his information cannot have been derived from the fountain of all truth and knowledge.

But more directly opposed to Divine revelation—to its spirit as well as its letter, and especially to that portion of it now under consideration—are all those crude theories and speculations largely countenanced at present, contrived to account for the formation of worlds and systems, on mere natural laws, without the agency or intervention of a present and Personal Creator, and which would deduce by insensible gradations from a monad or a monkey, man, whom we are taught to regard as made in the image of God, and so pre-eminently distinguished from all other creatures.

Weapons have thus been industriously collected from the various departments of human inquiry for the assault of this portion of Scripture. But in the meantime, and in view of all that has been or can be urged, against the character and credibility of this ancient document, which occupies the front of the Bible, one or two general remarks may advantageously be hazarded in regard to the difficulties which the intelligent reader of this portion of sacred history may naturally be led to expect, and the prospect he may entertain of their being in due time satisfactorily obviated or resolved.

In the first place, it is readily admitted that there are difficulties which present themselves to the student and interpreter of the first three chapters of Genesis, that are perhaps more numerous and formidable than any to be met with in any other portion of Scripture of similar compass. But this of itself should be no matter of surprise, considering the mighty problems of which these chapters treat, the comprehensive brevity with which the intimations are enunciated, the particular purpose they are designed to serve, and the peculiar place which they occupy at the commencement of a revelation of God's will and ways to man, which, as it advances, brightens and expands, as the dawn of morning into noonday.

But, secondly, it is not too much to affirm that, on the other hand, it will be found on a closer investigation that the difficulties are not so formidable, or the obscurities so deep as they are sometimes represented to be, and that the arguments on which the assailants are wont to rely, are not of such a kind as need seriously alarm the friends of the Bible, or furnish its adversaries with grounds for gratulation or triumph. Judging from the experience of the past, and especially of the last few years, there is reasonable ground for the assurance that the time is not far distant when not a few of the difficulties and contradictions alleged to exist, shall finally and for ever disappear.

Lastly, there are numerous and valid reasons to justify the conclusion that the weapons borrowed from the arsenal of heathen antiquity, and as well those furnished by modern criticism and science, for the assault of the history of Creation and the Fall, will yet be converted into serviceable instruments for its defence. This at least is only in accordance with the invariable experience of the past, in reference to the oft-repeated attacks made upon the Bible, but out of whose momentary darknesses it has again and again emerged with augmented light and lustre. The evidences of Scripture are multiplying and brightening day by day, and never were its credentials so many and strong as at the present hour. Archæological studies are furnishing a tongue and interpretation to many hitherto dumb witnesses, whose testimonies are found most unexpectedly to be favourable to the Sacred Volume, although, while silent, they were confidently appealed to as witnesses against it. Thus Egypt and Assyria, their painted monuments and chiselled marbles and gorgeous halls, are pouring in rich contributions in attestation of its historic credibility. The result cannot be otherwise in the case of the physical sciences, as in their several departments they become strengthened and solidified, and have their facts disentangled from fancies and airy speculations. As the desert mounds of Nineveh or Nimroud, now opened up to the light of day, re-echo with the story of the deeds of the long-buried Sargons and Sennacheribs, so it will be in a far higher sense with the stone volumes and adamantine pillars on which the Creator has inscribed in lasting characters a record of his works on our globe in ages long past, when these are fully unfolded. This record for its preservation He has hid deep in earth and ocean, and although long unknown and unnoticed, it is now being produced and deciphered with results which, whatever may have been hastily and erroneously supposed to be their tendency, and the doubts thereby thrown on a particular *interpretation* of the first chapter of Genesis, have even already wonderfully enlarged and corrected our conceptions of creation,[1] and therewith our views of the scope of the Mosaic narrative itself.

In accordance with the preceding classification of objections as Critical, Archæological, and Scientific, the three sections which immediately follow are devoted to—(Sect. iii.) A vindication of the internal unity of these chapters from the attacks of the *fragmentary* criticism ; (Sect. iv.) A comparison of the biblical account of Creation with heathen Cosmogonies, in order to show the distinguishing peculiarities of the former ; and, (Sect. v.) A comparison of the biblical account of Creation with the findings of modern Science, with the view of showing that there is no contradiction between the works, and what claims to be the word, of the Creator and Governor of the Universe.

SECT. III.—THE INTERNAL UNITY OF GENESIS I.-III.

The destructive criticism of the " Document," " Fragment," or, according to its more recent development, " Complementary Hypothesis," has found in Genesis abundant scope for its vocation. This hypothesis, as its name implies, proceeds on the supposition that the Pentateuch consists of a number of documents or fragments collected, combined, or wrought up, with more or less care, into the form in which it now appears. It originated, as already remarked, in an attempt to account for the change in the names of God noticeable in different sections. This was assumed to be conclusive evidence of a diversity of authorship. Accordingly, every section or paragraph in which

---

[1] " From the effects," says a distinguished geologist, " produced upon my own mind through the study of these imperishable records, I am indeed led to hope that my readers will adhere to the views which, in common with many contemporaries, I entertain of the succession of life. For, he who looks to a beginning, and traces thenceforward a rise in the scale of being, until that period is reached when man appeared upon the earth, must acknowledge in such works repeated manifestations of design, and unanswerable proofs of the superintendence of a Creator."—Murchison's *Siluria*, p. 483. Lond. 1854.

the name ELOHIM occurs, was marked off as belonging to one original document, to be designated the " Elohim-document." The sections or paragraphs, on the contrary, with the name JEHOVAH, were assigned to another and later author, whose production was to be distinguished in critical terminology as the " Jehovah-document." How these documents are related to one another is a point on which the critics are not agreed : hence the various forms of the hypothesis—the " document-hypothesis," properly so called, and its " complementary" modification. According to the one system, the two documents are distinct and *independent;* but according to the other, Genesis consists of an Elohim-document, but gone over by an editor who supplies supplementary details where the original is defective, or breaks off abruptly. The chief exponent of this view, now pronounced the only tenable one, is Tuch, who, to a limited extent, is followed even by Delitzsch, the most recent commentator on Genesis.

Besides the argument resting on the change of the Divine names, another but subordinate support to this hypothesis is derived from a supposed diversity of style in the two classes of passages, arranged on the principle already announced. Various expressions, single and combined, words and phrases, peculiarities of a grammatical and rhetorical character, and even of an historical and ethical nature, are produced as characteristics of the one author or of the other. It also, no doubt, materially adds to the fancied strength and stability of the structure, when, as in the case of the first and second chapters of Genesis, the critics believe that they have discovered palpable contradictions.

Happily, the theory thus briefly sketched, or the criticism which gave birth to it, is no longer the rash and reckless thing it was at an earlier stage of its history, but is sobered with years, and that to a degree which procures its reception among British theologians, just as it is falling into disrepute in the land of its birth. Still, it exercises sufficient influence to render not unnecessary an examination of its bearing on the present subject.[1]

---

[1] " About this time also I had perceived, (what I afterwards learned the Germans to have more fully investigated,) that the two different accounts of the creation are distinguished by the appellations given to the Divine Creator. I did not see

I.—INTERCHANGE OF THE DIVINE NAMES, AN ARGUMENT OF THE DOCUMENT-HYPOTHESIS.

The interchange of the Divine names in the Pentateuch was taken notice of at an early period. Among the Christian Fathers, Tertullian, Chrysostom, and Augustine, offered explanations of this interchange in respect to the first sections of Genesis. It was not, however, till the Document-hypothesis called attention to the matter, that it was made the subject of special investigation. This has been done at great length, and with much learning, by Hengstenberg, Dreschler, Kurtz, and others, in works directed to the defence of the integrity of the Pentateuch, and the unity of its parts.[1] But with much that is excellent in these productions, it must be admitted that there is also not a little which is arbitrary and untenable. It is, however, satisfactorily established, that whilst there is an important difference in the signification of the names Elohim and Jehovah, the interchange is not accidental or external, but of design; and that in whatever way the purpose may be explained, it gives no countenance to any alleged diversity of authorship. It is in their endeavours to explain the historian's object in selecting the one name or the other, that these authors principally fail in carrying conviction; while perhaps also, the distinction drawn between the two names is too artificial and refined, savouring more of the subtleties of a German philosophy than of the theology of the Bible.

Here, it may be remarked—and the point has not been sufficiently adverted to in discussions on the subject—that in its application to the first two sections of Genesis, the Document-hypothesis is decidedly at fault. The change there is not between Elohim and Jehovah, as in other cases, but between Elohim, which is constant and exclusive in the first section, and the compound form, Jehovah-Elohim, in the second, with only three exceptions, (Gen. iii. 1, 3, 5,) where in the mouth of

how to resist the inference, that the book is made up of heterogeneous documents, and was not put forth by the direct dictation of the Spirit to Moses."—Newman's *Phases of Faith*, fourth edition, 1854, p. 67.

[1] *Hengstenberg*, Beiträge zur Einleitung ins alte Testament, 1836. Band ii. pp. 180-414. *Dreschler*, Die Einheit u. Aechtheit der Genesis, 1838. *Kurtz*, Beiträge zur Vertheidigung u. Begründung der Einheit d. Pentateuchs, 1844. Die Einheit der Genesis, 1846.

the serpent and of the woman it is Elohim. This compound form of the Divine name is found *twenty* times in this section,—in chap. ii. *eleven*, and in chap. iii. *nine* times,—but is elsewhere of very rare occurrence. It is used only *once* again in the Penta- teuch, in Exod. ix. 30 ; and, exclusive of this section of Genesis, there are but three passages in the Hebrew Scriptures, viz., 2 Sam. vii. 22, 25, 1 Chron. xvii. 16, 17, and 2 Chron. vi. 41, 42, where it occurs *twice* in the same connected narrative.

1. *Etymology and import of Elohim.*

The etymology of the term אֱלוֹהַּ, *Elohah*, the plural of which is Elohim, the common Hebrew designation of the Divine Being, is involved in much obscurity ; and, as a natural con- sequence, great diversity of opinion exists among writers who have considered the subject. It is unnecessary to notice above one or two of the more probable views entertained regarding its derivation. The one perhaps most extensively received, is that which assumes a root, אלה, obsolete in Hebrew, but pre- served in the Arabic *aliha*, signifying *coluit, adoravit ;* and intransitively, *stupuit, pavore correptus fuit.* According to this view, אֱלוֹהַּ is an infinitive form like צְחֹק, *an object of laugh- ter*, Gen. xxi. 6 ; בּוּז, *an object of contempt*, Isa. xlix. 7, and thus signifies *the object of dread* or *adoration*, the *dread* or *adorable One*, equivalent to the Greek σέβας or σέβασμα. The advo- cates of this view, in confirmation of its soundness, refer to פַּחַד, *the object of fear*, a designation of God in Gen. xxxi. 42, 53. And Hengstenberg, who adopts this derivation, remarks,[1]— " It appears peculiarly suitable, if we keep in view the histo- rical use of the name Elohim. This name always appears to be the widest and most general, and for this reason we are naturally led to such a derivation. The feeling of fear is the lowest which can exist in reference to God, and merely in respect of this feeling is God marked by this designation. He is the great unknown which infuses fear. Of his interior nature nothing is expressed ; the name is merely relative, **and, as** such, superficial ; for the deepest relations of God to man, those which proceed from his holiness and love, are not included in the name." However descriptive these remarks may be of the experience of mankind in general, of the nature and attri- butes of God, they are far from being a correct representation

[1] Beiträge, vol. ii. p. 260. Ryland's Translation, vol. i. p. 267.

of the communion and intercourse which appears from Genesis to have existed between God and man at the beginning, when, so far as can be gathered from the history, the name Elohim only was known. Even in later and patriarchal times, how utterly incongruous with the state of matters depicted in Scripture is the assertion, that " the deepest relations of God to man, those which proceed from his holiness and love, are not included in the name Elohim !" To select only one instance, (Gen. v. 22,) " Enoch walked with THE ELOHIM ;" having, as the Apostle declares, (Heb. xi. 5,) " this testimony, that he pleased God."

In direct opposition to the etymology given above, others maintain that the verb assumed as a root was formed later than the noun, and took its meaning from it. They therefore propose a root אוּל, signifying *to be strong, powerful*. From this is derived, in the first instance, אֵל, *the strong*, or *mighty one*, a name of God of frequent occurrence ; from this again אָלַה, *to be strong* ; אֱלוֹהַּ, the word in question ; אֵלָה, *an oak*, or *terebinth*, so called from its strength, with several other words of similar signification. This derivation, which has the advantage of preserving the connexion between EL and ELOHAH, has found supporters among the older writers in Saadias (Arabic version of the Pentateuch) and Abusaides, while in modern times it has commanded the assent of men such as Gesenius, Fürst, Kurtz, and Delitzsch, not to mention many others. It is also strikingly confirmed by internal considerations. What, in his intercourse with God the Creator of all, and in his survey of the creation around him, would so soon impress the mind of man as the mighty *power* which called all things into existence ?[1] Besides, the feeling of fear or reverence is not of a primary but secondary nature ; for it rests on the belief that the object towards which it is cherished has *power* to injure or to aid.

---

[1] The early poet of the " Veda," " the first literary document of the Arian race," has discovered in his own breast, says Dr. Max. Müller, " a power that wants a name, a power nearer to him than all the gods of nature, a power that is never mute when he prays, never absent when he fears and trembles. . . . The only name he can find for this mysterious power is *Brahma*, for *brahma* means originally force, will, wish, and the propulsive power of creation. But this impersonal *brahma*, too, as soon as it is named, grows into something strange and divine. It becomes *Brahmanaspati*, the Lord of power, an epithet applicable to many gods in their toils and their victories."—Bunsen's *Phil. of Univ. Hist.* vol. i. p. 134.

The same uncertainty prevails regarding the import of the plural termination of Elohim, in which form the word most usually, and in the earlier prose compositions, exclusively, appears. Many, following Peter Lombard, find in it an intimation of the doctrine of the Trinity : on which Calvin remarks, —" Parum solida mihi videtur tantæ rei probatio."[1] German Rationalists maintain that it is the remains of an ancient Hebrew polytheism,—a view fully refuted by Hengstenberg. Rabbinical writers in general explain the usage by what they call the *pluralis majestaticus*, according to which, terms denoting relations of *power* or *greatness* are placed in the plural,—a rule which the best Hebrew grammarians affirm has no existence. Another view of the matter has been put forth by Hengstenberg, in which he is followed by Dreschler.[2] According to these writers, the plural in Elohim answers the same purpose as the accumulation of the Divine names in other passages, as in Josh. xxii. 22, or the thrice *holy* in Isa. vi. 3 It calls attention to the infinite riches and the inexhaustible fulness in the one Divine Being, so that, though men may imagine innumerable gods, and invest them with perfections, yet all these are contained in the one Elohim. Taking Elohah in the sense of the *mighty One*, Elohim, in the view of Delitzsch,[3] is intensive ; " the idea of the mighty One is, so to speak, internally multiplied in order to express its highest power, the Almighty, as קְדֹשִׁים, *the most Holy*, Prov. ix. 10 ; Hos. xii. 1, (E. V. xi. 12)." This is as probable as any of the numerous opinions entertained respecting this usage.

2. *Etymology and import of Jehovah.*

On this question there does not exist much diversity of opinion. The origin of the name Jehovah, or more correctly written *Jahveh*—for the vowels affixed to this word in the Hebrew text belong not to it but to *Adonai*—is almost universally acknowledged to be found in the root הוה, an old form of היה, equivalent to the Greek φῦναι, *to be, to exist*. יהוה is thus the regularly formed *future* in Kal. This etymology is placed beyond dispute by the passages of Scripture in which a derivation of the name is expressed or implied, particularly Exod iii. 14. There Moses, having made inquiry after God's name

[1] Comm. in Gen. chap. i. 1.　　[2] Die Einheit u. Aechtheit, p. 14.
[3] Die Genesis ausgelegt, 1852, p. 22.

receives the answer, " I am that I am—אֶהְיֶה אֲשֶׁר אֶהְיֶה (God speaking of himself in the first person) ; and he said, Thus shalt thou say to the children of Israel, I AM (אֶהְיֶה) hath sent me to you." In the next verse this is changed into, " Say to the children of Israel, JEHOVAH (יהוה) God of your fathers, . . . hath sent me to you."[1]

Taking this for the true etymology of the name Jehovah, it is necessary to inquire into the precise idea thus conveyed. Hengstenberg, who has largely examined the subject, concludes that the name represents God as " *the Being, the existing One*, or *absolute Being*." " If God be he who is, that is always the same, the unchangeable, he is also *the Being*, or *the absolute Being*, and if he be the absolute Being, then is he also the unchangeable, as it is inferred (Mal. iii. 6) from ' I am Jehovah, that I change not.' Every creature remains not like itself, but is continually changing under circumstances. God only, because he is THE BEING, is always the same ; and because he is always the same, is THE BEING." This has been objected to as far too abstract an idea, unsuited to the character of Scripture, and the occasion on which the name was formally announced. Others, again, as Baumgarten[2] and Delitzsch,[3] lay more stress on the *future* form of the word, and consider it as denoting not so much *the Being*, as one *becoming* or *going to be*, (der Werdende,) referring this not to the Divine nature or essence, but to the revelation of it: in short, that it designates the Divine Being as the God of historical revelation : He who in times past appeared to patriarchs and prophets, and was known as Jehovah God of the Israelitish fathers, (Exod. iii. 15,) but who should " in the fulness of time" be more gloriously manifested. This view is not a little countenanced by the fact, that in the New Testament the name Jehovah, or its equivalent, occurs only in the Apocalypse, a book which still points to the future of Christ's kingdom. There, indeed, the

---

[1] Another view is advanced by Ewald, (Geschichte d. Volkes Israel, vol. ii. p. 204. 2te Ausg. 1853,) but it merits little consideration. Assuming that in Gen. xix. 24, מאת יהוה is explained by the next clause, " out of heaven," and comparing Mic. v. 6, [E. V. v. 7] " a dew from Jehovah," with the Homeric phrase " snow ἐκ Διός," and the Latin *sub Jove*, the author concludes that Jehovah signifies *heaven* and the *God of heaven*.

[2] Theologischer Commentar zum Pentateuch, 1843, vol. i. p. 30.

[3] Die biblisch-prophetische Theologie, 1845, p. 120.

name undoubtedly appears in the circumlocution, "who is, and was, and comes," (Rev. i. 4, 8 ; iv. 8) ; but even there, in and after chap. xi. 17, according to the best MSS., the predicate ὁ ἐρχόμενος, *who comes*, is dropped after the *was* and *is*, because " the future of God's kingdom had become present, the coming had come."[1]

3. *The relation of Elohim and Jehovah.*

Much of the fine-spun distinctions of German orthodox writers on this subject must, it is apprehended, be rejected, equally with the superficialities of the Neologians. Whatever may be the relation of the two names, it does not appear that much light is thrown on the matter by the definition : " Elohim is the *God of the beginning* and of the *end*, the Creator and the Judge ; Jehovah is the *God of the middle*, of the development lying in the midst between the beginning and the end."[2] Nor is there much to recommend it in the view that Elohim is the more general, and Jehovah the more deep and discriminating name of the Godhead. But still more reprehensible is the distinction, according to which Elohim is an *appellative*, while Jehovah is the *proper name* of the only true God worshipped in Israel.[3]

The distinction of the two names appears to consist in the manner, and not in the degree, by which the Divine Being makes himself known. Elohim designates God as manifested in general, and intimates the relation which, as Creator, he sustains towards his creatures—the Mighty One, the Almighty ; Jehovah, the relation in which he stands to his fallen creature, man, to whom he has communicated his purpose of redemption. God reveals himself in creation and in his providential government, and it is difficult to estimate how fully God might be thus revealed to unfallen creatures, but it would still have been as Elohim. It is only in connexion with man's recovery from the Fall, that the Creator has made himself known as Jehovah, or *He that is to be manifested*, or to come. This will appear from the following considerations :—

(1.) Previous to the Fall and the promise of a Deliverer, the name Jehovah does not appear to have been known ; so that

---

[1] *Hengstenberg*, Com. on Revelation, vol. i. p. 67, Fairbairn's Translation.
[2] *Kurtz*, Die Einheit, p. 11.
[3] *Tiele*, in Studien u. Kritiken, 1852, p. 72.

it cannot be said with Baumgarten, that " the name Jehovah
has *survived* the Fall, and shines now in a new light, in the
light of grace and promise." Before the Fall, in every instance
where mention is made of God, it is as Elohim. Of course
such instances are very few, for the historian's own mode of
designating God as Elohim, or Jehovah-Elohim, must obviously
be excluded. The only passage, then, in which the true state
of the question appears, is Gen. iii. 1-5, " Now the serpent
was more subtile than any beast of the field which JEHOVAH-
ELOHIM (the historian's designation of God) had made. And
he said to the woman, Yea, hath ELOHIM said, Ye shall not eat
of every tree of the garden ? And the woman said unto the
serpent, We may eat of the fruit of the trees of the garden :
but of the fruit of the tree which is in the midst of the garden,
ELOHIM hath said, Ye shall not eat of it, neither shall ye touch
it, lest ye die. And the serpent said unto the woman, Ye
shall not surely die : for ELOHIM doth know, that in the
day ye eat thereof, then your eyes shall be opened ; and ye
shall be as ELOHIM (בֵּאלֹהִים), knowing good and evil." Dreschler's
note—" The irrational creature, the serpent, can know and speak
only of Elohim," is utterly worthless. Even the explanation of
Hengstenberg on this subject is unsatisfactory :—" The master
stroke of the tempter's policy was to change Jehovah into Elohim—the living, holy God, into a *nescio quod numen*. . . . The
woman should have employed the name Jehovah as an impene-
trable shield to repel the fiery darts of the wicked one. The use
of the name Elohim (*that this is not to be accounted for from
ignorance of the name Jehovah is proved by* ch. iv. 1) was the
beginning of her fall." The parenthetic clause is an assumption which has not the shadow of a foundation ; chap. iv. 1 evi-
dencing only the woman's knowledge, at a subsequent period,
previous to which she had been favoured with special communications from God.

(2.) But that passage shews, that soon *after* the Fall the
name Jehovah was known and in use. Whether justified or
not in tracing its origin to the revelation made at the Fall, it
is certain that the first indication of the knowledge of this
name is in Eve's exclamation on the birth of her first-born,
" I have gotten a man, Jehovah," which, whatever difficulties
may attach to it, or whatever may have been the views the

mother of mankind entertained regarding this first-born of women, must, according to strict philological rules, be thus rendered.[1] There can be little doubt, however, that the feelings which thus found expression were closely connected with the *promised Deliverer*, and that Eve somehow fancied that this her son was He—the יְהוָה that was to appear. By this it is by no means meant to affirm, that she was fully aware of the import of the name, or of the relation between Jehovah and Elohim. Indeed, the contrary appears from her grievous mistake. When, again, on the birth of Seth, Eve says, (Gen. iv. 25,) "*Elohim* hath given me another seed instead of Abel," there is no evidence to shew that her pious feelings, as Hengstenberg affirms, were less lively than on the former occasion— that they went no farther than an acknowledgment of God's general providence, while she saw in her first-born a blessed pledge of his grace. It would rather seem to be a correction of her previous painful mistake.

(3.) That *Jehovah* is the proper designation of God, as the Redeemer, and points especially to a *future* manifestation connected with redemption, is confirmed by Exod. vi. 2, 3, 6, 7. " Elohim spake to Moses, and said to him, I, Jehovah ; and I appeared to Abraham, to Isaac, and to Jacob, by El-Shadai ; but by my name Jehovah was I not known to them. . . . Wherefore say to the children of Israel, I, Jehovah, . . . I will redeem you. . . . I will take you to me for a people, and I will be to you a God (לֵאלֹהִים), and ye shall know that I, JEHOVAH, [am] *your* ELOHIM." This appearance of God in behalf of his people in Egypt, was an epoch in the history of redemption, and now for the first time was clearly revealed the relation of Jehovah and Elohim. The identity of persons represented by these names openly declared in this remarkable passage, may have been but dimly apprehended, or entirely overlooked by Eve ; but it was fully realized by Noah in the words, (Gen. ix. 26,) " Blessed be the Lord God of Shem " (יְהוָה אֱלֹהֵי שֵׁם), though again probably lost sight of in the immediately succeeding ages, when Divine truths were much corrupted and obscured. From the time of the Exodus, however, this particular truth, by an explicit revelation, is placed in the clearest

---

[1] See Part II., *Excursus*—" *On the First Promise.*"

light, and is henceforth never lost sight of, through the subsequent dispensations.

(4.) Accordingly, when Christ appeared as the promised Redeemer, he appropriated to himself forms of expression which could not fail to impress on his hearers the belief that he claimed to be regarded as the Jehovah of the prior revelations. Thus, John viii. 58, " Verily, verily, I say unto you, Before Abraham was, *I am*" (ἐγώ εἰμι), where there is not merely a claim to absolute and eternal being, but a reference also to the Divine appellation, (Exod. iii. 14,) which the LXX. render ἐγώ εἰμι ὁ ὤν. This, and numerous other passages which it is unnecessary to adduce, shew that, though, as already stated, the full name Jehovah occurs only in the Apocalypse, the idea itself holds an important place in other parts of the New Testament. He that in former ages and dispensations was known as ὁ ἐρχόμενος—" the coming One," (Matt. xi. 3,) now that in the fulness of time he has appeared, is constantly spoken of in the *present* or *past* tense by the New Testament writers, until the ὁ ἐρχόμενος again makes its appearance, in that portion of the Sacred Volume whose face is directed to the future, in that full and unmistakable form of expression which is universally admitted to be a paraphrase of the name Jehovah—Rev. i. 8 : " I am Alpha and Omega, the beginning and the ending, saith the Lord, *which is, and which was,* and which is to come, the Almighty." So chap. iv. 8 : " They rest not day and night, saying, Holy, holy, holy, Lord God Almighty, which was, and is, and is to come," where, and in the parallel passages, the expression *to come* refers to the future developments and triumphs of God's kingdom, when the Lord God Almighty, *who is, and was,* shall reign, having taken to him his great power (chap. xi. 17).

If the above be a correct view of the relation of Elohim and Jehovah, and if it be one of the main designs of the inspired writers to point out the personal identity thus undoubtedly existing, a very simple explanation can be given of the interchange of these names in the opening chapters of the Bible.

Throughout the first section of Genesis, the historian speaks of God only as ELOHIM, *the Almighty*—the character in which he is made known by creation, (Rom. i. 20,) and in which he was alone known to unfallen man. Utterly incorrect is the remark of Hengstenberg,—" The contents of this section are in general of a kind that the name Jehovah might have been suitably employed." Granted that the name Jehovah frequently designates the Creator of heaven and earth, it is only after the end proposed to himself by the writer of Genesis has been reached, that such is the case. In the first chapter, to designate the Divine Being as Jehovah, would have been altogether to defeat this purpose, which was to identify Elohim and Jehovah, the Creator and Redeemer, one of the most precious truths of the New Testament, but the germs of which are thus met with in Genesis. To attain his object, the writer must first distinctly settle the idea to be attached to the name Elohim.

In section *third*, beginning with chap. iv., the historian in his own person invariably uses the name Jehovah, but not until he has shewn that it was known and recognised, verse 1. Here, again, there is occasion to differ from Hengstenberg, when he says, that in most passages of this section, though Jehovah is in itself more suitable, yet Elohim might stand. As the writer of Genesis must, to attain his purpose, in the first section have used Elohim, so now, when he has entered on a new period of human history, and a new phase of revelation, wherein Jehovah is made known, he must employ that term in order to familiarize the reader with it, and so fix and define the idea.

Keeping this in view, the use in the intermediate section of the form Jehovah-Elohim is easily accounted for. In section *first*, the writer's purpose was to define the name Elohim, and in section *third*, Jehovah. Accordingly, to prepare for the transition, and especially to connect the two ideas, he invariably employs in the *second* section a designation equivalent to the phrase, *Jehovah who is Elohim.* That such is the object is evident from the fact, that when the transition is effected, and the idea firmly established, the compound designation is dropped. The writer has established the identity of Jehovah and Elohim, he has laid the foundation of the great principle of redemption, proclaimed by God in his communication to Moses (Exod. vi.)—a principle on which the Gospel sheds abundant light, in the acts and attributes of our glorious Redeemer.

The interchange of the Divine names, in the first three sections of Genesis, being thus shewn to be indicative of

design, not only is the foundation of the Document-hypothesis
thereby shattered, but the most incontrovertible proof is
thence deduced of the internal unity of these sections. It is
unnecessary to pursue this matter farther, but a few words
may be added in regard to the remainder of Genesis. After
the purpose of the historian, as stated above, had been attained,
it would seem that he, in a great measure, if not altogether, used
the names promiscuously, and this the rather to confirm the
idea of identity already established. This will account for the
remarks of Hengstenberg, already adverted to, that Jehovah
frequently appears as the Creator of heaven and earth. Besides, the change of Divine names in other parts of Scripture
shews plainly that the sacred writers did not always lay much
stress on their distinctive significance. Thus, in 2 Sam. vii.
18-25, in David's prayer before Jehovah, the form *Adonai-
Jehovah* occurs four times, followed by *Jehovah-Elohim* twice ;
while in the parallel passage, 1 Chron. xvii. 16, 17, the names
are in the order, *Jehovah-Elohim, Elohim, Jehovah-Elohim,
Jehovah.* No other satisfactory explanation of the interchange
of the Divine names in the Pentateuch has yet been given.
All the attempts of Hengstenberg, Dreschler, and others, to
account for it from the character of the contents of the respective sections are manifest, and in part admitted failures.

II.—DIVERSITY OF STYLE—AN ARGUMENT OF THE DOCUMENT-
HYPOTHESIS.

The diversity of style, in the first and second sections of
Genesis, has also been adduced in support of the view which represents them as the productions of two different authors, giving
distinct accounts of creation. A difference of style, however,
does not necessarily lead to this conclusion. Instead of being
indications of a diversity of authorship, it may be only the
natural result of a change of subject, or of the manner in
which the writer wishes to present that subject. Besides,
arguments of this sort can properly be resorted to, only where
the materials are of considerable extent, and the subjects
similar.

It is not to be admitted, though confidently affirmed by the
advocates of the Document-hypothesis, that there are two

narratives of creation. The first section of Genesis is a narrative of creation, properly so called,—a comprehensive, continuous, and entire sketch of creation, in all its fulness and extent. As Eichhorn[1] represents it, but for a totally different purpose, " There lies at the foundation of the first chapter a carefully designed plan, all whose parts are carried out with much art, whereby its appropriate place is assigned to every idea." The historian, in a few simple sentences, sketches, in prominent outline, his great subject, the creation of the universe, and more particularly the part of it designed for the residence of man. He does not pause in his lofty march to notice minutiæ, or distract the reader with details. He introduces the great First Cause operating by a simple fiat, and straightway describes the effects in rapid and consecutive order. But having reached that point in the narrative which tells of the creation of man, for whose dwelling-place earth was prepared, was clothed in beauty and replenished with life, and for whose instruction the volume of inspiration was written, the historian pauses, as it were, a moment—not to deviate from his straight and onward course, but to insert a mark, a *nota bene*, to arrest the reader's attention, and stimulate inquiry into matters which could not be fitly discussed at this stage, but which were to be introduced by way of appendix in the chapter that followed.

The second chapter, accordingly, is occupied with a detailed account of the creation of man, male and female, with full particulars as to his character and condition, his place in creation, and his relation to God. Whatever else is introduced is subordinate to this. In no sense, then, can these two chapters be viewed as distinct narratives of creation. The first is a narrative of creation in all its parts and proportions, but sketched, as already said, only in outline ; while the second is a filling up of one of the compartments of this grand picture. The second chapter consists of details, which could not well have been introduced into the first without marring its plan and symmetry, and yet could not be omitted without prejudice to the narrative of the Fall, which immediately succeeds it ; between which and the second chapter there is, by universal acknowledgment, an inseparable connexion.

[1] Einleitung in d. alte Testament, 1823, vol. iii. p. 40.

The second chapter, dealing as it does in details, describing creation not as a whole, but in one prominent particular,—is it reasonable to assume that it must conform to the style and oratorical structure of the first ? Is not the reverse of this a more natural conclusion, and is not a change of style befitting the change of subject ? In the present case, the most beautiful harmony is, in this respect, manifested and maintained. The spirit of the narration is one and identical throughout, though in every part its embodiment or drapery may not be the same. The writer of the second and third chapters of Genesis is none other than the writer of the first, for anything to the contrary to be inferred from the diversity of style.

With these remarks the matter might be dismissed, but as much stress is laid on peculiarities of expression said to be characteristic of the different writers, it may be well to examine these so far as applicable to the present subject. The following expressions peculiar to the Elohim document, so far as regards Gen. i.-iii., are taken from De Wette,[1] with an enumeration of the other passages of Genesis where they also occur.

Gen. i. 27. זָכָר וּנְקֵבָה, *male and female ;* v. 2, vi. 19, vii. 16, for which the Jehovah document uses אִישׁ וְאִשְׁתּוֹ, *man and his wife,* vii. 2, [De Wette omits to note that verse 3 has the other form.]

i. 22, 28. פְּרוּ וּרְבוּ, *be fruitful and multiply.* [The other passages, viii. 17, xvii. 20, xxviii. 3, xxxv. 11, xlvii. 27, xlviii. 4, are parallel as to combination of verbs, but not as to form.]

מִין, *kind,* or *species,* in the forms—

i. 11. מִינוֹ; ver. 12, 21, מִינֵהוּ; ver. 24, 25, מִינָהּ, vi. 20, vii 14. Additional expressions adduced by Knobel :[2]—

חַיָּה, *a beast,* ver. 28 ; חַיְתּ־דָאָרֶץ, *a wild beast,* ver. 24, 25, 30.

שָׁרַץ, *to swarm* with, and שֶׁרֶץ, *creatures that swarm,* ver. 21, 22.

רָמַשׂ, *to crawl;* and רֶמֶשׂ, *worms,* ver. 21, 24, 25, 26, 28, 30.

אָכְלָה, *food,* ver. 30 ; מִקְוֶה, *a place of assemblage,* ver. 10.

This list might be summarily disposed of, with the simple remark, that its contents do not tell the one way or the other.

[1] Einleitung in d. alte Test. 1852, p. 180.
[2] Die Genesis erklärt, 1852, p. 6.

Particular words and phrases occur in the first section, but not in the second, for the very obvious reason that, from the absence of similar ideas, they are not needed. To the objection that they recur in other passages assigned to the Elohim document, but not in those distinguished by the name Jehovah, it may be replied, either there is force in the argument drawn from the peculiarity of style in the first chapter, or there is little or no weight due to it. If the first alternative be admitted, it separates that chapter as well from the Elohim as from the other document. Indeed Eichhorn, the great reviver of the scheme, admits[1] that, strictly speaking, the Elohim document begins with chap. v. If, then, the first chapter be not connected with, nor form part of the document in question, nothing can be deduced from the circumstance that the above expressions are also found in it. But if the second alternative be admitted, and no weight attached to the diversity of style, the peculiarities of expression can avail nothing, in constituting a line of demarcation between sections otherwise connected. Further, there are specialities attaching to a narrative of creation, which distinguish it from all others, so that it need excite no surprise that the writer should have to avail himself of expressions not required in any other case, or under ordinary circumstances.

But a closer investigation will convince the reader that the expressions constantly and confidently appealed to, are not so peculiar to the Elohim document as is represented.

The phrase זכר ונקבה occurs in Gen. vii. 3, " a passage which," as Delitzsch remarks, "evidently stands in a Jehovistic context." Tuch gets over the difficulty, by boldly attributing the expression to a change introduced by the editor—the usual resort when facts will not square with theories. But farther, it has been shown by Kurtz,[2] from an examination as well of the etymology as of the usage, that this formula is by no means synonymous with איש ואשתו, as is generally assumed. The former expression regards the distinction of sex from its physical side, the latter considers it in an ethical relation, and as such, it *properly* applies only to man. In the use of the one or the other, design is evinced in selecting that which is the proper exponent of the sense.

---

[1] Einleitung, vol. iii. p. 110.   [2] Beiträge, pp. 79-89.

The combination פרו ורבו occurs only in passages assigned to the Elohim document, but is not always used there, in places where it might be expected. Thus Gen. i. 22, in blessing the fish, the two verbs are conjoined, but in blessing the fowl רבה only is used. It also occurs in Jer. iii. 16, xxiii. 3, Ezek. xxxvi. 11, proving that it was not peculiar to *one* author or age.

מין, always with לְ prefixed and with a pronominal affix, occurs only in the narrative of creation, the history of the flood, (Gen. vi.) and the Levitical precepts concerning food.—(Lev. xi.; Deut. xiv.) Out of the Pentateuch it is found only in Ezek. xlvii. 10, which shows how little stress can be fairly laid on this rare expression.

For חית-הארץ, the historian uses, in chaps. ii. and iii., חַיַּת הַשָּׂדֶה, *beast of the field.* Kurtz[1] thus accounts for the change : The word שדה does not occur in the first section, but is repeatedly used in the second, in the designation. of plants and animals, (Gen. ii. 5, 19, 20; iii. 1,) and this from the change in the writer's point of view. The scene of the second section is the garden in Eden, man's residence; and the contrast is between גַּן, *the garden,* and שָׂדֶה, *the out-field,* or between man in the garden, and the beasts in, or *of the field.* In the other case the contrast was between the sea and the *dry land,* and the living creatures of the one and of the other. Hence the use of אֶרֶץ.

שֶׁרֶץ and שֶׁרֶץ are excluded from the list by Delitzsch, a defender of the Document scheme: "although," he says, "onwards to Exod. vi. they occur in an Elohim connexion, yet שֶׁרֶץ (Exod. vii. 28) stands in a context considered to belong to the Jehovah document."

רֶמֶשׂ is found Gen. vi. 7, in what is admitted to belong to the Jehovah document.

אָכְלָה, but only in the form לְאָכְלָה, occurs again, Gen. vi. 21 ; ix. 3. The usual word for *food* is מַאֲכָל, Gen. ii. 9 ; iii. 6 ; vi. 21 ; xl. 17. According to Lee, the former expression should be rendered *eating* or *consuming,* and not *food.*

מִקְוֶה does not occur again in Genesis, but is found in Exod. vii. 19 ; Lev. xi. 36.

It has been farther objected to, that for בָּרָא, *to create,* of the first section, the second substitutes יָצַר, *to form.* But if chap.

---

[1] Beiträge, p. 103.

ii. 4, be reckoned to belong to the second section, then בּרא
occurs there, which Tuch as usual ascribes to the editor. In
Gen. ii. 7, grammatical reasons exclude this verb, but it occurs,
Gen. vi. 7, in a Jehovah section.

III.—THE ALLEGED CONTRADICTIONS OF CHAPTERS I. AND II.

These chiefly relate to the order of creation, as stated in the
two chapters. It is at once admitted that the arrangement of
the matter of the second chapter differs from that of the first ;
and farther, it is beyond question that the arrangement of the
first chapter is in the strict order of time. The only point in dispute is, whether the order of the second is also that of time, or
is not greatly modified by other considerations. To sustain the
allegation of contradictions, arising from diversity of arrangement, it must be shown that the order of time is intended to
be observed in the two cases. But this can be only maintained by mistaking entirely the nature and aim of the second
narrative. The second chapter does not run parallel with the
first, nor can it be called a continuation of it, for it does not take
up the history at the point where the other drops it. It is
properly an appendix to the first narrative, which, although
complete in itself, and sufficient to answer its own purpose, yet
omitted many things necessary to the elucidation of the history
of the Fall, or it may be equally regarded as the introduction to
that history. But whether viewed as an appendix to the one
narrative, or as an introduction to the other, it is a necessary link
in the chain. Its contents are accordingly laid out in groups ;
so that the parts and paragraphs thus constituted partly refer
to the preceding context, are partly related to one another,
and serve partly to introduce chapter third.[1] Even Tuch admits that in all this there may be traced a well-considered plan.

But to proceed to an examination of the more important
contradictions adduced. It is affirmed by the advocates of the
document theory,—

1. That chap. ii. 5-9 teaches, contrary to chap. i., that the
creation of man preceded that of plants. Tuch farther notices
the contrast in the way in which the production of plants is
here spoken of, compared with chap. i. :—" There, at the com-

---

[1] *Hävernick*, Einleitung in d. alte Test. 1836, I. ii. 214.

mand of God, the earth brings forth vegetation ; here it must
rain, that plants may spring up in a natural way."[1] But this
distinction is of no moment. The one statement differs from
the other, only in being more specific, and in referring to one
of the conditions, without which plants cannot exist. The
only difficulty lies in the supposed necessity of man's presence,
and by implication his existence prior to the growth of the
vegetable kingdom.

There is great diversity of opinion, as to where the second
section begins. The most probable supposition is, that it
commences in the middle of verse 4. " In the day that Jehovah-Elohim made," &c. Then is added, " And every shrub of
the field was not yet in the earth," i.e., according to a Hebrew
idiom, " no shrub of the field was yet in the earth, and no
herb of the field had yet sprung up, or sprouted." The reader
is thus carried back to a period of creation antecedent to the
vegetable productions. But this state of the earth is not to
continue,—so much is implied in טֶרֶם, not yet ; but is to be
remedied when the necessary conditions shall enter in : " For
Jehovah-Elohim had not caused it to rain upon the earth ;
and no man to till the ground." What, then, is the connexion
between rain and man in this statement relative to the
absence of plants ? Are the two agencies referred to as necessary conditions of vegetable existence? This can hardly be
affirmed, if only common sense be allowed to the writer of
Genesis. Mention is made of man, and the fact of his non-
existence at that period is adverted to, because his creation is
to be the main theme of this chapter ; and no mention would
have been made of the creation of plants, but for their connexion with man—adorning his dwelling-place, supplying him
with food, and serving to test his obedience. That such is the
case appears from verse 6 : "And a mist went up from the earth,
and watered the whole face of the ground," which was thus made
capable of supporting vegetable life. But without mentioning
its introduction, as might have been expected from verse 5,
and as would undoubtedly have been the case had the order of
time only been attended to, the historian proceeds straightway
to his main subject, the creation of man (ver. 7) ; with which
again is connected the preparation of the garden in Eden, and

---

[1] Kommentar üb. d. Genesis, 1838, p. 38.

his location in it ; and it is only after man is thus disposed of, that the writer returns (verse 9) to describe the plants passed over in verse 5. Then, again, after a digression as to the situation of the garden (verses 10-14), he returns to man and his connexion with it (ver. 15), incidentally touched on, verse 8. There are not, then, two contradictory accounts of the origin of the vegetable kingdom ; nor is there anything to shew that the second narrative conceived of it as posterior to the creation of man. The purport of this narrative is to shew, that the first glance of man fell on an earth adorned with all the gifts and blessings of a bountiful Creator. In order to obviate any difficulty or contradiction in the statements of the two chapters, it is not at all necessary to suppose that the herbs and trees had not attained to their full size,[1] or that the vegetable creation had not shone forth in its full beauty, until man was created,[2] or even to assume that the vegetable creation of chap. i. refers to the fossil flora, while that of chap. ii. 5-9 refers to the plants now existing.[3]

2. Another contradiction is said to occur in chap. ii. 18, 19, which, as is alleged, teaches that man was created previous to the lower animals. The difficulty lies in the two verbs, ויצר and ויבא, of the same tense, verse 19 : " Out of the ground the Lord God *formed* every beast of the field, and every fowl of the air, and *brought* them to Adam," &c.

The older versions and expositions, as also some modern writers, get over the difficulty by translating the first verb as a *pluperfect;* but for this there is no grammatical authority. Others assume a second creation of animals, and such as are more serviceable to man. Kurtz[4] proposes another solution, according to which he conceives that the passage is equivalent to ·" God brought the beasts, which he had formed, to Adam." He founds this on what he considers a Hebrew rule :—" Two consecutive imperfects, with *vau consec.* closely connected by unity of subject, (and mostly also by unity of object,) so fall under one point of view, that the progress intimated by the *vau consec.* is not conceived of through the first imperfect, but

---

[1] *Ranke,* Untersuchungen üb. d. Pentateuch, 1834, vol. i. p. 164.
[2] *Hävernick,* Einleitung, I. ii. 214.
[3] *Dreschler,* Die Einheit u. Aechtheit, p. 79.
[4] Die Einheit, p. 11.

through both combined. The emphasis of thought lies then on the *second* imperfect, and the *first* sinks into the subordinate place of a relative or parenthetic clause." Deut. xxxi. 9 is referred to as an example. Moses in his last days summons Joshua, and exhorts him to be of good courage, verses 7, 8 ; then is added, verse 9, " And Moses *wrote* (ויכתב) this law, and *gave* it (ויתנה) to the priests . . . and commanded them," &c. This does not imply that Moses wrote the law in the interval between his exhortation to Joshua, and the delivery of it to the priests. It is evidently this : Moses exhorted Joshua, and then committed to the priests the law which he had written, (previously to this transaction,) and exhorted them at its delivery, and in consequence of this trust. Whether this explanation be satisfactory or not, one thing is plain, that the idea most prominent in the mind of the historian was not the creation of the animals, but the fact of their being brought to Adam. Had it been his object to describe their creation, he has done so very cursorily, and has omitted to enumerate many and large classes of the animal world. But as it is plain, from a careful consideration of the second chapter, that no mention would have been made of the vegetable creation but for its connexion with man, so it is no less evident, that no notice would have been taken of the animal creation, but for the circumstance of their being brought to the man in furtherance of a purpose entertained towards him by the Creator.

3. A contradiction is pointed out in the statements of the two chapters regarding the origin of the winged tribes. Thus, according to Gen. i. 20, " God said, Let *the waters* bring forth abundantly the moving creature that hath life, and *fowl that may fly* above the earth," &c. But according to Gen. ii. 19, " And *out of the ground* the Lord God formed every beast of the field, and *every fowl of the air*." This contradiction is, however, easily explained. It is not found in the original, but is owing to a mistranslation of the first of the two passages in the English, and several other ancient and modern versions, as Onkelos, the LXX., the Vulgate, and Luther. The correct rendering is given in the margin of our Bible, and is that of Calvin, Junius, and Tremelius, Le Clerc, De Wette, and many others : " *Let fowl fly*," &c., ועוף יעופף, referring not to their origin, but to the sphere in which they were to move ;

while the design of the other passage is to shew the source whence the beasts and birds originated.

The above constitute the more important contradictions alleged to be found in these narratives. Assuming their reality, and the absence of any satisfactory solution of the difficulties thus presented against the internal unity of the chapters in question, if they avail anything in proof of a diversity of authorship, it is in favour of the earlier form of the Document-hypothesis, now given up as untenable by universal consent, and against the complementary scheme of Tuch, at present the only one in repute. But so far from being contradictions, the matters adverted to are rather indications of one author, with unity of design. The historian, having in the first chapter sufficiently settled all questions bearing on the *order* of creation, feels at greater liberty in the second to deviate from this arrangement wherever his plan required it, in the consciousness that he could do so without being misunderstood. The plan of the first is seen clearly only by the light of the second. By this it appears as a distinct, entire, and regular whole. But it is only by taking the two narratives together that the reasons are apparent which induced the writer to notice *one* particular, or omit *another*, in his first chapter. Many things necessary to the full understanding of the subsequent transactions, but there passed over in silence, would certainly have been introduced, had not the writer fully proposed to reserve them for the second chapter of his history.

So much, then, for the arguments of the *disintegrating* criticism in its bearing on the present chapters,—arguments resting on the change of Divine names, diversity of style, and historical contradictions. Taken singly or combined, it cannot be said that they contribute much, if anything, towards the accomplishment of the purpose contemplated by their authors. Indeed, the internal unity of this portion of Scripture, it is not too much to conclude, if not more clearly evinced and firmly established by the trial, has at least come harmless out of the ordeal.

SECT. IV.—THE BIBLICAL CREATION COMPARED WITH HEATHEN
COSMOGONIES.

It is well known to students of antiquity, that cosmogonies
and geogonies, or attempts to account for the origin of the
universe, and of the earth in particular, with its varied forms
of life, are met with among all ancient nations whose literature
or traditions have in any way been preserved. Such cosmogonies, in many cases, constituted an important part of the
sacred books of these nations, and were in all instances, perhaps, closely connected with their religious systems. These
facts have not escaped the notice of the enemies of the Bible ;
and, without farther examination, they at once conclude that
the account of Creation in Genesis stands on a level with the
myths and legends in question.[1] It is of importance, therefore, to examine the matter in order to test the soundness of
this conclusion, and see if one directly the reverse may not
reasonably be deduced from the same premises.

Granting that there are many remarkable similarities in the
biblical and non-biblical cosmogonies, it cannot be denied by
any one acquainted with the subject that there are also many
and wide diversities. In so far as the points of similarity are
concerned, it is now proposed to show that there are indications that the Mosaic narrative is truth and not fiction, while
the differences between it and the Heathen cosmogonies
attest this truth to be a revelation from God.

[1] Of this description, notwithstanding the disclaimer of the author to the effect
that he does not belong to the Orthodox, Infidel, or Rationalistic class of commentators, (Pref. p. vi.) is a work entitled—" Quæstiones Mosaicæ, or the First Part of
the Book of Genesis compared with the Remains of Ancient Religions." By
Osmond De Beauvour Priaulx, 2d ed., Lond. 1854. The principles of exposition
are thus stated : " I looked for his (Moses') view, not in the fables of the Talmud-
ists or in the ponderous tomes of commentators, but in the Vedas, the laws of
Menu, the Zendavesta, the Kings of China, the traditions of Greece, and the
legends and customs of half-civilized man. I found different nations uttering the
same cry, speaking the same thought, though not indeed in the same phrase, and
I made nation interpret the language of nation."—(Pp. vi. vii.) The result, according to this writer, is, that the cosmogony of Genesis is superior to that of Menu,
but still is only an invention of Moses or some of his predecessors (p. 45) ; while
the history of the Fall is " a fragment from the philosophy of the earliest ages,
which neither demands our belief, nor is necessary to our faith, but which is full of
instruction for us by the deep insight it gives into the simple creed of infant man."
—P. 92.

I.—ACCORDANCE OF ANCIENT COSMOGONIES WITH THE BIBLICAL.

The cosmogonies of heathenism differ widely from one another in form and character ; and yet on a closer view, it is found that they exhibit not a few points of internal relation with a remarkable sameness in their leading principles. This has been noticed and acknowledged by all who have given attention to the subject. To quote only the words of Tuch :— " However great the diversity of these theories of creation, it cannot but be observed that it is the same key-notes which, in the most varied harmonies, sound from the Ganges to the Nile, and even re-echo in the oldest philosophemes of the West."[1]. But it is not merely a resemblance among themselves which can be thus detected, there is also a remarkable accordance, in many particulars, with the Mosaic account of the Creation. This will appear from the subjoined abridgment of the Cosmogonies of the Egyptians, Phœnicians, Indians, and other ancient nations.

1. The account of the origin of the Universe given by Diodorus Siculus,[2] and which is regarded as the theory of the Egyptians, is in substance as follows. At the beginning heaven and earth were blended together, but afterwards the elements began to separate and the air to move. The fiery particles, owing to their levity, rose to the upper regions ; the muddy and turbid matter, after it had been incorporated with the humid, subsided by its own weight. By continued motion the watery parts separated and formed the sea : the more solid constituted the dry land. Warmed and fecundated by the sun, the earth still soft, produced different kinds of creatures, which, according as the fiery, watery, or earthy matter predominated in their constitution, became inhabitants of the sky, the water, or the land. Latterly the earth, more and more hardened by the sun and wind, could no longer produce any of the larger animals ; but they began to propagate by generation.[3] Another idea of the Egyptians was that there was boundless darkness in the abyss and a subtile spirit intellec-

---

[1] Kommentar üb. die Genesis, p. 5.

[2] Comp. Eusebius, Præparatio Evangelica, i. 7.

[3] With this agrees in general the scheme of Ovid ; only he admits that it was a god that arranged chaos into a world ; and also made man in the image of the gods, and appointed him ruler on earth. Metam. i. 5.

tual in power, existing in chaos. But the holy light broke
forth, and the elements were produced from among the sand
of a watery essence.[1]

2. The Phœnician Cosmogony given by Eusebius[2] from
Sanchoniathon, is as follows:—The first principle of the
Universe was a dark windy air and an eternal dark chaos.
Through the love of the spirit (πνεῦμα) to its own principles,
a mixture arose, and a connexion called *desire* (πόθος), the
beginning of all things. From this connexion of the spirit was
begotten *mot* (μῶτ), which, according to some, signified *mud*,
according to others, a corruption of a watery mixture, but is
probably a *feminine* form of מוֹ, *i.q.* מֵי, *water*. From this were
developed creatures in the shape of an egg, called *Zophasemin*,
a term generally considered as formed from צֹפֵי שָׁמַיִם, *the observers
of heaven*,[3] but by some taken to be compounded of צָפֶּה שׁ, *the
expanse of heaven*. Mōt and the stars began to shine. The
air being lighted up by the heat communicated to the earth
and sea, there arose winds and clouds; and the thunder of the
contending elements roused from slumber the creatures before
mentioned, which then, male and female, moved on the earth
and in the sea. Another form of this tradition is, that from
the wind *Kolpia*, κολπία, (קוֹל פִּי־יָה, *the sound of the mouth of Jah*,
or, according to others, קוֹל פִּיחַ, *the blowing of the wind*, or of the
spirit,[4]) and his wife Baau, Βάαυ, (בֹּהוּ), were brought forth two
mortals, Aiōn and Prōtogonos, and from these were produced
Genos and Genea who peopled Phœnicia. *Baau*, the producing principle in this tradition, is evidently the same as *Mōt*
of the other; *Kolpia*, the creative spirit, is πνεῦμα (רוּחַ מְרַחֶפֶת,
the brooding spirit, Gen. i. 2) of the other tradition, corresponding to the moving and moved air, which, according to
Diodorus, separated the elements.

3. The Babylonian Cosmogony, according to Berosus,[5] began
thus:—There was a time when all was darkness and water,
wherein moved frightful animals of compound forms; the ruler
of which was a woman named *Homōroka*, a term said to signify
the ocean. The supreme God, Bel, divided the darkness, and
cut the woman into two parts, out of which he formed heaven

---

[1] Wilkinson's *Ancient Egyptians*, 1847, vol. iv. p. 218.

[2] Præpar. Evang. i. 10. See Ewald, Abhandlung üb. d. Phönïkischen Ansichten
von der Weltschöpfung, 1851.   [3] Ewald, *l. c.* p. 37.

[4] Röth, Geschichte der Philosophie, i. 250.   [5] Eusebius, Chron. Armen. i. 22.

and earth. Bel cut off his own head ; and the gods, from the blood mixed with earth, formed men, who consequently partake of divine intelligence.

4. The fertile imagination of India produced cosmogonies of the most varied forms. One of the oldest is the teaching of Menù. According to this, at first all was dark ; the world still rested in the purpose of the Eternal, whose first thought created water, and in it the seed of life. This became an egg from which issued Brahma, the creative power who divided his own substance and became male and female. The waters are called *nárá*, because the production of Nara, or the spirit of God ; and since they were his first *ayana*, or place of motion, He is on this account named Náráyana, or, *moving on the waters*.[1] The mundane egg of this and other Eastern traditions,

[1] To this may be added a remarkable hymn from the Rig Veda—in a metrical version, by Dr. Max Müller, in Bunsen's *Phil. of Univ. Hist.*, i. 140. "In judging of it, says the translator, we should bear in mind that it was not written by a Gnostic or by a Pantheistic philosopher, but by a poet who felt all these doubts and problems as his own, without any wish to convince or to startle, only uttering what had been weighing on his own mind."

> " Nor Aught nor Nought existed ; yon bright sky
> Was not, nor heaven's broad woof outstretched above.
> What covered all ? what sheltered ? what concealed ?
> Was it the water's fathomless abyss ?
> There was not death—yet was there nought immortal :
> There was no confine betwixt day and night ;
> The only One breathed breathless by itself,
> Other than It there nothing since has been.
> Darkness there was, and all at first was veiled
> In gloom profound—an ocean without light ;
> The germ that still lay covered in the husk
> Burst forth, one nature, from the fervent heat.
> Then first came love upon it, the new spring
> Of mind—yea, poets in their hearts discerned,
> Pondering, this bond between created things
> And uncreated. Comes this spark from earth
> Piercing and all-pervading, or from heaven ?
> Then seeds were sown, and mighty powers arose—
> Nature below, and power and will above—
> Who knows the secret ? who proclaimed it here ?
> Whence, whence this manifold creation sprang ?
> The gods themselves came later into being—
> Who knows from whence this great creation sprang ?—
> He from whom all this great creation came,
> Whether his will created or was mute ?
> The Most High Seer that is in highest heaven,
> He knows it—or perchance even He knows not."

was also a doctrine of the Egyptians, from whom, probably, it was introduced by Orpheus to the knowledge of the Greeks.

5. To these cosmogonies may be added the traditions of the Etrurians and Parsees regarding the periods of creation. According to the Etrurian legends, God created in the first thousand years heaven and earth ; in the second, the vault of heaven ; in the third, the sea and the other waters of earth ; in the fourth, the sun, moon, and stars ; in the fifth, the inhabitants of the air, of the water, and of the land ; and in the sixth, man. The remaining six of the twelve thousand years of the supposed duration of the world will be the period of the human race.[1] So also the Persian traditions in the Zendavesta. Ormuzd, by his word Honover, created the visible Universe in six periods or thousands of years : First, the light between heaven and earth, together with the sky and the stars ; secondly, the waters which covered the earth were made to sink into its clefts, and clouds were formed ; thirdly, the earth was created, and, first, as its centre and heart, the highest mountain Albordj, afterwards the other mountains ; fourthly, the trees ; fifthly, the animals which all sprung from the primeval bull ; and sixthly, man, of whom the first was Kajomorts. At the close of each creative period, Ormuzd celebrated feasts with the heavenly inhabitants.[2] According to another tradition, preserved in a fragment of a Parsee MS. in the Bodleian Library, 3000 years passed before the earth was rendered useful ; for 3000 years Gayomorth dwelt alone in it : from the beginning of Gayomorth's reign to the resurrection are 6000 years. The same division is noticed by Theopompus, who states, six thousand years passed before the creation of the human race.[3] But besides the *long periods*, as they were styled by the ancient Persians, who had a particular term to designate them, it may be here added that there are found amongst almost all ancient nations traces of a week, or a period of seven days, and a character of sacredness attached to the number *seven* in general.

In these and other Cosmogonies which might be referred to, there is evidently much sameness, mixed up no doubt with much dissimilarity. The external form and features are very

---

[1] Suidas, Lexicon, *sub voce* Τυῤῥηνία.

[2] Rhode, Heilige Sage des Zendvolkes, 1820, pp. 213, 229.

[3] Zeitschrift d. Deutschen morgenländ. Gesellschaft, 1851, vol. v. p. 228.

unlike, but in all, points of relationship may be easily detected. Looking on these diversified and wide-spread traditions regarding the origin of things, in the light of witnesses of the beliefs generally, it may be, universally, entertained on that subject in ages long past, they are in many respects remarkable, but in nothing more so than in their unanimity as to certain fundamental ideas. When questioned separately, they doubtless give forth wild and incoherent utterances, but when brought together and their testimony compared, there is not a little that is both accordant with itself, and with the account of the creation which the Bible furnishes. To notice only a few particulars : there may be traced more or less distinctly in all, (1.) Intimations of a primeval darkness,[1] corresponding to the scriptural notice introductory to the work of creation, " there was darkness on the face of the deep." (2.) An unarranged chaos—an empty, desolate waste, or, according to the description in Genesis, " without form and void" (וָבֹהוּ תֹהוּ, *empty and desolate*), where may be particularly noticed the *Baau* of the Phœnician cosmogony. (3.) The preponderance of water in connexion with this state of things. (4.) The widely spread notions concerning the *mundane egg*, are evidently connected with the intimation in Genesis, " the Spirit of God moved (properly *brooded*) on the face of the waters ;" from which, it may be remarked, probably originated the symbolic designation of the Spirit as a *dove*. (5.) Another thing noticeable, especially in the Etrurian traditions, is the advance in creation from the imperfect to the higher and more perfect forms. And (6.) the origin of the animals from the earth, and man's likeness to the gods. The latter circumstance, in particular, is fully recognised by the classical writers of Greece and Rome ; being embodied in their fictions of Prometheus, who, forming men from clay, animated them with fire taken from heaven.

What account can be given of the dim but not doubtful accordance of these rude theories with the narrative of Creation in Genesis ? It cannot be the result of accident ; nor can it be shewn to have originated from anything in the nature of the case, nor in any general relation of the world to the human mind ; and yet, as Eichhorn remarks, " so great a resemblance

---

[1] In the Greek cosmogonies, *Night* is one of the first created beings—the daughter of Chaos, and the sister of Erebus, by whom she became the mother of Aether and Hemera.—Hesiod, *Theg.* 123.

in legends and conceptions is scarcely conceivable without a
common source."[1] Is it to be concluded, then, as is sometimes
done, that this common source is the biblical record ?[2] A
careful consideration of the subject will by no means warrant,
but rather preclude, any such conclusion ; for although the
influence of the Bible may have been felt by nations more or
less in the neighbourhood of the covenant people, yet it must
be seen and admitted, that these traditions are found also
among nations lying far beyond the range of such influences ;
and, moreover, that they can be traced back to the most remote
times. The only way of satisfactorily accounting for the phenomenon presented in the harmony of Cosmogonic theories, is
to regard it as the result of a primeval tradition extending
back to the cradle of the human race, but moulded in the
course of ages according to the tastes and tendencies of the
channels through which it was conveyed to the various regions
and tribes of earth.

But, it may be asked, what is gained for the confirmation of
Scripture from this collation of ancient Cosmogonies, for may
not its theory of creation be only one of the many to be met
with elsewhere,—or be only a tradition handed down through
the Israelitish nation, and, though preserved, it may be, in
greater purity than when passed through other hands, yet
added to and changed in the course of its transmission ? To
this it may be replied, were the matter even as here represented, enough is gained to prove, if not the entire historical
character of the Mosaic narrative, at least that it contains far
more truth than many modern critics are disposed to recognise.
The remarkable accordance of the biblical and non-biblical
Cosmogonies, in the particulars already indicated, incontestably
prove that they all rest on a basis of fact, however it may
have been discovered. But it is by contrasting the scriptural
narrative with the heathen Cosmogonies that the former is
seen in its proper light. By this its true historical character
will be vindicated, and it will approve itself as a revelation
from God,—not merely as the tradition of a primeval revelation made to the first man, but as an immediate revelation
vouchsafed to the writer of Genesis, who assigned to it the
chief place in his imperishable record.

[1] Einleitung, vol. iii. p. 20.
[2] Hävernick, in Cyclopædia of Biblical Literature, Art. *Genesis*, vol. i. p. 751.

II.—CONTRAST OF THE BIBLICAL AND NON-BIBLICAL COSMOGONIES.

Notwithstanding the points of agreement above indicated between the biblical and non-biblical cosmogonies, their differences are still more striking, affecting not merely the form, but the entire character of the subjects compared. In the first place, the simplicity of the Mosaic narrative of creation has called forth general admiration. Its superiority in this respect is thus acknowledged by Winer,[1]—" No other cosmogony of the ancient world can, as regards beauty and sublimity of style, be compared with the Mosaic." And by Knobel,[2]—" In comparison with the heathen cosmogonies, the praise, by general acknowledgment, is due to the simple and natural, worthy and sublime, Hebrew narrative." The heathen cosmogonies have but little symmetry of form, and much less consistency ; part disagreeing with part, and statement with statement, while withal they are enveloped in much that is misty and obscure, owing, no doubt, in some degree, to their imperfect state of preservation. But passing over generalities and minor distinctions, which relate more to the form than to the substance, it may be observed that,—

1. The Mosaic narrative of creation is distinguished from all other cosmogonies by the absence of everything fanciful or absurd. The heathen cosmogonies teem with absurdities, very partial instances only of which have been adduced in the preceding compendium. They manifest, without exception, the most gross ignorance of Nature, ascribing to matter powers and properties of the most ludicrous kind, and imposing upon the creative principle the necessity of having recourse to the most absurd expedients for effectuating its purposes or impulses. Even with the aid of an ancient and authentic tradition, which can be traced through all these theories, human reason, it is clearly demonstrated, is utterly inadequate to account for the creation of a world. But these ancient failures need not at all excite surprise, seeing how much, even in the *nineteenth* century, reason may be at fault in expounding the doctrine of Creation, when the Bible and its teaching are dis-

[1] Biblisch. Real-Wörterbuch, vol. i. p. 339.
[2] Die Genesis, p. 6. See also Gabler in Eichhorn's Urgeschichte, vol. i. pp. 30, 31.

carded. In illustration of this, it is enough to refer to such works as Oken's "Physio-Philosophy,"[1] and the "Vestiges of the Natural History of Creation."

The Hebrew narrative is entirely free of any such conceits. What so simple and grand as its opening announcement,— "In the beginning God created the heavens and the earth!" Indeed, the same characteristics belong to all its utterances. It carries the seal of truth on its very forehead. The historical matter which is related is replete with speculative thought and poetic glory, but is itself free from the influence of human fancies and philosophemes. In a field most inviting to speculation, where a thousand paths opened up on every side, and all presenting the most varied attractions, the writer carefully resists all such tendencies, and turns not aside to the right hand or to the left. He does not speculate, he does not give wing to imagination; nor does he pause to notice or discuss any of the numerous questions with which human curiosity has ever busied itself. In this, no less than in other particulars to be afterwards noticed, may be distinctly recognised the heavenly teacher, the Spirit of inspiration. Here, as in other parts of Scripture, He makes himself known, as well by what is left unsaid as by what is communicated. Most assuredly, were the writer of Genesis giving merely his own speculations or imaginings, or simply placing on record the traditions of his nation, he would have said more, by way of discussion or explanation, or mixed up with his narrative some sorry legends or wild fancies which could not fail to betray the source whence they sprung. That he has not done so, and that he has not penned a single statement which can offend right reason or good taste, or which clashes with any principle of revelation, plainly necessitates the conclusion, that what he recorded must have been received from above.

2. A distinguishing feature of the biblical creation is the fact, that it betrays nothing of a local or national character. All the non-biblical cosmogonies are not only marked by

---

[1] Of Oken's work, of which an English translation appeared in 1847, Professor Sedgwick thus speaks :—"All his pages on the structure of the earth give us little more than a compound mass of error, involved in a succession of assertions poured out with the utmost dogmatism, and without one syllable of reserve."—*Discourse on the Studies of the University of Cambridge*, 1850, p. cciv.

extravagant fancies, but exhibit in their form and structure various national characteristics, which prove that they must have grown up and assumed their peculiar conformations on the soil, and among the people to which they severally belong. As in the case of the Mythologies of the ancient nations, so also of their Cosmogonies—for the two are intimately related, there is discoverable the most marked impress, not only of the particular temperament of the human mind, but also of the physical characteristics of the locality. Thus, in the cosmogony of the Egyptians, for instance, the influence of the periodic inundations of the Nile is plainly discernible, while the Babylonian cosmogony no less evidently appears to have been constructed for Mesopotamia. The same local and national influences are particularly characteristic of the various theories of India and other ancient nations.[1]

No such modifying influences, however, can be detected in the Mosaic narrative of Creation. Here there is nothing local, nothing national. The narrative bears no traces of Egypt, or of the Arabian desert—the countries with which the writer was most familiar ;—the one his birthplace, the features and peculiarities of which must have made a deep and indelible impression on his memory ; the other the place where by far the greater portion of his life was spent in solitary musings, and political labours and anxieties. Even those parts of the narrative in which, if anywhere, might be expected traces of a national colouring, as the description of Eden, and its geographical position, are entirely free from anything that can be reckoned such. If the historian had in any way been influenced by local prejudices or national prepossessions, it is not at all improbable but that somehow or other he would have connected Eden, the birthplace of man, with the land set apart by God for the home of the covenant-people ; and that of the rivers that watered the garden and the surrounding regions, the Jordan would be one ; while the " goodly mountain" Lebanon, with its cedars and its snows, would in some way contribute a graceful ornament to the scene. In similar circumstances, there is little reason to doubt that the Hindoo would assign

---

[1] " In the cosmogonic myths of the Icelanders, as presented to us in the Edda, it is impossible not to perceive the influence of the peculiar locality of the Northern Scandinavians."—Bunsen's *Philosophy of Universal History*, vol. i. p. 80.

a prominent place to the Ganges, and the Egyptian to the
Nile, whether they drew on fancy for the embellishment
of the description, or only followed the traditions of their
country.

The only thing in this narrative that has been at all alleged
to betoken a national tendency, is the place occupied by the
institution of the Sabbath. It is maintained that the Sabbath
is entirely a Mosaic ordinance, and its connexion with creation
has been styled " a juridic myth."[1] This is not the place to
controvert these allegations, though it might be easily shewn
that they rest on assumptions utterly unwarranted. So far
has the attempt been carried to get rid of the Sabbath's connexion with creation, that many have not hesitated to affirm,
that the Hebrew cosmogony originally consisted of *eight* distinct acts of creation, and that it was only at a later period
the thought occurred to distribute them into six days, followed
by a Sabbath. This view, recently revived by Ewald,[2] has not
met with much reception even from writers of the same stamp.
" To take away the week-cycle and the Sabbath, were to
destroy the entire plan of the picture of creation," is the
remark of Tuch in reply to the same view as propounded at
an earlier period by Gabler, Ilgen, and other Rationalistic
writers.

3. The biblical creation is pre-eminently distinguished from
all other cosmogonies, by correct and worthy conceptions of the
Creator. The theories of heathenism proceed on the principle
either of excluding all Divine interposition in the creation of
the universe, assigning its original formation—if an origin be
admitted—or its present form, to the properties and dispositions of matter only ; or, if allowing the interposition of a
higher power, they make it to be some other than the Supreme
and Eternal God, some demiurgic principle. In some cases
it was assumed that the creative power acted under the
authority of the Supreme Being ; in others it was said to be
acting against him. In every instance, however, the ideas
entertained of a Creator, and of his perfections, intellectual
and moral, are exceedingly low, confused, and indistinct ; his
power being limited by the stubbornness of matter, or resisted

[1] De Wette, Einleitung, p. 172.
[2] Jahrbücher der Bib. Wissenschaft, 1849, pp. 86-94.

by some other hostile principle ; or creation is regarded not as a spontaneous product of the Divine will, but as a necessary act. The Bible, on the contrary, in its account of creation, rises infinitely above all such low and narrow views, and occupies a place peculiarly its own. It clearly and unequivocally ascribes creation in all its parts to the one living and true God, excluding the intervention of all secondary, or inimical co-ordinate principles between the Creator and his work. The Creator is independent, underived, and supreme : the universe in all its parts and combinations is derived and dependent, and has been called into being, simply at the pleasure of its omnipotent Maker. Matter has no will, can offer no resistance, but is formed and fashioned to the mind of the Creator and upholder of all. As if on purpose absolutely to exclude all ideas of an evil principle acting, whether by co-operation, subordination, or resistance, and to banish all misapprehensions as to the nature and character of the work, every part of the wonderful production, as it passed in review before its beneficent Author, is pronounced to be *good*, while the whole system, in its varied relations and complex arrangements, is found to be " very good."

It will be unnecessary to do more than advert to the objection sometimes urged against this narrative, on the ground that it conveys erroneous conceptions of God, by ascribing to him human characteristics, as when He is introduced *speaking*, *deliberating*, and *resting*. The objection, if valid, will apply to the whole of Scripture—to the New Testament as well as to the Old. The peculiarity of style complained of is not confined to this narrative, nor, indeed, to any particular book of the Bible, though prevailing more in the earlier than in the later writings ; and if Genesis contains a greater number of such expressions, it is because the earlier part of it relates more particularly to Divine operations and interpositions. But this style, so far from constituting a blot or blemish on Revelation, is, when correctly apprehended, an important testimony in its favour. The object of the Bible is to make God known to man ; but it is only through language derived from man's own mode of feeling and action, that correct conceptions of God can be conveyed.

4. The biblical narrative is distinguished from all other cosmogonies by its views of *creation*. This observation necessarily follows from the one immediately preceding, for wherever the ideas entertained of a Creator are inadequate—and such is the case in all non-biblical cosmogonies—there can be no correct conceptions of creation. This remark holds true also in every case where the right relation of mind and matter is unknown or unacknowledged.

From this point of view the various cosmogonies of heathenism, without much violence to their general form and character, will fall into two great classes. The one will consist of such as are more or less *Hylotheistic*, that is, such as deify matter, and are accordingly *Dualistic*. To this class may be reckoned the Phœnician, Egyptian, and Babylonian theories. The other will include all such as consider the universe as emanations of Deity, and are thus *Pantheistic*. To this class belong many, if not all, the cosmogonies of India.

The biblical creation is equally removed from both these extremes. It distinguishes between the Creator and the creature without the least hesitation or ambiguity ; and it is only by a perversion of its language that some have detected in it, or rather have forced upon it, the Indian notions of incarnation or emanation. It does, indeed, represent man as made in some intimate relation to his Maker—*created in the image of God ;* but the very terms in which this relation is announced, irrespective of the truths conveyed by the whole context and other collateral considerations, plainly declare that there was nothing farther removed from the purpose of the writer than to announce any participation in the Divine Essence, or in any way to represent man as an emanation of the Deity.

The distinguishing characteristic of the biblical cosmogony is, that it represents the pure and simple idea of a creation *from nothing*, without eternal matter and without demiurgic co-operation. " To the idea of a creation out of nothing," Hävernick remarks, " no ancient cosmogony has ever risen, neither in the myths nor the philosophemes of the ancient world. . . . By the peculiarity that the biblical cosmogony has for its fundamental idea, *a creation from nothing*, it is placed in a category distinct from all other ancient myths. Hence, recently, there appears, above all things, a disposition to deny that this is contained in the history of creation, but certainly without success."[1]

That the peculiarity just stated is a characteristic of the Mosaic narrative, has been disputed by two distinct classes of writers, though influenced by the most opposite motives. The one class is simply actuated by the desire to reduce the statements of the Bible to the level of other cosmogonies, while the design of the other is to bring the account of creation into harmony with the discoveries of the physical sciences. This latter class may be again subdivided—*first*, into such as consider that the doctrine of absolute creation is not taught in Scripture at all, and that it rests entirely on arguments of a metaphysical kind; and, *secondly*, into those who do not deny that in other passages, the Bible distinctly, or by implication, teaches the creation of the universe out of nothing, but maintain that this doctrine is not deducible from the term בָּרָא, which, in their view, imports a *renovation*, or *remodelling*, of the universe from matter already in existence, rather than an original *creation*, properly so called. As these views, whether for the one purpose or for the other, are extensively adopted and vigorously maintained, the matter will deserve a more extended examination than in other circumstances would be deemed necessary, although in any case the inquiry is not without importance.

The arguments on the negative side are usually put thus :—The leading import of the term ברא is twofold ;—1. The *production* or *effectuation* of *something new, rare, and wonderful ;* or the bringing something to pass in a striking and marvellous manner, as Numb. xvi. 30 ; Jer. xxxi. 22. 2. *The act of renovating, remodelling,* or *reconstituting, something already in existence.* In this sense it is used almost exclusively in the Scriptures in reference to the effects of the Divine influence in the moral or spiritual creation, as regeneration and sanctification, as in Ps. li. 10, " *Create* in me a clean heart, O God, and *renew* a right spirit within me," where, according to the parallelism and the nature of the case, ברא is equivalent to חדשׁ. In all these cases, it is remarked, the act implied by the word is exerted *upon a pre-existing substance*, and cannot therefore strictly signify *to create out of nothing.* And as in no other

[1] Einleitung, I. ii. 244 ; Cyc. Bib. Lit. vol. i. p. 750.

instance, if Gen. i. 1 be excepted, has the word necessarily or naturally this signification, it is at once inferred that there can be no sufficient ground for so interpreting it there.[1] To this is sometimes added the remark that the three terms, בָּרָא, to create, עָשָׂה, to make, and יָצַר, to form or fashion, are used indifferently and interchangeably ; and that there is therefore nothing in the import of the first to distinguish it from the others. The terms are so used, it is said, in many passages ; as e.g., Isa. xliii. 7, where they all three occur, applied to the same Divine act. The Septuagint renders ברא indifferently by ποιεῖν and κτίζειν. But especially in the account of the Creation, Gen. i., the verbs are used irrespectively in verses 7, 16, 21, 25, &c. ; and comparing Gen. i. 27 and ii. 7, man is said to have been created, yet he is also said to have been formed out of the dust of the ground. Again, in the Decalogue, Exod. xx. 11, the verb is עָשָׂה, made, not created. In Gen. i. the Septuagint has ἐποίησεν throughout.[2]

This, however, is by no means an adequate representation of the facts of the case, and particularly of the usage of the verb in question.

The verb ברא is derived, according to the best Hebraists, from a root of the form בר, which, in the harder modification פר, appears in a great number of stems, conveying the idea of hewing, splitting, &c. This primary signification is retained in the Piel of ברא, a conjugation which frequently preserves the primary sense. Thus in Ezek. xxiii. 47, " The company shall stone them with stones, and despatch them (בָּרָא, cut them down) with their swords ;" Josh. xvii. 15, " Get thee up to the wood and cut down (וּבֵרֵאתָ) for thyself there." In Ezek. xxi. 24, this verb signifies, according to Gesenius, to form, to fashion, i.q. יָצַר, but, according to Hävernick,[3] to engrave, to cut in. In all these instances it is implied that the act is accompanied with care, labour, and toil. But in Kal, on the contrary, it is the simple, unlaborious act, the product, properly speaking, of the Divine operation. God creates the heavens and the earth (Gen. i. 1), but creation is peculiar to him : it cannot be affirmed

---

[1] Bush, Notes on Genesis, vol. i. p. 27.
[2] Baden Powell, in Cyclop. Bib. Lit., Art. Creation, i. 477. See also Essays, p. 461.
[3] Commentar über Ezechiel, 1843, p. 340.

of any other being. Isa. xl. 26, " Lift up your eyes on high, and behold who hath *created* these." God is the *Creator* of Israel, Isa. xliii. 1 (compare Eccles. xii. 1) ; of the ends of the earth, Isa. xl. 28. He commanded, and the heavens with all their host were *created*, Ps. cxlviii. 5. *He creates* a new heaven and a new earth, Isa. lxv. 17. The expression is particularly used where God is said by a miraculous act to produce something which previously had no existence. See Isa. xli. 20 ; Jer. xxxi. 22. In this sense it is connected with חָדַשׁ, to *renew*, Ps. li. 12 ; civ. 30, " Thou sendest forth thy spirit, they are *created*, and thou *renewest* the face of the earth." In short, this is the proper and peculiar word for the true creating act of God.

Such are the limits of ברא ; but that the other and more general terms adverted to are frequently interchanged with it cannot be denied. This interchange does not of itself prove that the three terms are synonymous, but only that one or other can be used within certain limits, as occasion requires. So far from being synonymous, there is a wide distinction between them. The most general term of the three is עשׂה, while יצר approximates more to the idea of ברא ; the specific character of which will appear from the following observations :

(1.) How ברא differs from עשׂה, to *make*, may be plainly perceived from the concurrence of the two terms in Gen. ii. 3, " God blessed the seventh day and sanctified it ; because that in it he had rested from all his work which God *created to make*" (בָּרָא לַעֲשׂוֹת) ; or, according to the Vulgate, " quod creavit Deus ut faceret." On this passage L. de Dieu remarks, " Omnis creatio est effectio, sed non omnis effectio creatio." The distinction is evidently that between the original production and the subsequent conformation and arrangements of the universe.

(2.) The verb ברא, unlike the other two with which it is compared, never takes after it the accusative of the material out of which anything is formed. Thus in the case of עשׂה, Exod. xxxvii. 24, " He *made the altar of wood*" (עָשָׂה אֶת הַמִּזְבֵּחַ עֵץ) ; and of יצר, Gen. ii. 7, " The Lord God *formed man dust* of the ground," *i.e.*, *from* or *of dust*, וַיִּיצֶר הָאָדָם עָפָר. But ברא cannot be used in this connexion, and, accordingly, when the accusative of the material is to be designated, one of the other two verbs must be employed in its stead. Compare Gen. i. 27—" God *created* man in his own image : in the image of God *created* he him, male and female *created* he them," where ברא is repeated three times—with Gen. ii. 7, as given above. From this and other circumstances, it may be inferred that the interchange of these verbs is not owing to their being synonymous, but that the true reason is partly the grammatical exigencies of the language, and partly the desire of the writers for variety, so as thereby to amplify their descriptions. In other words, the substitution of the one term for the other, or the concurrence of two or more in the same sentence, is due to grammatical or oratorical considerations. To the latter is particularly to be referred such instances as Isa. xliii. 7, where the three verbs, *created, formed,* and *made,* occur.

(3.) Another peculiarity already incidentally adverted to is, that ברא is limited to Divine acts and operations. The other verbs can be used in reference to human as well as Divine acts, but this is exclusively confined to the works of God. This circumstance alone is sufficient to demonstrate the important distinction which exists between the terms compared. But there is another consideration which must not be overlooked, which is, that in its primary acceptation, this term, from the very nature of the case, can apply only to a single act of the Divine Being, the origination of the universe, Gen. i. 1 ; but in a secondary sense may extend to any other of the operations of God. This is enough to shew, that while in these latter cases the act expressed by the word is exerted on pre-existing matter, it by no means excludes the idea of *creation from nothing* in the only passage where the term can be used in its proper and primary signification.

But whatever weight may be due to the usage of the term, it is to be noted, that the question turns not so much on the sense of the verb taken alone and apart from the context, as on the way in which it is to be viewed in such a peculiar collocation as, " *In the beginning* God *created* the heavens and the earth." Granted, that in itself the term does not absolutely deny or affirm the presence of pre-existing matter, and that this can be inferred only from the context or the subject treated of, the question comes to be, What can be the meaning of the term here ? The expression, " in the beginning," evidently refers to the *beginning* of created existence, in contra-distinction to the eternal being of the Creator, and is thus an *absolute* beginning in and with time. An exact translation of בְּרֵאשִׁית is ἐν ἀρχῇ in John i. 1, with this difference, however, in the application, that in the latter case it does not refer to *an act done*, but to a *state existing* in the beginning, and therefore without beginning itself. With this distinction, the opening verse of the Bible is plainly the prototype and exemplar of the exordium of John's Gospel. Looking at the matter in this light, and with a special regard to the place which ברא occupies at the head of the narrative of creation, the *usus loquendi*, on which much stress is laid by parties on the opposite side, is at once disposed of, as also a remark already quoted: " As in no other instance throughout the Sacred Writings, if this passage be excepted, has the word necessarily or naturally this signifi-cation, we perceive no sufficient ground for so interpreting it here." On the contrary, it must be evident, from the con-siderations adduced, that there is ample ground for holding this to be a passage by itself, and distinct from all others, and for the conclusion arrived at by Hävernick, that it is only by the most forced exegetical means the idea of a creation out of nothing can be banished from the first verse of Genesis.

This conclusion is not a little confirmed by the fact, that it was in this light the doctrine of creation in Genesis was regarded from the earliest times. There is sufficient evidence to shew that the Samaritans held the doctrine of a creation out of nothing ;[1] and it is well known that the Jews formed a definition expressive of this truth : ἐξ οὐκ ὄντων, 2 Macc. vii. 28. It was not until the Platonic philosophy began to influence Jewish writers, that an opposite opinion was enter-tained, as may be seen from the Book of Wisdom, xi. 18: " Wisdom created the world out of shapeless matter," ἐξ ἀμόρφου ὕλης,—an idea which was carried out still farther by Philo and the Alexandrian school. The inspired writers of the New Testament, however, still adhered to the doctrine of creation from nothing, wherever they had occasion to refer to the subject. Thus, Heb. xi. 3, " By faith we understand that the worlds were formed by the word of God ; so that the things which are seen (τὰ βλεπόμενα) were not made from those which

---

[1] Carmen Samarit., i. 4; iii. 16, 17. Edid. Gesenius.

E

do appear ;" or, according to another rendering, which connects μὴ not with γεγονέναι, but with φαινομένων, " were made from those which do not appear ;" the same sentiment arising on either way. It is meant, that through faith we clearly apprehend that the world we see was not made out of apparent materials, from matter which had existed from eternity, but was produced out of nothing ; so that at God's fiat the material creation was brought into existence, and formed into the things we see. Rom. iv. 17, furnishes an instance of God's creative omnipotence, in his calling *the things that are not* as being, (as if they were,) τὰ μὴ ὄντα ὡς ὄντα. This, says Olshausen, is the *creative* call of the Almighty, by which, according to the analogy of the first act of creation, (Gen. i. 3,) he calls forth the concrete formations out of the general stream of life. So also John i. 3 : " All things were made by him ; and without him was not anything made that was made ;" where the second clause is not to be taken merely as a Hebraistic parallelism, but, as the best expositors maintain, " a distinct denial of the eternity and uncreatedness of matter, as held by the Gnostics." All except God is designated as *made*, and is considered as made through the Word, and thus the idea of a *second principle*, spiritual or material, is entirely excluded.

Following the teaching of the New Testament, the orthodox in the early Church firmly adhered to the doctrine of an absolute creation. But, as remarked in a previous section, the speculative tendencies of the Alexandrians could not be satisfied with the simple scriptural views, and, in particular, with the idea of the creation having taken place in time. Although Origen, however, had recourse to an allegorical interpretation of the work of the six days in order to find room for his notion of an *eternal* creation, he did not believe in the eternity of matter as a distinct and independent power ; and in this respect he differed from Hermogenes and the Gnostics. Yet these speculations were not founded on the Bible, but on the Platonic or Oriental philosophies. Not only does the Bible give no countenance to the notion of eternal or independent matter, but its entire teaching is diametrically opposed to it, from the first verse to the close. In this respect alone, there is an immense distinction between the Mosaic narrative of creation and all merely human speculations and theories, whether of ancient or of modern times.

From the examination instituted above, into the nature and character of the biblical creation, it must be apparent that no heathen cosmogony can bear comparison with it for simplicity, grandeur, and consistency. The Hebrew narrative contains all the elements of truth which lie at the foundation of all the myths of heathenism regarding the origin of the world and man, with the rigid exclusion of the extravagant fancies by which the whole of these traditions are grossly deformed. It contains all the scattered grains of the pure ore, without any tinge of the dross with which, in every other instance, it is mixed up, or almost concealed. The biblical account of the creation is consistent with itself—consistent with truth and enlightened reason—consistent with our highest conceptions of the Omniscient and Almighty Creator, and consistent with the entire teaching of the divinely-inspired Word. It has been well said,[1] " While philosophy was still breathing mist, and living in a chaos, the opening sentence of the Bible had been shining on the Hebrew mind for centuries, a ray direct from heaven.' Seeing the clouds and thick darkness which, on this subject, had settled down upon the earth, and distorted truth and man's apprehensions of it, whence otherwise could this light have come ? It is far easier to believe that Moses was taught the truths of creation, and the kindred subjects which he handles, directly by God himself, than that they are the result of his own sagacious speculations or discoveries, or of any eclectic power which he may have brought to operate on the heterogeneous compound of myths and marvels which existed in his day. " Such a deduction by the reflections of a sage," it has been remarked, " far transcends what we know of the sages of antiquity : such a lesson as is here furnished regarding the Creator, and, indeed, with the design to exclude all idolatry, we do not find even in much later times among the wisest and most cultivated nations : not even among the Greek philosophers. Such a geogony or cosmogony we seek for in vain among all ancient nations."[2]   And yet it has been attempted to account for all the excellencies and peculiarities of the

[1] Harris, Man-Primeval, 1849, p. 15.   [2] Jahn, Einleitung, 1803, II. i. 142.

biblical creation simply on the ground of the purer and more correct conceptions of the Divine Being in possession of the Hebrews, without first accounting for the origin of such conceptions, whether the offspring of the natural powers of the Hebrew mind, or of revelation from above; and, if the latter, without considering whether it be more unreasonable to conclude that the truths of creation have come from the same source. That explanation is obviously defective which would account, on natural grounds, for the superiority of the biblical creation from the circumstance of its being found among a people in the possession of a purer faith than that of any of the other nations of the ancient world, if the cause of this purity itself be unexplained, or be inexplicable on mere natural grounds. Such, however, is the explanation offered by Ewald,[1] who, in order to give more weight, if not consistency, to his theory, does not hesitate to bring down the composition of the biblical cosmogony to about the reign of David, as the period he conceives best suited for the full development of such ideas.

SECT. V.—THE BIBLICAL CREATION COMPARED WITH THE
RESULTS OF MODERN SCIENCE.

A very wide field for investigation here presents itself, and one on which many important and difficult questions have arisen, especially within recent years. It is not unnaturally suggested to those who have not given much attention to the subject, or who have looked at it from a partial point of view, that, admitting the incomparable superiority of the biblical creation in every respect over the cosmogonic theories of the ancient world, it may nevertheless be sadly eclipsed, if not confuted by the modern scientific discoveries which specially relate to creation and the physical revolutions of the earth and the Universe. This it is now proposed to consider; but in order to place the subject in a proper light, it will be necessary to submit a few preliminary remarks on the nature and aim of the physical truths contained in the Bible, and more especially in the account of the Creation.

First, It should be considered what the Bible, as a revela-

[1] Jahrbücher der Bib. Wissenschaft, 1848, p. 80.

tion from God, proposes to itself; and what accordingly the reader is justified in expecting from it. Inattention to this principle is often a great cause of confusion and disappointment, and consequently, of the many rash judgments passed upon the Sacred Word.

The Bible in no way professes to be a treatise or dissertation on science ; and, in particular, its narrative of Creation is not in the least designed to instruct the reader in physical truths, whether connected with Astronomy, Geology, Natural History, or any of the kindred sciences. Its purpose is entirely *moral ;* and it accordingly treats of the history of the universe, of the earth, and of man, only so far as it subserves that end. The information which it communicates on these subjects, has been vouchsafed to man not so much on account of his ignorance as of his sin. The Bible was written not to instruct him in physical truths, but in those which relate to the character and claims of his Creator, and to himself, as a fallen being, for whom mercy is designed.

Secondly, Such being the aim of the Bible, it may be reasonably assumed that its language and mode of describing natural phenomena will be suited to the lowest capacity. A book intended for the instruction of mankind, must speak a universal language—that of the people and of common life, and not the precise and scientific formulas and definitions of philosophers and the schools : otherwise it inevitably falls short of its object. As the Bible was written for all, so its language is level to all, and to a degree that bears the unmistakable impress of its omniscient Author. When it has occasion, as not unfrequently, to speak of any of the phenomena or objects of nature, it describes them by their appearance, rather than by their actual relations and forms : and thus it is that the description is so admirably adapted to every grade of civilisation and knowledge. On the contrary, were terms and expressions employed that are much insisted on by critical and philosophical objectors, it would prove itself anything but the work of God, because it would be, on that very account, unfitted for a place in the providential dispensation of the world.

Thirdly, The grand moral and remedial aim of the Bible is never for a moment lost sight of by any of the sacred writers.

This greatly influences the character and the contents, the structure and extent of their various narrations, and may be said to be the great principle on which was decided what should be inserted and what omitted in the history. From this point of view it may be well to look at the biblical creation, and the very limited space which it occupies in the Sacred Volume. Indeed, nothing intimates more plainly the views of the Divine Author of the Bible than the brevity with which that and other matters, naturally of the greatest interest and magnitude to man, are disposed of, to make room for others apparently of far less, but in reality and in the estimation of the Omniscient, of far more importance for man's spiritual and eternal wellbeing. The entire narrative of creation fills but a few short paragraphs ; and many of the mighty operations and the adjustments of immense portions of the Universe are despatched in a few simple words. How grand, how comprehensive, but, above all, how strikingly brief is the account of these subjects when compared with the full particulars, and minute details, and frequent iterations, of the story of grace and redemption which immediately follows the history. of Creation, and fills up the remainder of the Sacred Record !

It is of the utmost importance that this feature be attended to in any comparison of scientific discoveries and biblical statements ; and that due allowance be made for the plan, as well as for the purpose, of the inspired volume. This will not merely direct inquiry, it will also limit expectation, or rather it will correct, and so, in another point of view, materially enlarge it. So much is the mind influenced by prejudices or preconceptions in judging of the claims of Scripture, that while some refuse it their assent because they apprehend its statements are not in sufficient accordance with modern discoveries, others reject it, or doubt its age and authenticity, because it is found to accord with them too much. " If Genesis," says Eichhorn, " knew of a transformation of the earth after a general inundation, or a previous conflagration, such as philosophers *read in the records of nature*, I would doubt its authenticity and its age ; for such deep mysteries of nature would go beyond the horizon of hoary antiquity."[1] Objectors, in this respect, it may be truly said, are like the children in the market-place,

[1] Einleitung in das Alte Testament, vol. iii. p. 147.

whom neither piping nor mourning can satisfy ; " but Wisdom is justified of all her children" (Luke vii. 32-35).

Fourthly, But notwithstanding all these limitations, and particularly with the full recognition of the principle that the Bible was in no way designed to communicate scientific instruction, or supersede inquiry into physical facts and phenomena, yet on account of the sameness and consistency of all truth, it is to be inferred that the biblical statements, so far as they bear in that direction, shall not come into collision with any duly authenticated scientific or historical fact. This all believers in revelation must consistently maintain ; for to deny it were to give up the claims of the Bible to be the truth of God. The two volumes of Nature and Revelation must speak the same language, seeing that they claim to be the productions of one author, and He the immutable and omniscient One. It is only when either of the records, or both, are incorrectly read or rendered, that any collision or contradiction is possible. Misinterpretations of scriptural and scientific signs and symbols are of course exceedingly easy, and in certain low conditions of mental and moral culture they may be considered inevitable. There are difficulties connected with God's works as well as with his word ; and there may be difficulties —nay, with man's present knowledge, insurmountable difficulties—in bringing into clear and distinct harmony the testimonies of these two witnesses.[1]

That there are difficulties and apparent discrepancies in the Mosaic account of the Creation as compared with the conclusions of the physical sciences, no one who possesses the slightest acquaintance with the subject will deny. But let it be thoroughly understood that difficulties of reconciliation are not necessarily to be regarded as contradictions. It may be

[1] " There is no want of harmony between Scripture and Geology. The word and the works of God must be in unison, and the more we study both, the more they will be found to be in accordance. Any apparent want of correspondence proceeds either from imperfect interpretation of Scripture, or from incomplete knowledge of science. The changes in the globe have all preceded man's appearance on the scene. He is the characteristic of the present epoch, and he knows by revelation that the world is to undergo a further transformation, when the elements shall melt with fervent heat, and when all the present state of things shall be dissolved ere the ushering in of a new earth, wherein righteousness is to dwell."—*Encyclopædia Britannica*, 8th edit. 1854. Art. *Botany*, vol. v. p. 237.

well, however, to notice, and come to some understanding, as
to what really constitutes a discrepancy in the testimony of
two or more witnesses. Contradictions in such cases are either
seeming or real. They may originate from our limited acquaintance with the subject testified of, or with the testimony
itself, and are thus such as further information may be
expected to reconcile : or the depositions are so plainly and
palpably opposed to one another, that no amount of knowledge
can reconcile them. In this latter case, one or other of the
witnesses is unworthy of credit, or both may be in the same
position. But it may safely be affirmed that no such discord
is found to exist between the Bible and any authenticated
scientific result ; for,

Lastly, Already the difficulties are not so great, nor the
discrepancies so many, as they were even a few years ago
felt to be—a result brought about by no illegitimate means,
but solely by a full and free canvassing of the points in dispute—the progress of science and more correct interpretation.
Thus it happens that the imputations freely lavished on the
biblical creation by geology when an infant and immature
science, are now in a great measure, if not altogether, recalled.
This growing reconciliation, so to speak, between science and
Scripture, is a matter which deserves the most careful consideration in its bearing on the question of the biblical credibility.
Did the Mosaic cosmogony in any degree resemble the crude
theories of heathenism, the case must have been directly the
reverse ; for, with enlarged knowledge of nature and its operations, it would instinctively be felt that such a theory of the
Universe could not possibly be defended. This is no mere
conjecture or probable inference drawn from the nature of
things. It is the very process now going on in India, where
the Hindoo system, and the authority of its sacred books, a
compound of false science and false theology, are crumbling to
pieces before the literature and learning of the West. With
the Bible the case is otherwise. The rays of science and
Scripture are already uniting to form one rich halo of glory
around the throne of the Unchangeable and Eternal : the light
of science is helping to illumine the sacred page, and exalt
our conceptions of the greatness and power, the wisdom and
goodness, of the Author of Revelation ; and, on the other

hand, the light of Scripture is solemnizing the investigations of science into the awful depths of nature, where are traced in no dim or disputable characters in the ancient march of creation, the footsteps of Him whose goings forth have been from of old.

In examining the points of concord or of contradiction which, on the one hand or on the other, have been noticed in the testimonies of science and Scripture on the subject of Creation, the more natural course of procedure obviously is to consider the testimonies apart, with the view of deciding, not whether they are of equal extent or equally explicit, but whether, from their general character and bearing, there is evidence to conclude that the one witness is as credible and as accurately informed as the other. Further, it will be advantageous to the inquiry to begin with the consideration of the utterances of science as being more full and explicit, and as relating to matters pre-eminently its own. The admission that the testimony of science on matters pertaining to the structure and natural history of the Universe, or of the earth, is more full and explicit than that of Scripture, is one in no respect derogatory to the character of the latter, but the contrary, for the reasons already stated ; while such an admission will be found to contribute not a little towards correcting misconceptions, and repelling objections directed against the Sacred Record.

I.—SCIENTIFIC VIEWS OF CREATION.

1. *Science shews that there exists a very intimate relation between all the parts of the material universe.*—From careful and extended observation, it appears that not only are all the parts of the solar system intimately connected, but also that the system itself is linked to other systems, thus constituting parts of one stupendous whole. This renders it in the highest degree probable, that all the parts were simultaneously summoned into existence, or at least impressed with their present form and motions. This conclusion has more than probability in its favour, so far as regards the bodies which constitute the solar system, with which the present discussion has alone to do.

2. *Science further testifies that the universe is not eternal,*

but had a beginning.—Astronomical observations shew that a *resisting* medium, though rare, occupies the spaces in which the planets move, which must in time necessarily bring these movements to a close. This being the case, it is argued, " There must have been a commencement of the motions now going on in the solar system. Since these motions, when once begun, would be deranged and destroyed in a period which, however large, is yet finite, it is obvious we cannot carry their origin indefinitely backwards in the range of past duration."[1] But it is geology that places in the most commanding light the origin of the present order of things, so far as regards the earth. Looking into its stony records, and reading the history which time has inscribed upon them, this science announces that there was a period in the past when neither plants, nor animals, nor man, had an existence on the earth.[2]

3. *It is an induction of science and sound reasoning, that the beginning, whether of matter or motion, order or life, indicates the operation of an adequate cause.*—Various hypotheses have been invented in order to exclude creation in the proper sense of the term, but true science has ever pronounced them to be unsound and unsatisfactory. The Nebular hypothesis of Laplace, devised for the purpose of accounting for the formation and the motions of the planets and their satellites, if it be thereby intended to exclude the intervention of an *intelligent* cause, will, in this respect, be pronounced by true science to belong to the same category as the reveries of Diodorus the Sicilian and his Egyptian teachers, who conceived that the heavens and the earth were formed by the motion of the air and the ascent of fire. The same place is already assigned to the Development-hypothesis of Lamarck, and the author of the " Vestiges of the Natural History of Creation," which professes to account, on what it calls *natural laws,* for the origin of the varied forms and orders of organic life, vegetable and

---

[1] Whewell, Bridgewater Treatise, Lond. 1852, p. 177.

[2] " We can prove," says a distinguished geologist, " that man had a beginning, and that all the species contemporary with man, and many others which preceded, had also a beginning, and that, consequently, the present state of the organic world has not gone on from all eternity, as some philosophers have maintained."—Lyell, *Elementary Geology,* fourth edition, Lond. 1852, p. 500. " It is now beyond dispute, and is proved by the physical records of the earth, that all the visible forms of organic life had a beginning in time."—Sedgwick's *Discourse,* p. xvii.

animal, with which the earth is stored. It must not, therefore, be overlooked, in any judgment to be formed on the mutual bearing of science and Scripture, how, in such instances as those referred to, science, however her utterances may be worded, openly declares on the side of religion and the first article of faith ; and how, in particular, the facts of successive creations, which geology attests, furnish a complete refutation of the assumption of an eternal succession of generations, which was wont to occupy so large a space in the Theistic controversy, but which, previous to the rich discoveries of the natural sciences, could be debated only on the abstruse grounds of metaphysics and abstract argumentation.

4. *But although not eternal, the material universe, as presently constituted, has been in existence during untold ages.*— Astronomy furnishes most wonderful evidence of the inconceivably vast extent of the universe, and also remarkable, if not incontrovertible, proof of its great antiquity, from considerations regarding the transmission of light. Sir William Herschel was of opinion, that light required almost two millions of years to pass to the earth from the remotest luminous vapour reached by his forty-feet reflector : so many years ago, if this opinion, and the calculations on which it rests are to be received, this object must have existed in the sidereal heavens in order to emit those rays by which it is now perceived.[1] But any doubt as to the high antiquity of the system, or that portion of it in particular which, as his dwelling-place, comes more under the cognizance of man, is more than removed by the irresistible proofs adduced by another branch of science. The investigations of the geologist into the past history of the earth leave no room to doubt of its existence at an inconceivably remote period, and that not merely as a bare untenanted planet, but also as a theatre of life. It is admitted by all capable of observing the facts, and appreciating the reasoning, that the formation even of the strata nearest to the surface occupied vast periods in arriving at their present state.[2]

---

[1] Humboldt's Kosmos, Otte's Translation, vol. i. p. 144. Lond. 1849.

[2] " There can be no doubt that there have been successive deposits of stratified rocks, and successive creations of living beings. We see that animals and plants have gone through their different phases of existence, and that their remains, in all stages of growth and decay, have been imbedded in rocks superimposed upon each

5. *The earth has passed through several successive changes, and these have been improvements in its condition and capabilities as a habitable world.*—Whatever may be the hesitation felt in assigning a date to the origin of the earth, or determining its *absolute* age, there is none in fixing the relative age of the more important of its stratified formations, and in declaring that each of them was a work of time. The fossil remains furnish the clearest indications of a beginning of the various organizations with which at different periods in its history the earth was inhabited ; while change and progress meet the geological observer at every step of his investigations[1]—the slow majestic march of creation being upwards and onwards. Whatever may be conceived to have been the state of the earth in the first stage of its existence, whether aeriform or molten, or encircled by dark chaotic waters, it is certain that there was an absence of all organic existence. How long this state of matters continued there is no means of determining ; but in due time life was introduced : first vegetable,[2] and afterwards

other in regular succession. It is impossible to conceive that these were results of changes produced within the limits of a few days. Considering the depth of stratification, and the condition and nature of the living beings found in the strata at various depths, we must conclude (unless our senses are mocked by the phenomena presented to our view) that vast periods have elapsed since the Creator in the beginning created the heavens and the earth."—*Encyclopædia Britannica*, Art. *Botany*, vol. v. p. 237.

[1] See Murchison's *Siluria*, chap. xviii. pp. 459-468.

[2] As the priority of vegetable life is a point that has been somewhat controverted, it will be necessary to examine it more particularly. Thus Lyell, (Principles of Geology, eighth edition, 1850, p. 134 :)—" Traces of fossils referable to the animal kingdom make their appearance in strata of as early a date as any in which the impressions of plants have been detected." And still more decidedly, Professor Phillips, (Treatise on Geology in Cabinet Library, vol. i. p. 72 :)—" Those who expect, consistently with general probability, that the earliest indications of life on the globe should be of the vegetable kingdom, may be somewhat astonished to learn, that traces of plants are really not known in a distinct form in strata so ancient as those which contain the shells of *Brachiopoda* in the mountains of Wales, and that only fucoids are discovered in the Silurian system. What is calculated to add to this feeling of surprise, is the circumstance that in the next but one system which lies upon the Silurian, two of the formations are the repository of most enormous accumulations of fossil plants : for in these rocks principally lie the coal beds of Europe and America, which are nothing else than a mass of chemically altered vegetables." But these appearances are fully disposed of by various considerations, the force of which is admitted by geologists, and some of which are referred to in the chapter from which the last extract is taken. There it is remarked, that as the stratified rocks were formed chiefly on the bed of the sea, the remains of

animal life. As regards the farther progress of the earth's preparation for the reception of animal life, and the particular order or succession observed in the introduction of sentient beings on its surface, or into its seas, geologists are, upon the whole, agreed, that the fish preceded the reptile and the bird, and that these again preceded the mammiferous quadruped, and that the mammiferous quadruped preceded man.[1]

6. *Life, once begun on the earth, has been maintained without interruption.*—"From the origin of organic life," remarks Professor Phillips, "there is no break in the vast chain of organic development, till we reach the existing order of

terrestrial plants can only be expected to occur rarely; while the rarity of marine plants among the oceanic sediments is accounted for from the fact, that the most of these are natant, or confined to rocky shores. To this effect is the remark of Professor Sedgwick, (Discourse on the Studies of Cambridge, p. lxxii.)—"In order to speculate securely about the first beginnings of vegetable life, we ought to know more of the primeval condition of the earth than is, or ever will be, revealed to us by direct physical evidence. Our oldest Palæozoic strata appear to have been deposited in a deep ocean; and in such formations we have no right to look for the vegetable spoils of the land, even though we hypothetically admit their existence in as great abundance as during any after period." To this is to be added the consideration, that the cellular substance of the marine tribes of plants, and of many land plants also, as Dr. Lindley's experiments shew, would cause many of them utterly to perish under the slow accumulation of the strata. "The first created living material being belonged, it is believed, to that class of beings called cellular, and of which lichens and mosses are familiar examples."—(Kemp, *Natural History of Creation,* p. 3.) "Cellular plants have probably in a great measure been destroyed, or changed in their aspect, and hence their rarity."—(*Encyclopædia Britannica,* Art. *Botany,* vol. v. p. 233.) But farther, the priority of vegetable life is abundantly confirmed by considerations of another kind. "A moment's reflection will shew, that in the system of things which God has been pleased to constitute, animal life necessarily presupposes vegetation, and is, indeed, very much regulated in its extent by the quantity supplied. Vegetation is the ultimate support of animal life; for though some animals are carnivorous, those preyed on, if traced downwards, are found herbivorous; just as the herb itself derives its nourishment from the pre-existing inorganic elements. This is true of fishes and cetaceous animals which feed on the smaller plant-eating crustacea; and thus in the ocean, the phosphoric acid of inorganic nature is, by means of plants, carried over to animals."—(Harris, *Preadamite Earth,* p. 178.) It may, accordingly, be concluded with Professor Sedgwick, (*l. c.* p. lxxiii.)—"In the midst of much doubt and uncertainty, one thing, however, is clear, that some forms of vegetable life must have flourished at the commencement of our oldest Palæozoic strata; for no *fauna* could possibly exist without them." And also, (p. lix.)—"Should the place of the protozoic group be ever established, we may then expect to find within it the traces of that ancient flora which formed the necessary base of animal life."

[1] Miller, Footprints of the Creator, 1849, p. 283. See also Sedgwick's Discourse, p. ccxvii.

things ;—no one geological period, long or short, no one series
of stratified rocks is ever devoid of traces of life. The world,
once inhabited, has apparently never, for any ascertainable
period, been totally despoiled of its living wonders."[1]　And to
the same effect Sir Charles Lyell,—" In passing from the older
to the newer members of the tertiary system, we meet with
many chasms, but none which separate entirely, by a broad
line of demarcation, one state of the organic world from another.
There are no signs of an abrupt termination of one fauna and
flora, and the starting into life of new and wholly distinct
forms."　" There is no great chasm, no signs of a crisis, when
one class of organic beings was annihilated to give place suddenly to another."[2]

7. *Science testifies, in the most unequivocal manner, that
the appearance of man on the earth is comparatively a recent
event.*—Among all the facts of geology, there appears to be
none better established than the recent origin of man—recent
as compared with all the preceding creations, and particularly
with the age of the earth.　Thus Lyell :[3]—" I need not dwell
on the proofs of the low antiquity of our species, for it is not
controverted by any experienced geologist ; indeed, the real
difficulty consists in tracing back the signs of man's existence
on the earth to that comparatively modern period when species,
now his contemporaries, began greatly to predominate.　If
there be a difference of opinion respecting the occurrence in
certain deposits of the remains of man and his works, it is
always in reference to strata confessedly of the most modern
order ; and it is never pretended that our race co-existed with
assemblages of animals and plants, of which all, or even a
large proportion of the species, are extinct."　Or, to take the
most recent testimony on this point :—" We know not a single
fact in geology," remarks Hugh Miller, " amidst its magnificent accumulation of facts gathered from all quarters of the
earth, and by as laborious, skilful, and truth-loving observers
as have ever been united in the prosecution of human science,
that gives a shadow of support to the hypothesis that man's
history on the earth has extended beyond the ordinarily

---

[1] Quoted in Pye Smith's Scripture and Geology, p. 81.
[2] Principles of Geology, pp. 177, 179.
[3] Principles, p. 144.

assigned period of six thousand years. We know of no great name in the science who does not acknowledge it."[1]

8. Finally, *The introduction of man upon the earth is not only recent, but is the most recent act of Creation : scientific investigations supply no evidence of the creation of any species subsequent to man.*—With the introduction of man upon the earth creation came to a close : man is the last as he is the noblest production of creative power and intelligence. At least science has not been able to detect any trace of a subsequent creation, whether of plants or animals. So far as geological evidence extends, " no species or family of existences seems to have been introduced by creation into the present scene of being since the appearance of man." " The geologist finds no trace of post-Adamic creation."[2] To the same effect are the testimonies of the botanist and the zoologist in their own special departments; but it is unnecessary tô pursue further a question on which, as must be conceded with Lyell, the evidence, from the very nature of the case, is necessarily vague and incomplete.[3]

The facts adduced above may be considered as the first principles of science relative to the natural history of the universe, but particularly of the earth and its various inhabitants; and they are such as to whose truth all, or nearly all, scientific men are at one. The scientific testimonies and deductions thus presented have been arranged in the preceding scheme, with the view of serving not merely as references and guides in the subsequent examination of the scriptural declarations on

---

[1] Witness, Feb. 1, 1854. See also Wagner, Geschichte der Urwelt, p. 241, Leips. 1845. To these testimonies may be added that of another school : " Compared with many humbler animals, man is a being, as it were, of yesterday."— *Vestiges of the Natural History of Creation*, p. 110, tenth edition, 1853.

[2] Miller, Footprints, pp. 304, 307.

[3] Principles, pp. 681, 635. Sedgwick's testimony may be subjoined : " Revelation tells us that God created the heaven and the earth—that man was the last created of living beings—and that God then rested from his labours. Many learned heathens held that the order of nature, animate as well as inanimate, had been from eternity. Modern science gives us the truest elements of the religion of Nature, and proves that the order of Nature has not been eternal, and that man is a creature of the last and latest period. Science also tells us, that since the appearance of man, creative power in Nature appears to have been at rest."—*Discourse*, pp. cccv. cccvi.

the same subject, but also, it may be, to cast light on the interpretation of the sacred page in the way of suggestion or otherwise. One inference may, however, at present be legitimately drawn from the foregoing synopsis, that no science—no geological or astronomical speculations, and no physiological research, can give any distinct and satisfactory account of the origination of the world, or of its past and present flora and fauna. Science can point to a beginning of the several existences, but is unable to say how they were introduced on the previously vacant stage. Science can trace the progress and development of the earth upwards to the present order of things, and can again retrace the path which conducts nearly to the origin of all, but never reaches it. It is revelation alone which can supply reliable information on that point. "To assume that the evidence of the beginning or end of so vast a scheme lies within the reach of our philosophical inquiries, or even of our speculations, appears to be inconsistent with a just estimate of the relations which subsist between the finite powers of man and the attributes of an infinite and eternal Being." Such is the concluding sentence of Lyell's "Principles of Geology," and the idea which it expresses is in substance exceedingly just and appropriate if limited to man's own unaided powers of perception. For holding that it must be so limited, there is the highest authority, for it is plainly declared on Apostolic testimony that there are indubitable evidences of a beginning and also of an end, and they are pronounced *willingly ignorant* who disregard the fact, " that by the word of God the heavens were of old, and the earth standing out of the water, and in the water : whereby the world that then was, being overflowed with water, perished : but the heavens and the earth, which are now, by the same word are kept in store, reserved unto fire against the day of judgment and perdition of ungodly men" (2 Pet. iii. 5-7).

II.—SCRIPTURAL VIEWS OF CREATION.

1. *The Bible recognises the intimate connexion which subsists between the parts constituting the material universe.*—The opening sentence of the Bible not merely describes " the heavens and the earth" as the effects of a common Cause, but

also assigns to them a contemporaneous origin. " In the beginning God created *the heavens and the earth ;*" this, from its two most prominent constituent parts, being the common Hebrew designation of the material universe.[1] So also in various other passages of Scripture, the same connexion is observed and the same relation of time. Thus Ps. cii. 25, " Of old hast thou laid the foundation of the earth ; and the heavens are the work of thy hands ;" or, as rendered by the Apostle, Heb. i. 10, " Thou, Lord, *in the beginning* hast laid the foundation of the earth," &c. Indeed it is one of the main objects of the Bible to disclose and describe the close relationship between all the parts of creation, material and moral, as the productions of one originating mind.

2. *Scripture expressly teaches that the universe is not eternal, but had a beginning both as to matter and form.*—No declarations of the Bible are more plain and express than those which distinguish between the eternity of the Creator and the finitude of the creature as to time and space. Everything that exists had a beginning, but God : He is " without beginning of days or ending of duration." The very first word of revelation relates to the *beginning* of creation. Whatever ambiguity or doubt may be alleged to attach to the Hebrew term rendered *created,* considered in itself, is, as shewn in the preceding section, more than removed by the context, " *In the beginning* God *created* the heavens," &c. From the considerations there adduced, there can be no doubt that according to the whole tenor of Scripture, matter is conceived of as not eternal.

3. *If reason and science unite in testifying that the universe is the effect of an Intelligent Cause, the Bible teaches that this cause is God—the only living and true God.*—Scripture, unlike some systems of philosophy, does not exclude the Creator from his work : it will not recognise or tolerate laws, ordinances, or arrangements, which would shut out the Lawgiver, or remove him to a distance from his government. It distinctly teaches

---

[1] " The phrase ' the heavens and the earth,' though not always used by the sacred writers in the full sense, is the most comprehensive that the Hebrew language affords, to designate the universe of dependent being ; and, on account of the connexion, it requires to be so taken in this place."—Pye Smith, *Scripture and Geology,* p. 270. It would, however, seem rather to be limited to the material universe, for that is the subject immediately taken up in the narrative following.

F

that the Author of Creation in all its extent is a personal and ever present Creator—the living God, for the revelation of whose character and relation to man the Bible was written. The God of Creation, as seen in the light of the Sacred Scriptures, is not a mere Abstraction—a Power or an Intelligence —but a Personality clothed in every moral attribute and perfection.

4. *The Bible nowhere—from the first page to the last—assigns a date to the origin of the universe.*—It is of the utmost importance to attend to the statement advanced in this proposition relative to the antiquity of the universe or of the earth. Leaving out of view for the present all considerations arising from the demands which geology makes in behalf of a high antiquity for our planet, and taking cognizance only of the scriptural declarations, it may be safely affirmed as an undoubted truth, that neither in Genesis, nor in any other part or passage of the sacred record, is any determined period specified as that in which the earth began to be. If such a date can be detected anywhere, it must surely be in the narrative of the Creation with which the Bible opens, but no critical or hermeneutic skill can find it there. It is now, indeed, universally admitted by all who are competent to speak on the subject, that the expression, " In the beginning," with which the narrative and the volume itself open, leaves the matter quite undefined and unfixed. There are high authorities who even maintain that the first sentence of Genesis teaches only the priority of the material creation in respect to the immaterial, and render it, " *At first* God created the heavens and the earth."[1]   Anyhow no absolute date is assigned to this beginning or this first creation.   It was a mighty advance towards reconciling science and revelation, when it was perceived and announced that " the writings of Moses do not fix the antiquity of the globe ; and that if they fix anything at all, it is only the antiquity of the human species,"—a conclusion arrived at by the late Dr. Chalmers so early as 1804.[2]

---

[1] This is the rendering of the Arabic version of Saadias, and is recently adopted by Harris (Man Primeval, 1849, p. 481,) and Knobel (Die Genesis erklärt, 1852, p. 7.)

[2] See Life by Hanna, vol. i. p. 386.   At a subsequent period (1814) Dr. Chalmers writes :—" Shonld the phenomena compel us to assign a greater antiquity to the

So far is Scripture from limiting the past duration of the earth, that, on the contrary, not a few texts seem to assign a very high antiquity to its creation. " *Of old* hast thou laid the foundation of the earth," Ps. cii. 25.—" The Lord possessed me in the beginning of his way, *before his works of old*," Prov. viii. 22.

The preceding observations comprise matters of a more general, or of a negative character, as it may be called. They reveal no discrepancy between the sayings of Scripture and the discoveries of science ; but the farther prosecution of the subject will conduct to more marked and specific results, and in particular to the discovery—unexpected, perhaps, by many—of a wonderful accordance in the order of creation as described by Moses, and as written on the rocky strata of the earth. This proposition may be enunciated as follows :—

5. *The order of the successive creations in Genesis is the order of Geology, or, as it may be said, the order of God.*—As stated under the numerically corresponding proposition of the preceding head, scientific men are by no means agreed as to what was the original state of our planet, some considering it as gaseous, or as an incandescent mineral mass ; and others, that its matrix was water. Scripture carefully avoids all such theories. It gives no intimation or surmise regarding the first condition of the earth. All the information furnished by Scripture in connexion with the earlier stages of the earth's history, is, that it was " desolate and waste," without inhabitant, and destitute of every form of organized life—a fact abundantly illustrated by geological investigations—and encircled, whether at first or at a subsequent stage, by dark chaotic waters, תְּהוֹם, or *the deep*. How long this state of matters continued there is nothing in the narrative to indicate in the remotest degree. The results of the subsequent creating acts are " light," Gen. i. 3 ; an atmosphere, verse 6 ; the upheaval of the land from the bosom of the deep, verse 9 ; and the land thus laid bare in due course clothed with vegetation,

globe than to that work of days detailed in the book of Genesis, there is still one way of saving the credit of the literal history. The first creation of the earth and the heavens may have formed no part of that work. This took place at the *beginning,* and is described in the first verse of Genesis. It is not said when this beginning was."— *Select Works,* 1855, vol. v. p. 630.

" grass, herb yielding seed, and the tree yielding fruit," verse
11. Next, the waters are filled with animal life; birds are
also created at this stage, verse 20 ; after which follows the
creation of terrestrial animals, " cattle, creeping thing and
beast of the earth," verse 24 ; and last of all man, who was
made in the image of the Creator, verse 26.

6. *Life once begun on the earth has been ever since maintained
without pause or interruption.*—So says geology, and no intimation of a contrary nature is found in Scripture, or any
notice, expressed or implied of a creation, at least of a material
or organic creation, prior to that which is recorded in Genesis.
When difficulties connected with the discoveries of geology
began to press the interpreter of Scripture, their solution was
sought in the assumption that Genesis describes only a renovation of the earth after some desolating convulsion, and that
accordingly no reference is made to the ancient creations
whose remains are entombed in the rocks—to the order in
which they were introduced, or to the intervals in which they
succeeded one another, or how or when they perished, but only
to the vegetable and animal productions now in existence, and
introduced contemporaneously with man. But this assumption
is not in accordance either with the letter or spirit of the
narrative ; while geology emphatically asserts, that there is no
such break in the chain of being as is here implied.

7. *The creation of man is not only relatively the most recent,
it is the only one to which Scripture assigns an absolute date.*—
This date is determined from the genealogical tables of the
antediluvian and postdiluvian patriarchs in the line of Seth,
the son of Adam, and of Shem, the son of Noah. Notwithstanding some unimportant differences in the chronology of
the Hebrew text, the Samaritan recension and the Greek version, the period of the human race may be fixed at about 6000
years, a date which remarkably corresponds with the results
of science and historical investigations. " The Bible instructs
us," says Professor Sedgwick, " that man and other living
things have been placed but a few years upon the earth, and
the physical monuments of the world bear witness to the same
truth."[1] These are monuments, be it observed, which man

[1] Discourse on the Studies, &c., p. 110

has not been able to falsify or deface, and to this it is owing that they present a remarkable contrast to the lying chroni-cles of China, India, and Egypt, which claim a fabulous antiquity for their respective nations—an antiquity by which, some time ago, it was stoutly attempted to overthrow the authority of Scripture, because of the recent date therein assigned to the creation of man.

8. *With the introduction of man upon the earth creation came to a close.* Whatever uncertainty may attach to the declarations of science on this point, owing to a deficiency of evidence, nothing of the kind marks the testimony of Scrip-ture : " Thus the heavens and the earth were finished, and all the host of them. And on the seventh day God ended his work which he had made : and he rested on the seventh day from all his work which he had made." (Gen. ii. 1, 2.) The work proposed to himself by the Divine Architect being finished—perfected in all its parts—he ceased from further multiplying the objects of creation.

Such as now described is the order and course of creation set forth in the Sacred Volume ; and on a comparison with the results arrived at by scientific men, it must undoubtedly be felt, that the harmony subsisting between the ancient record in Genesis and modern discoveries, is in a great many parti-culars of a very remarkable kind. The striking similarity of views and statements thus evinced cannot be the result of accident ; and it would be equally preposterous to seek its ex-planation in any supposed physical knowledge possessed by Moses, or any of his contemporaries. Moses was no geologist, and yet he writes as if thoroughly acquainted with the sciences of the present day. Indeed, he writes in a way unattainable, even by philosophers, until within a recent period, as may be demonstrated from such productions as Burnet or Whiston's " Theory of the Earth," which appeared at the end of the seventeenth century. Without anticipating the results of a more extended examination of this question reserved for a subsequent section, it is not too much to assert, that the har-mony above traced, and the peculiarities of the Mosaic nar-rative of creation, both as regards manner and matter, are explicable only on the principle, that the Creator of the earth, of its rocks and mountains, its rivers and seas, plants and

animals, both extinct and living, is also the Author and Source
of this record of the wonderful production of his almig. ty power.

But here a serious difficulty arises, which may materially
interfere with such conclusions, and introduce discord into the
harmony which it has been attempted to establish. The difficulty consists in the period of time—six days—within which,
according to the narrative in Genesis, and still more expressly,
a statement in the Decalogue, (Exod. xx. 11,) the whole work
of Creation was begun and finished. In comparison with this
all other difficulties sink into insignificance, or admit of easy
explanation. Such, for instance, is the case with the frequently urged objection, that light was created on the first
day, but the sun, moon, and stars not until the fourth ; the
consideration of which may be safely omitted in the present
discussion, reserving the remainder of this section for an examination of the more popular and important of the schemes of
reconciliation proposed in regard to the days of creation, and
for an inquiry into the evidence, if any, which the narrative
itself, or any other portion of Scripture, may furnish, as to the
meaning of the days in this particular instance.

III.—MODES OF RECONCILIATION.

When an examination of the stratified appearance of the
earth first suggested the idea that its origin extended back to
a far higher date than was wont to be inferred from the Mosaic
history of the creation, various attempts were made to negative
the scientific conclusion. At one time, an explanation of these
appearances was found in an easy reference to the Deluge of
Noah, and the changes thereby induced in the relative position
of sea and land, when the organized fossils had been buried in
the solid strata. At another time it was suggested, that the
world may have been created in the state in which it is now
beheld—bearing on it seeming but not real indications of a
high antiquity, and of processes through which it never passed.
What are called *fossils*, it was alleged, never existed in any
other state—they were mere freaks of nature. All these fancies, however, are fast disappearing before more correct and
enlarged views of Nature, and the attempts at reconciling
Genesis and Geology, on any such principles, may be almost

numbered with the things that were. It will be necessary, therefore, to notice only the more recent and better attested explications, and such as accordingly command the greatest acceptance.

1. By one scheme of reconciliation, which is perhaps still, as it was recently, the most extensively received, the first verse of Genesis is taken to stand as a separate and independent sentence announcing an act of *creation*, properly so called. This creation, of which no particulars are furnished, and to which no date is assigned, is only remotely related to the creative acts forming the subject of the biblical record, in which no mention whatever is made of the changes and revolutions through which the earth has successively passed during the untold and almost interminable ages wherein lived and propagated and perished the various races of plants and animals, whose remains are carefully preserved in the fossiliferous strata. On the state of order and life to which these organic remains testify, there supervened, according to this theory, terrestrial convulsions which produced the chaos, or the confusion and emptiness described in Gen. i. 2, and out of which, in six days, the earth emerged in the order narrated, and was fitted for the reception of man. In a word, Genesis describes the present or the existing creation, and takes no cognizance of the creations which form the peculiar study of the geologist ; only it declares, that between the present and the past order of things, there intervened an awful blank, a chaotic period of death and darkness. It may be farther added, that by this theory the Divine mandate, " Let there be light," was fulfilled, when on the first day God had so far removed the dark, turbid vapours by which the earth was enveloped, as to allow some rays of the sun to penetrate the gloom, although it was not until the fourth day that these were so far dissipated as to allow the heavenly bodies to come fully into view.

But this scheme for reconciling Genesis and Geology is open to many and formidable objections. Waving for the present whatever may be urged against it from the Bible point of view, it is sufficient to remark, that the science whose deductions it seeks to harmonize with the Sacred Record, or rather to neutralize as a testimony against it, stubbornly refuses to submit to the process required in this adjustment. Among the various findings of geology enunciated on a previous page, there is none which appears to be sustained by better evidence than that which affirms, that " Life, once begun on the earth, has been maintained without interruption." Giving due consideration to this great principle of science, it must be felt that any scheme of reconciliation which, like the above, proposes to break the continuity of the chain of life by the intervention of an absolute blank, is one that cannot satisfy the requirements of the case.

2. To obviate this weighty objection, and to suit a more advanced state of the science, the scheme has been somewhat modified by the late Dr. Pye Smith. This author agrees with Buckland and others in viewing the first verse of Genesis as a distinct, independent sentence, referring to an act separated by a wide interval from what follows ; and he considers that it was during this interval, or untold and undetermined period, that the various stratifications, denudations, and upheavals took place, of which geology takes notice. But the description in verse 2, according to this amended scheme—and it is in this its peculiarity lies—does not embrace the earth in general, but only *a portion of its surface*, " brought into a condition of superficial ruin, or some kind of general disorder," at a comparatively recent date ;—" overflowed with water, and its atmosphere so turbid that extreme gloominess prevailed." " The Divine power acted through the laws of gravity and molecular attraction ; and, where necessary, in an immediate, extraordinary, or miraculous manner. The atmosphere over the region became so far cleared as to be pervious to light, though not yet properly transparent. In this process, the watery vapour collected into floating masses, the clouds, which the Hebrews expressed by the phrase, ' waters above the firmament.' Elevations of land took place by upheaving igneous force ; and, consequently, the waters flowed into the lower parts, producing lakes. The elevated land was now clothed with vegetation instantly created. By the fourth day the atmosphere over this district had become pellucid, and had there been a human eye to have beheld, the brightness of the sun would have been seen, and the other heavenly bodies after the sun was set. Animals were produced by immediate creation in this succession ; the inhabitants of the waters,

birds, and land animals ; all in the full vigour of their natures."[1]

Such is the carefully elaborated scheme of reconciliation proposed by Dr. Pye Smith ; and of which it has been remarked,[2] that " by leaving to the geologist in this country and elsewhere, save, mayhap, in some unknown Asiatic district, his unbroken series, it does not certainly conflict with the facts educed by geologic discovery." But notwithstanding the favourable testimony thus freely accorded by the geologist, the theory is open to objections of a very formidable kind from the opposite quarter.

On attentively considering the narrative of creation, it cannot but be instinctively felt, that the mode of explaining its language, and disposing of its statements by both the above schemes, but more particularly the last, falls immeasurably short of the end proposed, which was doubtless to interpret Scripture, and not to torture it. Can it be that by the term *darkness* is not to be understood " the absolute privation of light, but only a partial obscuration or gloom," and that the sublime command of Omnipotence, " Let there be light," does not at all imply that light was now first summoned into existence, but that the atmosphere became so far cleared as to be pervious to light, though not yet perfectly transparent? and yet, imperfect as this state of things was, it was such as to call forth the Divine approbation : " God saw the light that it was good." Most assuredly, if such assumptions are admissible, it is only by disregarding the plain import of language, and the sublime conceptions which have ever been entertained of this creating act. If the chaos be merely limited and local, the incongruity will be still more striking. Thus an eminent writer observes : " I have stumbled at the conception of a merely local and limited chaos, in which the darkness would be so complete, that when first penetrated by the light, that penetration could be described as actually a *making* or creation of light ; and that, while life obtained all around its precincts, could yet be thoroughly void of life."[3]

It is farther prejudicial to this view of a limited creation, that it demands that the term *earth* be taken in two distinct

[1] Scripture and Geology, pp. 270-280
[2] Miller, The Two Records, p. 16.   [3] Ibid., p. 17.

senses in the compass of two brief sentences, without any intimation to that effect ; in other words, that in the first verse it
signifies the whole globe, while in the second it must be
understood only of *a portion* of its surface. Without for a
moment questioning that in the Hebrew Scriptures the term
הָאָרֶץ is used in the latter signification, just as in the New
Testament the corresponding word γῆ denotes *a country,
region,* or *territory,* as well as the terrestrial globe—*the earth,*
as distinguished from the heavens, and that its greater or less
extent is to be gathered from the subject or context, it seems
a very doubtful, if not incredible, assumption, to maintain
that, without any qualifying note, any author, and least of all
an inspired writer, should, in the same breath, use the term in
two senses so widely different. This is more particularly the
case in the present instance, where, to all intents, *the earth* of
the first announcement evidently furnishes a definition of the
earth which forms the principal subject of the succeeding
narrative, in the course of which the same term does indeed
occur in another sense, but not without due intimation : verse
10, " God called the dry land earth."

The objection thus urged is not a mere matter of inference,
but is based on the express declarations of Scripture itself
regarding the extent of the creation therein described. At
the close of the sixth day, it is said, and with a pointed reference to the preceding narrative, " Thus the heavens and the
earth were finished, and all the host of them," Gen. ii. 1 ; a
statement which undoubtedly shews that the creation described
in the first chapter was not limited even to the earth, and far
less to a portion of it, but embraced *heaven and earth, and all
their hosts.* And still more strongly, if possible, and expressly
including the whole creating process in the operations of the
six days, is the declaration in the Decalogue, " In six days the
Lord made heaven and earth, the sea, and all that in them is,"
Exod. xx. 11. See also chap. xxxi. 17.

But another difficulty attends the theory of a merely local
creation. If, as is maintained by this scheme, other seas were
teeming with inhabitants, and other lands were clothed with
vegetation and filled with animal life, and other skies were pouring down golden light on field and forest, and were swept over
by the winged tribes, for what purpose, it may not unnaturally

be asked, must direct creative energies be put forth in the supposed depopulated region, and not rather leave the clearing of its atmosphere, and the peopling of its seas, and skies, and fields to the laws already in operation, and which were sufficient for all the requirements of the case? Why multiply miracles if they cannot be shewn to be necessary in the circumstances? If it be replied that the only new creation was man, and a few of the domesticated animals specially introduced for his use, the question then arises, In what light is the blessing to be regarded which was pronounced upon the newly created fishes and birds of this locality, " Be fruitful, and multiply, and fill the waters in the seas, and let fowl multiply in the earth ?" Gen. i. 22. Are the *seas* and *earth* here referred to the seas and earth of the circumscribed region—or are the terms to be understood generally, and so including seas and lands already peopled? If the terms are to be taken in the latter sense, why the blessing?—and if in the former, how do they harmonize with the similar blessing pronounced on man, " Be fruitful and multiply, and replenish the *earth*, and subdue it ; and have dominion over the fish of the *sea*, and over the fowl of the air, and over every living thing that moveth upon the earth," where the terms are evidently taken in the widest sense? But it is unnecessary to pursue the subject farther, as nothing but confusion and contradiction can come out of it.

3. A third mode of reconciliation proposed regards the narrative in Genesis as one connected whole, describing the various acts and evolutions of the one creating process from its beginning to its close. The various acts described from the *beginning*, which marked the origination of the heavens and the earth, onwards to the period when God finding all to be very good, and answering to his purpose, ceased from working, are, according to this view, links of one chain,—the successive parts of the one great drama of Omnipotent display, whereby the universe and the earth, as a part of it, have been brought into their present state. This view of the matter has the merit of preserving the simplicity and grandeur of the record of creation ; and at the same time accords well with the statement in the Decalogue, which expressly includes the whole creation in the six days. But, then, to meet the requirements of geology, and particularly its large demands on

time, a peculiar sense is ascribed to the word *day* as connected
with the creation : it is taken to signify a *period* of unknown
but immense duration. In this way it is conceived that the
creating process may have been indefinitely extended through
six periods, while its various phases succeeded one another in
the order which Moses describes ; an order which, as has been
shewn, is in remarkable accordance with the latest discoveries
of geology.

It was held in former times by Descartes, Whiston, De Luc,
and others, that the days of creation were not literal days, or
periods of twenty-four hours, but of vast, indefinite duration.
When more recently the discoveries of geology threatened to
impinge on Scripture, or its current interpretation, not a few
distinguished men, as Baron Cuvier, Professor Silliman of
America, and the late Professor Jameson of Edinburgh, adopted
this view as presenting the readiest solution of the difficulty.
Latterly, however, this mode of reconciliation has been very
much abandoned[1] for one or other of the schemes already
noticed, it being supposed that such an explication of the term
day had nothing to warrant it, but was rather excluded by the
specific mention of evening and morning as its constituent
parts. But the point seems worthy of re-examination, as the
view here presented has otherwise much to recommend it. If
it can be shewn that the days may, and, indeed, from various
considerations connected with the narrative itself, must be
taken in the extended sense, the reconciliation will be complete.[2]

IV.—THE DAYS OF CREATION.

Setting aside for the present all extraneous considerations,
and confining the attention to Scripture alone, it is proposed

---

[1] It would appear from a notice in the American *Bibliotheca Sacra*, April 1855,
p. 324, that it is revived by Professor Arnold Guyot.

[2] Before leaving this part of the subject, some notice must be taken of the well-
meant but evidently misapplied labour expended on a new cosmogonic theory in a
recent work, entitled " The Dynamical Theory of the formation of the Earth, based
on the assumption of its non-rotation during the whole period called ' the beginning.' " By Archibald Tucker Ritchie. Second edition, Lond. 1854, pp. 704.
The author's reverence for Scripture is commendable ; but not so his application of
its statements to supplement scientific deficiencies in what he calls his inductive
reasonings.

to inquire, whether anything in the narrative of creation, or in the term itself, forbids the extension of *day* beyond its literal and usual acceptation. This is particularly needed in a case such as the present, where the signification of a term in itself exceedingly simple may be greatly affected by the context. It will farther greatly simplify the discussion by clearing a foundation for any positive evidence, if, in the first place, it can be shewn that there is nothing which, expressly or by implication, excludes the extended meaning.

First, then, it is admitted on all hands, that both in the Old and New Testaments, the terms םוֹי and ἡμέρα are frequently used in the wider sense of *a period*, or time, as made up of days. But as Pye Smith remarks, " It is evident that this figurative use is employed, more generally indeed, in poetical or oratorical diction, but always when the connexion in any given instance makes it unquestionably manifest that a figurative sense is intended."[1]   From this, however, it is plain, that there is nothing in the word itself which necessarily limits its duration, which is the only point at present contended for.

But, *secondly*, neither does the context furnish any grounds for the limited duration of the days of creation. The mention made of " evening and morning," or, as it is sometimes improperly put, " alternations of day and night,"[2] is a point much insisted on as decisive of the question that only natural days are meant. This, however, is far from being the case ; for, in the first place, if the word *day* be used in a figurative sense, so must also the terms *evening* and *morning*. If any period, long or short, be designated in this way, as is not unusual, its close and commencement will naturally be described by the words in question. What more common than the expressions, the evening and morning of life, or of one's days ! But in the second place, any power which is thus supposed to belong to the combination, " the evening and the morning," in defining and limiting the *day*, arises solely from the rendering of the English Version, and will entirely disappear before a careful examination of the original. Instead of, " and the evening and the morning were the first day," and so on in the other instances, the Hebrew reads, " It was evening, it was morning,"

---

[1] Scripture and Geology, p. 201.
[2] Baden Powell in Cyclopædia of Biblical Literature, vol. i. p. 478.

&c. ; a form of expression which is by no means a circumlocution for *an entire day*, or any period of time. It merely indicates the succession of time, and the transition to a new day
of creating activity. Throughout the first section of Genesis,
the *vav consecutivum* of the Hebrew grammarians points out
only *the order of succession*, so that what stands first preceded
in time. In the present case, the order is thus :—" God said,
Be light ! Light was. God divided the light from the darkness. . . . It was evening, it was morning." All advances in
the narrative are in the strictest order of time, but without
any indication of its absolute duration. That no particular
period is fixed or defined, appears farther from the peculiar
arrangement of the terms, " evening, morning," and not
" morning, evening." This is usually explained or disposed of
by the remark, that darkness preceded the light ; to which
circumstance is also referred the Jewish custom of beginning
the civil day with the evening.[1] This explanation, however, is
not sufficient. Its fallacy will at once appear when it is considered, that the darkness which preceded the light, and which
was afterwards divided from it, is not called *evening* but *night ;*
and farther, that the expression, " it was evening," necessarily
presupposes a day or period of light, of which this was the
close. The day of creation cannot have begun with the evening, it must have begun with the morning,—a morning which
dawned at the instant when the Divine command went forth,
" Let there be light." Accordingly, the first mentioned morning must be understood not of the dawn of the *first*, but of the
second day.

But, again, in whatever sense " the evening and the morning"
may be taken, there is no ground to conclude that days of only
twenty-four hours are here meant. The natural day is measured by a revolution of the earth on its axis, as determined

---

[1] The Hebrews, as also many other ancient nations, began their civil day with
the evening—a custom founded, it is generally supposed, on the priority of darkness. Kurtz (Bibel und Astronomie, 3te Ausg., Berlin, 1853, p. 86) takes another
view of the matter. " It is based not on the first, but on the seventh day. The
day of labour naturally began with the morning, but the day of rest with the evening. As the Sabbath was the rule and measure for all religious and civil divisions
of time, and as the Sabbath naturally began with the close of the preceding day of
labour, so consistency, and the regulating character of that day, required the reckon-
ing of time in general to be conformed to it."

by the heavenly bodies. But with the full admission or belief of the earth's rotatory motion from the commencement of the system, or, at least, from the period indicated as the first day, it must also be received as expressly stated in the narrative, that not until the *fourth* day were the heavenly bodies brought into such a relation with the earth as to constitute them luminaries and *measurers* of time. In the absence, then, of these indices, how, it may be asked, was the length of the first three days to be determined, and what authority is there for the assumption that they must have been natural days? Now, if it should be found that these may have been other than natural days, analogy would extend the same character to the other three days of creation.

It is often assumed, however, from the case of the Sabbath, that the argument from analogy is entirely the other way, and that its whole weight is in favour of the natural days. The case is thus put :—The seventh, or Sabbath-day, which closed the week of creation, is a natural day, and it is, therefore, contrary to all the laws of grammar and language, to conceive that the six preceding and closely associated days must be taken in a sense so widely different. If the premises were as thus stated, no valid objection could lie to the conclusion ; but if it can be shewn that the assumption regarding the duration of the seventh day is unnecessary or unwarranted, and that instead of limiting the Sabbath of Genesis or of creation, it must, on the contrary, be greatly protracted, not only will the objection be obviated, but an immense advantage shall be obtained in favour of the view, that the days of creation extend over immense periods of time. But this falls to be considered under the next head.

Meanwhile it may be of some importance to notice in these preparatory remarks, that in the narrative of creation itself, and even in the compass of a single verse, the word *day* is used in two senses: first, for the period during which light prevails, or *day* as distinguished from *night;* and, secondly, for the *periods* of creation, whatever these may have been. Of the first usage a definition is given, verse 5, " God called the light day, and the darkness he called night ;" but so far as can be deduced from the preceding examination of the matter, the other appears to be absolutely undetermined. So

far everything tends to leave the nature and duration of the
days of Genesis an open question. For aught to the contrary
in the term itself, or in the context, God's *creating day* may be
something peculiar or pre-eminent, such as the יְהֹוָה יוֹם, or *the day
of the Lord*, Isa. ii. 12—the appointed time for the manifestation of his power and judgments—a day when, as the prophet
declares, " the stars of heaven, and the constellations thereof,
shall not give their light : the sun shall be darkened in his
going forth, and the moon shall not cause her light to shine,"
Isa. xiii. 9, 10, or such as the day of grace or salvation (2 Cor.
vi. 2) which God has mercifully extended to man.

V.—THE DAYS OF CREATION NOT NATURAL DAYS.

The principal objections to the view which insists on a wider
extension of the days of creation being so far obviated, it
remains to adduce any considerations which more directly
favour it, if they do not absolutely require its reception. But
here again, in order not to encumber the subject, some of the
more usual, but at best doubtful, arguments will be dispensed
with. Of this kind, for instance, is the frequent reference
made to Genesis ii. 4, where that is spoken of as accomplished
in a day, which yet according to the account given in the first
chapter, extended to *six* days. Nothing, however, can be
made of this, although the argument be countenanced by such
an eminent Hebraist as Delitzsch. The word used in the
instance referred to is not the simple noun, but compounded
with a preposition, בְּיוֹם, and, as such, an adverbial form equivalent to *when*, or *at the time when*.[1] But even allowing all
that is claimed for the expression, what is gained but the
irreconcilable contradiction in the two statements, that whereas
the one makes the creation of the heavens and the earth to
have occupied six *days* or periods, the other declares the work
to have been effected in *one*. It may also be advisable to dis-
miss, as not directly bearing on the subject, the often quoted
words of the Psalmist, to the effect that a thousand years in
God's sight are but as yesterday when it is past, (Ps. xc. 4,) or
the Apostolic admonition, " Be not ignorant of this one thing,
that one day is with the Lord as a thousand years, and a

[1] See Noldii Concord. Partic. Hebr. 1734, pp. 178, 953.

thousand years as one day," 2 Pet. iii. 8. There need be no hesitation, however, in dispensing with any aid derivable from statements of such doubtful application, as there are several more direct and reliable arguments.

1. It is deserving of notice, in any inquiry as to the nature of the days during which God carried on and completed his work of creation, that the language of the narrative in introducing the first of them is very peculiar. The cardinal *one* is employed, and not the ordinal *first.* " It was evening, it was morning, one day." The peculiarity is thus accounted for by a recent Jewish writer :—" The words, *one day,* are here used, not merely to point out the rank in the succession of days, but in order to convey, that the space of time thereby expressed was equal to the diurnal revolution of the earth round its axis, and that *evening* and *morning* spoken of in the text, were equal to what subsequently was called *one day.*"[1] Than this supposition nothing can be more unfounded. It rests merely on assertion, and that of the most extravagant kind. The generality of interpreters, however, satisfy themselves as to the peculiarity of this sentence, with a rule laid down by the Hebrew grammarians, that in many cases the cardinal numbers may be used instead of the ordinal : but as this rule is founded on the present passage, and some other examples of a nearly similar construction, it evidently explains nothing. It merely announces a fact, without inquiring into the causes in which it originated, or by which it is governed. It will therefore be necessary to examine the matter somewhat more minutely, and trace this peculiarity, if possible, to its source.

The significations of the Hebrew numeral אֶחָד, may be arranged as follows :—

(1.) Its most frequent use is as the cardinal number *one,* variously modified in sense according to the context in which it stands. Thus it comes to signify *some one, a certain one ;* and is sometimes an equivalent for the indefinite article, as נָבִיא אֶחָד, *a certain prophet,* or simply *a prophet,* as in the English version, 1 Kings xx. 3. So also Ezek. viii. 18, " When I had digged in the wall, behold פֶּתַח אֶחָד, *a door.*"

[1] The Sacred Scriptures in Hebrew and English. By De Sola, &c. Lond. 1844, vol. i. p. 2.

(2.) It is also used in particular cases as an ordinal, *first,* instead of the usual term רִאשׁוֹן; and the grammarians refer to the present passage (Gen. i. 5) as an example of this usage :[1] but that this is such a case is exceedingly doubtful. According to Gesenius,[2] the word is used as an ordinal only in enumerating the *days of the month,* and that with or without יוֹם, *day,* as in Gen. viii. 5, 13, Lev. xxiii. 24, Ezra x. 16, 17 ; but always with the preposition בְּ prefixed. The same usage prevails also in Arabic. In the enumeration of *years* another construction is employed, as שְׁנַת אַחַת, properly *the year of one,* for *the first year,* Dan. ix. 1, 2, Ezra i. 1. Except in the cases mentioned, says Gesenius, the numeral אֶחָד is never equivalent to רִאשׁוֹן, *the first.* That the passage now under consideration cannot be included in this usage might be at once assumed, but that its importance demands and justifies a more extended examination.

(3.) This term also signifies, by way of eminence, that which is *singular,* or *rare :* or, according to Gesenius, " *unicus* in suo genere, *eximius,* incomparabilis." Thus Ezek. vii. 5, רָעָה אַחַת רָעָה, " calamity, singular calamity," where for special emphasis the numeral precedes the noun. So also Cant. vi. 9, " My dove, my undefiled, is *one,* (אַחַת הִיא, unica est illa,) the *one,* אַחַת הִיא, of her mother," (unice, præ ceteris dilecta.) In this sense some have also understood Dan. viii. 3, " Then I lifted up mine eyes, and saw, and behold there stood before me a ram" (אַיִל אֶחָד), *a peculiar* or *remarkable* ram, *i.e.,* a ram of a singular description—one having two horns of unequal length. But in this instance it may be used merely for the indefinite article, as in the examples cited above.

Such, then, are the various significations of this Hebrew numeral ; and it appears that its use as an *ordinal* is very circumscribed, indeed so circumscribed as to exclude Gen. i. 5 from the cases where it is so used. It is confirmatory of this conclusion to find that the ancient versions regarded it as the cardinal *one* in this passage. Thus the LXX. render it ἡμέρα μία, and the Vulgate *dies unus.* But in support of the rendering *first day,* which is that of the English and most modern versions, an appeal is sometimes made to Gen. ii. 11 ; viii. 5, 13. But these passages prove nothing to the purpose : in the

[1] Ewald, Lehrbuch d. Hebr. Sprache, 1844, § 269, a.   [2] Thesaurus, p. 62.

first of them, שֵׁם הָאֶחָד may be simply, "the name of the one;" and besides, this case is quite distinct from that under consideration, inasmuch as the article is employed. The other references are just *the days of the month*, in which, as already stated, this usage is found, and to which, indeed, it is limited. But this furnishes no analogy to the very peculiar form, יום אחד, of Gen. i. 5, used in reference to the first of the creation days. There is at least something special in the use of the numeral in question in the present connexion; and there appears to be no way of accounting for it, but on the supposition, which, as already seen, is fully authorized by the use of the language, that it was intended to indicate that the evening and the morning spoken of belonged not to an ordinary, but to a peculiar day—a day *sui generis;* or, in other words, a period of indefinite duration.[1]

This view receives not a little confirmation from the remarkable fact, that long before geology was thought of, or any necessity arose for extending the age of the earth, the peculiar expression employed in connexion with the *first day* attracted considerable attention. Josephus thus remarks concerning it:—" This was, indeed, the first day; but Moses said it was *one day*,—the reason of which I am able to give even now; but because I have promised to give such reasons for all things in a treatise by itself, I have put off its exposition till that time."[2] Philo, according to his usual custom, detected strange mysteries in the expression. He observes, " When light came, and darkness retreated and yielded to it, and boundaries were set in the space between the two, namely, evening and morning, then of necessity the measure of time was immediately perfected, which also the Creator called ' day,' and He called it not ' the first day,' but ' one day;' and it is spoken of thus, on account of the single nature of the world perceptible only by the intellect, which has a single nature."[3] The same peculiarity of expression arrested also the attention of several of the Christian Fathers. Augustine, for instance, observes, " It is difficult, if not impossible, for us to conceive what sort of days these were."

But it is of more importance to inquire whether the Bible

[1] Bush, Notes on Genesis, vol. i. p. 32.　　[2] Antiquities, i. 1. 1.
[3] Philo's Works, Yonge's Translation, vol. i. p. 9.

itself furnishes any confirmation of the view which regards this expression as peculiar, and appropriate only to a particular acceptation of the word *day*. Now, it is remarkable, that there is one other example of the same phrase, and in a connexion which strongly confirms the above conclusion. It is in Zech. xiv. 6, 7 ; a passage which is thus rendered by Henderson in his Version of the Minor Prophets,—

> " And it shall be in that day
> That there shall not be the light of the precious orbs,
> But condensed darkness.
> But there shall be *one day*
> (It is known to Jehovah)
> When it shall not be day and night ;
> For at the time of evening there shall be light."

The translator's note on the passage is here subjoined :— " Verse 6. Now follows the prediction of a period of unmitigated calamity, which may be regarded as comprehending the long centuries of oppression, cruelty, mockery, and scorn, to which the Jews have been subjected ever since the destruction of Jerusalem. . . . Verse 7. Another period is here predicted, but one entirely different from the preceding—a day altogether *unique*, אֶחָד יוֹם, *one peculiar day*, the only one of its kind. Its peculiarity is to consist in the absence of the alternations of day and night. It is to be all day—a period of entire freedom from war, oppression, and other outward evils which induce affliction and wretchedness, interrupt the peace of the Church, and prevent the spread of truth and righteousness. Νὺξ γὰρ οὐκ ἔσται ἐκεῖ, Rev. xxi. 25. *The time of evening* does not refer to the close of the happy period just described, but to that of the preceding period of afflictive darkness. At the very time when a dark and gloomy day is expected to give way to a night of still greater darkness and obscurity, light shall suddenly break forth, the light of the one long day which is to be interrupted by no night. That this period is that of the Millennium, or the thousand years, the circumstances of which are described (Rev. xx. 3-7), I cannot entertain a doubt. The time of its commencement has been variously but fruitlessly calculated. The knowledge of it the Father hath reserved in his own power. ' It is known to Jehovah,' and, by implication, to him alone."[1]

[1] Henderson on the Minor Prophets, Lond. 1845, pp. 438, 439.

But whatever differences of opinion may be entertained regarding the particular period referred to by the prophet, there can be no question that the *one day* is the proper designation of a *peculiar day*, " *dies unicus,* prorsus singularis," (Maurer) ; " Ein einziges Tag, (De Wette) ; or " einzig in seiner Art," *the only one of its kind,* (Hitzig) ; and that the form of expression is strictly parallel with Gen. i. 5. The coincidence is certainly very striking, and naturally suggests the question, if prophecy, which depicts the far distant future, has, as thus evinced, its *unique* day, why may not also creation, which has to do with a remote past, whose days were completed long ere history began ?

2. There are, moreover, circumstances recorded in the narrative itself, more particularly in the portion of it which relates to the creation of man, which naturally suggest an extension of the period. On the supposition that only natural days are meant, a difficulty arises from an incident in the history, from which it is not easy to escape. The incident adverted to is the exercise, so to speak, assigned to Adam, which consisted in reviewing and bestowing names upon the animal creation, as brought to him by the Creator for that purpose.

The beasts were created on the sixth day ; and afterwards man, male and female, (Gen. i. 27.) But from the more detailed narrative of man's creation in chapter second, it appears that the woman was not formed contemporaneously with the man, though on the same day. Some time, however, elapsed between the two creations, and in the interval the beasts of the field and the fowl of the air were brought to Adam, by whom names were assigned to them. Now, in whatever light this circumstance may be understood, or however much the number of the animals may be limited—whether, as some writers suppose, the assemblage consisted of those creatures only which were within the precincts of the garden of Eden, or included others—is a matter of little importance for the present question ; and whatever ends or purposes this act and exercise may have been designed to serve—whether intended to assure man of the power and dominion over the animal creation conferred on him by his Maker, or, as seems to be intimated, to convince him of his solitary and singular condition, and shew to him the necessity, and awake in him the desire, of a partner for the completion of his happiness, one thing is in the highest degree probable, if it does not amount to certainty, that it must have been a work of time. It is, at least, exceedingly difficult to suppose, that the exercise, whatever it was, could have been comprised and completed within the space of a few hours, which, at the utmost, can be assumed if the sixth day on which all those events occurred was only an ordinary day.

Any difficulty which may be thus conceived to belong to the subject, is not to be got rid of in the manner sometimes suggested ; to take, for example, the solution proposed by Holden. This author fully recognises the difficulty. " It is not easy," he says, " to conceive how the naming of even the creatures of Paradise could be completed on the sixth day when Eve was made ;" and he subjoins in a note, " The history states that the concourse commenced *before* Eve was made, but not that it terminated *previously*."[1] The inaccuracy of this statement must at once appear from the most cursory examination of the narrative. That the transaction terminated before the creation of Eve is plainly indicated by the statement which announces the result of his review of the animal creation :—" And Adam gave names to all cattle, and to the fowl of the air, and to every beast of the field ; *but for Adam there was not found an help meet for him.*" Another view of this incident, so far as regards its place in the history, has recently been put forth, but in a form still more objectionable, by an American writer,[2] who maintains, that " it is not absolutely necessary to suppose that this naming of the animals took place on the sixth day, or before the formation of Eve, even though it is said, verse 20, *after* the account of the naming of the animals, ' for Adam there was not found an help meet for him,' any more than it is necessary to suppose, that the production of the beasts of the field out of the ground, and of the fowl of the air, was subsequent to the creation of man ; because in Gen. ii. 19, the production of the animals is again mentioned *after* the statement of the fact, that no suitable companion for man was found." This, however, is an entire misconception. The production of the animals is mentioned *not after the intimation of*

---

[1] Dissertation on the Fall, p. 99.
[2] Hamilton, The Pentateuch and its Assailants, Edin. 1852, pp. 126, 127.

the fact, that no suitable companion for man was found, *but only after the intimation of the Divine purpose* to provide such for him. " And the Lord God said, It is not good that the man should be alone, I will make him an help meet for him," verse 18. The two things are totally distinct. Before leaving this matter, reference may be made to a statement of Dr. Kitto —a statement exceedingly natural, and expressive of an idea likely to occur to a reader of the history, but on the author's supposition of natural days, and with the acknowledgment that Adam and Eve were created on the sixth day, strange and inconsistent. It is this:—" Adam was not long left by his indulgent Creator to that feeling of disappointment which he must have experienced when he realized the conviction, that there was not among the creatures of the earth one suited to be his companion. *As he one day* awoke from a deep sleep, which the Lord had caused to fall upon him, he saw before him a creature whom he at once recognised as the being his heart had sought," &c.[1]

These, and other difficulties of a like kind,—as, for instance, those connected with the assumed brief period of probation between the Creation and the Fall,—are easily explained, if it can be assumed that this sixth day of creation included in it many natural days. It may be farther noticed, as a striking characteristic of this portion of sacred history, how scanty is the information furnished respecting time. The order of events is carefully marked, but not so their dates, or the duration of the intervening periods. There is not, for example, the slightest intimation which can help to determine, with any certainty, the precise date of the Fall—an event in itself of the highest importance in man's spiritual history. In these circumstances, is it too much to conclude that the matter of dates and days and duration has been purposely left an open question ?

3. But it is when the history reaches the end of the creative operation, and describes the Sabbath of creation and the rest of God, that it furnishes the greatest confirmation of the view which regards the days as periods of immense duration. In noticing, under the preceding sectional subdivision, some of the arguments relied on as favourable to the representation of

---

[1] Daily Bible Illustrations, vol. i. p. 57.

the days of creation as ordinary days, it was observed that the Sabbath had been assumed to be a natural day, and from this it was argued that such also must be the other days. A caveat, however, was entered against this assumption as to the duration of the Sabbath; and it is now proposed to shew that it is utterly unwarranted, and that so far from limiting the Sabbath of Genesis to the length of an ordinary day, it must, on the contrary, be greatly protracted,—extended, in fact, to an immense period.

At the beginning of the second chapter of Genesis, it is recorded that the heavens and the earth were finished. The universe had been prepared, arranged, and perfected through a series of creative acts, the result of every one of which was *good*, and the entire combination *very good*. By these Almighty operations the heavens were garnished above, and the earth was constituted the fit dwelling-place of various orders of animated beings. During the preparatory and progressive processes of this great work, the laws impressed on animate and inanimate matter, vegetable and animal instincts, the order, also, and regularity of the planetary motions, and of the times and seasons, testified to the being and perfections of the Lawgiver, had there been any creature on earth of sufficient intelligence to understand the language. But it was not until man was introduced that any evidence of a moral government was afforded in this portion of God's dominions. The previous creations related only to physical arrangements or developments; but with the formation of man—a moral agent, and so distinguished from all prior existences, the work of creation was crowned and completed. The sixth day witnessed man's creation, and " on the seventh day God ended his work which he had made; and he rested on the seventh day from all his work which he had made" (Gen. ii. 2).

God *rested*, it is here said, on the seventh day, from all his work. He *ceased* (שָׁבַת) from farther adding to the objects of creation, or from putting forth any more creative energies. The idea of *cessation* or *rest*, here for the first time brought to view, occupies a very prominent place in the word of God, and in some form or other runs like a golden thread through the various dispensations under which man has been placed from the beginning, representing some great blessing prepared for, and proffered to him by the Creator. It is seen in Genesis in its germ or first principles—the Sabbatic rest of God when the work of creation was accomplished : it is seen also in the Divine institution of the Sabbath,—" the Sabbath was made *for man*," (Mark ii. 27 :) it is seen in the offer of the promised land to Israel, and its designation as a *rest*—the type of the better and unbroken *rest* above ; and it is seen in its fullest development in the Gospel dispensation, in the precious and explicit promises to the believer, of everlasting rest in heaven ; yea, an entrance into the very rest of God (Heb. iv. 1-11).

Tracing back this important idea to its source—the rest of God which succeeded the work of creation—it is now proposed to inquire, so far as it may afford aid or direction to the settlement of the question regarding the days of creation, what information Scripture supplies in respect to this Sabbath—its nature and duration.

(1.) *The nature of God's Sabbath.*—God rested, or, as the Hebrew term may be better rendered in this connexion, *ceased*, to avoid the danger of in any way applying to the Most High that which is predicable only of his creatures. " The Creator of the ends of the earth fainteth not, neither is weary," Isa. xi. 28. He ceased from his work, not because he was weary or needed repose, but because creation was finished, and proved to be very good. " The Lord rejoiced in the works of his hands ;" he calmly contemplated it in its beauty and grandeur and utility ; and it is of the sensations arising from this review the expression is to be understood, " He rested and *was refreshed*," Exod. xxx. 17. The rest of God signifies then the composure, the peace, the satisfaction and blessedness which he enjoys—a state and a disposition which, in order to bring down to human comprehension, is represented as the consequence of resting from labour.

But the rest of God is not a rest absolutely and from every work. It is not a rest of inactivity, but in a peculiar sense a rest in activity. " My Father," says the Son of God, " worketh hitherto (ἕως ἄρτι ἐργάζεται), and I work," John v. 17. By ἐργάζεσθαι, expositors maintain is meant the *operation* of God, as displayed in the preservation and governance of all parts of his creation ; and by ἕως ἄρτι, is expressed the perpetuity of that preservation and governance, unremittingly exerted for the safety and welfare of his creatures.[1] This is so far true; but it does not exhaust the force of the expression, for, as Olshausen well remarks, " in the spiritual world, the creative activity of God constantly continues." In that higher sphere there is a *new creation* (καινὴ κτίσις, 2 Cor. v. 17) ever going on. There is a restoring process, a building up from the ruins of the Fall—a Divine purpose and a Divine work in raising man to a higher level than that on which the material creation placed him. In this the Father *worketh ;* and this is the work which he hath committed to the Son—the work of the one is a reflex of that of the other—a work in which the profoundest rest is not excluded by the highest activity.

It was not until the first creation ceased that this new creating process began ; and it is not, like the former, exerted on dull senseless matter, but on the accountable and immortal soul of man. This spiritual creation, or saving and sanctifying operation, is the work of God's Sabbath-day, as the first was, so to speak, his week-day work.[2] And for the carrying on of this spiritual work in man and by man, God has specially appointed and prescribed to him the holy rest of the Sabbath, an arrangement by which is intimated, as Luther finely observes,—" Thou shouldst cease from thine own work, that God may carry on his work in thee."

(2.) *The duration of God's Sabbath-day.*—On this little need be said, for if the nature of the Sabbath of Creation, or the rest of God, has been at all correctly indicated in the preceding remarks, it must be at once apparent that its duration is not to be measured by that of the Sabbath appointed for man. God's Sabbath, which began when the work of creation was finished, has not yet reached its close. It thus includes in it all the Sabbaths and week-days of man from the dawn of his history. There is in the narrative itself what cannot but be regarded as a remarkable confirmation of this conclusion or conjecture. At the close of the notice of the seventh day, the usual formula is wanting : it is not added, as in all the other cases, " *it was evening, it was morning,* the seventh day." What can be the import of this, if not designed to teach that the Divine Sabbath has not yet come to an end, and that this

---

[1] Bloomfield, Greek Testament, vol. i. p. 418.
[2] See Miller, Footprints, p. 307, where this idea is well expressed.

one day comprehends the entire future of at least man's earthly history? Viewed in this light, it cannot be said that this Sabbath has even yet reached its noon; but there is abundant assurance of this, that it will brighten more and more into the perfect day—the day of glory, when the mystery of God shall be finished, and God shall be all in all.

Some writers go farther, and delight to trace out and apportion the Sabbatic rest of the Three Persons of the Blessed Trinity—the rest of the Father at the creation, the rest of God the Son which began with the Sabbath of his resurrection, (Heb. iv. 10,) and the rest or Sabbath of the Holy Ghost, which will begin with the future setting up of new heavens and a new earth.[1] But these distinctions, however just, are by no means necessary to the present purpose.

It remains only to add, that if the preceding be a correct interpretation of God's Sabbath, it necessarily and by analogy follows that the other days of the narrative of creation must be taken not in a limited or literal sense, but in a sense corresponding to that of the seventh—the great period of grace and salvation.

All the preceding arguments have been deduced from the expressed or implied intimations of Scripture, more particularly from considerations connected with the narrative of Creation itself; and no notice has been taken of any external collateral confirmation,—such, for example, as the long periods of the traditionary cosmogonies considered in the preceding section, especially the notions of the Etrurians and ancient Persians. But it may not be inappropriate, before concluding the subject, to consider briefly any allusion to such long periods of creation discoverable in the New Testament.

Something of this sort—some reference it may be to those long protracted periods, is probably involved in the language of the Apostle in Hebrews i. 2, " God hath in these last days spoken to us by his Son, whom he hath appointed heir of all things, by whom also he *made the worlds*," or, as it may with equal or perhaps greater propriety be rendered, *constituted the ages, τοὺς αἰῶνας ἐποίησεν* ; and again, Eph. iii. 11, " According to the eternal purpose which he purposed in Christ Jesus ;" or, " According to *the disposition of the ages (κατὰ πρόθεσιν*

[1] See Ebrard, Commentary on Hebrews.—*Translation.* Edin. 1853, p. 155.

τῶν αἰώνων) which he made," &c. It is admitted on all hands
that the primary meaning of αἰῶνες is *periods*, marked by
signal events in the Divine government, though it is contended
in controversy with the Socinians, that in Heb. i. 2, it signifies
the material universe. But the meaning thus assigned to the
word nowhere occurs in classical Greek, but is based entirely
on an assumed later Hebrew or Rabbinical use of the term
עוֹלָם, which in the Old Testament, however, has invariably reference to *time*. But admitting that in the passage quoted, as
also in Heb. xi. 3, the word does signify the world or universe,
there is nothing in this to exclude a reference, but rather the
reverse, to the successive and prolonged periods of its existence.[1]
Accordingly, in any point of view, this peculiar expression
must be admitted to have a favourable bearing on the results
arrived at through the previous arguments.

SECT. VI.—THE NARRATIVE OF THE FALL—ITS PURPORT AND
CHARACTER.

Having in the two preceding sections considered some of
the more remarkable features of the Mosaic account of the
creation of the earth and of man, its most noble and richly
endowed tenant ; having, in particular, shown the incomparable superiority of that most venerable record, in grandeur of
conception and truthfulness of statement, over all other ancient
cosmogonies, and having also evinced its striking accordance
with the scientific results of modern times, it is proposed
to appropriate this and the four subsequent sections to a review of the history of that mysterious moral blight which fell
upon this lower part of God's works and dominions, and
withered its beauties in their very spring. This examination
will embrace the following topics :—a consideration of the purport and character of the biblical narrative which immediately
succeeds that of the creation ; a review of some of the principal

---

[1] Owen on Heb. i. 2, says, " עוֹלָם signifies the ages of the world in their succession and duration, which are things secret and hidden." And again, " αἰῶνες, in
the plural number, ' the worlds,' so called, chap. xi. 3, by a mere enallage of number, as some suppose, or with respect to *the many ages of the world's duration*."—
Works. Edin., 1854, vol. xx. p. 75.

objections which have been urged against it; the confirmation which it finds in heathen traditions, and in facts historically and scientifically authenticated, but, above all, the corroboration yielded to its chief incidents and delineations by the views of temptation and sin which are disclosed in the New Testament,—the character of the former as more especially illustrated in the history of Christ—the second Adam, the Lord from heaven, " who was in all points tempted like as we are," and of the latter as it shall be fully developed in the person of Antichrist, " the *man of sin* and son of perdition."

At the outset of the proposed inquiry, attention must be directed to the purport of this narrative, and its precise bearing on the Creation, which, according to the historian's antecedent statement, had been completed and declared to be " very good;" and also on the question relative to the origin and existence of evil, which has been rightly termed the enigma of the universe. A due consideration of the purport of the present narrative would unquestionably prevent many mistakes and hasty conclusions, and moreover check unwarranted expectations of a solution from Scripture of all the difficulties of this question. With the precise subject on which it was the intention of the writer to communicate information, must also be considered the character of the narrative, or the manner in which the purpose is carried out, and the amount of information communicated on the specific object in view.

First, then, the great point of the narrative contained in the third chapter of Genesis, is to apprise the reader that a state of things which commenced with the introduction of moral government on the earth, and on which, as the historian had pointedly noticed, the Creator's eye rested with complacency, came to a sudden termination, which but for the merciful interposition of God, would have resulted in man's eternal and irretrievable ruin. The immediate occasion of this catastrophe was, it is plainly intimated, a failure on the part of man—a creature made in God's image, endowed with reason and understanding, intrusted with dominion over the earth, and whose every want was abundantly provided for—to render due obedience to the Divine will as expressed in law, to which as the creature of God he was amenable. Subordinate to this general announcement, yet of great importance to the subsequent history of man in connexion with the scheme of grace, the first disclosure of which forms also a leading principle in the narrative, is the manner in which the moral convulsion was brought about, with its circumstances and antecedents.

In order, however, to form a proper estimate of the very important subject thus briefly sketched, and bring out more definitely the precise purport of the narrative of man's first act of disobedience to the law of God, which involved the forfeiture of all blessings, and reduced him to a condition which is mysteriously and ominously termed " death," it is necessary to state in a few sentences how the problem relative to the present condition and character of the human race presents itself on natural and moral considerations.

That the present condition of man, viewed as a sentient and moral being, is, in various respects, one of wretchedness and misery, observation and experience conjointly testify. The human mind also instinctively feels that this state, considered in itself, presents something exceedingly anomalous, and greatly at variance with the conclusions deducible simply from the ideas entertained of the character of the Creator and Preserver of all, as a Being in the highest sense just and benevolent in all his conduct. So strong is this feeling, that it has at all times led the great majority of those who have earnestly considered the subject, to the irresistible conclusion that the present cannot have been the original state of man, however much they may have disagreed as to the manner and extent of the change thus admitted. There is a principle in the human constitution which distinctly testifies to a connexion between suffering and sin, or a violation of law, and proclaims that the miseries to which the race without exception are exposed, are to be viewed not as calamities simply, but punishments for misconduct. These conclusions are entirely independent of any Scriptural truth or testimony. The sinfulness of human nature is not a conviction primarily forced upon the mind by the Bible or any external witness—it originates within, so that those who have never been favoured with the revelation of the Gospel of Christ, admit the great principle on which the Gospel proceeds. Some vague recollections, moreover, of a mighty revolution in human

nature were preserved and widely circulated in heathen traditions. The poets of antiquity delighted to sing of a golden
age, distinguished by the absence of crime and exemption
from all suffering, when men enjoyed uninterrupted communion with the gods. The philosophers also of the ancient
world were fully cognizant of the fact of the moral corruption
of the race—a truth learned not from tradition or poetic pictures of the *past*, but from the painful experience of the
present, with which they themselves had to do.

But how to account on philosophical principles for the fact
thus acknowledged was, and has ever been, the great insolvable
problem. The various attempts of ancient times to trace up
evil to its source, proceeded on one or other of two misconceptions, the one injuriously affecting the nature of God, the
other virtually denying the reality of the evil of which an
explanation was sought. On the one hand, *eternity* was
ascribed to sin, and the difficulties connected with its ingress
into creation resolved into the principle of Dualism, which
plays so prominent a part in Oriental mythology ; on the
other hand, the difficulty was evaded by refusing to acknowledge evil as such, or in its character of sin. These two extremes were afterwards brought very prominently into view in
the controversies which arose in the early Christian Church
through the systems of the Manicheans and Pelagians respectively ; and they have since been frequently reproduced in one
form or another. But neither of these solutions was of a
nature to afford full satisfaction to the conscience, however
much it might impose upon the understanding. The same
may be said of their modern substitutes, in so far as they
would charge God with being the cause of evil, or in any way
accessory to it, or seek to exonerate man from the guilt which,
in spite of all sophistry, he cannot but feel.

Of the great problem involved in the *origin* of evil, which,
as just stated, has so long and fruitlessly engaged the attention of the thoughtful, Scripture offers no solution. This must
be distinctly considered, in any estimate to be formed of the
account of the first sin given in Genesis. This portion of
Scripture is not an account of the origin of evil in the universe, nor, strictly speaking, of its introduction into this
world, for it is obscurely but significantly intimated in the

history that evil, or the enemy of God, had already some footing in, some access to, or communication with the inferior creation, ere it asserted dominion over it in man, the representative of God on earth, and also of the creation; although of the manner and extent of that intercourse there is little of positive information. The presence of an enemy, however, is hinted at, in the narrative which immediately precedes that of man's melancholy apostasy. There is a premonition of the evil or the danger to be guarded against, in the duty assigned to Adam in connexion with the garden which God appointed for his habitation and intrusted to his care. " And the Lord God took the man, and placed him in the garden of Eden, *to dress it and to keep it*" (Gen. ii. 15). Man's duty in this respect was twofold—to cultivate the blissful, hallowed enclosure, and to *protect* or *guard* it from some evil, hostile Power, and not, as the expression is generally understood, merely from the incursions of animals. This consideration, it may be remarked in passing, may diminish the surprise often felt at the apparently abrupt manner in which the notice of the serpent is introduced at the opening of the record, which first clearly evinces the existence, and agency, and success, of the great adversary of man.

The narrative under consideration assumes the existence of evil prior to the transactions which form its subject, but offers no explanation of its origin. In respect of the questions *how* and *where* it first originated, the sacred historian maintains a profound silence. His object evidently is simply to tell of the spread of this contagion, and the manner in which it obtained a mastery over man, who, although made " upright," fell a victim to this destroyer. To this, and the intimation of a victory over this malignant Power, all other questions are secondary, or not entertained at all. On various points, however, which bear collaterally on the specific object of the history, there is shed a clear and convincing light; although the exposition may not be of a kind to satisfy all the demands of curiosity on the subject. This record, in continuation of the history of creation with special respect to its moral development, clearly teaches that the present character and condition of the human family, estranged from God and exposed to his righteous displeasure, is widely different from the original or creation state, and that the change has been induced through an act of disobedience on the part of the first man to the law of a bountiful and beneficent Creator. Accordingly, while the immediate and direct object of the narrative is to explain the spread of evil, or its origin in the limited sense just stated, and in especial to account for the miseries to which the highest, most honoured, and favoured of God's earthly creatures are constantly exposed, it no less clearly establishes as a fundamental principle, which finds a response in every human heart,—the connexion which subsists between moral and physical evil, or between sin and suffering, by tracing all the miseries and disquietudes of human nature to guiltiness before God. The history makes it plain that moral evil is the procuring cause of physical evil, and that by the sorrows and sufferings to which man is exposed, he is judicially punished. No doubt the physical evils and disorders introduced by the transgression, and incident to man in his present circumstances, occupy the most prominent place in the history of his first transgression, nevertheless its reference to a complete disarrangement of the moral system cannot be overlooked.

It is not clear, then, on what grounds Julius Müller maintains, that " as the entire narrative is directly to explain not the origin of *sin,* but that of *evil,* it tells us nothing expressly of *moral disorders* which had entered in with the first sin." This author, it must be stated, by no means denies that moral disorders did originate on the occasion and in the manner referred to by the historian ; all that he seems to assert or imply is, that they are not expressly mentioned in the narrative. The incorrectness, however, of this statement, if the distinction be anything more than a question of words, will be at once apparent. The fears which seized our first parents immediately on their transgression, and the attempts made, as the history particularly notices, to hide their shame from one another, and themselves from God, together with the ungenerous endeavours of Adam to transfer his guilt to the woman to whom he was united by the strongest possible ties, and whom he was bound to cherish as his own *flesh,* as he had himself but recently owned, and indirectly to charge even God himself as accessory to his ruin—unquestionably tell of moral disorders amounting to an entire revolution in man's feelings and apprehensions of

H

things. According to Julius Müller, the concealed attempt of
Adam to cast the guilt of his fall upon Eve, and then farther
upon God, hints at other offences which immediately followed
that first transgression. But this supposition, admitting it to
be well grounded, is utterly unnecessary, and does not in the
slightest degree alter the nature of the case; for whatever
offences followed, arose out of the original transgression, bore
its impress, and, to a certain extent, produced the same bitter
fruits. " But the Divine punitive judgment, Gen. iii. 16-19,"
adds this writer, " does not of course suspend over man, that
which as his perverted act, or as a conditioned state, he must
recognise as his culpableness, but that which exhibits itself as
a suffering inflicted upon him, misery, pain, and death."[1]
There is in this statement what cannot but be regarded as a
great though common misconception of what it terms the
Divine punitive judgment. That judgment did not, as is here
evidently assumed, consist merely in physical sufferings; in
particular, it is not to be determined, either as to its character
or consequences from the passage referred to, which is the
revelation of a remedial provision rather than the announcement of wrath and retribution, or a sentence of condemnation.
The true nature of the condemnation which overtook the
transgressor, is to be judged of from the original threatening
in the prohibition to eat of the tree of the knowledge of good
and evil: " In the day that thou eatest thereof thou shalt
surely die," (Gen. ii. 17.) The death thus threatened, and
which was in due course incurred, was most certainly a state,
and, by implication, a penalty, in which the sinner must have
recognised his culpableness or guilt. It was not physical evils
or disorders against which the warning voice of that Divine
premonition was directed, but moral evil—sin and estrangement from God.

    It is to be also noticed, as already incidentally adverted to,
how, with the account of man's ruin, there is connected in this
important chapter, and constituting one of the leading principles of the record, an intimation of a Divine purpose regarding the restoration of the transgressors and the defeat of the
Adversary, through whose machinations they were seduced
from allegiance to their Creator. Although horribly obscured

---

[1] Christian Doctrine of Sin, vol. ii. p. 433.

the prospect, and awfully ominous the cloud which had gathered round our fallen progenitors, Divine mercy, unsolicited and unexpected, disclosed a bright opening into the future, through which faith could enter in and be again blessed. God's promise of redemption, like the rainbow, gilded the thundery cloud of wrath which had gathered over Eden, or rather over the sinners' own souls, and threatened to overwhelm them everlastingly ; so that though the narrative opens in a way which excites fears and evil forebodings, the worst of which in its progress are fully realized, its concluding sentences, notwithstanding the numerous pains and privations announced, with the expulsion from Eden, shed down a sweet and benignant light on the otherwise dark and bewildering path of man's future history. Of so much importance is the principle now noticed in correctly estimating the nature of this record, that it may be with all safety affirmed, that were it not for the intimation which it contains of a restoration and recovery from the miserable condition into which sin plunged man, there is no reason to believe it would have been written either for his own information, or that of any other order of intelligent beings. On the same principles it may be that although there are in Scripture various intimations of a defection in the higher, spiritual world, a history of the angelic fall was, for aught that appears, never written, at least it has not been written for the use of man. Than these considerations, nothing more clearly shows the wholly practical aim and specific purpose of the present narrative. The disease is described so far only as was necessary to a correct apprehension of its nature and deadly character ; and if any significant intimations are added of the quarter whence it more immediately issued, all the information communicated is evidently with the view of shewing the suitableness of the remedy provided in the promise : " The seed of the woman shall bruise the head of the serpent."

The subject thus presented to notice is one whose importance, in a practical point of view, and as a matter of personal concern, cannot be overrated. The momentous and melancholy act of disobedience, by reason of which a new and disturbing element was introduced into the harmony of man's being and his relation to God, the source of all life and enjoyment, resulted in what, in theological language, is usually denominated the Fall,—a term expressive of all the changes, physical and moral, in man's constitution, consequent on his transgression. The expression, as thus used, does not occur in the Canonical Scriptures, but is found in the apocryphal writing styled " The Wisdom of Solomon." It is there said, (chap. x. 1,) " Wisdom preserved the first-formed father of the world that was created alone, and brought him out of his fall." But it is doubtful whether the term has been directly borrowed from this, or whether it be not more probably a translation of the Latin *lapsus*, as used by the Christian Fathers and the writers of the Reformation. This, however, is of no moment ; for whatever may be the designation given to the change induced in man's character and condition, it is one to which, under a variety of names and expressions, continual reference is made throughout the Scriptures, and which has stamped its universal and enduring features on the history of the Adamic race.

It would be utterly foreign to the present purpose to enter upon any examination, dogmatic or controversial, of the nature and character of the change thus occasioned in man's relation to all that is holy and good, and of the consequences, immediately or remotely, to which it has given birth ; or to discuss the many questions and controversies which have gathered round this central point of Theology. Such discussions properly belong to Systematic Theology ; and in treatises on that subject they usually occupy a very prominent place, under the heads or titles of the " Covenant of Works," the " Edenic or Adamic Dispensation," and " Original Sin." There are, however, several particulars comprehended under these general heads, the right exposition of which is so intimately connected with, and indeed so indispensable to, a correct apprehension of the narrative of the Fall, that they cannot be entirely overlooked, and yet, with very few exceptions, the consideration of them must be reserved for the expository portion of this work. Of this description are, for instance, the discussions connected with the penalty annexed to the transgression, and the sentence afterwards pronounced upon the guilty pair. So also the statement regarding the image of God in man, which has an important bearing on the nature and extent of the Fall, though occupying only a subordinate place in any discussions connected with the mere vindication of the historical and inspired character of the narrative. But as the present object is mainly exegetical, these matters will be discussed in a form and connexion different from that usually attended to in Treatises on Theology.

In the meantime, it is proposed simply to vindicate the narrative of the Fall from various misapprehensions, misrepresentations, or aspersions, to which it has been subjected. It may not be unnecessary, however, to observe, that this must not be confounded with the vindication of the doctrine of the Fall, or of the character of God in permitting evil to enter into his dominions and mar his works. The two subjects are totally distinct; and though the latter be undoubtedly one of the great difficulties of belief, yet not peculiarly of the belief in Christianity and the Bible, but in the being and perfections of God. Upon the consideration of the general question involved in the doctrine of a fall, save in a few passing remarks in the following section, where objections are stated, there is at present no intention whatever of entering; and from what has been observed on the purport and special bearing of the history in Genesis, it will be seen that such, in the circumstances, is not required.

The character of the narrative of the Fall, or the manner in which the sacred historian carries out the object which he proposed to himself, comes next to be considered. That object was, as already shewn, to connect the present with a past and perished order of things, by intimating how that which was created very *good* became very *evil*, and how a moral virus, from which spring all the miseries which embitter life, was communicated to the father of the human family. Considered in themselves, the intimations thus made regarding the defection of a moral creature, with the consequent forfeiture of all good, are exceedingly appalling, and, when viewed in their principles, perplexing in the highest degree. This portion of Scripture exhibits the terrestrial creation in man, its representative, breaking loose from God, and arraying itself against Him—the Almighty and Omniscient, whose power called it into existence, and whose pleasure continues it in being. But it is not in this painfully perplexing aspect that the Bible chiefly views the falling away of man from his original righteousness.   Although never losing sight of the culpableness essentially attaching to this perversion of the powers of free moral agents, it practically looks upon it as the disease of human nature for which the Gospel provides a remedy; and while it may be expected that those who have formed different systems, with regard to the nature of the remedy, will differ also as to the character of the disease, yet the subject, as presented in Scripture, is brought down from the airy heights of speculation and metaphysics, and is constituted an object of faith and practical religion, with special application to the conscience of the transgressor.

This mode of treating the subject is particularly exemplified in the narrative of the Fall, and forms one of its leading characteristics.   It has been already remarked, how the historian limits himself to one specific object, the spread of evil in this lower portion of God's dominions.   He assumes its existence in the universe, in the kingdom of the *good*, but does not attempt to lay bare the foundation on which it rests.   The aim is entirely practical, so that one of the first things which strikes the reader is the utter absence of aught having the least indication of a theorizing tendency, or a disposition to gratify mere curiosity.   This was a characteristic observable in the history of the Creation, but it is equally apparent in that of the Fall ; and yet, of all imaginable themes, what so inviting to speculation, what so prompting to questionings, as creation, and the origin and growth of evil among the works of the infinitely blessed, righteous, and holy God !   What were the immediate and remote causes of evil when all was very good ?   When, and where, and in what form, did it first betray its horrid and hateful character ?   What was the path of this destroyer through the universe—what its inroads on other worlds than this—and finally, to what power and stature did it attain before it attempted and succeeded in the subjugation of the human race ?   These, and innumerable other questions, pressed for a reply ; and when one calmly contemplates the matter in the light of reason and experience, and compares the history of the Fall in Genesis with the innumerable attempts made by wise and learned men to explain the origin of evil and fathom all its mysteries, and the unprofitable speculations which have thence resulted, the conclusion appears irresistible, that it required something more than mere human judgment, and caution, and modesty to withstand similar tendencies, in the manner and to the extent manifested in the third chapter of Genesis.

But, on the other hand, it may be thought that, in regard to various particulars, this reticence on the part of the writer has been carried too far. Even the practical reader may be disposed to desiderate more information on certain matters but slightly touched on, and upon which there is every reason to believe, had it suited the purpose of the historian, he could have thrown full light. But that purpose, influenced as it must undoubtedly have been by the particular circumstances of the case and of the times, especially the state of the Church when this history was written, must, in all fairness, be allowed to have weighed with the writer, both as to the extent of the information, and the mode in which it was to be imparted. This mode of presenting the subject with a reserve evidently intentional, is strikingly illustrated in the account given of the tempter, over whose true character and personality, for the time being, and perhaps owing to the strong tendency to idolatry which characterized the Israelites when this history was written, Divine wisdom saw it fit to draw a veil, to be removed only when circumstances so warranted.

Another matter to be taken into account, and which explains some of the difficulties and obscurities of the narrative, is the fact of its conciseness. It is not a memorial of the first human pair, or of all the incidents of their remarkable experience, but is limited to one transaction which determined their whole future history. It is only a leaf, so to speak, from the history of Adam ; and hence it is, that although in logical sequence the narrative of the Fall follows closely, and, indeed, is intimately connected with that of the creation of man, no intimation is given which can serve for connecting the two events in time, or determining the interval by which they were separated. All the information furnished by Scripture regarding the duration of the paradisaical and probationary state is limited to the intimation, inferential rather than express, yet not the less conclusive, that it came to an end previous to the birth, or even the conception, of any child of Adam. (Gen. iv. 1.) In these circumstances, it may be added, that it must be apparent the speculation largely indulged in by Christian as well as Jewish writers, who specify a particular day—the sixth or the seventh, the day of Adam's creation and union to Eve, the help-meet by Divine beneficence provided for him, or that immediately succeeding, as that of the Fall, or by those who more adventurously extend the state of innocence to a period of seven months,[1] is as unwise as it is unprofitable. The conclusions arrived at on this and similar questions furnish only additional grounds for doubt and disputation to those who not unfrequently confound the baseless inferences of expositors with the statements of the text. The prejudices which are often caused in this way will appear when some of the objections stated in the next section come under consideration. At present, attention is simply called to the fact, that there are many questions connected with the Fall, of which the duration of the state of innocence is only one, on which Scripture gives no information, and indeed may be said, in certain instances, studiously to withhold light, which, if vouchsafed, would, it may be presumed, greatly illustrate the narrative, and disclose to the earnest reader additional depths of Divine wisdom and grace, as contrasted with the supreme folly and wickedness of sin, though it may be also supposed that no explanations would suffice to silence the cavils of objectors bent only on wresting this narrative, as also the other Scriptures, to their own destruction (2 Pet. iii. 16).

The conciseness of the narrative, or its fragmentary character, so to speak, in an historical but not a literary point of view, also explains the manner in which it opens, apparently not at the beginning of the temptation, but near the crisis or catastrophe, —nothing being said of the gradual and guarded manner which, there is no doubt, marked the tempter's approach and proposals to the woman.

Another feature worthy of notice in the narrative of the Fall, as, indeed, throughout Scripture, is the circumstance, that notwithstanding the numerous objections to which, from its contents, and especially its form of description or delineation,

[1] An Essay on the Scheme and Conduct, Procedure and Extent, of Man's Redemption. By William Worthington. Second edition, Lond. 1748, p. 15.

it might seem to be exposed, nothing can be discovered on the part of the writer that deserves to be termed apologetic. There is no attempt made, or anxiety manifested, to bespeak indulgence, to disarm prejudice, or to explain away or smooth over anything that might give rise to objections on the part of an opponent, or one disposed to take offence. It is plain from the narrative, in all its bearings, that there is united in the writer the utmost candour and singleness of purpose, with the absence of all fear and misgiving. The difficulties and obscurities are permitted to remain : it may be as a trial or temptation bearing some faint resemblance to that which is the subject of the history itself—a temptation which, to the unbeliever, proves a snare or a stumblingblock ; but to the humble, heaven-taught Christian, becomes a salutary exercise of patience and faith,—of patience in waiting for future light to clear up obscurities, and of faith in receiving the narrative with all its difficulties, as composed through God's inspiration, and preserved by his providence, for remedying the grievous malady to which it ascribes all human wretchedness, when all other particulars regarding the first created man and father of the human family have perished from the memory of his descendants.

The characteristics thus far stated supply considerations justly entitled to weigh in any judgment that may be entertained of the nature and character of the matters recorded in the narrative of the Fall, and of their historical credibility, notwithstanding the difficulties which unquestionably encompass the subject. But another point to which still more weight is due in shewing the distinguishing peculiarity of this history, in respect to other theories formed upon the subject, is the way in which the true character of the Creator and the creature is manifested and maintained. The narrative, in accounting for the introduction and triumph of evil, never for an instant loses sight, or misrepresents the character, of the Creator, or of his responsible creature, either before or subsequent to his transgression of the Divine commandment. It never confounds the nature of things by calling evil good, or good evil. The broad lines of demarcation which separate these attributes or conditions are never, under any circumstances, overlooked. Everywhere the writer is found maintaining the most direct

opposition of good and evil. God is holy, just, and good : his
character is absolutely unspotted ; and the creature also, as
brought into being by Him, is *good*, in strong contrast to that
which, through apostasy, has become evil and depraved. In
entire accordance with this view of the character of God, and
of his creature as such, the temptation does not originate
within man himself, but comes to him from without ; yet not
from God, but from a source which declared itself to be the
enemy of all truth and righteousness. But to prevent any
mistake as to this being a power irresistible or independent,
God, in the condemnation of the tempter, is seen asserting
his supremacy, while he also concerns himself for the injury
done to his creatures. It is thus that the narrative, in a manner unapproached by any other hypothesis of the ancient
world, leaves untouched the character and perfections of the
One living and true God, without denying the reality of sin, as
well the criminality, as the rise and progress of which, as here
described, eminently accord with human consciousness, and
correct conceptions of the relation of Creator and creature.

SECT. VII.—OBJECTIONS TO THE ACCOUNT OF THE FALL
CONSIDERED.

The objections which have at different periods been advanced
against the biblical account of man's falling away from a state
of original righteousness, and the exceptions taken to various
incidents in that narration, or to inferences deduced from it,
are, as was stated in a previous section, exceedingly numerous.
But the opposition thus manifested will, when duly considered,
be no matter of astonishment. Indeed it could scarcely be
expected to be otherwise with a subject which in itself may be
said to be unfathomable to created intelligence, and certainly
to the human understanding as presently constituted, and
moreover involves so many and immense consequences bearing directly on man's present character, and his future and
eternal prospects. Judging from analogy and the nature of
things as witnessed in the fierce and prolonged controversies
waged on fields infinitely less important than that presented

in the chapter of man's history now under consideration, it could scarcely be expected but that a doctrine like that of the Fall, so humbling to human pride, so derogatory to all human assumptions and merits, would, in whatever form it should be delivered, call forth and encounter much and strong opposition. This spirit of opposition, again, would, it might be reasonably inferred, summon to its aid arguments and objections of every possible kind, from the contemptuous sneer of the materialist, who ridicules the reality of a Fall, to the subtle logic of the metaphysical pantheist, who confidently proclaims its impossibility.

But this opposition, when taken in connexion with the spirit of bitterness which is its usual accompaniment, can only be looked upon in whatever form it may appear, as in itself a witness to the truth of the doctrine it would call in question. Indeed, in one respect, what are all controversies, more especially religious controversies, and the mode in which they are too often conducted, but striking testimonies of the perverseness or prejudices of the human mind—a darkened understanding and a depraved heart? The pride and impatience which not unfrequently distinguish the objections and arguments brought to bear on the claims of Scripture to be the infallible Word of God, by which alone moral truth is to be decided and man's character tried, may be justly regarded as the natural and necessary consequences of the first act of transgression, or in another aspect as a disposition similar to that which resulted in the Fall : but in any point of view, indubitable indications of the alienation of the soul from God. It is by no means intended, in strict argumentation, to urge these considerations in proof of the doctrine of a Fall, or the account of it given in Genesis ; yet it is perfectly competent to present them in a light which has still an important bearing on the subject. If the Bible and its varied statements were universally and cordially welcomed, and God's laws cheerfully submitted to by man, instead of being as now in a great measure rejected and disobeyed, much of the evidence would be wanting which at present goes to confirm the scriptural account of human apostasy and alienation from God : so that, strictly speaking, the opposition adverted to is confirmatory rather than otherwise of the representation of human nature

contained in the third chapter of Genesis, and in the Scriptures throughout.

It would be as profitless, as it is obviously impossible, within
any reasonable limits, to enumerate, and much less to discuss
all, or even any considerable proportion of the multitudinous
objections which at various times, and under different forms,
have been brought to bear upon the present subject. Many of
the objections are in truth of a nature so trivial as not to
merit even a passing notice, and it is only matter of astonishment how men of understanding could be found seriously to
urge them. To give only one instance of such objections, reference may be made to Gen. iii. 7, " They sewed fig leaves
together, and made themselves aprons :" on which no less
learned and distinguished a man than Dr. Thomas Burnet,
author of the " Sacred Theory of the Earth," and other works,
with the view of discountenancing the literal interpretation,
seriously asks, whence could our first parents have procured
needles and thread ? This question, though frequently put, and
for sinister purposes, not contemplated by the author referred to,
is only a miserable criticism on the *translation* of a word which
in the original signifies to *fasten* or *connect* together in any way.
But passing over all such trifling conceits and captious observations, the more important and plausible of the objections which
have been advanced against this portion of Scripture, may be
conveniently arranged under these three heads :—

First, Objections which bear more directly on the doctrine
of the Fall, or the difficulties more or less connected with
all theories on the origin of evil, or a defection of the
creature from pristine innocence and uprightness.

Secondly, Objections having respect to the miraculous character of the history of the Fall in Genesis, and which,
originating in dislike or opposition to the miraculous in
all circumstances, apply in a measure, if not in an equal
degree, to other portions of Scripture as well as this.

Thirdly, Objections which specially apply to the third chapter of Genesis—to the *narrative* as contradistinguished
from the *doctrine* of the Fall, as referred to under the
first of these heads.

From the above synopsis, it will be at once apparent with
what particular class of objections it is at present purposed

more immediately to deal, seeing, as already intimated, that the object in view is not to establish or vindicate the *doctrine* of a Fall, or, it may be added, even to enter into any discussion of the philosophy or theology of miracles ; but taking for granted as truths avouched by independent and indubitable testimony, the reality of a Fall and the possibility of miracles, it is proposed simply to vindicate a character for soberness and consistency and credibility for that portion of Scripture in which the doctrine of man's apostasy from God is for the first time and circumstantially announced. Very few remarks will accordingly suffice for disposing of the numerous arguments and objections which come under the first two of the above heads. Without attempting an explication of the perplexities, or offering a reply to the arguments in question, it will, at the outset, be enough to shew that they are in reality as applicable, if not more so, to any other possible or conceivable explanation of the wretchedness and misery to which man is heir, in a system whose Author and Ruler is the infinitely just and benevolent God, as to that contained in Genesis : in other words, that the same difficulties press equally against natural as against revealed religion. In respect, again, to the objections of the third class, or those which more directly concern the narrative of the Fall in Genesis, it is confidently believed that on examination they will be found in the majority of instances to rest upon, or originate, in a misapprehension of its statements, not unfrequently countenanced by the dubious inferences of preachers and expositors, and by unquestioning popular beliefs.

In offering a few observations, with the view of disposing in the manner proposed, of the objections of the first class, or such as bear on the doctrine of the Fall, it is to be remarked, in the first place, that whatever difficulties may attach to the idea of a defection in the creation, the existence of moral cannot be questioned any more than that of physical evil. Men may, by subtle distinctions and sophistical definitions, impose upon themselves and others, but no amount of subtlety or sophistry can satisfy man that there is not something blameable in his conduct, and a cause of perturbation in his constitution. Even those theorists of the deistico-pelagian school of progress, who so attenuate the nature of sin as to destroy its real significance, cannot but admit its universal presence in human life. The very pantheist, too, who, to be consistent with his principles, is under the necessity of denying the existence of evil as such, must acknowledge that what the moral consciousness must condemn as sin, ever exhibits itself in human action and conduct: he knows of a contrast and conflict with the good, though he fancies he has made the grand discovery how to reconcile and even incorporate evil with good, as a necessary element of his world. In all such cases the name may be disclaimed, the disturbing element in question may not be called sin or transgression, but only a defect from the moral ideal, or some such complimentary designation ; nevertheless it is a power which persists in making itself felt and feared even by the most strenuous of its disputants. In the second place, no difficulty is removed by the denial of the doctrine of a Fall ; on the contrary, the difficulties are greatly multiplied and augmented, if a belief in the being and perfections of a Deity be retained. If human nature be not in a lapsed condition, why is it what it is ; and as it always must have been, although the product of wisdom and power, goodness and righteousness ? On what principle is man punished, and how is there that in man's bosom which pronounces him blameworthy ? Banish the Bible—get rid of its authority altogether, and yet no difficulty is thereby eliminated—not one step of progress is made in explaining the great mystery of human nature and human misery. Lastly, the objectors may be challenged to produce a more rational account of man's present condition than that contained in the Bible, and till they have succeeded in the undertaking, it is not too much to ask that the biblical account be allowed to remain.

The objections comprised under this head, then, although numerous and perplexing, are not of a nature to be much accounted of in their bearing on any scriptural truth or testimony, or any principle of revealed religion. If they prove anything, it is only the otherwise undeniable fact, admitted by none more readily than believers in the Bible, that human reason has not mastered the mighty and mysterious problems involved in the relation of Creator and creature. This ignorance by no means warrants the conclusion which would deny the possibility or the reality of a creature of God swerving from the path of original rectitude, without any reflection on the character of the Creator or his work as such ; more especially when the denial of the doctrine palpably involves more and greater difficulties than its admission. In this way may be fairly disposed of, if not answered, the strongest arguments usually and avowedly directed against the narrative of Genesis, but which in reality go to deny the doctrine of a Fall altogether, or the corruption of human nature, originating in the transgression of a Divine law by the first man, or in any other unknown and recondite cause.

Under this head, too, will fall to be reckoned, and to be similarly disposed of, a class of arguments closely connected with, but subordinate to those just stated. The arguments referred to are such as have for their object to deny or deride the doctrine of the existence and personality of a malignant Spirit, and his agency in temptation and on the souls of men.

Before, however, passing on to the next class of objections, as an instance of the arguments wherewith the narrative in Genesis is usually assailed, while they are in reality a denial of the existence of evil, reference may be made to that which is sometimes with great confidence deduced from the sentence passed upon the transgressors, (Gen. iii. 16-19.) That sentence, it is maintained, involves a false conception, for the punishments there said to be inflicted are the natural results of laws, arrangements, or dispositions of nature, which have God alone for their author, and are not therefore real evils : they are pains but not penalties.

This objection, in whatever form of words it may be stated, virtually amounts to a denial of the existence of evil, and is withal founded on a most fallacious process of reasoning. But the answer is simple. Granting that the pains and troubles to which man is exposed are the natural effects of appointed laws, and of the constitution under which he is placed by his Creator, and granting farther that " so far as these evils are merely physical, or bear a physical aspect, or are connected with other physical phenomena, they are not evils ;"[1] yet the matter assumes an entirely different appearance when viewed

---

[1] M'Cosh, Method of the Divine Government. Edin. 1850, p. 376.

in connexion with man—a moral agent, and originating in the purpose and executed by the power of a holy and benevolent Being, whom conscience declares to be our moral governor. No process of reasoning can ever prevail with the mind to regard the sufferings referred to as other than physical evils, and as the direct punishment of moral evil or sin.

The second class of objections are, as already stated, such as originate in opposition to, or involve a denial of all that is miraculous in the history of the Fall.

From the earliest times, miracles have proved in the hands of sceptics a fertile source of objections to Divine revelation, the earliest and the latest portions of which, as displaying more of a miraculous character, have especially afforded ample scope for hostile attacks. But happily now, through a larger and more correct acquaintance with the so-called laws of nature, of which the miracle was by the objectors alleged to be a violation which no testimony could accredit, combined with a better spirit of inquiry, these attacks have been very much turned aside, and have in consequence lost considerably their original impetus. It can now no longer be maintained by any laying claim to scientific acquirements, and a knowledge of nature's past operations, that a miracle is contrary to all experience. Geology, in particular, has largely contributed to bring about this result: it " has disclosed many new chapters in the world's history, and shown the existence of miracles earlier than chronological dates."[1] The miracles brought to light by science—miracles of creation demonstrable to the senses, and incontrovertible by any rules of logic or metaphysics, have procured at least a hearing for the miracles of Scripture. That miracles are impossible, will, accordingly, be now hardly maintained, and that they are not even improbable, has been more than established; the possibility and probability being converted into realities indelibly stamped on the medals of creation preserved in the great cabinet of nature. If, then, there have been miracles in creation, why should it be thought strange should they be met with on the higher field of revelation? and if the interpositions, immediate and direct, of the Creator and Moral Governor of the universe may be reasonably expected anywhere, or justified in any circum-

---

[1] Hitchcock, Religion of Geology, p. 279. See also Miller, Footprints, p. 248.

stances, surely it is in connexion with the transactions recorded in the opening pages of the Bible which treat of the infancy
of the human race, of times, and incidents, and conditions, both
physical and moral, differing widely from anything with which
at present we are or possibly can be conversant ; and to form a
correct judgment of which must, in the altered circumstances,
be exceedingly difficult if not impossible.

This simple observation ought of itself to go far towards
disposing of the class of objections now under consideration,
and neutralize any presumption against the credibility of the
transactions stated in the account of the Fall, so far as regards
their miraculous character and colouring. It has been well
remarked : " Whoever should be disposed to doubt that the
character of positive fact belongs to the historical account of
the first sin, because it contains something *miraculous*, would
shew his ignorance of the nature of the fact itself ; whoever
should desire that the first sin should come about in a natural
manner, would have the first sin itself regarded as a natural
thing, while, on the contrary, it was just that kind of thing
which is unnatural, and which has only become natural."[1]

Of the exceptions which, in this way, have been taken to
several incidents regarded as of a miraculous character, or, as
sometimes scoffingly styled by opposers, the *marvellous*, in the
biblical account of the Fall, with its immediate antecedents
and consequences, together with the particular machinery or
agency introduced, one or two instances may be shortly considered.

1. The objection urged against the scriptural account of the
origin of the human race, and more particularly in regard to
the formation of the woman, furnishes a remarkable instance
both of mistaken reasoning and misapplied merriment.[2]

In the origination of man there was undoubtedly a miracle,
and in that act, if anywhere, a miracle was required. In the
introduction of the human, as indeed of any other species,
whether of plant or animal, there was unquestionably something new—something which previously had no existence on
the earth, and therefore necessitating a departure from the

[1] Hävernick, Einleitung, I. ii. p. 252.
[2] Gabler, in Eichhorn's Urgeschichte, II. i. p. 121.

I

ordinary sequences or operations of nature, and an interposition in some way or other of the great Creative Cause; in short, a miracle. Any other supposition than this is irrational and absurd, whatever may be alleged to the contrary by the friends of the Development hypothesis. But farther, it must be no less evident, that in order to the safety and preservation of even their animal economy, there was a necessity that the first created human being, or beings, should be brought into existence in a state of maturity, and in the full exercise of their powers. Much more must this appear to be the case when account is taken of the various acts and exercises, not merely of a physical nature, but of an intellectual, moral, and religious kind, which it must be assumed were engaged in by man. " Who educated the first human pair ?" asks, in one of his sober moments, a leader of modern Pantheism ; " a spirit interested himself in them, as is laid down by an old, venerable, primeval document, which, taken together, contains the profoundest, the sublimest wisdom, and discloses results to which all philosophy must at last come." Farther, and in particular, so far from discerning anything ridiculous or absurd, as is frequently alleged in the scriptural representation of the woman's formation out of a part of the new-made man, heaven-taught philosophy will trace in it the most beautiful harmony with the laws of the creation, and the wisest adaptation to the sacred and social requirements of the case. Man himself was not formed from any new material, but from a new combination of pre-existing matter ; the woman, again, was formed from the man, as she was formed for him, and thus in her formation embodied all the prior laws of the creation ; but more especially she was thus placed, by the very constitution of her being, in the nearest and dearest relation to him for whom she was designed as a help-meet—a relation vividly realized in the experience of the first man at the moment that he gave utterance to the deep-felt emotion, " This is now bone of my bones, and flesh of my flesh : she shall be called woman, because she was taken out of man."

2. Another objection which may be properly classed under this head, is one founded on the immunity of our first parents from death and disease, in case of obedience to the Divine command, which charged them to abstain from the fruit of a

particular tree on pain of death.[1] In the threatening, " In the day that thou eatest thereof, thou shalt surely die," it is undoubtedly implied, that if man did not transgress the command, he should be exempted from all evils comprehended under the name *death*. To this it is often objected, that various considerations connected with man's constitution, animal and social, render such an exemption from death, or temporal dissolution, if not impossible, yet in the highest degree improbable. Two considerations are specially urged in regard to this point :—1. The physical organization of man necessarily implies progress, change, decay, and death ; and 2. The propagation of the race in conformity with the recorded blessing of creation, " Be fruitful and multiply, and replenish the earth," demands the removal of the successive races by death, as otherwise the earth would soon be overcrowded by its numerous tenants, or the law of generation must be suspended or repealed at no very distant date from its first enactment.

It is certainly true, as experience teaches, that decay, dissolution, or death, is a universal law of organic nature, as presently constituted ; and it is equally true, as physiology asserts, that this is a necessary law in the circumstances ; and it may farther be admitted, as established on incontrovertible evidence, that death, so far as the animal creation is concerned, was a law of organized beings prior to the apostasy, or even the creation of man. But none of these facts or findings by any means excludes the possibility of the functions of vegetable and animal organization going on for ever, without decay or death, if such had been the pleasure and purpose of the Creator. What is possible may, in certain circumstances and conditions, be probable ; and applying this to the case of man, and his presumed immunity from death, the probability may amount to a certainty, when it is considered what his place, according to the Divine purpose, is in creation, and in the whole future of the kingdom of God.

To the other consideration urged in the objection, it may be replied, there is certainly much force in this representation of the case ; and the difficulty therewith connected, if it were contemplated, or in any way maintained, by asserting for un-

[1] Gabler, in Eichhorn's Urgeschichte, II. i. p. 95. Newman, Phases of Faith, p. 69.

fallen man an exemption from death, that he was individually to continue for ever a denizen of the lower world, and was not in due time to be translated, generation after generation, to other spheres of existence in the vast universe of God. It is generally held by Christians that this would have been the case ; and as if to make the matter plain, at least to believers in the Bible, there are recorded more than one instance in the past dispensation of this kind of translation into another world without undergoing the change denominated death ; while there is the farther assurance, that in the future—the closing scene of the present order of things, this same change shall pass over many : " We shall not all sleep, but we shall all be changed, in a moment, in the twinkling of an eye, at the last trump : for the trumpet shall sound, and the dead shall be raised incorruptible, and we shall be changed." (1 Cor. xv. 51, 52.)

3. An objection is frequently taken to the part assigned to the serpent in the transaction ; whether regarded as the efficient, or merely the instrumental, cause of the Temptation and Fall. This objection presents itself in various aspects. Thus, it is said, assuming, as the narrative would evidently have it, that the tempter was nothing more than a natural serpent—a mere brute form—acts and exercises are ascribed to it which so far surpass the powers of any irrational creature, as to be explicable only on Esopian principles of interpretation. And, on the other hand, it is maintained, that to affirm the other alternative, and to suppose that the faculties of reason and speech then put in exercise were those of a higher hostile power actuating a serpent, or assuming its form, is to introduce a doctrine which strikes at the very root of the argument deduced from miracles, as furnishing peculiar attestations of a Divine revelation or mission, and which proceeds on the assumption that miracles can originate only with God, the supreme governor of the universe.

The whole subject, in its various bearings on the tempter-serpent, whether as the efficient or instrumental cause of man's ruin, will have to be considered fully in another connexion ; in the meantime, a few remarks will suffice for disposing of the objection in the two forms above presented. In regard to the one side of the argument, it is enough to observe, that as the writer of the narrative did not scruple, in the plainest and most direct manner, to ascribe extraordinary or supernatural powers and capacities to the serpent, this itself is a sufficient indication that he regarded it as more than the mere animal of that name. The other form of the objection ultimately resolves itself into the general question, Why did God permit the entrance of sin into his dominions? The bearing of the objection on the argument founded on miracles may, however, be briefly considered. If it must be assumed, as this objection evidently implies, that a miracle of itself, irrespective of any other consideration, proves the truth of a doctrine in support of which it is wrought, or of the statement which it would confirm, then assuredly there cannot have been a miracle in the case of the temptation, and in the communications of the serpent, for the statements then made were not only antagonistic to, but subversive of, the truth and testimony of God. On this view of the matter in general, it is sometimes maintained, that " it would evidently be inconsistent with the character of God to empower or to suffer wicked beings to work miracles in support of falsehood."[1] But numerous facts of Old and New Testament history cannot be easily reconciled with this assumption. The sacred writers make distinct mention of such things as " *lying* wonders" (2 Thess. ii. 9) ; so called, according to the ablest expositors, not because in themselves frauds and illusions, but because wrought in support of the kingdom of lies.[2] Olshausen characterizes these lying wonders as " astonishing, extraordinary operations in nature, which have their foundation only in the application of demoniac powers." To draw men from God and to evil is, he adds, to be imagined as the aim of these deceptions. Striking instances of the power and operations of evil spirits were witnessed during our Lord's life on earth. And if at that remarkable epoch in the history of the world, wicked spirits, as is expressly taught in the Gospels, had power or permission to produce preternatural effects on the minds and bodies of men, is it inconceivable that, at another and earlier period—another great crisis in the struggle of light and darkness, they might have

---

[1] Leonard Wood, in Cyclopædia of Biblical Literature, Art. *Miracles*, vol. ii. p. 347.

[2] See Trench, Notes on the Miracles, second edition, 1847, p. 21.

been suffered to produce the same or similar effects in and
upon irrational creatures ?   But however this may be, there is
undoubtedly more than a rhetorical figure in the declaration of
the Apostle, that " Satan himself is transformed into an angel
of light" (2 Cor. xi. 14) ; and if into an angel of light, why
not into any other suitable instrumentality ?

The objections hitherto considered bear more directly on the
subject of the Fall, and the truths therewith connected, and
accordingly press with almost equal weight against any form
of expression, or mode of narration, which might be selected
for communicating the same truths.   Those now to be stated
refer more particularly to the details and representations of the
transaction, as set forth in the narrative.

The third class of objections, as above arranged, are such as
more properly apply to the narrative of the Fall, as distinguished from the doctrine, or the truths communicated.   In
respect to these objections, it will be seen that they originate,
for the most part, in misapprehension of the statements of the
text, and turn on contradictions thus assumed between the
parts of the narrative itself, or between it and other established facts and conclusions.   A few only of the more important
objections of this kind can at present be noticed ; but these
may serve as specimens of a numerous, though not otherwise
formidable class.

1. It is objected, that the threatening of death was not
executed on the transgressors in the terms denounced.   The
penalty, as threatened, was, " In the day that thou eatest
thereof, thou shalt surely die :" but Adam lived more than
nine hundred years after eating the forbidden fruit ; and how,
it is asked, can this consist with the admitted immutability
of the eternal Lawgiver and Judge ?

This is an objection of long standing.   As early as the time
of Irenæus, the long reprieve or suspension of the sentence of
death on Adam, was felt to involve considerable difficulty ;
and, ever since, various explanations of it have been offered.
Irenæus himself enumerates no less than five different solutions current in his day.   It is unnecessary to advert to these,
or any of the other schemes, farther than to say, that the
whole difficulty, and supposed contradiction, rest entirely on a
misapprehension of what the threatened death really implied.

This was the forfeiture of all that pertains to a holy and happy existence, which the Scriptures emphatically denominate *life*. There is no ground whatever for the view on which the objection rests, which regards the penalty threatened as mere physical death, or as in any way contemplating the extinction of the physical life, or the termination of the earthly existence of man on the day of transgression. " Change, or separation of soul and body," as Jeremy Taylor remarks, " is but accidental to death ; death may be with or without either." It was so, in regard to the latter particular, in the case of Adam : on the day of his transgression he died, in accordance with the previous intimation of God, " who is not a man, that he should lie ; neither the son of man, that he should repent" (Numb. xxiii. 19). The transgressor died in the very act of sinning ; and died to the full extent of the death threatened. There was no delay in the judgment, no immediate mitigation of the sinner's doom ; although infinite mercy afterwards announced a remedy and remission.

2. The amount of the punishment is sometimes objected to as unreasonably severe, or exorbitant, considering the triviality of the offence ; and therefore it is alleged that the first sin must have been something other than eating of any particular prohibited fruit, as stated in the narrative : reason, it is asserted, demands that the crime be more proportioned to the punishment, if, as is stated, that was death.

Looked at in its true light, as rebellion against the Most High, and as a daring and deliberate renunciation of the Divine authority, and accordingly in its very essence a violation of the whole law, the first transgression must appear to be anything but a slight or trivial offence. The particular act by which the rebellious disposition was evinced does not affect the matter much one way or another. If anything, the unimportance, so to speak, of the object prohibited in the present instance, only enhanced the crime and the condemnation. Any other positive precept which it were possible to select as a test of obedience, would be open no doubt to similar, or perhaps weightier objections, on the part of transgressors disposed to cavil at what they regard as the *inequality* of God's ways (Ezek. xviii. 25) ; and if the selected test had been less indifferent, or required more self-denial than the one actually adopted, there need be little hesitation in affirming that it would be greatly decried on that very account. Nothing, however, is better fitted to prove a test of character and of absolute submission to law in its highest form than an act, the omission or commission of which is *in itself* indifferent, but to which attention is called by another will requiring or forbidding it.

3. Exception is also taken to the mysterious properties thought to be ascribed to the trees of knowledge and of life : in the one case, the power of communicating a knowledge of good and evil ; and in the other, of conferring immortality.

These must have been in every sense remarkable trees, if they were such as is here represented; but it will be found that the properties thus ascribed to them have had no existence save in the fancy of objectors and of some expositors. This, it must be acknowledged, is a case of the sort adverted to in the last section, wherein the fancies of expositors have contributed to raise objections against the credibility of the narrative. It was in no way to be wondered at that the superficial naturalism of such men as Gabler and Eichhorn, should trace the evil consequences resulting to man to the deleterious qualities of the forbidden fruit ; but it is matter of surprise to find evangelical divines seriously maintaining " that the fruit of this tree had the physical effect of rendering the understanding much more clear and forcible—that through it the intellectual powers were considerably enlarged, and man, consequently, endowed with faculties superior to those he possessed in his pristine condition."[1] The scriptural narrative, when properly considered, gives no countenance to such views. It is true, that on eating the forbidden fruit, it is said of the transgressors, that " their eyes were opened ;" but this result is not to be conceived of, as springing from any virtue in the tree, but entirely from the act of disobedience—the transgression of the command which constituted this tree forbidden. It is also true that attainments in the knowledge of good and evil from partaking of the forbidden fruit, were held forth as inducements to disobedience, but only in the artful representations of the Tempter. It is a similar misapprehension which ascribes to the Tree of Life the property of warding off death and conferring immortality—an opinion shared in by a writer

---

[1] Topham, Philosophy of the Fall, p. 59.

so judicious as Archbishop Whately, who even attributes to the influence of this tree the great longevity of the earliest generations of men,[1] notwithstanding the intimation that man was shut out from all access to it. The tree of life, according to the judgment of the soundest interpreters, was nothing more than a sign or seal of the Divine promise of life, properly so called, or everlasting blessedness to man when the period of his probation should come to a happy close. The reason assigned for the expulsion of man from Paradise after his apostasy, "lest he should take of the tree of life and eat and live for ever," whatever it may mean, cannot certainly, from reason and the nature of the case, imply that eating of this tree would have actually conferred immortality on the transgressor, and rendered nugatory the sentence which already doomed him to death; and if it does not imply this, nothing can be founded on the statement as to any inherent property in this tree. The simplest and most consistent view of the import of this expression would seem to be, that it was *fitting* —merciful as well as just, that man should be debarred from access to the *sign*, seeing that he had forfeited the thing signified.

4. It is also objected that the statement that vegetables constituted the only food of animals previous to the Fall, (Gen. i. 29, 30,) is in direct opposition to the facts brought to light, and firmly established by scientific investigations into the character and habits of the animals of the early world, many of which were extinct before the introduction of man.

It is undoubtedly true, that among a particular class of theologians it is held as an axiom, and indeed it may be regarded as the popular belief, that a great change—a revolution of habits and propensities, took place in the animal creation on the fall of man. In particular, it is believed that it was only after that catastrophe had disturbed the peace and harmony of creation that animals began to prey upon one another, the whole having previously been graminivorous. But notions of this sort, it may be affirmed, are indebted for their origin and acceptance more to the poets of ancient and

[1] Dissertation on the Rise, Progress, and Corruptions of Christianity.—*Encyclopædia Britannica*, 8th edit. vol. i. p. 453.

modern times, than to any biblical statements—they certainly
owe more to the poetic imagination of Milton for their place in
the popular belief, than to the simple history of Moses. The existence of carnivorous animals long before the fall or the creation
of man, is a truth too well established to require any argument
or evidence to be adduced here in its support ; and if Scripture
teaches otherwise, a difficulty, if not a contradiction, must be
at once confessed, however it may be explained. But no
intimation to that effect can be discovered within the compass
of the Sacred Volume, and certainly nothing of the kind can
be legitimately deduced from the passage above referred to
from the account of creation. All that that passage fairly imports is, that one part of the vegetable productions was assigned
to man, and another to other animals, while it by no means
precludes the idea that there might have been other tribes
requiring to be sustained by animal food.

5. Offence is not unfrequently taken at the curse pronounced
upon the serpent, as " a capricious punishment on a race of
brutes."[1] If the serpent was merely the instrument of another
power, how can it consist with justice, it is asked, to visit with
punishment the irrational and irresponsible reptile ?

The vindication of this punitive act is sometimes rested on
the doctrine of the sovereignty of God, who has a right to dispose of all his creatures in whatever way he sees meet.[2] But
this representation fails to carry conviction and satisfaction to
the mind ; for the act is evidently characterized not as one of
sovereignty but of judicial infliction, which must accordingly
be meted out with justice. Another mode of escape from the
difficulty is supposed to be found in denying that the sentence
on the serpent can be strictly regarded as a real punishment.
But this explanation also labours under as serious disadvantages as that already dismissed. The curse of God, which
constitutes the burden of the sentence, is most assuredly a
reality—a dread reality—a sore punishment wherever, and
however, it alights on any creature. There is no gainsaying
this. But is it certain that a curse was inflicted on the reptile
at all ? May it not be found that the simplest solution of the
difficulty is in the exclusion of the animal serpent, if not from
all share in the temptation, yet certainly from all direct par-

[1] Newman. Phases of Faith, p. 67.   [2] Holden, Dissertation, p. 128.

ticipation in the punishment that followed? Throughout the transaction, the serpent really present is described as an intelligent agent; and in the sentence pronounced, is addressed as a moral being. It is only on this supposition, and consequently, that the stroke of Divine vengeance fell not on an irrational and irresponsible creature, but on the moral agent which either actuated the serpent or assumed its form, that the sentence can be conceived of as reasonable or real. On this view of the matter, the whole scope or purport of the sentence would seem to be, to announce in language figurative, but conformable to the circumstances of the case, that from the degraded position to which the tempter had descended for the purpose of compassing man's ruin, he should never be able to rise, or throw off the gross and grovelling form he had assumed : in other words, the sentence, stripped of its metaphor, doomed him to the deepest degradation, and that perpetually.[1]

6. The origin of the various tribes of mankind in a single ancestral pair has recently been much disputed ; and this controversy has accordingly supplied arguments and objections to the Mosaic affirmation of the doctrine in the narratives of Creation and the Fall.

The unity and common origin of the human race, as expressly taught in the Bible, is not an isolated doctrine, but is connected in one way or another with all the fundamental truths of religion ; and yet looked at physically, it must be admitted that it is encompassed with many difficulties. Numerous appearances in natural history are strongly opposed to the dogma, and several distinguished scientific writers have boldly called it in question. But it is of importance to note, that with every disposition on the part of some of the opponents of the doctrine of the unity of the human race, to make the most of all facts and appearances in civil and natural history which favoured their own views, its falsity has never been established. The common origin of mankind has been questioned, but not disproved. It might therefore suffice to

[1] Leland, Answer to Christianity as Old as the Creation, Dublin, 1733, vol. ii. p. 516. " If there was a real serpent made use of, yet still it may be supposed that the curse was only and properly directed and designed against Satan, who actuated that creature, though couched in terms accommodated to the condition of the creature he actuated and assumed."

observe, until this be the case, that no valid objection can be brought against the credibility of the Bible on the point in question. It may, however, be added, without at present entering upon any discussion of the subject, that through enlarged acquaintance with the question on the part of naturalists and ethnographers, many of the difficulties are in course of removal, and the problem upon the whole is so far simplified, that the unity of mankind can now scarcely be maintained to involve an improbability. But the subject presents itself in another light, and one not less favourable to the credibility of the Mosaic writings. If, as already stated, and as strongly urged by the opponents of the biblical statements, there be so much apparently and antecedently unfavourable to the doctrine which ascribes the origin of mankind to a common parentage, how came it to pass that a writer like Moses, so cautious and circumspect, and, moreover, as some would say, so strongly imbued with Jewish exclusiveness, could fancy or defend such a dogma, looking at the circumstances of the case from his own point of view, if indebted only to his own reasonings and resources? It is not meant to urge this consideration as any test of the truth of the doctrine in question; but if its truth should be proved otherwise, the fact of its being held by Moses may undoubtedly be regarded as not a little confirmatory of the inspired character of the truths he taught.

The more pertinent of the objections urged against the doctrine of the Fall, and especially against the narrative in which that doctrine, in its causes and consequences, is delivered, have now been glanced at, or briefly considered. They have been brought together in the present section, for the twofold purpose of exhibiting their character and strength, and of indicating the points to which special attention must be directed in the exposition of the text, where also will be found fuller particulars and proofs of the more important positions in many cases tacitly assumed in the answers to objections and other controverted points, as stated above. There is, however, one other objection which must be noticed at greater length, and by way of appendix to this section, but of a kind distinct from any of the preceding; and which has reference not to any difficulties in the doctrine or details of the Fall, but to its origin, or the time and the occasion of its reception into the Jewish creed.

THE JEWISH DOCTRINE OF THE FALL NOT DERIVED FROM THE SYSTEM OF THE PARSEES.

It has been zealously maintained by not a few writers, that the doctrine of the Fall, or the interpretation now usually put upon the transaction recorded in the third chapter of Genesis, was utterly unknown in the earlier periods of the Israelitish history. It is admitted by the advocates of this view, that the Christian interpretation is that of the New Testament and of the later Jewish writers ; but it is denied that the doctrine was known, or acknowledged as an article of Jewish faith until the Captivity, and it is maintained that it originated in a mixture of oriental ideas with which the Israelites became familiar during the exile. More particularly, it is alleged that the doctrine of the existence of an evil spirit with which that of the Fall is intimately associated, is an importation into Jewish theology from the religious system of the ancient Persians, being nothing more than the Zoroastrian notions regarding the conflict of Ormuzd and Ahriman.[1]

This view is sometimes carried so far as even to deny the authenticity of the narrative in Genesis, and assign to its composition a date corresponding to the assumed requirements of the case, but more frequently it is satisfied with merely rejecting the interpretation, the authenticity being treated as a question of secondary concern. It is, however, only as a question of interpretation that the matter requires any serious examination here. As such, it assumes that the doctrine or details of the Fall, as at present understood, are not so much as alluded to in any Old Testament writings, except those composed during or after the Captivity.

But here it is necessary to premise, that in order to support those assumptions by the exclusion of all evidence of a contrary tendency, recourse is had to what must be called a

[1] Newman, Phases of Faith, p. 126.—" That *the serpent* in the early part of Genesis denoted the same Satan, is probable enough ; but this only goes to show, that that narrative is a legend imported from farther East, since it is certain that the subsequent Hebrew has no trace of such an Ahriman."

very illogical mode of procedure. Thus with regard to the existence of an evil spirit—a doctrine involved in that of the Fall, a date subsequent to the exile is frequently assigned to such compositions as make express mention of the being in question, and simply on that account; and then, again, from the absence of the idea in writings which, on the above principles of arrangement, are assigned a place prior to the Captivity, it is argued that it was not entertained at the earlier period. It is in this way that the Book of Job is often unceremoniously disposed of, or at all events its prologue, where it cannot be denied express mention is made of the great adversary of God and man.

But while strictly maintaining the acquaintance of the earliest Hebrew writers with the doctrine of an evil principle, it must be at the same time conceded, that they make little or no *express* mention of such agency, although fully implied in various acts and narrations. In the history of the Fall itself, there is no express mention of the presence of an evil spirit; but that the agency of such a being is indicated or assumed, the whole bearing and circumstances of the case abundantly testify. Indeed, throughout the Pentateuch, little or no express reference is made to beings of this kind, if the view be rejected which makes the obscure term *Azazel* (Lev. xvi. 8) to be the designation of some such creature. The first express and indubitable reference to an evil spirit is in the history of Saul, the first king of Israel : " The Spirit of the Lord departed from Saul, and an evil spirit from the Lord troubled him," (1 Sam. xvi. 14.) *The evil spirit* which troubled the unhappy monarch, from its being contrasted with the Spirit of the Lord, must evidently be a personality ; and not, as is sometimes represented, merely *madness* or *melancholy.* Coming down to a later period, to the time of Ahab (1 Kings xxii. 21, 22), mention is made of " a lying spirit," or *a spirit of falsehood* gone forth to deceive. Verse 21, " There came forth a spirit," or, as it is in the Hebrew, *the spirit ;* not, as Keil would have it, a personification of the principle of prophecy, a view which Thenius also adopts, but rather " a spiritual wicked principle," as was recognised by the older expositors, Grotius, Le Clerc, Vatable, Seb. Schmidt, and others, and as the very proposal made by the spirit itself sufficiently attests.

Turning to the Book of Job, which, whatever may be the doubts regarding its character, and the exact date of its composition, is unquestionably very old, as even its most resolute opponents have been forced to admit, we find mention made of a wicked spirit, styled by way of pre-eminence *Satan*, that is, *the enemy* or *adversary*. The same word which, in Job i. 6-12, ii. 1-7, occurs as a proper name, and with the Hebrew article, is used also as an appellative, as in Ps. cix. 6, " Let the *enemy* stand on his right hand." On which Hengstenberg remarks : " That the passage before us is the one from which the name of Satan, first used in Job, has been derived, is evident from the literal relation in which the verse before us stands to the second fundamental passage of Satan (Zech. iii. 1); the enemy of our psalm—a psalm in which *Satan* occurs more frequently than it does anywhere else—is the worthy representative, the visible emblem, of the Evil One."

Without determining what importance is due to this observation of Hengstenberg, particularly as regards the composition of the psalm prior to that of Job, it is of consequence for the present argument to notice, that the common designation of the Evil One in the Scriptures is strictly of Hebrew origin,—a fact which furnishes the strongest proof that the idea must be national, and not derived from without. Even Winer, who strongly maintains that the doctrine is of foreign origin, acknowledges that it cannot be denied that there were Jewish conceptions which served as connecting points for dogmatic Demonology, when it came to be developed at the time of the exile.[1]

The progressive development of this doctrine among the Hebrews, or, perhaps, more correctly, the greater freedom with which the later writers could allude to it, may be seen from a comparison of 2 Sam. xxiv. 1, with 1 Chron. xxi. 1. The reserved manner in which the subject is introduced or adverted to in the earlier Scriptures, may possibly be accounted for in a way similar to the equally remarkable silence there observed regarding a future state of existence, and the rewards and punishments therewith connected. Or it may have been with a view chiefly of preventing idolatry, to which the Israelites in the early periods of their history were exceedingly prone,

[1] Biblisches Realwörterbuch, *Art.* Satan, II. p. 384.

that so little is said regarding the existence or powers of demons—objects of special homage among several Gentile nations, who, in this respect, as opportunity occurred, found willing imitators among the Jews. But in whatever way the circumstance may be accounted for, it was not until the time drew nigh which should witness the advent of Him whose mission it was to destroy the works of the devil, that the evil principle, in his power and personality, was permitted to come fully into view. Until this important period approached, a veil was drawn over the subject ; but now that it is removed, the hints and silent intimations previously given stand forth in full expression, as may be seen when the history of the Fall is read with the apostolic commentaries on the tempter and temptation.

In regard, however, to the view which questions the existence or agency of such a being as the Satan of Scripture, and which is the actual basis of that more particularly under consideration, it will be sufficient to adduce the following remarks of Neander :—" The arguments of the Rationalists against the doctrine which teaches the existence of Satan, are either directed against a false and arbitrary conception of that doctrine, or else go upon the presupposition that evil could only have originated under conditions such as those under which human existence has developed itself : that it has its ground in the organism of human nature, e.g., in the opposition between reason and the propensities ; that *human* development must necessarily pass through it ; but that we cannot conceive of a steadfast tendency to evil in an intelligence endowed with the higher spiritual powers. Now it is precisely this view of evil which we most emphatically oppose, as directly contradictory to the essence of the gospel and of a theistico-ethical view of the world ; and, on the contrary, we hold fast, as the only doctrine which meets man's moral and religious interests, that doctrine which is the ground of the conception of Satan, and according to which evil is represented as the rebellion of a created will against the Divine law, as an act of free-will not otherwise to be explained, and the intelligence as determined by the will."[1]

After what has thus been said on the main argument in the

[1] Neander's Life of Christ, London edition, 1851, p. 79, *note*.

theory, which holds the doctrine of the Fall to be of foreign origin, and of comparatively late growth, little need be added regarding the alleged absence from the early Scriptures of all reference to its history, as set forth in Genesis. This omission, however, is more in appearance than in reality. What, it may be asked, is the whole of the Old Testament history, as it narrates the incessant struggle of the two principles of good and evil in the world and in man, but one continued reference to the Fall, through which this discord was introduced ? As a specific reference to that transaction, or its consequences to man, it is enough to adduce the belief entertained of an inward, hereditary depravity of human nature, at so early a period as that indicated by the *fifty-first* Psalm. The frequent allusions in the Book of Proverbs to the *tree of life*, are, upon the admission of Tuch, distinct references to the Fall ; and this is of the more importance, as coming from one who holds, in a modified form, the opinion now controverted. The later references in the prophetic writings need not be discussed, nor the passage in Eccles. vii. 29, where mention is made of man's original and better state, and then of his altered condition ; for the majority of these passages have, by the critics and controvertists on this particular point, a very late date assigned to them. Attention is, therefore, purposely confined to writings whose high antiquity is universally admitted, so as to avoid all discussions foreign to the main subject. Enough, however, it is believed, has been advanced to shew that from the earliest period there are not wanting intimations of the belief in a Fall, and in the existence of an evil principle.

But even were such intimations less numerous or explicit than is actually the case, it might be fairly urged, that it is exceedingly improbable that the latter dogma in particular, even if of foreign origin, should be introduced only at the late period of the exile, from intercourse with the Chaldeans or Persians, and not from the earlier and longer intercourse with Egypt, where the idea was strongly developed in the evil principle Typhon. If anything, however, were wanting in disproof of the opinion, that the doctrine of the Fall was derived from the Persians, it would be found in the fact that, as taught in the Bible, it differs essentially from all the systems of Parsism. The mythologies of these systems are broadly reflected in the teachings of the Gnostics and Manicheans, but to any reader of church history, it is needless to say how widely these diverged from the truths of the Bible and the doctrines of Christianity.

SECT. VIII.—THE INCIDENTS OF THE FALL TRACED IN TRADITION

The fables of the ancient world are in many cases as instructive as its philosophies, if not more so. They may be correctly regarded as important traditionary truths, although, in the majority of instances, so corrupted or disguised, as to be scarcely discernible, and requiring for their identification the closest scrutiny and comparison ; yet, even in such cases, they will be found, when carefully analyzed, to comprehend, in some form or other, various elements which bear an unmistakable relation to former habits and perceptions, and so furnish evidence regarding important transactions in the early history of the human race, the recollection of which might have otherwise perished. Amid the accumulation of myths and traditions handed down from the remotest ages, it might be reasonably expected that there should be found some traces of the Fall, provided it were a real, historical, and not altogether an imaginary event. It is undoubtedly a reasonable assumption, that a matter of such moment and magnitude as the Fall is represented to be, so productive of change in all the circumstances of man's lot, his relation to his Maker, and to the world around him, could not have passed away without leaving, in various ways, some traces of its occurrence,—nor have its memorials entirely obliterated from the monumental traditions of the past. These just expectations will, on examination, be nowise disappointed. The traditions of the Fall are neither few nor faint : they are numerous, and no less indubitable, in their relation to that moral catastrophe ; much more so—as from the nature of the case may be easily conceived—than those which were found to relate to the subject of Creation. In regard to the numerous and diversified myths and legends now to be considered, it will be found that, owing to the abundance of materials, and the distinct forms in which they have been preserved affording greater room for comparisons, there will be little difficulty in tracing the scattered and variously expressed ideas to a common source, and no danger in assigning their origin to some momentous catastrophe in the primeval history of man, whereby his character and his relation to God underwent a great change, exceedingly injurious in its consequences.

The more important notices bearing on this subject—and it is only a selection that can be presented—may be conveniently arranged under the following heads :—

1. *The original condition of man, physical and moral.*

The traditions of all ancient nations unite in testifying, that man's original condition differed widely from the state in which he now finds himself placed. This original condition, the traditions of the West, as preserved in the classic pages of the Greek and Roman authors, describe, under the designation of a " golden age," of which rich and glowing descriptions are found, especially in the poets, who agree in characterizing it as a period of innocence and bliss. According to the account given by Hesiod, one of the earliest of the Greek poets, in the first or golden age, men were like the gods, free from labours, troubles, cares, and all evils in general: they were in the full enjoyment of every blessing ; the earth yielded her fruits freely and abundantly, and men were beloved by the gods, with whom they held uninterrupted communion.[1]   With Hesiod's description of the first age of the human race, Ovid's essentially agrees, only that the latter notices more fully the moral goodness of the period,—the absence of sin as well as suffering.   It was a state of innocence as well as happiness,—the latter, indeed, being the result of the former.

> " Aurea prima sata est ætas, quæ vindice nullo,
> Sponte sua, sine lege fidem rectumque colebat.
> Pœna metusque aberant, nec verba minacia fixo
> Ære legebantur, nec supplex turba timebat
> Judicis ora sui, sed erant sine judice tuti."—*Metam.* i. 89.

By another Roman author, the state of this period is briefly characterized as a " *simplicitas mali nescia et adhuc astutiæ inexperta.*"[2]

Turning now to the Eastern traditions, which, from their

---

[1] Hesiod, *Opera et Dies*, 90, &c.   [2] Macrobius, *Somn. Scipionis*, ii. 10.

closer proximity to the cradle of the human race, may be supposed to have suffered less change than those of the West, the
same ideas, under a variety of forms, continually present themselves ; with the farther addition of most pointed references to
man's original dwelling-place. In the ancient Persian traditions, for example, there is found within the legend of a
golden age, also that of a paradise—the enclosed gardens of
Dschemschid, the *Ver*, as Anquetil, the author of the French
translation of the Zendavesta, calls it, and regarding which
Roth, a recent learned writer on the subject, remarks, " It
reminds us of the ancient Hebrew traditions of the garden in
Eden, only that in the latter case it was the first human pair,
and in the other, a select number of the human race that enjoyed the blessings of this paradise."[1] Man's original residence
is largely set forth in the Zend Books. It is described as a
place of many delights and felicities, and as the special creation
of Ormuzd. Mention is also made of its river and its sacred
trees, and, among others, the tree of life. According to the
description in the Vendidad, " Ormuzd spake to Sapetman
(*i.e.*, the excellent) Zoroaster : I have created, O Sapetman
Zoroaster, a place of delights and of abundance ; no one could
make its equal. Came not this region of pleasure from me, O
Sapetman Zoroaster ; no being could have created it ? It is
called Eerienè Vējô : it is more beautiful than the whole
world, wide as it is. Nothing can equal the charms of that
country of pleasure which I have created. The first habitation of blessedness and abundance which I, who am Ormuzd,
created, was Eerienè Vējô. Thereupon came Ahriman, preg-
nant with death, and prepared in the river which watered
Eerienè Vējô, the great serpent of winter that comes from
Dew."[2] In the *pleasure* and loveliness to which so much prominence is given in this description, there is, according to
Creutzer, an allusion to the Hebrew *Eden*, which also means
pleasure.[3]

The remarkable references made to Ahriman and the serpent, the destroyer of this delightful region, will be afterwards
considered, and confirmed by other testimonies ; meanwhile,

---

[1] Zeitschrift der Deutschen Morgenl. Gesellschaft, 1850, p. 421.
[2] Rosenmüller, Biblical Geography, Morren's Translation, vol. i. p. 51.
[3] Creuzer, Symbolik u. Mythologie, Leip. 1837, vol. i. p. 213.

attention may be shortly directed to the notions entertained regarding the river of paradise and the tree of life. " The Hindoos place the terrestrial paradise on the elevated plains of Bukhara the Lesser, where it is conceived there is a river which goes round Brahmápuri, or the town of Brahma ; then through a lake called Mansarovara. . . . From this lake come *four* rivers running towards the four corners of the world."[1] To the tree of life, again, frequent reference is made in these interesting legends of the olden world. In the Bundehesh it is said, " Among these trees is the white, salubrious, and fruitful *Hom :* it grows in the fountain of Arduisur, which springs from the throne of Ormuzd ; whoever drinks of the water, or the sap of this tree, becomes immortal." In the traditions of India also, mention is made of the tree of paradise, Kalpaurksham, which contains the drink and food of immortality. According to Persian ideas, Honover, the creative word of Ormuzd, was embodied under the name *Hom,*—a type of eternal blessing and prosperity, as a tree which was the crown of the vegetable kingdom, and was possessed of wonderful powers of vivification. A portion of this tree was accordingly essential in every offering.[2] The sacred tree occupies also, as is now well known, a very conspicuous place in the recently discovered Assyrian sculptures. Layard remarks, that the Zoroastrian Hom was likewise a common subject of Persian sculpture, and preserved almost, as represented on the Assyrian monuments, ᷓtil the Arab invasion. " The flowers on the earlier monuments" [of Nineveh], says this writer, " are either circular, with five or more petals, or resemble the Greek honeysuckle. From the constant introduction of the tree ornamented with them into groups, representing the performance of religious ceremonies, there cannot be a doubt that they were symbolical, and were invested with a sacred character. The sacred tree, or tree of life, so universally recognised in Eastern systems of theology, is called to mind, and we are naturally led to refer the traditions connected with it to a common origin." The author then adds in a note, " We have the tree of life of Genesis, and the sacred tree of the Hindhus, with its

[1] Wilford, Asiatic Researches, vol. vi. p. 488, quoted in Rosenmüller, *loc. cit.* p. 53.

[2] Creuzer, Symbolik u. Mythologie, vol. i. p. 224.

accompanying figures—a group almost identical with the illustrations of the Fall in our old Bibles."[1]

2. *The change which ensued.*

The state of innocence and happiness above described, it is universally admitted, did not long continue, but was succeeded by another in which crime, violence, and misery prevailed. Men despised the gods, became proud, disobedient, and profane, and were, accordingly, for their wickedness, subjected to various evils. The corruption of morals and manners, notwithstanding many tokens of Divine displeasure and retribution, went on increasing, until, in the fourth or iron age, according to some traditions, it attained to such a height that Jupiter, wearied out by the many provocations, sent at length a flood to destroy the guilty race. Such are the accounts furnished by the Greek and Latin writers of the degeneracy of the period which succeeded the primeval or golden age. All the traditions agree in representing that the miseries with which the world and the human race are afflicted—the pains, diseases, and deaths, have been introduced or occasioned by the apostasy of man, or his criminal disobedience to the commands of the gods. Some of the traditions even go so far as to specify the particular act of disobedience through which all these disasters ensued. It was a criminal curiosity prying into that which was concealed, or a snatching at the forbidden, which, according to the Greek and Roman poets, wrought the misery of the human race. Thus Horace—

" Audax omnia perpeti,
Gens humana ruit per vetitum nefas :
Audax Japeti genus
Ignem fraude mala gentibus intulit."—*Od.* I. iii. 25.

In the Bundehesch of the Persians, there is an account of the sad end of the golden age through the overthrow of the renowned Dschemschid. Iran has its paradise and its fall. The golden age has terminated, its blessings have disappeared from the earth ; but who could have disturbed the peace, and destroyed the paradise, and who could have overthrown its noble ruler, but the enemy of all good, the destructive serpent Zohak ? The legend farther adds, that Dschemschid drew down the curse upon himself, because in his vanity he desired to be like

[1] Nineveh and its Remains, vol. ii. p. 472.

God. But as Roth, the author already referred to, regards this as a later addition, it is not desirable to press it.[1] It may be, however, added, that according to a tradition of Thibet, it was desire to eat of a sweet herb, schimæ, that led to the change whence arose shame and the necessity of clothing.[2] The Dog-rib Indians of America, in a geographical relation widely different from the locality of the preceding legend, have a tradition of the fall of man, which they ascribe to disobedience in eating of a forbidden fruit.[3]

3. *The causes, instrumental and mediate, of this reverse.*

The causes of man's apostasy, or the means and the occasion whereby he was led into rebellion against the will of the Almighty Author of his being and happiness, have been variously explained or surmised in the legendary products of antiquity. This, as a necessary consequence of the great diversities in civilisation, mental and moral culture, and in the religious habits and beliefs of the nations among whom these traditions were entertained, is no more than might be expected. But it is of great importance to observe, that amid much that is confused, and in part contradictory, arising in great part from the changes which, in course of time, the traditions presented, the serpent or woman, in some connexion or other, was usually held as contributing to the present miserable condition of man.

According to Hesiod, Prometheus, whose name signifies " forethought," as that of his brother Epimetheus, also mentioned in this legend, denotes " afterthought," steals fire from heaven and teaches its use to mortals, although the father of the gods had denied it to them. Zeus, in order to punish men, caused Hephaestus to mould a virgin, Pandora, of earth, whom Athena adorned with all the charms calculated to entice mortals. Prometheus had cautioned his brother Epimetheus against accepting any present from Zeus, but Epimetheus, disregarding the advice, accepted Pandora, who was sent to him by Zeus, through the mediation of Hermes. Pandora, when brought into the house of Epimetheus, in her curiosity lifted the lid of the vessel in which the foresight of Prome-

[1] Zeitschrift der Deut. Morg. Gesellschaft, 1850, p. 429.
[2] Von Bohlen, Die Genesis, p. 39.
[3] Harcourt, Doctrine of the Deluge, vol. i. p. 34.

theus had concealed all the evils which might torment mortals in life. Diseases and sufferings of every kind now issued forth, but deceitful hope alone remained behind.[1] Æschylus,[2] however, regards this matter of Prometheus in another light. He knew of no evil resulting to mankind from the acts or interventions of Prometheus, but only supposes an attainment on the part of man to a state of higher standing and cultivation. The two ideas may, in a certain sense, be regarded as combined in the biblical narrative of the Fall, and the consequences accruing to man from the transgression.

In like manner, in the Eastern traditions, woman is found occupying a position opposed to man. Thus Feridun, one of the heroes of ancient Persia, in his contest with Zohâk, the destructive serpent, finds women in the palace of the latter ; and so also in the Indian form of the same legend, the demon is represented as having women on his side, whom he even summons to his aid in the contest. This circumstance of the women is, as Roth remarks, the more worthy of notice, as the gods of the Veda have no wives.[3] According to another Persian tradition, Meschia and Meschiane, the parents of the human race, were at first innocent, but they allowed themselves to be seduced to evil by the Dews, that is, the spirits of Ahriman. They had been destined to happiness, on condition of their continuing humble, obedient, and pure ; but Ahriman deceived them, and drew them away from Ormuzd. They betook themselves to hunting, and drank milk, which proved hurtful to them. Afterwards Ahriman gave them fruit of which they ate ; and, in consequence, they lost a hundred blessings save one. Thereafter they obtained fire, partook of flesh, and presented offerings to Ized ; they made themselves clothes of skin, and built houses ; but they forgot to thank the author of their life.[4] Some of the particulars of this latter legend present too striking an accordance with incidents in the narrative of the Fall, to escape the notice of even the most sceptical on such points.

But it is when inquiring into, or considering more particu-

[1] Hesiod, *Opera et Dies*, 83, &c. *Theog.*, 583, &c.
[2] *Prom. Vinctus*, 107, 442.
[3] Zeitschrift der Deut. Morg. Gesellschaft, 1848, p. 227.
[4] Rhode, Heilige Sage des Zendvolks, p. 389.

larly, the instrumental cause of the alienation of man from his Maker and Moral Governor, that astonishment is felt at the almost universal mention which is made of the serpent in the traditions relative to the disappearance of the original blessings of earth. " Almost all the nations of Asia," remarks Von Bohlen, "assume the serpent to be a wicked being which has brought evil into the world." " Indeed, it is remarkable," adds Hävernick, after quoting this statement, " what a similarity is observable between the traditionary tales of Egypt, India, Persia, and even of the Northern nations, (which are again met with in the Orphic mysteries of the West,) and the old Hebrew narrative." In the old prophecy in Herodotus (book i. chap. 78) the serpent is called *the child of earth.* It was under the form of a serpent that, according to the tradition last referred to, Ahriman deceived the first human pair : and, according to another tradition, the serpent was expressly created by Ahriman for the destruction of the world. In the Zend books the serpent is the common attribute of that evil principle.[1] This serpent, *ashi-daháka,* had three throats, three tails, six eyes, and the strength of a thousand powers. The Hindoo mythology, again, makes it to be the great serpent *kali naga* which poisoned the waters of the river, and thereby spread death and destruction all around. This serpent is often represented in Hindoo paintings as swallowing men who are seen deliberately walking into its yawning mouth.

But not to multiply particulars, it must have been some confused notions of the history of the Fall, which gave rise in the case of the Phœnicians, Egyptians, and many other nations, to a serpent-worship. This very circumstance of religious honours being bestowed on the serpent, goes far to prove that the part assigned to the creature by these traditions, in reference to the introduction of evil, has had its rise in something other than, as is sometimes alleged, the mere feeling of antipathy with which the human race instinctively regard this abhorred reptile.

4. *Expectations of a recovery.*

The expectations of a deliverer and of a release from the present state of sin and suffering, which characterize many of these legends, must not be overlooked, and, in particular, the

---

[1] Creuzer, Symbolik, vol. i. pp. 212, 223, 250.

fact that such anticipations not unfrequently take the form of ultimate victory over the old deadly serpent. The remark of Wagner,[1] that the Mosaic account of the Creation and the Fall is distinguished from the heathen mythologies by the hope of a restoration of the original blessed state, cannot therefore be taken absolutely. It is true that in the Bible alone this hope is set in its right position, and that the light which it thence emits is pure and unmixed, but an attentive examination of the longings, hopes, and fears, of the ancient nations of the earth, as embodied in their mythological legends, and in their poetry and songs, will leave no room to doubt that the ray of light which first broke in, according to the scriptural narrative, on the darkened hour which succeeded the apostasy, was no mere apprehension of the fancy, or a fiction of the Hebrew legislator,—seeing that among the widely dispersed nations of the earth it continued, though variously refracted, to shine down on man, sustaining him amid the labours and weariness of the present, and stimulating his aspirations after a better future. However much this ray of hope may have been shorn of its glories by the gross mediums through which it passed, it was never absolutely obscured ; but with the recollection of a golden age of the past, there was somehow connected the anticipation of a golden age of the future.

In the remarks about to be offered regarding the hopes thus cherished, it is intended to confine the attention to the more ancient traditions, or to such as are found among nations which may be supposed to have been uninfluenced by the promises and prophecies of the Hebrew oracles. Accordingly, much stress is not to be laid on the strong anticipations regarding a coming Deliverer, which prevailed in various parts of the Roman world about the time of our Lord's advent, as these may have in a great measure originated through the direct or indirect influence of the Bible, and intercourse with the Jewish nation. The poet Virgil, in particular, sings of a time when the golden age shall be restored ; when Astrea shall return to earth to bless mankind, when the serpent shall die, and also every poisonous plant ; but to this it is not necessary farther to advert.

It is, as already remarked, particularly worthy of note, that

[1] Geschichte der Urwelt, p. 516. Leips. 1845.

the expected deliverance is usually represented, in the more ancient traditions, as a victory over the serpent, issuing even in its death. And farther, it is to be observed, that the deliverer and conqueror in such cases is one that stands in an intimate relation to the Deity, being in many traditions represented as his son, or a special gift of the gods to men. Thus, in the legends of India, Krishna, an incarnation of Vishnu, the preserving principle, attacks the mighty serpent, and tramples on its head until the monster is totally overwhelmed. The Persian Feridun, or according to the Zendavesta Thraêtôna, who vanquished the poisonous serpent which devoured men and cattle, was a special gift of the gods vouchsafed to mortals for worshipping *Homa*. The same renowned hero appears in the Vedas under the name Trita, but there he is represented as a being of Divine nature.

The Western counterpart to these triumphs of Krishna, Thraêtôna, and Trita, may be discovered in the labours and deliverances wrought by Hercules and Apollo, who were also sons of the Deity. Of the various labours ascribed to Hercules, that which stands most closely connected with the present subject, was his fetching the golden apples from the gardens of the Hesperides. According to the legend, the garden, wherein grew golden apples on a mysterious tree watched by the serpent or dragon Ladon, had been shut in by lofty mountains in some remote and concealed region, because an oracle had intimated that a son of the Deity would carry off the sacred fruit. Hercules, however, notwithstanding these precautions, discovered the situation of the garden, obtained access to it, and, having slain the dragon, carried off the precious fruit. On this myth Dr. Kitto well remarks, " Here we have a strange mixture of the internal and external incidents of Paradise : the ideas of the primeval people viewing from without the Eden from which they were excluded, and coveting its golden fruits."[1] But the legend is no less interesting for this confusion of ideas, which evidently betokens the various modifying influences to which the simple truth was subjected in the course of traditionary transmission.

But the great averter of evil in the Greek mythology was Apollo, the son of Zeus, who was regarded as the source of the

[1] Daily Bible Illustrations, vol. i. p. 69.

powers exercised by his son. It is related of him, that four days after his birth he destroyed the dragon Python, which had pursued his mother during her wanderings, before she reached Delos. This Python, ancient legends affirm, was a serpent bred out of the slime that remained after Deucalion's deluge, and was worshipped as a god at Delphi. Eminent authorities derive the name of the monster from a Hebrew root signifying *to deceive.* If this etymology be correct, it is curious enough, as Harcourt observes, that the name should so accurately coincide with a title so well becoming that arch-deceiver, who contrived to mingle the worship of himself with all other deviations from the true religion.[1] It may be farther stated, that this very name Python occurs also in the New Testament, (Acts xvi. 16,) as in some way connected with the great deceiver of mankind.

Ideas similar to those now adduced are also met with in the Egyptian mythology, but the victor is the Younger Horus of that Pantheon. " It was probably," says Wilkinson, " in consequence of his victories over the enemy of mankind, that he was so often identified with Apollo, the story of whose combat with the serpent Pytho is derived from Egyptian mythology. Aphôphis, or Apôp, which in Egyptian signifies *a giant,* was the name given to the serpent, of which Horus is represented as the destroyer. The destruction of the serpent by the god, who, standing in a boat, pierces its head with a spear as it rises above the water, forms a frequent subject of representation on the monuments."[2]

In other quarters far apart from those now referred to, legends nearly identical with those regarding Apollo and Horus, the destroyers of the serpent, are to be met with. Thus, in the traditions of the Scandinavian north, the same ideas are expressed in the legends regarding the deity Thor, who, with his mace, bruises the head of the great serpent.

Before concluding this cursory survey of the legendary myths of the ancient world regarding the ruin and hoped-for deliverance of the human race, mention must be made of a minor, but perhaps no less significant incident, than any of those already referred to. In the Persian legends of Feridun, or

[1] Doctrine of the Deluge, vol. i. p. 366.
[2] Wilkinson's Ancient Egyptians, vol. iv. pp. 395, 435.

Thraêtôna, so frequently quoted above, a skin forms the banner under which the hero fights, and overcomes the serpent. The skin, (carma,) adds Roth, in commenting on this circumstance, is, in the old religion of the Persians, the important sacrificial vessel used in the preparation of the Soma, a symbol of the drink itself through whose power God overcomes the dragon.[1] And, it may be added, may there not be discerned in this some obscure idea relative to the institution of sacrifice in connexion with the fall and promised restoration of man, the animals first offered furnishing, by their skins, as is generally believed by Christian interpreters, clothing for the naked, guilty pair?

SECT. IX.—THE INCIDENTS OF THE FALL TESTED BY FACTS.

Besides the comparison just instituted between the biblical account of man's apostasy from God, and the mythological legends of antiquity regarding a great revolution in human conduct and happiness, which have been found to present a remarkable accordance with the more important circumstances of that event, as set forth in Genesis, another and no less important line of inquiry and comparison may also be pursued in this matter. According to the Scripture representation of the Fall, it was of a character which must have undoubtedly left many permanent impressions; and these not merely on the memory, as things of speculation, or as germs of mythological teachings and traditions, but deep signatures imprinted on nature and the constitution of man. Like as the mighty avalanche which, descending from some Alpine heights, or the lava torrent of fire belched out from some yawning volcano, carrying death and destruction into the midst of sunny, smiling plains, is long after remembered in its desolating effects ; or, as regards those other awful phenomena of nature—earthquakes and hurricanes—which derange and depopulate the face of earth, and to the intensity and direction of whose force, the crumbled rocks, the torn-up mountains, the trees and the habitations of man, thrown about in wild confusion, bear abundant testimony, long after the convulsions themselves have subsided or passed

[1] Zeitschrift der Deut. Morg. Gesellschaft, 1848, p. 227.

away,—so in the case of the Fall, the appearances now to be noticed.

Avoiding as much as possible all fanciful analogies, and confining the following observations to a few of the most important, characteristic, and indubitable phenomena, it is yet confidently expected, that the conclusions fairly deducible from the investigations of the last section will be greatly confirmed by the appeal now to be made to the human consciousness, and the facts of history and science. It must, however, be again premised, that it is not intended to allude so much to the many indications within and around us, which continually testify that we ourselves are fallen creatures, and have our dwelling in a fallen world, as to the facts and phenomena which bear more directly on the account of the Fall contained in Genesis ; and for this obvious reason, that there might have been a defection of the creature from God, some disarrangement or disorganization in the moral system, and yet this be accounted for on some other principle, and traced to some other cause, than that assigned in the Bible. The latter might be merely an attempt, as is often actually alleged, on the part of a careful observer, to explain the origin and nature of the phenomena of the case by a theory adapted as much as possible to the circumstances.

While carefully excluding on this view, as inapplicable to the present purpose, all such evidence as merely goes to prove that man is a *ruin*, and not as at first created and fashioned by the great Architect of the Universe, it will be, however, apposite, and of some importance, to consider anything which may tend to shew the *character* of the ruin, or the parts and proportions serving to indicate what the original and entire structure was. To adopt the language of a recent writer : " The ruins of a palace differ from the ruins of a hut. In the former, the work of desolation may be more complete than in the latter ; but we find here and there in the one what we cannot find in the other—a column or statue of surpassing beauty, indicating what the building was when it came forth from the hands of its maker. Not only so, but a palace in ruins is a grander object than a hut when entire." Applying these principles to the case of ruined humanity, enough appears in the structure of the soul, and in the inscriptions still legible on its walls and portals, to prove that this was once a palace of the Great King ; yea, a very temple in which the Divinity of heaven was enshrined and adored. Man is a ruined, fallen creature. This is a truth evident and unde-niable ; but it does not require much argumentation, and but little examination of the still majestic ruin, to shew, that in strictest accordance with the biblical representation, man was made in the image of God. The truth thus indicated by numerous and distinct evidences, did not altogether escape the notice of the wisest and most observant of the ancient heathen world. Their poets and philosophers are found giving frequent utterance to the sentiment. An expression of this kind is adduced by the Apostle Paul in his address to the philosophic Athenians : " As certain also of your own poets have said, For we are also his offspring ;" that is, as the preceding con-text shews, the offspring of God, (Acts xvii. 28.) But nowhere is the truth laid down so clearly and emphatically as in the words of Moses : " So God created man in his own image ; in the image of God created he him." In the heathen concep-tions of this truth, there was, for the most part, a lamentable confounding of the divine and the human, the former being reduced to the level of the latter ; or the soul of man regarded as an offshoot or emanation of deity ; but no trace of these errors can be recognised, as already stated, in any part or representation of the Bible.

There is another general consideration intimately connected with the preceding truth regarding man's past or primeval condition, which properly falls to be taken into account in estimating the character of the Mosaic account of the Fall, and its consistency with otherwise authenticated facts or con-clusions bearing on this subject. This is the intimation which various appearances, connected with human consciousness and the external world, furnish respecting man's future, considered both as to his deserts and his destinies. So far as man's deserts are concerned, everything within and around him agrees in pronouncing and confirming his sentence of condemnation, while simultaneously calling up fearful presentiments of a still greater judgment to come. But notwithstanding these fears and forebodings, the case is not so utterly hopeless and dis-couraging when man's destinies are simply considered, apart from his deserving. In the biblical account of man's fall, the promise of a restoration or recovery occupies, as already shewn, no unimportant place. While taking the most accurate view of the present, or the state induced through sin, and fully alive to all its miseries and woes, its pains and privations, the writer of the narrative in Genesis, as by a Divine purpose or decree, inseparably links the future to the past; and although he does not describe this connexion so much in words, as embody it in acts and emblems of mercy and grace, yet he holds forth a future exceedingly bright, and as one exceedingly full of promise, and containing elements of great blessedness for man—the lost more than restored, the perished more than recovered, and, what is of unspeakable importance, the enemy of man's happiness entirely overthrown.

How do these, and other intimations of a like import, which are impressively taught in the promise regarding the seed of the woman—in the preservation of Paradise after the expulsion of its fallen tenants—in the preservation also of the Tree of Life, and in the location, in the now tenantless garden, of the Cherubim—a higher order of life, and in other incidents recorded in the history, it may be asked, accord with the lessons which are to be read elsewhere, inscribed on the broad page of nature? In that wide field, also, it may be confidently asserted, there are innumerable and unmistakable tokens which show, if only questioned and carefully examined, that God has not abandoned the works of his hands, and that he has not ceased to be specially interested in man. The inspection of the ruins—to continue the use of the figure already introduced—which taught how glorious the original structure was, affords at the same time certain and satisfactory indications not only of what it possibly may, but what it shall eventually become, in the hands of the great Author of being and blessedness. The indications of intended renovation, as presented in nature, are numerous, and, so far as they go, satisfactory. "The very preservation of this world in its present state," remarks Dr. M'Cosh, the author last quoted, " seems to show that God did not intend it merely as a place of punishment. Among the withered leaves on which we tread, there are to be found the seeds of a coming renovation, and these leaves are preserved for a time, that the seeds may germinate in the midst of them. In this world there are evidences of God's hatred to evil; there are also proofs of his disposition to mercy and grace. The human mind has ever been prone to fancy that this world is yet to be the theatre of great events, in which all the perfections of God's character are to be displayed." There are everywhere tokens of a long-continued controversy between good and evil, life and death; but, at the same time, there are indications of the final triumph of the former even on this earth. Notwithstanding much apparently to the contrary, the general tendency on the whole is upwards and onwards. All the analogies of nature, physical and moral, concur in this. Should it however be objected that we could not have discovered these truths from nature alone, nor have interpreted her inscriptions in this manner without the aid of Revelation, let the fact be accepted, and instead of its being an objection, it will be found to contain a proof of the heavenly origin of Scripture, if it thus help to a true interpretation of nature, her laws or anomalies.

There is a third particular which presents itself for consideration in connexion with the account of the Fall, and which, from its nature, may be supposed capable of furnishing more abundant matter of comparison than either of those already noticed. Between the past condition of man and of the earth he inhabits, and whence he draws his sustenance, and the promised restoration just referred to, there extends the present, chequered with its sufferings, sorrows, and joys. In the two aspects of the past and the future, already considered, the analogies of Nature with the representations in the history of the Fall, were chiefly of a moral or metaphysical character, but in the present case the illustrations will be drawn more from physical facts and phenomena. The comparison will be mainly occupied with the ideas conveyed in the condemnatory sentence which, according to the explicit testimony of the narrative, was passed by the Supreme Judge immediately after man's apostasy, upon all the parties concerned in the act of temptation and disobedience, and in the curse pronounced upon the earth on account of man.

1. *The punishment of the Serpent.*

Throughout the narrative of the temptation and fall, the tempter is invariably spoken of and referred to, as a serpent;

and in strict conformity with this representation, is the sentence which dooms him to irrevocable degradation, and that of the very deepest kind, because of his participation or agency in the seduction of man. " Because thou hast done this, thou art cursed above all cattle, and above every beast of the field ; upon thy belly shalt thou go, and dust shalt thou eat all the days of thy life," (Gen. iii. 14.) As already remarked in another connexion, it is not at all necessary to suppose that this curse had any direct reference to the natural serpent, save in so far as the figurative language was borrowed from its peculiar form, habits, and mode of locomotion. It is therefore unnecessary to suppose, as is frequently done, that the serpent tribe was subjected on the occasion in question to any kind of transformation or degradation ; and, consequently, it is quite needless to consider, with the view either of answering or arguing the very flippant demand frequently urged in reference to the statement, *upon thy belly shalt thou go,*—" how else did it go before ?"—or the objection, that serpents do not eat dust. The degradation announced and enacted in the primeval curse was in the spiritual and unseen world, and not in the physical creation or animal economy ; and yet it is of importance to the present subject to find, from the testimonies of the geologist and physiologist, that there are not wanting remarkable and unmistakable indications of analogous degradations in the physical world, or deflections from the progressive course of creation. The degradations of the one creation may be set over against the degradations of the other, and it may not be too much to assume that the Creator and Preserver of man, who has shown himself so deeply interested in the moral and religious instruction of the human race, may have designed the degradations palpable to the senses, which naturalists discover in the physical creation, to serve as types or representations of degradations not discernible by the senses, but not the less real in the higher spiritual world.

In whatever light it may be viewed, it is certainly a very striking fact, to which attention is called by the observant author of the " Footprints of the Creator," that " when naturalists and anatomists give their readiest and most prominent instance of degradation among the denizens of the natural world, it is this very order of footless reptiles—the serpents—that they select. So far as the geologist yet knows, the Ophidians did not appear during the secondary ages, when the monarchs of creation belonged to the reptilian division, but were ushered upon the scene in the times of the Tertiary deposits, when the Mammalian dynasty had supplanted that of the Iguanodon and Megalosaurus. The degradation of the Ophidians consists in the absence of limbs—an absence total in by much the greater number of their families, and represented in others, as in the boas and pythons, by mere abortive hinder limbs concealed in the skin ; but they are thus not only *monsters through defect of parts*, if I may so express myself, but also *monsters through redundancy*, as a vegetative repetition of vertebra and ribs to the number of three or four hundred, forms the special contrivance by which the want of these is compensated."[1] When the fact, as stated by the highest authorities in physiology, is considered, that " in the true serpents the locomotive power is entirely withdrawn from the limbs,"[2] the declaration of Genesis, " upon thy belly shalt thou go," receives special emphasis. But whatever one may be disposed to make of the coincidence which here holds in respect to a phenomenon in nature, and a statement of the Sacred Word ; and however the physical may, in this striking particular, typify the spiritual in the transaction, there is not only in this, but in other important facts and testimonies, sufficient to show that the two fields of observation are closely related " by those threads of analogical connexion which run through the tissue of Creation and Providence, and impart to it that character of unity which speaks of the single producing mind."

There is another particular in the sentence passed upon the serpent, on which a few remarks must be made, although it will be more fully considered in the sequel—the enmity interposed between the tempter and the tempted : " I will put enmity between thee and the woman." To understand this in any way of the inveterate antipathy with which mankind universally regard the whole serpent tribe, is a notion too puerile to require refutation ; for if the announcement were merely this, it would be utterly unworthy of the occasion and of a place in the sacred history. There is, indeed, an antipathy,

[1] Miller, Footprints, p. 157.
[2] Carpenter, Comparative Physiology, London, 1854, p. 80.

an inveterate hate, cherished by man towards this class of reptiles; and such is the nature of this feeling, that it may be safely pronounced an instinct of our nature. As such, while its primary end may be to serve as a premonition of danger, it may have been also intended to shadow forth the more deeply rooted and eternal enmity interposed at the Fall by a merciful Creator between man and the old serpent, the devil, and which in various ways is ever since being perpetually manifested.

2. *The punishment of the Human Transgressors.*

In considering the sentence pronounced upon our first parents after they were found guilty of violating the law of God, attention must be separately directed to the cases of the woman and of the man; for although participating in the common guilt, yet various circumstances connected with their previous position and future prospects, as divinely determined and declared, called for different modes of punishment in the two cases.

The sentence passed upon the woman, who was the first in the transgression, and accordingly the first in the judgment after the serpent, contains in it three elements of misery. These are, the infliction of peculiar pain in child-bearing, the intimation of a predominant desire on her part towards her husband, and subjection to his authority, (Gen. iii. 16.) Or, according to another interpretation of the passage, which regards the last clause as explanatory or complementary of the second—the two being thus expressive of the exercise of authority owned and submitted to—the case of the woman may be characterized in two words, as one of suffering and subjection.

How peculiarly applicable this punishment was in the case and circumstances of the mother of mankind, will form the subject of after consideration; at present it is proposed simply to inquire, how or to what extent is the destiny of woman, as thus represented, verified by observation and the experience of the sex.

The most careful examination of this subject will establish it as a plain and incontrovertible fact, that the sentence said to be pronounced on the first human transgressor, describes to the very letter the universal experience of woman. Her case as a wife and mother is in the highest degree peculiar : it is in truth an anomaly in the creation. It did not escape the notice of an eminent philosopher of antiquity, while continued and more extended observation has served only to corroborate the conclusion, that woman is the only mother under heaven subject to the severity of suffering connected with conception and parturition. Although varying in degree in different circumstances and in individual cases, the sentence of the Fall, " in sorrow thou shalt bring forth children," is proved to be a universal and irreversible law of humanity. What reason, it may be asked, can exist for this marked peculiarity ? If these sufferings pertain to the original constitution of things, they appear to be sadly at variance with our best conceptions of the wisdom and beneficence of the Creator : but if we discern in them traces or tokens of a punitive character, and must assign to them a moral cause, what more reasonable or probable than the one stated in the history of the Fall ? " Why should woman—a partaker with man of a rational soul, fitted to be both his companion and his peer, endowed with all that distinguishes humanity from the brutes, and fits mankind to enjoy a supremacy over everything that is on the earth—be thus subjected to pangs and perils which no other living creature suffers ? The same Almighty Power which constituted other animals differently, and made their propagation scarcely in any degree a matter of suffering, could not want the ability, and could be as little destitute of the will, to form the noblest of animated natures, so as to secure the continuance of the race ordinarily, without that intensity of suffering, that protraction of pangs, and that preceding uneasiness, which marks human parturition. The noblest and highest nature of all would appear to be unequally treated, if this had been an original and not a superinduced condition. The facts themselves must be ascribed either to the primitive and arbitrary arrangement of the Sovereign Power—and would then appear to want equity and benevolence—or they must be admitted to have a punitive character and a moral cause, and so to comport harmoniously with the Mosaic narrative, and add greatly to its probability."[1]

But woman was doomed as a wife to subjection as well as

[1] Redford, Holy Scripture Verified, London, 1853, p. 67.

peculiar sufferings : and in attestation of the truth of this part
of her sentence, reference need only be made to the facts of her
history. These will show to what a state of social depression
she had been reduced during the long period which preceded
Christianity, and how deeply degraded her condition is still, in
all heathen countries which have not felt the influences of
what may be truly called this *woman-ennobling* religion. The
inequality, subjection, or degradation, which, in various forms
and degrees, is incident to woman, is not discoverable in the
female of any other species which roams the woods or pastures
the fields. This anomaly cannot surely be set down to reason,
—its use or abuse ; and yet, explain it as one may, woman's
condition, however it may be ameliorated by the advancement
of society in civilisation and morals, presents something peculiar and permanent. Various circumstances may contribute to
moderate the authority on the one side, and especially to
improve the mode in which it is expressed, but nothing has
been able to obliterate the feeling of dependence on the other.
" Even when Christianity improves and elevates the character,
both of man and woman, it does not obliterate the general
facts of her sorrow and subjection, but leaves these as an
inscription legible to every eye ; and yet one which can be
interpreted and reconciled with the goodness and wisdom of
the Creator, only by the light of the Mosaic narrative, and
which as natural facts, could have been traced in woman's
history exclusively by the finger of the Almighty."[1]
    In the sentence passed upon man, as represented by Adam,
the head and father of the family, the only element to be here
noticed is that which doomed him to a life of laborious toil :
" In the sweat of thy face shalt thou eat bread, till thou return
to the ground," (Gen. iii. 19.) Some other particulars comprehended in the case of man will be more conveniently
considered in connexion with the curse with which the ground
was visited for his sake.
    In considering the severe and exhausting toil to which man
is subjected in extracting from the soil the means of supporting his animal life, his case, it cannot fail to be observed,
exhibits something strikingly peculiar. The supply which
nature spontaneously yields to man's animal wants is scanty
────────────
[1] Redford, Holy Scripture Verified, p. 69.

and precarious, and is in many cases of the lowest and coarsest description. To all other creatures the earth of her own accord and in exuberance supplies food. The great granary of nature is theirs, and is stored for their use. They sow not, neither do they reap, nor gather into barns, yet God feedeth them ; that which He gives them they gather. He opens his hand, they are filled with good, (Matt. vi. 26 ; Ps. civ. 28.) To man, on the contrary, the earth furnishes a sure and suitable aliment only by hard and forcing labour, as the whole economy of agriculture and horticulture, or any other form of tillage, sufficiently shows. The soil has to be broken up and triturated by much and long-continued toil : foreign matter requires to be constantly supplied in the form of manures and composts, in order to keep up or restore the fertility, and then the serviceable and suitable seed has to be sown and covered in. Add to all this the consideration that the very plants and cereals which constitute the staple of man's food, appear to have been reclaimed with much care from a wild and comparatively worthless state, and would most certainly, if left to themselves, and without constant attention and culture, speedily degenerate into a condition utterly unfitted for the purposes which they are now made to subserve in the economy of nature,—and it will be at once seen that labour is the very law of man's being as at present constituted ; and that his progress and the propagation of the race, in every physical and moral point of view, depend on a willing and practical submission to it.

But do we not see in this stern necessity of labour—not merely of exercise—for this may have been allotted to man from the beginning and demanded by his physical constitution, (Gen. ii. 15,) but toilsome, sorrowful, and exhausting labour, such as causes his sweat or very substance to exude—something strongly at variance with man's original supremacy and lordship over the earth, and thus a condition of things explicable only on the principle announced in the history of the Fall ?

3. *The curse on the ground.*

The curse which the Supreme Judge pronounced upon the ground, forms an essential part of man's punishment as necessitating or contributing to the severe labour already considered. " Cursed is the ground for thy sake ; in sorrow shalt thou eat of it all the days of thy life. Thorns also and thistles shall it bring forth to thee ; and thou shalt eat the herb of the field," (Gen. iii. 17, 18.) The ground is cursed in its relation to man and on his account, and to this circumstance must be assigned, if not the whole, yet the principal cause of the laborious toil to which man is sentenced in procuring the necessary supply for his physical wants,—" in sorrow shalt thou eat of it."

The curse should manifest itself especially in the production of thorns and thistles, noxious weeds, alike exhaustive of the soil and troublesome in their eradication. In what other respects the power of the curse should be felt, it is not expressly declared, but it may be legitimately inferred, that sterility, or diminished powers of production, would form an important constituent. Sterility may have been induced in a variety of ways ; in particular, it may have been occasioned by the sources whence fertility arises, whence the ammonia and other substances entering into the composition of plants, and therefore essential for their growth, are derived, being so clogged, closed up, or changed, as to be no longer available for the purposes of man. But in whatever mode, and to whatever extent, it may be supposed the natural producing powers of the earth have been diminished, it would be utterly inapposite and inconclusive to point, as evidences of the curse, to the numerous deserts and barren regions of the present earth, as contrasted with the exuberant vegetation and gorgeous flora with which, at an earlier period of its history, it was clothed ; for wastes and deserts may have existed previously, and, no doubt, from the evidence of the case, actually did exist, contemporaneous with the rich vegetation in question, which flourished and also disappeared at an era long anterior to that of man. Nevertheless, the rich vegetation of a former period shews what the earth is capable of producing under conditions different from the present. We are treading, however, on surer ground, when confining our illustrations or evidences to *the thorns and thistles* expressly mentioned in the text ; and which, indeed, throughout the Scriptures, are always regarded as the very types of the curse, the removal of which, again, from a sin-laden and sorrowing creation, is set forth in figures descriptive of the disappearance of briers and thorns.   See Isa. lv. 13 ; Ezek. xxviii. 24.

What, then, is the nature of thorns and thistles ? What is their place in the vegetable economy ? and can these productions be said to furnish any indications which may serve to connect them with a primeval curse upon the ground, or a physical degeneracy thereby induced ? On these various points, it is satisfactory to be able to adduce the testimonies of able scientific writers. Thus, in regard to thorns, Professor Henslow of Cambridge states : " When a bud is *imperfectly developed*, it sometimes becomes a short branch, very hard and sharp at the extremity, and is then called a ' thorn.' We must not, however, confound the ' prickle' with the thorn. The former of these is a mere prolongation of cellular tissue from the bark, and may be considered as a compound kind of pubescence ; whilst the thorn, containing both wood and bark, is an organ of the same description as the branch itself. ' Spines' originate in the transformation of leaves." On this last point the author further observes : " Some leaves, which do not freely develop in the usual manner, assume a dry hardened appearance, and pass into spines, as in the common furze ; just as some *abortive* branches have been stated to assume the character of thorns. In the berberry all the intermediate states between a well-developed leaf and the hard spine may be distinctly traced on vigorous suckers of a year's growth."[1] To the same purpose are the remarks of another distinguished botanist. " Branches are produced," says Professor Balfour, " in the form of buds, which are connected with the centre of the woody stem. . . . But, owing to various causes, it is rare to find all the buds properly developed. Many lie dormant, and do not make their appearance as branches unless some injury has been done to the plant ; others are altered into thorns ; others, after increasing to a certain extent, die, and leave knots in the stem. That thorns are, in reality, *undeveloped* branches, is shewn by the fact, that they are connected with the centre of the stem, that they bear leaves in other circumstances, and that *under cultivation* they often become true branches. Many plants are thorny in their wild state, which are not so under cultivation, owing to this transforma-

[1] Descriptive and Physiological Botany, pp. 53, 71.

tion. Thorns, as of the hawthorn, differ totally from prickles, such as occur in the rose. The latter are merely connected with the surface of the plant, and are considered as an altered condition of the leaves, which become hardened in their structure."

The same author proceeds : " May we not see in the production of injurious thorns, an arresting of the fiat of the Almighty in the formation of branches, and thus *a blight passed on this part of creation,* a standing memorial of the effects of sin on what was declared at first to be very good ? The same remark may be made in regard to prickles, which are well seen in the brier and bramble, and which may be considered as an alteration in the development of hairs, a change on them which is associated with injury to man."[1]

Similar evidences of degeneration are also discerned in the thistle, another representative of the productions of the curse on the ground. Thus, the author last quoted observes : " In the case of such plants as the thistle, dandelion, artichoke, and others, which belong to the large division called Composites, which have numerous small flowers on a common head, the calyx is united to the fruit, and appears at the upper part of it in the form of hairs or pappus. This is a *degeneration* of the calyx, which is made subservient to the scattering of the seed, and in the case of thistles is the means of diffusing extensively these noxious weeds." " The injury which thistles and plants like them cause to fields is very great, owing to the mode in which the fruit is scattered by the winds, and the altered hairy calyx is the means employed for doing so. May we not see in this the curse of thistles ? (Gen. iii. 18.) The calyx is not developed as in other plants, but is *abortive, blighted,* as it were, and changed into hairs, which, as already shewn, indicate degeneration. Thus thistles add to the sweat and toil of man in the cultivation of the soil."[2]

The noxious orders of plants, of which thorns and thistles are the representatives, are troublesome and injurious on many accounts, but especially from their numbers, powers of multiplication, and tenacity of life. The order of Composites, to which the thistle belongs, is the largest and most generally

[1] Balfour, Phyto-Theology, Edin. 1851, pp. 110, 111
[2] Phyto-Theology, pp. 145-147.

diffused of all known tribes of plants. There are now as many species belonging to the order as there were known plants in the whole world in the time of Linnæus, and almost all have the hairy calyx. Thistles themselves are generally distributed. Their powers of multiplication, too, are exceedingly great, owing not merely to the facilities of transport and diffusion which their peculiar structure provides, but also to the multitude of seeds which they produce. The number of seeds yielded by a single plant of the common spear-thistle, for instance, has been estimated at about 24,000. Add to this the extraordinary vitality, under all circumstances of climate and seasons, possessed by these plants sown only by Nature's own hand, and it may be easily conceived, that unless kept in check by man and some other provisions of the beneficent Creator, they would speedily overrun the earth. All are familiar with the fact, that when weeds effect an entrance into the space appropriated to cultivated species, the latter are starved in their growth, and soon destroyed.

The analogies which have been thus shewn to subsist between the Mosaic narrative of the Fall in its most important features, and various facts and phenomena observable from a close inspection of Nature, are, to say the least, not a little remarkable. On the supposition that this ancient record is merely a poetical fiction, a philosophical speculation, or allegorical representation of some dubious and obscure transaction, real or fancied, in the history of the world, or of a transition in the state of man, prosperous or the reverse, these analogies are utterly unaccountable. They are, moreover, incompatible with anything short of literal, historical realities, as set forth in the narration. On any other view it must be shewn, either that the analogy does not exist, or that it is accidental ; or finally, that the natural appearances above described are so simple and apparent, that they could not have escaped the notice of the writer of Genesis. On the last supposition it may be maintained, that these phenomena have been seized on, and applied as illustrations or confirmations of the subject, or, as it may be more plausibly affirmed, that it is to a knowledge of such facts, whether read in the human consciousness, or on the broad page of external nature, or to the impressions which they made on an inquiring mind, that the origin of the narrative is to be ascribed, which is thus only a philosophical attempt to account for these natural appearances. But the least consideration must convince any one who calmly examines the subject, that any of these hypotheses is too gratuitous or absurd to merit a lengthened refutation. For, in the first place, the resemblances and the lines of connexion are too striking and strong to be summarily disposed of by a denial of their existence; while, again, they hold in too many and minute particulars to be the result of accident. But the view which, admitting the reality of the analogies referred to, regards the circumstance only as a proof of the power of observation or skilful adaptation on the part of the writer, or as the inciting cause of his speculations, is beset, if possible, with still greater difficulties, and rests on more gratuitous assumptions than either of the others.

In regard to these several allegations, it may be sufficient to remark, in the first place, that many of the facts on which the analogies are grounded, although now so plain when once pointed out, were entirely unknown and unnoticed for many ages : indeed, it required the scientific inductions of the present century to place some of them in their true light. It is certainly anything but likely that Moses, or any other of his day, was possessed of such powers of observation and induction as are implied in this supposed acquaintance with nature, and the various forms and most hidden aspects of creation ; and particularly, that he should be able to describe these appearances so accurately, and furnish, if not the true, yet so plausible an explanation of their origin as, it must be admitted, is supplied in the narrative of the Fall.

But, secondly, the analogies instanced above, must be reckoned among what writers or the Scripture Evidences are accustomed to call " undesigned coincidences," and on which they accordingly lay much stress. A careful examination of the narrative will shew, that not the slightest hint or intimation is furnished to the reader, that any such correspondence exists between the facts of nature and the scriptural statements. From anything that can be gathered from the simple unvarnished narration, it cannot even be made to appear that the writer himself was conscious of its existence, far less that he troubled himself with the matter at all, or was concerned for the impression which it might make upon the reader. Upon a full and impartial view of the case, the simplest and most satisfactory conclusion attainable on the subject of these analogies, and the only way of escape from the difficulties and contradictions with which the question is otherwise encompassed, is to look upon them as unmistakable tokens of the identity of authorship in the two productions compared— Nature, and the narrative of the Fall in Genesis ; both being alike upon this shewing the product of God, the Creator and Governor of man, the one being his work, and the other his word.

SECT. X.—TEMPTATION AND THE FALL IN THE LIGHT OF THE NEW TESTAMENT.

It will be the object of a subsequent section to point out the very intimate relation which exists between the ideas of the Creation and Fall as set forth in Genesis, and the scheme of doctrines unfolded and applied in the New Testament by our Lord and his Apostles, and shew, in particular, how the doctrine of the Fall is necessarily assumed as a first principle in all the intimations of salvation through Christ. It will, therefore, be unnecessary to refer at present to the more general and manifest correspondence which, as must be admitted by all who possess the least acquaintance with Scripture, holds on the subject between the earliest and latest portion of the Sacred Volume, while it will better subserve the purpose more immediately in view, to trace out some of the less obvious points of contact, and carry over into the purely scriptural domain the investigation pursued in the last section with respect to the analogies discoverable between the biblical narrative of the Fall, and Creation in some of its moral and physical aspects.

If the analogies found to exist between Nature and Scripture prove, that while the one is the work, the other is the word of God, the analogies discernible between the different parts of the Sacred Volume itself, whether styled the Old or the New Testament, will no less plainly evince the whole to be the expression of one mind, and shew that but one Spirit pervades the Bible from Genesis to the Apocalypse. " The analogy of religion, natural and revealed, to the constitution and course of nature," has been ably established by the immortal work of Bishop Butler, in which he has rendered eminent service to Christianity and the Bible ; and yet it may be affirmed, that equal, if not greater results, may be obtained in tracing the analogy of one portion of Scripture with another, though separated by many ages, and distinguished by many external peculiarities, and in establishing the wonderful harmony of the whole. That such analogies exist will be at once apparent from a careful examination of the subject, besides being plainly announced in various passages of the New Testament. To refer only to one or two instances, where analogies of this kind are announced or adverted to, and such as relate particularly to the history of the Fall, there is that notable passage, (Rom. v. 12-19,) where the Apostle discusses the bringing in of reconciliation and life through the obedience of Christ, in its analogy to the bringing in of sin and death through the disobedience of Adam, who is, in particular, declared to have been " a figure or *type* of him that was to come," elsewhere expressly styled " the last Adam." (1 Cor. xv. 45.) This analogy the Apostle traces out in many particulars connected with the two Adams, singled out as the heads of humanity in the two dispensations—the two poles on which turn the history and destinies of the human race, described by the same Apostle in another passage as " the *first* man of the earth, earthy ; the *second* man, the Lord from heaven ;" where it is also declared, that " as we have borne the image of the earthy, we shall also bear the image of the heavenly." (1 Cor. xv. 47-49.)

Did the prescribed limits admit, it would conduct into a highly interesting and useful field of investigation to pursue at length, and into various particulars, the analogical harmony of what must be regarded by every Christian reader as the two great discoveries of revelation, which respect the very momentous facts of the ruin and restoration of man, whether as unfolded in the Old or in the New Testament, and which supplies an argument strongly corroborative of the truth of both doctrines. This analogy might be traced in various directions. It might be shown how the sin, which first revealed itself in Eden, was the sin from which Christ came to save, while the death there incurred was that to which he as the surety of sinners submitted ; and how the gospel in its mode of justification, as announced to the first human transgressors, is the very gospel of the New Testament of Christ and his apostles. In particular, it might be shown how the scheme of grace established through the second Adam, preserves the inviolability of the law first published in Paradise, and since proclaimed through every subsequent dispensation—" the soul that sinneth it shall die ;" and how with the inviolability of the law are manifested and maintained all the perfections of the Lawgiver, who is seen to be " a just God whilst justifying the ungodly;" and farther, how, while making provision for reinstating the sinner in the favour of God, it is through a restoration to the Divine image: " Beholding as in a glass the glory of the Lord, we are changed into the same image, from glory to glory, even as by the Spirit of the Lord :" and all these great results effected through the intervention of that Adam who was made a quickening Spirit, (1 Cor. xv. 45.) Instead, however, of entering at present upon any general examination of the great questions thus announced, which would itself require a volume, it is proposed to single out two particulars intimately connected with the history of the first transgression ; and first, on the ground of the *typical* relation affirmed by the Apostle in a passage already quoted, to exist between Adam and Christ, to consider the necessity whereby, as stated in another passage, " in all things it behoved" the latter " to be made like to his brethren ;" but this similarity only in one aspect, his *temptation*, through which " he is able to succour them that are tempted," and of which it is farther affirmed, " he was in all points tempted like as we are, yet without sin." (Heb. ii. 14-18 ; iv. 15.) And, secondly, to compare the views disclosed in the New Testament regarding the course, the consequences, and the nature of sin, the last as particularly manifested in the character and claims of Antichrist, *the man of sin*, with the representation given of it in the history of the Fall.

There are two remarkable temptations described in the Bible, that of Adam in the beginning of the Old Testament, and that of Christ at the beginning of the New. There are no

doubt numerous other instances of temptation recorded ; for in
one point of view, what is the Bible but the history of the
trials or temptations of frail humanity, sometimes triumphing,
but in the majority of cases succumbing to the tempter : some
of these being incidentally adverted to and others accompanied
with details, but none of them bearing any but the remotest
similitude to either of the two just specified, which occupy a
place peculiarly their own. Not to insist on other distinguishing
features, it is sufficient to remark that, with the exception of
these two, all the other temptations recorded were " such as is
common to man," (1 Cor. x. 13,) being the temptations of
individuals who were members of fallen humanity, while the
two in question were the temptations of such as the Scriptures
affirm to have been upright and innocent, the one by creation,
the other essentially and always so, being " holy, harmless,
undefiled, and separate from sinners." But while these two
temptations differ widely from all others upon record, there is
manifested a striking analogy between themselves in various
points to be presently stated, the one being in fact the counterpart of the other. With a remarkable dissimilarity in the
conduct and external condition of the tempted in the two
cases, productive of the most opposite results, there is also a
sameness which brings out only more clearly that in the case
of Christ it was the old conflict waged over anew, but that
now the ground lost by the failure of the first Adam was more
than recovered by the fortitude of the second.[1]

1. The place which the second temptation occupies in the
New Testament and in the history of Christ, strikingly corresponds with that of the first in the older volume, or in the
history of the primeval man formed in the image of God, and
so in a sense *his son*, (Luke iii. 38.) Reference will be made
in a subsequent section to the correspondence between the
opening pages of the Old and of the New Testaments, both
beginning with a *genesis* or *generation*, the one to renew the
other, or remedy the disorder induced through sin ; but no less
striking is the circumstance that much the same place in the
Books of Genesis and of Matthew is occupied with the narrative

[1] Bengel (Gnomon Novi Test. in Matt. iv. 2):—" Conferri potest haec tentatio
cum illa quae describitur Gen. iii. *Tentator simili arte usus est ;* sed quam pro-
toplasti rem male gesserant, eam Christus restituit."

of two temptations, nothing similar to which again occurs in the whole history of humanity. The place of the one temptation in the history of our Lord, at the very outset of his public, official career, exactly corresponds to that of the other in the history of the first made man. A temptation forms the initial chapter, as it were, in the respective histories of the first and second Adam, and stands as an introduction at the head of the two dispensations. Although it is foreign to the present purpose to inquire what light the temptation of the second Adam, the Lord from heaven, is fitted to cast on the question, why God permits the innocent and the holy, who stand to him in the relation of sons, to be tempted by evil, yet it may be remarked that it would appear from the place which temptation is thus seen to occupy in the past and present economies, to be in some way or other a necessity of humanity, or a necessity in establishing a character for righteousness. From other intimations of Scripture, it may be inferred that the same law extends to the whole moral creation : why this necessity should have existed it is needless at present to speculate. It was no doubt, however, in accordance with this discipline, that when the Lord from heaven was " made under the law," (Gal. iv. 4,) he must be " led up of the Spirit into the wilderness,"—*driven*, as it is said in another place, (Mark i. 12,)—" to be tempted of the devil," (Matt. iv. 4.)

2. The conduct of the tempter, or the plan pursued by him, is the same in the two cases under consideration. His primary object was to raise doubts in the minds of the objects of his attack, in order to shake their faith in God, and their feeling of absolute dependence on him. In the one case the insinuation is, " Yea, hath God said ye shall not eat of every tree in the garden ?" in the other, " If thou be the Son of God, command that these stones be made bread." The terms of address in the two temptations are dissimilar, but the spirit and purport are essentially the same ; while in both alike the appeal is to the sensual appetites. Indeed, the mode of attack which proved so fatally successful in Paradise, is so frequently enacted, and with the same results, in the history of man, that it has passed into a proverb, " what begins in doubt ends in disobedience." There is another feature in the opening addresses of the tempter deserving of remark in analogical con-

M

siderations such as the present. In both there is reference to
a saying or declaration of God. In the one case this is fully
expressed, " Yea, hath God said ?" in the other it is no less
plainly implied. " If thou be the Son of God" obviously
alludes to the testimony which was vouchsafed to Christ at his
baptism, immediately preceding the temptation, when God in
a voice from heaven declared, " This is my beloved Son, in
whom I am well pleased."[1]

3. The character and the very form of the two temptations
are remarkably alike. The numerous and varied temptations by
which the human mind may be assailed, assume essentially one
or other of two forms. They address themselves either to the
desires, or to the *fears*, of the tempted, presenting something
to be obtained and enjoyed as an element of happiness, or else
to be shunned and preserved from, as causing misery or distress.
Our Lord at the outset of his public life and ministry was
tempted through the medium of *desire ;* but this failing to
turn him aside from the course on which he had entered, the
great adversary made another and last attempt on him towards
the close of his earthly labours. At the conclusion of the first
temptation, one evangelist remarks, " Then the devil leaveth
him," (Matt. iv. 11 ;) but another more pointedly mentions,
" When the devil had ended all the temptation, he departed
from him *for a season,*" (Luke iv. 13,) an expression obviously
intimating that the conflict should be again renewed, as was
actually the case in Gethsemane, but in another form. Although
of this last mighty struggle but scanty details are furnished,
probably as not possessing the same deep significance as the
first in the history and undertaking of the God-man, yet
information enough is given to show the power with which the
Saviour had to contend, (Luke xxii. 53 ; John xiv. 30,) and the
particular form of temptation to which he was subjected. It
was the same malignant enemy whom he had encountered and
foiled in the wilderness, that presented himself again in Gethsemane, but in this renewed assault the form of the temptation
was changed, being addressed to Christ's *fears* in association

[1] Bengel, Gnomon in Matth. iv. 3 :—" Et dubitat Satanas, et in dubitationem
conatur adducere ; vera eripere, falsa persuadere. Conditione solicitat, quod de
cœlo cap. iii. 17, categorice pronunciatum fuerat."

with the sufferings and death in prospect, and from which nature of itself would instinctively be ready to recoil.

In every possible form, then, the Saviour and representative of sinners was personally tempted, but at present the comparison instituted respects only the first of his great temptations which, from the full particulars furnished concerning it, and the prominence given to it in the Gospels, is seen to occupy a place by itself in the economy of redemption, and as constituting a part of the necessary equipment of the Redeemer for his high undertaking as the representative of man, who had not merely been tempted but seduced. This temptation, as already remarked, approached Christ in an address to his desires—sensual, intellectual, and spiritual—and without entering into details, it may be observed as particularly worthy of note, that in the three successive appeals made to our Lord's desires during this first temptation, are clearly indicated the three principal forces by which, according to apostolic testimony, sin or the world uniformly exerts its influence, " the lust of the flesh, the lust of the eyes, and the pride of life," (1 John ii. 16.) But what is still more noticeable, as strongly indicative of the analogy between the two temptations, is the fact that the same three elements were combined in the temptation which issued in the apostasy of man, with the additional circumstance that the general form of the temptation was the same.

Throughout the conference recorded in the narrative of the Fall, the tempter addressed himself solely to man's desires, and this procedure succeeded so well that recourse was not needed to the second mode of attack, which, moreover, in the circumstances of unfallen man who had nothing to fear, might not have been so suitable. But however this may be, is it too much to suggest that the plan adopted in the temptation of man proving so successful, the devil was thereby emboldened to repeat it in precisely the same form with Christ? There the circumstances were widely different from those of Adam : obedience and suffering were both before the Saviour, not as alternatives to be chosen, but to be embraced together ; and this diversity of circumstances may be supposed to render the temptation to the *desires* or to the *fears* equally appropriate ; but, in the first instance, the former mode of attack was chosen, corresponding to the temptation of man. Farther, and more particularly, the three forces by which our Lord was separately and successively assailed were, in the apprehension of the woman who had credulously listened to the evil suggestions of the enemy of truth and righteousness, concentrated in one object—the forbidden and now coveted fruit. The lust of the flesh, which proved ineffectual when presented to our Lord, is here called into exercise by the assumption that " the tree was good for food." The lust of the eye was dazzled by the " pleasant appearance" of the tree, although perhaps in that respect not distinguished from any other of the productions of the garden. The pride of life appeared in that bold presumption which daringly aspired to equal God in knowledge, and calculated on immunity in the way of sin or dereliction of duty. Indeed it might be supposed that the threefold division, according to which, in a passage already quoted, the apostle arranges the evil influences at work in the world, is based upon the words of the ancient record, " when the woman saw that the tree was good for food, and that it was pleasant to the eyes, and a tree to be desired to make one wise, she took of the fruit thereof and did eat, and gave also to her husband with her, and he did eat." But, farther, in the transaction recorded in Genesis, the immediate aim of the tempter was to persuade the objects of his assault to eat of *forbidden* fruit or food, and in the other and in the first place, to procure food in an *unfit* and so a forbidden way : " Command that these stones be made bread ;" but in both cases the ultimate aim was to secure a violation of the Divine law, whether as expressed in a special command or precept, or as merely implied in the constitution of things, or in any other appointments of nature or providence.

4. The conduct of the tempted in the two instances, affords important matter for comparison. The particulars already noticed show a remarkable correspondence in the two transactions ; but here begins the strong contrast by which they are distinguished. The conduct of the tempted is directly the opposite in the two cases, and accordingly produces results of the greatest contrariety. In the one, yielding to the temptation leads to sin and death, with their concomitants, shame and fear ; in the other, resistance discomfits the wicked one,— " then the devil departed from him "—agreeably to the apostolic

intimation, " resist the devil and he will flee from you ;" and not only so, but ultimately retrieves the ruin and disorder introduced through man's failure in the first temptation. But notwithstanding the painful contrast presented by the first Adam, it is to be noticed of the two cases alike, that the temptation came from without, and not from within, and beyond question from the same source, although in the case of our Lord the character and personality of the tempter are more openly unfolded. But, farther, notwithstanding the diversity of the results, the two temptations are similar, insomuch as they stand in the history of the individuals as decisive events, determining character, and such as in copy may be witnessed in every-day life, which by their native tendency give a direction to all succeeding actions. As, after Adam's first act of disobedience, all subsequent sin was nothing but the unfolding of that original sin ; so the Saviour's first victory laid the foundation of all his subsequent triumphs over evil, and may be said to have been the grand point on which depended the destinies of redemption. Regarding himself, Christ afterwards remarked, " The prince of this world cometh and hath nothing in me ;" that is, has no point of appliance whereon to fasten his attack, (John xiv. 30 ;) how much this may have been owing to the successful resistance offered to the first Satanic onset it is not easy to say, although, to judge from analogy, that was the crisis in our Lord's history.

5. The scene of the temptations and the situation of the tempted, also present strong points of contrast. These, however, only bring out more strikingly the peculiar relation of the two transactions. The scene of the first temptation was in Eden—the garden of delights, which God had specially planted for man—his representative on earth. Unfallen man, in an unfallen world, inhabited that plentifully stored and select dwelling-place, having thus all his wants abundantly provided for by his Beneficent Creator. But man's sin subverted that order of things : he is expelled Paradise, and made to inhabit the outfield of creation, and find there the supplies which his necessities required. The scene of the second temptation is accordingly in direct contrast to that of the first, but in striking analogy with the new order of things ; the literalities in the two cases bringing out more vividly the great moral

differences which they typified. It is no longer paradise with
its refreshing shades, and its sweet and abundant fruit : it is
" the wilderness" whither Christ is driven, and in striking
harmony with the scene and the situation, it is said, " he was
an hungered ;" the desert furnishing no provision for him who
came to remove the curse which rested on creation, and make
the wilderness and the solitary places glad. And as if to bring
out more strongly the contrast in the two cases, the evangelist
Mark observes, " And he was there in the wilderness forty
days tempted of Satan ; and was *with the wild beasts ;* and the
angels ministered to him." On which Olshausen, after Usteri,
truly as well as beautifully remarks—" This circumstance has
a typical meaning ; because it is meant to represent Jesus as
the restorer of paradise. Adam fell in paradise and made it a
wilderness : Jesus conquered in the wilderness and made it a
paradise, where the beasts lost their wildness, and angels took
up their abode."

In reading the narrative of man's temptation and fall with
the light of the New Testament, another point worthy of consideration is the harmony which exists in the representations
contained in the earliest and latest Scriptures regarding sin—
its progress, tendency, and nature.

The course or progress of sin, as set forth in the New Testament, from its rise in temptation to its final issue in death,
presents a strong analogy with the facts recorded in the ancient
history relative to the temptation and first entrance of evil.
This is very obvious from a statement of the Apostle James
regarding the source of temptation, in which he strongly repels
the insinuation, that God is in any sense the author of it, or
accessory to man's seduction : " Let no man say, when he is
tempted, I am tempted of God ; for God cannot be tempted
with evil, neither tempteth he any man. But every man is
tempted when he is drawn away of his own lust, and enticed."
This is the source of temptation in fallen man ; for it is of
such the Apostle evidently here treats. But being so enticed,
whether by external solicitations, as in the case of the first
temptation, or subsequently by the sinful desires and devices
of the heart itself, the course of temptation, when yielded to,
is always the same : " When lust hath conceived, it bringeth

forth sin ; and sin, when it is finished, bringeth forth death."
(James i. 13-15.) Than these words nothing can better express the truths so painfully and prominently brought into
view in the history of the primeval temptation, and of the
first experience of fallen humanity. To the same effect is the
statement of another Apostle, that " the end of sin," that in
which it terminates, " is death ;" or, regarded in another
aspect, " the wages of sin is death," (Rom. vi. 21-23 ;) with
which may be compared the original threatening, " In the day
that thou eatest thereof thou shalt surely die."

The tendency of sin as a *departure* from the living God,
(Heb. iii. 12,) which, if unchecked, would go on increasing for
ever, is forcibly exemplified in the conduct of the first transgressors. Their hiding themselves from that glorious Being
whom they were conscious of offending, was a fact which embodied all the representations of the New Testament regarding
the aberration of the sinner—representations, it may be remarked, in strict harmony with physical and moral truths—
while the fact that God himself must go in pursuit of the fugi-
tives ere they can be recovered, has its counterpart in the
mission of Christ, and is the basis on which rest some of his
most touching parables ; as, for instance, that of the man who
went in quest of the sheep that had gone astray, (Luke xv. 4.)
Such is the nature of the first departure from the path of
order or law, that it precludes the possibility of a disposition
to return, originating in the erring subject itself.

But that which more particularly merits attention as furnishing a remarkable analogy between the oldest and latest
discoveries of Scripture, is the disclosures made regarding the
nature of sin as first manifested in man, and described in the
narrative of the Fall, and as set forth in the New Testament.
Keeping in view the distinction between the form of all sin as
disobedience to the authority, or transgression of the law of
God, and its essence or originating principle, sin at first revealed itself according to the narrative in Genesis, as the
perversion and predominancy of the sensational impulse on
the one hand, and as usurpation and arrogance on the other.
The latter element, indeed, in the form of pride, or impatience
of authority or restraint, may be properly regarded as the
moving principle in the transgression ; for it may be justly

concluded, that that which rendered the forbidden fruit so very desirable in the estimation of the woman, was the very circumstance that it was *forbidden*, and as such was suggestive of law and authority on the one hand, and obedient subjection, with restraint, on the other; similar it may be to the experience of the Apostle, " I had not known sin, but by the law; for I had not known lust, except the law had said, Thou shalt not covet," (Rom. vii. 7.[1]) Of this disposition of the mother of mankind, induced through his previous representations, the tempter was not slow to take advantage : he held out to her the promise, " Ye shall be as God,"—independent, released from restraint and subjection of every kind.

This representation of sin on its first appearance, and in its leading principle, is in entire conformity with innumerable facts attested by observation and experience in the life of the transgressors of the Divine law. It is also in conformity with the teaching of our Lord and his Apostles on the subject, which is only a faithful and correct description of this everyday experience. Reference has already been made to a parable of our Lord illustrative of the tendency of sin in flying away from the centre of all good ; there are also parables of the same Heavenly Teacher descriptive of the disposition from which that tendency springs. An example is furnished in the parable of the Prodigal Son, in striking accordance with the preceding representation. " The abandoning of his father's house on the part of the son points at once," as Olshausen remarks, " to man's falling away from God, out of which the whole of his other backsliding gradually develops itself." But it is of special importance to notice how the disposition which resulted in such wretchedness and folly first manifested itself in the request, " Father, give me the portion of goods that falleth to me." " What does this request mean," asks Trench in his Notes on this parable, " when we come to give it its spiritual significance ? It is the expression of man's desire to be

---

[1] Müller, Doctrine of Sin, vol. ii. p. 179 : "The narrative in the Book of Genesis, of the primeval sin of our first parents, makes it in the most determinate manner prominent, that the consciousness of the forbidding law—therefore the consciousness of a possible act which absolutely ought not to be committed—precedes the resolve to sin, not merely by Gen. ii. 17, but still more expressly by Gen. iii. 3. And Rom. vii. 7-9, says the same of the beginnings of real sin in us."

independent of God, to be a god to himself, (Gen. iii. 5,) and to lay out his life according to his own will, and for his own pleasure. It is man growing weary of living upon God, and upon his fulness, and desiring to take the ordering of his life into his own hands, and believing that he can be a fountain of blessedness to himself. All the subsequent sins of the younger son are included in this one, as in their germ,—are but the unfolding of this, the sin of sins."[1]

But farther, and more particularly, with the first germ of sin, as thus viewed, corresponds its highest development. Sin, as such, remains in every dispensation ever true to itself, and to the character in which it was originally set forth by the earliest biblical writer in the history of the Fall, only with this very significant difference, that what in the germ is a promise on the part of the tempter, " Ye shall be as God," and a desire on the part of the tempted to secure so pleasing a privilege, appears, when sin has attained its full maturity, to be preferred in the form of an actual claim, blasphemously assuming the functions and prerogatives of Deity. Thus the Apostle Paul, in describing the completely developed form in which in the person of Antichrist sin shall appear at the concluding scene in this world's history, sets forth " *the man of sin,* the son of perdition," as presenting claims to unconditional dignity and independence, and to the homage which belongs only to the Supreme God.

It would lead into too wide a field of discussion to consider the various particulars to which the Apostle calls attention in the important passage referred to ; one or two observations must suffice. The Apostle's words are : " Who opposeth and exalteth himself above all that is called God, or that is worshipped ; so that he, *as God, sitteth in the temple of God, shewing himself that he is God,*" (2 Thess. ii. 4.) For the present purpose, it is quite unnecessary to inquire to what particular power or principle this description applies, farther than that it is *Antichrist*—the great opponent of the Redeemer ; or the *man of sin,* in whom sin is, as it were, embodied. Sin, throughout the various stages of its history, manifests itself in new and ever-changing forms, but in Antichrist it finally issues in downright self-deification, and thus discloses its inmost nature

[1] Notes on the Parables, Third Edition, 1847, p. 394.

or essence. In conformity with this leading idea in his character, Antichrist is afterwards described (verse 8) as the wicked or *lawless* one, whose nature is, that he acknowledges no law, no higher will, but as selfishness personified, will have his own will recognised as the one only law. "No one can fail," observes Julius Müller, "to mark the correspondence between this *mystery of iniquity* and the words, ' Ye shall be as God,' in the history of the Fall."[1] This correspondence will be seen to be more striking and deeply significant when it is farther considered, that the revelation of the man of sin is necessarily preceded by, or connected with, a remarkable apostasy or falling away from God and the truth. (Verse 3.)

For certain features somewhat similar to those here ascribed to Antichrist, reference might also be made to the earlier description found in the Book of Daniel, where the same power of evil is represented as a king that "shall do according to his will, and shall exalt himself, and shall magnify himself above every god," (chap. xi. 36;) and also to the account contained in the Apocalypse, where it is prophesied how an image of Antichrist will be vivified by pretended miracles, and the adoration of that image required on pain of death, (Rev. xiii. 15.) But it is unnecessary to enlarge; for it thus evidently appears that the history of the Fall, in describing the first beginning of sin, reveals its real nature so definitely and distinctly, as to present a most remarkable accordance with that which is more fully declared in the later Scriptures.

SECT. XI.—SCRIPTURAL REFERENCES TO THE NARRATIVES OF CREATION AND THE FALL.

The observations contained in the preceding section have disclosed some features of the mutual dependence between the earliest and the latest portions of Scripture with respect to the Fall; a subject which it was proposed to examine farther, including also the doctrine of Creation. As an important preliminary in the matter, the present section will be occupied with a classification of the more important references by subsequent writers of Scripture to the specific incidents and state-

[1] Doctrine of Sin, vol. i. p. 145.

ments of the *narratives* of Creation and of the Fall. This will shew more clearly than any general reasoning the important place which the first three chapters of Genesis occupy in the later writings; and it will be particularly useful in proving in what sense their contents were understood by the Church, both Jewish and Christian.

The references in the Old Testament, it will be found, are not so specific and express as those in the New: this is particularly the case with regard to the narrative of the Fall, as was observed in a former section. This, however, admits of easy explanation. " The historical writers of the Old Testament," says Bishop Sherlock, " were never led within view of this ancient story by the occurrences in which they are concerned; from them, consequently, no light is to be expected. Moral writers had sometimes occasion to reflect on the state of the world, and to consider how things came into the state and condition in which they found them: prophets, likewise, who were teachers of religion, were in the same case; from these we may expect some assistance." And again : " If we find less than it may seem reasonable to expect from these writers on the subject of the Fall, and the promise made to Adam, there is a plain reason to be given why it is so; for the great promises made to David of a Son, ' whose kingdom should endure for ever,' had eclipsed all the ancient hopes, and so entirely possessed the mind of the Psalmist and of his son Solomon, that they seldom look higher than the immediate promises of God to themselves. . . . The case was much the same with the succeeding prophets ; they were ministers of new declarations made by God, and had no occasion to treat of the old. And of the later writers, none treat expressly of this subject ; if ever they mention it, it is only occasionally, and *in transitu.* All the help, therefore, to be had in this case must come from hints and allusions, and ways of speaking, which refer to ancient things, and shew the writer's sense concerning them."[1] Yet these hints and allusions are numerous, and for the present purpose exceedingly important as links in the great chain of historical testimony which connects the first page of Genesis with the last of Revelation.

[1] Works, vol. iv. pp. 155. 178.

(A) *Distinct and indisputable references.*

Before entering upon the comparison of particulars, it may be noticed generally, that the historical narrative of Creation in Genesis (chap. i.) has a poetical echo or counterpart in the Book of Psalms—viz., Ps. civ. Instead, however, of quoting or commenting at any length on the psalmist's descriptions, it is preferable to give the remarks of Hengstenberg as presenting an epitome of this sacred lyric. " According to the general relation of the whole psalm-poetry, and also of prophecy, to the Books of Moses, it cannot but be that the psalmist, in the praise of God from nature, hung very closely upon the first book (section) of Genesis. The description follows in general the succession of the several days of creation: the first and second, verses 2-5 ; the third, verses 6-18 ; the fourth, verses 19-23 ; the fifth, verses 24-26 ; and an allusion to the seventh in verse 31. The deviations are occasioned, not only by the difference between the poet and the historian, and by the circumstance that the psalmist has before his eyes the creation perpetually prolonged in the preservation of the world, while the historian describes the act of creation merely in itself, but also by the fact, that the psalmist has proposed to himself not the general object to represent the greatness of God universally in nature, but the special object to set forth the greatness of God in the care which he takes of living beings. This affords an explanation of the circumstance, that in the succession of days no mention is made of the sixth, which is occupied with the creation of these beings."

I.—*Particular attributes and acts of Creation.*

1. *Its antiquity and unity.*—Gen. i. 1, " In the beginning God created the heavens and the earth."
   Ps. cii. 25, " Of old hast thou laid the foundation of the earth, and the heavens are the work of thy hands."
   Heb. i. 10, " Thou, Lord, in the beginning, hast laid the foundations of the earth," &c.
   Obs.—These passages are adduced, not particularly as references to Gen. i. 1, but as conveying similar ideas.
2. *Light.*—Gen. i. 3, " God said, Be light."

2 Cor. iv. 6, " God, who commanded the light to shine out of darkness, hath shined in our hearts," &c.

Obs.—The Apostle institutes a parallel between creation and regeneration ; in the latter, as in the former, light is the first product.

3. *The collection of the waters.*—Gen. i. 9, " God said, Let the waters be gathered together to one place."

Ps. xxxiii. 7, " He gathereth the waters of the sea together as an heap : he layeth up the depth in storehouses."

Ps. civ. 8, 9, " The *place* which thou hast founded for them. Thou hast set a bound that they may not pass over ; that they turn not again to cover the earth."

Prov. viii. 29, " He gave to the sea his decree, that the waters should not pass his commandment."

4. *The celestial luminaries.*—Gen. i. 16, " God made two great lights ; the greater light to rule the day, and the lesser light to rule the night ; the stars also."

Ps. cxxxvi. 7, 9, " To him that made great lights : the sun to rule by day ; the moon and the stars to rule by night."

5. *The purpose of these luminaries.*—Gen. i. 14, " Let them be for signs and for *seasons.*"

Ps. civ. 19, " He appointed the moon for *seasons ;* the sun knoweth his going down."

Obs.—The word rendered *seasons* in the two passages, means *set* or *appointed times—tempora statuta.* " It is clear from the second parallel clause, and from the expansion in verses 20-23 of the psalm, that the fundamental difference of day and night, on which all others depend, is here brought particularly into view. Compare, ' to divide between day and night,' which in Gen. i. 14 precedes, and ' to serve for signs and for seasons,' **and** ' to divide between the light and the darkness' of verse 18."—*Hengstenberg.*

6. *The mode of Creation—a Divine mandate or fiat.*—Gen. i. 3, &c., " God said, Let there be," &c.

Ps. xxxiii. 8, 9, " Let all the earth fear the Lord : let all the inhabitants of the world stand in awe of him. For he spake, and it was done : he commanded, and it stood fast."

(With particular reference to Gen. ii. 1, the psalmist says,)
Verse 6, " Through the word of the Lord were the
heavens made, and all their hosts by the breath of his
mouth."

Obs.—" In the history of the creation, to which this verse,
as well as verses 7 and 9, generally refer, the creation is
described as the work of the Spirit of God and his Word.
First, the *Spirit of God* moved upon the face of the waters,
then God *said.* We may also suppose that the Spirit and the
power of God are here represented by the figure of breath,
because that in man is the first sign of life."—*Hengstenberg.*

II.—*Eden and its accompaniments.*

1. *Its garden.*—Gen. ii. 8, " The Lord God planted a garden
    eastward in Eden."
  Gen. xiii. 10, " The plain of Jordan was as the garden of
    the Lord."
  Joel ii. 3, " The land is as the garden of Eden before
    them, and behind them a desolate wilderness."
  Isaiah li. 3, " He will make her wilderness like Eden, and
    her desert like the garden of the Lord."
  Ezek. xxviii. 13, " In Eden, the garden of God."
  Obs.—" Eden, as a proper name, the garden of Jehovah,
the paradise, as the Septuagint renders it, both in Isaiah and
in Gen. ii. 8, is the grand historical and yet ideal designation
of the most consummate terrene excellence."—*Alexander on
Isaiah, l. c.* In the passage from Joel, " the contrast between
the beauty of paradise and the desolation of a desert, is ex-
quisitely forcible and affecting."—*Henderson.*
2. *Its river.*—Gen. ii. 10, " And a river went out of Eden
    to water the garden."
  Ps. xxxvi. 8, " They shall be abundantly satisfied with
    the fatness of thy house ; and thou shalt make them
    drink of the *river of thy pleasures,*" עֲדָנֶיךָ נַחַל, the river
    of thy Eden.
  Obs.—" In the stream, which of old watered the garden of
Eden for the good of man, the psalmist saw the type of that
stream of bliss with which God's love never ceases to refresh
his people."—*Hengstenberg.* Another reference is Rev. xxii. 1,

" He shewed me a pure river of water of life," &c. " The type of the river here is the river that at first watered paradise. That allusion is made to that admits of less doubt, as here, precisely as in Gen. ii. 9, 10, the river and the trees are placed in immediate connexion with each other."—*Hengstenberg.*

3. *Its trees.*—Gen. ii. 9, " Every tree that is pleasant to the sight and good for food."

Ezek. xxxi. 8, 9, " The cedars in the garden of God could not hide him ; the fir trees were not like his boughs, and the chesnut trees were not like his branches, nor any tree in the garden of God was like unto him in his beauty. I have made him fair by the multitude of his branches : so that all the trees of Eden that were in the garden of God envied him." See also verses 16, 18.

4. *The tree of life.*—Gen. ii. 9, " The tree of life in the midst of the garden."

Prov. iii. 18, " She is a tree of life to them that lay hold upon her ;" xi. 30, " The fruit of the righteous is a tree of life." See also chap. xiii. 12 ; xv. 4.

Rev. ii. 7, " The tree of life which is in the midst of the paradise of God." So also chap. xxii. 2, 14 ; Ezek. xlvii. 7.

Obs.—" If we fail to perceive that the tree in Ezekiel is the tree of life, we violently tear his prophecy from its connexion with Gen. ii. 9, iii. 22, on the one hand, and with Rev. xxii. 2, on the other. The *variety* of the trees in Ezekiel, and here on both sides of the river, seems to present an important deviation from the representation given in Genesis, where only *one* tree of life is spoken of. But this latter point admits of some doubt. It is said ' the tree of life which is in the midst of the garden,' and at any rate it had conjoined with it as a type, ' every tree that is pleasant to the sight and good for food,' which the Lord is said, in the preceding context, to have made to spring out of the earth, and which we can suppose, according to verse 10, to have grown on the banks of the river. We must still think of these trees as trees of life in the more general sense, the tree of life only as such in the highest degree."—*Hengstenberg.* A more satisfactory explanation, however, of this deviation from the original description can be given. See Excursus iv., " *On the trees of knowledge and of life.*"

CREATION AND THE FALL.

5. *The gold and precious stones of Eden.*—Gen. ii. 11, 12,
"Havilah, where there is gold; and the gold of that
land is good : there is bdellium and the onyx stone."
Ezek. xxviii. 13, "Thou hast been in Eden the garden of
God : every precious stone was thy covering, the
sardius, topaz, and the diamond, the beryl, the onyx,
and the jasper, the sapphire, the emerald, and the
carbuncle, and gold."

Obs.—"The representation of the King of Tyre as the
normal or perfect man, not unnaturally led the prophet back
to the garden of Eden, where the man that really was such
had his abode. . . . But occupying such a blessed region, all
objects of natural preciousness and beauty of course lay at the
king's command; and as we are told in Genesis of the gold
and the jewels, with which that land originally abounded, so
here the prophet speaks of them as forming the very apparel
of the king."—*Fairbairn, Exposition of Ezekiel.*

6. *Its cherubim.*—Gen. iii. 24, "He placed at the east of
the garden of Eden cherubim and a flaming sword."
Ezek. xxviii. 14, "Thou art the anointed cherub that
covereth ; and I have set thee so ; thou wast upon the
holy mountain of God ; thou hast walked up and
down in the midst of the stones of fire."

Obs.—The reference of the prophet to the passage in Genesis
cannot be doubted. It immediately follows the representation
of the King of Tyre as occupying the garden of Eden *in
the day of his creation,* verse 13—perfect in his beauty till
iniquity was found in him, verse 15 ; but because of sin, he
will be cast out as profane from the mountain of God, and
destroyed from amidst the stones of fire, verse 16 : a reference
to the expulsion of man from the garden. Even the cherub, if
found guilty, shall be expelled.

III.—*Man, his Creation and Condition.*

1. *Formed of the dust of the ground.*—Gen. ii. 7, "The Lord
God formed man of the dust of the ground." See also
chap. iii. 19.
Eccles. xii. 7, "The dust shall return to the earth as it was."
1 Cor. xv. 47, "The first man is of the earth, earthy."

2. *Animated by the breath of God.*—Gen. ii. 7, " God breathed into his nostrils the breath of life; and man became
a living soul."

Job xxxiii. 4, " The Spirit of God hath made me, and
the breath of the Almighty hath given me life."

1 Cor. xv. 45, " And so it is written, The first man Adam
was made a living soul."

3. *Created in the image of God.*—Gen. i. 27, " God created
man in his own image : in the image of God created
he him."

1 Cor. xi. 7, " He (the man) is the image and glory of
God."

James iii. 9, " Men, who are made after the similitude
of God."

Obs.—The uprightness of man's original nature, which his
creation in the image of God implies, is referred to Eccles. vii.
29, " God made man upright," and more indirectly in the
" historical parable" regarding the King of Tyre, Ezek. xxviii.
15, already adverted to.

4. *Created male and female.*—Gen. i. 27, " Male and female
created he them."

Matt. xix. 4, " Have ye not read, that he which made
them at the beginning, made them male and female ?"

Mark x. 6, " From the beginning of the creation God
made them male and female."

Obs.—" Our Lord here refers to the Mosaic account of the
creation as the historical fact of the first creation of man, and
grounds his argument on the *literal expressions* of that narrative."—*Alford, Greek Test.*

5. *The names and order of creation of the first pair.*—
1 Tim. ii. 13, " Adam was first formed, then Eve."

6. *The mode and purpose of the woman's creation.*—1 Cor.
xi. 8, 9, " For the man is not of the woman ; but the
woman of the man. Neither was the man created for
the woman ; but the woman for the man."

Obs.—" In this passage, besides the *manner* of creation, ἐκ
τοῦ ἀνδρός, the *occasion* of creation, διὰ τὸν ἄνδρα, is insisted
on."—*Alford.* " In order to place the subjection of the
woman to man more clearly in view, the Apostle borrows an
argument from the second chapter of Genesis. The fact that

the woman was formed out of the rib of the man, and was
destined to be his helper, is employed by Paul for this purpose.
This sort of argument would appear singular in these days,
but evidently only because we have not accustomed ourselves
to read the Holy Scriptures, especially the Old Testament, so
literally."—*Olshausen.*

7. *The institution of marriage.*—Gen. ii. 22-24, " The Lord
   God brought the woman to the man. And Adam said,
   This is now bone of my bones, and flesh of my flesh :
   she shall be called Woman, because she was taken out
   of Man. Therefore shall a man leave his father and
   his mother, and shall cleave unto his wife ; and they
   shall be one flesh."

   Matt. xix. 4-6, " Have ye not read, that he which made
   them at the beginning, made them male and female ;
   and said, For this cause shall a man leave father and
   mother, and shall cleave unto his wife ; and they twain
   shall be one flesh ? Wherefore they are no more twain,
   but one flesh. What therefore God hath joined together," &c.

   1 Cor. vi. 16, " For the two (saith he) shall be one flesh."

   Eph. v. 31, " For this cause shall a man leave his father
   and mother, and shall be joined unto his wife, and they
   two shall be one flesh."

Obs.—" According to the narrative of Genesis, the words in
question are spoken by Adam, yet our Lord refers them to
God, and correctly, in as far as he is, by his Spirit, the Author
of Scripture, and the individuals who speak are to be regarded
merely as the organs of his Spirit. Only on this supposition
is there any force in the argument drawn from Adam's words."
—*Olshausen.* On Matt. xix. 4-6, Alford writes : " On these
verses we may remark, (1.) That our Lord refers to the Mosaic
account of the creation as *the historical fact* of the first creation
of man ; and grounds his argument on the *literal* expressions
of that narrative. (2.) That he cites from both the first and
second chapters of Genesis, and in immediate connexion ; thus
shewing them to be consecutive parts of a continuous narrative, which, from their different diction and apparent repetition, they have sometimes been supposed not to be. (3.) That
he quotes, as *spoken by the Creator,* the words in Gen. ii. 24,

which were actually said by Adam ; they must, therefore, be understood, as said in prophecy, *divino afflatu*, which, indeed, the terms made use of in themselves would require, since the relations alluded to by these terms did not yet exist. Augustin de Nupt., ii. 4 : ' Deus utique per hominem dixit quod homo prophetando prædixit.' (4.) That the force of the argument consists in the *previous unity* of male and female, not indeed organically, but by implication, in Adam. Thus it is said in Gen. i 27, not ἄνδρα καὶ γυναῖκα ἐποίησεν αὐτούς, but ἄρσεν καὶ θῆλυ ἐποίησεν αὐτούς—' He made them (man, as a race) male and female :' but then the male and the female were implicitly shut up in one ; and, therefore, after the creation of woman from man, when one man and one woman were united in marriage, they should be *one flesh, because* woman was taken out of man."

8. *Man's dominion over creation.*—Gen. i. 28, " Have dominion over the fish of the sea, and over the fowl of the air, and over every living thing that moveth upon the earth."

Psalm viii. 6-8, " Thou madest him to have dominion over the works of thy hands ; thou hast put all things under his feet : all sheep and oxen, yea, and the beasts of the field ; the fowl of the air, and the fish of the sea, and whatsoever passeth through the paths of the seas."

Obs.—" The psalm stands in the closest connexion with the first chapter of Genesis. What is written there of the dignity with which God invested man over the works of his hands, whom he placed as his representative on earth, and endowed with the lordship of creation, that is here made the subject of contemplation and praise."—*Hengstenberg.*

9. *Man in Eden surrounded with all delights.*—Ezek. xxviii. 13, " In Eden, the garden of God, thou wast ; every precious stone was thy covering . . . . *the service of thy tambourines and of thy females was prepared with thee* in the day when thou wast created."

Obs.—" I think, with Hävernick, that the objects denoted here are the musical instruments, tambourines, and the women who played on them ; and that this peculiar word, נקבה, *female,* rather than any other, was used because of the reference which the passage bears to Gen. i. 27, ' male and female created he them.' Tambourines, and female musicians to play on them, were provided for this King of Tyre on the day of his creation ; that is, from the very first, from the period of his being a king, he was surrounded with the customary pleasures, as well as the peculiar treasure, of kings. The royal house of Tyre had not, like many others, to work its way with difficulty, and through arduous struggles, but started at once into the full possession of royal power and splendour ; no sooner formed, than, like Adam, surrounded with fitting attendants and paradisiacal delights. So already Michaelis : ' All things poured in around thee, which could minister to thy necessities, thy comfort, or even thy pleasure, as they did formerly to Adam in the garden of Eden, which God granted to him.'"—*Fairbairn.*

IV.—*The Fall—its Concomitants and Consequences.*

1. *The instrument of the temptation—the serpent.*—2 Cor. xi. 3, " The serpent beguiled Eve through his *subtlety.*" *Obs.*—" We are perfectly justified in concluding from this mention of the Fall, that Paul spoke of it as the history of an actual occurrence."—*Olshausen.* " He takes for granted that the Corinthians recognised the agency of Satan in the (well-known) serpent ; see verses 13-15, where his *transformation* for the sake of deceit is alluded to."—*Alford.*

2. *The woman, the first transgressor.*—1 Tim. ii. 14, " Adam was not deceived ; but the woman, being deceived, was in the transgression."

Obs.—" Compare what is narrated in Gen. iii. 12, respecting the introduction of sin, and the order in which the punishment was declared against the parties concerned, and it will be found exactly to agree with what the Apostle here says. The connexion at Rom. v. 12, &c., is quite different. There the Apostle is speaking of how sin was brought into the world by the first sin, how the sin and death of the race were thus brought about ; and in this case it is the sin of the man, as the passage itself shews, through which the first sin has become the sin of the race."—*Wiesinger.*

3. *The curse on the serpent.*—Gen. iii. 14, " Dust shalt thou eat all the days of thy life."

Isaiah lxv. 25, " The wolf and the lamb shall feed together, and the lion shall eat straw like the bullock :
and *dust shall be the serpent's meat.*"

Obs.—" Vitringa understands the last clause to mean, that
the original curse upon the serpent who deceived Eve shall be
fully executed. (Compare Rev. xx. 1-3.) He refers to some
of his contemporaries as explaining it to mean, that the serpent should henceforth prey only upon low and earthly men ;
but the true sense seems to be, that in accordance with his
ancient doom, he shall be rendered harmless, robbed of his
favourite nutriment, and made to bite the dust at the feet of
his conqueror."—*Alexander.* It is more probable that the
allusion is to the *perpetuity* of the sentence. " The meaning
of the declaration, as used here, is probably, that dust should
continue to be the food of the serpent. The sentence on him
should be perpetual. He should not be injurious to man—
either by tempting him again, or by the venom of his fangs."
—*Barnes.*

4. *The sentence on the woman.*—Gen. iii. 16, " In sorrow
thou shalt bring forth children ; and thy desire shall
be to thy husband, and he shall rule over thee."

1 Tim. ii. 11-15, " Let the woman learn in silence with
all subjection. But I suffer not a woman to teach,
nor to usurp authority over the man, but to be in
silence. For Adam was first formed, then Eve. And
Adam was not deceived ; but the woman, being deceived, was in the transgression. Notwithstanding,
she shall be saved in child-bearing, if they continue,"
&c.

1 Cor. xiv. 34, " They are commanded to be under obedience, as also saith the law."

Obs.—" The Apostle adds the words ' through child-bearing,'
with no other object than just to point out to the woman her
proper sphere of duty ; and in particular how this position has
been assigned to her in consequence of the Fall."—*Wiesinger.*
The *law* referred to in 1 Cor. xiv. 34, Olshausen and Alford
take to be Gen. iii. 16.

5. *The ground cursed for man's sake.*—Gen. iii. 17, 18,
" Cursed is the ground for thy sake. . . . Thorns also,
and thistles, shall it bring forth to thee."

Gen. v. 29, " This same shall comfort us concerning our work and toil of our hands, because of the ground which the Lord hath cursed."

Rom. viii. 20, 21, " For the creature was made subject to vanity, not willingly, but by reason of him who hath subjected the same in hope ; because the creature itself also shall be delivered from the bondage of corruption," &c.

Obs.—" The expression *subjected* points, in a manner not to be mistaken, to an historical event ; originally the creation was free, but it ceased to be so. That here the fall of man, and the curse attaching to it, is alluded to, cannot be doubted." —*Olshausen*. Thorns and thistles are continually referred to as types of desolation and the curse. Hos. x. 8, " The thorn and the thistle shall come up on their altars." See also Heb. vi. 7, 8.

V.—*Restoration and Recovery.*

Preliminary remark.—It must be premised that, on this subject, although it constitutes the great theme of Scripture, and as such is continually adverted to by the sacred writers, and placed by the prophets, but especially by our Lord and his Apostles, in the clearest light, and in the most intimate connexion with the doctrine of the Fall, there are but few direct or explicit references to the record of that event. But this is easily accounted for from the fact, that the narrative of the Fall does not supply details on this particular point ; the intimation of the recovery being chiefly contained in the promised victory over the serpent by the seed of the woman. It is the germ only of the doctrine that is exhibited, and as such does not shew the same naked and marked correspondence with the development contained in the later Scriptures, as has been seen in the particulars already noticed.

1. *Man's dominion over creation restored.*—Isa. xi. 6, " The wolf also shall dwell with the lamb, and the leopard shall lie down with the kid ; and the calf, and the young lion, and the fatling together ; and *a little child shall lead them.*"

2. *Victory over the adversary.*—Rom. xvi. 20, " The God of peace shall bruise Satan under your feet shortly."

Obs.—It is held by the ablest expositors, that this intimation is an allusion to the primeval promise, (Gen. iii. 15.) Olshausen, Bloomfield, and Alford, are decided upon the point. The references in the designations, " the old serpent, called the Devil and Satan," (Rev. xii. 9, xx. 2,) the abridgment of his power, and his final confinement in the lake of fire and brimstone, are equally manifest.

3. *The Deliverer.*—Gal. iv. 4, " When the fulness of the time was come, God sent forth his Son, *made of a woman.*"

Obs.—" This language implies, that there was something peculiar in the fact that *he* was born of a woman; and that there was some special reason why that fact should be made prominently a matter of record. The promise was, (Gen. iii. 15,) that the Messiah should be the ' seed,' or the descendant of woman; and Paul probably here alludes to the fulfilment of that promise."—*Barnes.*

4. *Paradise restored, reopened by Christ.*—Luke xxiii. 43, " Jesus said to him, Verily I say unto thee, To-day shalt thou be with me in paradise."

Rev. ii. 7, " To him that overcometh will I give to eat of the tree of life, which is in the midst of the paradise of God."

Obs.—" Paradise is used of the *garden of Eden* by the LXX., Gen. ii. 8, &c., and subsequently became, in the Jewish theology, the name for that part of Hades, the abode of the dead, where the souls of the righteous await the resurrection. It was also the name for a supernal or heavenly abode. See 2 Cor. xii. 4; Rev. ii. 7. The *former of these* is, I believe, here (Luke xxiii. 43) primarily to be understood; but only as *introductory, and that immediately, to the latter.* By the death of Christ only was *Paradise* first opened, in the *true sense of the word.* He himself, when speaking of Lazarus, (Luke xvi. 22,) does not place him in Paradise, but in Abraham's bosom —in that place which the Jews called Paradise, but by an anticipation which our Lord did not sanction."—*Alford.*

5. *Death destroyed.*—Isa. xxv. 8, " He will swallow up death in victory; and the Lord God will wipe away tears from off all faces."

(B) *Doubtful or Disputed References.*

1. Isa. xliii. 27, " Thy first father hath sinned, and thy teachers have transgressed against me."

Obs.—Many ancient and modern expositors, among the latter Hitzig, Umbreit, and Knobel, understand the reference in the first clause to be to Adam, as the father of the human race. But this has been objected to, as he was not peculiarly the father of the Jews to whom the words are addressed. " To this it may be answered," says Alexander, " that if the guilt of the national progenitor would prove the point in question, much more would it be established by the fact of their belonging to a guilty race."

2. Job xxxi. 33, " If I have covered my transgression as Adam, (marg., *after the manner of men*,) by hiding mine iniquity in my bosom."

Obs.—It is not easy to determine which is the correct translation, that of the text or margin, as either will accord with the Hebrew. The majority of interpreters read " as man," or " as men," and consider the reference to be to the common practice of the guilty to attempt to cloak their offences ; but Schultens, Rosenmüller, and other eminent authorities, render it as in the English Version, and consider it as referring to the attempt of Adam to hide his sin from God after the Fall, (Gen. iii. 7, 8.) In favour of the latter view, Barnes remarks : " (1.) That there can be little or no doubt that that transaction was known to Job by tradition. (2.) It furnished him a pertinent and striking illustration of the point before him. (3.) The illustration is, by supposing that it refers to Adam, much more striking than on the other supposition. It is true, that men often attempt to conceal their guilt, and that it may be set down as a fact very general in its character ; but still it is not *so* universal that there are no exceptions. But here was a specific and well-known case, and one which, as it was the first, so it was the most sad and melancholy instance that had ever occurred of an attempt to conceal guilt. It was not an attempt to hide it from *man*—for there was no other man to witness it —but an attempt to hide it from *God*. From such an attempt Job says he was free "

3. Hos. vi. 7, " But they, like men, (or, *like Adam,*) have transgressed the covenant."

Obs.—There is the same ambiguity here as in the last passage, and accordingly the same diversity of opinion among translators and expositors. Some, as Jarchi, Jerome, Grotius, Rosenmüller, Newcome, and Hitzig, regard it as a proper name, and suppose the reference to be to the conduct of Adam in transgressing the Divine commandment ; but very many, as Kimchi, Tremelius, Calvin, Ewald, Gesenius (*Thesaurus*), De Wette, Henderson, Maurer, Simson, take it to be an appellative, and interpret the passage of the treacherous violations of contracts among mankind.

4. Job xii. 16, " With God is strength and wisdom ; the deceived and the deceiver are his."

Obs.—" If nothing more is meant by this than that the cunning man, as well as the weak man, is under the power of God, it is an observation that needed not to have been prefaced with an express declaration of God's great wisdom and power ; nor should it be placed, as it is, among the greatest works of Providence, the creation of the world, the destroying it by the flood, the settling and enlarging the nations of the earth, and straitening them again : in the midst of these great accounts of Providence stands this observation, the deceived and the deceiver are his.' This, therefore, must be something relating to the general condition of mankind, and must be understood to be an instance of God's providence in the great affairs of the world. And for this reason it is very probable that the words were meant of the fall of man through the cunning of the tempter. It was directly to the purpose of the Book of Job to assert and maintain the superiority of God over the deceiver, who, by this very means of bringing evil into the world, had grown up, in the opinion of many, into a rival of the power and majesty of God."—*Sherlock.*

5. Job xxvi. 13, " By his Spirit he hath garnished the heavens ; his hand hath formed the crooked serpent."

Obs.—" How come these disagreeable ideas to be joined together ? How comes the forming of a crooked serpent to be mentioned as an instance of Almighty power, and to be set, as it were, on an equal footing with the creation of the heavens, and all the host of them ? . . . If we consider the state of reli-

gion in the world when this book was penned, it will help to
clear this matter up. The oldest notion, in opposition to the
supremacy of the Creator, is, that of two independent principles; and the only kind of idolatry mentioned in the Book
of Job, (and it was of all others the most ancient,) is the worship
of the sun and moon and heavenly host; from this Job vindi-
cates himself, (chap. xxxi.) Suppose now Job to be acquainted
with the fall of man, and the part ascribed to the serpent in
the introduction of evil, and see how aptly the parts do cohere.
In opposition to the idolatrous practice of his time, he asserts
God to be the maker of all the host of heaven: ' By his Spirit
hath he garnished the heavens.' In opposition to the false
notion of two independent principles, he asserts God to be the
maker of him who was the first author of evil: ' His hand
hath formed the crooked serpent.' "—*Sherlock.*

6. Mal. ii. 15, " And did he not make one? Yet had he
the residue of the Spirit. And wherefore one? That
he might seek a godly seed."

Obs.—Henderson understands this of the *one flesh*, or conjugal body, into which the first couple were formed. (Gen. ii.)

(c) *Verbal and Idiomatic Allusions.*

These in themselves may not be of much importance, but
they will serve to shew the familiarity of the subsequent
writers of Scripture with these very ancient documents.

1. Isa. lix. 2, " Your iniquities *have separated between
you and your God,*"—הָיוּ מַבְדִּלִים בֵּינֵכֶם לְבֵין אֱלֹהֵיכֶם

וִיהִי מַבְדִּיל בֵּין מַיִם לָמָיִם—Gen. i. 6.

Obs.—Hitzig points out here an allusion to the separation
of the waters effected by the firmament, (Gen. i. 6.) " This
is the more remarkable, because it may be likewise traced in
the construction of the *preposition*, both the modes of employ-
ing it which there occur being here combined."—*Alexander.*

2. Isa. lxiv. 8, " We are the clay, and thou art our *potter;*
and we are all the work of thy hand."

Obs.—The allusion to Gen. ii. 7, " The Lord God *formed*
man (*moulded* or *fashioned* as the potter, this being the verb
from which is derived the substantive of the other passage) of
the dust of the ground," is evident.

3. Numb. xvi. 22; xxvii. 16; " The God of the spirits of all flesh."

Obs.—This designation of God is plainly founded on Gen. ii. 7, where the Creator is said to have breathed into the first man—the father of the race—the breath or *spirit* of life. So also in the narrative of creation (Gen. ii. 1) is found the origin of the appellation *Jehovah Sabaoth*, although the name itself does not occur in the Pentateuch.

4. Isa. xlv. 18, " God himself that formed the earth . . . . he created it not *in vain*, (or, *not to be empty ;*) he formed it to be inhabited."

Obs.—The reference is to Gen. i. 2 ; but still more express is the reference in Jer. iv. 24, where occurs the *combination* of terms used in describing the primeval chaos.

5. Psalm l. 10, " Every *beast* of the forest is mine."

Obs.—There is here a peculiar grammatical form borrowed from Gen. i. 24. See Exposition on the passage.

6. Psalm xc. 3, " Thou turnest man to destruction ; and sayest, *Return, ye children of men.*"

Obs.—" Gen. iii. 19 is undeniably alluded to here."—*Hengstenberg.* See also Psalm civ. 29 ; Job x. 9.

7. Psalm cxxvii. 2, " It is vain for you to rise up early, to sit up late, to eat *the bread of sorrows.*"

Obs.—" The words rest on Gen. iii. 17: ' In bitter labour shalt thou eat of it,' (the produce of the earth.)"—*Hengstenberg.*

It is unnecessary farther to multiply quotations : the above will serve as a specimen of the numerous allusions, more or less explicit, in various parts of the Old Testament, to Gen. i.-iii. Additional examples will be found in the Exposition.

SECT. XII.—CREATION AND THE FALL AS RELATED TO
SCRIPTURE IN GENERAL.

A very superficial examination even of the contents of Genesis, cannot fail to produce in the mind of the reader the conviction that if that book is to occupy a place in the Bible at all, its appropriate place is at the beginning of the Sacred Volume. But it may be farther unhesitatingly maintained, that the careful reader of Scripture, looking at the matter simply from a literary point of view, will be speedily convinced that Genesis forms not merely a fit but an indispensable introduction to the collection of writings which follows it. In such a case, uninfluenced by prejudice or predilection, the conclusion will appear most natural, if not irresistible, that it is not through mere accident that this book stands at the head of the canon. The plan or purpose also of the arrangement followed in the disposition or structure of the canon itself, may be not a little illustrated by the circumstance that the New Testament, no less than the older volume, begins with a book of *Genesis*—" The book of the *generation* of Jesus Christ," (Matt. i. 1.) Compare Gen. v. 1, " This is the book of the generations of Adam."

What holds true in this respect of Genesis as a whole, will be found to be equally true of its opening chapters, and, in particular, of the narratives of Creation and the Fall. The matters there recorded are of a nature so fundamental, that if they are to be introduced into or treated of in Scripture at all, their appropriate place must be found in its opening or introductory book ; and for the same reason, not in the last but first pages of that book, or, in other words, the only appropriate place for these narratives is that which they now occupy at the very commencement of what purports to be a revelation from God to man. But the proposition which it is now proposed to establish goes farther, and maintains that the narratives of Creation and the Fall constitute an integral and indispensable part of the Sacred Volume, and that their insertion in the first pages of Genesis is not merely appropriate, if they are to have a place at all, but also necessary for the attainment of the great ends and purposes for which it may be supposed the Bible was written and intrusted to man : in short, that Scripture, as a rule of life and duty, would be incomplete were these narratives wanting.

This may, no doubt, by many be considered to be an undertaking almost, if not altogether, uncalled for ; but a very moderate acquaintance with the many forms of opposition which this particular portion of Scripture has encountered in times past, and with the adverse influences at present specially in operation, will at once show that this unfortunately is not the case.

Reference has already been made to the denial of the internal unity of these chapters ; but here it is necessary to notice that in addition to this, and as part of the policy of those who strive by all conceivable means to depreciate the importance of these narratives, it is sometimes alleged that their insertion at the beginning of the Bible is owing to accident, or to the caprice of some ancient compiler ; or if a purpose be admitted, it is limited to a desire to imitate the sacred books of other nations, as the Puranas or Epos of India, which begin with cosmogonic theories : but in either case they are represented as a fly-leaf which has but a very slender connexion with the volume to which it has been attached, which would not greatly mar the integrity, nor perplex the subject of the succeeding record, were it entirely torn away.

Rationalism and infidelity are often very illogical in their reasonings ; nor is it too much to affirm that their conclusions are not unfrequently based on very inadequate arguments, and even sometimes on nothing better than the confident assertions of those who give them utterance. Anyhow it does not require much acquaintance with the Bible, and the plan of its composition and arrangement, to furnish powerful arguments, fitted to demonstrate that the reasons usually assigned by rationalism for the place occupied by the first chapters of Genesis, are exceedingly fallacious and absurd, and that the relation of this portion of Scripture to the Bible in general, as represented in these assumptions, is in the highest degree preposterous. A view less satisfactory than those adverted to can hardly be conceived of, nor does it appear to be a matter of extreme or unsurmountable difficulty to place this subject in a light which will better approve itself to the understanding of the inquirer seeking an explanation of the fact why the volume wherein God reveals his character, and states his claims on man, begins by representing Him as the Creator and Governor of all.

The arrangement, no less than the matter of Scripture, must, it may be reasonably inferred, accord with the purpose of God in connexion with revelation ; and in many cases, indeed, this accordance can be clearly and satisfactorily evinced from that purpose, as disclosed in the Bible. This, it is fully apprehended, can be shown to be the case with regard to the narratives now under consideration. It will, it is believed, appear to the entire satisfaction of all who can apprehend and appreciate the continuity and harmony of revealed truth, that they hold an important, indeed a fundamental place, in the scriptural system, and that the various threads which form the tissue of the record of Creation and the Fall, are intertwined with the facts and the framework of the entire Sacred Volume, in such a manner as to constitute the most intimate connexion with what may be denominated the past, the present, and the future of the Bible; or, in other words, its history, its theology, and its prophecy.

1. The opening chapters of Genesis are inseparably connected with the history contained in the Bible, and are indispensable to a clear and correct conception of that narrative, which, without the information there communicated, would prove an unintelligible fragment, wanting a beginning as well as a key to its elucidation.

In taking up any ancient history excepting that in the Bible, the reader is painfully impressed with the feeling that he possesses only a fragment, broken off he knows not where or how— a story without a beginning, some pages or chapters wanting, which no ingenuity or conjecture can supply in a manner to inspire full confidence in their genuineness and integrity. In all such matters, however firm at times the footing may be felt to be, the student, in tracing back the course of history, invariably comes to find himself on the brink of a chasm, of which he cannot discern the other side, owing to the thick clouds and darkness which have settled down upon it. Towards that other side—that obscure past—man's inquiring spirit and searching eye are ever and anxiously directed, but with very unsatisfactory results, for at that point the light of secular history altogether fails. There are not wanting, it is true, legends in abundance relative to the dawn of humanity, but of so contradictory a character as would seem absolutely to defy all attempts to connect or combine them into any consistent or harmonious whole, although, when placed in the light of Scripture history, these complex and confused ideas present in numerous instances the outlines of historical truths, much dimmed, no doubt, in their transmission, and hideously distorted by the mediums through which they are seen.

With the history preserved in the Bible, and with it alone, the case is entirely otherwise. Here there is a *beginning* both of the history of man and of the earth which he inhabits; and this beginning, however the matter may be denied or misrepresented by such as can discern or admit nothing credible in Scripture, because of its peculiar claims, is set forth in distinct and definite form, and with all the features of a living reality. No misshapen monsters, no hideous, grotesque figures, ever cross the path of the reader of this history. Every feeling of dissatisfaction and disappointment is entirely removed in its perusal; for it is seen to be a history consistent and connected, not losing itself in a misty mythological past—for there is no such thing as a Hebrew mythology in any sense of the term—but connected throughout with the initial announcement, " God saw the light that it was good: and the evening and the morning were the *first day*" of creation, and of the earth's history introductory to that of man and his all-important concerns. This is not the place to enter upon any general vindication of the sacred history from the misrepresentations and objections to which it has been exposed; suffice it to say, that not one of its statements has yet been contradicted or disproved by any well-authenticated fact; while, on the other hand, all the truths of history and tradition unite in certifying to the credibility of this record. In regard, however, to the portion of sacred history comprised in the narratives of Creation and the Fall, this has been sufficiently evinced and verified in the preceding sections; it is only necessary to observe here how these narratives form the first link of the long and uninterrupted chain of Bible history.

Taking up at any point the history of the covenant people to whom God intrusted his truth and his testimonies, and whose story occupies so large a space in his Holy Word, the reader can trace back the whole historic line till it reaches the first father of the human family, whom it connects in a peculiar manner with God, not merely as his noblest creature, but as his earthly representative. Looking, for instance, at this people, as described in the first pages of Exodus, bowed down under their burdens, and beaten by the taskmasters of Pharaoh, and if it be asked how or whence came they into their present situation among strangers on the banks of the Nile, it is only

necessary to turn back a few pages to Genesis, to see the
caravan coming down from Palestine, called even then, by
anticipation, the land of the Hebrews, though actually possessing little more than a sepulchre in it, and to see also the
waggons which Joseph sent up from Egypt to carry Israel and
the little ones thither. A few pages still farther back, and
the reader converses in the groves of Mamre with Abraham,
the great ancestor of the company that was seen going down
to Egypt, and is apprised of the purpose of that journey and
of the promise of a return thence : or he may trace the wanderings of this patriarch himself from the country of the
Euphrates into the land promised and pointed out to him by
God. Still farther back, and the national history blends with
the universal, and as such it is the history of man, although
still with special reference to one chosen line. Continuing
thus to trace upwards the historic course, is reached " Enos,
who was the son of Seth, who was the son of Adam, who was
the son of God," (Luke iii. 38)—the great centre from which,
according to the invariable testimony of Scripture, radiate all
the lines of history and humanity.

Pursuing an opposite path, the reader of this history is conducted to a Second Adam, who occupies a place in many respects
remarkably analogous to that of the man with whom the history
commenced. In particular, it may be seen that the two are
related by the laws of generation and descent. But after what
has been already said upon this point in a former section, it is
unnecessary to pursue the subject farther, having simply
called attention to the *historical* connexion of the first and
second Adam, which, it may be truly said, is the great aim of
the Bible history to establish by its register of names, and
apparently dry genealogical catalogues.

2. The matters recorded in these first chapters of Genesis,
are as intimately connected with, and as indispensable to the
theology of the Bible, as it is possible for them to be in the
case of its history.

In the account of the Creation and of the Fall are laid the
foundations of the Bible doctrines as well as of the Bible history ; for *Creator* is the first and fundamental relation of God
to man : on creation is based his proprietary rights and his
consequent dominion over the creature which owes its exist-

ence solely to the Divine will. Now it does not require any laboured argumentation to show that for the knowledge of God as *Creator*, and of the relation thereby sustained to him, man must be indebted mainly if not altogether to revelation. To whatever extent it may be allowed that the idea of the existence of God, as a supernatural or Supreme Being, may be forced upon the human mind by attention to the phenomena of the world within us, and of the greater but not more wonderful world around us, it would appear that the idea thus originated will represent God in the character of Lawgiver and Judge rather than in his primary relation of Creator, on which indeed his other functions depend. Notwithstanding the large concessions made in previous sections to the claims of science, and the acknowledgment of its noble testimonies in behalf of creation, it is not at all certain whether, by mere reasoning, apart from all communications from above, man could have ever arrived at the idea of a Creator or creation in any proper sense of the terms; and it assuredly makes this matter extremely doubtful, when it is considered how, as already shown, the pure idea was corrupted or lost among the heathen nations of the earth without exception. But at all events, apart from the Bible, the doctrine of creation must necessarily have been very confused and indistinct. Conscience, while express and explicit in urging God's inalienable claims on man, is not equally communicative in regard to the foundation on which these claims rest.

To meet this first and felt want of responsible creatures, the doctrine of creation must necessarily find a place in any system or book which, like the Bible, purports to be a revelation of God to man, and in that character and capacity may be reasonably supposed to embrace all necessary truth. And again, reasoning from the fundamental character of the doctrine, the probability is that its place will be at or near the first page of any such book. The facts of the case are in entire harmony with these conclusions; for it appears that while nothing is said, or, from the nature of the case, could be appropriately said, by way of proof of the being of God—the first principle of all religion, whether natural or revealed—the volume of Scripture opens with the no less important intimation, " In the beginning God created the heavens and the earth."

Upon this intimation and its accompanying statements, in the first and second chapters of Genesis, is founded the entire doctrine of the Old Testament on the subject of creation, together with all the solemn and sublime ascriptions of adoration and praise to the Creator, which are found in the prophetical writings, in the Psalms, and in the book of Job. Not only, however, the Old Testament doctrine of creation, but also that of the New, is reared on this narrative, for the teaching of the two parts of the volume is, upon this as upon other subjects, essentially the same, the only difference being, that in the later dispensation, from its very nature and design, creation is particularly described as the work of the Word, who was *in the beginning, was with God, and was God,* (see John i. 1-3; Col. i. 16.) But if the praises of the Old Testament saints and seers were founded on creation, and were in a manner echoing notes of the narrative in Genesis, no less is it the case in the New Testament, where the adoring hymn of praise, as sung by the celestial choir, is described in the words, " Thou art worthy, O Lord, to receive glory, and honour, and power : for thou hast created all things, and for thy pleasure they are and were created." (Rev. iv. 11.)

But the doctrine of creation itself occupies no isolated position in the scheme of revealed truth embraced in the Scriptures. On the contrary, it is most intimately related to all the truths and teachings of the Bible. Upon this point it is satisfactory to be able to adduce the testimony of Neander. " Already, in the history of the heresies," says this distinguished writer, " we have spoken of the close connexion between the doctrine of God, as the absolutely free Creator of the universe, and the whole peculiar essence of Christianity ; and of the strong antithesis which this doctrine must have presented to the existing modes of thought which had been derived from antiquity. The Apostle Paul sums up the Christian theism, as the belief in one God, from whom, by whom, and to whom all things exist ; and the threefold relation here expressed of all existing things to God, denotes, at the same time, the close connexion between the Christian doctrines of creation, redemption, and sanctification, as well as the close connexion between the doctrine of creation and the ethical element ; for the phrase, ' to him,' which assigns to the Chris-

tian system of morals its province and its fundamental principle, presupposes the ' from him ;' and the phrase, ' by him,'
denotes the synthesis or mediation of them both. Hence, as
we saw in the history of the Gnostic sects, the corruptions of
the Christian doctrine of the creation which proceeded from
the reaction of the spirit of the ancient world, must superin-
duce corruptions also of the doctrine of redemption and of the
system of morals."[1]

The importance, in short, of the doctrine of creation cannot
be easily overrated. It may in fact be regarded as the root or
the trunk of the tree from which spring, as so many diverging
branches, the other doctrines of revelation. This doctrine,
accordingly, stands at the head of the Bible—largely and
legibly written on its first page—serving, as already shown,
not merely as an introduction to the Scripture history, but
also and chiefly as the first and fundamental article in its
theology. It is this which at all secures to it a place in the
sacred writings; for how important soever this truth may be
in itself, and however edifying to be made acquainted with
incidents and events which occurred on the earth previous
to man's existence on it, or to be told how by successive acts
of creative energy and goodness, the dwelling-place was gradually prepared and duly furnished for the reception of its
coming tenants, it is only when the narrative comes to describe
man—made in the image of God and constituted the head of
the terrestrial system—that it rises into its true significance,
and is seen to attain to its chief end. This plainly appears
from the manner and arrangement of the narrative, every
feature clearly evincing that it is with man as a moral and
responsible being that it has to do. The creation of the
heavens and the earth, light and life, and the latter in various
forms and gradations, both vegetable and animal, are preparatory to the introduction of man, who has been well styled the
crown or capital of the creation column, after whose completion
all is declared to be " very good,"—a declaration in which is
emphatically announced the important truth, " God made man
upright."

Man's character, and his condition " under the law" of his
Creator, are next more fully described in the ancient record,

[1] Neander, Church History, vol. ii. pp. 311, 312.

in order to prepare for a correct understanding of the account that follows of his fall into sin. It must be self-evident that this momentous event, in its nature and extent, could never be accurately comprehended, without the information communicated in the previous chapters on the creation and on man's place in it. It was above all needful that this truth should be announced and fully known, that the *fall* in creation, or the disorder now witnessed in the moral system, was preceded by a state regarding which the Holy and Omniscient declared his approbation ; and also this other truth, that the sin with which all, without exception, are so painfully familiar, is not the necessary or legitimate result of the original constitution bestowed upon man ; and, moreover, that the sorrows and sufferings which stand to him in such close companionship do not spring from the law of creation, but have been induced through his disobedience to the commands of God. It was needful that these truths should be known, because of their bearing as well on God's character as on the present condition and future prospects of man—a fallen being—but in his circumstances capable of redemption, owing to the manner in which his ruin was effected.

With the doctrine of Creation is thus inseparably linked that of the Fall, together with all the scriptural declarations respecting the evils, both physical and moral, thereby introduced into the world, entailed upon the human race, and transmitted from sire to son throughout all generations. On the doctrine of man's fall, again, is reared the doctrine of his recovery. The one supplies not indeed the condition, but the occasion of the other. Man is convicted and condemned, and the very ground is cursed on his account ; but the very sentence of condemnation is preceded by an intimation of deliverance. Man, now guilty and depraved, is expelled from the garden of delights—the scene of his innocence and of his sin—which thus becomes a paradise lost ; but amidst the doubts and darkness which, as previously remarked, had in these circumstances settled down upon the earth, there breaks forth one bright ray which hopefully points to a paradise restored. As a happy augury of this restoration, it is of importance to find that the blessed effects of the Divine intimation of mercy are strongly depicted in an act of faith described in the memorable words,—" Adam called his wife's name Eve, because she was the mother of all living," (Gen. iii. 20 ;) an incident to which further reference will be afterwards made.

If then, in this narrative, there is seen the outburst of that fountain of depravity whose streams have deluged and desolated the earth, and poisoned the whole human family, no less distinctly may be discerned the germ of that promised power which shall heal this fountain and stay its baneful streams. If the third chapter of Genesis points to the origin of sin, and records the sentence which, on account of it, condemns the guilty to death, no less does it announce a Saviour to deliver from the sin and the death thereby incurred. Without the sin recorded in that chapter, there had been no substitution, no sacrifice, no gospel, no grace—arrangements unknown, because unneeded in a state of innocence, and so there would not have been made known to principalities and powers in heavenly places, by the Church, the manifold wisdom of God as now displayed, (Eph. iii. 16.) If, then, all the denunciations against sin, and all the warnings to the sinner, which are contained in the Bible, point to the narrative of the Fall, equally so do the invitations to seek the Lord, with all the accompanying offers of pardon and peace. If all the crimes and outrages ever perpetrated on earth find their origin and explanation in the history of the Fall, no less all the law-honouring acts and the propitiatory sacrifice of the Saviour and Surety of sinners. If we can there "scern our relation to the first Adam, with the nature and amount of the obligation which that relation involves, we shall by these lessons be also prepared for the New Testament doctrine of the Second Adam, the Lord from heaven, and prepared too for the apostolic commentary on the relation in which, through the grace of God, we stand to our second Head, who has assumed the human nature, and will ever retain it, associated with the Divine. In one word, all the peculiar doctrines of Christianity and the Bible cluster round the narrative of the Fall, and find their explanation in its statements.

Such, then, is the place which the truths announced in the chapters on Creation and the Fall hold with respect to the scheme of doctrine revealed in the Bible, and the provision made in the Gospel for the sanctification and salvation of fallen man. The relation being such as is here represented, it is but reasonable to suppose that the scenes depicted, and the transactions recorded, in the first three chapters of Genesis, will be frequently referred to by the subsequent writers of Scripture, and employed as illustrations of their subjects, or as first principles in their reasonings and argumentations. This supposition is fully borne out by the facts of the case as regards both the Old and New Testament Scriptures presented in the last section. The incidents and issues recorded in those early chapters were, it has been clearly seen, known to the prophets of the Old Testament, and to all the apostles and teachers of the New, and to the Great Teacher himself, by all of whom their literal historical character was unhesitatingly taken for granted. The principles established in the older record lie at the foundation of all their reasonings. This is particularly conspicuous in the writings of the Apostle Paul. He at least was not conscious of any flaw in his argument ; nor did he anticipate the possibility of any objection to the legitimacy of his assumptions, or to the strict historical veracity of the facts on which he proceeded when, addressing himself to the conscience and understanding of Jews and Gentiles, he reasoned of sin and of death, the wages of sin, and also of deliverance from both. But the position is greatly strengthened by the fact, that from the beginning of the Bible to its close, no other theory is proposed or even adverted to, in order to account for the introduction of sin and suffering into the world, or to explain the present and perplexing state of things. Mention is repeatedly made of the rise of evil as described in Genesis, but no reference is ever made to any other scheme. It cannot be too much insisted on that the Scriptures may be searched in vain to detect a single allusion or expression which can by any possibility be construed as a reference to any other originating cause than that recorded in the third chapter of Genesis. No trace can be detected of any contradictory principles. Paul, or any other of the apostles, knew of no other way of accounting for the origin and prevalence of sin among mankind, and the necessity thence arising for a Saviour to deliver from it.

3. These chapters of Genesis, comprising the account of the creation of the world and the fall of man, have also an impor-

tant bearing on the prophecy of the Bible, as well as on its history and theology. This statement, although applicable to both parts of the Sacred Volume, is intended to apply, not so much to the prophecy of the Old Testament, and the bright visions of a future which gladdened the hearts and sustained the spirits of the children of God during a past and preparatory dispensation, as to the prophetic announcements of the New Testament, and especially that glorious period still future, connected with man's destiny and dwelling-place, as described in the closing pages of the Apocalypse. It might be useful and interesting to consider the hopes and prospects of the past which found their realization in the advent of Christ, the promised "seed of the woman," and to mark the influence which the remembrance of Edenic beauty and Edenic bliss exercised on the prophetic pictures of the then coming age, when God should again in very deed dwell with men upon the earth delivered from the curse ; but, looking back from our present advanced position in the economy of grace, these prophecies and predictions may be in a manner classed with the Bible history, while space would fail for an enlarged induction of particulars.

It has not escaped the notice of the students of God's word, that, as in the great revolutions of nature witnessed on earth, and in the sidereal heavens, and also in the dispensations of Providence, s   in like manner, in the system of Revelation there are to ᷓ discerned unmistakable indications of cycles or full periods, which, after a complete revolution, come round to the point whence they set out.[1] The preceding observations have had for their object the elucidation of the relation of the first chapters of the Bible—the starting-point of revelation, so to speak—to those which immediately follow, and to the Scriptures in general ; but no less striking and intimate will the relation appear which holds between the first and the last chapters of the sacred writings,—between the history of the past, as given by Moses, and the visions of the future opened up to the view of the rapt seer of Patmos,—although in other respects widely different, and separated by an interval marked by two entire dispensations. It will be found not only that there is no contradiction or contrast, but also that the great

[1] Douglas, The Structure of Prophecy, 2d edit. p. 26, Edin. 1852.

cycle of revelation or Scripture is completed, that the last pages of the Apocalypse have come round to the first pages of Genesis in their subject and mode of representation. In particular, it may be observed that as the Bible begins with an account of creation, so also does it close. It commenced with the intimation, "In the beginning God created the heavens and the earth;" but as sin has dimmed the lustre and destroyed the harmony of these glorious productions of almighty wisdom and power, near the close of the Bible is a corresponding announcement of a creation entirely new, and freed from the curse and corruptions of the present: "And I saw a new heaven and a new earth, for the first heaven and the first earth were passed away, and there was no more sea," (Rev. xi. 1.) This correspondence is not merely a general one, but extends to various particulars. Thus, in Genesis, after the account of the Creation follows that of the Fall, including the curse pronounced upon the serpent, and upon the ground, and the sentence of death passed upon man, and the sorrows, sufferings, and toils therein involved. In the last announcements of the Bible this state of matters is entirely rectified, with the exception of the condemnation of the serpent, whose condition had been declared irremediable—the curse is disannulled, and death itself destroyed. "There shall be no more curse," (Rev. xxii. 3,) "and there shall be no more death, neither sorrow nor crying, neither shall there be any more pain: for the former things are passed away. And he that sat upon the throne said, Behold, *I make all things new,*" (Chap. xxi. 4, 5.) As, again, in Genesis, man is seen cast out of Paradise, and precautions taken to prevent his return thither, "lest he should put forth his hand and take of the tree of life," which, because of his transgression, was not to be enjoyed, but was constituted also a *forbidden* fruit, so, in the new dispensation which the last chapters of the Bible introduce, the attainder of Eden is removed: "To him that overcometh will I give to eat of the tree of life which is in the midst of the paradise of God," (Rev. ii. 7,) and a way of access opened up to the restored paradise: "Blessed are they that do his commandments, that they may have a right to the tree of life, and may enter in through the gates into the city," (Rev. xxii. 14.) As it was for disobedience man was banished Paradise and forbidden the tree of life, so it is obedience that secures his return thither, and his restoration to more than the forfeited blessings of the primeval state.

But it is unnecessary to enter intó further details, for it must be obvious that between the opening and the concluding chapters of the Bible, although, as already remarked, separated in time by an interval which comprises two dispensations, and which, it may be added, witnessed many vicissitudes in human affairs and in modes of thought, the analogy is unmistakable, and the correspondence complete : matters by a complete revolution have come round again to the point of departure, answering to the original description, " very good." Nay more, creation is raised to a higher platform, and put upon a more stable foundation than at the first, through the undertaking of the Deliverer promised ere the expulsion of the guilty transgressors from Paradise. Redemption through "the seed of the woman" has more than corrected the error, and more than restored the ruins of the Fall. It has vindicated the Divine character from the foul aspersions cast upon it by the Wicked One—aspersions in which man also acquiesced when he accepted the testimony of the Old Serpent rather than the infallible word of God. It has, moreover, shown how God can bring good out of evil ; how His counsel shall stand, and He shall do all His pleasure. Accordingly, almost the closing sentences of the volume dedicated to the great theme of redemption are occupied in proclaiming that the work and mystery of God are finished. To quote the testimony of by no means a fanciful writer :—" Thus the beginning and the end of the Bible lend their authority in support of each other. The transaction recorded in the beginning explains the reason of many expressions which occur in the progress of Scripture ; and the description which forms the conclusion reflects light upon the opening. Whatever opinion we may entertain of the third chapter of Genesis when we read it singly, it swells in our conceptions as we advance ; and all its meaning and its importance become manifest, when we recognise the features of this early transaction in that magnificent scene by which the mystery of God shall be finished."[1]

If such, then, be the relation of these first chapters of Gene-

[1] Hill, Lectures in Divinity, B. IV., chap. i. § 1.

sis at the very opening of the Bible to all that follows, and if the matters there recorded occupy in the system of revealed truth and in the plan of redemption the important place above indicated, all doubt must be at once removed as to their forming an integral part of Scripture. Any contrary supposition leads at once to the most absurd conclusions. Can it be for a moment seriously maintained that the narrative of creation, with which the volume begins, was inserted merely in imitation of the sacred books of heathenism—or that this narrative and that of the Fall, with which it is so intimately connected, are nothing more than fly-leaves picked up, one knows not where, and placed in the front of the Hebrew Scriptures, one knows not why nor how ? In the first place, it has been shown how these narratives are inseparably connected with the history in the Bible, so that to take them away, or deny their historical character, would be enough to render incomplete and unintelligible, not merely the history of the Hebrews, but the history of man, and much more, the entire history of redemption through Christ, in whom the history and the hope of the Old Testament culminate. In any way, the rejection of these chapters is equivalent to wrenching off the most important link in the chain of human history—the link which, through the first Adam, connects man with his Maker, and which again connects the second Adam with the first.

But, secondly, take away these chapters, or, what amounts to the same thing, deny their historical character, and what, in consequence, is the position in which the reader of Scripture is placed in regard to its doctrines, especially those which bear more directly on man's character, and his wants as a moral being ? Sin is in the world, but how did it enter, or in what way is the fact to be accounted for, that its virus has infected the whole human race ? Sorrows, sufferings, and death enter into the universal lot of humanity, and conscience in some way or other invariably connects these evils with sin. But these, and innumerable other questions and enigmas, are utterly inexplicable without the information furnished in the first chapters of Genesis. Again, it is a New Testament doctrine, or rather its fundamental theme, that satisfaction has been rendered to a violated law by Christ, in his character of the representative of man ; but without the information furnished in the history of the Fall, even this is inexplicable and perplexing; for, reject the doctrine of the Fall, or deny man's apostasy from God, and what need of satisfaction or atonement? In this way would be rendered unintelligible, and even nugatory, the great teachings of the Bible; while the apostolic reasonings would be subverted, or entirely swept away, having no foundation to rest on. The truths unfolded in these narratives may be traced in their workings and counter-workings from Genesis to the last pages of the Apocalypse, which completes the canon of Scripture, and they constitute the first principles of our holy religion—the very foundations on which, through Christ, the whole system of salvation is built. The Gospel, in all its grace, and in all its suitableness to the case and character of fallen man, is itself merely the principles of the third chapter of Genesis developed and applied so as to restore and perpetuate the union between God and man, who was at first created in the Divine image.

But, thirdly, a connexion of a very close, though not equally vital character as that just noticed, has been shewn to exist between the most important incidents of these very ancient narratives, and the most recent prophetic announcements, but to this it is unnecessary again to refer. The conclusions to be deduced from the relationship manifested in such a variety of ways, are utterly opposed to the views which would, by any mode of representation, seek to disparage this portion of Scripture. If—to recapitulate the result of the preceding observations—by any possibility the first chapters of Genesis can be regarded as fragments or fly-leaves, how came they to be so linked with the history of the Bible,—how came they to constitute the fundamental articles in its theology, the correlates in its prophecy, and to be interwoven with its varied contents in every possible way? And farther, but only in passing, as this matter will be resumed, and more fully considered in the next section—if the matters recorded in these ancient documents are merely fanciful representations, or poetical or allegorical figures, how came they to be regarded by all the subsequent writers of Scripture, whenever they were led to allude to them, as literal, veritable facts?—for that such is the case, the numerous quotations adduced in the preceding section have made it abundantly plain, and that they should be so received without at any time a suspicion being entertained to the contrary ? These questions are utterly unanswerable on any supposition which would raise the slightest doubt as to the genuineness of these narratives, and to their claims to be received as integral portions of the Sacred Scriptures. If, then, on account of any difficulties attaching to their interpretation, or connected with their acceptance in a literal, historical sense, whether arising from scientific discoveries or any other cause, one statement even of these narratives were given up or sacrificed, it must be at once apparent that such a surrender is not unattended with danger, but may involve a necessity for the abandonment of much more than was at first reckoned on. If there be difficulties in defending the Bible because these narratives form a part of it, it is not too much to affirm that it would involve far more difficulties, both as regards the vindication of its authority, and the interpretation of its contents, were the opening chapters away. So far, then, from acknowledging the necessity or expediency of sacrificing the narratives of Creation and the Fall, or of abandoning the literal interpretation of these ancient, but in no sense antiquated records, in order to be able to retain faith in the Bible or in Genesis, the reader, on a dispassionate view of all the facts of the case, must feel that they constitute an integral and essential portion of the volume.

SECT. XIII.—CONCLUSION—THE NARRATIVES OF CREATION AND THE FALL HISTORICAL AND INSPIRED.

It only remains, under this division of the subject, to sum up the results of the preceding investigations into the character and the claims of the portion of Scripture containing the account of the creation and of man's fall, in view of the various forms of opposition which it has at different times encountered, adding such observations as shall serve to connect and bring out more distinctly the conclusions arrived at under the several heads of inquiry relative to its historical form and inspired origin.

By the brief historical review of the various interpretations of the first three chapters of Genesis at the outset of the present work, the way was in a manner prepared for the discussion which followed, and still further cleared and determined by the succeeding observations on the leading objections urged against these chapters, the place and importance of which, in a controversial point of view at least, was thereby fully established.

In vindicating the character of the chapters in question from the various and vexatious accusations preferred against them, it was found necessary, in the first place, to defend their internal unity, which had been very determinedly assailed. Accordingly, it was shewn that there is no valid ground whatever for the view, variously modified, which considers these three chapters of Genesis as made up of fragments, or as a compilation of the productions of different authors and ages. On the contrary, it appeared that one at least, and that the most important of the arguments employed to substantiate the fragmentary character of Genesis—that founded on the changes of the Divine names, not only failed, but in its application to the chapters under consideration told directly the other way. The diversity of style, and the alleged contradictions between the first and second chapters, employed in furtherance of the same purpose, were also, it is believed, satisfactorily accounted for, so that the internal unity of the narratives was fully vindicated from aught that can be considered derogatory to the character of the work as the production of a single mind carrying out one grand design. But here, it may be added, were the facts of the case otherwise, and such as inevitably to lead to the conclusion that Genesis, or the early part of it, is a compilation from pre-existing documents, this need not necessarily detract from its genuineness and authenticity as an historical work, and composed under the direction of the Divine Spirit. Many excellent persons, taking that view of the matter, feel no anxiety about the Document-hypothesis, in, at least, its mildest form. One who views the matter in that light remarks: " Nothing to a philosophic mind can give a greater value to the writings of Moses than to behold him, under the guidance of the Holy Spirit, carefully gathering up the fragments of ancient history and early inspiration, whether in Genesis or Job, and giving them a permanent form, which was to last unto the end of time ; previous to his announcing the

Law given upon Mount Sinai, and committing to writing the typical dispensation of the Jews."[1]

The next two sections were devoted to the consideration exclusively of the narrative of the Creation ; the one viewing it in the light of the past, and contrasting its simple statements with various cosmogonic theories of heathenism ; the other considering it in the light of the present, and comparing it with the magnificent results of scientific research into the history of the earth, and the processes by which it was successively brought into its present condition. From both these sources most satisfactory results were obtained in favour of the Mosaic narrative. Its incomparable superiority, in every possible respect, over all other systems of ancient times, was clearly evinced. It was found to be consistent with itself— consistent with truth and enlightened reason, and consistent with our highest conceptions of the character of the Great Author of all being. But no less strikingly was evinced the remarkable accordance of the biblical narrative of the Creation with the discoveries of modern science. On this point it was remarked, that on a comparison with the results arrived at by scientific men, it must undoubtedly be felt, that the harmony subsisting between the ancient record in Genesis and modern discoveries, is in a great many particulars of a very remarkable kind.

An examination and comparison somewhat similar was also instituted in regard to the narrative of the Fall. It was in the first place compared with various traditions which evidently referred to some great moral revolution in the early history of man, corresponding in character and consequences with what the Fall purports to have been. And farther, the narrative was compared with various facts and phenomena in nature of a moral and physical character, which find their proper explanation only in such a catastrophe as is there described. From both these sources of information, most important testimonies were derived confirmatory of the truthfulness and accuracy of the statements and representations of the Hebrew narrative of man's apostasy from God.

Following up the subject of the internal unity of these chapters, attention was subsequently directed to the connexion

---

[1] Douglas, The Structure of Prophecy, p. 26.

clearly discernible between them and the remainder of the volume in which they stand. First, there was pointed out a remarkable analogy between several particulars in the narrative of the Fall and the representations of temptation and sin in the New Testament. Next, it was shown that the incidents recorded in the first pages of the Bible have such a bearing on God's government, moral and mediatorial, and on man's condition under that rule, that they are constantly referred to by the subsequent writers of Scripture, both of the Old and New Testaments, as illustrations, or as first principles in their reasonings, warnings, and exhortations. Farther, and more particularly, it was evinced that the contents of these chapters are so inseparably interwoven with the substance and not merely the language of the Bible in every possible way, with its history, its theology, and its prophecy, that they cannot be severed from it without reducing the whole to an unintelligible chaotic mass. To offer violence to the narratives of Creation and the Fall, it was shown, is to offer violence to the entire Scripture revelation, so close and complex are the bonds of union between it and the introductory statements of Genesis. The continuity of parts resembles not merely that which subsists between the body and an external member, the severance of which might not destroy or even endanger the vital action, but that of the bones and ligaments which give form and coherency to the structure.

This was an important point reached in vindicating for those narratives a place in the Sacred Scriptures. In ordinary circumstances, it would have sufficed to show that any document forms an essential and inseparable part of what is usually received as the oracles of the living God, in order to entitle it to all the reverence accorded to the volume of which it constitutes a part; but as this seems, most assuredly with strange inconsistency, to have been viewed as an exceptionable case by some who receive the later Scriptures, and more particularly as there are numerous parties disposed to give little consideration to the authority of Scripture at all, it was considered necessary to examine the matter farther, and on other grounds.

Notwithstanding the important place which, on the slightest examination, these chapters must be seen to occupy in the

Bible, and notwithstanding the express recognition and sanction accorded to their contents by prophets and apostles and by our Lord himself, to no other portion of the Sacred Volume has equal opposition been manifested, or a greater disposition evinced to deny their claims to inspiration, and evacuate their literal, historical character by resolving them into allegories, myths, poetic fictions, or philosophical speculations.

In the first place, then, it will be necessary to consider the bearing of the preceding investigations on the question affecting the literal, historical character of the contents of the first three chapters of Genesis; and, secondly, how far they may have contributed to determine their inspired origin.

The review of the attacks to which these narratives have been subjected, and of the history of their interpretation, showed in general that the various deviations from, or evasions of the literal, historical sense, have had their origin in grounds connected more or less with philosophical speculations or infidel tendencies. This much, however, may be said in favour of the allegorical interpretation—the earliest departure, apparently, from the literal historical sense—that it may, in a certain sense, consist with a reverence for Scripture and a belief in its inspired origin. But with this must terminate any favourable acknowledgment of the allegorical mode of viewing Scripture, particularly the narratives of Creation and the Fall. A comparison of the various expositions of this description brings out very distinctly what might have been inferred à priori, that there are no fixed principles—no settled rules, nothing to help to fix or define the symbols—in short, nothing at best but his own fancy to guide the interpreter. In a word, this method of exposition makes a complete chaos of Scripture, and goes far to subvert its authority altogether.

Various arguments might have been advanced in disproof of the allegorical mode of viewing these chapters, but this was considered unnecessary, owing to the circumstance just stated, of the conflicting and self-contradictory expositions thus produced affording sufficient evidence that there was nothing in the text to give them any countenance. But if this consideration is not sufficient to dispose of the allegorical interpretation, the preceding comparison of the narratives with ancient remains and modern scientific deductions, has disclosed such a substratum of solid fact, such a reality, and, at the same time, such a literality, in the statements, that by no possibility can they be resolved into allegorical figures or poetic fancies. To this may be added the consideration which to many will be held decisive of its literal historical character, that no part of the early chapters of Genesis was ever taken in any other acceptation by the writers of the Old or New Testament. Viewed as a simple matter of fact, this should satisfy all that the narratives plainly purport to be history, and have all the appearance of it, although it may not be so decisive of the value to be attached to that history.

But if the allegorical mode of viewing the contents of these chapters be unsatisfactory and utterly irreconcilable with the accordance manifested between them and the facts and phenomena adverted to, and also with the use made of them by the Lord and his Apostles, much more is this the case with some of the other views recently substituted in its place.

The view which regards these narratives as a philosophical speculation of the author of Genesis, or some other oriental sage on the origin and present constitution of things, necessarily and consistently rejects all claims to a source higher than human reasoning ; but irrespective of this, which is not the point immediately under consideration, it labours, as has been shown, under the serious disadvantage of assuming a degree of knowledge in ancient times regarding nature—its operations and laws—much at variance with what is known from the best sources, to have been actually the case. In nothing were the philosophers of antiquity more deficient than in an acquaintance with physical truths and the system of the universe, while the statements of Genesis respecting the creation can bear comparison with any production of modern times. This view is farther and more particularly discountenanced by the results of the comparison instituted between the biblical narrative of creation and the remains of heathen cosmogonies. That comparison and the correspondence, in various particulars, thence educed, disclosed such a universality, and at the same time community of conceptions on the subject of Creation among nations far apart from one another, as clearly proved that they could not have originated in the way suggested by this theory, or at any period subsequent to the first dispersion of the human race.

Whether it be owing to a better acquaintance with, and a juster appreciation of, the remains of heathen antiquity surviving in the form of myths and legends, or to the clearer and more commanding light in which modern science has placed the biblical account of the Creation, or to some other undetermined cause, it is certain that the above view which regards the matter as a philosophical speculation, is at present, equally with the allegorical, falling into disrepute before the more popular mythical theory which by several German writers has been indiscriminately applied to all ancient writings, and which supposes the narratives of Creation and the Fall to be a selection from, or a transcript of, the early legends common to mankind.

Of this theory, it may in strictness be said, that it explains nothing. It allows, indeed, that there is some truth lying at the foundation of these narratives—some facts which gave rise to the traditions common to the Bible and the ancient world, but what these facts are it has not determined, nor does it offer any explanation of their character, their connexion, or their origin. In taking into account the universality of the traditions bearing on the creation and the fall of man, the mythical theory has so far a decided advantage over the philosopheme ; but then its first difficulty is satisfactorily to explain the cause of the marked dissimilarity which in various and most important points of view is seen to exist between the biblical narratives and the traditions with which they are compared, and, secondly, to explain what were the facts and phenomena out of which these legends were evolved. But waving further objections to this very untenable representation, not of the origin of the facts or fancies recorded in the early chapters of Genesis, for this the theory does not profess to explain, but of their currency among the Israelites, and their subsequent reception into their sacred books, what Julius Müller urges against the philosopheme is equally applicable to the myth—the view he himself is disposed to favour :—" Surely it were not to be seen what dogmatic use could be made of it by Christian theology."

The only simple and consistent course, in the circumstances, is that which either receives or rejects the whole historical character of this portion of Scripture. There is no principle on which the allegories can be expounded, no rule by which it can, with any certainty or satisfaction, be determined what is fact and what is to be pronounced fiction in legends which, on the above showing, cannot be traced to any definite source, nor be made to subserve any important purpose through their reception into the sacred Canon.

But, more particularly, it may be asked, if the subject and the substance of these chapters be merely fictions or fancies, though with a substratum of truth, how came they to be linked to the Bible by the close ties above indicated, and how came their true character never to be suspected by any of the subsequent writers of Scripture, by whom the statements made regarding the creation and the fall in these earliest records have been unreservedly regarded as literal historical verities? "It is very difficult," remarks Julius Müller, "to comprehend how the deeply meditative piety of an Israelite, if it attached its poesy to the holy traditions respecting the first parents of the human race, should have ventured to represent the same as history, or how, perhaps contrary to the intention of its author, such a misunderstanding was able to arise." But, again, if these narratives be fictions, what, it may be asked, in the Bible are facts? How are the former to be distinguished from the latter, and where, at what chapter and book, is the line of demarcation to be drawn between a so-called Hebrew mythology and the Hebrew history, if it be allowed that there is anything historical at all in the Old Testament Scriptures? If these simple statements, bearing on their very front all the characteristics of historical truths and literal realities, must be pronounced myths, or classed with poetry, it would certainly be exceedingly difficult, if not impossible, to show that there are in the Bible any historical truth at all. It is a leading principle of Scripture, that all its doctrines stand in an essential relation to its facts, and the important bearing of the facts of these narratives, assumed to be such by prophets and apostles, has been fully evinced; but if the very foundations be distrusted, what confidence can be reposed in the strength and stability of the superstructure?

The simple fact, however, that the literal, historical character of these narratives is so emphatically endorsed by the subsequent writers of Scripture is itself sufficient to satisfy all who are impressed with a due reverence for the Word of God, and who can intelligently appreciate the testimony of its inspired authors. To all such it must appear a perfectly legitimate inference that every argument which proves the inspiration of the New Testament, or any of its parts, bears indirectly on the character and claims of the earlier records to which it lends its sanction. At present the discussion is in great part with a different class of opposers, and one with whom the name of an apostle, or the authority of inspiration, weighs but little. It will therefore be well to establish, if possible, from another point of view, the historical character of these early documents before vindicating for them a place among the productions of the " holy men of God who spake as they were moved by the Holy Ghost."

Irrespective, then, of the sanction accorded to these narratives by the other writers of Scripture, and looking at them, in the first instance, merely as productions of a very high antiquity, is there any reason to conclude that they are fictions or philosophemes—beautiful but baseless speculations, or with only such a foundation as dim and dubious legends, or reasonable conjecture supplied? Heathen antiquity has been questioned on this point, so also has modern science in the comparisons above instituted, first regarding the narrative of the Creation, and next that of the Fall, but in neither case has the response been such as would in any way seem to countenance such a conclusion. Indeed, it must be evident that the results of the investigations and comparisons conducted in departments of human knowledge specially selected, be it observed, by the supporters of the views which would decry the authority of the scriptural records, for their presumed favourable bearing on the case, lead to an entirely opposite result.

The comparison of the biblical records with the remains of heathen cosmogonies, and the still more distinct traces of a fall, which ancient traditions and mythological legends furnish, has made it plain that there are various marked and unmistakable features common to the Bible and the *unwritten* history of the earth and man, which, although in the latter case grievously dimmed and distorted, indicate a common parentage, and point to a period when the now scattered nations and families of the earth were one—a period such as the Scriptures represent as that of Noah, or of Adam the first father of the human race.

The universality of these traditions, and their similarity in the main, farther prove that there must have been some foundation of truth, some reality or historical facts from which they sprung, but the extent of which cannot with certainty be determined from an examination of the traditions alone. Here, however, the discoveries of modern science opportunely come to our aid, and confirm the conclusions which may be reasonably deduced from the character and consistency of the traditions themselves. The history of Creation has been inscribed in records more durable than ever-shifting traditions, or even books, which are not absolutely exempt from corruption ; and science—from the reading of that register of his mighty operations kept by the Creator himself—demonstrates that the germs of the multifarious traditions which bear on the subject of creation are truths, and especially that the form in which these traditions, so to speak for the present, are preserved in the Bible, is truth without any mixture of error. Keeping in view the object of the biblical narrative of Creation, which is, as was distinctly stated, to communicate not scientific truths, but moral and religious instruction, and that in language necessarily adapted to the lowest capacity if this object was to be attained, few can deny that it exhibits a wonderful harmony with the facts of the earth's history and the period of man, as these have been recently brought to light through a careful and laborious deciphering of the deeply imbedded stony record. Indeed, a close and critical comparison of the statements of the Bible in all their simplicity, with the discoveries of the physical sciences, shows on the part of the former, an acquaintance with the history and course of Creation such as science itself could not boast of until within a very recent period.

So much for the literal, historical character of these venerable documents. But while distinctly claiming for them such an acceptation, it is only on the principle laid down at the very outset of this disquisition, where was stated and defined the sense in which the terms *literal* and *historical* were predicated of this portion of Scripture. It is necessary to revert to

that distinction, inasmuch as it was found that by neglecting
the simple principles which ought to regulate the interpretation of all language, and by unnaturally straining every statement of these narratives into a jejune literalism, not only were
unnecessary difficulties raised in the path of the reader, but
the statements themselves converted into puerilities unbe-
fitting the occasion on which they were uttered, and the
character of the record in which they are preserved.

If it be thus shown that the matters treated of in these
biblical narratives are facts true to nature, and to the physical
and moral history of man ; and farther, that a general acquaintance with these facts, and acquiescence in them as such, can
be traced back to the very early period in the history of the
human race, which, irrespective of any biblical testimony, the
existence and universality of the traditions upon this subject
have been shown to determine, the next question that arises
is, how came these truths to be discovered, and to form so
deep an impression on the human mind and memory ? By
what medium—observation, reasoning, or revelation—have
these truths come to the knowledge of mankind ; or to simplify the matter, and state it in accordance with a preceding
conclusion—to the knowledge of the first man ?

A part, no doubt, of these truths, common to Scripture and
tradition, is referable to memory, as incidents of personal
experience. Such, for instance, are those which relate to the
history of the Fall, and some of its antecedents. But another,
and for the present purpose a very important part of the
information which the knowledge of these facts implies, cannot certainly have originated in observation or experience.
The great truths of creation taught, though in a deeply mys-
tified and doubtful form, by tradition, but in the Bible disposed in proper order and light, obviously belong to this class.
The whole of the first section of Genesis, and a part of the
second, treat of times and transactions, conditions and results,
connected with Divine operations, which no human eye had
seen, and which, therefore, could not come within the range of
man's experience or memory. It needs but little consideration
of the nature of the case to make it manifest, that, in order to
arrive at a correct acquaintance with various particulars in
this pre-Adamic history, there was need of other means than

are at present at the command of man for obtaining information of the past, seeing that in this instance the transactions were entirely unexperienced and unrecorded in any human register, and were, moreover, of such a character as to furnish little ground for their ready apprehension as necessary or axiomatic truths.

The narrative of the Creation has been sometimes taken to be the expression of the knowledge which the first man had of what preceded his own creation. This may, in a sense, and to a certain extent, be true. Such knowledge was undoubtedly possessed by the first man, and to it is to be referred the truths found amid the confused traditionary memorials on the subject; but whether it equalled or exceeded in amount that comprehended in the narrative of Genesis, cannot be determined. But however this may be, it is quite another thing to argue that such knowledge might be acquired by the first man without the necessity of a special revelation ;[1] and, again, that the biblical narrative is simply a record of this knowledge handed down by tradition. It is maintained that this acquaintance with the past history of the earth, and with former creations, might have been the result of observation, just as similar knowledge is acquired at the present day, an examination of the earth's surface and rocky strata furnishing a history of the order and mode of its formation. But as regards this, it is not too much to say that the reasoning is utterly unsatisfactory, the assumptions gratuitous, and the conclusion delusive. It ascribes to the first man powers and capacities which there is no reason to conclude he possessed, and places him in a relation to the creation, and indirectly to the Creator, in which revelation of any kind may be pronounced superfluous. Even now, with all the accumulated experience of a greatly protracted past, and with the most careful and long continued observation, not of one, but of a multitude of inquiring minds, the progress of discovery in the path of physical truth is slow, and a correct knowledge of nature is only now beginning to be attained. In the infancy of the human race, and even in a state of innocence, whatever may be the assumed capacities of unfallen man, creation must have presented a dark enigma, which demanded for its solution more than his

---

[1] Hofmann, *Der Schriftbeweis.* Nördlingen, 1852, vol. i. p. 232.

own reasoning powers. Without entering on any discussion of the matter, it may be fairly argued that in the infancy of the human race, extraordinary communications from the Deity were vouchsafed on grounds even of physical and moral necessity ; and if such communications there were, is there anything more probable than that to these, man was indebted for his information as well regarding the creation as the Creator and Governor, to whose laws and administration he was amenable ? An acquaintance with the *origin* of things must be obtained by immediate revelation from God, or it must be for ever unknown.

But passing over the question regarding the source of the primitive information, and of the truths lying at the foundation of the traditional cosmogonies, as bearing only indirectly on the present subject, which is an inquiry into the origin of the present form of the biblical narrative of creation, it is of more importance in this point of view to direct attention to the fact, that in the course of transmission through a long succession of ages, and by their translation, as it were, into the various languages of the earth, and the various modifying influences thus brought to bear upon them, the original ideas have been so moulded and mixed up with the grossest absurdities and superstitions, that it requires the most careful comparisons and nicest analysis to determine even approximately what is fact and what is fiction in this conglomeration of ideas.

Farther, it is of the utmost importance to take into consideration the very decided contrast, clearly evinced in the preceding pages, which the biblical narratives of Creation and the Fall bear to all the heathen traditions and mythologies. This contrast brought out very distinctly the unapproachable superiority of the former in every point of view. This was shown to be particularly the case in regard to the narrative of the Creation, but it is even more striking in the account of the Fall, although from the multiplicity of particulars, and the far deeper impression which the events connected with the Fall made upon the human mind, this contrast, at first sight, might not appear so clearly defined. What has already been said of the narrative of the Creation, may be equally applied to that of the Fall. These narratives contain all the elements of truth which lie at the foundation of all the myths and legends of heathenism regarding the origin of the world and the past and present condition of man, without any one of the numerous and extravagant fancies and absurdities by which, without exception, all these traditions are so grossly deformed. They contain all the scattered grains of the pure ore, without any tinge of the dross with which, in every other instance, it is mixed up, or almost concealed. These narratives are consistent with themselves—consistent with truth and right reason—consistent with our highest and holiest conceptions of the Almighty Creator, and consistent with the entire teaching of the divinely-inspired Word.

This is a highly interesting feature in these earliest biblical records, and, on any view that may be taken of the matter, must greatly influence the inquiry into their origin. It incontestably proves, in the first place, that the narratives of Genesis are not a mere transcript or a careless compilation of heathen testimonies and traditions.

But even where this last point is conceded, it may be still urged, that the early chapters of Genesis are only a carefully transcribed copy of the traditional history of the early ages of the earth and of man, as preserved in Israel, and transmitted in the patriarchal line, which thus secured for it the greater purity by which it is distinguished. The case is sometimes thus put, and summarily disposed of. But the mere circumstance that the traditions were transmitted in this line, of itself scarcely furnishes a sufficient guarantee against changes and corruptions, more or less extensive, during the many ages that elapsed before they were committed to writing; and so, of course, it cannot be admitted as a full explanation of the absolute, and not merely relative purity, of the biblical records, and of their entire freedom from all that is false, fanciful, and absurd.

Nor does it sufficiently account for the purity and consistency of the Hebrew ideas relative to the Creation and Fall, as compared with the traditions of other nations, to say that the former were at a very early period committed to writing, and were in these circumstances preserved from the many chances and changes to which the unrecorded traditions of the other nations were long exposed. This representation of the case is certainly true in a measure, and were the question, as

remarked above, one only of relative purity, it might go far
to furnish the requisite answer ; but it will by no means
account for the many peculiarities by which the biblical narratives are so remarkably distinguished. The circumstance that
the Hebrew traditions were associated with a purer theology,
has also been adduced in explanation of this remarkable phenomenon, but this is not one that at all tends to diminish
the difficulty, or to account for the differences to which reference has been so frequently made. The doctrine of the unity
of God, as held by the Israelites, has, in particular, been
adduced in explanation of their correct and consistent views
of creation. But this is palpably no explanation ; for the
origin of the one doctrine requires as much to be accounted
for as that of the other. This purer theology, the peculiar
privilege and possession of the Israelites, without question,
rested upon, and was kept alive only by, special revelation
from above, if any weight be due to the records, the genuineness and authenticity of the earliest portion of which are now
being discussed ; and if thus revelation must be admitted in
the one case, there is nothing to be gained by excluding it in
the other.

But again, on the supposition that the narratives of Creation and the Fall, as found in Genesis, and whose historical
character and credibility have, it is believed, been satisfactorily
established, are simply a transcript of unauthenticated Hebrew
traditions, or a compilation from those of the other nations of
the earth, there are numerous and weighty difficulties which
must be obviated before this view of the matter can, with any
degree of satisfaction, be accepted—a view which has been
evidently devised for the purpose of dispensing with Revelation, and which, in order to be consistent, must also exclude
or dispense with all supernatural endowments on the part of
the copyist or compiler.

First, on the supposition that the matters recorded in the
narratives in question are an assemblage or a selection of traditions floating on the stream of time, and wafted down from
some remote but unknown era, how came the author, by whom
they were collected and committed to writing, to form so correct an estimate of their value as is manifested in the fact,
that he gathered them up, and selected them from amidst

what must be supposed a mass of similar or dissimilar legends, —to give them a place and an importance in his history which are fully awarded to them by every subsequent statement of the Holy Scriptures ?

Secondly, on what eclectic principles, and by what rule or process of reasoning did the author proceed, when, with such consummate skill and unrivalled discernment, he contrived to separate the true, as well in history as in theology, from all that was fictitious and false, and succeeded so admirably in giving to the former only a place in his narrative ?

Thirdly, how did the writer or compiler of the narratives of Creation and the Fall manage so to rise above the limited horizon of knowledge, not merely of his own age, but of nume- rous succeeding centuries, and to emancipate himself so com- pletely from the disturbing influences of his time, whether of ignorance or of prejudice, as to be enabled to avoid the false in theory no less than the false in fact ; and not only so, but, it may be added, how did he contrive, on so very extended a field as is presented in Creation and the Fall, and amid such a multiplicity of statements, to express himself in a way to which no other document of ancient times furnishes a parallel, and also in terms to which the brilliant discoveries of modern science afford not the shadow of a contradiction, but, on the contrary, most material and unexpected corroboration ?

These, and various other difficulties which present them- selves in connexion with this matter, are utterly inexplicable on the theory that the narratives of Genesis are not the pro- duction of Divine inspiration, but that their author or compiler was indebted solely to his own powers of reasoning and reflec- tion. For in whatever light the matter may be viewed, the task thus assumed, and so successfully executed by the writer, was so vast and peculiar, that it unquestionably demanded powers and capacities on his part, so incomparably superior to those of his contemporaries, as to imply scarcely less than the inspiration now claimed for him ; or if, on the other hand, he was not, by some extraordinary gifts and endowments, immea- surably raised above the level of his contemporaries, the facts of the case, in these circumstances, and on this supposition, claim an amount of knowledge, and an acquaintance with nature for that early age, so unsupported by any fact, so unsanctioned by any analogy, as, to say the least, must be declared utterly incredible.

The case has by a recent French writer been thus stated : " The cosmogony of Moses, simple, clear, and natural, is evidently the result of learned research. The author of this system, respecting the origin of the earth and the heavens, must necessarily have devoted himself to profound meditations on the history of the globe ; and it is certain that geology must, in his day, have reached an extraordinary point of perfection for the historian to follow, as Moses has done, step by step, all the mysteries of that creation."[1]

All this might be readily regarded as an ironical refutation of the views which would dispense with the aid of Revelation in the matter, but it was by no means so intended by the author. On the contrary, it was soberly meant as a simple explanation of the origin of the Mosaic narrative of creation. Accepting the unequivocal testimony rendered by the learned author to the truthfulness of the narrative, and to its harmony with scientific discoveries, it may be remarked, that geology must have assuredly reached an extraordinary point of perfection at that early period, and Moses must have been a geologist inferior to none of the present day if he did not learn the facts which he records relative to the world's history from some other source than the study of organic remains, and the order of the stratifications ; or if he did not otherwise learn to estimate and arrange the facts supplied, it may be at second hand, by ancient and often perplexing traditions, and so to build up the scattered and fragmentary materials into the beautiful and well-proportioned structure which the opening pages of Genesis present.

If it were necessary to discuss the matter farther, it might be shewn, that not only geology, but all the kindred sciences, must come into requisition, and that, too, in almost their present perfection, if inspiration is to be dispensed with in the case ; and thus there would be no end to the extravagant demands to be made on our credulity, when all the difficulties could be at once simply and satisfactorily disposed of by admitting that the writer was not left to his own resources, or those of his age, but was guided and governed in his composi-

[1] Henri, Egypt Pharaonique, vol. i. p. 155.

tion by the Spirit of the omniscient God. A favourite supposition, however, with those who, when it serves their turn, are not unwilling to ascribe any amount of knowledge to a writer of Scripture, provided only it be of an earthly kind, is, that the source of the remarkable knowledge evinced by Moses in the narrative of creation, is to be traced to the Egyptians, in all whose wisdom he was learned, (Acts vii. 22.) But it is sufficient to observe, that whatever Moses may have borrowed from the Egyptians or their schools, it is certain he could have obtained from that quarter but exceedingly little aid, if any, towards the construction of a cosmogony.

But assuming to the utmost imaginable extent the early progress of physical knowledge, and the proficiency of Moses in respect to all the subjects to which he directly or incidentally adverts, the assumption is utterly inadequate to account for the care and the circumspection displayed throughout this vast and most recondite subject. No false step—no erroneous turn—no falter can be instanced in the narrative from the starting-point in the history, " In the beginning God created the heavens and the earth," till it reaches the majestic close, " God saw everything that he had made, and behold, it was very good." The same is equally true in respect to the narrative of the Fall. On the two great and mysterious subjects of which he thus treats, the writer is not like one hazarding a guess, or darkly and doubtfully feeling his way. Through the fields of creation and moral government, a condition of innocence and a state of sin, he walks abroad with calmness, confidence, and courage. Nothing short of Divine power and direction could have conducted him so safely and securely through those wide and bewildering regions; but whether the Divine communications thus received were exercised simply and solely in teaching the writer of Genesis to gather up the fragmentary truths which he found imbedded in tradition and obscured by the dust of ages, and set them anew and in due order in the pages of his imperishable record, or whether, as may be conceived more probable, they were directed in communicating the matter by a new revelation, need not be determined ; for, in an inquiry such as the present, the determination of the particular mode of revelation is of comparatively little moment. On either of the alternatives, the inspired

origin of these narratives is fully asserted ; while their literal
historical character has been previously evinced. " If," to
quote from a recent writer, " Moses compiled Genesis either
wholly or in part from previously existing documents, he was
divinely inspired to select, arrange, to alter, expunge, or add
to these documents, *as truth demanded.* If he received the
facts as handed down by oral tradition, he was, in like manner,
guided of God to receive and to record the truth, the whole
truth needed in the case, and *nothing but the truth.* And if
Moses wrote the whole as communicated directly to him by
inspiration alone, then the very truth necessary to be known
in the case, and the truth alone, pure and free from all admixture of error, must have been the result of his authorship."[1]

And now, in drawing this matter to a close, the result of
the preceding attempt to vindicate the historical and inspired
character of the first three chapters of Genesis, if it has
effected anything, has, it is believed, shown that, notwithstanding every form of opposition, this portion of the most
ancient of existing literary muniments can appeal and approve
itself to every dispassionate and unprejudiced inquirer ; and,
in particular, that it will be found by all who reverence and
can recognise Scripture, to speak a language and to breathe a
spirit strictly conformable with the most recent and best
attested productions of inspiration ; that by the student of
antiquity, it will be found to explain, in an eminently consistent manner, the origin and meaning of many of the perplexing legends which lie scattered and apparently unconnected
over the classic page ; and by the man of science, to demonstrate that the Creator of the earth is also the writer of its
history, as well in the pages of the Bible as on its own rocky
bosom, the one record confirming and elucidating the other ;
while both unite in testimony and in tributes of praise to " the
Lord of Hosts, who is wonderful in counsel, and excellent in
working," and in declaring of themselves, " Lo these are parts
of his ways ; but how little a portion is heard of him ! " while
they testify of Him, " the thunder of whose power who can
understand ?"

[1] Hamilton, The Pentateuch and its Assailants, p. 131.

PART SECOND.

PART SECOND.

AN EXPOSITION OF THE FIRST THREE CHAPTERS OF GENESIS.

PREFATORY OBSERVATIONS.

RELEASED from the consideration of wearisome controversies and disputations regarding the authority to be conceded to this portion of Scripture, and the sense in which it is to be understood, the examination of the record itself can now be approached, with, it is believed, considerable advantages derived from that discussion. Not the least of these is a greatly deepened conviction of the strength and stability of the basis of revelation furnished by the opening chapters of Genesis—a conviction similar to that of the Psalmist when he declared, " Concerning thy testimonies, I have known of old that thou hast founded them for ever." This was particularly felt in considering the strong contrast presented by the immutability of the Record itself, and the absence of all doubt or misgiving on the part of its writer, when compared with the transitory character of human expositions, as well of natural phenomena as revealed truths, and the unnecessary fears of the friends of the latter when the progress of discovery threatened to clash with *their* modes of thought.

In consonance with the conclusions above arrived at, the following exposition will, it must be observed, have for its object to discover not the mind of erring and ignorant man, but of the infallible Spirit of God. For the right prosecution of so important an inquiry, the preceding disquisition has furnished some aids in the way of suggestion and caution, one or two of which it will be well briefly to state, in these prefatory

o

observations, even at the risk of giving expression only to truths, of some of which the importance is perhaps already generally recognised.

If any reflection more than another has been awakened by the conflicting interpretations which came under review, and the fallacious notions entertained regarding various particulars in the history of the Creation and the Fall, it is the necessity of keeping close to the letter of Scripture, and explaining it by the ordinary rules of language—taking care, however, that the result does not contradict the analogy of faith, and also, it must be added, the analogy of nature, both in a physical and moral aspect.

While the fundamental principles of exposition should be the strict historico-grammatical, the analogy of faith must by no means be lost sight of, notwithstanding the disparagement with which its application to such a purpose is viewed by many, and the abuse to which, it must be admitted, it is liable. If, as is evinced in the preceding pages, it is one mind, with one object, which pervades the Bible, from Genesis to the Apocalypse, it may be safely presumed that nothing can afford better aid than the later and admittedly clearer statements for expounding the earlier and more obscure.

The analogy of nature, as elucidated by the labours of scientific men, will also usefully contribute to the exposition of the Word of God, particularly of such portions of it as relate to other than strictly spiritual truths. With regard to the latter, Scripture is the only source of information; but for attaining to an acquaintance with the former, the Creator has put within the reach of man other means besides his own unerring revelation. He has spread the book of nature before the eyes of his rational creation, to confirm and illustrate the book of grace. It may therefore be affirmed, that as that interpretation is to be rejected which broadly contradicts an article of faith, so also is that interpretation open to suspicion which is opposed to any properly authenticated finding of science, and it demands, to say the least, a very careful reconsideration. The Bible, with its truths, eternal and unchangeable as its Great Author himself, has nothing to fear, but much to gain, from the progress of knowledge, particularly that which concerns God's works. It may, without presump tion, be affirmed, that the first chapter of Genesis, for instance, would not have been understood to the extent it now is, without the light unintentionally reflected upon it by the studies of the geologist, and the direction thereby given to the scriptural interpreter, still necessarily proceeding with his labours according to strict philological rules.

The use of these principles in the way proposed, assumes that the language of Scripture is in itself unambiguous and intelligible, though liable to be misunderstood and perverted by the dulness and prejudices of its readers, and if properly adhered to, will have the effect of equally avoiding allegorical fancies, superficial literalisms, and all figments of a *double sense.* The principles themselves can be consistently questioned only by such as deny the inspiration of the Record, or the harmony of all truth. Of course, it is only on the supposition that the whole Bible is the Word of God, and that the universe also is possessed of a reality and truthfulness, that the adjuncts above specified—the analogy of faith and the analogy of nature—can be deemed safe and legitimate auxiliaries in the interpretation of Scripture, and this supposition is at the same time a sufficient vindication of their being so applied.

SECT. I.—THE CREATION OF THE HEAVENS AND THE EARTH,
GEN. I.-II. 3.

§ 1. *Introduction to the Work of the Six Days,* Gen. i. 1, 2.

The first section of Genesis narrates the creation of the heavens and the earth, with all their hosts. The doctrine of creation is a fundamental article of religion. It is one, however, on which reason or experience can furnish little or no light; for creation antedates man, and lies beyond the sphere of his observation. (See Job xxxviii. 4.) To Revelation alone we are indebted for any reliable information on this subject, so that it is " through faith we understand that the worlds were framed by the word of God," (Heb. xi. 3.) God's revelation of himself to man, accordingly, opens with the announcement, *In the beginning God created the heavens and the earth.*

These simple but majestic words disclose, on the highest

authority, matters of the utmost importance to man as a moral being, and as the creature of God; for that it is in a moral and religious, and not in a physical aspect, they are to be viewed, is evident from the place which they thus occupy. This authoritative declaration puts the plainest reader of Scripture in possession of truths but dimly apprehended by the wisest of the heathen philosophers, notwithstanding the anxiety with which they inquired into such things. It is of importance, however, to notice as well the particulars on which this first sentence of the Bible gives no information, as those on which it furnishes definite and distinct statements. Thus, on the question of time, or the date of the production here described, there is no intimation. The expression, *in the beginning*, fixes nothing as to the antiquity of the creation: it merely asserts that the Creator, at some point or period in the flow of past duration, called into being things which previously had no existence. As this position has been already somewhat discussed in the former part of this volume, it is unnecessary to enlarge upon it farther in this place, particularly as it is now very generally conceded. The same silence is observed also with respect to the mode of creation, and many other questions on which curiosity may desire information, or science be able to throw light.

The opening announcement of Genesis teaches, simply and distinctly,—1. That the world is not eternal, either as to matter or form. By the exclusion of *eternal matter*, the Scripture doctrine of creation is distinguished from all the forms of heathenism; as it is also, 2. By the other truth, that the world is not the product of accident or necessity, but owes its origin to the will of an intelligent, free, and almighty Agent—ELOHIM, the Supreme God, who, as the succeeding narrative repeatedly intimates, called all things into being by the " word" of his power; or as it is elsewhere described, " He spake, and it was done; he commanded, and it stood fast," (Psalm xxxiii. 9.) 3. That the act of creation at the beginning comprehended *the heavens and the earth ;* or, according to the etymology of the terms, " the high (the heights) and the low," the usual Hebrew periphrasis for *the universe,* for which the language had no single word. For the illustration of these and other particulars comprised in this verse, the reader is referred to various observations in the preceding sections, particularly for the meaning of the word rendered *created*, and of the Divine name *Elohim*, which is exclusively used in the first section of Genesis. With regard to *creation*, it was fully shewn that the whole weight of Scripture evidence bears out the interpretation, that the first sentence of Genesis teaches the origination of matter—the elementary bodies of the chemist; but it is to be added, it farther teaches, that the matter so created was distributed into distinct masses throughout space, to form the nucleus of worlds and systems.

But what is the relation of the first verse to the narrative at the head of which it stands ? Is it to be viewed as occupying a place apart—a first general announcement or title, and so a summary of the chapter, or as the first creating act in the series ? It is not easy to determine which of these alternatives is to be chosen. Much may be said on both sides of the question, the decision of which, though apparently of little moment, yet in reality greatly affects the view which expositors take of the whole narrative. The first is the opinion most generally entertained by such as would reconcile Genesis and geology. The grounds on which it is urged are, (1.) That general statements of this kind are of frequent occurrence in Scripture, as, for example, in this very history, (Gen. i. 27, compared with ii. 7, 18 ;) and (2.) That in the course of the narrative the creation of the heavens (verse 8) and of the earth (verse 10) is particularly r ntioned,—a circumstance which, it is thought, proves that these names were not applied to the product of the first creative act. On the other hand, this view is pronounced to be in direct opposition to the context, which clearly indicates a continuity in the discourse. Verse 2 begins, *And the earth*, &c. ; and this, according to the preceding view, is the beginning of the narrative ; but no history can begin with the Hebrew *vav*, whether taken in the sense of *but* or *and*. Exod. i. 1, to which reference is sometimes made, is not an exception ; for this is not a *beginning*, but a continuation of the history of Genesis. Farther, taking verse 1 to be merely a title or summary of contents, the first object presented to view is the earth in a state of *desolation and emptiness*, (verse 2,) which would readily induce belief in an *eternal chaos* —a notion utterly opposed to the whole tenor of the Bible ;

but which is effectually excluded when this chaos, whatever may have been its character and duration, is seen to be bounded by the first creative act in verse 1, an operation not limited to the mere creation of matter, but continued until matter assumed forms which, although not finished, might yet be properly designated as " the heavens and the earth." This is distinctly stated as regards the " earth," which is so called when in the condition described in verse 2 ; a circumstance which completely sets aside the assumption, that the names *heaven* and *earth* are applicable only to a more advanced state of things.

Without dwelling on other considerations favourable to the view which preserves the continuity of the account of the creation from the origination of " the heavens and the earth" down to the period when they were declared to be finished, it is of more consequence to observe, that no special necessity calls for the separation, and no real difficulty is removed even when it is assumed.

It is thus evident, that the first verse cannot be so well taken for a title, as an introduction to the six days' work, and which, with the reserve characteristic of Scripture as a revelation of moral and not of physical truths, silently conducts the reader to a period when the state of the earth was as described in verse 2 : *And the earth was without form, and void; and darkness was upon the face of the deep.*

In the announcement of the previous verse the *heavens* were included, but here the description is limited to the *earth*, as the part of the universe destined to form the residence of man, with whom, and with whose history and wants, the Scriptures have directly to do. The earth is described as תֹהוּ וָבֹהוּ, *emptiness and vacuity; ·κένωμα καὶ οὐδέν, Aquila ; κενὸν καὶ οὐδέν, Theodotion ;* inanis et vacua, *Vulg. ;* the synonymes being combined, as is frequently the case in Hebrew, to give intensity to the idea. The same combination as here is used by Jeremiah (chap. iv. 23) to set forth the completeness of his country's desolation through the Babylonian invasion :--

" I saw the land,
And behold ! it was *waste and empty :*
And the heavens, and they had no light.
I saw the mountains,

And behold! they trembled,
And all the hills shook vehemently.
I saw, and behold! there was no man,
And all the birds of the air had fled.
I saw, and behold! the fruitful land had been turned into the desert,
And all its cities were broken down,
Before Jehovah, before the fury of his anger."—*Henderson's Translation.*

This description is quoted as a poetical amplification of the idea expressed in Gen. i. 2. " All is represented," says Henderson, " as one complete scene of solitude and desolation, no vestige of the human or of the feathered creation is to be seen."

The picture of the primeval dreariness and desolation is farther deepened by the intimation, *darkness was upon the face of the deep.* This is not the darkness which was afterwards so far subdued and bounded by the light, as to be called *night,* (verse 5;) but the primeval darkness into which no ray of light had ever penetrated. It lay upon the *face* or *surface* of the *deep;* that is, the vast collection or mass of waters in which the earth was also enveloped—covered as with a garment, (Psalm civ. 6.) The name תהום (from הום, *to perturb*) is frequently applied to the sea, because of its tossing and roaring, (see Psalm xlii. 8;) but here it denotes the dark chaotic waters of the universal ocean. The rendering of the LXX. (ἄβυσσος) corresponds to the Hebrew, as Tuch remarks, neither in etymology nor in sense; so that there is no room for comparison with the cosmological notions of the Greeks regarding the *abyss.*

The state of the earth, as here described, was one from which all life was absent; even the first conditions of life were wanting. An important question, however, arises—Is this a description of the earth in its original state, or at an after period in its history, when, through some such convulsion as geology indicates, disorder and death succeeded a former state of order and life? Many adopt the latter supposition, and maintain that the terms descriptive of the desolation are elsewhere applied to devastations of previously fertile and populous regions, (Job xxxiv. 11; Jer. iv. 23;) and are such as a " Hebrew writer would naturally use to express the wreck and ruins of a former world, if such a one were supposed to have existed."—(*Bush.*) This may be true, but, in the absence of all evidence, the supposition of an earlier world is not to be admitted, or a reference to it by the writer of Genesis. But it is urged, that such a rude chaotic mass ill accords with the character of the productions of God, of which it is said, " He formed the earth, and made it; he hath established it, he *created it not in vain,* or *desolate,*" (Isa. xlv. 18.) According to Bush, " the action denoted by the word *created* did not result in the state denoted by the word *desolate,* but the reverse : ' He formed it to be inhabited.'" This argument proceeds on an entire misapprehension. The chaotic state of the earth is in no respect at variance with the most correct conceptions of a work of God, not intended to be perfected instantaneously, but through successive stages. The Almighty, had He pleased, could have at once perfected and peopled the universe, but, in his infinite wisdom, He adopted another mode of operation, and one which necessarily entailed imperfection and incompleteness more or less on all the progressive steps of the process. But it is unnecessary to argue the matter; for the rendering, " the earth *became,*" &c., is totally inadmissible: this would have required וַתְּהִי הָאָרֶץ, instead of וְהָאָרֶץ הָיְתָה ; and farther, to prevent ambiguity, the preposition לְ would have been probably conjoined with the verb. This removes all ground for the opinion, that it is not the original but a subsequent state of the earth that is described; and so all room for the strange views of Baumgarten, Kurtz, and others, who, following the reveries of Jacob Böhme, ascribe this chaotic state to the fall of the angels.

The duration of this chaotic condition cannot be determined from anything expressed or implied in the narrative, which is equally silent respecting any natural processes which may have been going on in the interval; but that it was a short period, or one of inactivity, there is no reason to conclude from anything known from Nature or Revelation of the operations of God. There was a pledge, however, in the character of the Creator, that this state of matters should not always be —an assurance extending also to His higher operations, that He will *perform* the good work *begun,* (Phil. i. 6.) In the universal darkness and desolation which prevailed, one omen appeared of a coming change : *The Spirit of God moved upon the face of the waters.* To take רוּחַ אֱלֹהִים for *a strong wind,* as is done by Dathe, Vater, and Schumann, after Onkelos, Saadias, Aben Ezra, and other Jewish expositors, is an interpretation of which Calvin well remarks :—" Adeo frigidum est ut refutatione nulla indigeat." The Hebrew can be undoubtedly rendered *wind* as well as *spirit*, but how can it signify wind, in the present connexion, before the atmosphere was created? It is, moreover, an entire mistake to assume, that here, and in similar cases, the addition of the Divine name is designed to give intensity to the idea, or supply the place of a *superlative* in Hebrew. Besides, the expression מְרַחֶפֶת, which is the participle Piel of רָחַף, *to flutter* or *hover*, as a bird over her young, (Deut. xxxii. 11,) is not at all applicable to the character or action of the wind. While for these, and other reasons, the idea of *wind* is excluded, it is yet doubtful whether the allusion be to the Holy Spirit as a personal distinction in the Godhead, or merely to the Divine power and energy in general, as the source of life, from which creation draws its renovating powers, and without which all flesh withers, and all life returns to dust. (Job xxxiv. 14; Psalm civ. 29, 30.) But the difference may be more a matter of words than a reality; for although in the Old Testament the Spirit's personality is but dimly indicated, and his operations referred to more in a physical than in a moral aspect, yet the acts predicated of the Holy Spirit by the New Testament, warrant the conclusion that it was this Divine Agent who operated through all the dispensations, communicating light, order, and life to the dark chaotic mass, and cherishing the vital spark He first enkindled : his office in connexion with the old creation being thus analogous with the part he acts in the new and spiritual economy. In the words of Dr. Owen : " Without him all was a dead sea, a confused deep, with darkness upon it, able to bring forth nothing, nor more prepared to bring forth any one thing than another; but by the moving of the Spirit of God upon it, the principles of all those kinds, sorts, and forms of things, which, in an inconceivable variety, make up its host and ornament, were communicated unto it."[1]

[1] A Discourse concerning the Holy Spirit.— *Works*, iii. 98.

§ 2. *The First Day of Creation*, Gen. i. 3-5.

There is some difficulty in determining where the operations of the first day may be said to begin ; whether with the originating act described in verse 1, or with the creation of the light announced in verse 3. The statement of Exod. xx. 11, " In six days the Lord made heaven and earth, the sea, and all that in them is," favours, if anything, the first view. But the consideration that the works of the other days uniformly begin with the formula, *And God said*, strongly countenances the supposition that the work of the first day begins at verse 3, where the same expression is used, " *And God said*, Let there be light."

But however this may be, in due time the voice of the Almighty broke in upon the dark void—*Be light*—words which, taken in connexion with the equally short and simple terms in which the fulfilment of the Divine command is narrated, have ever been adduced as one of the finest examples of the sublime. Of far more interest, however, than anything connected with rhetorical forms, is the fact here announced, and to which frequent reference is made in the subsequent Scriptures. By this act of creation, the psalmist describes God as covering himself in light like to a garment, (Psalm civ. 2 ;) and an apostle founds on it a parallel between creation and regeneration : " God, who commanded the light to shine out of darkness, hath shined in our hearts, to give the light of the knowledge of the glory of God in the face of Jesus Christ."

The terms *God said*, which introduce this and the subsequent acts and epochs of creation, are usually considered as only an anthropology. It would, however, be more correct to recognise in the expression the germ of the doctrine of the Divine Word, traces of which may be found in several passages of the Old Testament, but the full development of which was reserved to the prologue of John's Gospel, between which and the opening of the history of creation in Genesis there is a strong analogy. The whole form and expression of the Old Testament revelation was that of the *word of God ;* and as here, " *God said*, Let there be light," so *spoken* commands, openly or in vision, were the communications of God to man. It is the *Word* in the law—the *Word* in the prophets—the *Word* in the gospel; in short, the *Word* in all God's dealings with his people. (See Isa. xl. 8; lv. 10, 11; Jer. xxiii. 29.)

Verse 4, *And God saw the light, that it was good.* God sees and judges of things as they really are. In the other cases, it is more the state or condition induced by the creating word that meets the Divine approbation; but here it is the object created that is *good:* perhaps as the one object in nature which forms the fittest representation of the Creator himself, who is *light,* and in whom there is no darkness at all, (1 John i. 5;) and of the *true light,* which lighteth every man, (John i. 9.) This complacency of the Creator, or rejoicing in his works, (Psalm civ. 31,) intimates not merely that the work was good, or answered the intended purpose, and was thus indicative of wisdom and power, but more particularly that the Creator is not a cold, unimpassioned abstraction, but a Being moved and affected by the contemplation of the beautiful and the good. This relation of Creator and creature furnishes a strong plea in the prayer of faith: " O Lord, forsake not the works of thine own hands," (Psalm cxxxviii. 8.)

And God separated between the light and between the darkness, בֵּין...וּבֵין, *between and between,* a common Hebrew construction with verbs of *separating, judging,* or *estimating,* between two opposite persons or things. The sense is given correctly in the English version, " God divided the light from the darkness." But it is not so easy to understand in what this particular operation consisted. It must mean more than *distinguished* between light and darkness; for that was effected by the creation of light—an element in itself the direct opposite of darkness. Nor can it mean that now the light was separated from the gross medium in which it had been previously bound up; for that this had been sufficiently accomplished in the act of creation is evident from the Divine satisfaction already expressed. The division now introduced must refer to the succession of light and darkness, and the arrangements made for causing and continuing it. The alternation of light and darkness depends at present, as is well known, on the relation of the earth to the sun; but there is no means of determining on what it depended previous to the period when the sun was constituted *the light* or luminary of its dependent planets, (verses 14, 16.) It is necessary to notice the distinction made in Hebrew, and particularly in this narrative, between light in itself, and the bodies into which it is collected, or from which it is emitted—אוֹר, *light,* and מָאוֹר, *the place of light,* the luminary; and farther, the early date assigned to the creation of light, three days or epochs, before the illumination of the heavenly orbs.

This latter circumstance had been long pointed to by the enemies of revelation as unmistakable evidence of entire ignorance of nature and its laws. It is now found, however, that the ignorance was on the part of the objectors, and not of the Author of the narrative of Creation. Modern science has fully substantiated this, though it has lacked the power of placing the subject in a better position than it was left by Moses thousands of years ago. The question is still as unanswerable as when proposed in the time of Job,—" Where is the way where light dwelleth? and as for darkness, where is the place thereof, that thou shouldest take it to the bound thereof, and that thou shouldest know the paths to the house thereof?" After all the vast discoveries of science, who knows what light is—what supplies it, or prevents it from being exhausted? The philosopher has been able to measure its flight, and investigate its action upon matter in the various phenomena of transmission, reflection, refraction, colour, polarization, and vision; but no theory hitherto devised is sufficient to explain its nature and account for all its phenomena. It is found, however, that from whatever source light is procured—whether from chemical action, electrical, calorific, or vital excitation—sources independent of the solar rays—it is the same in character, and differs only in intensity.

Light and darkness being divided, and bounds set to the extent and duration of each, the next thing needed to be recorded was, verse 5, *God called the light day, and the darkness he called night.* The two periods of time constituted by the arrangement already intimated, are to be distinguished by the names *day* and *night:* ל קָרָא, *acclamare alicui,* or more fully with שֵׁם, *a name,* Gen. ii. 20, xxvi. 18; therefore *to name,* verses 8, 10, chap. xxxi. 47. But as man did not yet exist, to whom these names could have any significance, and as God does not require articulate sounds to express his will or designate his works, the occurrence of these names is not a little remarkable.   Bush would explain it thus :—" For the most part by God's ' calling' a thing by a particular name, is meant rather a *declaration of the nature, character,* or *qualities of the thing* named, than the mere bestowment of an appellation by which it should ordinarily be known.   In the present case, therefore, it is probably to be understood that there was something in the import of the word יוֹם, *day,* which rendered it a peculiarly appropriate term by which to express the diurnal continuance of light, and one that He would have to be employed by men for this purpose when they should be created, and should begin to express their thoughts by language." Allowing the appropriateness of the term for the object to be designated, the conferring of names in the present instance, as well as in the other cases mentioned in this chapter, rests on a deeper foundation than is thus supposed : it may have been intended rather to convey the idea of God's sovereignty and absolute control over all the parts of nature, its ordinances and arrangements ; just as afterwards, in token of man's delegated rule in the lower creation, he was directed by the Creator and Owner of all, to give names to the animals around him, (Gen. ii. 19, 20.)   The idea may be then that expressed by the Psalmist in his address to God,—" The day is thine, the night also is thine : thou hast prepared the light and the sun.   Thou hast set all the borders of the earth : thou hast made summer and winter."   And in reference to the naming of the heavens, the earth, and the seas, (verses 8-10,) it may be that it is said,— " Thou rulest the raging of the sea : when the waves thereof arise, thou stillest them.   The heavens are thine, the earth also is thine ; as for the world, and the fulness thereof, thou hast founded them," (Ps. lxxiv. 16, 17 ; lxxxix. 9, 11.)   But there may have been a special propriety in bestowing a name on the darkness, and so declaring the Creator's relation to it ; and this in order to preclude the idea of the darkness being a defect in the creation—something which the Almighty could not remedy—and also the supposition of any independent, opposing power in the universe.   " I am the Lord, and there is none else.   I form the light, and create darkness : I make peace and create evil : I the Lord do all these things," (Isa. xlv. 6, 7.)

And the evening and the morning were the first day: but literally, *It was evening, it was morning, one day.* There are two mistakes frequently committed in interpreting this expression. The one is by maintaining that the evening is mentioned first, because darkness preceded the light, and was that out of which it emerged. But this is the idea conveyed by *morning,* בֹּקֶר properly *the breaking of the early dawn,* or as in English, " the break of day." On the contrary, *evening* (עֶרֶב) was so called from the *setting* or departing of the light or the sun, which thus presupposes the priority of light or day of which this is the close. The other and more important error is the assumption that the above expression is equivalent to the later Hebrew compound, עֶרֶב בֹּקֶר, *evening—morning,* (Dan. viii. 14,) or the Greek νυχθήμερον, (2 Cor. xi. 25 ;) and as such denotes *a whole day,* as made up of evening and morning. But for this there is no evidence. In the first place, expositors are not agreed as to the meaning of the term used in Daniel; and it is only on the supposition that the *evening* and the *morning* of the narrative of the creation constitute a day, and that this, too, is the origin of the phraseology in the other case, that it has been concluded that it there signifies a civil day. Even were it shown on independent grounds, that the expression in Daniel is to be taken in the sense supposed, still there would have been wanting evidence to connect it with the entirely dissimilar construction in the history of the creation. Here there is no reference to time or duration at all, as made up of civil days. *It was evening,* simply intimates that in accordance with the Divine ordination previously mentioned, the time marked by the prevalence of light drew to a close ; evening and night settled down upon the scene ; or, more definitely, that the particular period during which the omnific word directly operated came to an end, leaving it undetermined whether that period comprised one or more, few or many alternations of the natural light and darkness. *It was morning*—the darkness was again dissipated by a new dawn—the opening of a new day of creating activity. In regard to the duration neither of the day nor of the night is the slightest intimation given, for as yet there was no index to the great horologe of nature. But, besides, these were strictly God's days. Man's days are only a derivation and symbol of the archetypal days of creation: the only thing which at all bears comparison with them is the *day*, or appointed course of Christ's working on earth, of which he himself said, " I must work the works of him that sent me, while it is day : the night cometh when no man can work," (John ix. 4.) The fact of the succession is the only one determined, for no sun, moon, or stars, shone down upon the earth still desolate, but subjected to influences which must greatly modify this state of things, and which were only waiting the Divine appliance to introduce order and the most diversified forms of life in the succession and at the intervals which should approve themselves to Infinite Wisdom.

§ 3. *The Second Day of Creation*, Gen. i. 6-8.

After the subjugation of the darkness on the first day by the creation of light and the division of time into day and night, the next step in the work of preparing and perfecting the earth, according to the Divine plan, was the subjugation of the waters in which it was still enveloped. This was partially done on the second day by the interposition of the firmament between the waters. The waters had been previously mentioned in connexion with the primeval darkness as covering the earth, while masses of watery vapour must doubtless have formed another envelope. Ver. 6. *And God said, Let there be a firmament in the midst of the waters,* רָקִיעַ, (from the root רָקַע,) *an expansion,* a term used of anything stretched or spread out ; here, and in Ps. xix. 2 ; cl. i. ; Dan. xii. 3, *the expanse* of heaven or the sky ; and in Ezek. i. 22-26 ; x. 1, *a canopy.* The verb means primarily *to stamp, to extend,* or *spread out* by stamping, and then simply *to spread out,* as Ps. cxxxvi. 6, " God stretched out the earth above the waters." (See also Isa. xlii. 5 ; xliv. 24.) The idea of anything *firm* or *solid,* as expressed in the versions of the LXX., Aquila, Theodotion, and Symmachus, by στερέωμα, and of the Vulg. by *firmamentum,* whence the English *firmament,* does not necessarily belong to the Hebrew, and there is nothing to countenance the notion sometimes ascribed to the sacred writers, that " they supposed that at a moderate distance above the flight of birds there was a solid concave hemisphere, a kind of dome, transparent, in which the stars were fixed as lamps ; and containing openings to be used or closed as was necessary."¹ The sacred writers describe the things of the natural world according to their appearances, and often employ, no doubt, bold and highly poetical figures, as when speaking of the sky as " a molten mirror" borne up by the high mountains, called, therefore, the foundations and pillars of heaven, (Job xxxvii. 18 ; xxvii. 11 ; 2 Sam. xxii. 8 ;) but these are nothing more than figures, and are not to be construed as supposed realities ; for if, in the present instance, it be said that the firmament bears up the waters, it is also said, " He bindeth up the waters in his thick clouds, and the cloud is not rent under them," (Job xxvi. 8.)

The firmament, or expanse, was placed *in the midst of the waters*, or rather *between* the waters, for the purpose of forming and preserving a separation between them ; " *let it divide*," or form a continuous division, מַבְדִּיל וַיְהִי—the *participle* with הָיָה expresses *continuance*, (comp. Gen. iv. 17 ; xxxvii. 23,) "between waters in respect to waters." The construction, בֵּין ··· לְ, is a rarer form than בֵּין ··· וּבֵין, already noticed, but the sense is the same, (see Isa. lix. 2.)

Verse 7 records the complete realization of the Divine purpose : *And God made the expanse, and divided the waters which are under the expanse from the waters which are above the expanse ; and it was so.* What the Divine will purposed, the Divine power performed. The last clause, "and it was so," is added to show the complete accord between the work and the conception of it in the Creative mind, and also to declare the permanence of the arrangement here introduced.

Verse 8. *And God called the expanse Heaven. It was evening, it was morning, the second day.* The word *heaven*, as already remarked, denotes in Hebrew the higher regions in general ; but distinguished by degrees, as in the expression, *the heaven of heavens*, or the highest heavens, (Ps. cxlviii. 4,) and a lower degree in the expression, " fowl of the heavens," or as in the English version, " fowl of the air," (Gen. i. 26.) It is in this latter sense *heaven* is evidently here used. The " expanse" or " heaven" is the Hebrew designation of the atmosphere, and the formation of this elastic medium, with all its

¹ Pye Smith, Scripture and Geology, p. 264.

wonderful properties of collecting, supporting, and transporting water in the shape of clouds, was the work of the second day. " The waters above the firmament," or " the heavens," (Ps. cxlviii. 4,) are then the watery vapours suspended in the atmosphere, carried about in the form of clouds, and by condensation poured down on the earth as rain.

Some recent writers, among whom may be mentioned Delitzsch, maintain that by "the waters above the firmament" more is implied than the water suspended in the atmosphere. They consider that they were the material out of which the heavenly bodies were formed on the fourth day, and, in support of this view, they appeal to the low specific gravity of some of the planets. But if anything were wanting in disproof of this fanciful idea, it would be found in the fact that the Psalmist speaks of those waters as still existing as such, (Ps. cxlviii. 4,) which would have been impossible had they formed the substratum out of which the planetary bodies were constituted. On the passage of the Psalm referred to, Hengstenberg remarks :—" The waters above the heavens can only be, according to the original passage, (Gen. i. 7,) the clouds. Of other heavenly waters Scripture knows nothing. If, therefore, we hold it as certain, that in the first member the highest heavens are mentioned, in the second the clouds, we must also hold that the parallelism is not a mere synonym, but that the highest regions of heaven and the lowest are set in opposition to each other. The mere heaven as contradistinguished from the highest heaven, can only be the lower heaven."

At the close of this day's work the LXX. adds the usual formula of approbation : " And God saw that it was good." But this interpolation is entirely gratuitous. The words are wanting in the original, possibly to intimate that the whole arrangement with respect to the waters was not yet completed, but was to be farther carried out on a subsequent day.

In reviewing the operations and results of the first two epochs of creation, the first thought that will probably arise is, how little has yet been accomplished of the great work ! If so, it may be well to consider that the glorious Being engaged on the work of creation is One who is not limited to time, but has an eternity wherein to operate ; for with Him a thousand years are as one day, and one day as a thousand years ; and farther.

that long preparation characterizes all His works. But again, in the creation of light, and in the investiture of the earth with an atmosphere, principles most powerful and comprehensive were put in operation, and it can only be from ignorance or inattention to this that the thought originates which would regard the results of the first and second days as bearing but a small proportion to the operations of the succeeding days. It is clearly proved, however, from these first acts of creation, that the Author of the universe is a God of order, and that if the stupendous wonders of nature evince almighty power, the orderly arrangement no less evinces Omniscience on the part of Him by whose will and wisdom all was originated and ordained.

From all that is known of light—the production of the first day, of its operations in all the combinations of matter, and of its functions in regard to all that constitutes the life and enjoyment of every form of organized being, we are justly led to consider it as a principle acting a chief part in the grand economy of nature, so much so that without its influence no world could be inhabited, and no animated being could subsist in the manner it now does.

Light is thus the first condition of life. Plants and animals alike proclaim that the continuance of their functions is absolutely dependent upon it. But not only life, order also, or inorganic form, is in various ways greatly influenced by this universal agent. In the process of crystallization this is particularly marked. But without entering into details on this vast and inviting subject, totally unsuited to the occasion, it cannot but appear to be in remarkable harmony with all the deductions of science to find that in the biblical scheme the first place is assigned to its creation.

But of scarcely less importance, for the existence of organized life on the earth, is the atmosphere—the work of the second day—its various properties so nicely adapted to the exigencies of nature, and its constituent parts so duly proportioned for the sustenance of vegetable and animal life. How many mysteries of science are still unresolved in the single function here ascribed to the atmosphere, of supporting the floating vapour, and keeping in suspense a fluid of greater specific gravity than itself! The formation of clouds, and their condensation into rain, are still questions to which science has not furnished a satisfactory answer; and the matter is yet as fraught with wonder as when, in the days of Job, it was asked, " Dost thou know the balancings of the clouds, the wondrous works of him who is perfect in knowledge?" and when the greatness of God was considered to be manifested in the distillation of the rain-drops: " Behold, God is great, and we know him not ; neither can the number of his years be searched out. For he maketh small the drops of water: they pour down rain according to the vapour thereof, which the clouds do drop and distil upon man abundantly."

§ 4. *The Third Day of Creation*, Gen. i. 9-13.

The third day witnessed the accomplishment of two other important operations more immediately connected with the surface of the earth. The first was the farther subjugation of the waters, which led to the arrangement into dry land and seas ; and the second was the creation of vegetable life on the land thus laid bare from its watery covering. As the work advances it becomes more and more definite, and shews more distinctly the end proposed to himself by the Creator. The relations already established between light and darkness, between day and night, and also between the earth and the atmosphere, the terrestrial waters and the clouds, were the fundamental conditions of all life in the lower creation ; and these being adjusted, arrangements more immediately connected with the introduction of life are now to be proceeded with.

Verse 9. *And God said, Let the waters under the heaven be gathered together unto one place, and let the dry land appear.* The mass of waters which yet covered the surface of the globe is called " the waters under the heaven," in reference to the arrangement introduced on the second day. They are henceforth to be brought into a narrower compass : יִקָּווּ הַמַּיִם, *let the waters gather themselves.* קָוָה, cognate with קָוָא, (Exod. xv. 8,) signifies primarily *to draw together ;* Niph., *to draw one's-self together, to assemble,* (Jer. iii. 17.) From this is derived מִקְוֶה, in the phrase מִקְוֵה הַמַּיִם, (verse 10,) which Tuch takes to mean, " the *place* of assembling of the waters ;" but the usual ren-

dering, in which Gesenius concurs, is, " the collection of
waters." The expression, *one place*, is not to be understood
in the strictest sense ; it implies no more than that the waters
were to be collected into one vast body, and to occupy an
appropriate place by themselves, so as to allow a portion of the
earth's surface to be dry. The hollows and depths into which
the waters by their natural gravitation sunk, in accordance
with this arrangement, are elsewhere described as " a place
founded for them," (Psalm civ. 8 ;) but of the convulsions and
upheavals which prepared it, the narrative of Genesis takes no
notice, though distinctly referred to in the psalmist's account
of the creation. *Let the dry land appear ;* הַיַּבָּשָׁה, similar to
the Greek ἡ ξηρά, is that which is habitually or usually *dry*,
applied to the land as opposed to the sea.   תֵּרָאֶה is to be taken
as jussive, compare Gen. xli. 34.   The full realization of the
Divine purpose is recorded in the simple announcement, *And
it was so ;* without, as in the other cases, the repetition in
another form of the creative command.

Verse 10. *And God called the dry land Earth; and the
gathering together of the waters called he Seas : and God saw
that it was good.*   The expression of the Creator's approval,
which was wanting at the close of the second day's work, is
here inserted, in attestation that the arrangements which
regarded the waters were now completed.   The same expression is repeated in reference to the second great act of this
day, (verse 12.)

To the act of creation which resulted in the separation of
the land from the water by giving to the latter its appropriate
bounds, there are frequent references in Scripture, furnishing
some of its grandest images.   Thus God demands of Job :
" Who shut up the sea with doors, when it brake forth, as if it
had issued out of the womb ? when I made the cloud the garment thereof, and thick darkness a swaddling-band for it, and
brake up for it my decreed place, and set bars and doors, and
said, Hitherto shalt thou come, but no further, and here shall
thy proud waves be stayed ?"   Similar allusions occur in Psalm
xxxiii. 7, and Prov. viii. 29, but the most striking reference to
this transaction of Genesis is found in Psalm civ. 6-9, already
adverted to : " Thou coveredst it (the earth) with the deep as
with a garment : the waters stood above the mountains.   At

thy rebuke they fled; at the voice of thy thunder they hasted away. They go up by the mountains; they go down by the valleys unto the place which thou hast founded for them. Thou hast set a bound that they may not pass over; that they turn not again to cover the earth."

We have now reached that place in the history of creation which may be considered the starting-point of all scientific investigations; and which forms the hitherto impassable barrier between the known and the unknown in geology. This science builds all its reliable conclusions, regarding succession and duration, on that crystalline floor of the earth termed *primary*, consisting of igneous rocks, beneath which no explorations have been made. But the manner in which Scripture keeps aloof from all theories connected with the processes of formation, is particularly exemplified in the account of the third day's work. To this period must unquestionably be referred the elevation of the mountain ranges, with the endless variety of hill and dale, which diversifies the earth's surface, and the differences of level on which depend the relative distribution of land and water, the flow of fountains and rivers, a healthy state of the atmosphere, and various other essentials to the life and beauty of this lower world. But of all these movements no notice is taken by the sacred historian; and it is left to the philosopher to discover and describe them as best he may. The psalmist's account of this day's work, above quoted, enters somewhat into details, and makes mention of the mountains; but expositors are not agreed whether the allusion be merely to the fact of their existence, or to their origination. Hengstenberg, and after him Kurtz, maintain that the language of verse 8 cannot refer to the origin of the mountains, as, according to verse 6, they were already in existence. But Rosenmüller, De Wette, Ewald, and others, render verse 8 as in the margin of the English Version, " the mountains rise, the valleys sink ;" or, as Delitzsch proposes, " the mountains rise, the waters sink into the valleys, to the place," &c. This gets rid of the objection, that in verse 7, as well as in verse 9, the water is the principal subject. Utterly unwarranted is Hengstenberg's farther remark : " The mountains existed also, according to Gen. i., before the work of the six days. To the third day belonged only the *appearing* of the dry land, not its *formation :*

the work of that day consisted only in this, that, as at the deluge, the waters retired from the earth, ' the dry land *appeared.*'" On the contrary, the work of the six days included, as already stated, the formation of the earth itself, and therefore the formation of its mountains.

But whether the language of the psalm refers to the existence of the mountains, or, as is more probable, to their origin, as they might be seen emerging from the waters, it cannot in any case be adduced, as is done by A. Wagner,[1] as an argument in favour of one geological theory rather than another. It describes the effects, not the cause—the appearing of the mountain ranges, and not the physical agency to which the phenomenon was due.

But that the separation of the dry land from the super-incumbent waters was effected through the instrumentality of means and long-continued processes, there is no reason to doubt. For information, however, upon this point, recourse must be had to another quarter than Scripture. The appearances presented by the shattered and upheaved crust of the earth indicate the operation of mighty and long-continued forces, producing convulsions, it has been said, " of such terrible potency, that those of the historic ages would be mere ripples of its surface in comparison." Through the mighty agency which the Creator set in motion on the third day, the mountain tops, bare rocky points, probably first emerged from the deep ; islands and continents were gradually formed as the dry land was elevated above the oceanic level.

With the distribution and adjustment of the dry land and water, the inorganic terrestrial arrangements were completed, and all was ready for the reception of organic life. There was light, an atmosphere, dry land, and a wonderful combination of means for distilling and distributing fresh water, all which were essential to the existence of a terrestrial flora and fauna ; and it is a matter of some importance to consider where, and in what form, life is represented to have commenced. Owing to lack of evidence, easily explicable from the nature of the case, science refuses to pronounce a decided judgment regarding the first of organized forms. But various considerations preponderate in favour of the precedence of vegetable life.

[1] Geschichte der Urwelt, p. 481.

The known dependence, directly or indirectly, as regards food, of the animal on the vegetable kingdom, is a particularly strong testimony to the conclusion, that vegetable life was the first summoned into existence, but whether in the ocean or on the earth cannot be determined. It is, moreover, to be remarked, that the biblical record makes no mention of the marine flora.

Verse 11. *And God said, Let the earth bring forth grass, the herb yielding seed, and the fruit tree yielding fruit after its kind, whose seed is in itself, upon the earth: and it was so.* No sooner is the earth relieved from its load of waters, than the creative energy is displayed in clothing it with a living robe of verdure, composed of the beautiful and endlessly diversified productions of the vegetable kingdom. And as progressive development in general characterizes this history, so in particular this portion of it. Three orders of vegetable productions are here enumerated, the characteristic distinctions of which are carefully attended to in the Hebrew writings, although not to be regarded as precise scientific definitions :— 1. דֶּשֶׁא, from which is derived the verb הִדְשִׁיא, also occurring here, *to put forth young grass,* is in general, *young grass, tender herbage,* 2 Sam. xxiii. 4, which appears when *the old grass* (חָצִיר) has departed, Prov. xxvii. 25, adorns the meadows, Ps. xxiii. 2, and furnishes pasture, Job vi. 5. It signifies, in particular, the smaller perennial herbs, which, according to the opinion of the ancients, were produced without seed, αὐτόματοι. 2. עֵשֶׂב (comp. Prov. xxvii. 25) is distinguished by the characteristic of "yielding seed," as a higher order ; assigned to man for food, Gen. i. 29, and evidently including the productions of agriculture, chap. iii. 18, and as such distinguished from חָצִיר, the food of cattle, Ps. civ. 14. Sometimes, however, the term is used in a wider sense of the smaller vegetable productions in general, Gen. i. 30. 3. עֵץ פְּרִי, *fruit tree* in the widest sense—comprehending not merely " fruit trees" properly so called, but all that produce seed-fruit. The advance is plain from the grass and the herbage to the tree which yields, literally *makes* fruit, עֹשֶׂה־פְּרִי, a common Hebrew idiom, which is imitated in the New Testament expression, καρπὸν ποιεῖν. So also the tree is said *to make* branches, (Job xiv. 9.) The distributive לְמִינוֹ, *according to its kind* or *species,* is to be connected with עֵץ, *tree :* and בּוֹ, *in it,* refers to פְּרִי, *fruit ; i.e.,* whose seed is in its fruit.

Verses 12, 13. *And the earth brought forth grass, and herb yielding seed after its kind, and the tree yielding fruit whose seed was in it,· after its kind : and God saw that it was good. It was evening, it was morning, the third day.* Naturalists conclude, and with great probability, that the first created of organized substances belonged to the class of plants called cellular, and of which lichens and mosses are familiar examples. These inferior organisms may have supplied the first step towards rendering the bare, desolate rock, a fertile and productive soil. But however this may be, before the close of the third day of creation, the earth, in obedience to the Divine command, had brought forth the various kinds of vegetable productions above represented, from the humblest creeper to the stately tree, and with full provision for the perpetuation of their respective species. How fully this command was carried out, how abundant and luxurious were the productions of that early period, there are ample means of showing in the fossil flora. To quote the graphic description of a highly competent authority :—" In the first, or Palæozoic division, we find corals, crustaceans, molluscs, fishes, and, in its later formations, a few reptiles. But none of these classes of organisms give its leading character to the Palæozoic, they do not constitute its prominent feature, or render it more remarkable as a scene of life than any of the divisions which followed. That which chiefly distinguished the Palæozoic from the secondary and tertiary periods, was its gorgeous flora. It was emphatically the period of plants,—' of herbs yielding seed after their kind.' In no other age did the world ever witness such a flora ; the youth of the earth was peculiarly a green and umbrageous youth—a youth of dusk and tangled forests, of huge pines and stately araucarians, of the reed-like calamite, the tall tree-fern, the sculptured sigillaria, and the hirsute lepidodendron. Wherever dry land, or shallow lake, or running stream appeared, from where Melville Island now spreads out its ice-wastes, under the star of the Pole, to where the arid plains of Australia lie solitary, beneath the bright cross of the south, a rank and luxuriant herbage cumbered every foot-breadth of the dank and steaming soil ; and even to distant planets our earth must have shone through the enveloping cloud with a green and delicate ray. . . . . The geologic evidence is so complete as to be patent to all, that the first great period of organized being was, as described in the Mosaic record, peculiarly a period of herbs and trees, ' yielding seed after their kind.'"[1] The system of rocks, termed by geologists the carboniferous, constitutes a remarkable group, consisting of a series of deposits of great extent, and of which the coal occupies a thickness on an average of one hundred and fifty feet. Coal is proved to be of vegetable origin, whether examined by the microscope, or submitted to chemical tests. Whatever differences may exist among the learned on such subjects, regarding the mode of deposit, there can be none respecting the endless multitude of plants which must have gone to the formation, or which must have lived and died in various localities during the deposition of the strata in which they have been stored up by Divine Providence for the service of man.

The two works which occupied the third day, though in themselves entirely distinct, are yet closely connected. This is shown in the fact, that, as at the Creation, so it continues to be the case still, no sooner is any rocky islet laid bare than the powers of nature, in accordance with the principle originally established, are at work to form a soil and to effect the other necessary preparations for the abode of life.

It is unnecessary to do more than simply advert to the recent and popular doctrine of centres of creation, whether in regard to the origin of plants or of animals, as on the supposition either of its truth or falsity, it in nowise affects or interferes with anything contained in this narrative, where, with the single exception of man, no intimation is given as to what numbers, or in what localities, the original types of life were summoned into existence. As noticed already, more than once, the absence, too, of such intimations is a distinguishing characteristic of Scripture, and one which incontestably proves it not to have proceeded from man, who could not fail, from ignorance or inadvertence, to introduce some of his own speculations and theories, which that subtle searcher, time, would assuredly pronounce to be utterly unfounded.

[1] Miller, The Two Records, pp. 20, 21.

§ 5. *The Fourth Day of Creation,* Gen. i. 14-19.

The works of the last three days of Creation form a remarkable parallel with those of the first three, which were occupied with the production of light, the arrangement of the atmosphere, and of the terrestrial waters, and the covering of the earth's surface with vegetable life. The works of the three remaining days consist in farther perfecting these arrangements. The fourth day is occupied with regulating the light created on the first day—collecting it into the heavenly orbs which are henceforth to illumine the earth. The fifth day sees the waters and the air replenished with living creatures ; and the sixth witnesses the introduction of the terrestrial animals, including man, the head of the family, on the earth, on the third day laid bare from the waters and stored with vegetable life.

The arrangement instituted with regard to the light on the first day hitherto served all the wants of the earth ; but on the fourth day this was superseded by another arrangement, that which we now witness and enjoy. Verses 14, 15. *And God said, Let there be lights in the firmament of the heaven, to divide the day from the night : and let them be for signs, and for seasons, and for days and years. And let them be for lights in the firmament of the heaven, to give light upon the earth : and it was so.*

The purpose to be answered by these lights—מְאֹרֹת, properly *where light is, the place of light,* (Ps. lxiv. 16,) φωστῆρες, as rendered by Aquila and the LXX, and *luminaria* by the Vulgate—was, as regarded the earth, threefold :—1. " To divide between the day and between the night," verse 14, or according to another statement, " between the light and between the darkness," verse 18, and thus to continue the separation formed on the first day. 2. To serve as indices of time : signs, seasons, days, and years : וְהָיוּ לְאֹתֹת וּלְמוֹעֲדִים וּלְיָמִים וְשָׁנִים. This last clause of verse 14, has been the subject of a variety of interpretations. Some, as Rosenmüller, Gesenius, De Wette, and Baumgarten, take the first two terms for the grammatical figure *hendiadys,* and render the clause, " they shall serve for signs for the seasons, and for the days and years ;" or, according to another rendering, adopted by Schumann and Maurer, " for signs of the times, as well of the days as of the years :" while others, again, desirous of avoiding the hendiadys, render it variously : " for signs, and indeed for appointed times, and for days and years," (Vater ;) or " for signs, as well for the times as also for the days and years," (Tuch ;) or more simply, according to the English Version given above, which in this adheres to the old translations, which are also followed by Luther, Calvin, Mercer, Piscator, and Delitzsch. So great a diversity of interpretations demands a careful examination of the terms.

The primary signification of אוֹת, is anything *engraved* or *indented,* and then a *mark,* (Gen. iv. 15 ; 2 Kings xx. 8 ;) joined with מוֹפֵת, in the common expression, " signs and won- ders," it means *a portent,* a sign of warning or instruction, (Isa. viii. 18 ; xx. 3.) It is used in very many senses of a secondary kind ; but it is in one or other of the significations now assigned to it that it is evidently used in the present passage. The heavenly bodies have served as *marks* to tra- vellers and voyagers, and particularly in ancient times, before the discovery of the mariner's compass, (see Acts xxvii. 20.) But they have chiefly served as *marks* or *signs* of important changes and occurrences in the kingdom of Providence. A star conducted the wise men to the cradle of the infant Savi- our ; and the sun, moon, and stars shall by signs presage the second advent of the Son of Man : " There shall be signs in the sun, and in the moon, and in the stars ; and upon the earth distress of nations, with perplexity ; the sea and the waves roaring," (Luke xxi. 25.) Farther, the heavenly bodies shall serve for regulating *the fixed, set times,* (מוֹעֲדִים, from יָעַד, *to indicate, to define,* or *fix,*) periods of longer or shorter duration, and of which the causes and limits are such as are not entirely dependent on the planetary motions as are the day and the year, but on these, in connexion with other con- ditions, relations, and occurrences. Thus the word is used of seed-time and harvest, the time or period of pregnancy and birth, the time of the migration of birds, and of the Hebrew fasts and festivals, &c. Thus, " He appointed the moon for *seasons;* the sun knoweth his going down," (Psalm civ. 19.) It was by the moon, in particular, that the time of the passover and other feasts was fixed. The relation of the heavenly bodies to *days* and *years* is simple, and needs no farther explication. To the various relations which the heavens sustain to the earth, as regulating the affairs of man, and influencing the seasons and vicissitudes around him, reference is made in the question proposed by the Almighty to Job: " Knowest thou the ordinances of heaven ? canst thou set the dominion thereof in the earth ?" (Job xxxviii. 33.) This dominion, whatever it may be, is as yet but little understood ; and if too much influence was in former times attributed to it, the probability is that too little is ascribed to it now. 3. The third purpose to be served by the celestial luminaries was " to give light upon the earth," and which had previously been supplied by some other arrangement, but of what nature the sacred historian has not thought it necessary to say.

Verse 16. *And God made two great lights ; the greater light to rule the day, and the lesser light to rule the night : the stars also.*—The two great lights are naturally the sun and the moon—the one absolutely great, the other only relatively so ; but both properly called great, considered only with reference to the quantity of light which they furnish to the earth, the only point of view in which they are here considered. God *made* them : the verb is עשה, *made, constituted,* or *appointed.* This by no means necessarily implies that these bodies were created on the present occasion, but only constituted luminaries,—the heavenly lamps, so to speak, previously prepared, were now lighted up. Their creation, in conjunction with the earth, took place " in the beginning," at which period, it may be also presumed, all the planetary motions began. But these revolutions, previous to the fourth day, though performed about a common centre, as at present, could not be properly said to be about a sun ; for as yet the great central body had not been made the storehouse of light for its dependent system. It may be also supposed that, like the earth itself, the sidereal and planetary bodies were in the interval undergoing a preparation for the various offices they were designed to serve, in the great economy of nature, and that it was only on the fourth day of creation they were fitted for acting as depositories or dispensers of light. The supposition of a progressive preparation, by consolidation or otherwise, of the cosmical bodies which people the immensity of space, is in strict accordance with astronomical conclusions, apart and independently of the Nebular hypothesis; and this again confers, at least, a great degree of probability on the other suppositions advanced, whether light be conceived of as centred in the body of the sun, or resident only in its atmosphere. One thing, however, science clearly demonstrates, that lighting and heating by a central sun have no necessary connexion with the system, and may be something superinduced on the original constitution and gravitating arrangements of the universe.[1]

But, passing over discussions of this kind, nothing shews more clearly the nature and design of this record of creation than the manner in which mention is made of the stars. The innumerable hosts marshalled in the sky, scattered over the immensity of space, nearly all of which, on the shewing of astronomers, are suns, and the centres of systems, and in comparison to which the earth is in magnitude but as a speck, are summarily disposed of by the remark, " and stars," as if the sole end of their creation had been to gladden the eye of man by their nocturnal sparkling—a proof, at once, exclaims the sceptic, of the erroneous and contracted views of the writer. This might be true had his object been to produce a treatise or dissertation on astronomy; but keeping in view the professed aim of the narration, there is not the smallest room for any such insinuation.

Verse 17. *And God set them in the firmament of the heaven, to give light upon the earth.*—It is solely on account of the relation these heavenly bodies bear to the earth, and of the service they discharge to it, that notice is here taken of them. God *set* or *placed* these glorious orbs *in the sky*—the language being according to the appearance presented. The same term that expresses this arrangement is used in Psalm viii. 1 : " Who hast *set* thy glory above the heavens," where God is said to have clothed or crowned the heavens with his glory, in that He has set in them the sun, moon, and stars, as proofs of his almighty power and greatness. The place assigned to them, " the firmament of heaven," compared with verse 7, shews how indefinitely these expressions are used in Scripture.

---

[1] Whewell, Bridgewater Treatise, p. 146.

Verses 18, 19. *And to rule over the day and over the night, and to divide the light from the darkness : and God saw that it was good. It was evening, it was morning, the fourth day.*— The accomplishment of the work of the fourth day is described more in detail, and with greater deviation from the narrative of the Divine purpose regarding it, than is the case with any of the other days. Special notice is taken of the office to be discharged by these luminaries in *ruling* the day and night respectively, and in separating the light from the darkness. This leads Delitzsch to observe : " The separation of light from darkness is the great end of the whole work of the six days ; and the history of every creature, and all the mystery of the stars, is involved in this, that they serve to divide the light from the darkness. God is *Elohim of hosts :* the stars are his hosts that he leads to battle against darkness. The stars are involved in the quarrel that is to be decided on the earth in humanity. Eternity will manifest what is meant by the stars being called lights." But however this may be, or whether there be any mystery at all in the matter, the Divine approbation seals the work of the fourth day ; and so permanent and regular have these ordinances and arrangements been ever since the Creator gave to them their constitution and commission, that they are appealed to by himself as illustrations of the stability of the covenant He has entered into with His people. " Thus saith the Lord, who giveth the sun for a light by day, and the ordinances of the moon and of the stars for a light by night, who divideth the sea when the waves thereof roar ; The Lord of hosts is his name : If those ordinances depart from before me, saith the Lord, then the seed of Israel also shall cease from being a nation before me for ever." And again : " Thus saith the Lord, If ye can break my covenant of the day, and my covenant of the night, and that there should not be day and night in their season ; then may also my covenant be broken with David my servant, that he should not have a son to reign upon his throne ; and with the Levites the priests, my ministers." (Jer. xxxi. 35, 36 ; xxxiii. 20, 21.)

The view taken of the work of the fourth day, which considers it as consisting in the concentration in the heavenly orbs of the light created on the first day, is far more agreeable to the text and the whole tenor of the narrative, than that which conceives of it as the clearing of the atmosphere and rolling away the clouds that prevented the heavenly bodies from being seen. Science, as already remarked, clearly demonstrates that there is no necessary connexion between light and the chief source whence it now emanates, contrary to what the present order of things would naturally lead a casual observer to conclude. Now the very fact that Moses mentions the creation of light so long before he refers to the sun, so far from being a proof of ignorance, or of contradiction in his narrative, as is frequently alleged, is evidence rather of his being guided by an influence far superior to his own reasoning or observation.

But while scientific investigation has demonstrated that there is no necessary connexion between light and the sun, and that light is the same from whatever source it issues, whether from the glow-worm in the hedge, or from the remotest nebula in the heavens, the most careful analysis and research have failed to penetrate the mystery in which its nature is shrouded. " We know much of the mysterious influences of this great agent, but we know nothing of the principle itself. The solar beam has been tortured through prismatic glasses and natural crystals; every chemical agent has been tried upon it, every electrical force in the most excited state brought to bear upon its operations, with a view to the discovery of the most refined of earthly agencies; but it has passed through every trial without revealing its secrets, and even the effects which it produces in its path are unexplained problems, still to tax the intellect of man."[1] But it may be interesting to observe, that an examination of the visual organs of the earliest animal remains, proves that light, as far as it can thus be traced back in time, was of the same nature and properties as that which is now shed down upon the earth. The eye of the fossil trilobite shows that the mutual relations of light to the eye, and of the eye to light, were the same at the period when these crustaceans inhabited the primeval seas, as at this moment; that the atmosphere did not differ materially from its present condition, and that the waters must have been pure and transparent enough to allow the passage of light.

[1] Hunt, The Poetry of Science, Lond. 1854, p. 164.

It is to be farther noticed, that it was in the period denominated the fourth day that the *seasons* originated, which are
so intimately connected with the present constitution of the
earth, and particularly as regards vegetable and animal existence. An examination of the earliest history of the earth
recorded in the fossiliferous strata, shows that at that primeval
period the earth's temperature must have been much higher
and more uniform than at present ; that tropical vegetation,
and consequently tropical heat, prevailed within what are now
the temperate and even the arctic zones. It is not at all
improbable that mighty changes may in this respect have been
introduced through the arrangement of the heavenly bodies on
the fourth day. That this high and uniform temperature
reached down to a period when the earth was tenanted by
living creatures, and consequently, beyond the fourth day of
Genesis, does not offer any valid objection to this supposition,
will appear, so soon as it is considered that the solar arrangement only commenced with the fourth day, and that it may
have required for its full adjustment and the complete development of its effects, not merely that but the succeeding period.
This is not without countenance from the observed motions of
particular bodies belonging to the solar system—the comets,
variations in whose motions and periods of revolution, prove that
heavenly bodies revolving round the same sun as our earth, do
not necessarily come into existence stamped at once with the laws
by which they are to be governed throughout all time to come.

But the character and constitution of the seasons are intimately connected with, and indeed dependent, in a measure,
on the length of the day and of the year—measures of time
introduced, we are expressly told, at the same time with the
appointment of the seasons. The day, it is well known, is one
revolution of the earth upon its axis, and the year is the time
employed by the same planet in performing its revolution
round the sun, both periods being determined from the observation of the heavenly bodies. It must accordingly be
evident that before these bodies came into view, the measures
of time denoted by days and years could not have existed ;
and hence that when the term *day* had been previously employed to designate a period of *light*, it must have been
entirely indefinite as to its duration.

An observation may be added on Laplace's objection to the view which ascribes to the Creator the purpose of having given the moon to the earth to afford light during the night. This, he remarks, cannot have been so intended, for we are often deprived at the same time of the light of the sun and the moon; and he points out how the moon might have been placed so as to be always *full*. On this Whewell observes,— " That the light of the moon affords, *to a certain extent,* a supplement to the light of the sun, will hardly be denied. If we take man in a condition in which he uses artificial light scantily only, or not at all, there can be no doubt that the moonlight nights are for him a very important addition to the time of day-light. And as a small proportion only of the whole number of nights are without some portion of moonlight, the fact that sometimes both luminaries are invisible very little diminishes the value of this advantage. Why we have not more moonlight, either in duration or in quantity, is an inquiry which a philosopher could hardly be tempted to enter upon, by any success which has attended previous speculations of a similar nature. Why should not the moon be ten times as large as she is? Why should not the pupil of man's eye be ten times as large as it is, so as to receive more of the light which does arrive? We do not conceive that our inability to answer the latter question prevents our knowing that the eye was made for seeing: nor does our inability to answer the former disturb our persuasion that the moon was made to give light upon the earth."

The same author continues—" Laplace suggests that if the moon had been placed at a certain distance beyond the earth, it would have revolved about the sun in the same time as the earth does, and would have always presented to us a full moon. For this purpose it must have been about four times as far from us as it really is; and would, therefore, other things remaining unchanged, have only been one *sixteenth* as large to the eye as our present full moon. We shall not dwell on the discussion of this suggestion, for the reason just intimated. But we may observe that in such a system as Laplace proposes, it is not yet proved, we believe, that the arrangement would be stable, under the influence of the disturbing forces. And we may add, that such an arrangement, ın which the motion of one body has a *co-ordinate* reference to two others, as the motion of the moon on this hypothesis would have to the sun and the earth, neither motion being subordinate to the other, is contrary to the whole known analogy of cosmical phenomena, and therefore has no claim to our notice as a subject of discussion."[1]

§ 6. *The Fifth Day of Creation*, Gen. i. 20-23.

The course of creation on the fifth day takes an important step in advance. The operations of the preceding days, and especially the work of the fourth, were arrangements of a most stupendous character, indicative of the highest wisdom and power; but with the exception of the vegetable creation—the lowest form of life—all had hitherto been confined to the origination and orderly adjustment of inanimate matter. Until the fifth day, there was no life in the higher sense of the term, and no enjoyment on the earth. The forests, which profusely covered the earth, were not yet enlivened by the hum of insect or the song of bird; no shadow save that of the darkening clouds floated over the woods or fields, no reptile bathed in the shallows, or basked in the sunshine, and no fish sported in the seas or rivers of the primeval earth, before the morning of the fifth day. But behold now, at the creating word, new forms and an entirely new order of beings are ushered in, occupying in the scale of creation, as compared with anything previously summoned into existence, a place higher than the heavens are higher than the earth! What a mystery is life, even in the mollusc, and how it transcends all that concerns magnitudes and motions, whether on the earth or in the sidereal heavens!

It may not be easy strictly to reconcile these statements with some of the appearances presented to the geologist, and the occurrence of animal life in the Palæozoic rocks; but there are various considerations which materially diminish the difficulty. One is the obscurity which still shrouds the first dawning of life, and the improbability that science has yet detected the place of the protozoic group. Another considera-

[1] Whewell, Bridgewater Treatise, pp. 148, 149.

tion, is the continuity which marks all the works and arrangements of nature, not broken off in the abrupt manner which
scientific classification and nomenclature render necessary. It
is thus a general resemblance only that can be expected in the
two records of creation, and it may remain for farther investigation to render it more specific and complete. In the meantime, however, it is enough to observe, that all accessible
evidence concurs in connecting the commencement of animal
life with the sea.

Verse 20. *And God said, Let the waters bring forth abundantly the moving creature that hath life, and let fowl fly above
the earth on the face of the firmament of heaven.*—As already
remarked, the work of the fifth day carries on and completes
that of the second, which consisted in the partial adjustment
of the waters and the formation of the atmosphere. By the
intervening arrangements and operations, these two elements
were doubtless prepared for the reception of animal life : the
temperature of the waters was sufficiently lowered, probably
by the cosmical order introduced on the fourth day, and the
atmosphere was sufficiently deprived of its superabundance of
carbon, by the profuse vegetation created on the third day, as
to render it respirable and capable of supporting life in the
animal tribes about to be ushered into existence. The priority
of the vegetable to the animal creation was undoubtedly a
necessity as regards the supply of food, but also, it is probable,
no less essential in this other point of view ; for, so far as can
be judged of the atmosphere of the early world, its condition
was such as unfitted it for animals possessed of true lungs.
Plants may be considered the great laboratories of nature, which
convert the inorganic materials of the air and the soil into
nourishment for the animal creation, and keep up the proper
balance of the atmosphere, and render it fit for the processes
of respiration. On this nice adjustment, it may be satisfactory
to quote the remarks of a distinguished chemist :—" Since we
know that animals consume oxygen, replacing it by carbonic
acid, that plants consume carbonic acid, replacing it by oxygen,
and that carbonic acid contains its own volume of oxygen, we
see that there is a balance between animal and vegetable life,
which are mutually dependent, each restoring to the air what
the other has removed, and consuming what the other has

produced, and thus preserving constant the composition of the air; each while living in it rendering it fit for the life of the other. · Should any cause suddenly increase the amount of one of them—and some causes, such as volcanic action, and the combustion of fuel in manufactures, &c., do tend to increase that of carbonic acid—the vegetable kingdom instantly seizes on it more luxuriantly, purifies the air, and at the same time produces more food for animals, so that an increase of the food of plants (carbonic acid) causing an increase of vegetation, is followed by an increase of food for animals and of animal life, and thus the balance is kept up between the animal and vegetable worlds by means of oxygen and carbonic acid, the atmosphere being the scene of action."[1]

And here, it is worthy of notice, as illustrative of the part performed by the plants of the primeval world in preparing for the entrance of animal life, that it was not until the rank and luxurious vegetation of the early eras gradually gave way, never more to be restored in such profusion and preponderancy, that animals appeared in any considerable numbers. An examination of the fossiliferous strata proves that the temperature had so far sunk, or the atmosphere had been so despoiled of its carbon, or other changes had supervened as to give a decided check to the growth of plants, but on the other hand introducing conditions highly favourable to the existence of animals at the period which heard the Creative mandate, יִשְׁרְצוּ הַמַּיִם שֶׁרֶץ נֶפֶשׁ חַיָּה—*Let the waters swarm with swarms—animated* or *breathing beings.*

Animal life thus began in the waters; for "the rapidly multiplying" or "swarming" creatures now summoned into existence are farther characterized and specified as "a breath of life," that is, an animated being—a term applied to any living creature, including man, (Gen. ii. 7.) In the present case it comprehends all the inhabitants of the waters, from the lowest to the highest forms; although it is not to be supposed that such were introduced simultaneously.

The succeeding clause of the verse in which mention is made of birds, or, more correctly, "winged creatures" in general, the next form of life, is ambiguous. It may be rendered, as in the English and many other versions, ancient and modern, "and

[1] Professor Gregory in Encyclopædia Britannica, *Art.* Chemistry, vol. vi. p. 464.

fowl that may fly," thus implying that they were produced out of the waters; or it may with equal propriety be rendered, " let fowl fly," the reference not being to the element from which they were taken, but to that in which they were destined to move. This translation is, however, preferable, as it removes any contradiction between the statement here made and the intimation in Gen. ii. 19, that the birds were formed from the ground. The place of the bird's flight, עַל־הָאָרֶץ עַל־פְּנֵי · רְקִיעַ הַשָּׁמַיִם, in the English version, " above the earth in the open firmament of heaven," has been variously understood. The only difficulty is as to the precise idea expressed in the words *upon the face*, or *upon the surface*, of the expanse. This, according to Von Bohlen, Baumgarten, and others, means *above* the firmament; because, as it is said of the clouds, that they are above the firmament, so it may be said of the birds. Had the construction simply been עַל־רְקִיעַ, this view would have been correct, for certainly the proper meaning of the Hebrew preposition here used is *over* or *above*, as in the first clause of the same sentence, *above the earth ;* but the sense is modified by the introduction of the term *surface*, and we have to consider what is meant by the *surface* of the firmament. Tuch and Delitzsch take this to be the *concave* surface of the azure vault, or, optically considered, the side turned towards the earth; and there can be little difficulty in adopting this as the only correct view, conformable to popular ideas and the apprehension of mankind.

The history farther goes on to narrate how, at the word of Omnipotence, this purpose was fulfilled; and how the waters and the air were, in due course, tenanted with living creatures. Of the inhabitants of the water, special mention is made of one class, called in the English version " great whales," but which in the original signifies merely " the long-extended creatures."

Verse 21. *And God created great whales, and every living creature that moveth, which the waters brought forth abundantly, after their kind, and every winged fowl after its kind : and God saw that it was good.*—When the sacred writer describes the first act which results in *life*, he has recourse to the verb *created*, which had not been employed since mention was made of the origination of the universe in the beginning. It is now used in reference to the origin of the first living beings, as if to distinguish, in a marked and peculiar manner, this act from the operations which immediately preceded, which had respect only to the adjustment of inanimate matter. The same term is employed in the account of the formation of man, (verse 27.) In the creative command addressed to the waters, all the inhabitants of this element were spoken of collectively: here, however, two classes are particularly speci-fied,—" the great tinninim," and " the living creature that *creeps*," the " remes." Although the rendering of the English version here and in verse 20 is the same, *moving* or *moveth*, the Hebrew of the two passages is different, neither of which is aptly expressed by the term in question. The word impro-perly rendered *whales* is used of the serpent, (Exod. vii. 9, 10, 12; Deut. xxxii. 33; Psalm xci. 13;) of the crocodile, the symbol of Egypt, (Isa. li. 9; Ezek. xxix. 3; Psalm lxxiv. 13;) and of sea-monsters in general, (Job vii. 12; Psalm cxlviii. 7;) but is never specially applied to fishes. According to the ety-mology of the term, it signifies the *long-stretched* or *extended*, being derived from a root *tan*, which, according to Tuch, means, in Sanscrit and Semitic, " to expand" or " extend," and in its purest form appears in Hebrew as תנן. It is remarkably appropriate to the gigantic aquatic and amphibious reptiles which, as geology shews, played so conspicuous a part in the early history of the earth. רָמַשׂ, *to creep, to crawl*, (Gen. vii. 21,) especially used of creeping animals, (compare Gen. ix. 2;) hence רֶמֶשׂ הָאֲדָמָה, (verse 25;) chap. vii. 14, " creepers of the ground," generally thus used to denote the smaller kinds of land animals; but here, as also in Psalm lxix. 35, applied to the smaller aquatic tribes. These generic terms include many orders and species, created each after *its kind*, and forming the countless dwellers of the deep, concerning which the psalmist observes: " O Lord, how manifold are thy works! in wisdom hast thou made them all: the earth is full of thy riches. So is this great and wide sea, wherein are *things creeping* innumerable, both small and great beasts." (Psalm civ. 24, 25.)

In close connexion with the dwellers of the deep, mention is made of the winged creatures, כָּל־עוֹף כָּנָף לְמִינֵהוּ, *every winged fowl*, or more literally, *every flier of wing after its kind*, (omne volatile, *Vulg.,*) as brought into existence on the fifth day. This designation is undoubtedly properly used of birds, (Psalm lxxviii. 27,) but is probably here used in a wider sense, and may include flying insects, (Delitzsch,) but it is doubtful whether it can be made to embrace the winged reptiles of the geologist. The productions of this day also approve themselves as "good" to the eye of Omniscience.

But, as if farther to express the Divine complacency, and assign a special place and purpose to life even in these its lowest manifestations, and particularly to stamp a permanency on the stream which now began to flow from "the Fountain of Life," (Psalm xxxvi. 9,) and which was destined to deepen and expand as the work of creation proceeded, Heaven's *enriching blessing* (Prov. x. 22) is pronounced on these, the first of living creatures. Verse 22. *And God blessed them, saying, Be fruitful, and multiply, and fill the waters in the seas, and let fowl multiply in the earth.*

The first blessing pronounced on earth had respect to the continuance of the living tribes from generation to generation, and to their increase, so as to fill the residences respectively assigned to them. The paronomastic combination, פְּרוּ וּרְבוּ, *be fruitful and multiply,* became a regular formula of blessing; compare Gen. xxxv. 11, with xxiv. 60, xlviii. 4. פָּרָה, properly *to sprout, to bring forth fruit,* is here used of animal fruitfulness, as in ᵀᵒᵈ. i. 7, xxiii. 30, and so פְּרִי, *fruit,* (Psalm xxi. 11,) or, ᵣ re fully, פְּרִי בֶּטֶן, *the fruit of the womb,* (Gen. xxx. 2.) How effectual this blessing proved is seen in the almost boundless increase of animated beings with which every portion of the globe is peopled—the air, the waters, and the dry land, and their continued preservation amid many violent terrestrial changes. It is one of the best established of the deductions of the geologist, that from the period when life first began on our planet, it has been maintained without interruption to the present hour—no epoch, long or short, can be pointed to as destitute of the memorials of animal life since it first awoke in the waters. Individuals perished in rapid succession; and myriads simultaneously ceased to exist, destroyed by extraordinary convulsions of nature—even families and entire species passed away; but other families and forms of life took the place of the perished, and so the living chain advanced ; for as link after link fell away at the one extremity, new links were successively added to the other, until the present order of creation was reached. The geologist farther shews, from the quantity of the remains imbedded in their rocky sepulchres, how very prolific life was in the freshness of its youth. The mountain limestone, for instance, a thousand feet in thickness, and extending for many miles, consists of nothing else than the remains of coralline and testaceous forms compressed into hard masses. So also in regard to other rocks, which are found to be little else than a conglomerate of animal remains. But not only these lower orders, vertebrate forms of life also flourished profusely in the ancient seas, as is fully attested by the immense platforms of death presented by the rocks of various localities.[1] What is all this, it may be asked —though a voice from the dead, from the grave of creation— but an unimpeachable witness to the potency of the Divine blessing, " Be fruitful, and multiply," which was spoken at the beginning ?

This era of creation in due time came to a close, but only to be succeeded by another. It was again " evening ;" but much of the work of creation remained unaccomplished, and so on the evening there followed a " morning," ushering in a new day of creative energy. Verse 23. *It was evening, it was morning, the fifth day.*

The period of creation which had thus closed, is what the geologist distinctively calls the *age of reptiles ;* and it is instructive to observe how remarkable is the agreement between the description of the productions of the fifth day and the geology of the great Saurian era. The reptiles of the sea, and the reptiles of the land, numerous and gigantic as they then existed, could not be described by any term more appropriate than that employed by Moses in his account of the animals of that period—*the great tinninim,* which, as already remarked, is very unaptly rendered *great whales.* Could any term be more suitable than *long-stretched* to characterize the Ichthyosaur which geologists tell us was thirty feet long, having the head of a crocodile, the body of a fish, and the general conformation of a lizard ; or the Plesiosaur, possessed of a long neck like the

---

[1] See Miller, The Old Red Sandstone, p. 276. Edin. 1850.

body of a serpent; or the gigantic Iguanodon, a lizard reckoned to have been sixty feet long?

The geologist farther shews, that while this period of creation was distinguished by its huge creeping things—winged and wingless reptiles, and its enormous monsters of the deep, there are also indications of the presence of gigantic birds by the impressions of their footprints on the rocks, which then, of course, existed as mud. " In North America, ancient indications of the existence of the feathered tribes have been detected; the fossil footmarks of a great variety of species, of various sizes, some larger than the ostrich, others smaller than the plover, having been observed. These bipeds have left marks of their footsteps on strata of an age decidedly intermediate between the lias and the coal." Thus, in the early ages under consideration, " there were terrestrial, winged, and aquatic reptiles. There were iguanodons walking on the land, pterodactyles winging their way through the air, monitors and crocodiles in the rivers, and ichthyosaurs and plesiosaurs in the ocean."[1] At the same time, the feathered tribes skimmed along the sky, or waded in the marshes and the shallows of lakes and seas. The contemporaneous, or nearly contemporaneous, creation of the inhabitants of the ocean and the air, and also the early date of their origin as disclosed by geology, are facts in remarkable keeping with the Mosaic account of the works of the fifth day; and it is questionable if any of our geologists, with all the facts of the case before him, as brought to light by his favourite science, could in so brief a compass furnish so full and accurate a description as that of Moses, written long before geology began its wonderful explorations, or was even dreamed of as a science.

§ 7. *The Sixth Day of Creation*, Gen. i. 24-31.

The course of creation is still onward and upward. Higher and nobler forms of life had already succeeded lower organisms, as witnessed in the advance from the plant to even the lowest types of animal life and the most limited enjoyment in beings appropriately termed the " swarming creatures," that have

[1] Lyell, Principles of Geology, pp. 135, 136.

life, whose introduction took place at the dawn of the fifth day, and from these onwards to the great sea-monsters and reptiles, and again to the feathered tribes. But although the seas, the rivers, and the skies were thus profusely peopled with their respective inhabitants, one very large and important portion of creation was still destitute of its proper denizens,— and that a portion of the earth specially fitted for sustaining life in its highest form. The dry land, which so early as the third day had been wrested from the deep, and then arrayed in the most beautiful of vegetable robes, was still destitute of the animals which are peculiarly its own. This want, however, the creation of the sixth day entirely obviates. At this stage of the great work, accordingly, was introduced the innumerable variety of land animals,—the mammiferous quadrupeds. But, above all, this day witnessed the birth of man—a being differing from all the preceding creations, not merely in degree but in kind—a being possessed of properties exclusively his own, distinguished not only as the highest type of animal life, but as cast in a mould entirely different from that of any other creature. With the introduction of man upon the earth the mighty works of creation came to a close, as if to shew that in him the apex of the pyramid had been reached, and nature had received her crown.

The works of the sixth, or last day of creation, are then the introduction of the animals which people the dry land, according to their various classes and kinds, (verses 24, 25 ;) and the creation of man, in regard to whose formation in the image of God, the Creator is represented as deliberating or consulting, (verses 26-28.) Next follows a notice of a grant of food to man and the lower animals, (verse 30 ;) with the Creator's complacency, " very good," on a review of the whole operations and arrangements now concluded, (verse 31.)

Verses 24, 25. *And God said, Let the earth bring forth the living creature after its kind, and cattle after their kind, and creeping thing, and beast of the earth after its kind : and it was so. And God made the beast of the earth after its kind, and cattle after their kind, and everything that creepeth upon the earth after its kind : and God saw that it was good.*—The work of the sixth day, as already noticed, forms a parallel with, while at the same time a continuation of, that of the third day. Accordingly, the words with which verse 24 opens, " Let the earth bring forth," חּוֹצֵא הָאָרֶץ, correspond to וַתּוֹצֵא הָאָרֶץ, verse 12, where the production of the plants is described. But farther, in this account of the animal creation it is not to be overlooked, that in every case the most express mention is made of the *species* or kind; for with this funda-mental law of existence the order of increase is so connected as to constitute the successive generations a strict copy of the first exemplar, as is held to be the case by the ablest naturalists. " The original creation of distinct and predetermined species," says an eminent authority, " is the rational and well-founded belief of all who have studied the subject with attention, un-biassed by any prejudice in favour of imaginative views, which have no foundation in the facts of nature. . . . Omnipotence, the first, the greatest, and indeed the only truly creative power, formed the species of animals; and the influence of man and of physical agents has produced the varieties. But it is only superficial characters which either the one or the other of these ulterior causes has the power of modifying. The basis of organization, or real specific mould, remains unalterable, though a thousand circumstances constantly tend to produce variations in the external forms."[1]   Again, it is to be re-marked, that although the earth and the waters were com-manded *to bring forth* respectively the creatures which should inhabit them, yet, in describing the actual execution of the work, it is not said that the earth created, or the waters created, their several tenants, but that *God created* them, one and all. No creative power was in any degree delegated to the insensate elements. Omnipotence alone was adequate to the result, whether that was man or the minutest infusoria, and by Omnipotence only was it effected.

It thus appears that Scripture knows nothing of the trans-mutation of species, equivocal generation, or creation by natural laws—terms much insisted on at the present day. In every instance where a new order of beings is said to be introduced, Scripture invariably ascribes its production to a direct action or interposition of the Creator and Preserver of all, and in this it commends itself to the most enlightened reason and the

[1] Encyclopædia Britannica, Eighth Edition, *Art.* Animal Kingdom, vol. iii. pp. 173, 174.

soundest philosophy. If the object of some modern speculations be to remove to the greatest possible distance the Creator
of the universe, and consign him to an Epicurean indifferentism
and repose, the express purpose of Scripture, on the contrary,
is to bring him near to his creatures, and to shew the interest
which he continues to cherish towards the works of his hands.
From the contrast thus presented, nothing can be plainer than
the fact, that the God of the Bible is an infinitely more worthy
and loving Being than the First Great Cause in all such systems of philosophy.

The " living creature," (see on verse 20,) which is here the
common name of all land animals, comprehends, in accordance
with the usual Hebrew division, three classes :—(1.) בְּהֵמָה ;
(2.) רֶמֶשׂ ; (3.) חַיְתוֹ־אֶרֶץ. The *first* is the *Behemah*, a term which
literally signifies " the *dumb* animal," and denotes the larger
quadrupeds, and more commonly the domestic animals of the
flocks and herds, (Gen. xlvii. 18 ;) and also the beasts of
burden, (Gen. xxxiv. 23 ; xxxvi. 6.) Sometimes, however, the
word is applied to the wild animals ; but this is only in poetry,
and where it is followed for the most part by the expressions,
" the earth," (Isa. xviii. 6 ;) " the field," (1 Sam. xvii. 44 ;) or
" the wood," (Mic. v. 7,) denoting their peculiar localities or
places of abode. The *second* class is the *Remes*, which comprehends here, according to its usual signification, the smaller
animals of the dry land, particularly such as *creep* or *crawl*,
(Deut. iv. 8 ; Hos. ii. 18.) The third class is the *Chayah*, or
more definitely with the adjunct *of the earth* as here, or *of the
field*, (Gen. ii. 19,) denoting such animals as live at large—the
wild beasts in contradistinction to the tame. The term is frequently used of the beasts of prey, (1 Sam. xvii. 46 ; Ezek.
xxix. 5, xxxiv. 28 ; Psalm lxxix. 2 ;) here, however, it is more
comprehensive, from the relation which it bears to *Behemah*.
The termination of the *status constructus* ı in חַיְתוֹ־אֶרֶץ, is an
old and rare form : in prose preserved only in this word ;
but from *this passage* it is, according to Ewald,[1] repeated
in the same word in Psalm l. 10 ; civ. 11, 20 ; Zeph. ii. 14 ;
Isa. lvi. 9.

That these zoological divisions are merely a popular classification, laying no claims to scientific accuracy or precision, it

---

[1] *Lehrbuch der Hebräischen Sprache.* Leip. 1844, sect. 211 *b*.

is scarcely necessary to remark ; nevertheless, they sufficiently determine the great characteristics of the terrestrial fauna. On the subject of classification, however, it may be observed, as a very remarkable fact, that the arrangement of the animal system which, after much error and confusion, naturalists have on scientific principles been led to adopt, as the right and natural one, was that according to which, as taught in the Mosaic narrative, creation proceeded at the first. " Cuvier decided, that in the vertebral division, fishes should be placed at the bottom of the scale, reptiles next in place, birds next, then the irrational mammals, and man at the head of all. And not many years after, it was discovered by the geologists, that the fishes had appeared first in the order of time, then the reptiles, then birds, then the irrational mammals, and finally, as at once the lord of creation, and as, in at least this lower world, its crowning effort, reasoning man, the delegated monarch of the whole."[1]

A *threefold* division or classification, both as regards method and matter, occupies a very important place throughout the narrative of creation. The six days themselves are arranged into two divisions of three and three, distinguished by many things in common, particularly by the fact, that the terminal member of each was occupied with two great works, and con- stituting, as has been shewn, a remarkable parallel. The vegetable kingdom—the production of the third day—is arranged under a threefold division ; the fourth day is occu- pied with the arrangements connected with the heavenly bodies, which are distributed into sun, moon, and stars ; and the fifth day may be also viewed in the same light, seeing that its productions were, (1.) The great monsters of the deep ; (2.) The smaller aquatic animals ; and (3.) The winged tribes. The threefold division of the first work of the sixth day has been already noticed. This arrangement is, at least, more than accidental ; and although it may not be easy to give a satisfactory explanation of the principle on which it proceeds, there is enough to shew that the narrative was formed on a plan,—a consideration fitted to obviate any objections, on the ground that the botanical and zoological subdivisions are not sufficiently numerous and distinct, or that the writer was

[1] Hugh Miller in " Witness," July 14, 1855.

guided solely by the popular but imperfect, and necessarily erroneous views of Nature, which prevailed among the Hebrews as among other ancient nations.

Another consideration which may correct or modify our ideas relative to the order of creation, as announced in this narrative, and particularly of the subdivisions of any one work or day, is the fact, that in verse 25, which describes the creation of the land animals, the order is, " beast of the earth, cattle, and creeping things ;" whereas in the creative command, (verse 24,) the arrangement had been " cattle, and creeping thing, and beast of the earth." Perhaps, however, in cases of this kind, where there is any appearance of diversity in the statements, the actual order of creation is to be settled from the description of the work as accomplished. But whatever may have been the sequence in which the work of the sixth day proceeded previous to the appearance of man, the description furnished by the revealed and written word remarkably harmonizes with the story told by the rocks of what is called the tertiary formation. The geologist, as he enters on this period, is introduced, as it were, into a new world. The huge monsters which distinguished " the age of reptiles" have passed away, and a new order of beings start into life, constituting the van of the present zoology of our planet. The tertiary age—the third and last of the great geological periods—was peculiarly the age of great mammalian quadrupeds, including the " beasts of the earth and the behemah." The mammiferous remains preserved in various localities, particularly in the eocene formations of the Paris basin, shew that at this period the earth was the theatre of an extensive creation of the highest forms of animal life, and at first chiefly of a class now represented by the tapir of South America. Another group of the Paris fossils exhibits a slight approach to the deer tribe. In the higher strata only of this period occur the first abundant traces of what is properly termed " cattle." This era also witnessed the introduction of a new variety of " creeping thing." No traces of the true serpent occur in the secondary formation, but the tertiary period presents them of the size of the boa. There was also, at this period, abundance of marine mammalia, seals, dolphins, and whales. But amid all these new creations, there is as yet no trace of man or of his works.

And the reason is obvious ; for of this latest creation he is the very last.

> " Neu regio foret ulla suis animantibus orba,
> Astra tenent cœleste solum formæque deorum,
> Cesserunt nitidis habitandæ piscibus undæ,
> Terra feras cepit, volucres agitabilis aër.
> Sanctius his animal mentisque capacius altæ
> Deerat adhuc, et quod dominari in cetera posset.
> Natus homo est."[1]

Within the range of human science, there is not a single fact which, in reality, or even in appearance, opposes the testimony of Scripture, which is that also of tradition, relative to man's place in the order of creation.   On the contrary, geologists, who of all others are most directly led to the consideration of such subjects, and whose pursuits were for a long time looked upon as unfavourable to the character of the Mosaic history of creation, have, it may be said, unanimously come to the conclusion, that the formation of man was the last of the great operations connected with the preparation and peopling of the earth ; and, moreover, that it is an event of comparatively recent date.   On this point, it may be observed, that the objectors to the Mosaic chronology having been thus dislodged from the strong position which, for a while, geology promised to furnish them, are now content to resort to the more doubtful and indefinite testimonies contained in the Indian and Chinese claims of their respective nations, to an antiquity, in comparison to which, the duration of the human race, as attested by all reliable evidence, sinks into insignificance.

On the sixth and last day of creation, man is solemnly introduced into his future dwelling-place, after all needful preparation and provision has been made by the beneficent Creator for the comforts as well as the necessities of this the highest and noblest denizen of earth.   Verse 26. *And God said, Let us make man in our image, after our likeness ; and let them have dominion over the fish of the sea, and over the fowl of the air, and over the cattle, and over all the earth, and over every creeping thing that creepeth upon the earth.*

Man's creation is distinguished not merely by the place

---

[1] Ovid, Metam., lib. i. 72.

which it occupies as the last of the great series of creative acts, but also, and particularly, by the Divine counsel or deliberation by which it was preceded, וַיֹּאמֶר אֱלֹהִים נַעֲשֶׂה אָדָם בְּצַלְמֵנוּ כִּדְמוּתֵנוּ. There is in this a solemn and significant pause in the onward and uniform flow of the narrative of the sequences of cause and effect. It is no longer the usual, " Let there be," or, " Let the waters or the earth bring forth," but a solemn act of deliberation, " Let us make,"—an expression, however, not implying any doubt or difficulty on the part of the Creator, (Isa. xl. 13, 14,) but simply intimating, in the most forcible terms, the distinguished character of the creature now about to be introduced.

It is, in the first place, of importance to consider to whom this language is addressed by the Divine speaker. Phraseology somewhat similar occurs in one or two other instances. Thus, in Gen. iii. 22, " Jehovah-Elohim said, Behold the man has become as *one of us.*" Chap. xi. 7, " Come, *we will go down*, and there *we will confound* their language." And Isa. vi. 8, " And I heard the voice of the Lord, saying, Whom shall I send, and who shall go for *us ?*" Various explanations have been offered of this usage apparently so opposed to the simple monotheistic views of the Hebrews ; but, for the most part, they deserve little or no consideration. This is particularly the case with regard to the notions of some of the Jewish Rabbis, who consider that the language of the Creator at the formation of man was addressed to the earth or to the angels, (Targ. Jonath. Jarchi,) a view which, strange to say, commends itself to Delitzsch. The same remark applies to the supposition of several German Rationalists, that these plural forms are the remains of a pre-Mosaic polytheism, (Vogel, Herder.) Another and more plausible explanation is by what many Hebrew grammarians call a " Pluralis Majestaticus," which means that God here uses the language common and appropriate to a sovereign prince. This view, put forth by Aben Ezra and other Jewish writers, has found much acceptance with British Unitarians, as Priestley and others. It is adopted by Schumann, and by Knobel, the most recent Rationalistic commentator on Genesis, who refers for illustration of this usage to Ezra iv. 18 ; 1 Macc. x. 19 ; xi. 31 ; xv. 9. But Hitzig, another writer of the same school, had previously denied the existence of such an idiom among the orientals, ancient or modern, and Dr. Pye Smith perhaps more correctly remarks, that " we have no reason to think that this style had been brought into use in the days of Moses, nor till many ages afterwards, when the simplicity of earlier times gave way to the degeneracy and arrogance of princes."[1] This is fully corroborated by the fact that Knobel could produce no earlier instance of this style than from the times of Ezra. But all difficulty will at once vanish by merely conceding that these expressions relate to a plurality of persons in the Godhead—a doctrine fully revealed in the New Testament, but no less certainly taught in the Old. In no other way can a satisfactory explanation be given of these and other remarkable peculiarities of language in respect to the acts and attributes of God occurring in the Hebrew Scriptures. It is not meant to affirm that the plural names and expressions found in the earlier portions of Scripture are of themselves sufficient evidence of the doctrine of the Trinity, but only lay a foundation for it. Seeing, however, that the doctrine is afterwards explicitly taught, it is perfectly legitimate to explain the early usage in conformity with it.

The being whose creation was thus formally and solemnly gone about is *man*, in Hebrew *Adam*—a term employed as the generic name of the human race, and also, in certain circumstances, as the proper name of the first individual. Here it is used in reference to the race, as is evident from the whole context, but especially the absence of the *article*, thus differing from all the instances, nineteen in number, in the second and third chapters, where it signifies *the man*, the first male human being. As to the etymology of the term nothing certain has been determined among the many conjectures on the subject. The common derivation, that of Kimchi, Rosenmüller, and others, is from אֲדָמָה, *the ground*, so that אָדָם means *the earthy*, referring to man's origin. This is objected to as a reversing of etymological rules, inasmuch as it derives the simple from the more complex. Others, as Gesenius, Tuch, Hupfeld, following Josephus, derive both terms, אָדָם and אֲדָמָה, from a root אָדַם, *to be red*, referring to the colour of the first man, as formed of *red* earth. But it is hardly conceivable that a matter so trivial as the colour of man's body, admitting it to be as thus supposed,

[1] Scripture Testimony to the Messiah, vol. i. p. 325. Lond. 1847.

should be chosen as his distinguishing characteristic rather than some quality not common to him with the lower animals. Other etymologies have been proposed by Ludolph from the Ethiopic, and by Sir W. Jones from the Sanscrit, but as they have not obtained much acceptance, they need not be farther specified. The most recent conjecture is that of Meier and Fürst, who propose a root *Adam* not occurring in Hebrew, but in Arabic signifying *to bring together, to hold together*, to bind or connect firmly, and from which has been derived a large class of words, in all of which the primary idea is something, the parts of which are closely connected, materially or socially.[1] But, amid so much uncertainty, it is next to impossible to arrive at any sure or satisfactory conclusions. See farther on chap. ii. 7.

The Creator's deliberation intimated that some distinguishing dignity was intended for man ; what this was the words which immediately followed fully determine : " Let us make man *in our image, after our likeness.*" This will be more fully considered in the sequel. Let it suffice at present to remark that it implied that man should be distinguished from all other creatures of the earth by his possession of *personality*. He is made the revelation and representative of the living and true God. That which in the dispensation of grace has been realized by the Son of God—the second Adam, was in part assigned to man at the creation. Farther, in virtue of this dignified office, he is invested with dominion over the creation, and the living beings in the various elements. To this original constitution the Psalmist refers : " What is man, that thou art mindful of him ? and the son of man, that thou visitest him ? For thou hast made him a little lower than the angels, (or rather, *thou makest him to want little of a Divine standing,*) and hast crowned him with glory and honour. Thou madest him to have dominion over the works of thy hands ; thou hast put all things under his feet : all sheep and oxen, yea, and the beasts of the field, the fowl of the air, and the fish of the sea, and whatsover passeth through the paths of the seas," (Ps.

---

[1] Meier, Hebräisches Wurzelwörterbuch, Mannheim, 1845, p. 359. See also Fürst, Hebräisches u. Chaldäisches Handwörterbuch, p. 23. Leipzig, 1851. This etymology is adopted by Hofmann, *Art.* Adam, in Herzog's Real-Encyklopädie, vol. i. p. 116. Stuttgart, 1853.

viii. 4-8.)   On this Hengstenberg remarks : " That what is here ascribed to man belongs to him still in a certain degree even since the fall, as is implied in the frequent use of the *future* denoting the *present*, is shown, not only by Gen. ix. 2, but also by daily experience. No creature is so strong, so savage, so alert, but that man, though relatively one of the weakest creatures, in process of time becomes its master ; compare James iii. 7. Nevertheless there is a vast difference in this respect between *before* and *since* the Fall. Before that event, the obedience of all creatures towards the appointed vicegerent of God, was a spontaneous one : after it, his subjects revolted against *him*, as he against *his* Lord.   He must maintain against them, as against the resisting earth, a hard conflict, must on all hands employ art and cunning, and though, on the whole, he remains conqueror in the warfare, yet, in particulars, he has to suffer many defeats."

The purpose entertained by the Creator concerning man is duly accomplished.   Verse 27, *So God created man in his own image, in the image of God created he him : male and female created he them.*—The style of this verse has often been remarked as very peculiar.   Ewald and Delitzsch take it to be expressive of joyful emotion.   The former observes : " The language moves on unusually strong in joyful tremor, as if the thought could not be expressed with sufficient vivacity." " The Lord," says the Psalmist, " shall rejoice in his works ;" and it may well be conceived that at the creation of man, there was some of that satisfaction which attended the advent of the Second Adam—an occasion as to which the Apostle observes : " When he bringeth in the first-begotten into the world, he saith, And let all the angels of God worship him," (Heb. i. 6.)

Another peculiarity in the account of man's creation is the mention made of the difference of sexes, " male and female created he them."   This fact was equally true in the case of the other creatures, but it is only here it is specially noticed—another proof of the dignity of man, and of the Creator's interest in him.   But more particularly is it an intimation, as Luther remarks, that " the woman was also created by God, and made a partaker of the Divine image, and of dominion over all."   And he adds, " We should observe from this expression that the woman should not be excluded from any honour of human nature, although she is a weaker vessel than the man."

It is to be noticed that the account of man's creation in this chapter has regard to the race and not to the first individual, or the first human pair. That forms the principal subject of the second chapter, where it is described in detail. Here, however, it is simply the origination of the race as such that is announced : " Let us make *man* . . . . and *let them* have dominion," followed by a specification of *sexual* differences, but not of the number of individuals or pairs then created. It is from inattention to this that some fancy they discover contradictions in the account of man's creation in the two chapters, and particularly as to the interval which is stated in the second chapter to have elapsed between the creation of (in that case, *the man*) the first man and the woman. While every appearance of contradiction in the two narratives will completely vanish so soon as their different objects are considered, it may be well to notice how the account of the woman's creation illustrates the series of creative acts recorded in the first chapter. Without the information supplied by the second narrative it would be naturally assumed that the creation of the woman was contemporaneous with that of the man ; but with this additional light, it is at once seen that such a conclusion does not necessarily follow from the original statement. So in the other acts of creation, when several subjects are mentioned as the productions of a particular day, it need not be inferred that they were created at the same instant, or were contemporaneous in any stricter sense than dating their origin from the same period of creation. Thus, when God said, " Let the earth bring forth grass, the herb yielding seed, and the fruit-tree yielding fruit," &c., and when this is said to be realized, it is not necessary to suppose that these three classes of vegetable productions began their existence at once and together. It is enough to assume that they were all brought into being within the period distinguished as the third day, and so also with respect to the productions of the other days.

On the creation of man follows the Divine blessing—a blessing more full and emphatic than that pronounced on any previous creature. Verse 28, *And God blessed them, and God said unto them*—(they are personally addressed, intimating intelligence on their part, and thus the blessing is more direct than in verse 22)—*Be fruitful, and multiply, and replenish the earth, and subdue it : and have dominion over the fish of the sea, and over the fowl of the air, and over every living thing that moveth upon the earth.*

This blessing contains three distinct elements. Besides the capacity of propagating and multiplying the species so as to fill the earth—an endowment common to him with the other living creatures, man was qualified and called on to *subdue* the earth, כָּבַשׁ, to tread upon, or *trample under foot*, (comp. Josh. x. 24,) conveying the idea of complete victory, similar to Ps. cx. 1, "Until I make thine enemies thy footstool." The subjugation of the earth here evidently means its being made subservient in every possible way to the use and comfort of man by the art of navigation, the operations of agriculture, mining, metallurgy, and road-making, and everything which contributes to the welfare of the individual and of the community, and to the realization of the Divine purpose as to the multiplication of the species and the replenishment of the earth, and now the farther purpose of preparing the way of the Lord, and making straight in the desert a highway for our God, (Isa. xl. 3.) This dominion is not to be limited to inorganic matter, or the elements or occult powers of nature, but it is to extend to all the denizens of earth, to many of which, though man is far inferior in strength and agility, and as to his physical constitution in several respects inferior to all of them, especially as to the means of procuring food or repelling attacks, yet he is, by this blessing, and the endowments contained in it, the undisputed lord of creation. Man is empowered to *exercise dominion over* (וּרְדוּ בְּ imperative Kal of רָדָה, of the same import as כָּבַשׁ, applied to the treading of the wine-press, Joel iv. 13, [Eng. Ver. iii. 13 ;] then to rule over, Lev. xxvi. 17 ; בְּ is properly *local*, referring to that whereupon one sets foot) the fish of the sea, (דְּגַת הַיָּם, otherwise דְּגֵי חַיָּם, chap. ix. 2 ; Ps. viii. 9,) the fowl of the air, and every living thing that moveth upon the earth—in a word, the inhabitants of all the elements. It is in consequence of this lordship bestowed upon man that "the spoils of all nature are in daily requisition for his most common uses, yielded with more or less readiness, or wrested with reluctance from the mine, the forest, the ocean, and the air."[1]

---

[1] Herschel, Preliminary Discourse, p. 3.

To man and the other animals a grant is made of their appropriate food, indispensable to their sustenance. Verses 29, 30, *And God said, Behold, I have given you every herb bearing seed, which is upon the face of all the earth, and every tree, in the which is the fruit of a tree yielding seed, to you it shall be for food. And to every beast of the earth, and to every fowl of the air, and to everything that creepeth upon the earth wherein there is life, I have given every green herb for food : and it was so.*—The mention of man's food as a special and express gift of the Creator is intended to inculcate several important truths. It is not to be viewed as a mere permission to man and the other animals to partake of their necessary and appropriate nourishment, this being fully conceded by the natural wants belonging to their constitution. In regard to man, the permission and also the power of supplying himself with food from the ground must have been comprised in the mastery over creation already conferred upon him ; and as to the other animals, it is but reasonable to suppose that previous to this grant they partook freely of what the Creator's bounty had provided, and His wisdom adapted for them. The reason why mention is made of the provision for man's physical necessities may have been simply to serve as a memorial of his dependence. He had been appointed head of the creation, but only with a delegated authority—a truth he might be prone to forget. But to be told that the first necessaries of his existence were the gifts of his Sovereign was well fitted to remind him of his absolute dependence every time he sought to appease the cravings of hunger. If the matter is looked at in this light, it forms a part of the great discipline which has been in operation ever since, necessary in a state of innocence, but still more in a state of sin, and which was particularly manifested in the history of Israel. " The Lord thy God bringeth thee into a good land ; a land of wheat, and barley, and vines, and fig-trees, and pomegranates ; a land of oil-olive and honey ; a land wherein thou shalt eat bread without scarceness, thou shalt not lack anything in it. . . . . When thou hast eaten and art full, then thou shalt bless the Lord thy God, for the good land which he hath given thee. Beware that thou forget not the Lord thy God ; . . . . lest when thou hast eaten and art full, ... then thine heart be lifted up, and thou forget the Lord thy God, ... and thou say in thine heart, My power and the might of mine hand hath gotten me this wealth. But thou shalt remember the Lord thy God, for he it is that giveth thee power to get wealth," &c. (Deut. viii. 7-18.) Here then is the germ of that all-important principle which was placed in its true light by our Lord'. declaration :—" It is written, Man shall not live by bread alone, but by every word that proceedeth out of the mouth of God," (Matt. iv. 4.)

But besides teaching man his dependence on God, this grant of food was a pledge to him of a continued supply for his wants. This assurance is particularly expressed by the preterite נָתַתִּי, *I have given*, (compare chap. xv. 18 ; xvii. 20 ; and see Ewald, § 135, c,) and it may have been necessary for the following reason. At the first creation of animal life, a blessing was pronounced insuring propagation and continuance. Not so, however, in the case of the vegetable creation, as being perhaps incongruous in the circumstances ; but any deficiency in this respect is now supplied, and an assurance given of the continuation of the vegetable tribes from the relation which, by express Divine appointment, they are henceforward to sustain to the animal kingdom.

And further, this special mention of a grant to man of the vegetable productions may have been designed to connect the first narrative of creation with the second, and more particularly with the selected test of man's obedience. The limitation of a single tree may be thus considered in connexion with the Creator's absolute right of circumscribing His sovereign gift to any extent that seemed good.

It is frequently argued from this passage, that neither man nor beast lived on animal food previous to the Fall. It is assumed from chap. ix. 3, where the grant is enlarged, that up to the flood man lived entirely on vegetables. This may have been the case, and yet furnish no reason for concluding that the original grant implied a prohibition of animal food. First, this grant is not, properly speaking, *permissive* in regard to food, much less can it be construed as a partial limitation. But, secondly, the grant is directly to man, the animals being introduced only incidentally, so that were it the case that man's food was limited and prescribed, there is no reason to conclude that it must be so with all other creatures. Thirdly, from the general terms used, it is plain that nothing more is to be inferred than the close relation of the vegetable and animal kingdoms, or the fact that plants are the ultimate support of all animal life. So comprehensive is the grant to man—" every herb bearing seed, every tree wherein is the fruit of a tree yielding seed"—as to include many productions in no way immediately serviceable to him. On the other hand, if there be limitation, all animals, exclusive of man, are to be confined to the green herb, יֶרֶק עֵשֶׂב, *the green of herb*, herbage or grass.

Verse 31, *And God saw everything that he had made, and behold, it was very good. It was evening, it was morning, the sixth day.*—Six times during the progress of the great work did the Almighty pause to contemplate, as it were, the successive steps of His undertaking, and on each occasion He had reason to express His satisfaction, for the work was " good," all the arrangements, adjustments, and productions entirely corresponding to the Divine plan. But now that the work is completed, the Creator's satisfaction is more intense than before. What was formerly declared to be " good," in its individual parts, is now, as a whole, " very good." " God saw all that he had made : and lo, very good." Nought defective or redundant, all in proper place, in due order and subordination, and man, God's representative, invested with authority over the whole. This " very good" which followed the creation of man, is the declaration of Wisdom when, " rejoicing in the habitable part of the earth, her delights were with the sons of men," (Prov. viii. 31.)

EXCURSUS I.—MAN THE IMAGE OF GOD.

The discussion of this subject usually occupies a large place in Dogmatic Theology, and, from its bearing on such questions as the nature and extent of the Fall, original sin, and the imputed righteousness of Christ, it has formed a fertile source of controversy among the disciples of rival schools and systems. Although properly belonging to another department, yet the ideas involved in the representation of man as God's image cannot be overlooked or disposed of by a few remarks in an exposition of the narratives of Creation and the Fall. The observations, however, to be offered will partake more of a historical and exegetical character, with but little reference to systems.

1. It is first of all necessary to settle the import of the expressions, the "image" and "likeness of God," considered in themselves and as predicated of the first man. The terms themselves offer no difficulty : צֶלֶם primarily signifies *a shadow,* (Ps. xxxix. 7,) and then *an image,* from the shadow's resemblance to the body from which it is projected. The other term employed דְּמוּת, (from a root, דָּמָה, *to bring together, to compare, or liken,*) signifies *a comparison, likeness,* or *similitude.* Thus, Isa. xl. 18, "To whom *will ye liken* (תְּדַמְּיוּן) God, or what *likeness* (דְּמוּת) will ye compare to him?" The two words would seem to be nearly synonymous ; if there be any distinction it is this, the latter is more definite, intimating a resemblance in the parts and proportions, the former referring to the more general form or delineation, the shadowy outline, as it were.

But how are the terms to be understood when, as in Gen. i. 26, occurring together ?—as expressive of two distinct though connected ideas, or as only a Hebrew form of intensity ? The former view is that of many expositors. The Fathers of the Christian Church in particular held that there were two distinct ideas in this representation. Inasmuch as there is a great difference between the mere natural dispositions and their development by the free use of the powers granted to man, Irenæus, and especially Clement and Origen, distinguished between the image of God and resemblance to God, as that the latter can only be obtained by a mental conflict, in an ethical point of view, or is only bestowed on man, in a religious aspect, as a gift of sovereign mercy through union with Christ. Or the *image* was taken for the spiritual, moral endowments belonging to the very nature of man ; but the *likeness* for the Godlike perfection after which man had to strive as after that to which he was destined.[1]

But that this distinction was arbitrary and unsupported by Scripture will immediately appear from the fact that in other passages wherein reference is made to man's original constitution, the terms occur singly—sometimes the one and sometimes the other. In Gen. v. 1, only דְּמוּת ; in chap. x. 6, only

---

[1] See Hagenbach, History of Doctrines, vol. i. p. 145. Müller, The Christian Doctrine of Sin, vol. ii. p. 390.

צֶלֶם; but more particularly צֶלֶם only occurs in Gen. i. 27, which describes the realization of the Divine purpose announced in the preceding verse. The distinction also of the renderings of the LXX., εἰκών and ὁμοίωσις, is not maintained throughout, εἰκών being used for דְּמוּת, Gen. v. 1. For these reasons it must be held with the old Protestant theologians, in opposition to Bellarmin and other Roman Catholic writers, that the combination of the synonyms serves no discoverable end other than giving a more definite and express determination of the idea, as a likeness or resemblance in every possible respect.[1]

But, however this likeness of the creature to the Creator may be conceived of, or whatever may be its properties, it is to be observed that it is predicated of man as such—a being constituted by the union of body and soul. While, without doubt, it savours of the grossest materialism to restrict the image of God to man's bodily form and features, there may be also an error in the opposite extreme which refers this solely to man's soul, or his intellectual and moral nature. It is not enough to urge that " God is a spirit," without bodily parts or proportions, for this is sufficiently met by the reply that man is not *man* conceived of simply as a spirit, but a spirit in union with a material form, and that it is of man as thus constituted it is said, " Let us make *man* in our image," &c.[2] Farther, Scripture does not hesitate to ascribe *form* to God; and in such a way as cannot be explained simply on the principles of anthropomorphism, for this itself must have some foundation on which to rest. There is a form belonging to the *God of revelation*, in which his manifestations must be concentrated, that

---

[1] See Calvin, *Institutio Chris. Relig.*, Lib. i. cap. xv. 3. A distinction has been proposed by Hävernick, (Vorlesungen üb. die Theologie des Alten Testaments, p. 81. Erlangen, 1848,) to the effect that the *image* is the concrete, and the *likeness* the abstract, designation of the idea. This view is adopted by Hofmann, (Der Schriftbeweis, p. 251,) and by Schœberlein, the most recent writer on the subject, (Herzog's Real-Encyklopädie, *Art.* Ebenbild Gottes, vol. iii. p. 614: Stuttgard, 1855,) but it is too metaphysical to be of any practical value, even if correct.

[2] Owen, (Discourse concerning the Holy Spirit, *Works*, vol. iii. p. 417):—" That our entire nature was originally created in the *image* of God I have proved before, and it is by all acknowledged. Our whole souls, in the rectitude of all their faculties and powers, in order unto the life of God and his enjoyment, did bear his image. Nor was it confined unto the soul only; the body also, not as to its shape, figure, or natural use, but as an *essential part* of our nature, was interested in the image of God by a participation of original righteousness."

He may be recognised by men. Moses saw the *form* of Jehovah, תְּמוּנָה, (Num. xii. 8 ; compare Ex. xxiv. 10,) the same word which occurs in Job iv. 16, descriptive of the appearance in the night-vision of Eliphaz : " It stood still, but I could not discern the form thereof : an *image* (a form) was before mine eyes." That which will satisfy the Psalmist is the expectation of seeing the *form* of Jehovah. " I shall behold thy face in righteousness, satisfy myself when I awake with *thy form.*" (Ps. xvii. 15.) " This hope of the righteous," says Hengstenberg, " of satisfying themselves with the form of the Lord, grows out of the same feeling of need, which the appearances of God under a corporeal veil in the time of the fathers served to meet, and which had its highest satisfaction in the Word being made man. There is so strong a craving in the human heart for a *near, human God,* that anticipating the incarnation of God, it figuratively transferred to him corporeity, lent to him *form,* that it might love him very intimately, and comfort itself with a place in his heart." But there must have been something more in this than a mere figure, or a strong human craving with nothing to satisfy it ; but this will be better seen after it has been settled wherein the image of God consists ; and to this we now proceed.

The combination of the terms " image" and "likeness" intimates, as already observed, a likeness or resemblance in every possible respect, that is to say, every way possible for the finite and created to adumbrate the Infinite and Uncreated. But beyond this, the narrative in Genesis affords little direct aid to the present inquiry. It is only from comparisons with other scriptural intimations, and the analogies of the case, that there is a prospect of attaining to correct conclusions. The fundamental idea, however, is simply that "the image of God" is that whereby He, the *invisible* One, reveals himself or comes to view. Thus, in a way, creation in general is such an image of God ; " for the invisible things of him from the creation of the world are clearly seen, being understood by the things that are made, even his eternal power and Godhead," (Rom. i. 20.) And so all creatures, some more, some less, are expressive images of the great Author of being. And thus, too, it may be conceived that all the objects in the animal and vegetable creation with which Christ compares himself, as the lion, the lamb, the vine, are possessed of some property fitting them to shadow forth, though dimly, some quality, excellence, or disposition in their glorious Archetype. But man is specifically different from, and is exalted above, all natural beings around him, though in his physical organization, he includes in their highest and most perfect forms, the types of creation, in such a way as constitutes him "a compendium of all animated nature, and of kin to every creature that lives."[1] Man possesses personality, and accordingly in him the image of God attains its highest style, and has all its scattered rays concentrated. Man is in a special and peculiar manner God's representative on earth—the highest creature-revelation of the Creator of all. The other orders of existences may be able "to reveal God and his eternal thoughts ; but images of God those beings only are able to be, who are a revelation of God not merely for others, but also for themselves, who in general not merely *are*, but also are *for themselves*, who are conscious of themselves, and therefore also are conscious of God."[2]

Man is thus a reflex of the Divine powers and properties— an embodiment of the Divine ideas, he is possessed of consciousness, will, and power ; but above all, he was created in a state of moral excellence or *uprightness*, (Eccles. viii. 29.) He is, in fact, a creator, and also a governor invested with lordship over the other inhabitants of the earth. The Socinians, in part also the Arminians, understand by the Divine image merely this dominion. That this stands in essential connexion with the Divine image cannot be doubted ; but the connexion is not one of identity, but of cause and effect.

Yet, from the connexion thus subsisting between the Divine image in man and his dominion over nature, it will appear how important is the physical organization of the human being to the idea of the Divine image. It is the pedestal on which that image stands, for on this peculiar organization it greatly depends that man is what he is. Nor is it at all unreasonable to suppose that this embodiment in highest physical type of a Divine idea stands in some mysterious, unexplained, and perhaps inexplicable relation to what the Scriptures regard as the *form of God*, in the passages already cited.

[1] Miller, Footprints of the Creator, p. 290.
[2] Müller, Doctrine of Sin, vol. ii. p. 394.

But however this may be, the image of God in man was a true likeness of the great Original; yet still dim and shadowy —an outline faithful to the capacity of the subject, but infinitely remote from the reality, as must at once appear from the essential distinction of Creator and creature. At best the image was of the earth, earthy. But Scripture speaks of its being raised to a higher platform, and that, too, in the person of man—the Son of man—the Lord from heaven. He, in the highest sense, is said to be "the image of God," "the image of the invisible God," "the brightness of the Father's glory, and the express image of his person," χαρακτὴρ τῆς ὑποστάσεως αὐτοῦ, the image or counterpart of God's essence or being, (2 Cor. iv. 4; Col. i. 15; Heb. i. 3.) So express is this likeness, so marked in every line and lineament, so perfect, pure, and unclouded, that this man can testify of himself, "If ye had known me, ye should have known my Father also, ... he that hath seen me hath seen the Father," (John xiv. 7-9.) And thus God in living concentration appears, and has appeared only in Jesus Christ—the man of his right hand, the Son of man whom He made strong for himself, and to whose image He hath predestinated His people to be conformed, (Ps. lxxx. 17; Rom. viii. 21.)

For determining how Christ is the image of God, the New Testament affords ample information; and accordingly it is from what is said of the person of the Redeemer, the Head of restored humanity, the second Adam, rather than from any indirect intimations of the image to be borne by the redeemed themselves, that it can with certainty be determined wherein it consisted in the first Adam, the head of unfallen humanity. It is simply by comparing the scriptural representation of Adam and Christ, and not by any metaphysical subtilties, that it can be verified whether, and how far, the above view of the image of God in man accords with what is so much more plainly indicated respecting Christ, only bearing in mind that he is not the image of God, as *formed* in it, like Adam; and, moreover, that he is the image of God's essence, as well as of his character and perfections.

Now, according to Paul's representation, Christ, as the image of God, is πρωτότοκος πάσης κτίσεως, (Col. i. 15,) an expression variously interpreted, but which there are the best reasons for

rendering, " the head of the entire creation," and in which may
be detected a tacit comparison with Adam, who was head only
of the earthly creation, and in this held only a delegated trust,
while Christ exercises authority, universal and in his own
right, as the Creator and Preserver of all, (verses 16, 17.) Accordingly, he is every way fitted for the discharge of the required functions, being endowed with *all fulness*, (verse 19,)
or, as the Apostle afterwards more fully states, πᾶν τὸ πλή-
ρωμα τῆς θεότητος, "the totality of the Divine vital powers,"
(Col. ii. 9.) It is thus as possessed of all Divine properties,
and *in the full manifestation of the same*, that Christ is the
image of the *invisible* God. Thus, too, the first Adam is to
be viewed, according to his creature capacities, God's representative on earth, a revelation of God to himself as well as
to others ; the head of creation, and, as such, liberally endowed with all qualifications, physical, intellectual, and moral,
necessary for the proper discharge of his high and glorious
vocation.

2. Another important question is, How the image of God in
the first man is related to the New Testament representation
of the same in the *new man* or new creation in Christ?

Two passages in particular are usually referred to as definitions of the expression, " the image of God." " That ye put
off, concerning the former conversation, the old man, which is
corrupt according to the deceitful lusts ; and be renewed in
the spirit of your mind; and that ye put on the new man, which
after God is created in righteousness and true holiness," (Eph.
iv. 22-24.) Again, "Ye have put off the old man with his
deeds, and have put on the new man, which is renewed in
knowledge after the image of him that created him," (Col. iii.
9, 10.) It is not clear that the first of these passages refers
to the Divine image. Some, as Bloomfield, render it, "in conformity to the will of God ;" but others, of whom may be mentioned Olshausen, with greater probability, infer from the
parallel passage that κατὰ Θεὸν stands for κατ' εἰκόνα Θεοῦ.
In this representation of the Divine image, or some at least of
its specific tokens, there may, no doubt, be a reference to the
case of the first man, and yet not the reference usually supposed. That takes it to be a definition of the image of God in
man, not, indeed, as if the words applied directly to man's *past*

but to his *future* in Christ; but it is inferred that what the redeemed shall be when restored to God's image, such Adam must have been while yet unfallen.

This mode of reasoning is open, however, to several objections, and it should, in particular, be considered that—

(1.) The passages in question, taken singly or combined, express only *some* features of the Divine image in the new man —the second creation in Christ. The first passage exhibits the image of God in its ethical aspect, δικαιοσύνη denoting the right relation inwardly between the powers of the soul, and outwardly to men and circumstances; while ὁσιότης points to the integrity of the spiritual life, and the piety towards God which this implies. The other passage presents the same Divine image, but merely in its intellectual aspect, as consisting in *knowledge*.[1]

(2.) In applying to Adam this description of the Divine image, it is assumed that the new creation is essentially only the *restoration* of man's character and condition as existing prior to the Fall. But the *new* creation is a far higher form of humanity than the *old*. The Divine image in Adam was rudimental only; in the other case it is the full development— what Adam would have attained to by perseverance in the path of duty. "Indisputably," says Müller, "the Divine image, which follows from redemption, stands essentially in connexion with the image which man bears from the creation; the former is only the realization of the latter; man has only been made a partaker of the one in order that he may attain to the other, if not in the direct course of faithful persistency in the fellowship of God, then in the circuitous way of redemption; but

[1] Hofmann considers that neither of these passages has anything to do with the question regarding the image of God in the first man. "In the former passage," he says, "according to the arrangement of the words, ἐν δικαιοσύνῃ καὶ ὁσιότητι τῆς ἀληθείας is to be connected with ἐνδύσασθαι, and not with κτισθέντα, and κατὰ Θεὸν is not to be explained by κατ' εἰκόνα τοῦ Θεοῦ, but is to be understood of man as created by the Divine method, in contrast to man as continued by human generation. In the other passage, κατ' εἰκόνα τοῦ κτίσαντος αὐτόν is not to be connected with ἀνακαινούμενον, since it is an unsound and arbitrary interpretation to consider ἐπίγνωσις as meaning a knowledge of God or of salvation; and if it be supposed to designate the spiritual nature of man in one of its aspects, this limitation of the meaning of the word is the less justified by the polemic object of the epistle against presumptuous knowledge, as then a more precise definition of the knowledge meant could not have been dispensed with."—Der Schriftbeweis, p. 252.

from the nature of this connexion it follows that the contents of the two notions is not the same."[1]

To these considerations, particularly the latter, sufficient importance has perhaps not been attached by writers on this subject. Certain it is, that the qualifications necessarily resorted to by such as would identify the apostolic descriptions of man renewed, with the Mosaic account of man unfallen, go very far to destroy the identity contended for. Thus Calvin, on Eph. iv. 24:—" Quod de creatione subjicitur, tam ad primam creationem hominis, quam ad reformationem, quæ fit Christi gratia, referri potest; utraque expositio vera erit. Nam et initio creatus fuit Adam ad imaginem Dei, ut justitiam Dei quasi in speculo repræsentaret ; sed quoniam imago illa deleta est per peccatum, ideo nunc in Christo instaurari oportet. Nec sane aliud est regeneratio piorum, quam reformatio imaginis Dei in illis ; quemadmodum 2 Cor. iii. 18, dictum est. Quamquam *longe uberior est ac potentior Dei gratia in hac secunda creatione quam prima fuerit ;* sed hoc tantum respicit Scriptura, quod summa nostra perfectio sit conformitas et similitudo, quæ nobis est cum Deo. Ad eam vero quum formatus esset Adam, perdidit quod acceperat; nobis igitur per Christum restitui necesse est. Quare huc spectare docet regenerationem, ut ex errore reducamur ad eum finem ad quem sumus conditi."

The principal reason for adverting to this question here, and insisting on the diversity in the two cases, is the circumstance that the views frequently advanced by preachers and expositors regarding the condition of Adam, are plainly inconsistent with the tenor of the narrative in Genesis. That unfallen man, from the moment of his creation, was *potentially* such as the Apostle represents the new man to be *actually*, is certainly to be concluded from all that is written concerning the state of innocence, especially from the idea of the Divine image ; but this is all that can with safety be affirmed regarding man's character, ere his powers were called into exercise through the probation to which he was subjected. This, however, implies no imperfection on his part, save that which necessarily attaches to capacities not fully expanded by exercise. But another reason for entering so largely in this place on the distinction in question, is the light it is fitted to shed on a

---

[1] Müller, Doctrine of Sin, vol. ii. pp. 392, 393.

difficult and greatly misunderstood statement of God regarding man subsequent to the Fall, Gen. iii. 22 : " And the Lord God said, Behold, the man is become as one of us, to know good and evil ;" but on which see the Exposition.

3. The image of God, how affected by the Fall, is the next point to be considered. This is a subject on which the most conflicting opinions are entertained ; one extreme regarding the image of God as utterly defaced, and the other as strenuously denying that any deterioration in that respect was induced through the Fall. This diversity of opinion is the result of vague and unfixed ideas of the nature of the Fall itself, but more particularly arises from the different views entertained by expositors as to what constituted the Divine image, some taking it in a wider, and others in a more limited sense.

Thus, according to Hofmann : " It is not the resemblance to God which is borne by a moral, holy being, as appears from the context in which is described the creation, not of the man Adam as distinguished from the now sinful race, but of humanity as distinguished from the animal world. Gen. v. 3 affords at least a confirmation of this view. The subject of that passage is not the moral resemblance between the sons of Adam and their father, but the similarity of father and son, by means of which the race so long as it is naturally propagated and not produced by the unnatural depravity mentioned in Gen. vi. 1, remains like itself, and the same as created by God."[1]

Others, on the contrary, limiting the idea to the moral condition of the first man, view it as lost through the Fall ; while a third class makes a distinction between the natural and the moral image. Thus President Edwards : " As there are two kinds of attributes in God, according to our way of conceiving of him, his moral attributes, which are summed up in his holiness, and his natural attributes of strength, knowledge, &c., that constitute the greatness of God ; so there is a twofold image of God in man, his moral or spiritual image, which is his holiness, that is the image of God's moral excellency, (which image was lost by the Fall,) and God's natural image, consisting in man's reason and understanding, his natural ability

---

[1] Hofmann, Der Schriftbeweis, p. 251.

U

and dominion over the creatures, which is the image of God's natural attribute."[1]

Of the texts usually appealed to in this discussion, one of the most important is Gen. v. 3,—" Adam lived an hundred and thirty years, and begat a son *in his own likeness, after his image.*" Here, it is usually said, there is no longer mention of the image of God : fallen man begets a son, but it is in his own image, plainly intimating that the image in which he was created is lost and no longer his.   On the other hand, it is held that this inference is unwarranted by the text or context, the purport of which is that God created man in his own image, (verse 1,) and then, without mention of any intervening change, it is added, Adam begat a son in his own image, which is thus nothing other than that in which he was created.   This position is thought to be strengthened by Gen. ix. 6, " Whoso sheddeth man's blood, by man shall his blood be shed : *for in the image of God made he man.*"   The reason here given prohibitory of the violation of human life assumes that man still bears God's image as a seal of inviolability.   So plain is this, that Calvin admits, " Si quis objiciat imaginem illam deletam esse : solutio facilis est, manere adhuc aliquid residuum, ut præstet non parva dignitate homo."   But if this *residuum* be such that it can be fitly called the Divine image, the question is settled.

Another text implying the permanence of the Divine image is James iii. 9, where it is said that *men* (τοὺς ἀνθρώπους) are made καθ᾽ ὁμοίωσιν Θεοῦ (after the similitude of God.)

These are all the passages which bear directly on the subject, and their testimony upon the whole, it must be admitted, is in favour of the view which maintains that the Divine image in man has not been lost or obliterated.   This, however, by no means goes to disprove that a grievous disorder in man's moral state was introduced through the Fall, but only that the idea expressed by the image of God is not to be limited wholly, or even chiefly, to man's moral character, and his consequent relation to God.   Of the entire revolution in his moral nature, and relation to the Author of his being, the history of the Fall itself gives ample evidence.   But as, notwithstanding that change, he is still said to bear the image of God, it must be

---

[1] Treatise concerning Religious Affections, Part III. ; *Works*, vol. iii. p. 102 : New York, 1844. See also Freedom of the Will, Part I. sect. v. ; *Works*, vol. ii. pp. 19, 20.

held that that had respect to more than his original uprightness, and yet even in this more general aspect the image, though not destroyed, has been greatly dimmed. It may, in fact, be said to be another image and yet the same ; another, because so obscured and distorted, and deficient in many of the features which constituted it a symmetrical whole. Like a tarnished mirror, or a ruffled lake, man reflects the image irregular and broken—indistinct in feature and form, but still so far true to its ground lines—its fundamental character, that it is not wholly impossible to recognise the original. Thus it may be that while in one sense the son begotten by Adam is viewed as bearing God's image, in another sense he may be more properly said to bear the image of his fallen progenitor, so much has human nature deflected from its pristine uprightness. Thus, Bishop Patrick :—" For *his own likeness and image,* wherein this son was begotten, seems to be opposed to the *likeness and image of God,* wherein Adam was made, which, though not quite lost, was lamentably defaced."[1]

One or two other passages may be noticed which bear, though only indirectly, on this subject. Thus, 1 Cor. xi. 7, " Man is the image and glory of God." From the scope of the Apostle's argument, it appears that this refers to the authority and domi-nion with which man was invested at the creation. This, the Apostle intimates, is still retained, and man is to be regarded as God's representative. Again, 1 Cor. xv. 49, " As we have borne (*and do bear, ἐφορέσαμεν*) the image of the earthy, we shall also bear the image of the heavenly." This does not re-fer so much to our resembling Adam in moral character, as appears from verse 45, but rather applies to the fact that we are, like him, subject to sickness, frailty, sorrow, and death ; but shall at the resurrection resemble Christ in our glorified and immortal frames.[2] The distinction is evidently between the animal body of creation and the spiritual body of the re-surrection. " The Apostle dwells on the fact, that there is such an animal body and such a spiritual body—shows how these two organizations are produced, and in what order they are possessed by those who are Christ's."[3]

---

[1] A Commentary upon Genesis, p. 112. Lond. 1704.

[2] See Bloomfield, Greek Testament, *in loc.*

[3] Brown, The Resurrection of Life, p. 197. Edin. 1852.

This is a mere outline of what is in truth a very extensive as well as important subject. It is believed, however, that the conclusions deduced from the data furnished in the Old Testament regarding the Divine image in man serve to reconcile the exposition of two apparently contradictory classes of passages, one affirming the loss and the other the permanency of that image, while they fully harmonize with the representations of the New Testament on the subject, particularly with what the Apostle Paul propounds regarding the full realization of the idea in the *new* man. The knowledge, righteousness and holiness adverted to by the Apostle were undoubtedly affected in a special degree by the Fall ; and this may have been the reason why he particularizes these characteristics as restored in the new creature.

§ 8. *The Sabbath of Creation,* Gen. ii. 1-3.

The works of God differ in many respects from man's undertakings, but in nothing more than in the certainty of their being finished. Eternity shall not witness any unfinished structure of God, any defeated purpose or thwarted plan. The work whose commencement and progress the preceding chapter described is now said to be completed, and with this is connected the sabbatic rest of God.

Verse 1. *Thus the heavens and the earth were finished, and all the host of them.*—" In the beginning God created the heavens and the earth," but these were not at once the orderly adjusted structures which in time they became. " The earth," in particular, " was without form, and void,"—no life on its surface, no lights in its skies. The same must have been the case, there is every reason to conclude, with the other mighty masses of matter which fill the immensity of space. How these were being prepared, and whether in the same order and to the same extent as the earth, we are not informed, and it is vain to conjecture. So much, however, is certain, that by the fourth day of creation they were brought into a condition to convey light to the earth, and by the close of the sixth day everything connected with the heavens and the earth was so forwarded, that it could be said, " The heavens and the earth were finished," the mighty structure was completed, the deep and broad foundations of which had been laid "in the beginning." But the fabric is not merely reared, but ornamented and tenanted by organic forms, in some of which are embodied intellectual and moral existences. So much is certainly included in the *host* of the heavens and the earth ; but whether the term צָבָא, *host*, which is properly used only of heaven, as a designation of the stars and the angels, but here by the grammatical figure *Zeugma*, applied also to the earth, comprises other intellectual and moral creatures besides man, cannot be easily determined. Scripture gives ample evidence of the existence of such beings, but their *genesis* it does not record, and yet the fact may be here intimated that they were in existence previous to the close of the sixth day, and the other fact, that all without exception derived their being from God. This is countenanced by the general terms employed, "all their host," that is, of the heavens and the earth, but particularly by the reference to this passage in Neh. ix. 6, "Thou, even thou art Lord alone : thou hast made heaven, the heaven of heavens, with all their host : the earth and all that are therein, the seas and all therein, and thou preservest them all : *and all the host of heaven worshippeth thee.*" Thus understood, the intimation contained in this passage is identical with that of the New Testament, "All things were made by him ; and without him was not anything made that was made," (John i. 3.) The announcement of this truth here is very significant, as in the course of the history mention is to be made of a being whose character and conduct might possibly give rise to the apprehension that he could not have been a creature of God.

Verses 2, 3. *And on the seventh day God ended his work which he had made, and he rested on the seventh day from all his work which he had made. And God blessed the seventh day, and sanctified it : because that in it he had rested from all his work which God created to make.*—Some ancient translations, as the LXX., the Syriac, and the Samaritan recension, so stumbled at the connexion of *ended* with the *seventh* day, as implying that part of the work of creation was performed on it, that they unwarrantably altered the text so as to read *on the sixth day.* Modern writers, as Calvin, Drusius, Le Clerc, Rosenmüller, and Tiele, avoiding such arbitrary expedients, would escape the difficulty by rendering the verb, *had finished*, but this, besides being ungrammatical, in reality contributes nothing to the end contemplated. Others, again, take the *Piel* conjugation in this case as *declaring* or *pronouncing* a thing *to be finished*. But none of these expedients is necessary when it is perceived that, as shown by Vater and Tuch, the verb כָּלָה, followed by מִן, simply means to cease to *prosecute* or *carry on* any matter; in which sense it is frequently used, (Exod. xxxiv. 33; 1 Sam. x. 13; Ezek. xliii. 23.) Or, with Baumgarten, the *rest* of the seventh day itself may be considered the *perfecting* of the creation. In any case, cessation and rest filled up the seventh day.

The seventh day, it may be justly supposed, was no less important in the view of the Creator, and for the history of the world, than any of those which preceded it. Indeed, it may be affirmed that the highest place belongs to the day which witnessed the completion of the great work so long in progress. The end has been reached; and if in the means there were afforded intimations of the Creator's desires and delights, much more now in the end towards which from the beginning all things tended. The *cessation* or *rest* of this day is not to be regarded as a mere negation, for as such it could not be God's rest. The figure is borrowed from human life and labours, but it is of deep significance. Man, even, cannot be said absolutely to rest, for when the eye is closed in slumber on the labours and commotions of the outer world, then begin, with more or less consciousness, creations in the world within. How much less, then, can it apply to God, the Spring of life and activity! His *rest* consists in a cessation from creating acts: "He rested from all his work which he had made;" and He did so simply because it was made.

The *rest* of God cannot then refer to His works in general, for of these the Son declares, "My Father worketh hitherto, and I work," (John v. 17,) and to the same purpose is the language of the Prophet: "The everlasting God, the Lord, the Creator of the ends of the earth, fainteth not, neither is weary," (Is. xl. 28.) It may rather be viewed as a transition from one kind of work to another. What the work is on which the Creator now entered is easily determined: it is the work of world-preserving, as through the preceding periods it was the work of world-creating

that engaged the Divine mind. The world, the universe of
dependent being, had in creation been made as perfect, it may
be conceived, as omnipotence and omniscience could render a
creature ; and yet it may be the Creator's design still farther
to advance the works of His hands, and bring His moral creatures, especially those formed in His own image, into closer
connexion with himself. But, on the supposition that they
were already as perfect as creation could make them, any farther
advance or elevation in the scale of being must be attained by
other than physical laws or the powers by which these are set
and sustained in operation ; it must be sought in that moral
government which, so far as regards earth, began with the
creation of the human race. The creative mandates which had
previously gone forth were simply, " Let there be," and the
implicit but blind obedience of universal nature followed
according to the announcement, " And it was so." Now, however, God's dominion is greatly extended : His subjects are of
a higher rank : His voice is no longer directed exclusively to
unconscious matter or to irrational brutes. He can now demand and receive willing and intelligent homage ; yea, there
are creatures who can reciprocate His affection, who can rejoice
in His favour, and be saddened by His frown.

The *rest* of God is thus an entrance upon a work more elevated and holy in its character than any of the preceding, for
its object is to make the creature more like to the Holy One
himself. As the cessation from one work in order to begin
another, the rest of God in creation has an exact counterpart
in Christ's work in redemption. Christ had his work—the
work which the Father gave him to do, (John xvii. 4 ;) and
though a trying and toilsome undertaking, he brought it to
such a state that he could affirm, " It is finished," (John xix.
30)—words which form a remarkable parallel to Gen. ii. 1, 2,
and which, while constituting the closing amen to the Saviour's
life and labours in all that pertained to his sufferings and his
satisfaction to the claims of his undertaking, were no less
truly the announcement of his entrance on a new life and new
works in the kingdom of God ; just as in Rev. xxi. 6, " It is
done " constitutes the transition to the full development of
that kingdom where all things shall be made new.

In rest after labour, and especially when the work is completed, there is satisfaction, and this in proportion as the work comes up to the plan and purpose of its author. In every human work there is much imperfection, and regrets and disappointments mingle with our joys; but no such ingredients could possibly mar the satisfaction of God as he rejoiced in the works of his hands, when, on the seventh day, " He rested from all his works ;" or, as it is elsewhere said, " On the seventh day he rested and was refreshed," (Ex. xxxi. 17 ;) and no pains or disappointments shall disturb the blessed rest of the Saviour, for " he shall see of the travail of his soul, and shall be satisfied," (Is. liii. 11,) for he, too, rests in a sabbatic manner as God does. " He who hath entered into his rest, himself rested from his works as God from his," (Heb. iv. 10.)

The Sabbatic rest of the Creator was also designed for the creature. It was God's purpose that creation should keep the Sabbath with him, and participate in the calm and composure of that hallowed state. This is fully shown in several parts of Scripture, particularly in Hebrews, chap. iv., where the apostle gives an inspired commentary on Psalm xcv., with special reference to the *rest* there spoken of. But the same truth is distinctly stated in the first section of Genesis. Into the rest of God, its blessedness and sanctity, man might at first enter, so soon as he had finished the work assigned to him by the Creator. This will appear from various considerations connected with this narrative.

1. The position which the Sabbath occupies in the history immediately after the creation of man, shows that the arrangement had a special reference to his benefit. There can be no doubt that it is on the narrative of creation and the truths therein embodied that our Lord founds the deeply significant declaration, " The Sabbath was made on account of man, (διὰ τὸν ἄνθρωπον,) not man on account of the Sabbath," (Mark ii. 27.) So the beatific repose which it typified was by the Creator specially designed for man.

2. There was also given at the creation a pledge of the **permanency** of this rest : " God blessed the seventh day." In the course of this history repeated mention was made of God's *blessing*. He blessed the first living creatures which the waters brought forth, and he blessed man, the last and noblest of his works ; thus comprehending in the Paternal blessing,

life from the humblest to the highest form. This blessing it was which, as already shown, secured and assured the continuance of life on the earth, notwithstanding any appearances to the contrary, and any apprehensions that might arise from the operation of laws which affected all organic existence. If, then, in these cases the Divine blessing is to be considered as a pledge of permanence and perpetuity in the midst of change, it may be fairly regarded in the same light when applied to the seventh day, which was designed to be typical of the rest of God and of the creation. God *blessed* it, and thereby stamped upon it a character of permanent endurance—a rest that could not be broken, and into which no disquietude could enter, whatever the attempts to mar the works of God, and introduce discord into the harmony of the universe. Thus considered, the Divine blessing on the dispensation now begun was in the highest degree encouraging in itself, but especially in connexion with the moral catastrophe, the record of which immediately follows. The work of creation concluded, and pronounced to be "very good," the Creator and Governor of the universe, in full view of the evil and disorder about to be introduced, blessed the seventh day, in which he had rested from all his work, and in so doing gave a pledge of the triumph of holiness and happiness—how truly, the Apostle intimates when he says, "There *remaineth* therefore a *rest* to the people of God," σαββατισμός, *a Sabbatic rest*, one truly corresponding to the rest of God when the work of creation was finished. But still farther to show the permanency of this rest, and its exemption from change, the seventh day is not characterized by the vicissitudes of evening and morning. It was thus recognised by Augustin, when, at the close of his *Confessions*, addressing himself to God, he remarks : " Dies septimus sine vespera est nec habet occasum, quia sanctificasti eum ad permansionem sempiternam."

3. Farther, God *sanctified* (וַיְקַדֵּשׁ, *set apart*) the seventh day from common to sacred purposes. What the purposes are to which it was thus dedicated, appear from the reasons assigned for the separation, as well as from the blessing : " because that in it he had rested from all his work." It is for the purpose of carrying out and realizing the idea of rest, not with respect to God, for He had entered on it : but with respect to man,

for whom also it was prepared. In order to man's participation in it he must be able to rest from his works as God did from His. This, however, needs labour and preparation, and in lapsed human nature, concurrence in the works of God in the prosecution of his gracious design respecting the soul. The blessing was a pledge of the security of this rest, while the sanctification pointed out this day as a preparation for the rest, and showed also the necessity for such preparation.

EXCURSUS II.—THE WEEKLY DIVISION OF TIME—ITS CONNEXION
WITH CREATION.

It is frequently urged by Rationalists and others, desirous of depreciating the Bible, that its account of the Creation has been constructed mainly with the design of furnishing a Divine sanction to the Jewish Sabbath, and that to this alone is to be referred the distribution of the creating acts among six days followed by a day of rest.[1] But this allegation is fully met by the fact, that the division of time into weeks or periods of seven days, was not peculiar to the Jews, but was a universal custom, and much older than the time of Moses, or of the composition of the earliest portion of the Hebrew Scriptures.

1. The week or cycle of seven days is an ancient and universal division of time. In the earliest notices of the human race, for which we are solely indebted to the Bible, peculiar mention is made of the number *seven*. " Whosoever slayeth Cain, vengeance shall be taken on him *seven*-fold." " If Cain shall be avenged *seven*-fold, truly Lamech *seventy* and *seven*-fold," (Gen. iv. 15, 24.) The mystical or proverbial character here ascribed to *seven* and its multiples, is maintained throughout the Scriptures. Its use in connexion with time is first strikingly brought out in the history of the flood. An earlier passage in the history of Cain and Abel (Gen. iv. 3) is sometimes adduced, but inconclusively, as referring to a seventh or Sabbath day. It cannot be shown that the expression, " in the end of the days," refers to the end of the *week* and not to the end of the *year*, as is evidently the case in 2 Sam. xiv.

[1] Winer, Biblisches Realwörterbuch, *Art.* Sabbath, vol. ii. p. 347.

26.[1] In the narrative of the flood, however, mention is made of four days as succeeding one another at stated intervals of seven days. They are distinguished as the days on which the raven was sent out of the ark once, and the dove three times, (Gen. viii. 6-12.) That this division of time was known in Patriarchal times, is evident from the facts recorded respecting Jacob, who, marrying two wives, first fulfilled the bridal *week* (שָׁבֻעַ from שֶׁבַע, *seven*, like ἑβδομάς) of the one, and then of the other, (Gen. xxix. 27, 28, compare Judg. xiv. 12, 17.) Seven days was also in ancient times the usual period of mourning. Thus they made public lamentation for Jacob *seven* days, (Gen. l. 10,) and for a like period the friends of the afflicted Patriarch of Uz sat with him in his distress, in silence upon the ground, (Job ii. 13.)

Coming down to the period when profane history begins to shed light on the character and customs of antiquity, there are innumerable indications of the *sacredness* of the number seven, and of the division of time into weeks. The ancient Persians, for instance, the nations of India, and the old German tribes, regarded seven as a sacred number.[2] And in particular, Hesiod, Homer, and Callimachus, apply the epithet *holy* to the seventh day. Lucian says the seventh day is given to schoolboys as a holiday. Eusebius declares that " almost all the philosophers and poets acknowledge the seventh day as holy." And Porphyry states, that " the Phœnicians consecrated one day in seven as holy." [3]

But besides this general estimation of *seven* and the *seventh* day, a weekly division of time was in general use. It is certain that the Egyptians were acquainted with this mode of computing time: Dio Cassius, indeed, ascribes to them the invention of this cycle. So also were the Assyrians, the Babylonians, the Chinese, and the nations of India. Traces of the same usage have also been detected by Oldendorf among the tribes inhabiting the interior of Africa. Nay, farther, it has been met with among the American nations of the West. But it is unnecessary to multiply evidence on this head ; Josephus had long ago affirmed that there was scarcely any nation,

[1] Jennings, Jewish Antiquities, p. 410. Lond. 1823.
[2] Winer, Bib. R. W., *Art.* Zahlen, vol. ii. p. 714.
[3] Cox, Biblical Antiquities, p. 245. Lond. 1852.

Greek or barbarian, but in some degree acknowledged or conformed to a seventh day's cessation from labour.[1]

2. What account can be given of the origin of a custom so ancient and so universal? Its antiquity shows beyond all question that the notion was not borrowed from any Jewish source, or from the Mosaic institutions. Any doubt on this subject must be removed by the other consideration, that this division of time was in use among nations at the greatest distance from one another; and of many of whom it cannot be said that they were in any way influenced by the Hebrew legislator.

Another element to be considered in any theory proposed to account for the origin and prevalence of this custom, is, that it was not confined to nations which had greatly advanced in civilisation, but was also in use among tribes in various stages of knowledge and refinement. This evidently necessitates the conclusion that if this division of time be not of a character to force itself on the attention of mankind, owing to some palpable connexion with the constitution of nature or the organization of man, it must have been transmitted from the ancestors of the human race, and spread abroad with the dispersion of the nations. Thus in regard to the division of time into months or *moons,* the cause is at once obvious, and is such as must have universally commended itself. The same would hold true of a cycle of *ten* days: its origin would be immediately referred to the fact that man has ten digits, and which has originated the decimal scale of notation. But that a period so obvious and convenient was not in use, is in itself a strong confirmation of the original acceptance of a weekly division of time.

But can it be said that, apart from all traditions regarding the order and arrangements of creation, the weekly division of time possesses qualities or relations strong and palpable enough to commend its universal adoption? Many learned men do not hesitate to reply in the affirmative; and Anti-Sabbatarians eagerly avail themselves of the testimony. But how do they attempt to explain it?

Some writers, as Acosta and Humboldt, find the origin of the week in the number of the primary planets as known to

[1] Contra Apionem, lib. ii. cap. 40.

the ancients.[1] The only evidence, however, in support of this theory is, that the days of the week were by many nations named after the planets. These names originated in astrological notions : and it is enough to say that such notions were not so ancient or so universal as that division of time whose origin they are supposed to explain. With the Jews in particular, and many other nations, no designation of the days of the week was in use, save the ordinal numbers, *first, second,* &c.

Not satisfied with this explanation, Ideler, a learned writer on chronology, refers the origin of the week to the circumstance that the quarter of the moon consists of about seven days, (properly $7\frac{3}{8}$,) the *lunar* month naturally dividing itself into four such periods.[2] This account of the matter, Winer characterizes as highly probable ; and it has also found a strenuous defender in Professor Baden Powell.[3] But although more plausible than the view already referred to, it labours under serious disadvantages. First, the lunar month of about $29\frac{1}{2}$ days does not admit of any exact subdivision, and *seven* is only a remote approximation to such ; so much so, that the days of the week would be continually varying from the corresponding phases of the moon. But, again, *four* is not so natural and obvious a division as to be generally suggestive. Seeing that *ten* is so convenient a numeral, how did it never occur to any, taking the month at 30 days, to divide it into *tens ?* Besides the week, the Peruvians are said to have had a cycle of *nine* days, but this is not the approximate and natural third of a lunation, and therefore does anything but show, as Baden Powell alleges, " the common origin of both." Periods of 14 or 15 days might also with great probability be referred to the increase and decrease of the moon ; but for the origin of the week no theory has been proposed which can for a moment admit of comparison with the view which sees in it a memorial of creation—known through tradition long before the composition of Genesis or the Hebrew cosmogony. Besides, no other theory professes to account for the sacred character attached to the numeral *seven,* and, in particular, to the *seventh* day.

[1] Cyclopædia Bib. Lit., *Art.* Sabbath, vol. ii. p. 655.
[2] Handbuch der Mathemat. u. tech. Chronologie, vol. i. p. 60. Berlin, 1825.
[3] Cyc. Bib. Lit., *loc. cit.*

SECT. II.—DETAILED ACCOUNT OF THE CREATION OF MAN,
Gen. ii. 4-25.

§ 9. *Transition from the First to the Second Narrative,*
Gen. ii. 4.

The second chapter of Genesis is not strictly a continuation of the narrative begun in the first, but rather a transition from that chapter to the third, or from the history of creation to that of the creature, considered in a moral point of view. The blessing and sanctification of the seventh day which followed the close of creation, intimated a purpose on the part of the Creator still farther to ennoble it and draw it closer to himself. This was to be effected in and through humanity— the only personal existence on earth, and which, as formed in the Divine image, and invested with dominion over nature, was at once the representative of the Creator and the creature. Nevertheless, in the general record of creation, how little is absolutely communicated in regard to man, his creation, his character, or his condition; although these matters occupy relatively a large space in a narrative designed to describe in a few sentences the creation of the heavens and the earth with all their host. And yet, again, the information thus communicated respecting man is of such a nature, and is conveyed in such a manner as irresistibly to lead to the conclusion that the historian is not done with the subject in his first section. This expectation is justified, and the curiosity is satisfied, by the particular account of the creation and original condition of man which immediately follows; while nothing shows more clearly that the object of the writer was entirely moral and religious, than to find that this account of man, and of his location on the earth, covers nearly as large a space as the foregoing account of the creation of the universe.

In its relation to the first section, the second may be viewed as an enlarged monograph on Gen. i. 26-29, and, as such, consisting of details which could not be conveniently inserted there. Thus there is an account of the origin of the first human being, verse 7, a notice of the pleasant residence assigned to him by the Creator, and of its situation, verses

8-15, of the provision made for his sustenance, verse 19, and also of the creation of the woman, and of her relation to the man, verses 18, 21-25.

But it is in relation to the history of the Fall, and as furnishing materials for the correct understanding of that melancholy occurrence, that this narrative assumes a special importance. Already, in the general history of creation, there were terms employed which, although not expressly, yet by implication, may be regarded as pointing to the altered state of things induced by man's apostasy : such perhaps is the particular mention made of man as created in the image of God, and most probably the " very good" with which, at the conclusion of His work, the Creator declared its character and gave expression to his own gratification. But it is in the second chapter that the premonitions and preliminaries of the Fall are most abundant and particular. It might be shewn, verse by verse, how the two chapters supplement and explain one another; and how their mutual relation is such, that they are fitly described by Herder " as two sides of one and the same humanity." One or two examples may however suffice. Thus the scene of the third chapter is laid in a garden—the residence of a human pair—but from which on transgression they are expelled. The second chapter answers all such questions as, What and where was the garden, who and whence its inhabitants? Again, the account of the Fall begins with a reference to a Divine permission, and also a prohibition, to partake of the fruit of certain trees in the garden : the previous narrative had fully prepared the reader for this incident by specifying man's liberty, and its limitation in respect to one tree in the garden. Once more, the intimation, " They were both naked, the man and his wife, and were not ashamed," (chap. ii. 25,) is in marked contrast to what is said of their state after transgression : " They knew that they were naked, and they sewed fig-leaves together, and made themselves aprons ;" and the confession of Adam, " I was afraid because I was naked," (chap. iii. 7, 10.)

But notwithstanding the seemingly well-defined limits between the first and second sections of Genesis, and the marked difference of style which distinguishes the two narratives, critics and interpreters are not a little perplexed in determining where the one really ends and the other begins. The difficulty is in regard to chap. ii. 4, whether as a subscription it is to be connected with the preceding narrative, or as a superscription with what follows ; or whether it partly belongs to the one and partly to the other, for the three views have found able defenders. Practically the question may be deemed by many of little importance, whatever interest it may possess for the Biblical critic. Any importance attaching to it in this respect is mainly due to its forming a battle-ground in the controversy regarding the unity of Genesis ; but even here its importance has been overrated, for those who are ranged on opposite sides in that controversy are not unfrequently agreed in their views regarding this question. And yet, in a practical point of view, the place assigned to this verse may so affect its interpretation as to justify a somewhat extended examination.

The older expositors, for the most part, so far as they noticed the division of the two sections, considered this verse as the conclusion of the first section, principally because as a superscription of the second, the title would be directly opposed to the contents, inasmuch as no mention is made of the heavens, but only of the earth in the second section. But the document hypothesis of Astruc and Eichhorn gave prominence to the view already advanced by Vitringa, who connected this verse with the second section, mainly on the ground that it contains the Divine name, Jehovah-Elohim, peculiar to that section. The recent reaction against that hypothesis has revived the older view, and Ranke, Tiele, and Hävernick labour to show that chap. ii. 4 belongs to the first section. In this, however, they are opposed by Hengstenberg and Kurtz, equally zealous opponents of the document hypothesis, while, on the contrary, they obtain the concurrence of some of its advocates, as Tuch, Ewald, and Stähelin. Dreschler differs from both parties, as he holds that the first half of the verse belongs to the first section as a recapitulation of its contents, and an intimation that the history of creation was concluded ; and he considers that the new section begins with the words, " In the day that," &c.

In proof of this passage forming a superscription to the second section, it is argued that in all the other instances where the formula, " These are the generations," or its equivalent,

" The book of the generations," occurs in the Pentateuch, eleven times besides the present passage, it is as a superscription or title to what follows. And farther, it is urged that תּוֹלְדוֹת is not used in reference to an account of the birth or origin of a person or thing, but only of procreation and development ; the *genitive* connected with the term always denoting the assumed beginning, and itself the genealogical, or generally the historical progress of this beginning. The word, says Kurtz, never signifies history in the common sense of the term, without direct reference to genealogies.

But these arguments do not possess, as Delitzsch remarks, the weight usually ascribed to them. In the first place, although the words with which the verse begins usually commence a new section, yet, if anywhere, in the present instance there may have been occasion for a departure from this practice, inasmuch as the preceding important section is destitute of a title. Farther, the pronoun *Elle* (*these*) can refer equally well to what precedes as to what follows, as is evident from many instances in this history ; as Gen. x. 5, 20, 31, 32, and, in particular, the concluding subscriptions of Leviticus and Numbers. As to the second argument, it is remarked that, in the narrative of the creation, " the heavens and the earth " are considered not merely as existences, but as the gradually developed productions of the Creative word. And it may be added, with respect to the two arguments, that the expression, " the generations of the *heavens and the earth*," involves a peculiarity not common to any of the other instances which are brought into comparison with it.

These remarks, although not sufficient to prove that this verse must form the conclusion of the first section, yet show that there is no insuperable objection to that supposition, should other considerations require it. Such considerations are, on the other hand, detected in the fact that, while this verse purports to be the generation of the *heavens* no less than of the earth, the subject of the second narrative is exclusively the earth, and, in particular, man, with the arrangements made on his behalf ; while, on the contrary, it is very apposite to the first narrative, which describes the origin, progress, and completion of the heavens and the earth.

None of the proposed explanations of this formidable objection can be pronounced very satisfactory. Gabler takes "the heavens and the earth," as equivalent to *the world*, or the earth and its atmosphere, according to Gen. i. 8; Rosenmüller, as a *synecdoche* of the whole for a part; as *kosmos* and *mundus* are frequently used of the earth alone, so he supposes may the Hebrew equivalent הַשָּׁמַיִם וְהָאָרֶץ. But this can only take place where the universal idea is expressed by a single term, and never where recourse is had to a circumlocution formed by the juxtaposition of the constituent parts. Baumgarten, again, finds an explanation in man's relation to the world. "We have found much in the preceding history," he says, "which pointed to a further development of the creation, but the true initial point of all the development to be expected presents itself to us in man. Accordingly, in a narrative of the further evolution of heaven and earth, it is quite natural if the discourse is of man." To this Kurtz objects that it places in the background the idea of generation so prominent in *toledoth*. Kurtz's own explanation has respect to two points; first, how inorganic matter can be considered as *generative;* and secondly, how not only earth, but heaven also, stands related to man. But the learned disquisition of this ingenious writer has utterly failed to establish either of his propositions, that man is a *production of nature;* or that, being such, he may be properly considered a production of *heaven and earth*, from the close connexion in which these two parts of creation stand to one another in the first section of Genesis.

It thus appears, that whatever alternative be adopted with respect to the verse under consideration, neither is exempt from considerable difficulties; but if in any degree, these are greater on the view that it forms the title of the second narrative. But then, on the other hand, if it be transferred to the preceding section, the second must begin at verse 5, in a form, as Tuch and Kurtz remark, exceedingly abrupt, and so opposed to the genius of the language that the former of these writers pronounces it impossible. In these circumstances, the view of Dreschler, already referred to, though it has not met with much acceptance, promises a simple solution of the difficulty. The first part of the sentence—*These are the generations* (or *genesis*, as it is in the LXX.) *of the heavens and the earth when they were created*, (literally, *in their creation*)—is to be joined with the preceding history of the creation, while the remai der, "In the day of Jehovah-Elohim's making earth and hea.en," belongs to what follows, forming not merely the commencement of the paragraph, but also of the sentence in verse 5, notwithstanding the Masoretic punctuation.

Simplicity is not the only merit of this scheme. It satisfactorily disposes of the difficulty arising from the definition "heaven and earth," when the verse was taken to belong to the second narrative. It also removes the objection to a commencement so unnatural as that furnished in verse 5. Indeed Tuch, who assigns the whole verse to the second section, says the narrative begins with, "In the day," &c., a division which De Wette also follows in his translation. This division farther brings out very distinctly the difference of plan and purpose in the two narratives. Throughout the first narrative the usual form, "the heavens and the earth," is invariably used ; but here the exceedingly rare one, "earth and heavens," (occurring again only in Ps. cxlviii. 13,) as if on purpose at the very outset to apprise the reader that there is now a change of subject. The name Jehovah-Elohim, also, which occurs here for the first time, is in entire keeping with the remainder of the section.[1] Lastly, thus considered, the commencement of the two sections is somewhat analogous : "In the beginning," &c., and "In the day," &c., the difference being only in the opposite or changed circumstances of the two cases.

§ 10. *Introduction to the History of Man's Creation,* Gen. ii. 4-6.

In order to connect this narrative with the preceding, and at the same time form a fitting introduction to the detailed account of man's creation here to be presented, the point of view is thrown back to a period in the history of the earth when no shrub or herb clothed its sterile surface ; and when even the first conditions of vegetable life had no existence. Verses 4, 5. *In the day that the Lord God made earth and heaven there was no shrub of the field yet in the earth, and no herb of the field had yet sprouted, for the Lord God had not*

[1] For the import of Jehovah-Elohim see above, pp. 31-37.

caused it to rain upon the earth ; and man was not, to till the ground.

This describes a state of the earth's surface absolutely bare and barren. שִׂיחַ, *a shrub* or *bush*, here joined with עֵשֶׂב, *an herb*, to comprise the whole vegetable kingdom. טֶרֶם, (an adverb formed from שׂם, after the manner of *segolate* nouns,) followed by the *future*, is equivalent to *nondum* with the *pluperfect*, (Gen. xix. 4, xxiv. 45 ; Ex. ix. 30.) Latterly, it was used as a conjunction, in the sense of *priusquam*,[1] as it is taken in this instance, but incorrectly, by the English version after the translations of the LXX. and Vulgate. The literal rendering of the passage is : " Every shrub of the field was not yet," that is, *no shrub of the field was yet*, for such is the force of בֹל----טֶרֶם ; and so in the parallel clause. Even the necessary conditions of vegetation and growth were absent : there was no rain. Tuch, Knobel, and others of the same school, affirm that two reasons are assigned for the absence of vegetation at this period : the want of rain to moisten, and of man to cultivate, the soil ; but this is not correct. From anything known of the writer of Genesis, there is no reason to conclude that he could be guilty of the gross error of supposing that moisture and tillage are co-ordinate conditions of vegetable existence. The absence of man is noticed in close connexion with the absence of rain, but only because it was the writer's design to show how the wants then existing were to be supplied. The expression, *not yet*, intimates that the state of matters described was not to continue, but that plants, and man, too, were to be introduced in due course.

The time to which this description corresponds was *the day* in which were made *earth and heaven*. It was evidently prior to the Creative mandate, " Let the earth bring forth grass," &c. (chap. i. 11,) uttered, it may be supposed, towards the close of the third day, and after the dry land had emerged from the deep. The term בְּיוֹם is usually taken adverbially, as a general designation of time, *then, when ;* but the passages referred to by Tuch (Gen. v. 1 ; Ps. xviii. 1) do not fully bear out this view. In the present instance, however, there is no occasion to depart from the literal meaning of the term, *in the day*, for this does not refer, as is often supposed, to the whole process of creation which extended to six days or periods, but

[1] Noldius, Concordan. Partic. Heb. *Jenæ*, 1734, p. 339.

to certain specific arrangements. It is not the *creation of the heavens and the earth*, but the *making of earth and heaven* that is here spoken of. The former expression was the usual designation of the universe, the other may mean no more than the *dry land and the atmosphere*, (chap. i. 8, 10.) It may be objected that these were the works not of one day, but of two. But then it should be considered, that in the narrative of creation these two works, which in one point of view referred entirely to the waters, are not merely described as immediately succeeding one another in order, but are regarded as parts of one and the same operation, for it was not until the dry land was separated from the waters that the Creator pronounced the work to be " good."

Had it been the writer's intention to treat merely of the creation of man, without reference to the state of the earth at the period when he was introduced upon it, it would have been sufficient to begin the present section of his narrative with the sixth day. But the historian's purpose was also to describe man's appointed dwelling-place, the garden in Eden, and how it was planted with every goodly tree, and furnished by the all-bountiful Creator with all that was necessary for man, or conducive to his happiness. Hence the reference at the outset to the vegetable kingdom, as if to intimate that all the protracted preparations were mainly for man ; and that, as shall appear in the course of the history, by the fruits of the ground his wants should be supplied and his obedience tested.

On the due disposition of the atmosphere and dry land (fully described in chap. i. 6-10) followed the meteorological processes which are indispensable to the existence of plants. Ver. 6. *And a mist ascended from the earth and watered the whole face of the ground.* The *imperfect* יַעֲלֶה, conjoined with וְהִשְׁקָה, the *perfect,* denotes an operation commenced and continued, the two actions being connected as cause and effect, (Ewald, § 332, *b* ;) the vapour *ascended,* and so *watered* the ground, being returned in the form of rain, as may be concluded from verse 5. It is not meant, as is sometimes supposed, that the *mist* supplied the absence of rain, (Rosenmüller,) but was itself changed into rain, the want of which had been already noticed : and thus God " caused it to rain upon the earth," " The clouds pour down rain according to the vapour thereof," (Job xxxvi. 27.)

But although the historian notices the preparation thus made for the existence and growth of plants, he does not expressly mention their creation, but leaves it to be inferred from the preceding section, while he directly proceeds with his main subject, the formation of man. It is very singular that, with the exception of the one note in the introduction, already adverted to, there is no reference to time throughout this narrative ; but it is evident that onward from this point all belongs to the sixth day.

§ 11. *The Creation of the First Man*, Gen. ii. 7.

And the Lord God formed the man of the dust of the ground, and breathed into his nostrils the breath of life : and the man became an animated being.—This is not a statement of the fact of man's formation, but of the manner of it, as is plain from the use of the verb וַיִּיצֶר, *formed*, or *fashioned* as the potter moulds or models the clay, (Isa. lxiv. 8.) Of the manner of man's creation the previous narrative said nothing, but only showed that he was constituted of a far higher nature than the beings around him. But now, at the opening of this his moral history, it was necessary to know somewhat more regarding his origin, in order to understand the relation in which, by the law of his being, he stood to God and to the creation.

This master-work of creation consisted of two Divine acts, the formation of the human body, and the communication of life to it. As regards the former, it was made עָפָר מִן־הָאֲדָמָה, *dust from the ground*, *i.e.*, from or of dust of the ground : the *accusative* of the *material* being used after a verb of *making*, (see Ex. xxxvii. 24 ; xxxviii. 3 ; and Ewald, § 284, *a*.) This simple representation of the constituents of the human body is in strict accordance with the results of chemical and physiological investigations. The nomenclature and the analysis of the philosopher may be more accurate and minute than the popular phraseology of Moses, yet the results are the same. It is well known, from chemical analysis, that the animal body is composed, in the inscrutable manner called *organization*, of carbon, hydrogen, oxygen, nitrogen, lime, iron, sulphur, and phosphorus—substances which, in their various combinations, form a very large part of the solid ground.[1]

The view taken of the constitution of the human body in Genesis [2] is frequently referred to in other parts of Scripture. Man is said to be formed of the clay, (Job xxxiii. 6,) of the dust, (Eccles. iii. 20; xii. 7;) and death is spoken of as a return to the dust, (Job x. 9; xxxiv. 15; Ps. cxlvi. 4.) So also in the New Testament, "the first man" is described as "of the earth, earthy," (1 Cor. xv. 47.)

But besides the body which, although of a nobler mould, is yet common to man with the lower animals, there is another and a distinguishing principle imparted to him by the Almighty breathing into his nostrils the breath of life. The inspiration is said to be through the *nostrils*, (אַפַּיִם dual of אַף, *the nose*, so called, according to Fürst, from its being the most prominent part of the face,) because the function of respiration is chiefly visible in this part of the human frame, and the breath is the expression and the index of the life within. It is in this second act of the Creator that the first finds its necessary completion, and the result of the two is that "the man becomes a living soul," (Eng. Ver.,) or more correctly "an animated being," an expression already met with, as applied to the lower animals, (Gen. i. 21,) and equivalent to ψυχή ζῶσα, 1 Cor. xv. 45.

Wherein, then, it may be asked, consists the distinguishing superiority of man over all the other inhabitants of the earth in this notice respecting his formation, if the expression נֶפֶשׁ חַיָּה, does not point him out as endowed with *personality?* This has been variously answered. Some make the distinction to consist in נִשְׁמַת חַיִּים, *the breath of lives*, bestowed on man, and

---

[1] Encyclop. Brit. *Art.* Chemistry, vol. vi. p. 501.—"The elements of organic bodies are the same as those which constitute the inorganic world, save that the relative proportions are different, and that few comparatively of the elements can enter into the composition of organic compounds. The chief mass of such compounds is formed of only four elements, carbon, hydrogen, nitrogen, and oxygen; frequently of carbon, hydrogen, and oxygen alone; sometimes of carbon and hydrogen only. In every case of an organized structure, however, or of any substance capable of being formed into such a structure or tissue, there are not only the four elements just mentioned, but also sulphur, and several mineral salts in small proportion, but equally essential with the rest."

[2] The classical reader will recognise the parallel presented by the descriptions of the Poets, *e.g.*, Ovid, *Metam.* lib. i. 82; Juvenal, *Sat.* xiv. 35; Hesiod, *Opera et dies*, 61, 70.

the way in which it is expressly said to have been conferred. Others conceive that no such distinction is made in this passage which treats of man only in a physical relation, his moral character having been sufficiently indicated in chap. i. 26, 27.[1] Perhaps the truth lies between these two extremes. That the expression, *the breath of lives,* in itself implies no peculiar excellency in man, is evident from Gen. vii. 22, where it is so used as to include the lower animals, and yet the way in which the principle of life is said to be imparted to man may have been designed to denote a special pre-eminence on his part.[2] This is very much confirmed by the numerous references in other parts of Scripture to this divinely communicated vital principle. Thus, Job xxxii. 8, " But there is a spirit in man, and the inspiration (*breath*) of the Almighty giveth them understanding." Chap. xxxiii. 4, " The Spirit of God hath made me, and the breath of the Almighty hath given me life." But in Job xxvii. 3, the reference is merely to physical life : " all the while my breath is in me, and the Spirit of God is in my nostrils." Isaiah xlii. 5, " Thus saith God the Lord, he that created the heavens, and stretched them out ; he that spread forth the earth, and that which cometh out of it ; he that giveth breath unto the people upon it, and spirit to them that walk therein." Eccles. iii. 21, makes a distinction between " the spirit of man" (רוּחַ, synonymous with נְשָׁמָה,) that " goeth upward, and the spirit of the beast that goeth downward." Again, chap. xii. 7, " The dust shall return to the earth as it was, and the spirit shall return unto God who gave it." If then no particular stress is to be laid on the expression, " breath of lives," yet it must not be overlooked that in the formation of man the communication of life is described as a

---

[1] Calvin :—Quicquid sentiant plerique veterum, subscribere eorum sententiæ non dubito qui de animali hominis vita locum hunc exponunt : atque ita flatum interpretor, quem spiritum vitalem nominant. Siquis objiciat, non debuisse igitur discrimen poni inter hominem et cætera animantia, quum hic nihil referat Moses nisi quod omnibus simul commune est : respondeo, quamvis hic tantum memoretur inferior animæ facultas, quæ corpus inspirat, et illi dat vigorem et motum : non tamen obstare quin gradum suum obtineat anima, ideoque seorsum poni debuerit. De flatu primum loquitur Moses : deinde subjicit, datam esse animam homini qua viveret, sensuque et motu esset præditus. Jam virtutes humanæ animæ scimus plures esse ac varias. Quare nihil absurdi si nunc unam tantum attingat Moses : partem vero intellectualem omittat, cujus mentio primo capite facta est.

[2] Delitzsch, Die biblisch-prophetische Theologie, p. 190. Leip. 1845.

peculiar and distinct act of God. But it may be remarked that, in the second chapter, man's dignity and supremacy are not so much expressed in words, as implied in the several acts ascribed to him, and the provision made by the Creator on his account. He is described throughout this narrative as the one object of God's peculiar care, towards whom his attentions are directed, and in whom his delights are centered; all which circumstances are in beautiful harmony with the solemn purpose intimated in the preceding chapter, " Let us make man in our own image."

It is farther to be noticed that this account of the formation of man relates only to the individual—the first human being—THE MAN, and not like chap. i. 26, 27, to the race as represented by, and so included in the first ancestral pair. It is from overlooking this fact, that charges of contradiction with respect to this particular are rashly preferred against the history. It is true the first narrative does not specify the *numbers*, but only the *sexes*, of the original creation, but this information is fully supplied by the supplemental narrative.

Reference was already made to the uncertainty regarding the etymology of the Hebrew term, by which the race of mankind, and its first sole representative, the subject of this history, were designated. It may, however, be necessary to add, that there is no evidence whatever to support the conclusion that it has any connexion with *red*, as denoting a particular race. The relation between *Adam*, and *adamah* the *ground*, on the other hand, though not an etymological one, is deserving of consideration, as it is plainly indicated in the present passage. Farther, and more particularly, to take the expression as equivalent to the *Adamites*,[1] is contrary to the entire genius of the language: and certainly no Hebrew scholar would so understand it.

§ 12. *The Garden, Man's appointed Residence—its Productions, Situation, and his Office in Connexion with it*, Gen. ii. 8-15.

The state of the earth when man was introduced upon it, was widely different from that described in verse 5, when

---

[1] Journal of Sacred Literature, Jan. 1855, pp. 436, 449.

there was no plant on its surface yet unmoistened by fertilizing showers. At this later period, the earth is adorned with graceful and goodly trees, and there are fountains and rills and rivers. It might be fitly said of the world with which at this time God held close and uninterrupted intercourse, " Thou visitest the earth, and waterest it : thou greatly enrichest it with the river of God, which is full of water : thou preparest them corn, when thou hast so provided for it. Thou waterest the ridges thereof abundantly : thou settlest the furrows thereof : thou makest it soft with showers : thou blessest the springing thereof," (Ps. lxv. 9, 10.) But such was the distinguishing kindness exercised by the Beneficent Creator towards man, that not satisfied with the common bounties which nature furnished for his other creatures, He makes a special provision for him : verse 8, *And the Lord God planted a garden eastward in Eden ; and there he put the man whom he had formed.*

Eden, עֵדֶן, (compare the Greek ἡδονή, *voluptas,* which it greatly resembles in sound and sense,) signifies both in Arabic and Hebrew, *delight, tenderness, loveliness.* Some render גַּן־בְּעֵדֶן, " a garden in a pleasant region," or, according to the Vulgate, *paradisus voluptatis.* But that *Eden* is in this place the proper name of a district, is evident from its being said, Gen. iv. 6, that Nod lay to the east of Eden. The word occurs as an appellative for *pleasures* or *delights,* but only in the plural, Ps. xxxvi. 9 ; 2 Sam. i. 24. With a slight difference in the punctuation (עֶדֶן) the same word is used as the name of some other localities ; see 2 Kings xix. 12 ; Isaiah xxxvii. 12 ; Amos i. 5 ; most probably so denominated from their pleasant situation and appearance. In particular, the place referred to by the Prophet Amos was a pleasant valley in the neighbourhood of Damascus, greatly famed by Arab writers.

For more accurately defining the place of man's abode *in Eden,* which may have been an extensive country, the historian adds מִקֶּדֶם, *from the east,* equivalent to the English phrase, " on the east, or eastwards," and the Latin " ab occasu." The LXX. rightly considering the reference to space or geographical situation, renders it κατ᾽ ἀνατολάς, but other ancient versions erroneously refer it to time. Aquila ἀπὸ ἀρχῆς : Theodotion, ἐν πρώτοις ; and the Vulg., *a principio—*

a sense indeed which the expression admits, but only in later and poetical usage, Ps. lxxiv. 12; lxxvii. 6, 12. In the *eastward* of this choice region God plants *a garden*, a protected place, an enclosure, גַּן, (from גָּנַן, *to guard* or *protect*,) in contradistinction to שָׂדֶה, *the field* or *open country*. The Hebrew term applies to all enclosures for trees, herbs, fruits, or flowers. In the select locality, Eden, the Creator farther selects and sets apart—marks off and encloses a pleasant residence for his newly-formed son. The garden or residence set apart for man is rendered in the Samaritan recension, פרדים, by the LXX. and Symmachus, παράδεισος, and by the Vulg. *paradisus*, whence our *paradise;* but the etymology of this term is involved in obscurity. A Hebrew form, פַּרְדֵּם, occurs in Neh. ii. 8, Eccles. ii. 5, and Cant. iv. 13, meaning *a garden*, but it is evidently of foreign origin.

The garden was richly stored with the various vegetable productions which could contribute to man's happiness. **Verse 9,** *And out of the ground made the Lord God to grow every tree that is pleasant to the sight and good for food.*—A twofold object was kept in view: ornament was no less attended to than utility,—a characteristic which indeed marks all the productions of God. נֶחְמָד לְמַרְאֶה, *lovely to see,* compare chap. iii. 6. This sacred spot was the concentration of all that was beautiful and blooming in the young world, to such a degree that " the garden of the Lord" became a proverbial expression for denoting a state of the highest fruitfulness and fertility. It was the grand historical and yet ideal designation of the most consummate terrene excellence, as in Isaiah li. 3, " For the Lord shall comfort Zion, he will comfort all her waste places ; and he will make her wilderness like Eden and her desert like the garden of the Lord."

Of the goodly trees which the Divine planter caused to spring up in the garden, special mention is made of two: *The tree of life also in the midst of the garden, and the tree of the knowledge of good and evil.* The reason why these trees are particularly specified, fully appears in the course of the history.

The situation of the garden is next described (verses 10-14) in connexion with the river and its four streams, by which Eden and the neighbouring countries were watered. **Verse 10,**

*And a river went out of Eden to water the garden ; and from
thence it was parted, and became four heads.*—To the river of
Eden there are frequent allusions in Scripture.   It furnished
some of the finest imagery for Psalmists and Prophets, when
setting forth the blessedness resulting from living in communion with God, or dwelling in his glorious habitation.   Thus
in Ps. xlvi. 4, mention is made of " a river, the streams
whereof shall make glad the city of God, the holy place of the
tabernacles of the Most High."   And more directly Ps. xxxvi.
8, " They shall be abundantly satisfied with the fatness of thy
house ; and thou shalt make them drink of the river of thy
pleasures."   So in Ezek. xlvii., Zech. xiv. 8, for representing
the diffusion of the blessings of salvation over the earth, the
image evidently resting on Gen. ii. 10, is that of a stream
which, issuing from Jerusalem, refreshes the parched and
desolate region around.[1]   In the New Testament, also, John
iv. 18 ; and in the description of the heavenly paradise, Rev.
xxii. 1, " He showed me a pure river of water of life, clear
as crystal, proceeding out of the throne of God and of the
Lamb."

It cannot with certainty be concluded from the narrative in
Genesis, whether the source of the river was within the garden
or outside of it, although the latter was most probably the
case.   It sprung up, however, in Eden, flowed through, and so
watered the garden.   That this highly favoured soil was
abundantly supplied with the means of irrigation, so very
essential in oriental climes, may be certainly inferred from the
comparison contained in Gen. xiii. 10, " All the plain of Jordan was well watered everywhere, before the Lord destroyed
Sodom and Gomorrah, even as the garden of the Lord."   At
the place where the river issued from the garden, (מִשָּׁם, *from
there,*) it separated and became (הָיָה לְ, *to become into*) four
(רָאשִׁים) *heads* or *beginnings :* not " had four fountains," (Michaelis,) or main streams.   In the same manner this term is
used of the *beginning* of the way, or the place where two roads
part, Ezek. xvi. 25 ; xxi. 24 [21].   The streams are called
" beginnings," considered with reference to the place where
they originated or assumed separate existence, but in their
farther course they are designated " rivers," verses 13, 14.

[1] See Hengstenberg, Christologie, 2te Ausg., vol. ii. p. 604. Berlin, 1855.

Farther, the four branches are named, and their courses pointed out by a notice of the countries which they bordered, except in the case of the fourth, where the name only is given, the Euphrates, evidently being so well known as not to require any additional specification.   Verse 11, *The name of the first* [arm or branch] *is Pishon : that is it which compasseth the whole land of Chavila.*   It is not necessary to conceive that the river completely encircled the district here named, for סבב is frequently used in the sense of fetching a compass or sweeping round one side or border, (Num. xxi. 4 ; Jud. xi. 18.)   Chavila is next described by its natural productions.   Verses 11, 12, *Where there is gold.   And the gold of that land is good : there is bdellium and the onyx-stone.*   Chavila is here distinguished not only as a place of gold, that is where gold was found, and of a very pure quality, but from the article before זהב, as the land of *the gold,* the land which chiefly produced gold.   Besides the gold, two other productions are mentioned : the one is the *b'dolach,* to the appearance of which, the manna is compared, (Num. xi. 7,) and which must therefore have been well known to the Hebrews, although its nature cannot now be determined. The word does not occur except in these two passages, and it is a question with interpreters whether it denotes a mineral or vegetable production.   By the LXX. it was considered a precious stone, and translated in the present passage by ἄνθραξ, and in Num. xi. 7, by κρύσταλλος.   The Jewish Rabbins considered it to mean *pearls,* a view adopted by Bochart and Gesenius.   But an older and more probable opinion found in Aquila, Symmachus, Theodotion, and which Josephus also follows, is that *b'dolach* is the *bdellion,* an aromatic and precious gum, which issues from a tree growing in Arabia, India, Media, and particularly Bactriana.   The other production of Chavila was the stone *shoham,* by which many of the older authorities understand the *Onyx,* (LXX. on Ex. xxxix. 13 ; Job xxviii. 16 ; Aquila on Ex. xxv. 7 ; xxxv. 9, &c. ; Theod. and Sym. on the same passages, and Gen. ii. 12,) or the Sardonyx, (Aquila on Gen. ii. 12 ; Vulg. on Job xxviii. 16,) or the Sardius, (LXX. on Ex. xxv. 7 ; xxxv. 9.)   Others, as the Targums, Saadias, the Arabic of Erpenius, and Josephus, take it to be the *Beryl,* a precious stone of a sea-green colour.

Verses 13, 14, *And the name of the second river is Gihon : the*

*same is it that compasseth the whole land of Cush. And the name
of the third river is Hiddekel : that is it which goeth towards
the east of Assyria.*—This last expression has occasioned some
difficulty. The Hiddekel is by universal consent the Tigris,
but the country commonly known as Assyria lies on the east
side of that river, not on the west. The Hebrew phrase קִדְמַת
אַשּׁוּר has accordingly been rendered by Michaelis and others,
" before Assyria," in respect to the writer's point of view on the
west of the Tigris ; but this is opposed to the idiom of the language, for in the other passages where קִדְמָה occurs, (Gen. iv.
16 ; 1 Sam. xiii. 5 ; Ezek. xxxix. 11,) it undoubtedly denotes
towards the east. Another explanation is, that this is not to
be understood of Assyria proper, but of the whole region extending from the Mediterranean to the Tigris. In Gen. xxv.
18, the territory of the Ishmaelites is described as east of Egypt,
" as thou goest to Assyria," which, however, could only be
reached through Mesopotamia or Babylonia. This is considered
as strongly confirmatory of the opinion that in the present instance the Assyrian provinces of Mesopotamia and Babylonia
are meant.

And the fourth river is Euphrates. This was so well known
to the Hebrews as not to require any additional marks of determination. It is frequently referred to in Scripture as " the
river," (Ex. xxiii. 31 ; Isa. viii. 7,) as being by far the most
important stream in Western Asia ; and in Deut. i. 7 it is
termed " the great river."

After this extended digression on the geographical situation
of the garden, the historian reverts to the point on which he
had touched in verse 8, the location of man in the garden, and
now farther intimates his office in connexion with it. Verse
15, *And the Lord God took the man, and put him into the garden of Eden to dress it, and to keep it.*

Man was not created in the garden, but was introduced into
it. It was not his birthplace or native soil. He was not born
heir, so to speak, to this patrimony : it was in every sense a
gift of God, which might be recalled if he proved unworthy of
it, as was soon, indeed, found to be the case. A twofold office
was assigned to the man in connexion with the garden into
which he was thus, sometime after his creation, transferred.
First, it was appointed to him, *to labour* or *cultivate it*, לְעָבְדָהּ,

(see verse 5,) including therein all the operations of tillage, and of training all the vegetable productions necessary to his subsistence, or which served to beautify the situation and rejoice the sight. Simple labour was not a part of the curse incurred by man on transgression, but was appointed to him from the first. It was only wearisome, exhausting toil which commenced after the Fall in consequence of the curse pronounced upon the ground. At his creation man was appointed to " subdue the earth," (chap. i. 28,) and in this work of subjugation a commencement is to be made with the garden of Eden, by diligently bringing to light the latent powers of its soil and regulating their exercise. But, secondly, the man was appointed to *keep* the garden, as well as to cultivate it. This cannot refer, as is sometimes supposed, to the same or similar acts and exercises as those already noticed. The ideas conveyed by the two verbs עָבַד and שָׁמַר are totally distinct. Nor does the latter term simply mean *to keep possession :* it is rather to be taken, in the present case, *to watch* or *guard* from any hostile attack, a sense in which this verb is frequently used. But this assumes the existence of some evil and inimical power, meditating harm not so much to the garden as to the possessor of it. Thus viewed, there is here a Divine premonition or warning to the man, the inhabitant of Eden, of the nature of the danger to which he was exposed, and of the quarter whence it might proceed. The pure idea of creation would forbid the seeking of this inimical power in the creature as such. A hostile power can only proceed from a wicked will which has broken loose from God. As to this there can be no doubt, from the disclosures presently made in the history, (Baumgarten.) As well the term שָׁמַר as עָבַד points back to כְּבָשׁ, (chap. i. 28,) but it is much less than this which is here demanded of the first man ; he is not so much called upon *to tread* the wicked One *under foot,* as to hinder his approach.

EXCURSUS III.—THE SITUATION OF EDEN.

On the situation of Eden, and its memorable garden, the first and favourite residence of man, innumerable dissertations have been written. But notwithstanding the labour expended in determining this most interesting[1] and ancient of geographical problems, the results have not been very satisfactory. This may at first sight appear somewhat inexplicable, considering the copious and apparently definite details furnished regarding the locality ; but a careful examination of the subject will at least moderate the reader's expectations and surprise.

The designation of the garden as "eastward in Eden," is of course very indefinite, whatever may have been the writer's point of view. But it may be supposed that this indefiniteness is more than compensated by the mention of no less than four noted rivers which had a peculiar relation to one another, and to the river which watered the garden. Besides the obscurities connected with the geographical notes in general, and the natural productions specified as abounding in the neighbourhood of the rivers, one main difficulty is to ascertain two of the four streams enumerated—the Pishon and Gihon, and particularly to discover any one spot on the earth at present fully answering to all the conditions of the case, as these are usually understood. The true state of the problem will, however, be better understood from a review of the principal theories which have been formed on the subject.

Respecting two of the rivers of Paradise there is no question: the Hiddekel and the Phrath are by all admitted to be the Tigris and Euphrates. It would, accordingly, seem most natural in this investigation to set out from these fixed points, as the most likely method of arriving at correct conclusions in the attempt to identify the two remaining streams.

Keeping, however, these fixed points in view, the great difficulty consists in bringing the Tigris and Euphrates into such a relation to two other rivers that the four can be regarded as *heads* or *arms* proceeding from *one* main stream. Of the writers on this subject, only a few have attempted a solution of this special difficulty. Among these are Calvin, Huet, Bochart, Steph. Morinus, J. Vorst ; and of English authors, Patrick and Wells.[2] These are upon the whole agreed, and

---

[1] Quamquam non sit terrestris Paradisi situs inter ea, quæ ad cœlestis Paradisi ingressum cognosci prorsus debent; habet tamen ejus cognitio præter alios usus hunc fructum, ut Mosis historia rite a nobis intelligatur.—Marck. *Historia Paradisi,* Lib. I. cap. xiv. ? i. p. 134. Amst. 1705.

[2] *Huet,* Tractatus de situ Paradisi terrestris, Amst. 1698: (also in Ugolini Thesaurus, vii. 501.) *Morinus,* Dissertatio de Paradiso terrestri ; Ugol. vii. 633.

thus understand the description. "It (the river of Paradise) divided itself from thence (*i.e.*, issuing out of the garden) into four rivers — two towards the north, and two towards the south." According to this view, Pishon and Gihon are the two principal mouths of the Schat-al-Arab, the name given to the united stream of the Tigris and Euphrates. Huet, Bochart, and Morinus regarded the western branch as the Pishon, and the eastern as the Gihon. Calvin maintained the reverse of this. Cush was supposed to be the modern Persian Chusistan, or the country of the Susii, called also Kissioi ; but, according to Calvin, Cush was Arabia. Eden was thus to be sought in the district of Korna, where the Euphrates and Tigris unite.

Against this view many strong objections may be urged. 1. Cush, which occurs so often in the Old Testament as a geographical designation, is, upon the above supposition, applied to a country which is so named nowhere else. 2. It cannot be shown that the two principal mouths of the Schat-al-Arab existed at a very remote period, and even were it otherwise, they are hardly of so much importance as to be spoken of in the same way as the Euphrates and Tigris before their junction. "The union of the Tigris and the Euphrates," says Lyell, "must undoubtedly have been one of the modern geographical changes on our earth." 3. The above interpretation of Gen. ii. 10 is very unnatural. The figurative expression *heads* cannot be so understood ; and farther, as Le Clerc observes, אצי, *issued* or *went out*, can only apply to the direction in which the river flows, (see Ezek. xlvii. 1, 8, 12,) and so excludes all reference to the upper course or courses before junction.

But more objectionable than this was the theory of J. Hopkinson,[1] who considered Paradise to be situated about Babylon, and in order to make up the number of four rivers proceeding from one stream, he included two of the canals of the Euphrates —Nahar Malca and Maarsares. The former, proceeding east-

---

Bochart, Epistola de Paradisi situ, Ugol. vii. 627. *Vorst*, Dissertatio de Paradiso, Ugolinus, vii. 695. *Wells*, Historical Geography of the Old and New Testament, [Oxford, 1809.] A very good summary of the views of foreign writers is contained in Winer's Realwörterbuch, 3te Ausg. *Art.* Eden, vol. i. pp. 284-294, to which the author has been much indebted.

[1] Descriptio Paradisi, Leyd. 1593, [Ugolinus, vii. 607.]

ward, was presumed to be the Pishon, so that Chavila must be Susiana ; the latter, proceeding in a western direction, was the Gihon, and so Cush was Arabia. This gives a more natural interpretation of Gen. ii. 10 than that of the preceding theory; but then, 1. It is utterly inconceivable that, in any description of Paradise, two artificial canals should be enumerated with the Euphrates and Tigris. But, admitting these canals to be natural rivers, they do not possess so prominent and peculiar a character as would lead to their being thus distinguished, in a country so intersected by streams. 2. Of the Nahar Malca, whose course, moreover, is not accurately known, it can hardly be said that it flows round the land of Chavila ; for it enters the Tigris, which forms for a great distance the boundary of Susiana. 3. The identity of Chavila and Susiana rests only on the previous assumption regarding the Pishon.

To avoid the difficulty presented from regarding the four rivers as *connected*, attempts have, on the other hand, been made to deduce from the Hebrew an entirely different sense: or it has been assumed that the description no longer strictly applies, inasmuch as the course of the rivers must have greatly changed during the lapse of ages.

Thus, Verbrugge [1] takes נָהָר to mean a multitude of waters and fountains in Eden, and, proceeding on that supposition, deems it only necessary to discover some district in Asia abounding in fountains. Much the same view is taken by Pye Smith, who remarks, " The multitude of droppings and trick-lings, rills and streamlets, [from the surrounding hills,] having one beneficial design, and ever tending to confluence, would, in the mind of a primeval writer, readily coalesce into a singular term, a river. We have an appropriate example in Ps. lxv. 10, where the aggregate of showers is called ' the river of God, full of water.' " [2] In regard to this, it should be noticed that, irrespective of the distinction between poetical expressions and a simple prose style, it does not appear that, in the passage adduced, the Psalmist at all referred to the aggregate of showers when he mentioned " the river of God," but only to the source whence the showers proceed.

The other mode of escape from the difficulties of the subject,

---

[1] Oratio de situ Paradisi in Observv. de Nomin. Hebr. plur. Num. p. 11.
[2] Cyc. Bib. Lit. *Art.* Paradise, vol. ii. p. 471.

by supposing great geological changes, either at the flood or at a period subsequent to the composition of Genesis, facilitates the task of the investigator, inasmuch as he is thereby relieved from the necessity of identifying the Mosaic description with the present geographical aspect of the country; but it may be said to remove that description almost, if not entirely, out of the way. Yet this view of the matter has commended itself to many distinguished writers, as Le Clerc, Reland,[1] and recently Baumgarten; although early objected to by Calvin, so far as regarded the changes on the earth's surface previous to Moses:—
"Adde quod topographiam suam Moses (meo quidem judicio) ad suæ ætatis captum accommodavit."

Le Clerc held the Pishon to be the Chrysorrhoas, which, rising in the neighbourhood of Damascus, flowed through a land of gold, as may be inferred from its name. But the arguments, philological and otherwise, upon which this opinion is founded, are worthy of no consideration. For Chavila, Le Clerc refers to 1 Sam. xv. 7, where it is spoken of in connexion with "Shur, that is over against Egypt," and so not far from Cœlesyria: Cush is Cassiotis in Syria, Gihon the Orontes, and, accordingly, Eden was situated in Syria. Reland understood by the Pishon the Phasis, which rises in the Moschian mountains, and is mentioned by Strabo in connexion with the anciently famous gold-land Colchis (Chavila:) the Gihon is the Araxes, which, still frequently called *Jihoon-el-Ras*, rises in Armenia, and falls into the Caspian sea: Cush, the country of the Cossæi, who are said to have dwelt in the neighbourhood of Media and the Caspian sea. According to this representation, the four rivers had their origin in the Armenian mountains, and thus, in *one district* at least, which is thought to answer sufficiently all the conditions of the problem. Eden, on this supposition, was Armenia. This also was the view of Calmet; and is in general adopted by the English authors, Hales, Faber, and Pye Smith.

J. D. Michaelis originated another hypothesis.[2] Though doubtful as to some of the names, he was inclined to consider the Gihon to be the Oxus of the ancients, which still bears the

---

[1] *Le Clerc*, Commentarius in Genesin, Amst. 1693, p. 19. *Reland*, De situ Paradisi tenestris in Dissertt. Miscel., vol. i. Traj. 1706, [Ugol. vii. 581.]

[2] Supplementa ad Lexica Hebraica, Gothing. 1784-92.

name *Jihoon, i.e.*, the stream, similar to the Hebrew designation which comes from a verb, signifying *to break* or *issue forth*, Job xl. 18, [23]. Cush, Michaelis compares with a city Chath on the Oxus, which occupied the site of the modern Balkh. Chavila, he identifies with the nation called Chwalisker or Chwalisser, on the Caspian. Pishon, although Michaelis does not say so, is in that case the Araxes. Jahn in general agrees with Michaelis, only he takes Pishon to be the Phasis.[1]

Hammer[2] finds the Mosaic paradise in the Bactrian table-land. Pishon is the Sihon or Jaxartes which rises near the city Cha, and surrounds the land Ilah, where there were mines of gold and precious stones, and where also bdellium was found. Chavila is thus Chowaresm, and Gihon must be the Oxus in the neighbourhood of the Jaxartes, and which rises in the country Kush or Hindukush. Link[3] takes Cush to be the country about the Caucasus : Pishon is the Phasis, Gihon the Kur, and as the sources of the four rivers lie at no great distance from one another, he thus discovers Paradise in the high lands of Armenia and Grusinia, the native country of fruit-trees and many species of grain.

All the preceding theories classed under this second head, have this in common, that they understand the biblical description of Paradise as distinctly pointing to a particular region in Asia, which, although no longer strictly answering to all the particulars, lay somewhere on the borders of the Euphrates and Tigris ; and then starting from the sources of these rivers, the hypotheses in question seek to connect the obscure names, Chavila, Cush, Pishon, and Gihon, with names of a similar sound in Syria, Armenia, Persia, and the environs of the Caspian sea. But it may be observed in general that nothing can be more deceptive than conclusions deduced from supposed etymological similarities in oriental names of rivers or districts. This will be seen to be particularly the case with the rivers and countries mentioned in the geographical account of Paradise. Thus Gihon, or, according to the Arabic, Jihoon, certainly, and probably Pishon, were used as appellatives, alone or as prefixes, signifying *a stream* in general ; just as the

---

[1] Bibl. Archäologie, vol. i. p. 27. Wien, 1796.
[2] Wiener, Jahrbücher d. Lit. 1820, ix. 21.
[3] Urwelt, i. 307.

old British *Avon* of the same meaning has become the proper name of several rivers in England, Wales, and Scotland.

More particularly it is to be noticed with respect to the preceding theories—1. That although Cush in Scripture is a comprehensive, yet it is not a variable geographical designation, and therefore there is no warrant for giving it a new and special meaning, as is done by Le Clerc, Reland, Michaelis, and others. 2. That the Chavila of 1 Sam. xv. 7, is to be sought for in Arabia, and so cannot have been washed by the Chrysorrhoas. 3. That it appears from more recent observation, that the Phasis of the ancients has its rise not in Armenia, but in the Caucasus, a discovery which entirely overthrows Reland's theory. And, 4. That it is exceedingly unsafe to identify Chavila, as Michaelis attempts, with a name or a nation which does not appear in any ancient author.

In these circumstances, after so many fruitless attempts to arrive at any definite conclusions on the subject, it need occasion no surprise that Rationalistic writers should pronounce the geographical description of Paradise mythical, and class it with the Greek myths of the gardens of the Hesperides, the islands of the Blessed, or the journey of Io. It is admitted by these writers, that an ancient tradition regarding the primitive seat of the human race in Western Asia, may have supplied the germ of the description which grew into its present form out of the free combination of known and half-known, and so unknown, geographical elements like the Greek legends adverted to ; so that the expectation of finding Paradise on the map of the earth is pronounced as reasonable as to hope for the discovery of the gardens of the Hesperides, or what is supposed to approach nearer the Hebrew tradition, the Indian mountain Meru, whence four streams were said to issue to water the whole earth. This view was put forth in Britain in a modified form by the writers of the " Universal History :" " We are to consider Paradise described according to Moses' notion of things, and that imperfect knowledge of the world which they had in those early times." [1]

But even where the mythical view is adopted in all its extent, there are found writers like Sickler, Buttmann, and

---

[1] Ancient Universal History, vol. i. p. 118. Lond. 1747.

Hartmann,[1] diligently employed in settling what rivers and lands may have been probably meant in the description. And though a review of the theories thus put forward may contribute little to the elucidation of the subject, it will be useful in a historical point of view, while it will farther show the wanton violence done to the text, and the crude notions attributed to it.

Sickler supposes that the author of the myth understood by the *river*, the Caspian sea, which in his apprehension was an immense stream from the east. The first principal river is Pishon, which surrounded the whole of the then known earth from the east even to the Nile. The second principal river was the Atlantic ocean, the Mediterranean and Black seas, including the Phasis : this, in the view of the writer, enclosed the whole earth from the West to the Nile. The third and fourth rivers, the Tigris and Euphrates, are merely land-streams, (*Landflüsse*,) which indeed divide one country from another, but can surround none. Eden is thus to be sought near the Caspian sea, where there are many fruitful and pleasant districts.

According to Buttmann, the myth of Paradise was introduced to the West from Southern Asia. The original poet conceived the four greatest rivers of the earth known to him as issuing from one quarter, and as branches of one main stream. In the middle of Southern Asia, the author was well acquainted with the Indus and the Ganges ; and the Shat-al-Arab, (the combined Euphrates and Tigris, named through the transportation of the myth towards Western Asia, the Euphrates, from the principal stream known there,) towards the west, and Irabatti in Ava and Pegu, towards the east, bounded the world, as known to him. It is unnecessary, however, to descend to particulars.

Hartmann, again, regards the whole of the second chapter of Genesis as a product of the Babylonian or Persian period, and he finds Paradise in Northern India, in the celebrated vale of Kashmir. As this valley is encircled by a chain of impassable snowy mountains, where all the northern rivers which fall into the Oxus, and all the southern rivers constituting the Indus,

---

[1] *Sickler*, Augusti Theol. Monatschrift, I. i. p. 1. *Buttmann*, Mythologus I. 63-121 ; Berlin, 1828. *Hartmann*, Aufklärung über Asien, vol. i. p. 249.

have their origin, while the valley itself is watered by the river Behnt, (Hydaspes,) it might easily happen, this author thinks, that an ancient tradition would by degrees be so modified as to make the several rivers originate in one stream rather than in one mountain range.   Then the Hebrew writer enumerated, as the four rivers of Paradise, such as seemed to him the greatest, and so most worthy of the distinction.   Gihon is the Oxus, Pishon the Phasis; Chavila is to be recognised in Colchis, and Cush in Bactria or Balkh.

Ewald has recently propounded another theory on this inexhaustible subject.   " The description of Paradise as regards its origin," he says, " will never be rightly recognised, or the four rivers correctly determined, until it is admitted that the names of the four streams have been entirely changed, and partly in course of the tradition.   The Pishon and the Gihon are the Indus and the Ganges; and instead of two rivers originally corresponding better to these, there were added to them in the transit of the tradition to the Hebrews in Palestine, the Euphrates and Tigris, with which they were better . acquainted."[1]

Equally vague, fanciful, and absurd as these conceptions of the situation of Paradise, was the view entertained by Josephus, who says, " The garden was watered by one river, which . went round about the whole earth, and was parted into four parts.   Phiso , which denotes a multitude, running into India, makes its exi 'nto the sea, and is by the Greeks called Ganges. Euphrates also, as well as Tigris, goes down into the Red Sea, ... Geon runs through Egypt, and denotes what arises from the East, which the Greeks call Nile."   Not only Josephus, but several of the Fathers of the early Church, particularly Epiphanius, Theophilus, and Philostorgus, were of opinion that Gihon meant the Nile.   And of Rabbinical writers favourable to this view may be mentioned Kimchi and Abarbanel ; but according to Nachmanides, Rabbi Saadias Gaon and Rashi, Pishon is the Nile.   In modern times the notion that Gihon is the Nile, or more strictly the river of Nubia and Ethiopia, different from *Jeor*, the Nile of Egypt, has found supporters in Schulthess, Gesenius, Fürst, Bertheau, and others.   The idea, so far as it can be traced back, seems to have originated with the

---

[1] Geschichte des Volkes Israel, 2te Ausg., vol. i. p. 377.

Jews of Alexandria, who, to all appearance, were led to entertain it for no other reason than that they naturally took Cush
to be the African Ethiopia. But, however this may be, the
notion was introduced into the Septuagint translation, where
in Jer. ii. 18, Γηών is used for שִׁחוֹר, which undoubtedly means
the Nile. The same Greek term also occurs in the Apocryphal
Ecclesiasticus (xxiv. 27,) in a connexion which leads Gesenius,
Hitzig, and others, to think that it applies to the Nile; but
this is exceedingly improbable. The passage with its context
is as follows :—Speaking of the law of Moses, the writer says,
"It overflows with wisdom like the Pishon, and like the Tigris
in the days of spring: it is filled with understanding as the
Euphrates, and as the Jordan in the days of harvest: it sheds
instruction *as the light*, (ἐκφαίνων ὡς φῶς, which, as the work
is a translation from the Hebrew, is by many considered to be
a false reading of כְּאוֹר for כִּיאֹר, as Amos viii. 8, and that it should
be *as the Jeor or Nile*,) and as the Gihon in the days of vin-
tage." Either way, however, identity is excluded.

The above appears to be all that can be said in favour of the
view which identifies the Gihon with the Nile. It is true the
Ethiopians call the Nile Gejōn and Gewōn, but this goes for
nothing, as there is the authority of Ludolph for stating that
this designation originated from the use of the Septuagint, and
from the biblical interpretation.[1]

On the other hand, the view thus set forth supposes that the
writer of the description of Paradise must have imagined that
the Nile originates in Asia, near the Euphrates and the Tigris.
This is quite conceivable to the defenders of this theory, and
they adduce passages from classic authors, showing that the
Greeks also fancied a connexion between the Nile and the
rivers of Asia. But apart from the inspiration claimed for the
writer of Genesis, it is utterly inconceivable that one who on
every other point shows much critical discernment, and particularly one like Moses intimately acquainted with Egypt and
Ethiopia, could by any considerations be led to suppose that
the Nile rose in the north of Asia.

To obviate the difficulty which presents itself on the above
view of the matter, if the smallest discernment be allowed to

---

[1] Historia Æthiopica, Lib. I. 8. *Franc.* 1681. Lexicon Æthiop. p. 544.

the writer of Genesis, Bertheau[1] has recourse to the expedient of geological changes to account for the striking differences between the present and the past geographical aspect of the case. But, admitting such changes to the utmost reasonable extent, it may be safely affirmed that no changes which geologists can discern on the earth's surface, subsequent to the human period, are at all sufficient to account for such a mighty revolution in the courses of the rivers of Asia and Africa as this theory demands. And it is no less strange that a writer like Delitzsch should be reduced to the dilemma in which he acknowledges, " I do not venture to maintain that Moses conceived that the Nile had its source in Asia, but I do not venture to deny it."

Thus far in review of the more prominent of the almost interminable theories advanced, with more or less confidence, regarding the situation of Paradise. With the exclusion of the view which holds the description to be entirely or partly mythical, the other theories may be divided into two classes : first, such as consider Eden to have been situated somewhere near the sources of the Tigris and the Euphrates, and thus in Armenia ; and, secondly, such as place it in Babylonia, at the junction of these two streams. Of none, however, of the schemes proposed can it be said that it answers all the conditions of the problem, save in a very remote degree. As regards two of the rivers specified, no certain conclusions can be deduced from anything that has hitherto been advanced on the subject, and all that can be safely affirmed is, that Eden must be sought in the neighbourhood of the two known rivers, and, so far as probability can determine, near their source.

This result cannot be pronounced very specific or satisfactory, but, after so much laborious research by the critic and antiquarian, it must be felt that until our acquaintance with the geography of Central Asia is considerably enlarged, it is all that can be reasonably expected. At present our knowledge of these localities is limited and imperfect, and it will be far safer, in the circumstances, to admit that at present the problem cannot be solved, than attempt to add to the number of

---

[1] Die der Beschreibung der Lage des Paradieses zu Grunde liegenden geograph. Anschauungen, Gött. 1848.

crude hypotheses. But, imperfect as our knowledge is of the physical conformation of the countries watered by the Euphrates and Tigris, and of the contiguous regions, more particularly those to the north, it enables us to say that these localities have been the subject of important geological changes at a comparatively modern period. The *recent* union, as Lyell pronounces it, of the Euphrates and Tigris has been already adverted to. It may be farther stated that other important changes are known to have taken place in the course of the former of these streams. And what is of more importance in its bearing on the present question is a fact testified by the most eminent geologists, that in, and in the neighbourhood of the region where we are approximately led to seek the place of Paradise, great alterations have occurred in the relative distribution of land and water. It is held by writers qualified to form an opinion on the subject, that in the neighbourhood of the Caspian and Aral seas there existed at some remote period a vast inland sea of brackish water as large as the present Mediterranean, and of which the Caspian and Aral are the diminished type. "The former existence of an interior sea, which occupied a great part of the lower regions of Asia, has been long believed by modern Chinese geographers, not only from tradition, but from the actual phenomena which the surface of the earth now presents to us."[1] And Lyell gives a prominent place among the regions of "subterranean disturbance" to that which extends through a large part of Central Asia to the Azores, or from China and Tartary through Lake Aral and the Caspian to the Caucasus, and the countries bordering the Black Sea.

But while admitting that a full solution of the problem is at present unattainable, it will hardly suffice to take refuge in the view which regards the description as applicable to an antediluvian state of things, and not to the time of Moses. A description so full and circumstantial, in a narrative where other important matters are passed over with the utmost brevity, cannot have been inserted without an important purpose, which, whatever it may be, is hardly compatible with geographical relations which had ceased long before the period when Moses wrote. It is much more reasonable to conclude that the fulness of de-

[1] North British Review, May 1846, pp. 194, 195.

tails was designed to give such a description of the locality that, whatever its condition may have been in the time of Moses, its geographical situation might be traced in some future age. That this shall be realized there is every reason to believe ; and, judging from what is going on at present, and what is doing to advance our acquaintance with remote countries and times, such a result may be attained at no distant day. And, should this be the case, there will be found another proof among the many of a similar kind already accumulated, that Moses was in this, as in other things, led by the Spirit of God, in describing the situation of the first dwelling-place of man.

§ 13. *The Divine Prohibition addressed to Man, and the Purpose entertained towards him*, Gen. ii. 16-18.

Man has had assigned to him a residence and an occupation. He has been placed by the Creator in the garden of Eden to cultivate and to guard it. For this latter part of his duty he required special instructions : he needed to be told whence danger might be apprehended, and how it should be warded off. Accordingly, the Creator is here introduced as the Instructor of his moral creature, making known to him the Divine will, and encouraging him in duty by the intimation of a purpose entertained towards him of farther adding to his happiness. In the whole of the Divine procedure relative to this matter, respect is had to man's appetencies and capacities, physical, moral, and social.

In regard to man's physical wants, and the abundant provision made for them (comp. ver. 9) it is said, ver. 16, *And the Lord God commanded the man, saying, Of every tree in the garden thou mayest freely eat.* וַיְצַו עַל־הָאָדָם—" He charged it upon the man," that is, laid upon him a command, Gen. xxviii. 1 ; but the *accusative* of the person is the more common construction, Gen. iii. 11 ; xxvi. 11. Although the matter in itself is to be viewed rather as a permission, and not strictly a command, yet it takes this particular form from the prohibition which follows, and with which it is intimately connected. The form of conveyance is of the most liberal kind, מִכֹּל עֵץ־הַגָּן אָכֹל

בֹאכֵל—" Of every tree of the garden *thou canst* or *mayest eat*," freely or without restriction, save that which is immediately specified. " A very liberal concession, which was abundantly sufficient to demonstrate that it was not envy (of which the Divine nature is not capable) which moved their Creator to abridge our first parents' liberty in one particular," (Patrick.)

With regard, however, to the moral character and capacities of man, it is added, ver. 17, *But of the tree of the knowledge of good and evil, thou shalt not eat of it : for in the day that thou eatest thereof thou shalt surely die.*—In the words " thou shalt" and " thou shalt not," are heard the first utterances of a moral law, and the intimation that the Creator has become the Governor, and that the creature has risen to the rank of subject.

This is obviously not a place to enter upon any discussion of the questions connected with the federal relation of the first man, or the position which he sustained with respect to his posterity. Nor will it be necessary to advance anything in vindication of the Divine procedure, in placing man in a state of probation, or of the particular mode in which his character was to be determined ; although it might be easily shown that the positive precept given to man, enjoining him to abstain from the fruit of a particular tree, was in nowise fitted to ensnare or seduce him, as is sometimes irreverently represented, but was, on the contrary, adapted to preserve him from destruction, and to confirm him in innocence and the image of God. A few observations may, however, be appropriately offered on the prohibition itself, and the reason by which it is enforced.

In considering the prohibition, it is of importance to notice not only what it is in itself, but also the relation in which it stands both to what precedes, and to what follows it in the narrative. The prohibition was limited to the fruit of a single tree: the Divine provision and permission embraced all the other trees with which the garden was stored. And farther, it is to be remarked that the single exception was founded on the previous liberal grant. God did not ask, or reserve, but on the ground of His own free gift. And, while exercising His prerogative as the Moral Governor, it is evident from the words which immediately follow, that He did so with all the tenderness of a Father, and in such a manner as plainly showed that the good of the creature was designed no less than the glory of the Creator.

The law thus established in Eden is enforced, and its infringement guarded against by the announcement of the fatal consequences to ensue on transgression: "thou shalt surely die"—מוֹת תָּמוּת, compare Gen. xxvi. 11: the *infinitive* before the *finite* verb, expresses *the certainty* and *reality* of the event. (See Gen. xviii. 10, 18; xxii. 17; xxviii. 22.) The penalty attached to law is designed not so much as a punishment as a preventative of transgression. It was certainly so in the present case; and, when it is objected that it was unreasonably severe and disproportioned to the offence, the fact is overlooked that its very severity, irrespective of other considerations, fitted it the better to check disobedience. But, although the penalty alone is expressly mentioned, it is to be considered in connexion with the promise which secured blessedness to man in the event of obedience. "In the day thou eatest thereof thou shalt surely die," obviously implied that *life* would be the sure reward of faithfully abstaining from the forbidden tree. But the same truth was still more strongly brought out by the fact that the tree of life and the tree of the knowledge of good and evil— the one permitted and the other prohibited—stood in juxtaposition in the garden; a circumstance which spoke the language which was afterwards addressed by Moses to Israel:—"I have set before you life and death, blessing and cursing; therefore choose life, that both thou and thy seed may live," (Deut. xxx. 19.) It was with the design and the desire that man should live, that such instructions and admonitions, in word and deed, were addressed to him by his Beneficent Creator and Governor, and not with the view merely of abridging his liberty or limiting his choice.

But this subject may be viewed in another aspect. The penalty here attached to the transgression of a Divine command depends not on an arbitrary imposition; nor has it respect to any specific or prescribed obligation only, but extends equally to every violation of the law, and does so as a necessity of the moral constitution of things. Death, as here denounced, would have been the inevitable consequence of any failure on the part of a moral creature, independently of the consideration of the penalty being previously intimated or not. That

God so plainly announced the penalty of transgression to man, not leaving it to be inferred by the moral consciousness, was a special act of kindness. But the fact that He did so had no respect to the enactment of the penalty, which rested, as already said, on principles of an entirely different kind. The announcement, "In the day that thou eatest thereof thou shalt surely die," like the more general announcement, at a subsequent period, "The soul that sinneth it shall die," (Ezek. xviii. 4,) republished in the New Testament, in the words, "The wages of sin is death," (Rom. vi. 23,) is the proclamation of a principle of eternal and unchangeable obligation.

Everything connected with this law—the language in which it was conveyed, the place where it was enacted, and the penalty annexed to it—combines to illustrate and magnify the lovingkindness of God. But more particularly does this appear when viewed in connexion with the farther provision which God immediately intimates it is his design to make for man's happiness, verse 18 : *And the Lord God said, It is not good that the man should be alone ; I will make him a help meet for him.*

The view thus expressed as that which the Creator took of man's solitary condition, points back to a period anterior to the close of the sixth day, when the state of everything was such that it was pronounced to be "very good." "It is not good," as here spoken by God, corresponds in sense with the absence in chap. i. 8, of the usual expression of approbation, "And God saw that it was good;" and the absence of which, in that instance, is, as already remarked, to be regarded as indicative of the incompleteness of the work. So also in this passage : the Divine ideas to be embodied in man's creation and social constitution are not yet fully expressed. "It is not good, the being of the man alone," or "that the man be alone;" לְבַדּוֹ, *in his separation,* or *solitary state.* According to the constitution given to him, man is a social, as well as a sentient and moral being; but the all-bountiful Creator will wisely consider and supply all his wants, nay more, He will even anticipate his wishes. The desire of social intercourse would doubtless be among the first of which the new-formed man was conscious ; but he might not well know what it was, and far less have any idea of how it could be gratified before the Divine purpose was intimated, "I will make him a help meet for him."

These words form an instructive supplement to chap. i. 26, where it was said, " Let us," or " we will make ;" but here, " I will make." If the one expression implied a plurality in the Godhead, the other shows the Creator to be *one*—the one living and true God. Nothing can more strongly express the kind intentions of God towards man, than the words, " I will make ;" more particularly when viewed in relation to the gift which his creative hand is to bestow, עֵזֶר כְּנֶגְדּוֹ, *a help*, (סְמַךְ, *support*, Onkelos,) *i.e.*, *a helper*, (abstract for concrete, Ezek. xii. 14, Job xxxi. 21,) *corresponding to him*, or *like to him*. The term כְּנֶגְדּוֹ, occurring only here and in verse 20, has given great and unnecessary trouble to the critics who refer to the Syriac, Ethiopic, and the other cognate languages, for its interpretation.[1] In exceedingly bad taste are the conclusions of Gabler, Rosenmüller, and some others. The Greek versions give the sense correctly : Aquila, ὡς κατέναντι αὐτοῦ ; Symmachus, ἄντικρυς αὐτοῦ ; LXX., κατ᾽ αὐτόν, and in verse 20, ὅμοιος αὐτῷ. The *help* about to be given to the man was one adapted to him in all respects. In a word, this gift shall be, as it were, another self.

EXCURSUS IV.—THE TREES OF KNOWLEDGE AND OF LIFE.

Of the many trees " pleasant to the sight and good for food," with which God stored and beautified the earthly paradise, two are specially distinguished by name—" the tree of the knowledge of good and evil," and " the tree of life." They are thus specified because of their important relation to the history of the temptation and fall. Farther, as befitting their character, they were planted in a conspicuous and commanding situation—" in the midst of the garden." Passing over many frivolous speculations indulged in on this subject, it may be desirable, though at the risk of anticipating somewhat that more properly belongs to the subsequent history of the Fall, to bring together into one view all that can be gathered from Scripture regarding the number, the names, the peculiar properties, and the typical character of these remarkable vegetable productions.

1. *The number of the Trees.*—In considering this question,

---

[1] See a long discussion by Gabler in Eichhorn's Urgeschichte, vol. iii. p. 165.

it may be remarked, that it is sometimes maintained they were not two distinct productions ; but only one tree distinguished by two different names.[1] The chief argument in support of this view is the place assigned to the trees—"*the midst of the garden.*" But that this is not to be taken in its strictest sense, must be self-evident. The only matter worthy of consideration is, Were the trees specified limited to two individual plants, or is the term עֵץ, *tree,* to be taken as a *collective,* and so comprehending a species under the respective names ? The latter view, particularly in reference to the tree of life, is advocated by several eminent authorities, as Witsius, Kennicott, and recently Hengstenberg.[2] But all the circumstances of the case are plainly opposed to it ; as the plain grammatical construction of the words alike in the case of the two trees, the authority of the ancient versions so far as they go, the references to the tree of life in the following chapter and in subsequent passages of Scripture, and the locality it is stated to have occupied, although, strange to say, from the expression, " the tree of life which is in the midst of the garden," Hengstenberg would infer that other trees of the same kind were planted in other situations—an inference than which nothing can be more forced and unnatural.

But the argument most insisted on by the advocates of this opinion is the implied or express references to the tree of life, not as one but as many, in the descriptions of the glorious future occurring in Ezekiel and in the Apocalypse, (Ezek. xlvii. xlvii. 12 ; Rev. xxii. 2.) It is true that these descriptions, more particularly the latter, borrow their imagery from the terrestrial paradise of Genesis—its river and its tree of life. It is also true that the tree of life is spoken of not as a single plant, but as many : " In the midst of the street of it and on either side the river, was there the tree of life." It abounded everywhere, on the banks of the river, and in all the streets. But then the disparity of the two cases is overlooked. If this were attended to, the differences in the description of the past

---

[1] Pye, The Moral System of Moses. Lond., 1770. See also De Sola, the Sacred Scriptures in Hebrew and English, p. 21.

[2] *Witsius,* De Œconomia Fœderum, lib. i. cap. vi. 11. *Kennicott,* Two Dissertations, 2d edit. Oxford, 1747. *Hengstenberg,* Commentary on Revelation, vol. ii. p. 357.

and future paradise would strongly discountenance the view which regards the tree of life in Genesis as a species and not a single production.

In Genesis, the description is of the earthly paradise, and the provision made for one human pair; in Ezekiel and the Apocalypse, the description is of the new and glorified earth, or of the heavenly paradise, whose boundaries and blessedness shall so far surpass the limited confines and resources of Eden, as the differences in the nature and necessities of the two cases imperatively require. So while one tree of life was adequate for all the wants of Eden, it was very fitting that in the altered circumstances of the case, it should be said that the tree was greatly multiplied, when its food and medicine are no longer for a single pair, but for the *nations*—the multitude of the redeemed; and not only the tree multiplied, but also its returns of fruit. " It bore twelve fruit-harvests or crops, (not as in Luther, the English, and other versions, *twelve manner of fruits*,) rendering its fruit in each month." This view of the case is farther strengthened by the consideration, that in the heavenly paradise the tree of life seems to be the common tree of the place, no mention at least being made of any other.

2. *The names of the two Trees.*—Did the appellations by which alone these trees are known in the Bible, originally belong to them, or are they used proleptically, having originated from the subsequent events in the history? For the supposition that the names are used proleptically, there does not appear to be the slightest evidence. The only thing that seems to favour such a supposition is, that Eve speaks of " the tree of the knowledge of good and evil," without naming it, merely as " the tree in the midst of the garden," (Gen. iii. 3.) But it is too much to assume from this that she was ignorant of its name, particularly as in the prohibition addressed to Adam it is distinctly specified. A more important, and withal more difficult point to determine, is the precise purport of these appellations.

The one is " the tree of life," or rather, " the tree of *the* life," עֵץ הַחַיִּים, (compare ξύλον τῆς ζωῆς, Rev. ii. 7, xx. 19.) The explanation is utterly inadequate which represents this as a mere Hebraism for *a living tree*, that is, a tree of undecaying

z

vitality, and so ever flourishing and fruitful; or a tree producing wholesome fruit.[1] Nor does it come up to the full import
of the term to say that the tree was thus named from its conveying immortality, renovated health and vigour to all who
partook of its salubrious fruit. It is not merely to unimpaired
vigour and immortality, as such, that reference is made in this
peculiar designation : it is to *life—the life*, as the insertion of
the article throughout this narrative shows ; life absolutely, in
the highest and scriptural sense, holiness, bliss, and everlasting
communion with God. But the determination of the question, whether the tree actually conferred life, or merely confirmed it as a pledge—in either case, of course, by Divine
appointment—must be reserved to the next head.

The other remarkable production of the garden was the
prohibited tree, called " the tree of the knowledge of good
and evil," עֵץ הַדַּעַת טוֹב וָרָע, *the tree of the knowing* (the verbal
noun followed by the accusative, which here limits its range
to) *good and evil*. It is first necessary to settle the import of
the expression " to know," or " the knowledge of good and
evil." It is said of children that " they know not good and
evil," (Deut. i. 39,) with which may be compared (Isaiah vii.
16,) " Before the child shall know to refuse the evil and choose
the good." So also of the aged, reduced as it were to second
childhood, " I am this day fourscore years old : can I discern
between good and evil ?" (2 Sam. xix. 35,) although here the
expression is somewhat different in form. On the other hand
it is said of David, " As an angel of God, so is my lord the
king to *discern* (שָׁמַע) good and evil ;" " my lord is wise,
according to the wisdom of an angel of God, to know all that
is in the earth," (2 Sam. xiv. 17, 20; see also 1 Kings iii. 9.)
From the preceding usage, it may be concluded that the expression relates to distinctions of every kind, but especially
moral distinctions, and to a power or capacity of perceiving
them. But how this can be predicated of a tree, and, in particular, how and to whom this tree furnished the power of
discerning moral actions and judging of moral character, is
now to be determined.

3. *The peculiar properties and purposes of the Trees of Life
and of Knowledge.*—These two particulars are here conjoined,

---

[1] Geddes, Translation of the Bible, vol. i. p. 4.

on the ground that, apart from the purpose they were selected to serve in connexion with the probation of man, and his preparation for glorifying and enjoying God, it does not appear, from anything narrated in the history, that we are warranted in assuming that these trees were possessed of any physical, intrinsic properties, distinguishing them from the other productions of the garden, any of which might have served the purpose equally well, had God so willed.

In particular, there is no evidence to substantiate the notion that the tree of knowledge was possessed of any noxious properties, to the effects of which are sometimes ascribed the disorders, both physical and moral, which ensued in man's constitution after partaking of its fruit;[1] or the notion which assigns to it properties of an opposite kind, fitted to clarify the understanding and enlarge the intellectual powers.[2] But equally destitute of authority is the view frequently taken of the tree of life, which regards it as fitted to prolong life or confer immortality,[3] notwithstanding the proof supposed to lie in the intimation, that the expulsion of man from the garden was designed to prevent this contingency : " Lest he put forth his hand, and take also of the tree of life, *and eat, and live for ever.*"

If it were to be supposed that the tree of *life* was so called from any power it possessed of conferring life, it must also, by parity of reasoning, be assumed that the other tree conveyed wisdom ; but then arises the difficulty, if not the contradiction, that the virtue of the one was obtained by eating of the fruit, and that of the other by abstaining from it ; unless the other, but more perplexing, view be taken, that man's knowledge would be, and actually was, augmented by acting in disobedience to the command of God. It does not, however, appear in any way probable, that the tree of life was fitted or designed to confer life, or prolong the existence of those who partook of its fruit.[4] Adam was already in possession of life, physical

---

[1] [Barrington] Essay on the several Dispensations of God, 2d ed. p. 20. Lond. 1732.

[2] Josephus, Antiq., Book i. chap. 1, § 4. Knobel, Genesis erklärt, p. 25.

[3] Essay on the several Dispensations, p. 18. Fairbairn, Typology of Scripture, vol. i. p. 288. Edin. 1845.

[4] Calvin :—" Arbori autem vitæ nomen indidit, non quod vitam homini conferret, qua jam ante præditus erat: sed ut symbolum ac memoriale esset vitæ divinitus acceptæ."

and spiritual : he enjoyed the favour of God, which is *life*, and this would have been continued on condition of unswerving obedience to the law of his Creator. Of the continuance of life and the enjoyment of God's favour on these terms, the tree of life was a token and pledge, sensible and near at hand ; so that every time man partook of it, his faith in God and reliance on his promise would be refreshed and invigorated. Man's apostasy put an end to this arrangement ; and thereafter the ordinance of the tree of life could no longer answer the purpose for which it was designed. Lest, however, the transgressor should be deluded by false hopes, and betrayed by futile contrivances only to his destruction, mercy judged it necessary that, by expulsion from the garden, he should be placed beyond the reach of the now obsolete ordinance.

In regard to the tree of knowledge, again, the case would seem to be this. As Adam was already in possession of life, irrespective of the tree of that name, so also it must be supposed he was possessed of the knowledge of good and evil, or the power of discerning moral actions. It cannot therefore be said that it was by abstaining from this tree in conformity with the command that he should attain to this capacity, or, on the other hand, that it was through transgression he actually did attain to it, as is sometimes unwarrantably concluded from the Divine declaration after man's apostasy, " Behold, the man is become as one of us, to know good and evil."

This tree, through the prohibition attached to it, and the contrast, " thou mayest eat," and " thou shalt not eat," (Gen. ii. 16, 17,) ever exhibited to Adam the rightful authority and law of God, and was fitted to keep in his view the great and broad distinctions of right and wrong. An important difference in the cases of the two trees was this :—The virtue of the tree of life was to be known only by partaking of it, and so was necessarily limited to man. But this limitation did not necessarily attach to the other tree. The Divine purposes in respect to it would have been fully answered, whether man had partaken of it or not. But while it is not conceivable that in any case it could increase man's own knowledge, it would serve as an index or a power to other intelligences throughout the universe whereby to judge of his moral character, in some such way as is affirmed of the Church, that it makes known to principalities and powers the manifold wisdom of God, (Eph. ii. 10.)

Could the tree in any way impart to our first parents the knowledge of good and evil, the Tempter's promise could not be considered a lie, and yet we know that he was a liar from the beginning. It was in the transference to man of what was intended for other intelligences, or converting what was properly a test of character, into a medium of conveying knowledge to the parties themselves, that the lie of the Tempter may be supposed to consist. It is true that in the woman's apprehension, the tree was one " to be desired to make one wise ;" but this supposed excellence was only of her own imagination perverted by the suggestions of the Destroyer. It is true, also, that after the perpetration of the crime, the transgressors had their eyes opened, and they knew that they were naked ; but this is rather to be considered an intimation of a change of state than of advance in knowledge : they were made conscious of their degradation and misery. It may be admitted that by this act of disobedience they were made to know or experience evil ; but in no sense can it be said that in this way they came to know good ; and had the tree been simply called " the tree of the knowledge of evil," it were easy to understand how applicable would be the designation in that respect. But it is the tree of the knowledge of good and evil ; and good man must have known independently of it, as he must also have known as a moral being the eternal distinction between right and wrong.

4. *The typical character of the Tree of Life.*—The tree of the knowledge of good and evil had fully answered the purpose for which it had been set apart. From the nature of that purpose it could not be otherwise, whatever man's conduct might prove to be. The purpose being accomplished, the tree henceforward passes entirely out of view : it is never again mentioned in Scripture. But it is otherwise with the tree of life. Its purpose had been frustrated ; the pledge which by Divine appointment centered in it, was suspended, and, as regarded the first economy, utterly disannulled. Not so, however, God's eternal counsels respecting the blessings to be conferred on man : the life forfeited shall be again restored.

Accordingly the tree of life is preserved for man's future use. Its name and memorial must by no means perish, but remain as a type of the blessings about to be conferred. It is, however, to assume an entirely new character; yielding not merely food, but according to the necessities of the case, food and medicine,—" The fruit thereof shall be for meat, and the leaf thereof for medicine;" " The leaves of the tree were for the healing of the nations," (Ezek. xlvii. 12 ; Rev. xxii. 2.)   Death, with every kind of disorder, has been introduced through sin, and although at the beginning it was enough that by a divine pledge and promise this tree continued and confirmed life, now it must needs *confer* life, and recover such as are dead in trespasses and sins.

But, in this case, it rises from the sphere of the material and created to that of the spiritual, uncreated, and eternal, and is thus a typical representation of that Adorable One of whom it is said, " In him was life, and the life was the light of men," (John i. 4,) and who himself declares, in a figure somewhat akin to the present, "*I am the bread of life ;* he that cometh to me shall never hunger, and he that believeth on me shall never thirst," (John vi. 35 ;) and of this bread of life he says, " The bread of God is he who cometh down *from heaven* and giveth life unto the world," (John vi. 33.)   Indeed, in the restored Paradise all is life: the trees, as already remarked, are all trees of life, and the very river which watered the earthly Paradise, and imparted to it freshness and beauty, is here raised to the quality of " a pure river of water of life, clear as crystal, proceeding out of the throne of God and of the Lamb," (Rev. xxii. 1.)   And it had been long before declared, " everything shall live whither the river cometh," (Ezek. xlvii. 9.)

Finally, as it was through disobedience the privilege to partake of the tree of life was forfeited, and Adam was excluded from the very precincts of the garden, it is only through obedience these rights and immunities shall be restored.   Thus, it is declared, " Blessed are they that do His commandments, that they may have right to the tree of life, and may enter in through the gates into the city."   The foremost of these commandments is to believe on the name of the Son of God, who hath, by His own perfect obedience, recovered for sinners the blessings forfeited in Adam, and who has specially promised, " To him that overcometh will I give to eat of the tree of life which is in the midst of the Paradise of God."

§ 14. *Man's Relation to the Animal World,* Gen. ii. 19, 20.

The preceding section might have been appropriately headed, " Man's relation to the Creator," as the present represents his relation to the creature as represented in its highest forms of animal life. Means had been already taken to teach man his dependence on God, and how he stood related to Him as a Moral Governor ; and he is now to be instructed as to the supremacy with which he was invested over the creation, and the excellencies which distinguished him from every other inhabitant of the earth. The order in which he is taught these lessons so essential to his wellbeing is, as might be expected, in conformity with God's usual administration, or the rule, that " the fear of the Lord is the instruction of wisdom ; and before honour is humility," (Prov. xv. 33.) When man had been taught his own dependent place, it was then that he was qualified for the announcement of his honours, and for sustaining them aright.

Verses 19, 20. *And out of the ground the Lord God formed every beast of the field, and every fowl of the air, and brought them to the man, to see what he would call them : and whatsoever the man called every living creature, that was the name thereof. And the man gave names to all cattle, and to the fowl of the air, and to every beast of the field, but for man he did not find a help meet for him.*

Exception is sometimes taken to this statement, as assigning to the creation of the animals a place subsequent to that of man, contrary to the arrangement of the first chapter ; and several, to avoid this difficulty, assume that this is the account of a second creation of animals in man's immediate neighbourhood, and it may be under his eye. The truth, however, is, that this is not properly an account of the creation of the animals. As already remarked on man's formation, noticed in this chapter, it is a statement not of the fact, but only of the mode of creation ; and so also of the vegetable productions, there is no account of their creation, except so far as concerns the garden of Eden. In like manner, there would have been no mention of the animals, but for the relation which they are represented as sustaining to the man. This statement, then, in the first place, is to be taken as a commentary on chap. i. 28—" Have dominion over the fish of the sea and over the fowl of the air, and over every living thing that moveth upon the earth."

This dominion was to be expressed by a very significant action. The Creator brought the creatures which He had formed to the man, " to see what he would call them "—an act which plainly intimated to him that by the Creator he was invested with sovereignty over all the animate creation. It was an act of solemn investiture with the high authority which God committed to man's hands : it was, as Philo designates it, τὸ ἔργον σοφίας καὶ βασιλείας.[1]

But another and no less important end to be served by this transaction was to show to the man how signally he differed from every living thing around him. The other creatures so far resembled him as to the material out of which their bodies were formed—" Out of the ground the Lord God formed every beast of the field," &c. But here the similarity ends ; and, as if to mark this more distinctly, the historian makes no mention of the vital principle in the lower animals, what it is, or how or whence it came. Accordingly, the result of this careful review of animated nature, of its constitution and capacities, was that the man found no help meet for him. He found among the vast assemblage no being corresponding to לְאָדָם, to man, that is, to himself as man. There was none in creation like to him in character and susceptibilities ; he was the only one of his kind. It is frequently affirmed that the chief design of this transaction was to awaken in the man a sense of his solitary condition, and a desire for a partner fitted to complete his happiness. But this does not appear from the narrative ; though no doubt it was fitted to effect this, if the desire had not been already and otherwise awakened. But whether this had been the case, or whether it was only by the contemplation of the animal economy that man was brought to a consciousness of his anomalous condition, certain it is that the transaction in which he is here said to have participated was

[1] De Mundi Opificio, § 52.

every way fitted to convince him that creation could not furnish the companion which he needed ; and that, if this want too is to be supplied, it must be like the others by a direct gift from God. This conviction would, at all events, dispose him to prize more adequately the blessing, and recognise the beneficence of the Giver of all good.

Objections of a zoological character are urged against this representation of bringing the animals to the man in Eden, where, it is said, even if miraculously congregated, some of them must be miraculously sustained, seeing that the climate and its productions must be unsuitable to many of the creatures of the earth. Various explanations have been offered. Sometimes reference is made to a similar case in the history of Noah ; but this is obviously no explanation. Another method is to take the Hebrew כל not in its usual sense, *all* or *every ;* but, as it is sometimes evidently used, for *many* or *much ;* and, accordingly, that the expressions, " every beast of the field " and " every fowl of the air," may only denote of the field and climate of Paradise.[1] It will be more satisfactory, however, if it can be shown that the objection rests only on a misapprehension of the narrative, which by no means affirms that all the creatures, or even many of them, were congregated before the man. " Out of the ground the Lord God formed every beast of the field, and fowl of the air, and *brought to the man,*" not " brought *them,*" as in the English version, but " brought to the man," which is evidently equivalent to *brought of them,* the universal *every* referring only to the formation. Should it, however, be objected that the next verse adds, " the man gave names to all cattle," &c., this will admit of easy explanation, for the correct rendering of the passage is, " to all *the cattle,*" evidently to as many as were thus brought before him. The transaction under consideration was entirely of a symbolical character, and it needed not the concourse of the whole creation to give effect to it : it was enough that its representatives appeared. Accordingly, although no mention is made of the various classes and kinds of aquatic creatures, yet the productions of the fifth and sixth days, that is, the entire animate creation, are duly represented by the fowl of the air and the beast of the field. Already there was granted to the man

[1] Holden, Dissertation on the Fall, p. 98.

power over the vegetable productions, verse 16, corresponding to the intimation in chap. i. 29, " I have given you every herb bearing seed," &c.   And now all living creatures are delivered into his hand, agreeably to the Creator's purpose expressed at man's creation, chap. i. 26, or, as the psalmist describes it, " Thou madest him to have dominion over the works of thy hands : thou hast put all things under his feet," (Ps. viii. 6.)

These coincidences shew how intimately the narrative of the second chapter is related to that of the first ; and how, more-over, in all its parts it refers directly or indirectly to man, to his creation, the preparations made for him, and the constitu-tion under which he was placed.   And the whole facts thus recorded in all the amplification of detail, are in strict harmony with the brief notices in the general narrative, the one supple-menting and elucidating the other.

§ 15. *The Creation of the Woman, and her Relation to the Man,* Gen. ii. 21-25.

What Adam could not find for himself to complete his hap-piness, is supplied directly by the Creator, in accordance with the purpose already announced, " I will make him a help meet for him."   The desire for companionship and social inter-course had been awakened in man's bosom.   He felt a void in his existence, but saw no prospect of its being filled up.   Al-though God's purposes and promises of kindness anticipate the wishes of the creature, yet He awakens the feeling of want before bestowing the blessing.   So it was in the present instance. He had seen man's need : He expressed his determination with respect to it ; and now that the man himself is cognizant of his condition, and ready to welcome the provision about to be made for him, the Creator proceeds to give effect to His purpose.

The particulars comprised in this important paragraph are, 1. The mode of the woman's formation, verses 21, 22.   2. Her introduction by the Creator to the man, ver. 22[b].   3. The man's reflections on the occasion, in respect to the woman's origin, and their mutual relation, verses 23, 24.   4. The peculiar cir-cumstances of condition and character of this heaven-united pair, verse 25.

The mode of the woman's formation, verses 21, 22. *And the Lord God caused a deep sleep to fall upon the man, and he slept; and He took one of his ribs, and shut up the flesh in its stead. And the Lord God formed the rib which He took from the man into a woman.*

How simple the record of this fact, and yet every line is charged with truths of the highest interest, as bearing on the mutual relations of man and woman—husband and wife. No other passage in the Bible, however, has furnished more scope for the profane wit of the scorner and the sceptic. The mystery of the narrative is not to be denied, and yet it may be asked, Is the formation of the man himself from the dust of the ground, or the continued procreation of the race any whit less mysterious than the creation of the woman?[1] This particular account of the formation of the woman was needed not merely to explain and confirm the ordinance of marriage, but also to explain various incidents and allusions in the following history of the Fall.

"The sleep of a labouring man is sweet," (Eccles. v. 12.) This was no doubt pre-eminently the case with the sleep of Paradise. The man had finished the first work to which he had been called : he had exercised the faculties which God had given him, and, for the first time, his dominion over the creatures of the earth. He had searched for a being like to himself, and fitted for companionship; but although he found none such, yet his search has not been in vain, seeing that he is thereby made aware of the distinguished, if solitary and singular position which he occupied. He may have been weary of the search when the sleep of heaven settled down upon his eyes ; and, while thus resting in the arms of his Creator, that object was found for him, in quest of which he himself had searched in vain. It was thus that to the first man was realized the declaration of the psalmist, " So gives he to his beloved in sleep," (Ps. cxxvii. 2,) without human co-operation or even observation. The woman was given to the man as a pure gift of God, as Delitzsch remarks, a tender, veiled mystery.

The " deep sleep," תַּרְדֵּמָה, which God *caused to fall* (וַיַּפֵּל Hiph. of נָפַל) upon the man is not an *ecstasy*, ἔκστασις, as the **LXX.** render it. In the present instance it was supernatural, inas-

---

[1] Schröder, Das erste Buch Mose Ausgelegt, p. 37. Berlin, 1846.

much as it was not the result of natural weariness arising from
the work just completed, but of a Divine appliance which
sweetly lulled to rest the usual activity of nature. This "deep
sleep" God sometimes sends in a way of judgment, (see Job
xxix. 10,) but here it was manifestly the reverse. The word
simply means *sound repose*, and is frequently used without any
express reference to Divine agency, though such may be implied,
(Gen. xv. 12 ; 1 Sam. xxvi. 12 ; Job iv. 13.) In consequence
of the divinely-sent repose, it is added, "and he slept," perhaps
to intimate that in appearance it did not differ from ordinary
slumber.

"He took one of his ribs." Hofmann,[1] and after him Baumgarten, take צֵלָע to denote an independent and separable part of
a whole, and they suppose that in the present case it does not
mean *a rib*, but some easily separable portion about the abdo-
men in the first-formed human being. But this idea is not
compatible with the mention made of the part, whatever it was,
as one of several, one of his צְלָעוֹת ; and as one only was taken
for the formation of the woman, the others must still belong
to the man's male posterity. There is no reason whatever to
call for or warrant a departure from the usual acceptation of
the term צֵלָע, which, somewhat like the Greek πλευρά and
πλευρόν, primarily means *a side*, then *a side bone, a rib*. It
means *a rib* also in Arabic, Syriac, and Chaldee ; and it is so
understood here by the old translators and by interpreters in
general. The rib being removed, its place was supplied by
flesh : "He closed flesh in its place," וַיִּסְגֹּר בָּשָׂר תַּחְתֶּנָּה, that is,
either inserted flesh in the void thus occasioned, or by compres-
sion closed up the wound.

The rib thus taken from the man, the Lord God made into,
literally *builded*, (וַיִּבֶן,) into a woman ; on which expression Calvin remarks :—"Consulto etiam usus est Moses ædificandi verbo,
ut doceret in mulieris persona tandem absolutum fuisse huma-
num genus, quod prius inchoato ædificio simile est." Or the
figure may probably refer to the part of the female in *building*
up the family. Thus in Ruth iv. 11, "The Lord make the
woman that is come into thine house like Rachel, and like
Leah, which two did *build* the house of Israel." (See also Gen.
xvi. 2 ; xxx. 3 in the original, and marginal readings of the

---

[1] Weissagung und Erfullung, vol. i. p. 65. Nordl. 1841.

English version.) Farther, it is not without the deepest significance that the portion of matter which at the bidding of Omnipotence was wondrously expanded and fashioned into the human form of one who was to be united to the man by the closest and tenderest ties of nature and affection, is represented to have been taken from a region contiguous to his heart.

The Creator conducts this newly-formed creature to the man. Verse 22[b]. *And he brought her to the man.* וַיְבִאֶהָ, *led, conducted,* that is, presented her to the man. "It can scarcely be supposed that she was, after her formation, taken to a distance from Adam, and then reconducted into his presence. It is far more rational to understand the term of simply presenting her to him on the spot where she was created, which was doubtless the same where Adam was reposing at the time. The word implies, moreover, the solemn bestowment of her in the bonds of the marriage covenant, which is hence called 'the covenant of God,' (Prov. ii. 17,) implying that He is the author of this sacred institution," (Bush.) "God himself," says Bishop Patrick, "made the espousals (if I may so speak) between them, and joined them together in marriage." Than the act described in the few and simple words, "He brought her to the man," what could have been better adapted to set the seal of God upon an ordinance first instituted in Paradise ! It was, no doubt, to this act, and the important truth of which it was symbolic, that our Lord referred when he said, with all the weight of Divine authority, "What, therefore, God hath joined together, let not man put asunder," (Matt. xix. 6.) With these high and heavenly sanctions, well might the apostle Paul characterize marriage as "honourable," (Heb. xii. 4.) But not only this, there may be farther recognised in the present act the marvellous kindness and condescension of God, who not merely creates the blessing but moreover puts it into the man's hand.

The man's reflections when presented with the woman, verses 23, 24, *And the man said, This is now bone of my bones, and flesh of my flesh : she shall be called Woman, because she was taken out of man. Therefore shall a man leave his father and his mother, and shall cleave to his wife, and they shall be one flesh.*

This language is strongly expressive of deep and sudden emotion—joy at an unexpected discovery : " The man said,

הַפַּעַם זֹאת, *this is the stroke,* or *this is it* at length," (Gen. xxix. 34,) as he saw the anxiously sought object before him. He had gone to sleep with the feeling, the result of careful observation, that " there was not found a help meet for him," and he awakes to the agreeable discovery that this object has at length been found. The thrice repeated זֹאת, *this,* in verse 23, is very characteristic. It vividly points to the woman on whom in joyful astonishment the man's eye now rests with the full power of first love, as in rapture he exclaims, " Bone of my bones, and flesh of my flesh!" (Delitzsch.) He at once, as by intuition, recognises her origin, her character, and entire conformity to himself. The Lord had taken from him a part, but now restored it to him as a whole. The part taken away was simply matter, the gift bestowed was a second mind corresponding in every respect to the first. This immediate and correct recognition of the woman by the man, must have been the result of Divine enlightenment. The close intercourse which he enjoyed with God the Creator, solved to him the enigma of the woman's creation, and therewith her nature and the mystery of marriage.

Still, however, he was conscious of his own divinely determined and declared superiority, or of the truth that, as described by an Apostle, " the head of the woman is the man," (1 Cor. xi. 3.) This appears from the very significant fact that he bestowed upon her a name : " This shall be called *woman,* אִשָּׁה, because this was taken from the man, אִישׁ." The etymological connexion of the two names is necessarily very much lost sight of in the versions : Symmachus renders אִשָּׁה by ἀνδρίς, and the Vulgate uses the inapposite term *virago.* Luther has männinn, (*maness.*) According to Festus on the word *querquetulanœ,* women were by the ancient Romans called *virœ.* Here, too, it is to be noticed, that the man himself assumes another designation : formerly he was known only as הָאָדָם, a term which, as already shown, probably had regard to his origin ; now he is, for the first time, distinguished as אִישׁ, a term which Gesenius[1] supposes to denote man's *authority* or *rule,* as in the Sanscrit, *ischa,* vir, dominus, and *ischi, ischani,* mulier. Meier,[2] on the contrary, regards it as a desigtion of man as a *social* being, or *living in society.* With so

---

[1] Thesaurus, p. 86.   [2] Heb. Wurzelwörterbuch, p. 306.

much obscurity respecting the etymology of the term, nothing can with certainty be affirmed as to its meaning. It is evident, however, that a new relation has now commenced, and that the first human being is henceforth *man*, in contradistinction to *woman*.

Whether the words which follow in verse 24 are to be taken as conveying the remarks of the historian on the language of the man in the preceding verse, or as a continuation of the same, it is not easy to determine, although various considerations are decidedly in favour of the latter view. The words are referred to by our Lord, and are quoted as the language of the Creator himself, (Matt. xix. 4-6.) This, however, does not necessarily imply that it was spoken *directly* by God. It intimates that it was an utterance of divine inspiration, but leaves it undetermined whether it is to be ascribed to Adam or to the writer of the narrative. In favour of the view which regards the remark as proceeding from the historian, it is urged that it is his custom to weave into the narrative reflections beginning with the formula, עַל־כֵּן, *therefore*, which is used in the present case, and various passages are cited in confirmation of the statement, *e.g.*, Gen. x. 9; xxvi. 33; xxxii. 33. But the instances thus referred to, it must be remarked, are not at all parallel with the present: they do not immediately succeed a previous discourse or quotation, and so are in no danger of being mistaken for a part of it. Here, however, the case is otherwise, and as there is no expressed or implied intimation to the contrary, it is safer to consider the words as a continuation of the reflections of Adam on the occasion. That he speaks of *father* and *mother*, shows that it was a matter which he conceived related to the future, and to his posterity, as much as to himself. His ideas of a posterity and of the parental relations, need occasion no difficulty when the primeval blessing (chap. i. 28) is considered, of the import of which he must assuredly have been aware.

But whatever may be concluded as to the origin of the words, the truths which they embody are of the highest importance, as is evident from the view taken of them by our blessed Lord in his argumentation with the Jews. עַל־כֵּן, *i.q.*, ἕνεκα τούτου, (Matt. xix. 5,) *therefore, on this account*, that is, because woman was taken out of man, referring to the previous combination, and to the union now again effected, but in a far higher form: " A man shall leave his father and his mother, and shall cleave to his wife." What thus holds true of the man, applies also, and in a special manner, to the woman, (see Ps. xlv. 10.) But the man only is here spoken of, and his duty in regard to his wife particularly insisted on ; because he, the first created, naturally feels himself more independent and free, while the woman already, from her origin, constitution, and character, appears to be drawn towards the man, and to be urged by weakness as well as by affection. *And they shall be one flesh*, or, as our Lord expounds it, " and they twain shall be one flesh : so that they are no more twain, but one flesh," (Mark x. 8.) This is the essential bond of union in marriage, and that which gives it its indissoluble character, constituting a union which man cannot, and which God only can dissever. " Marriage in its ideal form," says Olshausen, " appears as a union of the entire nature of man in the feeling of love out of which all union (which consists in giving and receiving) proceeds. It presupposes unity and conjunction of soul and spirit." But on this Stier observes :—" The bodily union is not only the foundation of, it is also that which is alone essential to marriage, which indeed can be sweetened and hallowed, and certainly should always be so by love and affection, but yet without which it subsists as marriage. See the distinction in 1 Cor. vi. 16, 17. *One flesh*, that is, one person, one man within the limits of their united life in the flesh, for this world; but beyond these limits, the death of the flesh severs the marriage. In this alone lies the justice of a *second* marriage, which in no way breaks off the unity of spirit with the former spouse now departed."[1]

This important subject is also treated of by the Apostle Paul, but in another aspect. He represents the union between husband and wife, as described in the case of the first created pair, as typical of the union subsisting between Christ and his Church, which is frequently spoken of as his *bride*. " So ought men to love their wives as their own bodies: he that loveth his wife loveth himself. For no man ever hated his own flesh ; but nourisheth and cherisheth it, even as the Lord the church ; for we are members of his body, of his flesh, and

[1] Die Reden des Herrn Jesu, 2te Ausg., vol. ii. p. 267. Barmen, 1852.

of his bones. For this cause shall a man leave his father and mother, and shall be joined unto his wife, and they two shall be one flesh. This is a great mystery ; but I speak concerning Christ and the church," (Eph. v. 28-32.)

To the institution of marriage as founded, according to the narrative of Genesis, on the *one flesh*, or conjugal body into which the first pair were formed, it is supposed that the Prophet Malachi refers, (chap. ii. 15,) where reproving his countrymen for the practice of divorce,—

> " Yet did he not make one ?
> Though he had the residue of the spirit ;
> And why the one ?
> That he might seek a goodly seed :
> Therefore take heed to your spirit,
> That none act unfaithfully to the wife of his youth." [1]

Notice may be here taken of the confirmation afforded to this original law of creation, so important to the social constitution of mankind, by the remarkable fact of the equality of the sexes born into the world. As at the beginning of the human race one man and one woman only were created for one another, so by a series of wonderful adjustments, independent of man's will, and even beyond his cognizance, the same numerical proportion has upon the whole been maintained ever since.

The state, physical and moral, of this primeval pair, is next described. Verse 25. *And they were both naked, the man and his wife, and were not ashamed.*—הָאָדָם וְאִשְׁתּוֹ, " the man and his wife ;" the woman is now *the woman* or *wife* of the man. Dr. Pye Smith [2] objects to the common interpretation of this description of the two human beings seeing no incongruity in the total destitution of artificial clothing. His objections are partly moral and partly physical. It seems impossible, he thinks, for the state of mind and habits to exist which evidently belonged to the then state of man, without a correct sensibility to proprieties and decencies. And he farther adds that the action of the sun's rays, the range of temperature through the day and the night, exposure to insects, &c., would render some protective clothing indispensable. For these con-

---

[1] Henderson, The Minor Prophets, p. 454.
[2] Cyc. Bib. Lit., *Art.* Adam, vol. i. p. 62.

siderations the author in question takes עָרוֹם to import not *absolute* but *partial nudity.* Any objection from Gen. iii. 7, 10, 11, he meets with the remark, that in consequence of the transgression, the clothing was disgracefully injured !

It is unnecessary to reply to these statements, farther than to say, that they are warranted neither by *feeling* nor by *facts.* Admitting that there are difficulties in the matter as understood literally, it is evident that that sense is nevertheless required by the references in chapter third, which cannot be explained by the strange supposition of Pye Smith given above. As regards the *feelings* of proprieties or decencies, we are incompetent judges, the present condition of man offering nothing that can be compared with the primeval state of innocence ; and as regards *facts,* it is known that tribes of the human race go naked at the present day without suffering much if any inconvenience. But the state here described referred not so much to the physical as to the moral condition of our first parents : the former is noticed, only so far as it was unattended by these feelings of fear and shame, which manifested themselves so soon as sin interrupted the innocent existence, by disturbing the harmony of their moral nature. Shame first entered in with sin ; as did also distrust and disunion. There could be no shame while a feeling of perfect unity endured, while the two were in the strictest sense, one flesh.

Passing over all objections of this sort, it is of importance to notice how the state of innocence is briefly but forcibly characterized by the concluding words of this narrative, " they were not ashamed," which form an exceedingly appropriate transition to the history of the Fall, whereby the original relation between the Creator and His moral creatures, and the relation of the latter to one another, was totally subverted. The narrative has distinctly shown that the first human beings were possessed of a language, of powers of reasoning and reflection, and that their acts and exercises were those of adults and not of children. If, at the same time, there was an entire absence of fear and shame, it must accordingly have been the result not of infantile immaturity, but of true moral and social harmony in the bosom of innocence.

EXCURSUS V.—MAN ONE FAMILY.

Though by his physical organization man is allied to the animal creation, and so takes his place in the classification of the zoologist, yet he is not merely a higher or more perfect form of animal, but is essentially distinguished from all the other creatures of the earth. With the exception of the disciples of Maillet and Lamarck, this is universally admitted by all qualified to express an opinion on the subject. But besides this distinction between man and every other creature, there are differences between individuals and families of mankind. These are partly physical and partly mental. The physical distinctions consist in diversities of colour, of bodily conformation, especially the form of the skull and the features of the countenance, differences in the texture of the hair, &c. The mental distinctions are exhibited in peculiarities of manners and customs, and particularly in the endless variety of languages and dialects.

These appearances and peculiarities, constituting such a marked diversity in the human race, could not fail to be a fertile subject of discussion, and more especially is it a question whether this diversity be of a nature to prove a difference of species incompatible with a common origin, or merely to constitute different varieties of the same species. Though no doubt a legitimate subject for scientific investigation, the matter would present but little interest save for its moral and religious aspect. Unfortunately with many, it is a sufficient ground for the rejection of a doctrine, that the Bible affirms it. Voltaire and the French infidels derided the idea that all men are descended from a common parentage, and it was inducement enough to do so that it was expressly taught in a book to which they refused to listen, and whose authority they deemed must in every case be set aside. Much the same may be said of the views more recently put forth on this subject by the German Rationalists, Ballenstedt and Bretschneider, though they bear the name of *theologians*, and whose writings are as remarkable for hostility to the sacred records, or the Hebrew myths, as they call them, as for want of scientific acquaintance with the subject which they discuss.[1] Lately, however, another class of disputants has appeared—men of whom it must be said, that whatever may be their views of Christianity and the Bible, they have at least qualified themselves for expressing a judgment on questions purely scientific. Among such opponents of the doctrine of the unity of the human species are Burmeister in Germany, and Agassiz, Morton, and Nott in America; in which latter country, from political considerations and domestic arrangements, a ready welcome has been given to any view which ascribes to the coloured population a distinct origin and a natural inferiority.

Although the decision of this question must be sought mainly on the field of natural science, yet it is of importance to notice, in the first place, the testimony of Scripture on this subject; not, of course, because that testimony will avail much with many of those who deny the unity of the race, but because it will show, to all disposed to reverence Scripture doctrine, the importance of the question at issue, and the express terms in which it is there affirmed.

I. *The Scriptural account of the origin of Mankind.*—The intimations of Scripture on this subject are neither few nor ambiguous. The account of the Creation derives all mankind from a primeval pair, destined by the Creator through their offspring to replenish and subdue the earth. Nothing can be plainer than the testimony of this narrative, that Adam and Eve were the only human dwellers on this earth until the birth of their children. The whole tenor of the history is opposed to any other previous or subsequent creation of human beings. Nothing to the contrary can be inferred from what is said of Cain fearing to be slain by any with whom he might come in contact—that he had a wife and was the builder of a city—for all this refers to a period when, through the first human pair, the population may have considerably increased, although, from the brevity of the history, this circumstance is not expressly stated. But all questions of this nature are set at rest by the intimation that, by the deluge, the whole human race, with the exception of Noah and his family, perished from the earth. (Luke xvii. 27.)

[1] Tholuck, in Herzog's Real-Encyklopädie, *Art.* Abstammung des Menschengeschlechts, vol. i. p. 85.

From the three sons of Noah the earth was re-peopled, and mention is made of the nations which sprung from them respectively, and of the cause which led to their dispersion, previous to which the whole earth was of one language and of one speech, (Gen. ix. 19 ; chap. x. ;) and to which, also, allusion is made in Deut. xxxii. 8 : "When the Most High divided to the nations their inheritance, when He separated the sons of Adam, he set the bounds of the people according to the number of the children of Israel."

The account of the origin of mankind given in Genesis, and referred to in other parts of the Old Testament, (e.g. Mal. ii. 15,) is fully endorsed by New Testament authority. Christ refers to it as the foundation of the marriage institute, introducing his remarks with "have ye not read ?" (Matt. xix. 4.) The unity of the human race is insisted on in Paul's address at Athens as strongly as words can express it : " God hath made of one blood (ἐξ ἑνὸς αἵματος, of one kindred) all nations of men for to dwell on all the face of the earth," (Acts xvii. 26.) The pointedness of the apostle's statement will be more apparent when it is considered that the Athenians regarded themselves as sprung from their native soil, and as a people highly exalted above all others.

But it is not as a bare historical fact that the New Testament views the unity of mankind ; it is the very foundation of the cardinal doctrine of Christianity — the atonement through Christ. It is on the assumption that all men are descended from the first Adam, and involved in his guilt, that the atonement proceeds, and the offers addressed to sinners of the blessings procured by the second Adam, the new head of *humanity*, (Rom. v. 14, 19.) The denial of this doctrine, then, involves more than the rejection of so-called Hebrew myths. It is practically a rejection of Christianity, and, in a personal point of view, raises doubts which on this theory are from their nature incapable of solution. For, if there be any tribe not descended from Adam, how can any individual assure himself or those around him of this connexion, and so of any title to participate in the blessings of the gospel ?

II. *Scientific Conclusions regarding the Origin of Mankind.*— In settling questions of specific unity there is a difficulty, owing to the indeterminate ideas attached to the term species in classification and the character of its criteria. The most essential characteristic of species is usually admitted to be similarity or dissimilarity of descent. This, however, is often utterly beyond the reach of the inquirer. It is a *cause*, and, when hidden, can be judged of only by its effects; but such conclusions must partake more of the character of inferences than of settled facts. What naturalists, accordingly, chiefly rely on in investigations of this kind is the fact that individuals only of the same species produce by their union fertile offspring.

The opponents of the doctrine of the unity of the human species deny the validity of this criterion, or resort to some other principle of classification, such as that founded on embryology, or the comparative development of animals as shown by the fœtus. But more than this; it is now no longer agreed that unity of species proves unity of origin. Agassiz, while in words admitting the specific unity of mankind, maintains that the races are so distinct and dissimilar, and at the same time are so related to their present geographical locations, that, like the flora and fauna around them, they must have originated at various centres of creation.

It is of importance to attend to the new phase which the controversy has thus assumed, for on this view the unity of origin, as distinct from the unity of species, has ceased to be a question of natural history. But, although the two questions are distinct, they are not entirely independent; for though, as thus stated, the unity of species does not prove the unity of origin, yet, if the unity of species be disproved, the unity of origin falls too. The preliminary or general inquiry must be, are the peculiarities which mark the tribes and nations of the earth such as prove or render probable that there must have been more than one ancestral pair? in other words, are the peculiarities so permanent and invariable, so independent of all known modifying causes, that they can have resulted only from original descent?

The subject may be considered from three points of view— the physiological, philological, and historical. The unity of the species must be decided mainly by physiological principles; the unity of origin, by philological and historical considerations.

1. *Physiological considerations.* — The physical peculiarities

which distinguish the various races or varieties of mankind consist chiefly in the hue of the skin, the texture of the hair, and the form of the skull. Looking at the extreme types denoted, for instance, by the colours white, black, red, with their concomitant peculiarities, it may occasion considerable doubt whether any one of these could originate from another. Further observation, however, shews that the transitions are not so abrupt as in this representation, and that between these extremes of hue and anatomical structure, there are *means* whence the transition proceeds by insensible gradations. To this is to be ascribed the fact that, in grouping mankind into races, naturalists have never been able to agree as to the number of such.

(1.) *Differences in colour.*—It is proved by microscopic anatomy that the colour of the skin exists in the epidermis only, and is the result of the admixture of pigment cells with the ordinary epidermic cells. The former withdraw from the blood, and elaborate in their cavities colouring matter of various shades, so that the different hues depend on the relative quantity of these cells, and the colour of the pigment deposited therein. " If we examine," says Dr. Hall, " the skin of the negro anatomically, we shall find no structure peculiar to it ; for the very same dark cells are found in the fairest of mankind." [1]

Whether or not the peculiarities of colour be referable entirely to natural causes, there is no doubt that they are greatly dependent on climate. Of this there is abundant proof. The Jews, for instance, dispersed through the colder countries of Europe, have in some degree assumed the lighter complexion, and the yellow, red, and brown hair of the people among whom they dwell. On the contrary, in the hotter climes of the East, they approximate to the jet black of the Hindoo. These transitions are the more noticeable in the case of the Jew, as they cannot have been the result of intermarriages or amalgamation of races. So also the descendants of the early Portuguese settlers in India have become in many instances as dark as the native races around them. Nor are there wanting examples of fair races becoming dark, without any considerable change in their external conditions. And further, there are daily ex-

[1] Introduction to Pickering's " Races of Man," p. xliv. Lond. 1850.

amples of the development of pigment cells in particular parts of the body. Thus, the tan or summer freckle, the result of the action of the sun and light, is an aggregation of brown or red pigment cells.[1] In some nations and individuals there is a greater predisposition than in others to the secretion of the dark-coloured pigment. Thus, a Jew is sooner darkened than a Saxon or a Celt, and individuals with black hair assume very readily a yellow or brownish hue of complexion on exposure to the sun.

(2.) *The texture of the hair.*—By this not only are the white and black races distinguished from each other, but the latter particularly among themselves. The Indian, for example, may be as black as the negro, but he has no such crisp, woolly hair. Of the eleven races into which Pickering divides mankind, five have the hair straight or flowing ; in the others it is more or less crisped, and in two of them, the Negrillo and the Negro, it resembles wool.[2] Yet microscopic examination has shown that it is not really such ; but were it otherwise, this peculiarity would by no means prove a distinct stock, unless constantly presented by all the nations of negro descent, and restricted to them alone, which is not the case. Indeed Europeans are not unfrequently to be met with having hair as black and woolly as that of the negro. And, farther, that the texture of the hair is no safe criterion of specific distinctions, is shown by the fact that there are breeds of domesticated animals which have wool, while others of the same species, under different influences of climate or food, are covered with hair.

(3.) The conformation of the cranium may be supposed to be a more reliable guide to the naturalist in his classification, than either the hue of the skin or the texture of the hair. Upon this, indeed, some of the chief classifications have proceeded since the time of Camper and Blumenbach. The leading types of configuration of the skull are, according to the most usual division, the oval, the spherical, and the elliptical ; but Retzius, a German anatomist, has recently proposed two classes only— round and long skulls. But whatever may be the classification adopted, it is admitted even by Burmeister, a zealous defender of the doctrine of the diversity of the human species, that the

---

[1] Hall, Introduction to Pickering, p. xlviii.
[2] The Races of Man, pp. 3, 175.

application of this principle to the zoological separation of the races of mankind leads to unnatural segregations or collocations.[1]

Farther, it appears that the cranial peculiarities are far from constant in the several nations of one race, or even in the several individuals of one nation ; and that, external conditions being changed, they are liable to alterations—depending much on the different habits of life and modes of procuring food.[2] These and other facts bearing on the same point, prove that these typical forms are not permanent, and have therefore no weight in proving a specific distinction of races.

Any of the above peculiarities applied singly to prove specific differences, if it proves anything, proves too much : from the insensible shades of transition it will prove the species to be numerically indefinite and incalculable ; and, applied collectively, the tests come into mutual conflict and introduce confusion, the testimony of one neutralizing that of the other. There are, however, subsidiary arguments employed to show the necessity of the origination of mankind in various localities —such as the difficulty of the means and the absence of inducements for transport into regions so inaccessible and inhospitable as many of those now inhabited by man. But arguments of this sort are not entitled to a place when the decision of the question is referred to science.

Before concluding this part of the subject, notice must be taken of two additional considerations which decidedly favour the view of the unity of species.

First, Nature, while maintaining a specific unity, permits varieties within a certain range. The operation of this law is abundantly indicated in plants as well as in animals ; designed evidently for effecting a beautiful and combined diversity, but chiefly for permitting the adaptation of organic life to the varied external circumstances and conditions of the earth's surface. Man is the most widely diffused of any creature on the earth, inhabiting all climes, from the equator to the poles, and no doubt he was destined for such a wide and diversified range of existence. To this the diversity of races has greatly contributed. " It may be questioned," says Pickering, " whether any one of the races existing singly would, up to the pre-

---

[1] Geschichte der Schöpfung, 4te Ausg. p. 576. Leipz. 1851.

[2] Hall, Introduction to Pickering, p. li.

sent day, have extended itself over the whole surface of the globe."[1]

Next to man in range of habitation are the domesticated animals which contribute to his wants or pleasures—particularly his faithful attendant, the dog. In these, too, the most marked and numerous varieties are found, far exceeding anything met with among wild animals. But, in these cases, the question of specific unity or diversity is rarely, if ever, mooted ; naturalists accepting creatures marked by more striking dissimilarities than any which distinguish the human races, as varieties, and not as distinct species. If this be admissible in regard to these lower forms of life created chiefly for man's use, and endued with powers of conforming to the altered circumstances into which they are brought as the companions of his migrations, do not reason and analogy commend and even require the application of the same principles to the case of man himself?

Secondly, While admitting varieties, nature will not go beyond certain fixed limits. If the former law serves to introduce variety with harmony among the numerous orders of life with which the earth is peopled, this is no less fitted to prevent confusion and the utter eversion of species and genera. Nature has set up an impassable barrier between the different species which prevents their permanent intermixture. This is the law of hybridity, or the sterility which marks the offspring of individuals of different species brought by constraint into unnatural connexion.

Judged by this law, the present question is at once settled. All the races of mankind are fitted for free and permanent amalgamation—satisfactory evidence of their specific unity, unless man be an exception to all other living creatures. Such is the force of this argument, that repeated attempts have been made, but unsuccessfully, to weaken it by reported instances of exception to the law of hybridity. Recently it is evaded altogether by the admission of the specific unity to the exclusion of the unity of origin. A favourite argument on the other side, is that no new races of men are springing up at present : and that the strong characteristics of the negro, for instance, were as developed in the earliest ages of historical record as

[1] The Races of Man, p. 289.

they are now after a lapse of three thousand years, while after generations of domestication in America, the unmixed descendants of Africans remain true to the negro type.

To this it is replied that, in the infancy of the race, and when circumstances must have differed much from the present more settled order of nature, there may have existed greater predispositions to change, and stronger influences to effect it. Again, in regard to the slaves in America, the period of observation is too short to admit of any marked diversity; while it is also found that varieties, once introduced, become so far permanent, and do not revert to the original type.

But America, with its one aboriginal race extending nearly over the whole continent, is appealed to as a proof how little influence climate exerts in producing varieties. This is so far true, and a serious objection to any theory that holds the diversities to be entirely the result of climatic influences, which are, in fact, only a small part of the aggregation of causes in operation. But, on the other hand, this fact presents an insuperable difficulty, on the theory of centres of creation as advanced by Agassiz.

Most of the objections to the sufficiency of natural causes accounting for the diversity of races, arise from viewing one or other of the extremes, instead of assuming a mean from which the various races have diverged. But, admitting that natural causes cannot adequately explain the present appearances, recourse must be had to supernatural causes, that is, Divine interpositions. This must be admitted on any theory save that of Maillet and Lamarck. The opponents of specific unity refer the diversities to distinct acts of creation. But is this necessary; or is it philosophical to evoke a greater cause, when it cannot be proved that a less might not suffice? If recourse must be had to supernatural causes, it is more reasonable to suppose that the Creator originally implanted certain predispositions to be manifested in the progress of the race, or at a subsequent period introduced changes to facilitate the dispersion of the nations, than that by distinct acts of creation he introduced the varieties.

2. *Philological considerations.* — The contributions to this subject by Philology are exceedingly valuable. Recently, much has been effected in a comparison of languages, the study being

greatly facilitated, and its boundaries enlarged by a careful examination of ancient monuments, and by the accounts of travellers and missionaries regarding tongues and tribes previously unknown.

Language, or the power of communicating thought by articulate and conventional sounds, is a common property of man. There is no tribe, however degraded in intellect and morals, but is possessed of this medium of communication. But language is also peculiar to man. Brutes, no doubt, can communicate with one another by signs or sounds, but language, strictly speaking, they have not. This, then, separates man into an order by himself; while, at the same time, it shews that all the races of men, however they may differ in complexion, in form or feature, or in moral and intellectual attainments, are yet possessed of a common nature, and are, in every sense, members of humanity.

In this common and peculiar attribute of man there exists, as is well known, the greatest diversity. His languages and dialects are far more numerous than the shades of colour on his body. This was wont to be adduced in proof of the diversity of species or of origin. But, as a test of specific difference, it has entirely failed, being difficult of application, and often leading to the most unexpected results. It was found that nations, proved by physical characteristics to belong to one race, differ widely in language; while nations which wonderfully agree in language, exhibit in all other respects but an extremely remote connexion. Another result, however, emerged from the further investigation of this subject. In the midst of the bewildering diversity of languages and dialects, the comparative philologist has succeeded in pointing out many affinities and lines of connexion. To a certain extent this fact was recognised long ago, and the principal languages were reduced into something like a system, and arranged into families, yet with few apparent bonds of union. Now, however, the matter is more simplified. Analogies, previously hidden or obscured, have been brought clearly into view, and these again have led to other unexpected coincidences. So numerous are the affinities thus brought to light between languages at first sight remarkable only for their contrasts, and so comprehensive the principle, that the most eminent philologists can account for the fact only on the assumption that all the existing languages are the remains, variously modified, of one primeval tongue. But this, again, assumes that, whatever view may be taken of the origin of language, or of the nature of its modifying causes, the nations now separated from one another by great geographical barriers were at some former period very closely connected. One primeval language evidently points to family relations, and proves a unity of origin as respects the scattered tribes and families of the earth.

This conclusion can be evaded only by supposing that the affinity of languages is the result not of family connexion, but of subsequent intercourse between the nations, or of accident. But the fact of a primeval language has been established on strictly scientific data, and has commanded the assent of such men as Klaproth, Humboldt, and Bunsen. "The universal affinity of language," says Klaproth, "is placed in so strong a light that it must be considered by all as completely demonstrated. It appears inexplicable on any other hypothesis than that of admitting fragments of a primary language to exist through all the languages of the Old and New World." So, also, Frederick von Schlegel: "Much as all these languages differ from each other, they appear, after all, to be merely branches of one common stem." [1] And more recently, Bunsen: "As far as the organic languages of Asia and Europe are concerned, the human race is of one kindred, of one descent." "Our historical researches respecting language have led us to facts which seemed to oblige us to assume the common historical origin of the great families into which we found the nations of Asia and Europe to coalesce. The four families of Turanians and Iranians, of Khamites and Shemites, reduced themselves to two, and these again possessed such mutual material affinities as can neither be explained as accidental, nor as being so by a natural external necessity ; but they must be historical, and therefore imply a common descent." "The Asiatic origin of all these (American) tribes is as fully proved as the unity of family among themselves." [2]

[1] The Philosophy of History, p. 92. Lond. 1847.

[2] Phil. of Univ. Hist. vol. ii. pp. 4, 99, 112. But it should be added that these results, founded on the philological researches of Professor Max Müller of Oxford, are called in question by Professor Pott of Halle in the Zeitschrift der Deutschen morgenländischen Gesellschaft, p. 405. Leipz. 1855.

The difficulty of determining this common stem in no way affects the question at issue. It is satisfactory to find that the whole tendency of linguistic inquiries is so strongly in favour of the unity of mankind, and that many learned men, some it may be undesignedly and some unwillingly, have fully confirmed another intimation of Scripture, that there was a time when the whole earth was of one language and of one speech, before mankind was dispersed upon its surface. Here, moreover, may be noticed a fact established by the philologist, confirmatory of a tripartite division of mankind proposed by some of the ablest naturalists, and confirmatory, it may be said, of the biblical account of the *three* sons of Noah, by whom the earth was re-peopled after the flood. Before reaching the final result represented in *one* primeval language, the philologist was enabled to arrange all languages into three great divisions, corresponding to the three great families of mankind inhabiting the three continents of the Old World, or more particularly spreading from the north of Europe to the tropic lands of Asia and Africa—thus embracing all the nations who have played the most conspicuous part in the world's history—a part strikingly in accordance with the blessings bestowed by Noah on his sons respectively.

3. *Historical considerations.* — From history in its strict sense, whether recorded in books or sculptured on monuments, little information can be derived relative to the origin of mankind. The only history, the biblical, which, in fact, treats of this subject, is purposely excluded from present consideration, inasmuch as it is the testimony of Scripture regarding it that, in a manner, is called in question. But while excluding direct biblical testimony, it is quite admissible to refer to it in proof of the information possessed by the writers of Scripture, or of the views entertained at the time of its composition. Thus, it cannot be doubted that Moses, the accredited author of Genesis, was fully aware of the great diversities among mankind. During his sojourn in Egypt and the desert of Arabia, he must have come in contact with various races distinguished by strong peculiarities, and yet he did not hesitate to assign a common origin to all the families of the earth—a circumstance which shows that at that early period the matter did not present itself as a difficulty.

But there are not wanting historical records of another character : such are the truths and testimonies preserved in tradition, and in popular usages and superstitions, which, in most instances, have survived the recollection of their origin. Now, if many of these be seen to converge to one point from various parts of the earth's circumference, that point must be the centre of the circle, the central point from which all such traditions, usages, and superstitions have radiated.[1]

(1.) *Traditions common to the nations of the earth.*—The more important only of these need be referred to, such as those in connexion with the Creation, the Fall, and the Deluge. Of the traditions bearing on Creation and the Fall, sufficient notice has been already taken in the preceding pages, where it was shown that there was no way of accounting for the essential agreement of these wide-spread notions but on the supposition of a common origin referable to the first seat of the human race. The information on the subject of creation and the fall, diffused among the nations of the earth, is of such a nature and character, so utterly beyond the reach of invention, so consistent with itself and with the results of modern science, that children must have received it from their parents, and so upwards to one ancestral pair. In addition to what has been already stated concerning these initial transactions in human history, it might be interesting to notice the general unanimity of tradition respecting some other particulars of the period from the Fall to the Deluge : such as the names and the longevity of the patriarchs, their arts and inventions,—but this the present limits forbid.

The tradition, however, most widely diffused, and most uniform in its dispersion, is, as might be anticipated, that of the flood,—a catastrophe which must have had a striking effect on the mind, and, being of more recent date, was better retained in the memory. The traditions on this subject have been collected by Bryant, Faber, and Harcourt, and although in these compilations there is much that is fanciful, there is yet enough to show how widely the memorials of the more important circumstances had spread, and how faithfully they were preserved among nations and tribes situated at the widest distances from one another, and differing greatly in civilisation,

[1] Harcourt, Doctrine of the Deluge, vol. i. p. 47.

religion, manners, language, and modes of thought. Such a community of tradition, were it even limited to one or two particulars, would merit attention in an inquiry into the mutual relation of mankind, but when taken in connexion with the other testimonies on the Creation and the Fall, the matter is inexplicable on any theory which denies to mankind a common origin.

(2.) *Popular customs and religious usages and superstitions common to mankind.*—Of the numerous and strong points of contact presented to the view on this wide and interesting field of inquiry, only one or two can be noticed—specimens of independent and concurring testimonies which admit of being indefinitely multiplied.

The weekly division of time, and the sacredness of the number *seven* in general, is a remarkable instance of this kind; but this has been already considered. Another usage—religious or superstitious—which leads to similar conclusions with the tradition of the Fall, in which it doubtless originated, was the serpent-worship. "In almost every pagan nation the serpent has been the object of idolatrous veneration, which may be presumed to have arisen from some tradition concerning that reptile in Paradise. It cannot be conceived how mankind could be brought to pay divine adoration to an animal so loathsome and disgusting, and to which there seems a natural antipathy in the human species, except from some traditionary record of its instrumentality in the Fall: yet the fact is certain of its being regarded with religious veneration all over the world."[1]

But of more importance still are the views which were held regarding atonement, with the universal practice of animal sacrifice founded thereon. "It is notorious that all nations, Jews and Heathens, before the time of Christ, entertained the notion, that the displeasure of the offended Deity was to be averted by the sacrifice of an animal; and that, to the shedding of blood, they imputed their pardon and reconciliation. In the explication of so strange a notion, and of the universality of its extent, unassisted reason must confess itself totally at a loss. And, accordingly, we find Pythagoras, Plato, Porphyry, and other reflecting heathens, express their wonder *how*

[1] Holden, Dissertation on the Fall, pp. 159, 160.

an institution so dismal and big with absurdity could have spread through the world." To these remarks of Archbishop Magee[1] may be added a statement by Faber, another able writer on this subject : " I have always thought, and still think, that a universal accordance in matters purely arbitrary evinces, of necessity, that these matters had a common origin. Now, if this principle be just, the universal accordance of the pagan world in the purely arbitrary doctrine of an atonement and in the purely arbitrary practice of piacular sacrifice, invincibly demonstrates that *that* doctrine and *that* practice could not, in point of fact, have been independently struck out by all the nations of the world in their insulated state, but that the doctrine and practice in question must have been derived by all nations from some one common origin, to which the ancestors of all nations must have had an equally easy access."[2]

(3.) To the considerations arising from universal or widespread traditions, usages, or superstitions, may be added others of a similar tendency. For instance, the various circumstances of a historical or mythical character which point to Western Asia as the cradle of the human race. " The uniform and universal testimony of history traces up all the nations of the earth, like streams, to a common fountain, and it places that fountain in some oriental country in or near the tropics."[3]

But not only in regard to the locality of the dispersion of the race, but also in a great measure in regard to its chronology, is there a wonderful harmony between history and tradition. To quote from Sir W. Jones :—" Thus have we proved that the inhabitants of Asia, and, consequently, as it might be proved, of the whole earth, sprang from three branches of one stem : and that these branches have shot into their present state of luxuriance in a period comparatively short, is apparent from a fact universally acknowledged, that we find no certain monument, or even probable tradition, of nations planted, empires and states raised, laws enacted, cities built, navigation improved, commerce encouraged, arts invented, or letters contrived, above twelve, or, at the most, fifteen or sixteen centuries before the birth of Christ."

[1] On the Atonement, *Works*, vol. i. p. 359. Lond. 1842.
[2] Treatise on the Origin of Expiatory Sacrifice, p. 50. Lond. 1827
[3] Smyth, Unity of the Human Races, p. 226. Edin. 1851.

It is unnecessary to pursue this subject farther. Enough has been advanced to shew that, notwithstanding any appearances to the contrary, mankind constitute but one family. The testimony of Scripture on this point is fully sustained by the evidence of science, physical, philological, and historical. All the lines of philosophical and antiquarian investigation converge to one point or centre whence the nations have been dispersed over the earth, and unite to prove, that although thus scattered, they are the children of one ancestral pair—the Adam and Eve of the Bible.

EXCURSUS VI.—DEATH BEFORE THE FALL.

The notions entertained of the primeval constitution of the earth and animated nature are, in many instances, exceedingly crude and confused—the result mainly of fanciful representations of a golden age exempt from all pain and suffering, and in which there was not even place for changes of climate or of seasons, for the war of elements, biting frosts, or chilling winds. Death, in particular, is supposed to have been absolutely excluded, by all accustomed to regard it as, in every case, the fruit of man's transgression. But of the numerous facts disclosed by science while exploring the Creator's works and wonders in ages long past, not one is supported by stronger evidence than that which shews, that long anterior to the fall or creation of man, death was busy at its work of destruction. That this discovery, however, is not at variance with any statement of the Bible, as the enemies of Revelation would wish, or its friends might fear, or with any conclusion deducible, in particular, from the narratives of creation and the fall, will appear from the following considerations :—

1. Death is a universal law, from the operation of which, in the present constitution of things, no organized being is exempt. Every living thing on earth must succumb to this power. The grass withers, the flower fades ; and not only these short-lived productions, which are proverbial of what is frail and fleeting, but the strongest, stateliest, and most enduring trees of the forest, must yield to decay and death. Rising higher in the scale of life, the same inexorable law is ever encountered—in

the insect ephemera, whose life-span extends but to a few hours of a summer eve ; yet no less certain in the nobler types of animal existence in the ocean, in the air, and on the earth, and last of all in man, of whom it is affirmed, " It is appointed unto all men once to die." From this appointment only two individuals of the race are known to have been hitherto exempted—Enoch and Elijah, who, nevertheless, underwent a change equivalent or analogous to death. Death is thus a shadow which ever follows in the wake of life ; but differs in this, that it never fails to overpower the substance.   " No perfection of organism, no completeness in the supply of the conditions of existence, can prevent any living individual from at last failing to derive the means of maintenance from those conditions, and from falling into a state of decay and dissolution."

2. Death is a constant law, and has been in operation from the beginning.   The state of matters above described is no innovation—no breaking in on another and different state of existence.   There is incontestable evidence to prove, that long before the era of man, life and death were dwellers on the earth, where they waged incessant war.   True, life is older than death, but by no great period ; while it is from death, or the records preserved in and by it, that our knowledge is wholly derived in regard to the antiquity of life, and to the various forms in which it was once manifested.   These records from the sepulchres of perished creations incontrovertibly prove, that then as now, birth, growth, decay, and dissolution succeeded one another in a continued round ; and that, as at present, one part of creation warred with and preyed upon another.   In the whole past record of life on the earth, there is no indication of a time when death's ravages were unknown, operating by natural decay, or by violent convulsions and catastrophes of nature, or of a period during which, as some fancy, the whole animal creation lived in mutual harmony, when as yet there were no beasts or birds of prey, but all without distinction cropped the herbage, or subsisted on grains and fruits.

A moderate acquaintance with physical science, and particularly with the character and organization of the animal creation, will suffice to commend this view of the matter, by shewing not merely the fallacy, but the impossibility, which attaches to

the opinion, that the fall of man occasioned an entire transformation of tastes and tendencies in the animal economy and
constitution ; an opinion tolerable enough as a fiction of poetry,
but unworthy and injurious as an article in a theological creed.

(1.) The anatomical structure of the carnivora shews that
they cannot have originally conformed to the habits of the tribes
which still obtain their food from the vegetable kingdom.   Between animals of the herbivorous and carnivorous classes there
is the greatest difference of organic structure.   This difference is
not confined to one or two parts, but extends more or less to all
the organs and the general conformation of the creature—as
the organs of vision, prehension, mastication, and digestion ;
and so distinct and consistent is the respective conformation,
that from the examination of but even a small part of the
skeleton of an unknown animal, the comparative anatomist can
determine to which of the two classes the animal must have
belonged.   So decisive is this evidence as to an original difference of habits, that there is no alternative but to admit that
beasts and birds of prey lived from the beginning on the kind
of food on which they subsist at present, or to assume, without
the shadow of evidence, and in opposition to all the analogies
of nature, that they have undergone a transformation so complete as properly to deserve the name of a new creation.

(2.) This is corroborated by the testimony of the fossiliferous
strata.   The oldest of the sedimentary rocks contain in vast
numbers the remains of animals which must have lived and
died at a period so remote, that the mind can with difficulty
approximate to it.   These all tell a story of the long and
ancient reign of death, while stratum after stratum exhibits it
as the successive platform of life.   Individuals had their day ;
and so also species.   One after another appeared and disappeared, only to make way for other forms of life suited by
the Creator for the varying conditions of existence on the
earth.   These records also tell how animal devoured animal as
a means of subsistence.   It is curious, too, to find, how the
evidence of this fact is preserved in the very stomach of the
devourer.   In some of the strata, in the Lias for instance, are
found reptiles of extraordinary size and structure, as the
Ichthyosaurs, which lived and perished many ages before
man's creation.   These reptiles shew their carnivorous char-

acter not only in the structure of their jaws and teeth, " the half-digested remains of fishes and reptiles, found within their skeletons, indicate the precise nature of their food."[1] Indeed, it would thus appear that these monsters of the ancient world did not hesitate to devour the smaller and weaker of their own species.[2]

(3.) There is nothing in Scripture at variance with the view which the above facts present. There are numerous passages where the introduction of death into the world is spoken of, and its origin ascribed to man's sin ; but the reference in these cases will be found to be exclusively to death as related to the human race. As regards its power over the inferior creatures Scripture is entirely silent ; yet its existence may be considered as tacitly assumed in the history of creation. The passages which speak of the entrance of death are the following :—

Gen. iii. 19, " Dust thou art, and unto dust shalt thou return." This announcement to Adam after the Fall is entirely silent as to the presence or absence of death in the lower creation. It may imply, that he was familiar with the phenomenon of dissolution, but it cannot be construed as involving irresponsible beings in a fate from which they had been previously exempt.

Rom. v. 12, " By one man sin entered into the world, and death by sin, and so death passed upon all men," &c. Here the entrance of death is distinctly ascribed to Adam's transgression, but the clause, " so death passed upon all men," limits *the death* thus introduced, and shows that the apostle referred simply to death as related to man.

1 Cor. xv. 21, " For since by man came death, by man came also the resurrection of the dead." Here, also, the reference is exclusively to man, as appears from the contrast instituted between " death " and the " resurrection." This is put beyond doubt by the words subjoined : " For as in Adam all die, even so in Christ shall all be made alive."

Rom. viii. 20, 22, " The creature was made subject to vanity, not willingly, but by reason of Him who hath subjected the same in hope. For we know that the whole creation groaneth and travaileth in pain together until now." It is frequently

[1] Lyell, Elements of Geology, p. 276. 4th edit. Lond. 1852.
[2] Burmeister, Geschichte der Schöpfung, p. 495.

assumed that this is an intimation that all the sufferings of creation, its subjection to vanity, and its groaning in pain, are the result of the Fall. But it is to be remarked, (1.) That interpreters are not agreed as to whether the terms, "the creature" and "the whole creation," refer to two distinct objects, or to the same, and then whether to the rational or irrational part of creation. (2.) This subjection to vanity is not ascribed to man's sin, but to God's appointment. (3.) If the reference be to the curse on the ground for man's sin, the effects of which were sterility and the growth of noxious weeds, this does not justify the conclusion that pain, suffering, and death then entered in for the first time.

This is the sum of the information which the Scriptures furnish on the origin of death. That it is limited to the case of man is not to be wondered at, seeing how much man's place and position differed from that of all other creatures, and his life and death from theirs. It is from inattention to these essential distinctions that much of the confusion has arisen with which this subject is surrounded.

The portions of Scripture supposed to countenance the notion that, previous to the Fall, all animals were graminivorous, are, (1.) The grant of food at the creation limited to vegetable productions, (Gen. i. 29, 30.) But that this is not conclusive, the following considerations shew :—*First*, The grant is directly to man, the lower animals being mentioned only incidentally ; and so when it is subsequently enlarged man only is included, (Gen. ix. 3.) *Secondly*, The animals concerned in this grant can be considered only in a limited sense ; for of one large class, the monsters of the deep, there is no mention. Besides that general terms, as here, must not be taken absolutely, is evident from Gen. ix. 3, where it is said, " Every moving thing that liveth shall be meat for you." In the original grant of food it is therefore reasonable to conclude that only a particular class of animals was meant—such, probably, as were in closest relation to man—while the other tribes, from their creation, used the food congenial to their nature, without any explicit grant but that implied in their instincts and necessities. (2.) Passages from the prophetic writings, descriptive of a blessed, peaceful future, are adduced in support of this notion. Thus Isa. xi. 6-8, where it is predicted that " the wolf shall dwell with the lamb, and the leopard lie down with the kid," and "the lion shall eat straw like the ox." But by no process of legitimate interpretation can any support be found here for the notion in question. For these prophetic intimations are entirely figurative, and have respect not to a physical but to a moral future, for it is made to depend on the earth being full of the knowledge of the Lord. But, besides the unwarrantable assumption of literalities, there is another in the supposition that the future, thus viewed, is only the restitution of the original state of creation ; or that the unfallen past must have corresponded to this fanciful restored future.

3. Death is a necessary law of organized beings. Life and death are great mysteries, which are known only by their actings. Of the numerous points of difference between dead, inorganic matter, and that endued with vitality, whether in plant or animal, there are two of primary importance—assimilation, on which depends the growth of the individual, and propagation, whereon depends the continuance of the race. Considered on both these principles, death is a necessary law of organization.

(1.) Death is necessary, from the law of assimilation. By assimilation is meant that continued process by which plants and animals separate their appropriate food from all other particles of matter, and incorporate it into their own substance. This process consists of two parts : the absorption of new matter is accompanied by a constant, uninterrupted separation of the dead, *effete* matter,[1] so that a continued decay or dissolution attends the actings of life. Vegetables derive a part of their nutriment from inorganic matter ; but animals can find nourishment only in substances which had life, vegetable or animal. From dead organic matter the living structure derives its requisite support, but these supplies cannot insure a perpetuity of existence. " All individual vital action is essentially temporary in its nature ; and every living thing must die." [2] " After a certain period, the vessels which convey the nutritive materials, and elaborate the proximate principles, become choked with incrementitious matter, assimilation is performed

[1] See Carpenter, Principles of Comparative Physiology, p. 127.   4th edit.   London, 1854.
[2] Kemp, Nat. Hist. of Creation, p. 113.

imperfectly, and gradually the vital energies are overpowered, and yield up their charge to the disorganizing power of chemical agencies." [1]

(2.) Death is necessary from the law of propagation. The propagation of the race is the second grand characteristic under the present constitution of things. By the operation of this law imposed upon creation at the beginning, the earth would speedily be overstocked, were no provision made for removing by death, or something equivalent to it, the successive generations brought into being. In the absence of this, how were the surplus population to be disposed of? Were the inferior creatures, in some such way as it may be conceived with regard to man, to be removed to some other scenes and higher states of existence? Or, if continued on earth, was the law of propagation to be repealed or suspended when the numbers had advanced to a ratio commensurate with the capacities of the earth or the supply of food? Or, finally, are these creatures fitted for immortality? Probably few of these considerations have occurred to those who argue that death had no place in the world previous to man's fall. But the absurdities flowing from such a notion need not be farther insisted on.

4. Death is a benevolent law. If death be a necessary ordinance of organic life, it must have entered into the original plan of creation, and so evince not merely design but benevolence, notwithstanding difficulties in the existence of pain and suffering irrespective of moral desert.

(1.) In regard to the animal creation, as a whole, the present constitution secures the greatest possible amount of enjoyment. It secures a continuous succession of young creatures, in which animal enjoyment is at its highest. This exuberance of joy reacts upon the older of the species; besides the instincts and delights which the parental relation draws forth and gratifies. Farther, it secures, through a diversity of food, the greatest possible amount of contemporaneous animal existence.

(2.) It is chiefly, however, in its bearing on man that death is to be viewed under the present dispensation as a benevolent arrangement, though essentially of a penal character. In its bearing alike on the individual and the community, death is a part of the remedial economy. As regards the individual,

[1] Hitchcock, Religion of Geology, p. 75.

death is fitted perpetually to remind him of his fallen, ruined condition. The certainty of leaving this world at no distant day, develops in one class all the better qualities of the *new man*, tempers their joys and moderates their sorrows. On the other hand, death is eminently fitted to check the natural propensities of the wicked by the fear which it inspires, and the limited time which it affords for maturing and putting into execution schemes of vice and villany. Again, as regards the community, death is a benevolent law. While it no doubt sunders the sweetest, tenderest, and most endearing ties of humanity, it at the same time draws forth all the deepest sympathies of the heart—sympathies which constitute the very bond of society. Unlike the instinct implanted in many species of animals, which gives them a presentiment of death, and leads them to hide away in some obscure retreat to die unnoticed, death and its precursory symptoms in man draw more closely all the ties of kindred and of kindness, and call into exercise the tenderest affections, beneficial to the *subject* and the *object*, and to the community at large. As death, too, cuts short the plots of tyrants and the enemies of mankind, it acts beneficially to the race. With the present limited prospect of life, how many are the projects for subjugating nations, for crushing liberty, for usurping the rights of conscience, for oppressing the poor, for accumulating property, adding house to house, and field to field, till there be no room left for a rival on the earth ! What would the state of matters be, individually and socially, with the prospect of an earthly immortality, or even with the longevity which was granted before the flood ? It is death, and the abbreviation of man's sojourn here, that prevents the recurrence of a state of things of which it was said, that " all flesh had corrupted his way upon the earth, and the earth was filled with violence." The matter is seen in its proper light, only when the mind is brought to consider what earth would have been had a terrestrial immortality been permitted to its human inhabitants after the Fall —and the idea is quite compatible with a state of condemnation, and indeed it may be said to be that state realized and intensified—earth would in that case have resembled hell.

As there are no intimations by which to determine the duration of the state of innocence described at the close of the preceding chapter, speculation on the subject is altogether vain. It is of importance, however, to know that a state of innocence did thus precede the present condition of sin and suffering, which is thereby proved not to have been originally inherent in the constitution of man, and so not a necessity of his being; and it is of importance, too, to be possessed of a history of man's temptation and fall. Scripture affords several intimations of a fall in the invisible world, (2 Pet. ii. 4; Jude 6,) and which must have preceded that of man, but when or how that defection took place is nowhere expressly affirmed. A history of angels, or of their fall, has not been written, and in this respect there is a distinction between their case and that of man—a distinction resting no doubt on the Divine purpose of redemption regarding the latter.

Of man's fall there is a full account, not indeed such as affords an answer to many questions which curiosity will suggest, but to all to which Divine goodness and omniscience saw meet to reply. Among other important truths which may be learned from this narrative, it teaches that though God had prepared a test of man's obedience, yet the temptation came not from Him. Nor did it originate in man himself. He was tempted from without, and seduced into transgression; and in this it may be conceived lies the possibility of the restoration purposed and promised by God. The same characteristics of the Divine Being and principles of government manifested throughout the Scriptures, particularly the method whereby He brings good out of evil, are conspicuously displayed in the narrative of the Fall. At the same time, the character and conduct of the great adversary of God and man, as represented in this portion of Scripture, are in entire conformity with the information which the New Testament furnishes regarding the enemy who sowed tares among the good seed. In reading the history of the Fall, after the account of the Creation, as it came from the hand of God, the conviction is irresistible, " An enemy hath done this," (Matt. xiii. 39.) For while recording an event in its consequences most disastrous to man, and which, by proving the want of stability in a creature so highly honoured and blessed, might seem to reflect on the character of the Creator himself, this history will be found to vindicate the procedure of the Divine Being both in the work of creation and in the government of the world.

§ 16. *The Temptation and First Sin,* Gen. iii. 1-6.

The previous history was simply that of man and of creation as subordinated and subservient to him. At this point, how-ever, man's history begins to be mysteriously blended with that of a principle occupying a place and manifesting a dis-position alien from all that the previous narrative would natur-ally lead us to anticipate. The appearance of this principle at this stage of the history is sudden, but not altogether unex-pected, when viewed in connexion, as already shewn, with the charge committed to man on his being introduced into the garden, (chap. ii. 15.) The origin of the being in question it might not at first be easy to determine, although the character of the lower creation, and its subjection to man, were sufficient to show that this was no creature of earth; while, on the other hand, the language to which it gave utterance, plainly wanted the seal and attestation of heaven. Anyhow, this phenomenon argued disorder and disaffection somewhere in the creation, and as such should have sufficed to put the keeper of the garden on his guard.

The Tempter described, and the mode of his attack, verse 1. *Now the serpent was more subtle than any beast of the field which the Lord God had made. And he said to the woman, Yea, hath God said, Ye shall not eat of any tree in the garden ?*

In order to diminish the difficulties of this history, some writers take the *serpent*, according to New Testament usage, to be a symbolical designation of the Spirit of Evil; but that it applied to a serpent properly so called, or what appeared to be such, is evident as well from other considerations, as from the comparison with " the beasts of the field." Moreover, we stand here on purely historical ground, however mysterious some of the circumstances may seem, (2 Cor. xi. 3 ; 1 Tim. ii. 13, 14.)   But not the less was the serpent the mere instrument of an invisible higher power, who, notwithstanding his cunning and disguise, so far betrays himself by his conduct and conversation, as to leave no doubt regarding his person. Several critics of no mean note render הַנָּחָשׁ, *a certain serpent,* but this is by other equally eminent authorities pronounced to be unwarranted.   That the Hebrew *article* has not unfrequently this force cannot indeed be questioned, but that it is not necessarily to be so taken in the present instance is shown from Numb. xxi. 9 ; Eccles. x. 11 ; Amos v. 19 ; ix. 3, &c.   On this argument, therefore, if it stood alone, it would be unwise greatly to insist.   But there are other considerations which concur in pointing out the serpent of the temptation as distinct from all other creatures.   Thus to urge at present only the opening announcement of the narrative, there is, first, the preeminent subtlety ascribed to this serpent over " all the beasts of the field," a comparison which, taken in conjunction with the words superadded, " which the Lord God had made," seems to be an intimation that the reptile in question was no creature of earth, or one that received its form from God.   The serpent, it may be remarked, is by no means distinguished for sagacity or subtlety, and yet in all languages it is symbolical of such attributes, (see Matt. x. 16,) no doubt from its early connexion with the destinies of mankind.   " The serpent was subtle (עָרוּם, *cunning, crafty,* Job v. 12; xv. 5) above or in comparison with all the beasts of the field."   This term may have been used to mark the contrast between the character of this creature and that of the objects of his attack.   These were עֲרוּם, *naked,* (chap. ii. 25,) implying a state of innocence and simplicity, the Tempter was עָרוּם, ($\pi\alpha\nu o\hat{\upsilon}\rho\gamma o\varsigma$, Aquila, compare 2 Cor. xi. 3,) cunning and malignant.   The craftiness of the serpent appeared in the choice of the object and the mode of attack.   He addressed himself to the woman as the more susceptible, because the more dependent and *weaker* of the two, (1 Pet. iii. 7 ;) and perhaps she had heard of the Divine prohibition only from her husband, and not directly from God himself, although however received, she was fully aware of its existence and import.

The abrupt manner in which the conversation of the serpent

with the woman is introduced, shews that the reader is not
presented with the beginning of it. The first words of the
colloquy recorded contain a question, אַף כִּי, "etiamne? verumne
quod?" according to Noldius; "a question of astonishment,"
as Tuch characterizes it; "*is it so, then, that God said,*" &c.;
intimating, as it were, that such a report had been noised
abroad, but that it seemed utterly incredible. But while apparently only asking information, the tempter took occasion
entirely to pervert the Divine prohibition: "Hath God said,
Ye shall not eat of all the trees in the garden?" that is,
according to the force of the *negative* before the *universal*
in Hebrew, *Ye shall not eat of any tree in the garden,* (Tuch,
Knobel, Ewald, § 313, *b.*) No; God had said directly the
reverse, (chap. ii. 16.) So much apparent ignorance, however,
of the purport of the Divine command, as completely to reverse
its terms, when taken in connexion with the knowledge of its
existence and of the language in which it was conveyed, was
a circumstance well fitted to shew to the woman that the ignorance was only assumed, and that there lurked an evil purpose
under it. But, instead of seeing this, she seeks, in her simplicity, to correct the misapprehension of the inquirer.

The woman corrects the serpent's mistake, verses 2, 3.
*And the woman said to the serpent, We may eat of the fruit of
the trees of the garden ; but of the fruit of the tree which is in
the midst of the garden, God hath said, Ye shall not eat of it,
neither shall ye touch it, lest ye die.*—It cannot be admitted
with Hengstenberg, that the use by the woman of the name
Elohim, instead of Jehovah, was the beginning of her fall; nor
can it be regarded as a depression and obscuration of the religious sentiment. (See above, p. 34.) The woman gives, upon
the whole correctly, the import of the Divine charge, though
with some slight variations from the original terms, some of
which, at least, betray the first risings of sin. In the first
place, her reply, " Of the fruit of the trees of the garden we
may eat," was not a sufficiently distinct and emphatic negative
to the serpent's insinuation, " Ye shall not eat of any tree in
the garden;" while it scarcely did justice to the large and
liberal grant of God, " Of every tree in the garden thou mayest
freely eat, but of the tree," &c. Secondly, to the Divine prohibition to eat of the tree, she adds, " And ye shall not touch

it,"—an addition which, according to some interpreters, *e.g.*, Delitzsch, reveals the fact, that a feeling of the severity of the inhibition, and dissatisfaction with its too great strictness, had already begun to operate. It is better, however, with Calvin, to regard it as the indication of an anxious and careful desire to observe the commandment. Perhaps it may have been a cherished purpose of Adam and his wife—and connected in the mind of the latter with the instructions received from her husband relative to this tree—not merely to abstain from the fruit, but, for greater security, not even to touch the tree itself. But, finally, that which chiefly indicates a change of disposition is the circumstance, that she passes over the threatened punishment more lightly than the original terms warranted : " In the day that thou eatest thereof thou shalt surely die," is, in the reply of the woman, reduced to the more contingent expression, פֶּן־תְּמֻתוּן—*lest ye die.* The particle פֶּן may point to a consequence as certain, *seeing ye shall,* or only as probable, *seeing ye may, lest.* There is evidently here some doubt or hesitancy concerning the threatened consequences of transgression. Death is no longer in the woman's estimation a certain, inevitable result of disobedience to the Divine law, but only a possible, or it may be a probable, contingency. The penalty is thus at once stripped of more than half its terrors. It is a thing to be risked, if there are any counterbalancing promises and prospects, if the chances, so to speak, are against the infliction of the punishment ; or it may be even submitted to in consideration of the greater gain to be secured by grasping at the thing forbidden.

This parleying of the woman with the enemy was exceedingly hazardous : it was, in fact, like standing on the very edge of the precipice. But the danger was still farther enhanced by the state of mind indicated by the woman's answer. Her position did not escape the notice of the tempter, who at once saw his advantage, and accordingly did not let slip the opportunity of following it up. Verses 4, 5. *And the serpent said to the woman, Ye shall not surely die : for God doth know, that in the day ye eat thereof, then your eyes shall be opened, and ye shall be as God, knowing good and evil.*

There is in this reply, first a direct and emphatic contradiction of the Divine declaration. The *negative* before the *infinitive*

in לְאִ־מוֹת תְּמֻתוּן, is an unusual form for מוֹת לֹא תְּמֻתוּן, and is an arrangement which occurs elsewhere only in poetry, e.g., לֹא־פָדֹה יִפְדֶּה,
(Ps. xlix. 8.)   In the present instance, it is evidently occasioned
by the terms of the penalty in chap. ii. 17.   The serpent's statement presents a remarkable contrast to the woman's uncertainty
about the threatening.   Here there is no hesitancy or ambiguity.   But it also exhibits a contrast no less remarkable with
the tempter's own previous doubt and ignorance of the Divine
command.   How has that ignorance, but so recently exhibited,
all at once given place to the highest confidence and assurance
in regard to a point which involves the whole character and
government of God?   It was a bold stroke, and one which the
tempter well knew must decide the controversy one way or
another: it must break off the conference, or secure to him
the victory.   The tempter speaks out, and reveals himself in
his true character, as he blasphemously gives the lie to God.
Now is the decisive moment for the mother of mankind: she
need no longer be at a loss as to the character of the being
with whom she holds converse; but she utters no prayer for
deliverance, and enters no protest against this Heaven-arraign-
ing temerity: she permits the speaker to proceed with his
ill-disguised falsehoods.

The tempter goes on to state the grounds of his startling
proposition.   But the arguments are as weak as the proposition was daring.   In support of it he can advance nothing
save his own bare assertion, " For God doth know that in the
day ye eat thereof your eyes shall be opened," &c.   He had
impugned the Divine veracity, and he can advance nothing in
behalf of his blasphemous assertion, but a farther impeachment of Divine goodness and love.   The particle כִּי, for, because,
in כִּי יֹדֵעַ אֱלֹהִים, shows that this was meant as a proof of the preceding statement, or as the ground of the Divine procedure in
interdicting a particular benefit to his creatures, and terrifying
them into acquiescence in his determinations, on the pain of
death.   It was not to preserve you from death, the serpent
urged, that this command was given, or out of any regard for
your welfare; but only because God knows that by partaking
of this fruit ye shall become like himself, and so ye are envi-
ously forbidden it.   God had other ends in view than the
happiness of His creatures, in giving forth such a command,

and annexing to it a penalty meant only to frighten. It was thus the tempter argued with the woman. When he boldly declared, " Ye shall not surely die," perhaps he did not mean it to be understood absolutely that God would not execute the threatened penalty, but only that through means of this tree they should be put in a position to escape His vengeance.

After thus making void the threatening of God, the tempter proceeds to substitute a blessing of his own in its stead. His promise begins with the very words of the Divine denunciation: " In the day ye eat thereof," compared with " In the day thou eatest thereof," (chap. ii. 17 ;) but the continuation and the conclusion fully attest it to be the promise of the devil, "Then your eyes shall be opened." פָּקַח, as here, is the usual term for opening the eyes, or of giving sight to the blind, (Isa. xxxv. 5,) and then figuratively applied to the act of raising one above his usual short-sightedness, or disclosing to him an object of which he was previously unconscious, (Gen. xxi. 19.) So also נִגְלָה עֵינַיִם, Numb. xxii. 31 ; and, on the contrary, the *blinding of the eyes* is an image of stupidity—an indisposition to perceive or understand the truth, (Isa. vi. 10.) " Opening the eyes " is here a promise of advancement from their low and limited condition under the law of their Creator, to a more correct and enlarged apprehension of things, and to such a degree that they should feel as if hitherto they had been walking about with eyes *closed* to the beauties and pleasures around them and within their reach. The promised blessing is farther explained, and placed in a still more attractive light by the intimation, וִהְיִיתֶם כֵּאלֹהִים יֹדְעֵי טוֹב וָרָע, "Ye shall be as God," *like Elohim :* not ὡς θεοί of the LXX., "sicut dii" of the Vulg., or " as gods " of the English version. The promise is, that they shall resemble the Supreme God, their Creator and Governor ; and this is farther amplified or illustrated by the assurance of their being put in possession of the knowledge of good and evil, that is, being made to participate in the *fulness* of knowledge. This last suggestion was exceedingly insidious. The tempter founded it on something which the woman had omitted in her answer, and at the same time, in accordance with the deceiver's usual procedure, on a perversion of the word of God. The woman had spoken only of " the tree in the midst of the garden ;"

though it had previously been designated by God as " the tree of the knowledge of good and evil," (chap. ii. 17.) The tempter carefully abstained from intimating his acquaintance with the name of the tree, but he alluded to it by mentioning its effects. " The tree of the knowledge of good and evil," he would insinuate, was so called from its excellent properties, of which those who eat of its fruit were sure to participate.

And yet, though every word of this statement was a lie, and every thought horrid blasphemy and rebellion against the Eternal Lawgiver and Judge, and might have been seen by the woman to be supported by no other evidence than the bold assertions of him who gave them utterance, the representations are believed, and the implied though not expressed counsel is followed. Verse 6. *And when the woman saw that the tree was good for food, and that it was pleasant to the eyes, and a tree to be desired to make wise, she took of the fruit thereof, and did eat ; and gave also to her husband with her, and he did eat.*

The act which was now consummated externally had already, in disposition and desire, been operating within. The woman's silence at the Satanic insinuations uttered in her presence against the character of God, was a virtual approval of, and assent to them : it was an internal fall which needed only the outward act to make it manifest. She had ceased to fear God's threatening and to cherish His love. There was an impatience of the Divine restraint, and a strong disposition, come what would, to snatch at the promised blessings now seen to centre in the forbidden fruit. There were, as apprehended by the woman, three attractions in the tree which combined to hurry her on in the path of transgression :—1. She " saw that the tree was good for food." Of this, however, she could have had no assurance or experience. It might, indeed, as afterwards stated, appear " pleasant to the eyes," but for aught that she knew it might prove not only unpleasant to the taste, but exceedingly deleterious to the system. She had known it only as a forbidden fruit, and could not possibly fathom all the reasons of its prohibition. Yet how exceedingly blinded and headlong is sin, and what fearful odds is it willing to encounter ! 2. The woman saw that the tree was " pleasant to the eyes," וְכִי תַאֲוָה־הוּא לָעֵינַיִם, *a desire or lust to the eyes.* It was not merely *desirable* or *pleasant*, but *a desire.* The desire was not simply

2 c

a property, but, as it were, its very nature, (Baumgarten.) This is what the Apostle John calls ἡ ἐπιθυμία τῶν ὀφθαλμῶν, (1 John ii. 16.) The former good was entirely fancied, and so, possibly, might have no real existence ; this, however, was a perceptible and so an actual, though, in this case, a perverted excellency. For, in this respect, were there not innumerable trees around "pleasant to the sight and good for food," (chap. ii. 9,) with the farther recommendation that they were not forbidden, but liberally assigned for the use of man ? But to the now distempered eye none so lovely or desirable as this one object, simply because it was forbidden ! " Stolen waters are sweet, and bread eaten in secret is pleasant," (Prov. ix. 17.) 3. But what particularly affected the first human transgressor, was the circumstance, learned only from the tempter, that it was " a tree to be desired to make wise"—נֶחְמָד הָעֵץ לְהַשְׂכִּיל. This is not to be taken in the sense of "lovely to the look," as in the Syriac, Onkelos, the Vulgate, " aspectuque delectabilis," and the similar renderings of De Wette, Tuch, Delitzsch, and Knobel, as if the expression were equivalent to נֶחְמָד לְמַרְאָה, (chap. ii. 9.) Tuch and Delitzsch refer to Psalm xli. 1, in support of the meaning they attach to this term, but that passage by no means bears out this view. " The more common meaning," says Hengstenberg, "and that which lies nearer the radical one of acting prudently, wisely, (Ps. ii. 10 ; 1 Sam. xviii. 14 ; Jer. xx. 11 ; xxiii. 5,) is in Psalm xli. 1 more suitable, and also recommended by the אֶל." Besides, the idea which these writers contend for had been already and more strongly expressed in the preceding clause, " pleasant to the eyes." הִשְׂכִּיל means to be wise, act wisely, or be instructed, Ps. ii. 10, and also to make wise, Ps. xxxii. 8. It is obviously in the latter sense that it is here used : the tree was desirable (נֶחְמָד, desiderabilis, part. Niph. of חָמַד) because of its making wise, ὡραῖόν ἐστι τοῦ κατανοῆσαι, (LXX.) It is so rendered also by Saadias, Rashi, Aben Ezra, and other Jewish writers ; by Luther, Le Clerc, Baumgarten, Eng. version, and by the recent Jewish translator, De Sola. Thus viewed, it forms a climax in the description which, by an enumeration of the circumstances that affected the woman, vividly sets forth the ever-growing power of unhallowed desire.

There was thus in the first temptation, as it presented itself at the beginning of the history of our race, a combination of the three elements which the Apostle John regards as the source of all after sins : " All that is in the world, the lust of the flesh, and the lust of the eyes, and the pride of life, is not of the Father, but is of the world," (1 John ii. 16.) How powerfully these principles wrought on this occasion, appears from the statement, " She took of the fruit thereof, and did eat." The heart followed the eyes, (Job xxxi. 7 ; Eccles. xi. 7,) and now the hand follows the heart. " Lust has conceived and brought forth sin," (Jam. i. 15,) in disobedience to, and as transgression of a known command of God. Disbelief of the Divine word, distrust of a proved Friend, and culpable credulity in the representations of an untried stranger, have led to this fatal result.

But more than this, as showing the true character of sin even from the beginning, the tempted becomes a tempter in turn : " and she gave also to her husband with her." She that had been given to the man to complete his happiness, and to be helpful to him in his divinely-appointed calling, is the first to involve him in rebellion against God. How soon and easily the greatest of blessings may, through sin, be transformed into the deadliest curse ! It is worthy of remark, that here, for the first time, the man is called the *husband* of the woman, אִישָׁהּ, *her man, her husband*. By this, the historian evidently designed to direct attention to the total perversion of the Divine ordinance of marriage which this conduct exhibited, and to show that the woman, designed as a help for her husband, became a hindrance, by becoming the agent of the tempter. The same truth is farther pointed out by the term, עִמָּהּ, *with her*, which is by some taken to intimate that Adam was present during this transaction, or at least towards its close ; but as this is not at all probable, it is better to consider the reference to be to the union or conjugal relation which subsisted between the parties. And the husband, on his part, was so far forgetful of God, and of the authority with which he was intrusted not only as the head of creation, but also and especially as the head of the woman, that at her solicitation he committed an act which the Supreme Governor had expressly forbidden him : " She gave also to her husband with her, and *he did eat*." Thus was the transgression completed. This act of the man, sanctioning and adopting the sin of the woman, was not merely a violation of the commandment relative to the forbidden fruit, but also a breach of the whole law, (James ii. 10 ;) and particularly was it an entire reversal of the original and prescribed relation of husband and wife, in which the former was appointed to rule and the latter to obey ; for here the man relinquishes his authority, and submits where he ought to command and to check.

In contrast with the full details of the woman's temptation and fall, it is remarkable with what brevity the man's sin is described. No mention whatever is made of the motives which influenced him in taking the fatal step here recorded. The history is silent as to whether he was drawn into the snare by the serpent's representations detailed to him by the woman, or by her own blandishing solicitations, or whether, as is sometimes supposed, he rushed into it with his eyes open, in order to share the fate of the partner of his life. When afterwards questioned as to the cause of transgression, the woman stated, " the serpent beguiled me," the man merely replied, " the woman gave me of the tree, and I did eat." The Apostle Paul indeed states that " Adam was not deceived ; but the woman, being deceived, was in the transgression," (1 Tim. ii. 14 ;) but it is doubtful whether by this he meant to intimate that when Adam partook of the fruit he was under no deception, or only that he was not deceived by the serpent. On any view of the case, sin is itself at all times a deception, and however the first man may have been led to the commission of it, there was absolutely nothing to palliate his conduct. He was, without question, every way more culpable than she on whom he would afterwards ungenerously charge his fall. But while passing over the motives which led the father of mankind into transgression of the Divine law, the historian is careful to record the consummation of the act : " he did eat," an act whereby " sin entered into the world, and death by sin," (Rom. v. 12)—an act inconceivably horrid and heinous, and one to which none other in the history of our sinful and fallen race can be compared, not even the crucifixion of the Lord from heaven—the second Adam, who came to deliver from the miseries caused by the first.

EXCURSUS VII.—THE TEMPTER-SERPENT.

Against none of the numerous incidents in the narrative of the Fall, have more cavilling objections been urged, than against the part assigned to the serpent in the transaction. The disposition thereby manifested has proceeded from the desire, either of proving the whole narrative an allegory, or of stamping it with the character of the Æsopian stories of talking and reasoning beasts and birds. It will be found, however, that the majority of these objections applies not so much to the scriptural statements, as to certain conclusions commonly deduced from them. And yet it must be admitted that many difficulties do attach to what is related of the tempter—difficulties perhaps inexplicable, and certainly greatly increased by the preconceptions of critics and commentators.

From the many points of view in which the matter has been regarded, there have necessarily sprung up the most conflicting opinions. Of these three only need be adverted to. The first attributes the temptation to the agency of the serpent alone : the second excludes the natural serpent from any participation in the transaction, and considers the name to be merely symbolical of the evil one ; and the third opinion, which may be regarded in a manner as a combination of the other two, holds the serpent to be the mere instrument of Satan, or himself transformed into a serpent.

Dismissing from consideration, in the meantime, all that may be urged for or against these opinions, or the comparative merits of each, it is proposed to prove, as the exposition of the simple scriptural account of the transaction, that the tempter that seduced the mother of mankind approached in the form of a serpent, but was not merely the reptile of that name, but a moral agent.

I. The tempter was a serpent in form and appearance. This is evident from the whole narrative, and so plain that it were superfluous to adduce arguments in its support, were it not that it has been strenuously denied that there was any serpent present, the name being merely a designation of the devil. But all argumentation, though far more cogent than any advanced on this point, must yield to the fact that the serpent of

the temptation is compared with " the beast of the field,"—
a fact which is in entire harmony with the curse pronounced
upon the tempter : " Thou art cursed above all cattle, and
above every beast of the field : upon thy belly shalt thou go,
and dust shalt thou eat all the days of thy life."

A reference to the participation of the serpent in the temptation, or at least to the curse it thereby incurred, is found in
Isaiah lxv. 25, " Dust shall be the serpent's meat :" an expression which, from the contrast instituted between the serpent and the other creatures of the earth, intimates, according
to Vitringa, that the original sentence shall be fully executed,
or perhaps more correctly, that it shall be perpetuated. The
presence and participation of the serpent in the temptation is
confirmed by New Testament authority : thus the Apostle
remarks, " As the serpent beguiled Eve through his subtilty,"
(2 Cor. xi. 3.) It is farther in accordance with, and is no doubt
the foundation of, all the heathen traditions relative to the
serpent ; and also by a strange perversion of the history, the
cause of the religious honours so largely bestowed on this
reptile, which nevertheless mankind hold in dread abhorrence.

That the name was employed merely as a designation of
Satan, there is not a shadow of evidence to show. Throughout
the Hebrew Scriptures he is never known by that name. The
theory has been proposed evidently with the view of obviating
some of the difficulties which are felt to attach to the agency
of a serpent in this transaction. But if it simplifies the matter, it comes at the same time into conflict with the letter of
Scripture ; and is recommended by no argument, but only by
the difficulties, the improbabilities, or the presumed impossi-
bilities, of the contrary supposition.

But while holding that the unmistakable meaning of the
narrative of the Fall necessitates the conclusion that the
tempter was a serpent, it is not to be inferred, as is sometimes
done, from the comparison with the " beast of the field," and
not with the " reptiles," that the serpent was at that time a
quadruped, or was a higher form of life than at present ; for,
in the first place, the distinction, denoted by these terms, is
not always attended to in Hebrew, " beast of the field" generally applying to wild creatures, in opposition to the tame or
domestic cattle ; and, secondly, the comparison extends only

to the attribute of *subtilty*. Neither is the conclusion justified which is usually drawn from the curse pronounced upon the serpent, as if it implied a degradation of the species, an alteration of their form and their mode of locomotion. The curse applied only to this particular serpent, and intimated a continuance of its then abject state.

That the serpent of the temptation was no ordinary serpent, is plainly evinced by the terms of the narrative. There is—
1. The manner in which it is designated, " *the* serpent," or " *that* serpent." As already stated in the exposition of the passage, the article is not always emphatic, and though it is taken so in the present case by the younger Vitringa, Pool, Horsley, and others, and is strongly countenanced by various examples in the Hebrew Scriptures, *e.g.*, Isa. vii. 14, " Behold a virgin," literally " the virgin ;" yet this argument, if unsupported by concurrent testimony, is certainly not conclusive. But such testimony is found in the farther description of this creature, thus :—2. The pre-eminent subtilty ascribed to the serpent, whether taken with some expositors in a good, or with others in a bad sense. It cannot be said of any of the numerous species of serpents, notwithstanding the statements of Bochart and others to the contrary, that they are more subtile than all the other irrational creatures. This is felt by the writers who, like Marck,[1] and more recently Hengstenberg,[2] take the wor as descriptive of the natural serpent, and who accordingly a mit that they apply more strictly to the being who actuated the serpent. Calvin, too, will have it that the subtilty spoken of was a characteristic of the natural serpent, but he would obviate the difficulty just stated, by the assumption that the serpent tribe has greatly deteriorated since the Fall : and so also Holden.[3] Others, with greater reason, limit the description to the real agent in the temptation, and consider that the serpent was said to be subtile only on account of the subtilty of him whose instrument it was. Of the writers who take this view of the matter may be mentioned Augustin[4]

---

[1] Historia Paradisi, lib. iii. cap. v. 7, p. 570.
[2] Christologie, vol. i. p. 7.
[3] Dissertation on the Fall. p. 399.
[4] De Genesi ad Literam, lib. xi. cap. 29. Proinde prudentissimus omnium bestiarum, hoc est astutissimus, ita dictus est serpens propter astutiam Diaboli qui in illo et de illo agebat dolum ; quemadmodum dicitur prudens vel astuta lingua, quam

and Theodoret among the Fathers. 3. The farther mention of the beasts of the field, as created by the Lord God, obviously points to some distinction between the creation of those animals and of this serpent, as if the latter had not received its being along with the creatures of the six days, according to the preceding history.

But on the supposition that the temptation proceeded from some creature of serpentine form, a question for consideration is, whether the speech of the serpent is to be regarded as a subjective or as an objective occurrence ; in other words, whether the language ascribed to the serpent was really uttered by it, and was audible to the external ear of Eve, or whether it existed only for her mental perception, she interpreting the words in the suggestive looks and actions of the reptile. " It is obvious at once," says Hengstenberg, in his observations on a somewhat similar incident—the speaking of Balaam's ass—" that as far as the case is concerned, both views are perfectly the same : the difference is purely *formal*. The distinction only becomes essential if the contrast of the internal and the external is changed into that of the real and the unreal, if the imagination is substituted for the vision."[1]

It may be that on either supposition the reality of the occurrence is maintained, and that the subjective view has the advantage of obviating some of the objections urged against the transaction ; but any merit in this respect is not sufficient to counterbalance the violence it does to the spirit as well as the letter of the narrative. The only real difficulty it removes is that connected with the familiarity and absence of surprise on the part of the woman at the phenomenon of a speaking reptile—a difficulty which most probably arises from the brevity of the narration, which omits the previous and preparatory approaches of the tempter, and records only the results. At all events, it is clear that the historian meant the narrative to be understood literally, for by the ascription of *subtilty* in its highest degree, he intimates a fitness on the part of the serpent for the work in which it engaged, while in the words of

prudens vel astutus movet ad aliquid prudenter astuteque suadendum. Non enim est haec vis seu virtus membri corporalis quod vocatur lingua, sed utique mentis quæ utitur ea.

[1] Balaam and his Prophecies, p. 376. Edin. 1848.

the curse, " Because thou hast done this," &c., there is expressed a purpose or design which involves conditions and
consequences incompatible with the subjective view of the
case.

II. The serpent of the temptation was not simply the reptile
of that name, but an intellectual and moral agent. That it
was so in the historian's apprehension at least, will not admit of
question. It not merely talks, it reasons upon matters relating
to God and man—it discourses of good and evil in a way to
indicate an acquaintance with the laws of nature and providence—argues against the Divine prohibition not to eat of the
tree in the midst of the garden, and conducts the argument
with such craftiness as to secure the victory over the woman.[1]
It is needless to state that no mere animal was capable of anything thus attributed to the serpent : and it is farther evident,
that whatever may have been the conceits of Josephus and the
Rabbinical writers as to the inferior animals being gifted with
speech before the Fall, not one of the Sacred writers for a
moment countenances such extravagant fancies. It is true,
that Moses does not say in so many words that the serpent was
possessed by a being of a higher nature, or that such a being
had assumed the serpent form, yet this is not the less implied.
Why the historian contented himself simply with the external
appearance, and did not more distinctly characterize the being
engaged in this unhallowed enterprise against God and man, it
may be difficult to determine. An opinion as probable as any,
and one which will account for the silence maintained throughout the Pentateuch relative to the existence and agency of
wicked spirits, is, that in an age so addicted to idolatry, intimations on such a subject would serve only to encourage the
propensity. But however this may be, so clear are the two
statements—first, of the presence of the serpent, and, secondly,
of its more than animal nature, that readers of the narrative
looking at the subject from one side only, see merely a serpent, while others from an opposite point of view discern only
an intellectual power.

So far it is plain, from the part enacted by the tempter-
serpent, that he was a rational being ; his moral agency is
farther evinced in the words which convey his penal sentence :

[1] Holden, Dissertation on the Fall, p. 142.

" Because thou hast done this thou art cursed,"—words which, unless addressed to a moral creature, have no meaning, and are utterly unworthy of the righteous Judge. The curse takes its shape from the assumed form of the tempter, but its whole weight falls only on the head of the *guilty*. It is in no sense to be considered as extending to the natural serpent, if such there was, or to the species in general. From confounding what is merely *formal* in the sentence pronounced on the tempter, with that which constitutes its essence, have arisen many of the difficulties of this subject.

If the narrative in Genesis proves that the tempter was a moral agent, it certainly leaves no room to doubt as to his moral character. The conversation with the woman at once stamps him as the arch-enemy of God and man—the liar from the beginning—not merely disposed to question God's goodness, but also prepared to contradict God's word. Any doubt on this subject will be entirely removed by the information furnished in the later Scriptures. There is no means of determining at what period this doctrine was first clearly recognised in the Jewish Church. A reference to it in Isa. lxv. 25, has been already noticed. In the apocryphal writings it is explicitly asserted, that the entrance of death into the world was through *the envy of the devil.* (Wisdom ii. 24.)

The teaching of our Lord and his apostles confirms and illustrates this meaning of the narrative in Genesis. In the Apocalypse, the great tempter is described as " the old serpent, who is called the Devil, and Satan, who deceiveth the whole world ;" " the dragon, that old serpent, which is the Devil, and Satan," (Rev. xii. 9 ; xx. 2.) The *old serpent* is evidently an allusion to the history of the Fall. " It refers," says Hengstenberg, " to the fact, that his appearance on earth was at an early stage of the world's history, and that he had long been employed in the work which is here attributed to him— that of opposing the Church." To the passage already quoted from the writings of Paul, in which there is reference to the serpent that deceived Eve, and which expresses a fear lest the Christians at Corinth should be led away from the simplicity of the Gospel, " through false apostles, deceitful workers, transforming themselves into the apostles of Christ," there is subjoined the remark, " and no marvel, for Satan himself is transformed into an angel of light." (2 Cor. xi. 3, 14.) But of more importance is the declaration of Christ: " Ye are of your father the devil, and the lusts of your father ye will do: he was a murderer from the beginning, (ἀνθρωποκτόνος ἀπ᾽ ἀρχῆς,) and abode not in the truth, because there is no truth in him. When he speaketh a lie, he speaketh of his own; for he is a liar, and the father of it." (John viii. 44.) The devil is here described as a murderer from the beginning. " If we compare this," says Olshausen, " with 1 John iii. 15, where the apostle expresses his profound view as to the nature of the spirit of murder—which he regards as identical with hatred— it cannot be doubted that the term ἀνθρωποκτόνος, (man-mur- derer,) used in respect to the author of evil himself, cannot refer to an isolated fact, an external murder—such as that committed by Cain, [as many commentators suppose]—but to the radical principle which produced this as well as all other murders. It is the seduction of the first man, and the infusion of the spirit of murder into him and his entire race, that is here viewed as the spiritual murder of a vast collection of life. In this sense it may be said literally to have taken place *from the beginning ;* and it forms a fine antithesis to the intended murder of the Redeemer as the second Adam, whose death was the source of life and happiness for all, whilst the death of the first Adam brought destruction on the whole human race." That our Lord's reference was to the first temptation is recog- nised by commentators in general, although some take it to be to the case of Cain—a view which, as Müller remarks, " stands at a disadvantage in comparison with the general interpreta- tion, in that it does not allow of the ἀπ᾽ ἀρχῆς being so strictly taken as the other, but still more by the narrative in Genesis not containing the slightest intimation of a seductive influence upon Cain."[1] " We must not overlook," says Olshausen, " the ἦν in our passage: it implies that the devil constantly main- tains the character which he manifested from the beginning of the history of man. It would add to the significance of the second statement which Christ makes respecting the devil: ἐν τῇ ἀληθείᾳ οὐχ ἔστηκεν, if ἔστηκεν might be translated, ' he continued not in the truth,' because this would presuppose a previous existence in it, and would accordingly indicate the

[1] Doctrine of Sin, vol. ii. p. 431.

fall of the devil from that original state of purity.   But it has
often been remarked, and, so far as the terms are concerned, it
is perfectly indubitable, that ἕστηκα and ἑστήκειν have the
significations ' I stand' and ' I am standing.'   Hence it appears, that here the Saviour describes only the actual state of
the Prince of Darkness."   This state is next described : *first*,
negatively, as one entirely alienated from the truth of God :
the devil's *lie* has become his very nature ; *second*, positively,
as speaking lies of *his own* (stores or resources) in such a
manner as emphatically characterizes him as ψεύστης, *a liar*,
and the father of falsehood.   There can hardly be a doubt but
that the *lie* here spoken of, in so close connexion with the
murder perpetrated at the beginning, is intended by our Lord
as a reference to the mode by which the tempter succeeded in
destroying man : the first murder was effected through the
first lie.

Combining the various intimations and references to this
transaction which occur in the New Testament, it may be said
with Dr. Pye Smith : " The summary of these passages presents almost a history of the Fall,—the tempter, his manifold
arts, his serpentine disguises, his falsehood, his restless activity, his bloodthirsty cruelty, and his early success in that
career of deception and destruction."[1]   Against these plain intimations of Scripture, it is of little purpose to urge considerations derived solely from our own preconceptions of propriety or
probability, for this were to assume the office of judges, and not
of interpreters of Scripture.   Yet this is the character of the
greater part of the objections to this portion of Holy Writ.

Thus, for instance, a recent writer remarks : " I can have
no conception, founded on anything like probability, as to how
the name ' serpent' came to be applied to the tempter, if we
reject the literal method of interpretation ;" and yet he adds,
" that we are to reject the literal method appears to me very
evident if we consider the following :—1. It appears contrary
to our ideas of God to think that he would have allowed the
devil to perform such a miracle (as either to cause a dumb
serpent to speak, or to assume a serpentine form) for such a
wicked purpose as to tempt an innocent couple.   2. It is not
likely that the devil would have assumed, or made use of such

[1] Cyclopædia of Biblical Literature, *Art.* Adam, vol. i. p. 64.

an unsightly shape, when assuming the appearance of an angel of light (if he must assume any appearance at all) might have contributed much more toward insuring success. 3. Hearing a dumb serpent speak would have struck the woman with surprise and terror, rather than prepare her mind to listen to its message. 4. The present construction of the serpent shews that it has no apparatus for walking erect or speaking, and geology shews that the serpents which existed before Adam were of the same construction as at present," &c.[1]

The first of these objections, if of any force, is equally valid against temptation in any form, as reflecting on God's character ; and yet we know that He not merely suffered man to be tempted, but suffered him also to fall. More particularly, if God permits Satan to transform himself, as Scripture testifies, into an angel of light, why not into a serpent, the design in both cases being the same—to deceive and betray ? No less gratuitous is the second objection, whether as to the improbability of Satan assuming the unsightly form of a serpent, or as to the probability that some other appearance would have served his purpose better. We know not but that this form was the most eligible—we know not that Satan was allowed a choice of instruments, and we know that the instrument he did employ, or the form he did assume, fully answered his purpose. The objection as to the absence of surprise or terror on the part of the woman has been already explained, from the fact, that we are not in possession of the whole conversation, and are not informed of the gradual and guarded approaches of the subtle adversary. But farther, the circumstances, internal and external, of the first woman differed so much from everything with which we are familiar, as to admit of no comparison with our feelings or fears. Fourthly, it is nowhere asserted that the serpent at any time walked erect, or possessed the organs or the gift of speech. But admitting that the mouth of the serpent is as incapable of forming articulate sounds as the mouth of the ass, this does not preclude the possibility of either of these dumb creatures having its mouth " opened" by a higher power. We know that a dumb ass, speaking with man's voice, forbade the madness of a prophet, (2 Pet. ii. 16 ;) only it was the Lord who opened the mouth of

[1] Journal of Sacred Literature, April 1854, p. 239.

the ass, in order to save a sinner, (Numb. xxii. 28;) but it was the devil who opened the mouth of the serpent, in order to ruin the innocent. This, however, leads to the much agitated controversy as to the power of evil spirits in working miracles; and on which a few remarks, additional to what has been already stated, (see above, p. 133,) may be offered with a particular view to the present subject.

It is often affirmed, that the admission that evil spirits are empowered to perform miracles, tends to confound the eternal distinction between truth and error, and subvert the argument from miracles as attestations of a Divine commission. "It must not be lightly assumed," says another writer on this subject, "that Satan has power so far to contravene the Divine appointments, as to produce an articulate voice from the mouth of a serpent. Evil spirits may be permitted to work out their own ends in accordance with the laws which the Almighty is pleased to regulate the universe, but caution is required in ascribing to them supernatural power, for the evidence which miracles furnish as *divine* attestations of truth, may, to say the least, be weakened by an unwarranted admission, that diabolical agency is competent to effect so great a deviation from the ordinary course of things, as to cause a serpent to speak."[1] As to this, however, it is safer to receive the testimony of Scripture regarding matters which it represents as facts, than to rely on any hypothesis, however much it may accord with our own preconceptions. Now, it cannot be questioned that Scripture attributes to Satan *miracles* by which he seeks to hinder or oppose the cause of God in the world. They are called "*lying* wonders," (2 Thess. ii. 9,) but this designation is not meant as a denial of their reality; it merely imports that they are wrought in furtherance of the cause of lies. "Antichrist's miracles," says Olshausen on this passage, "are grounded, not like Christ's in truth, but in falsehood, in that they are performed not in God's power, but in Satan's power." The first wonders of this kind, of which particular mention is made, were those wrought by the magicians of Egypt, changing, for instance, water into blood, and rods into serpents. That these were realities, and not mere tricks or juggleries, is borne out by the whole tenor of the narrative; and it shews farther, that

[1] Journal of Sacred Literature, January 1852, p. 352.

the magicians stood in relation to a spiritual kingdom, as truly as did Moses and Aaron.[1]

Our Lord gives assurance, that to such an extent shall the power of falsehood be manifested at the end of the world in " great signs and wonders," as to deceive, if it were possible, the very elect, (Matt. xxiv. 24.) It is also to be remarked, that Christ refers to an " hour and the power of darkness," (Luke xxii. 53)—a period when darkness should be, as it were, in the ascendant. Now, it is seen from the sacred records, that Satan's power is more enlarged, or that he is more active at particular epochs in the history of man and of redemption, and especially at the beginnings of new dispensations. It was thus at the deliverance from Egypt ; it was thus at the appearance of Christ in the flesh : it will be so, we are told, in the last days ; and that it had been so also at the creation, analogy alone would lead us to conclude. And if in the time of Christ evil spirits, in an extraordinary manner, took possession of the bodies of men, and in one case, with the Lord's permission, entered into the brute creation, may there not be seen in this a parallel to the power and the purpose of the tempter at the beginning of the history of mankind ?

To say that God will permit evil spirits to operate only in accordance with His established laws may be strictly true ; but from our ignorance of these laws, and of the nature and capacities of spiritual beings, this will determine little. If it be possible for evil spirits to change rods into serpents, or to take possession of swine, how can it be determined that it was beyond their power to take possession of a serpent, or assume its form ? It is true, that the entrance into the swine took place only after permission was sought and obtained. But the request was granted, though it was designed to counteract Christ's mission in the locality ; as the circumstances resulting from compliance with it proved it eventually did. In regard to the first temptation, too, permission to employ, or take possession of the serpent, is as much implied as in the case of the swine, and was granted in both cases in full view of all the consequences to the deceiver and to the deceived.

[1] Trench, Notes on the Miracles, p. 22.

§ 17. *First Fruits of Transgression—Shame and Fear,*
Gen. iii. 7, 8.

The Divine law has been violated, and in a way that leaves
no room to question the fact: a plain and positive precept has
been infringed; man has eaten of the tree concerning which
God had said, in terms not to be misunderstood, " Thou shalt
not eat of it." It now remains to be seen which is to prove
true, God's threatening, " In the day that thou eatest thereof
thou shalt surely die ;" or the serpent's prediction, " In the
day ye eat thereof, your eyes shall be opened ; and ye shall be
as God," &c.

The consequences of transgression were not slow in manifesting themselves in the guilty pair: verses 7, 8, *And the eyes
of them both were opened, and they knew that they were naked ;
and they fastened fig-leaves together, and made themselves
girdles. And they heard the voice of the Lord God walking in
the garden in the cool of the day : and the man and his wife
hid themselves from the presence of the Lord God amongst the
trees of the garden.*—From the first words of this description,
" the eyes of them both were opened," it might seem that the
serpent's promise was about to be realized. Have the Divine
terrors then turned out to be a mere phantom, is the righteous
government of God disannulled, are his judgments paralyzed,
and is the truth which is wanting in the word of heaven to be
found only in the declarations of hell ? This were surely
infinitely worse than the apostasy, or even the utter and irremediable ruin of the whole race of man ! " And they knew :"
this seems still to confirm the words of the serpent ; but as
the narrative proceeds, the matter is placed in its true aspect,
and the character of " liar and murderer" is stamped upon
the tempter of mankind. The deluded victims had indeed
their eyes opened, but it was to a sense of their wretchedness
and misery. They had been lulled into slumber, and they
dreamed of satisfaction and security, but they awoke to a
consciousness of want,—" they knew that they were naked,"—
without at once perhaps being fully aware of all that such a
discovery intimated. Like Samson, when aroused from his
sleep, and though conscious of the loss of his hair, still ignorant

of the full amount of blessings forfeited when he said, " I will go out, as at other times before, and shake myself :" while the historian adds, " And he wist not that the Lord was departed from him." (Judges xvi. 20.)

If any interval of time elapsed between the transgression of the man and of the woman, the case of the latter must in the meanwhile have been such as is described in Rom. vii. 9, " I was alive without the law once." The commandment was forgotten, its warning voice was unheeded, and it had not, in its character of a broken law, yet begun to condemn the transgressor. But no sooner was the act consummated by both, than, it is very probable, " the commandment came, sin revived, and the sinners died." That the coming of the commandment in its condemning power tarried until the issue of the probation of the man who was properly the responsible party, is seen from the fact, that it was upon his transgression, it is added, " the eyes of them both"—of the woman as well as of the man—" were opened."

And what is the great, the important discovery which they have made, and for which they dared the terrors of the Almighty ? " They knew that they were naked." This they must have known before ; but although previously known, the circumstance did not occasion the feelings of uneasiness of which they are now conscious. Formerly though naked they were not ashamed : and it is to a difference of feeling in this respect, rather than to the fact, that the historian adverts when he says, " they knew that they were naked." They had flattered themselves that by eating of the forbidden fruit they should be like God—that they should become lords, independent and free, but instead of this they have become the servants of sin. They have cast off God's authority, but they straightway find themselves under the dominion of another, in a manner which proves that the mastery of the spirit has ceased before the ascendency of sensuous desires and delights. The previously pure and subordinated desires have become transformed into passions, and the entire person has sunk into the character of *flesh* in the Scripture sense of the term—a state in which, as the apostle Paul teaches, " the motions of sins, which were by the law, did work in the members to bring forth fruit unto death," (Rom. vii. 5.) In the case of the first transgressors these motions were altogether strange, and withal painful and perplexing to a degree which gave rise to feelings of the deepest shame. So overpowering was this and the impulses from which it sprung, that they were glad to have recourse to external aid to supply, however feebly, the check previously furnished internally by the spirit's robe of innocence.

That which presented itself most readily for this purpose was girdles of fig-leaves. "They sewed," (Eng. version,) or better, *bound together*, "leaves of the fig-tree, (עֲלֵה תְאֵנָה, *collect*, as עֵץ הַגָּן, verse 8,) and made to themselves girdles," (חֲגֹרֹה, from חָגַר, to bind about : fully חֲגֹרָה עַל־חֲלָצַיִם, *a girdle upon the loins*, Isa. xxxii. 11.) תָּפַר, (the opposite of קָרַע, Eccles. iii. 7, *to tear*, or *rend asunder*,) means to connect or bind together, whether by sewing, tying, twisting, platting, or any other operation required by the nature of the things to be connected. Some writers suggest that as the leaves of the common fig-tree are not adapted for the purpose specified, the reference must be to the large leaves of the *pisang*, or *paradise fig-tree*. The leaves of this tree are often ten feet long, and of proportional breadth. But as Rosenmüller, and after him Winer, remarks, " there is no reason for supposing that any tree but the common fig-tree was intended, for it is expressly said that the leaves were ' sewed or bound together,' which is not so applicable to large leaves as to those of a moderate size."[1] This, however, is referred to, merely for the purpose of showing on what grounds charges of ignorance or inaccuracy are sometimes preferred against the sacred writers. Thus Knobel, on the present passage, assumes that the common fig-tree cannot have been meant, but only the pisang ; and then concludes that the writer could scarcely be aware of the great size of the leaves of this plant, when he stated that they were sewed together.

Besides the feelings of shame connected with the nakedness of the body, and from which deliverance was sought by the fig-leaf coverings, there were others springing from the same consciousness of nakedness, and manifested as terrors, or fears of the wrath due to sin. " And they heard the voice (the sound of the motion or footsteps) of the Lord God walking in

---

[1] Mineralogy and Botany of the Bible, p. 299. Edin. 1840. Winer, Real-Wörterbuch, vol. i. p. 369.

the garden in the cool of the day." " The voice of the Lord " is in Ps. xxix., by a beautiful poetic figure, applied to the thunder and the crashing storm by which to the dullest ear He proclaims his Majesty and Omnipotence, but it is not in this sense the expression is used here. Every feature of this scene is marked by calmness and repose. The place is paradise, and the time towards evening, " in the cool of the day," לְרוּחַ הַיּוֹם, *towards the breathing* or *blowing of the day*—that is, towards evening, when in eastern countries a cool, refreshing wind arises shortly before sunset, which pleasantly lowers the temperature of the heated air; compare חֹם הַיּוֹם, *the heat of the day*, Gen. xviii. 1, when the oriental seeks sheltered repose. Of the same import is the expression in Cant. ii. 17, יָפוּחַ הַיּוֹם, *the day blows*, that is, becomes cool, and which is farther defined as the time when " the shadows flee away," though Le Clerc takes it to refer to the morning, as he also, with Calvin, understands the passage descriptive of the scene in paradise. Among the older interpreters, Theodotion gives the sense most fully, ἐν τῷ πνεύματι πρὸς κατάψυξιν τῆς ἡμέρας. At this quiet and cooling hour, the Lord, as the owner of the garden, takes His accustomed rounds. The *Hithpael participle* מִתְהַלֵּךְ, (from הָלַךְ, *to go,*) *walking*, does not point to any specific spot, or refer to any particular purpose, but denotes wandering or walking about in a circle, or within certain bounds: it also implies a custom or usual course, as when it is said "Enoch *walked* with God," (Gen. v. 22,) where it is the same term that is used. The garden was thus the place of God's rest and delight—a place frequented by His presence, and where He held converse with the dresser and guardian of the hallowed spot. " The voice of God walking in the garden," is the sound of His footsteps, (see 1 Kings xiv. 6 ; 2 Kings vi. 32,) or the rustling of the leaves and tender branches as He moved among them : and this was no unusual or terrific sound, for at this period God in very deed dwelt with man upon the earth, the state of innocence resembling the blessed future of which it is said, " Behold, the tabernacle of God is with men, and he will dwell with them, and they shall be his people, and God himself shall be with them, and be their God," (Rev. xxi. 3 ;) and yet " the man and his wife hid themselves from the presence (or face) of the Lord God amongst the trees of the garden."

There was not, as on after occasions of the Divine manifestations, a great and strong wind to rend the mountains and break
in pieces the rocks before the Lord ; nor an earthquake nor a
fire, there was only a still small voice (1 Kings xix. 11, 12)
mingled with no louder sound than the sighing of the evening
breeze among the trees of Paradise, nevertheless it was sufficient to startle and put to flight the sinners. When Adam was
afterwards questioned about conduct so unusual as that shown
in hiding from God, whose approach had, on other occasions,
been hailed by him with joy and delight, he answered, " I was
afraid, because I was naked." It was fear prompted him to
such a course,—a fear originating in the same cause as the
shame.

The knowledge purchased by transgression, which at first,
and as regarded sensuous appetites, had resulted in feelings of
shame between the fallen pair themselves, now, at the approach
of God, led to fear and anguish before the Lawgiver and Judge.
The transgressors anticipate the judgment, and tremble in view
of the penalty incurred. They feel not only vile, but guilty,
the nakedness of the body being only an emblem of the state
of their souls now laid bare to the holy eye of God. " The
shame of their nakedness" had appeared, (Rev. iii. 18,) and
with it a consciousness of exposure to Divine wrath ; " they
hid themselves amongst the trees of the garden." This is so
far parallel with their girdles of fig-leaves that both intimated
their need of external aid and appliances to conceal their vile
and miserable condition ; but the hiding among the trees of
the garden farther intimated the conviction, that what sufficed
to cover their shame from one another, was not adequate to
hide it from God. In themselves, and in the end for which
they were had recourse to, the two modes of concealment were
essentially alike, and they illustrate the close connexion already
adverted to between the state of mind which gave rise to shame,
and that which expressed itself in fear of, and departure from
God.

The shame, and the means resorted to in order to keep in
check the motions from which it sprung, intimated, as already
said, that the *flesh* had obtained the ascendency over the *spirit*
or better part, that the mind had become *carnal*—a state which,
as described in the apostolic writings, exactly corresponds with

what may be inferred to have been the condition of our first parents when they fled at the approach of God—"The carnal mind is enmity against God," (Rom. viii. 7.) It is a departure from God, and at the same time a demand addressed to him, "Depart from us, for we desire not the knowledge of thy ways." The transgressors who hid themselves among the trees of Paradise shewed that they had lost all confidence in God as a friend, love to Him as a benefactor, and delight in communion with Him, and that fear and hate assumed the place once occupied by holy, heavenly desires. According to the testimony of the apostle last quoted, this state of mind is to be characterized as "death."—"For to be carnally-minded is death; but to be spiritually-minded is life and peace," (Rom. viii. 6.) So that it may be justly said, thus and then was fulfilled the Divine declaration, "In the day thou eatest thereof thou shalt surely die." It is true the transgressors were not smitten to the ground by any of the swift-winged arrows of the Almighty, as they put forth sacrilegious hands to take of the forbidden fruit, and that no convulsion or catastrophe of nature filled them with blank and unutterable horror. But there are other deaths and disorders than these, and as innocent and happy beings they might be exposed to a far heavier doom than anything which could affect merely the body; and so in and through the very act of transgression they died, for their innocence and their happiness then perished.

This view of the matter serves completely to reconcile a contradiction frequently alleged to exist between the penalty threatened in the event of man's disobedience to the command to abstain from the tree of knowledge, and that actually inflicted after the transgression. The penalty was, "In the day thou eatest thereof thou shalt surely die;" and this sentence, it is said, was superseded or suspended—a procedure at variance with the whole character of God as a Being of unswerving veracity. This, however, rests entirely on a misconception, and the contradiction wholly disappears when the terms of the sentence are rightly understood.

And here must be repudiated, as totally inadmissible, that mode of escape from the difficulty which assumes that *day* is used indefinitely for time in general,[1] or that, as it was the

---

[1] Krabbe, Die Lehre von der Sünde, p. 50. Hamburg, 1836.

Lord who denounced the sentence, and as with Him a thousand years are as one day, if Adam died within that period—and he lived but 930 years—the penalty was to all intents exhausted. Nor is it a correct view of the threatening to take it as merely intimating that, on the day of transgression, man would become mortal, liable to death; and that thus it was virtually fulfilled, although God deferred the execution of it. In support of this, reference is made to the threat held out by Solomon to Shimei: "It shall be that on the day thou goest out, and passest the brook Kidron, thou shalt know for certain that thou shalt surely die," (1 Kings ii. 37;) and yet he did not die immediately on violating the terms of his engagement.[1] But the two cases are not alike. Many circumstances may absolutely prevent, as in the case of Shimei, the immediate execution of a human sentence, but nothing can so delay a Divine threatening. It is not by such distinctions, but by attention to the *death* denounced in the sentence, that the difficulty will disappear.

The expression מוֹת תָּמוּת is literally "*dying, or by dying thou shalt die.*" This construction of the infinitive followed by a finite tense of the same verb is of common occurrence in Hebrew, and denotes assurance or certainty as to the act or event. The specific terms here employed are also frequently met with. Gesenius observes :—" Frequens formula de eo cui certa mors nunciatur."[2] It occurs, Gen. iii. 4 ; xx. 7 ; 1 Sam. xiv. 39, 44 ; xxii. 16 ; 2 Sam. xii. 14 ; xiv. 14; 1 Kings ii. 37, 42, &c., and frequently in Ezekiel, *e.g.* chap. iii. 18, on which Hävernick remarks : " God's old threatening continues to be repeated in the history of His people and of individuals." According to some Hebraists, however, it refers not so much to the *certainty* of the death threatened as to its *severity*— death in the strictest, fullest, most absolute sense of the term. But this is exceedingly doubtful : a comparison of the other occurrences of the formula decidedly favours the rendering of the English version, " Thou shalt surely die." Thus, in particular, Saul's declaration, " Though it be in Jonathan, my son, he shall surely die;" and again, " Saul answered, God do so and more also ; for thou shalt surely die, Jonathan," (1 Sam. xiv. 39, 44.) Here, if anywhere, the expression denotes the cer-

---

[1] Payne, Doctrine of Original Sin, p. 47, 2d edit. Lond. 1854.
[2] Thesaurus, p. 779.

tainty not the severity of the punishment. At the same time, its severity or extreme character is sufficiently indicated in the term *death*, which properly does not admit of degrees. Whatever, then, may be the import of the *death* first denounced against disobedience to the Divine law, so much is indubitable from the form of the threatening, that it was something of a penal character to follow immediately on transgression, and not anything, the actual infliction of which might be delayed for years or centuries. " No language could more forcibly convey the idea of instantaneous sequence between the commission of the crime and the endurance of the penalty, than that employed in the primal threatening."[1] Were it not to subserve a theory, it probably would never have been questioned, that the immediate infliction of the punishment was designed and expressed. But farther, from a consideration of all the circumstances of the case, the two following propositions may be maintained :—*First*, That the threatening did not comprehend annihilation, which would have been the de struction of the individual transgressor ; and *secondly*, That it did not comprise temporal death, which would have been equivalent, in this case, to the destruction of the human race.

On the first of these two points little need be said ; for the idea of annihilation is so absolutely excluded by everything we can learn or conceive of the character of the Creator, of the nature of His government, and its relation to intelligent and responsible agents, as to render that supposition untenable. The annihilation of the sinner, in fact, would involve an acknowledgment that moral government had failed, that the Sovereign of the universe had so far abdicated his functions, and that eternal law and justice had relinquished their claims by removing out of being the subjects of their authority.

But not less clearly can it be shewn, that it was not temporal death that was denounced in the threatening, " In the day thou eatest thereof thou shalt surely die." Some see in this mainly, or *only* temporal death—the disruption of the union of soul and body, and the dissolution of the latter.[2] But irrespective of other objections to which this view is open, the delay in the execution of the sentence must ever prove a

1 Alexander, Connexion of Old and New Testaments, p. 102. Lond. 1853.
2 Venema, Institutes of Theology, p. 436. Edin. 1850.

barrier to its reception by all who cannot be satisfied with the usual explanation, that " mercy granted a long respite." The idea of temporal death, moreover, immediately to follow the act of disobedience, and, for the reasons already stated, it is only as immediate it can be conceived of at all, is excluded by the following considerations :—

1. All the Divine arrangements respecting man, entered into prior to the prohibition to abstain from one tree in the garden, intimate a purpose and a provision in regard not merely to one, or at most two individuals, but to a race of human beings. Such, for instance, is the declaration, " It is not good that the man should be alone," and the announcement, " I will make him an help meet for him," with the realization of the Divine purpose in the creation of the woman, and the institution of marriage ; but above all the original blessing, " Be fruitful, and multiply, and replenish the earth, and subdue it." All these arrangements and ordinances indicated a purpose of permanency or continuance, if they did not furnish a pledge of it.

2. Temporal death is not an essential, but an accident of death in the scriptural sense of the term. From a careful examination of the scriptural usage of the terms *death* and *life*, it appears, that when used without qualification by the context, or the nature of the case, they signify, as well in the Old as in the New Testament, what in theological language is known as *spiritual* death and *spiritual* life, the former of which consists in estrangement from God, and exposure to his righteous displeasure. " By death," says President Edwards, who, from an extensive induction of passages, shews that the word is used in the sense now stated ; " by death was meant the same death which God esteemed to be the most proper punishment of the sin of mankind, and what he speaks of under that name, throughout the Scriptures, as the proper wages of the sin of man, and was always from the beginning understood to be so in the Church of God."[1] If anywhere in Scripture the word is used in its widest and most unrestricted sense, it is manifestly in the present passage, where mention is made of death for the first time ; and this state can, and does consist, with temporal life protracted to its utmost limits, as, on the other hand, temporal death does not fail in a manner to invade

[1] On Original Sin, *Works*, vol ii. p. 391.

spiritual life, and bring into subjection those who live and shall never die.

3. The death threatened, viewed as spiritual death, was a necessary consequence of transgression in the economy under which man was placed. It was the direct and immediate fruit of sin, agreeably to the doctrine of the apostle, "When lust hath conceived, it bringeth forth sin; and sin, when it is finished, bringeth forth death." (James i. 15.) So immediate and direct is this consequence, that it needed not the voice of the eternal Judge to pronounce sentence, and no extrinsic power needed to be put in requisition to carry it into execution. By the very constitution under which man was placed, the sentence of itself took effect; in the very act of disobedience his condemnation was pronounced. It required no arraignment of the transgressors, no direct judicial procedure, to carry home the conviction that they were guilty, and wretched, and miserable—that they had forfeited the Divine favour, which is *life*, (Ps. xxx. 5; lxiii. 3,) and had brought upon themselves, in all its aggravation, the death which had been denounced.

4. The interview between God and the guilty pair, subsequent to the Fall, was in no way connected with the execution of the primal threatening. The penalty therein involved had not only been incurred, but was inflicted and felt; and it needed not to be formally reaffirmed, or recalled to the sinner's remembrance. What interval elapsed between the transgression and the summons to meet with God cannot be determined. Probably it was but of short duration; while assuredly it was an interval of unspeakable anguish and anxiety. It pleased Divine mercy, however, to terminate this agonizing suspense, by the announcement of a purpose of restoration and recovery. In this interview God appears in mercy, and not for judgment— to save and not to destroy—to remove the curse already resting on man, not to bind it on. It is true, intimation is made to the fallen pair of sorrows, sufferings, and labours, as the future concomitants of their earthly lot; and, in particular, it is announced to Adam—though not to the exclusion from a similar fate of his companion in guilt—that he shall return to the dust out of which he was taken. It is this latter circumstance, coupled with a misapprehension of the character of the whole transaction, that has given rise, on the one hand, to the

notion, that the penalty fell far short of the threatening ; and
on the other, that as it was only temporal death that was inflicted, nothing more was included in the threatening. But
besides the general character of the transaction, the place
which the announcement occupies immediately after the intimation of mercy, demonstrates that man's temporal chastise-
ments are to be considered, not so much as portions of the
original penalty, as appliances, no doubt of a punitive, but, in
the altered circumstances, of a necessary and merciful dispensation, designed and adapted to remind man of his lost condition,
and beget in him desires after restoration to the favour and
fellowship of God.[1]

§ 18. *God's dealings with the transgressors : farther fruits of*
sin thereby brought to light, Gen. iii. 9-13.

Judgment has overtaken the guilty : for such is the perfection of God's government, physical and moral, that the violation of His law brings its own punishment, without recourse to
formalities of any kind. So soon as the authority of love and
righteousness is cast off, the dominion of sin begins. So it was
with the first transgressors. The commandment which was
ordained to life, (Rom. vii. 10,) intended as a warning from
transgression, and so a preventative of death, was now found
to be unto death. Sin when finished brought forth death,
and this would have continued to produce its natural and
necessary fruits, but for the merciful interposition of God at
this awful catastrophe in the moral history of our race : and
who by such an interposition has shown himself to be exceeding good in contrast with man, who had proved exceeding
evil, ungrateful, and unjust.

Several circumstances serve to show that it was God's purpose not to suffer man fully and for ever to eat of the bitter
fruit of his own misdoings. We gather this, or at least discern in man's constitution a capacity for deliverance, in the
first place, from the feelings of dissatisfaction and insecurity
awakened in the breast of the fallen pair. Shame and fear,
with the vain attempts to conquer or conceal these feelings,

___
[1] See Dods, Incarnation of the Eternal Word, pp. 552, 553. Lond. 1831.

may be considered as a protest against sin. These feelings, in the circumstances, were indeed no indications of true sorrow or penitence, and so the actings of grace: yet as the workings of nature they evinced that sin was a foreign element, and not co-natural to man. Had these feelings and fears no place, or were they lost or obliterated, a condition would result from which little good could be expected: but this was not the case then. Although by a continued course of sin man may attain to this hopeless and unhappy state of mind, it did not immediately follow the first act of disobedience. A state in which the sinner refuses to be ashamed, is one that betokens a habit of sin and a sad amount of effrontery, (Jer. iii. 3.)

Another circumstance more clearly indicative of God's merciful intentions towards his erring and rebellious children, was the fact of his going after them and seeking them out from the hiding-places whither they had fled, (Luke xv. 3.) Although this, or the other circumstance just adverted to, could not at the time be regarded by the guilty parties themselves as mercies, or merciful visitations, yet afterwards they could not fail to recognise in them tokens of unmitigated good. At the time indeed they would be content, yea, doubtless, exceeding glad, to be left alone in their hiding-place, but to be let alone and left alone would be to be left undone—unpitied, unpardoned, and lost. But in mercy God did not let them alone, or leave them to themselves or to the destroyer.

Verses 9-13. *And the Lord God called to the man, and said to him, Where art thou? And he said, I heard thy voice in the garden, and I was afraid, because I was naked; and I hid myself. And he said, Who told thee that thou wast naked? Hast thou eaten of the tree, whereof I commanded thee that thou shouldest not eat? And the man said, The woman whom thou gavest to be with me, she gave me of the tree and I did eat. And the Lord God said to the woman, What is this that thou hast done? And the woman said, The serpent beguiled me, and I did eat.*—It is usual to consider the proceedings here recorded as the solemn and searching investigations of the Divine Judge into the conduct of the transgressors of His law, previously to His passing upon them the sentence due to their crimes. The preceding remarks will have served in a measure to correct some misapprehensions on this point, and place the

Divine procedure in its true light; the essential object of the present interview being not the announcement of retribution, but a gracious intimation of mercy. But although the first appearance of God to man after the Fall was not for the purpose of judging or condemning, but was in accordance with what is affirmed afterwards of the mission of his Son Jesus Christ : " God sent not his Son into the world to condemn the world, but that the world through him might be saved," (John iii. 17 ;) yet in one point of view it may be considered as including a purpose of condemnation. This condemnation, however, was not a sentence to be pronounced by God upon the sinner, for this, to all intents and purposes, had been done already,—but a sentence to be pronounced by the sinner upon himself as a necessary preliminary to his justification. Considered as designed to bring home to the guilty a conviction of his sins, and thus to prepare him for the precious announcement of the pardon about to be conferred, God's dealings with our fallen progenitors are in entire harmony with His whole character and with His invariable procedure in such cases. But no less, on the other hand, are the attempts of the offenders to avert conviction by futile excuses and palliations of sin, in conformity with the usual practice and experience of men. In this latter aspect the incidents here recorded have been appropriately termed by Schröder, " a biography of conscience."

The first thing that requires notice, is the fact of God calling to the man, and his immediate appearance in compliance with the Divine summons. In the previous interviews and conversations between God and man, there is never any mention of God calling to or after him. Formerly the man was found in his place, or with hasty footsteps and bounding heart he hastened forward to meet his Maker whenever he heard his approach. But now he is absent from the accustomed spot—he is nowhere to be seen : this is explained by the fact that he hid himself amongst the trees of the garden. Verse 9, " And the Lord God called to the man and said to him, Where [art] thou ?" Now, for the first time, the well-known accents fell upon the sinner's ear. It is entirely to mistake the character of the scene and circumstances, to suppose that it was from God's *voice* properly so called that the transgressors fled, or that the Divine voice was waxing louder and louder, until at length in awful majesty it irresistibly summoned them into the presence of the Judge. On the contrary, it was now only, and for the first time, that the Creator asked, " Where art thou?" and this not in an angry, loud, or menacing tone, but as there is every reason to believe, in the soft and gentle accents of former times. But soft and gentle as was the voice, it was enough to compel the presence of the reluctant sinner. " Where art thou?" was a question that needed not to be repeated a second time : and this was a truth which, in the first place, it behoved the sinner to know. His vain attempts at concealment showed how much he needed to be taught the truth which was powerfully felt by the psalmist when he asked, " Whither shall I go from thy spirit? or whither shall I flee from thy presence?" And when he acknowledged, " Yea, the darkness hideth not from thee: but the night shineth as the day : the darkness and the light are both alike to thee," (Ps. cxxxix. 7-12.)

How much Adam needed to be taught this salutary lesson appears farther from his answer to the Lord's first inquiry,— an answer which reveals the painful fact of a complete change not only in the dispositions, but also in the perceptions of fallen man. He acknowledges that his absence from his wonted place and occupation in the garden was intentional : " I hid myself," (אֵחָבֵא, I fled so as to hide :) and with the farther acknowledgment that he hid himself from God. But while admitting the fact, with the usual disingenuousness of sin he attempts a deception as to the motives which prompted him to conduct so strange. Instead of honestly and at once confessing to the true state of things, and to his transgression as the real cause of his altered disposition, he merely mentions the effects, in the vain hope of thereby concealing the cause. That to which he ascribes his flight and attempted concealment from God was *fear*, originating in a perception of *nakedness :* " I was afraid, because I was naked, and I hid myself."

This, however, although meant as an excuse for his conduct, and an attempt to conceal his guilt, was virtually a revelation of it. The fear thus acknowledged was itself sufficient proof that love had fled, for, as an apostle remarks, " There is no fear in love," (1 John iv. 18.) To say that he feared the voice of

God disclosed a state of mind explicable only on one of three suppositions : first, that Adam had never heard God's voice before ; or, secondly, that it was now so changed, so awful, and terrific, so different from anything that he had previously experienced, as to strike him with alarm ; or, finally, that the change was not in God—His manner or motions—but entirely in the man himself. The first supposition is excluded by the ample information supplied, in the preceding narrative, as to the communion and intercourse between God and unfallen man, more intimate, indeed, than His subsequent converse with Moses, of which it is said, " The Lord spake to Moses face to face, as a man speaketh unto his friend," (Ex. xxxiii. 11.) The second supposition is excluded by the whole character of the scene, the calm and composure of which have been already noticed. It remains only to trace to man himself the entire change, and seek in it the cause of his present alarm. This is sufficiently proved by his own admission, " I was afraid because I was naked."

This fear, then, did not originate from any tempest in the world without ; it was not occasioned by any dark clouds or portents in the skies above, or any quaking of the earth under foot : the sun was calmly sinking as usual to his rest, and the soft breath of evening was reviving the drooping flowers of Paradise, at the time when the Almighty and Beneficent Creator visited His subjects, and asked the man formed in His image, "Where art thou ?" And yet the fear was not imaginary ; it was real and well grounded, and the more so that it sprung from something appertaining to the man himself, something personal, from which he could not escape or shake himself free. His case was such that he might be appropriately named "*Magor-Missabib*, fear round about," (Jer. xx. 3.) But although the fear was by Adam himself ascribed to a personal but bodily defect of which he had become conscious, it was nothing other than the feeling of guilt and consequent exposure, helpless and naked, to Divine wrath ; and, in whatever way he might try to hide the matter from God or from himself, conscience would not fail to connect it with the act of disobedience.

God, however, disregarding the evasions, takes the sinner at his word. Verse 11, " And he said, Who told thee that thou wast naked?" But, without waiting for a reply, and as if to remove all ground for further subterfuges, and so at once shut up the sinner to self-conviction and to the acknowledgment of his transgression of a known law, He proceeds to inquire, "Hast thou eaten of the tree whereof I commanded thee that thou shouldest not eat?" This was a question so pointed and precise as to admit only of an answer, yea or nay. The transgressor cannot deny the fact as thus placed before him. He feels that he must plead guilty of a violation of the law, and yet he is reluctant to own it. If he must make confession, he is resolved to postpone it to the last. Recourse is again had to palliations, and the answer to the question which might have been simple and direct, comes out only at the close of all that he can urge in his own defence. Verse 12, "And the man said, The woman whom thou gavest [to be] with me, she gave me of the tree, and I did eat."

This answer discloses another sad effect of sin. Man's love to God had already been displaced by fear and hatred, and now his love to his neighbour also gives way before feelings of self-preservation, or desires of alleviating the apprehended punishment, even though that neighbour is related to him, as he himself recently said, as bone of his bones and flesh of his flesh. Sin remorselessly bursts asunder all bands, even the sweetest, most hallowed, and endearing. "*The woman* gave me:" coldly, unfeelingly spoken! How altered the disposition from that which gave utterance to the memorable saying, "Therefore shall a man leave his father and his mother, and shall cleave to his wife; and they shall be one flesh." The present accusations indicate anything but a purpose to cleave to his wife; they are an unnatural, unmanly abandonment of her in her hour of greatest need.

But more than this; the offender does not even hesitate to make God himself accessory to his fall: "The woman *whom thou gavest* to be with me." Horrid, blasphemous insinuation of one that has not heeded the admonition, "Let no man say, when he is tempted, I am tempted of God; for God cannot be tempted with evil, neither tempteth he any man," (Jam. i. 13.) The most tenderly loved and anxiously longed for of God's gifts (Gen. ii. 18, 20) now becomes an abomination to the sinner, and a weapon in his hand wherewith to assail the character and kind intentions of the Giver, " 'The woman whom thou gavest,'—to her I owe my ruin and all the miseries of this dread hour; and she is thy gift." But enough: nothing shows more clearly the true character of sin than the accusations brought by the sinner against God—impious charges, in which Adam's descendants are found only too faithfully concurring.

Vain, however, are all prevarications and attempts to remove blame from off ourselves to some other—to our external circumstances or to God; for not only will these fail to satisfy the Righteous Judge, they will not satisfy conscience itself in the end. At last, when all evasions have failed, there is no alternative but to plead guilty, " I did eat :" confession is extorted, and he is condemned out of his own mouth.

Conviction being obtained, the blessed God, without noticing the excuses, which served no other purpose than of rendering the man's conduct more criminal and odious, proceeds to interrogate the woman as to her share in this transaction. Verse 13, " And the Lord God said to the woman, What is this that thou hast done ?" or, according to the LXX., Vulgate, Luther, and De Wette, " Why hast thou done this ?" מַה־זֹּאת עָשִׂית, the words being taken as intimating surprise or astonishment rather than as inquiring into the fact, (see Gen. xii. 18 ; xxvi. 10)—" And the woman said, The serpent beguiled me, and I did eat."

The process of conviction, in the case of the woman, is essentially the same as in that of the man ; only with her the matter is more speedily determined. The question also proposed to the woman differed considerably from that put to the man. The latter required a categorical answer, negative or affirmative, as to a fact ; the other admitted and required details or explanatory statements, the inquiry being into the grounds of the woman's procedure. But the same attempts at self-justification are not less apparent here, than in the case already considered. Not instructed by the ill success of Adam's pleas, his companion in guilt imitates his example. "The serpent beguiled me," is all, however, that she can urge in her own defence. It were something to the purpose could she say that the serpent compelled her to this act ; but such was not the case. The serpent beguiled her ; but not until she lent a too credulous ear to his flatteries and his false representations of God, of His character and commands, and of the duties owing to him by his creatures. While charging the serpent as the sole cause of her misconduct, the woman makes no mention of the motives, immediate and personal to herself, which were the true causes of her calamitous fall. She makes no mention of the unhallowed feelings with which she regarded the forbidden fruit, and which, rather than the serpent, urged her to put forth sinful hands. But when all attempts at extenuation have failed, the condemning acknowledgment must be as in the case of Adam, " I did eat." Though conducted, it may be, into their present position by different paths, and urged to transgression by different motives, the result in the two cases is alike, and as they sinned together, so are they together self-convicted and self-condemned.

§ 19. *God's condemnatory Sentence upon the Tempter,* Gen. iii. 14, 15.

The convictions of sin, and the self-condemnation now produced in the first transgressors, are allowed to do their work. Meanwhile, another scene opens of a totally different character from that just contemplated, but intended still further to prepare our fallen progenitors for the mercy which God had designed for them. If the Divine Being had, in the previous transaction, manifested himself as a Father moved with pity towards his erring children, He now shews that this has in no degree influenced His conduct as a Judge; for He appears in order to vindicate His law, His government, and character, grossly assailed in the temptation and the fall. He will shew His hatred of sin, and of all that leads to it.

But the sentence of condemnation will, in this instance, be passed, not on the deceived, but on the deceiver; and with regard to him it will be a sentence of judgment without mercy. Accordingly, there are no preliminary questionings, no examinations, no attempts to extort confession, to produce conviction or self-condemnation, as was remarkably exhibited in God's dealings with the sinners of mankind, but the Judge proceeds at once to pass sentence on the declared enemy of God and man. How or whence the serpent was summoned to the bar of Divine justice, the historian does not state ; but no doubt it

2

was the same irresistible voice which summoned Adam from among the trees of the garden, that now called the deceiver to confront his Judge—" the one Lawgiver, who is able to save and to destroy." (James iv. 12.) The Divine summons, to which no creature can refuse compliance, shews that " the deceived and the deceiver are his (God's)," (Job xii. 16)—alike subject to His authority, and amenable to His law.

But although the transaction now to be considered had a direct bearing only on the serpent as the cause of man's apostasy, yet it was not without important reference to man himself, and that over and above what related to his past connexion with the deceiver. It was solely on man's account that the sentence of condemnation was formally pronounced, and afterwards placed upon record ; for its purpose in this respect was to carry on and complete the work already begun in the human soul.

Verses 14, 15. *And the Lord God said to the serpent, Because thou hast done this, thou art cursed above all cattle, and above every beast of the field : upon thy belly shalt thou go, and dust shalt thou eat all the days of thy life. And I will put enmity between thee and the woman, and between thy seed and her seed : it shall bruise thy head, and thou shalt bruise his heel.* —Although no questions had been put to the serpent to elicit the reasons of his conduct, or afford room for explanations, or a denial of the facts charged against him, as in his case, and from his known character, altogether unnecessary, yet the righteous Judge, for the vindication of His own procedure, and in order to serve as a warning to others, but especially as an encouragement to fallen man, is careful to state the grounds of the condemnation : " Because thou hast done this;" that is, beguiled the woman, (for so he was charged, verse 13.) The deception thus practised included all the serpent's misrepresentations of God's character and law, all his lies and blasphemies, and every other malignant word and act which contributed to the murderous result which he effected. By this declaration, God will shew not merely His abhorrence of such conduct, but also how exceedingly dear to Him is the safety of His creatures who were thus betrayed into sin.

The sentence, in its nature and actings, is next announced. It is a *curse.* אָרוּר אַתָּה מִכָּל־הַבְּהֵמָה וּמִכֹּל חַיַּת הַשָּׂדֶה, " *accursed* art thou," &c. In no case is God's curse an empty or idle threat; but in the present instance it was designed to be pre-eminently severe. The comparison, " above all cattle," with its parallel clause, has been variously rendered : " *before*, or *above* all cattle," (Luther, Fagius, Eng. version, Rosenmüller, Delitzsch ;) *by* all cattle, (Dathe, Gesenius, Maurer, De Wette, Baumgarten ;) *from*, that is, separate and apart from all cattle, (Le Clerc, Von Bohlen, Tuch, Knobel.) The last appears to be the only admissible rendering ; the second is altogether ungrammatical ; and the first assumes that a curse had also been laid on the other creatures here enumerated. The particle מִן is thus taken, not in its strictly *comparative* sense, but as a disjunctive denoting selection and separation. Thus, (Deut. xiv. 2,) " The Lord hath chosen thee to be a peculiar people unto himself *above* all the nations (מִכֹּל הָעַמִּים, selected *from* all the nations) upon the earth." (Compare also Judges v. 24.) The curse upon the serpent was something marked, something to distinguish the deceiver of mankind from every other creature, and point him out as hateful to God, abhorred by men, and miserable in himself.

The serpent's curse consisted of three distinct parts or forms of punishment. He is condemned to go on his belly ; to eat dust; and to be regarded as an object of everlasting hate and hostility by the human race. The ideas couched under this figurative language are two, as shall be presently shewn : *first*, the perpetual degradation of the serpent, and *secondly*, his final overthrow ; understanding by the serpent the responsible agent who assumed that form, or actuated that animal as the fittest or readiest instrument wherewith to effect his diabolical purposes. As already stated, the terms of the curse are not to be considered as applying to the natural serpent at all, although it is from it that the language of the curse takes its form. All suppositions, then, of a change in the physical constitution of that reptile, from the period of the Fall, are to be rejected, seeing that, while forbidden by the natural history of the creature, they are not required or warranted by any statement of Scripture.

1. The perpetual and complete degradation of the tempter. The completeness of the degradation is forcibly expressed by being condemned to the humblest form of locomotion, and the

meanest kind of food : " Upon thy belly shalt thou go, and dust shalt thou eat." With the former of these expressions may be compared Ps. xliv. 25, " For our soul is bowed down to the dust ; our belly cleaveth unto the earth,"—a condition indicative, as explained by the context, of the sorest misery and oppression. Than the serpent trailing along upon the ground, no emblem can more aptly illustrate the character and condition of the apostate spirit who once occupied a place among the angels of God, but has been cast down to the earth, preparatory to his deeper plunge into the fiery lake. (Rev. xx. 10.) The other denunciation of eating dust expresses the same idea of degradation as the preceding ; but more in the way of misery, as of want and dissatisfaction. " Eating the dust," says Bush, " is but another term for grovelling in the dust; and this is equivalent to being reduced to a condition of meanness, shame, and contempt. Thus the prophet Micah, speaking of the nations being confounded, says, ' They shall lick the dust like a serpent,' (Mic. vii. 17 ;) that is, they shall be totally overthrown, and made vile, debased, and contemptible." But the expression " eating dust," denotes rather a state where one is reduced to the necessity of partaking of unsavoury, unsatisfactory food, and is thus equivalent to the saying, " filling his belly with the east wind," (Job xv. 2.) Applied to the tempter it denotes the highest intensity of a moral condition, of which the feelings of the prodigal may be considered a type : " When he would fain have filled his belly with the husks that the swine did eat," (Luke xv. 16 ;) but a faint type only, inasmuch as even the husks of the swine cannot, as an article of food, be compared to dust.

But this miserable degradation is not only complete, it is to be perpetuated—" all the days of thy life." There shall be no recovery from this fall, and no satisfaction in it. It is evidently to this that the prophet Isaiah refers when foretelling a glorious future of the earth and its inhabitants, he adds, " and dust shall be the serpent's meat," (Is. lxv. 25 ;) thus intimating that the blessings in which creation is to participate, shall not extend to the serpent of the fall, the deceiver and murderer of man : his curse is permanent and his condition is irremediable.

2. But a still heavier doom also impends over the tempter-

serpent, even complete ruin, and to make it more bitter, this is to be effected through the very party whose destruction he flattered himself to have secured. It is intimated to the tempter that God himself will avenge the wrongs done His people, verse 15, " I will put enmity between thee and the woman :" and thus the willing subjection of his victims shall cease. Farther, this enmity shall be perpetuated : it shall prove a standing quarrel, and shall involve other parties in the strife—the seed of the woman and the seed of the serpent. And, finally, though the contest be prolonged, and be attended with partial suffering to the conqueror—the seed of the woman —yet the victory over the serpent shall be complete. The seed of the woman " shall bruise thy head, and thou shalt bruise his heel." Reserving the full discussion of these particulars to the following Excursus, it remains to notice here how this announcement was fitted to affect not only the tempter, whose expectations, founded on his recent victory, were doomed to utter disappointment, but also his deluded victims, on whose doubts and darkness a ray of hope now shone.

That our first parents were present on the occasion of the serpent's judgment and condemnation, and that his sentence was pronounced in their hearing, is evident from the fact that this, and what immediately follows, where they themselves are addressed, form parts of one scene : Jehovah-Elohim, who is introduced at the commencement of the transaction, is not again mentic. 3d in the address to the woman and the man, the narrative being continued and connected simply by the expressions, " and he said," verses 16, 17. While then judgment was proceeding, every word that fell from the mouth of the Judge was fitted to strike like a thunderbolt all parties present as accomplices in the same reprehensible act. For though the words were not directed to our first parents themselves, yet they must have reacted on them : for no doubt they now felt themselves to be in the same condemnation. Their convictions of sin would thus be deepened, and their fears and anxieties awfully augmented, as they stood in trembling expectation of their own doom being next pronounced. It was only when the Judge proceeded, " I will put enmity between thee and the woman," that some faint gleam would dawn upon them, causing some indefinite expectation that the bonds into

which they had been drawn, and by which they were now
united to the serpent, might be broken, and that they should
escape as a bird out of the snare of the fowler, although of the
manner in which they were to be disposed of by their Sovereign
Judge, they could as yet form no conception. Their hopes
would, however, become more definite and distinct when they
heard that it was the woman's seed that was destined to effect
this deliverance for them, by completely vanquishing the
enemy to whom they owed their fall. But it was only so far
as they laid to their own hearts the words of the curse, or
recognised in it their own condemnation, that they were fitted
or entitled to appropriate the comforts flowing from the latter
part of the announcement. This was certainly the great aim
of the Judge, so far as the transaction regarded man. This,
while accounting for the mode in which God's merciful intentions regarding the human transgressors of His law were conveyed to them, and for the place which the blessing occupies
in relation to the curse, shows also that in this first publication
of the gospel, the same great principles were established, and
the same procedure followed as in the fuller revelations of the
New Testament. The whole transaction shows that the God
of the Old Testament, or the God of Adam and Eve in and
out of Paradise, is the God of the New Testament, the God
and Father of our Lord Jesus Christ ; and that neither His
character, nor His government, nor His law, has undergone any
change ; and that from the beginning as now, He was " just
while justifying the ungodly."

EXCURSUS VIII.—THE FIRST PROMISE—THE WOMAN'S SEED.

In the sense in which the promise or prophecy of the
woman's seed is usually understood among Christians, it forms.
the first, not merely in the order of time, but fundamentally,
of " the exceeding great and precious promises" of revelation.
It is the *protevangel*, the first intimation of mercy on the
part of the holy and righteous God to a sinful creature. The
declaration made immediately after the Fall, at the first interview between God and His rebellious subjects, as well the
deceiver as the deceived, held out to man an assurance of the

perpetual degradation and final destruction of the adversary, by whose craftiness he had suffered himself to be drawn from his allegiance to God. It is thus, as President Edwards remarks, " the first dawning of the light of the gospel on earth."

Regarded in this light, the announcement is eminently worthy of God, of the great occasion on which it was made, and of the solemn, judicial formalities with which it was attended ; in all of which, as throughout the dispensation then and thus introduced, the Righteous Judge shows himself " a just God and yet a Saviour." Laying aside, however, for the present, all considerations arising merely from the importance attached to the subject of inquiry, as tending only to bias the judgment, and dismissing also, as far as possible, the theories and preconceptions which have largely contributed to mystify a subject in itself exceedingly simple when read in the light of the New Testament, it is proposed in the *first* place to educe the simple ideas couched under the figurative phraseology of the announcement ; and, *secondly*, to bring to bear on it the light which subsequent revelations may be presumed to furnish, if the doctrine be the vital principle it is supposed.

I. The first thing that demands consideration is the *form* of the declaration : And in this, again, the first thing that strikes the reader is, that it was directed to the serpent—to the author of man's ruin, and not to man himself. " I will put enmity between thee and the woman," is the determination of the Eternal Judge before whom the tempter-serpent was arraigned for the part he acted in the apostasy of man. Again, it is to be remarked that this announcement takes the form of a judgment. It is expressly a curse without any mitigation or alleviating circumstance : it is a part, and a most important part, of the irrevocable sentence passed upon the seducer. The former part of the sentence intimated and sealed his lasting degradation, this announces his complete and final overthrow. The seed of the woman " shall bruise thy head,"— the head, it is well known, being the most vulnerable part of the serpent.

These considerations sufficiently account for the peculiar phraseology employed, and at the same time evince its admirable fitness for making the desired impression on all associated in the sin. And here it may be remarked that it is an idle and uncalled-for attempt, to settle how far the curse applied to the natural serpent, and how far to the direct agent in the temptation, when it is not certain, from anything expressed or implied, that it at all bore on the former—although it is on the form of the serpent the terms of the curse were moulded. The concurrence of a natural serpent in the temptation, or its participation in the curse, unless absolutely demanded by the narrative, which is by no means the case, for it speaks only of *the serpent*, only perplexes the subject by originating futile objections, which, in turn, draw forth very unsatisfactory answers.

But, although the announcement regarding the seed of the woman was formally addressed to the serpent, and so directly a curse, nevertheless it was an exceedingly precious promise to the deceived and fallen pair. The degradation and final overthrow of the enemy who, now that his wiles had succeeded, no doubt haughtily triumphed over his deluded victims, must afford comfort and consolation to them. Two important considerations contributed to this. *First,* The serpent was thus doomed as the cause of man's transgression—" Because thou hast done this, thou art cursed ;" *secondly,* God himself appeared as the avenger of their wrongs : " *I will put* enmity between thee and the woman ;" as if it had been said, " Vengeance is mine ; I will repay, saith the Lord," (Rom. xii. 19.) No doubt it was with the design of imparting encouragement to our fallen progenitors, and of awakening faith, hope, and penitence in their souls, that this merciful intimation preceded the sentence passed upon themselves ; while its character of free and sovereign grace must have been gloriously displayed by the consideration that it was made when unhoped-for and unasked.

But the particulars contained in this merciful and righteous announcement require to be more fully stated and illustrated.

1. It is intimated to the serpent, and indirectly to his victims, that their willing subjection to him shall cease ; enmity, henceforth, shall take the place of confidence. That this refers to the very criminal confidence but recently reposed in the serpent's representations is evident from the mention of the woman in the controversy about to ensue, and which also explains why she is thus introduced rather than the man.—"Adam

was not deceived, but the woman, being deceived, was in the transgression," (1 Tim. ii. 14.)

2. This implacable enmity shall prove a standing quarrel. It shall involve other parties in the strife—the seed of the woman and the seed of the serpent. This is an important addition to the list of the combatants. It is no longer with the woman, weak and yielding as she proved before his falsehood and flattery, that the serpent has to do, but with her seed, her representative, and, as it shall prove, her avenger.

To determine the sense of the terms, "the seed of the woman," and "the seed of the serpent," belongs properly to the second division of the subject. But one consideration connected with the mention of the woman's seed falls to be noticed in this place, as it afforded an additional intimation of mercy : this is the fact that the blessing of the creation, "Be fruitful, and multiply, and replenish the earth, and subdue it," was not forfeited or suspended ; which was farther confirmed by the sentence passed on the woman herself, "in sorrow shalt thou bring forth *children.*" Though it proves to the woman the occasion of intense suffering, which she must consider as the chastisement of her sin, yet she shall bear children, and give birth to a seed which shall maintain her quarrel with the serpent. Possibly it is to this that the apostle Paul refers, 1 Tim. ii. 15, a passage of great obscurity, and on the import of which commentators are much divided. With its preceding context it is, " Adam was not deceived, but the woman, being deceived, was in the transgression. *Notwithstanding she shall be saved in child-bearing* (διὰ τῆς τεκνογονίας, by or through the bearing of children) if they continue in faith," &c.

3. Though the contest be prolonged, victory is sure. In due time the serpent shall be worsted and destroyed, although the victory shall entail some suffering to the conqueror. הוּא יְשׁוּפְךָ רֹאשׁ וְאַתָּה תְּשׁוּפֶנּוּ עָקֵב—" He, or it, (the woman's seed,) shall bruise thy head, and thou shalt bruise his heel." The verb here rendered *bruise* occurs only in two other passages, (Job ix. 17 and Ps. cxxxix. 11,) and Hebraists are much divided as to its precise signification. Some, as J. D. Michaelis, Dathe, and Rosenmüller, compare it with an Arabic root of the same form, meaning *to see,* and accordingly take it in the sense of *watching* or *laying wait* with a hostile intention, *observare, insidiari.* Others,

as Umbreit [1] and Knobel, consider שׁוּף cognate with שָׁאַף, *to snap,
to snort at,* and hence to attack in a hostile manner. But the
great majority of interpreters, comparing it with a Chaldee
verb of the same form, give it the sense of *crushing* or *bruising.*
Of the earlier writers who held this view, may be mentioned
Luther, Grotius, and Le Clerc ; and, of the more recent, Tuch,
Baumgarten, Hengstenberg, and Delitzsch. On the passage in
the Psalms where this verb occurs, Hengstenberg remarks :—
" It signifies, in the two other passages where it is found, unquestionably *to bruise;* and this signification, which the LXX.
(καταπατήσει) and the Vulgate (conculcabit) retain also here,
will be found quite suitable, when we do not miss the proper
interpretation of the two preceding verses, and are not led
generally to suppose that the Psalmist had in view only a one-
sided application of the Divine omnipresence."

But whatever may be the primary signification of the term,
it no doubt imported something very destructive or deadly to
the serpent. The part of the serpent against which the action
shall be directed is the head, which is not merely the most
assailable, but is also known to be the most vulnerable, and
where, if properly directed, the blow insures death.[2] The full
import of the denunciation could not fail, at least as to its
consequences, to be understood by all parties, whatever uncertainty might attach at the time to the character of the defeat
or the agent by whom it should be achieved. " He shall bruise
thy head," would leave no room for doubt as to the issue of the
conflict then announced and begun.

But although the overthrow of the enemy is thus made sure
by the declared purpose of God, yet it shall not be effected
without injury to the person of the conqueror. In the struggle,
and possibly in the very act of trampling on its envenomed
head, the serpent shall succeed in bruising the victor's heel.
But the injury thus received, though it may be painful, is yet
of a trivial character, not affecting any vital organ, and so easily
admits of cure. For a time it may retard the triumphant
march of the conqueror, but it cannot prevent him from lifting
up his head, (Ps. cx. 7.)

[1] New Version of the Book of Job, vol. i. p. 184. Edin. 1836.
[2] Rosenmüller. " Ab iis qui serpentem occidere volunt, caput potissimum peti-
tur."—Scholia, vol. i. p. 117. Lips. 1821.

4. The conqueror of the serpent is the woman's seed. It must be mortifying to the serpent to be foiled and defeated in any way, but infinitely more so when this shall be effected by the party, or the representative of the party, over whom he but lately triumphed, and whom he confidently believed to be henceforth altogether his own.

So also, on the other hand, must the consolation be proportionally augmented which this intimation afforded to the parties who, at the serpent's instance, had been drawn into sin, and made to experience its bitter consequences. They had been trodden down in the very dust: but it is satisfactory to be told that the ensnaring tyrant shall be taken in his own wiles, that he himself shall bite the dust: it is more so to be told that at length he shall be deprived of all power of causing injury or annoyance; and much more comforting to be assured that all this shall be accomplished not by a stranger, but by a kinsman, by one to whom they shall stand related by the closest ties of blood—personal and parental—by one who is to be in some way pre-eminently distinguished as the seed of the woman.

One other observation may be introduced here. It is the statement of the fact, without, however, at present offering any explanation of it, that although the enmity is between the serpent and the woman, and their seed respectively, yet the final contest is between the woman's seed and the serpent only, the serpent's seed having, during the struggle, disappeared from view.

The result of the preceding remarks may be summed up in a few words. From the cloud of wrath which burst over the earth in the condemnatory sentence passed upon the father of lies, who contrived and compassed the ruin of man, there was reflected a ray of hope to the latter: not the less cheering that it emerged from that awful gloom, and not the less illustrative of the character of God. It was not the less a blessing that it was carried in the bosom of a curse, and not the less a deliverance that it proclaimed a dreadful destruction. The destruction takes its colour from the form and character of the being more immediately addressed, yet it is clear that the benefits to be recovered must correspond to those forfeited and lost, and thus be of a moral and spiritual nature. Accordingly, a preliminary requisite on the part of man is *enmity* to evil and the power of evil. This disposition, too, is mercifully induced by God, and preparation is made for continuing the strife until it terminate in the destruction of the adversary, by one in the form and with the nature of man.

So far in general both as to the form of this announcement or promise of the woman's seed, and as to what may be gathered from the terms in which it is conveyed, apart from other considerations. These, however, must now be brought to bear upon the subject in order to elucidate its specific import.

II. The import of the promise made to our first parents regarding the seed of the woman. Some particulars introduced into this Divine announcement are explicable, in a measure, from the narrative of the temptation alone, but there are others which can be correctly determined only by the fuller revelations which follow, especially the light of the New Testament. Of such is the precise determination of the terms, " seed of the serpent," and " seed of the woman," where it is a question whether the latter is to be understood of an individual, or of the race collectively.

It will be of importance to determine, in the first place, in what sense the promise was received by our first parents themselves, and happily there are incidents in their history which supply the desired information.

1. Their views of the promise, and their faith in the deliverer there announced, appear in the circumstance that Adam called his wife's name Eve, that is, *life*, because, as it is explained, " *she was the mother of all living.*" The name is remarkable in itself, but more especially from the occasion on which it was given. It was immediately after a sentence of *death* had been pronounced upon them both, that Adam conferred on his wife this new name. Had it been given at the creation, it might be understood as only implying that the first woman was to be the mother of mankind. But the name given at that time to the human female was *Isha*, or woman. A new name, in Scripture, implies a new relation ; and were such to be given to the woman after the Fall, and after the sentence of condemnation had been passed, it might be presumed to be, if implying any maternal relation at all, the " mother of all dead, or of a dying race." But it is the direct

opposite, " the mother of all living." The name thus evidently refers to something other than the melancholy state into which sin had plunged them : and what can that be but the antecedent promise of a deliverance to be wrought out by the woman's seed, and of a recovery of the *life* forfeited through disobedience ? " I think it exceedingly natural to suppose," remarks President Edwards, " that as Adam had given her her *first* name from the manner of her *creation*, so he gave her her new name from *redemption*, and as it were *new* creation, through the redeemer of her seed ; and that he should give her this name from that which comforted him, with respect to the curse which God had pronounced on him and the earth, as Lamech named Noah, Gen. v. 29, ' Saying, This same shall comfort us concerning our work and toil of our hands, because of the ground which the Lord hath cursed.' Accordingly he gave her this new name, not at her first creation, but immediately after the promise of a Redeemer of her seed."[1] The blessing of the creation now appeared to Adam in an entirely new light. In the first promise he saw *life* in death, and the woman made the medium of life to her posterity.

2. Another indication of the views held by our first parents on this promise, occurs in an incident connected with the birth of their first-born. The mother exclaims—קָנִיתִי אִישׁ אֶת־יְהֹוָה, " I have obtained a man, Jehovah," (Gen. iv. 1.) Whatever difficulties may attach to the truth thus conveyed, this is the literal, grammatical rendering of the words,[2] and not *from*, or *with*, or *by the help of Jehovah :* and they have been so rendered by many of the most eminent Hebraists of earlier and recent times. Any other interpretation is resorted to, only because of the foregone conclusion, that such precise conceptions of the person of the promised deliverer as these words imply were unaccountable in Eve's circumstances, and incompatible with the egregious mistake manifested in her application of the promise to Cain.[3] But how does the matter actually

---

[1] On Original Sin, part ii. chap. i. § 3.

[2] " There seems no option to an interpreter, who is resolved to follow faithfully the fair and strict grammatical signification of the words before him, but to translate the passage as it is given above."—Pye Smith, *Script. Testimony*, vol. i. p. 154.

[3] Tiele, Das erste Buch Mose's, p. 119. Erlang. 1836. Hofmann, Weissagung u. Erfüllung, vol. i. p. 77.

stand? The gracious promise made to our first parents informed them that the deliverer was to be a man. But the character of the enemy with whom he had to contend, with the decisive result of the contest, apart from farther intimations on the subject, must have convinced them of the need of more than human power ; and that to fulfil the expectations, the coming deliverer must be in a position different from their own. The faith reposed in the promise had been already exhibited in the name *Eve*: while doubtless their views were farther extended by the sacrificial rites which, there is every reason to believe, were by Divine appointment instituted immediately after the Fall. But supposing that there was no way of accounting for the correct and enlarged apprehension of the person of the Redeemer manifested by the first mother, that surely would be no sufficient reason for questioning its reality, or for explaining it away by forced interpretations of the language.

But while thus maintaining that, from a consideration of the circumstances of the case, and of the language employed, the conclusion is irresistible, that Eve recognised in her first-born the promised Redeemer, and in the Redeemer Jehovah, it would be too much to conclude that she was aware of the full import of this designation. It is to be observed that this is the first recorded instance of the use of the name Jehovah, which it is the object of the whole subsequent revelation fully to illustrate and define.

That Eve was mistaken in her application of the promise, does not in the least militate against her faith in it, or against her acquaintance with the person and the purpose therein revealed. The mistake was very natural in her circumstances, and indeed inevitable without express revelation to the contrary ; yet, error as it was, it showed the lively hope with which the first mother regarded the sure word of promise, and her ardent longing for the advent of the deliverer. But this mistake, which after events did so much to correct and embitter, though it checked the anticipations of a proximate deliverer, and so may have been the occasion of the name Jehovah being for a time almost lost sight of or forgotten, yet served to illustrate and realize some of the great truths of the Divine declaration. The disposition and murderous conduct of

Cain towards his brother, proved that the serpent had *seed* among men. Cain plainly proclaimed himself to be " of that wicked one," (1 John iii. 12,) a truth which must have been painfully impressed on the sorrowful parents. The contrast exhibited in the first two brothers, with the results that followed, fearfully illustrated and confirmed the words, " I will put enmity between thee and the woman, and *between thy seed and her seed.*" The effect of this discovery on the mind of the mother is exhibited in her remark on the birth of her next son, Gen. iv. 25, " She called his named Seth, for God hath appointed me *another seed* instead of Abel whom Cain slew." She had been taught to regard Abel as *her seed;* and now that he was slain, the Lord, true to His promise of maintaining the controversy with the serpent, has given her *another seed.*

It thus plainly appears, to quote the words of Dr. Pye Smith, " that Adam and Eve looked for the deliverer from sin and evil with deep anxiety and sanguine hope, that they believed that he would be a child of man, and that they had an obscure but yet strong impression, that, in some unknown and mysterious sense, he would be described as ' the man Jehovah.'"[1]

The sense in which this prophecy was understood in subsequent times is next to be considered.

Although there is no direct reference in the Old Testament to its specific form, yet the promise itself is never lost sight of, but is presented in such terms as suited the exigencies of the times, and served to gladden the hearts and sustain the faith of the people of God, and with such additional circumstances of family, time, and place, as would remove all uncertainty when it was fulfilled. It is unnecessary to notice these prophecies farther than to state that all, more or less distinctly, refer to a *twofold* nature in the person of the Redeemer, and that one particularly announces him as the offspring of a *virgin-mother,* and so pre-eminently the *seed of the woman.*

But even in the New Testament there is no direct reference to this promise, although there occur abundant intimations conclusive as to its meaning and its application directly to *that seed* of the woman to whom " gave all the prophets witness, that through his name whosoever believeth in him

[1] Scripture Testimony, vol. i. p. 157.

shall receive remission of sins," (Acts x. 45.) That Jesus Christ our Lord, who was made of the seed of David according to the flesh, and declared to be the Son of God with power, (Rom. i. 3, 4,) was the seed of the woman primarily referred to, is distinctly taught on apostolic authority. In illustration of this, notice may be taken of the explicatory remark of the apostle, (Gal. iii. 16,) on a similar promise made to Abraham of a *seed* in whom all the families of the earth should be blessed, (Gen. xxii. 18,) " Now to Abraham and his seed were the promises made. He saith not, And to seeds, as of many : but as of one, *And to thy seed, which is Christ.*" Whatever difficulties critics may detect in the apostle's mode of argumentation, he distinctly teaches that in the promise made to Abraham the reference was not to his descendants generally, nor yet to those in the line of Isaac, nor to his spiritual descendants, but to his illustrious descendant, Christ.[1]

Another observation of the same apostle is also worthy of notice, and may be considered a more direct testimony than the preceding : Gal. iv. 4, " When the fulness of the time was come, God sent forth his Son, *made of a woman.*" No doubt the apostle's primary object was to set forth the doctrine of the incarnation, by contrasting Christ's earthly humility with the majesty denoted by the name, " the Son of God," yet the expressions employed, " the fulness of time," and " made of a woman," were evidently designed to intimate that the first promise of the woman's seed, though dating back many ages past, was at length fulfilled.

The bearing of the first promise is put in a striking light by another apostle, who states that the great end of Christ's appearance in the flesh was to destroy the works of the devil, (1 John iii. 8.) This is the more striking that the reference cannot be considered direct, although the context leaves no room to doubt that the circumstances connected with the temptation and the fall were vividly present to the apostle's mind when he wrote,—" He that committeth sin is of the devil ; for the devil sinneth from the beginning. For this purpose the Son of God was manifested, that he might destroy the works of the devil." The same apostle, in the Apocalypse, besides passing allusions to the old serpent—his present hos-

---

[1] Brown, Exposition of Galatians, p. 144. Edin. 1853.

tility to all that is good and godlike—and his future overthrow, fills one chapter (xii.) with a detailed description of his enmity and rage at the prospect of the advent of one who shall terminate his dominion, all the symbols and imagery being borrowed from the narrative of the Fall. A few particulars only can be noticed, verses 1, 2, " There appeared a great wonder in heaven; a woman clothed with the sun. . . . . She being with child, cried travailing in birth, and pained to be delivered." The effects of the sentence, " In sorrow thou shalt bring forth children." Verse 3, " There appeared another wonder in heaven, and behold a great red dragon, having seven heads and ten horns, and seven crowns upon his heads." He is no longer merely the *subtile* serpent, but a *crowned* dragon, having obtained power over man by the Fall. Verses 4, 5, ... " The dragon stood before the woman ready to be delivered, to devour her child as soon as it was born. And she brought forth a man-child, who was to rule all nations with a rod of iron ; and her child was caught up to God, and to his throne." Notwithstanding the pains of parturition a living child sees the light, and notwithstanding the hostile attitude of the dragon the child is secure—caught up to God's throne, intimating a majesty equal to the divine. Verses 7-9, War in heaven—the old serpent and his adherents defeated and cast out : " they prevailed not." Verse 11, The servants of God overcome the dragon by the blood of the Lamb. Verse 12, The dragon has but a short time. Verse 13, Meanwhile he persecutes " the woman who brought forth the man." Verse 14, The woman is hid from his rage and is helped. Verse 17, " The dragon was *wroth* with the woman, and went to make war with the *remnant of her seed*, which keep the commandments of God, and have the testimony of Jesus Christ." Thus besides the man-child, the woman has other seed against whom the dragon is enraged : this is in complete harmony with all the revelations of God and with the history of the Church from the beginning.

While, then, in the first promise the primary reference is to Christ, who was manifested to destroy the works of the devil, it is not exclusively to him, but embraces " the remnant of the woman's seed," constituting the body of which Christ is the head—a body against which the serpent wages incessant war,

2 F

but who have the encouraging assurance of realizing in their own experience the triumph promised to the seed of the woman: "The God of peace shall bruise Satan under your feet shortly," (Rom. xvi. 20.)

By parity of reasoning, the designation "the seed of the serpent" obviously applies to all who are the willing subjects of that malignant Power, and who are associated with him in his work and warfare by similar dispositions, as hatred to truth and holiness. It thus includes that large class, "the children of disobedience," (Eph. ii. 2,) in whom the evil spirit works and exercises supreme authority; and who are called by the Baptist and by our Lord "serpents" and a "generation (progeny) of vipers," (Matt. iii. 7; xxiii. 33.) This relation, with the grounds on which it rests, is plainly declared in Christ's denunciations of the Jews—"Ye are of your father the devil, and the lusts of your father ye will do," (John viii. 44.) But "the seed of the serpent" probably includes also the evil spirits who fell with Satan—his "angels," and who co-operate with him and with wicked men in resisting Christ and His cause in the world.

It was remarked that the serpent's seed disappear before the final contest, which lies between the woman's seed and the serpent only, as if his helps and adherents were already disposed of and adjudged. With this agrees the intimation at the very close of the Bible, that on the defeat of Satan's representatives—the Antichristian Beast and his followers—his own judgment follows, (Rev. xx. 1-3.) The *old serpent*, the deceiver of the nations, is put under restraint for a season. The restraint being removed, he is again busy at his work of deception, and collects a great body of adherents. "And they went up on the breadth of the earth, and compassed the camp of the saints about, and the beloved city; and fire came down from heaven and *devoured them.*" Then it is added: "And the devil that deceived them was cast into the lake of fire and brimstone, where the beast and the false prophet are, and shall be tormented day and night for ever and ever." Upon this follow the general judgment and the close of the dispensation.

It remains to consider to what *the bruising of the heel* refers— whether to Christ's personal sufferings, in virtue of which he obtained the victory, when "through death he destroyed him that had the power of death," (Heb. ii. 14,) or to the obstacles thrown in the way of his cause. The former is the usual, and certainly the correct acceptation. The opposition to the Redeemer's cause had been announced in the preceding clause, and it is improbable that it should be resumed in the account of the final struggle and victory. Besides, it is likely, from the nature of the promise—a compendium of the entire subsequent revelation—that with the victory, some notice would be given of the mode in which it should be achieved. It is objected to this interpretation, that it destroys the antithesis of the passage—bruising the head being presumed to refer to the destruction of Satan's power, and not to any injury to his person.[1] But this is too limited a view of the results to Satan of this controversy ; there is not merely a destruction of power, but also the infliction of punishment—personal destruction so far as compatible with continued existence—the destruction of every source of happiness and satisfaction, with the embittering consciousness of utter detection and defeat. Another objection, that Christ's sufferings were of a nature so intense as to forbid the supposition that they could be compared to a wounded heel, rests on a misapprehension of the figure, the design of which is to contrast the consequences of the two cases, without reference to the intensity of suffering on either side. And let it also be observed, that however agonizing Christ's sufferings may have been, they were temporary in their duration, and in their extent could not reach to his head or higher part ; though he was " crucified and slain, God raised him up, having loosed the pains of death, because it was not possible that he should be holden of it," (Acts ii. 24.)

§ 20. *God's chastisement of the Woman and the Man.* Gen. iii. 16-19.

The connexion which subsisted between the tempter and the first human beings whom he had drawn into sin being declared at an end, God turns to the latter as the convicted transgressors of his law. Notwithstanding the assurance extended to them of a final deliverance from their miseries, by an arrangement

---

[1] Alexander, Connexion of Old and New Testaments, p. 182.

which admitted even of present pardon and peace, they must
be told that their altered character and condition made it fit,
and indeed necessary, that they should be treated differently
from what would have been the case had they maintained their
original integrity. And so, though with the announcement of
mercy the sentence of condemnation was suspended and in
part reversed, yet there was that in the disposition and nature
of the sinners which required severe discipline to eradicate or
correct.

The woman is first addressed ; not because the more guilty
of the two, (Delitzsch,) but because the first in the transgression ; and possibly also because of the relation which it was
just declared she should sustain to the destroyer and the deliverer, such honour requiring a speedy correction or counterpoise in what is to prove a permanent memorial of her compli-
city in the temptation. Verse 16, *To the woman he said, I
will greatly multiply thy sorrow and thy conception : in sorrow
shalt thou bring forth children ; and thy desire shall be to thy
husband, and he shall rule over thee.*

The lot of the woman as thus foretold shall comprise in it
two inflictions of a chastening character—severe bodily sufferings, and a feeling of weakness and dependence ; both having
reference to her share in the fall, and the deliverance from it.

By the law of creation, the woman was designed to be a
mother. This law was not repealed on transgression ; it was
indirectly reaffirmed when God expressed his determination to
make it the medium of deliverance to man, and of destruction
to the tempter. It is now directly reaffirmed to the woman
herself ; not, however, without express intimation of the sorrows
and sufferings which by Divine appointment it would entail
upon her.   הַרְבָּה אַרְבֶּה עִצְּבוֹנֵךְ וְהֵרֹנֵךְ—" I will greatly multiply (multiplying I will multiply) thy trouble and thy conception," *i.e.*,
the troubles or pains of thy conception, or, more probably, thy
troubles in general, and those connected with pregnancy and
parturition in particular.   עִצָּבוֹן, *painful, great labour*, as in
verse 17, and Gen. v. 29, " Our work and *toil* of our hands."
The *vav* may here serve, as it frequently does, for connecting
the more prominent and particular with the general, Ex. xviii.
10 ; Ps. xviii. 1 ; comp. Zech. ix. 9. The second idea is more
fully expressed in the next clause—בְּעֶצֶב תֵּלְדִי בָנִים, " with pain

shalt thou bear children," or literally *sons*. The pains of child-
birth were in Hebrew proverbial of the severest pangs, Is. xiii.
8 ; xxi. 3 ; Hos. xiii. 13 ; Mic. iv. 9. It is not without design
that *sons* are here specified, the reference being doubtless to
the terms of the promise. The woman's lot shall henceforth
be one of suffering, but not unmitigated, for the pain is that
of *birth*, and so shall be forgotten, " for joy that a man is born
into the world," (John xvi. 21.)

As the victory over the serpent shall be attended with suffering to the conqueror—the woman's seed—so also with
trouble to the woman herself. Every step towards the realization of the promised deliverance shall be one of pain. But as
it illustrates the Divine wisdom, that the proximate cause of
man's fall is made the medium of his recovery, so it no less
serves to magnify the Divine goodness and grace, to find that
the very word of threatening to the woman contains a promise
and a pledge of this blessed restoration. Farther, the painful
personal infliction with which the woman was visited, while
serving as a standing memorial of her transgression, was designed to work in her "holiness with sobriety," (1 Tim. ii. 15.)
It was no doubt a judicial retribution, but it was thus also and
especially a paternal training and chastisement.

The other concomitant of the woman's lot is a feeling of
weakness and dependence—" And thy desire shall be to thy
husband." By many modern expositors, (Rosenmüller, Tuch,
Schröder, Delitzsch, Knobel,) תְּשׁוּקָה, *desire*, is understood in a
sexual point of view, but it is better with Luther, Calvin, Le
Clerc, and others, to take it as expressing *deference* or *sub-
missiveness*, arising from a consciousness of *weakness* and dependence. This view is commended by two considerations ; first,
the feeling in question is represented as *peculiar to the woman ;*
and secondly, the same expression occurs, Gen. iv. 7, as denoting
the deference and obsequious respect of a younger to an elder
brother. The counterpart of the felt weakness and dependence
of the woman is the authority committed to the husband —" he
shall rule over thee." This authority, though often grievously,
shamefully, and criminally abused, is yet of Divine origin and
obligation. This is not merely, as is sometimes alleged, a prophecy ; it is an investiture. " It is the husband's part, nay
his duty, to rule. It is a relinquishment of the place which

God hath given him not to do it." [1] On account of the husband's authority, the wife was described in Hebrew as בְּעֻלָת בַּעַל, *the possessed,* or *the subjected one of a lord,* Gen. xx. 3 ; Deut. xx. 22 ; and the husband as בַּעַל אִשָּׁה, *lord of a woman,* Exod. xxi. 3.

The place thus assigned to the woman, which is distinctly recognised by the New Testament, (1 Cor. xiv. 34 ; Eph. v. 33 ; Col. iii. 18 ; 1 Tim. ii. 11, 12 ; 1 Pet. iii. 1, 6,) and indeed by the dictates of our nature, was fitted, as it was designed, to correct the disposition which led to the first transgression. The proper place of husband and wife respectively had been fixed by the law of creation (see 1 Cor. xi. 8, 9) and the ordinance of marriage. It was to the reversal of this due order of subordination and supremacy of the woman and the man respectively, that the Fall was in a great measure, if not altogether, owing. The woman affected independence of judgment and action ; she would be like God—her own will shall govern and her own wisdom direct her. And Adam, too, in an evil hour, "hearkened to the voice of his wife." The woman promised herself liberty, but she brought herself into subjection to the deceiver, and under the dominion of sin. In order to be delivered from this thraldom, she, as well as her husband, must be again brought under the lawful and loving rule of God, and, as a means to this end, under all divinely-constituted authority. Divine wisdom and goodness may be recognised in this provision. Of the woman it may be especially said, that *when she is weak she is strong ;* for it ever appears that when, in a spirit of meekness and modesty she advances to the discharge of her duties, and confines herself within the quiet circle assigned to her by God, her labours are abundant, and blessed to herself and others.

Next follows the sentence passed on the man, prefaced by a statement of his guilt, with a recital of the grounds of his condemnation. Verses 17-19, *And to man he said, Because thou hast hearkened to the voice of thy wife, and hast eaten of the tree of which I commanded thee, saying, Thou shalt not eat of it ; cursed is the ground for thy sake ; in sorrow shalt thou eat of it all the days of thy life. Thorns also and thistles shall it bring forth to thee ; and thou shalt eat the herb of the field. In*

[1] Chalmers, Sabbath Scripture Readings, vol. ii. p. 4. Edin. 1852.

the sweat of thy face shalt thou eat bread, till thou return to the
ground : for out of it wast thou taken : for dust thou art, and
to dust shalt thou return.

It is worthy of notice that here, for the first time in the
history, the first man appears as (אָדָם) *man,* and not (הָאָדָם) *the*
man, as in the other cases. In chap. ii. 20, the same form
occurred, but in quite another sense ; " for man (generically)
he did not find a help meet for him." The only instance parallel with the present is verse 21, " To man also and to his wife
did the Lord God make coats of skin." It is usual to explain
this anomaly by taking the word as a proper name ; but there
is no evidence that it was so used until after the birth of
Adam's children, Gen. iv. 25 ; v. 1, 3-5. It is better, however,
to regard it as indicative of the representative character of
Adam as *man,* or the head of humanity, which farther appears
from the sentence pronounced upon him.

The grounds of his condemnation are two. It was remarked
on verse 6, that the first transgression, besides violating an
express command of God, reversed the original and divinely-
appointed relation of the woman to the man. This is fully
brought out in the sentence of condemnation : " Because thou
hast hearkened to the voice of thy wife, and hast eaten of the
tree of which I commanded thee, saying, Thou shalt not eat of
it." Throughout this history, Adam is regarded as the head
of creation in general, and of the woman in particular, and as
properly the responsible party ; and as such he is dealt with.
To him the command was directly given, and to him the danger
of disobedience was directly made known. Accordingly, after
transgression, it is to him the inquiry is directed, " Where art
thou ?" and again, " Hast thou eaten of the tree whereof I
commanded thee that thou shouldest not eat ?" and, in his
case only, are the grounds of condemnation stated.

Adam was doubly guilty : his conduct was a dereliction of
the duty which he owed to the creature as well as to the Creator.
It was a reversal of all order, rule, and authority. He submitted where he ought to have commanded, and disobeyed
where he ought to have submitted. His sin may be described
in the words of the apostle : " He changed the truth of God
into a lie, and worshipped and served the creature more than
the Creator, who is blessed for ever, Amen," (Rom. i. 25.)

Accordingly, it is on man's account, and on his alone, that a curse is laid on creation : " Cursed is the ground for thy sake." The afflictions with which Adam was visited are painful and trying ; but they differ greatly in character and consequences from those allotted to the woman. Hers, though painful, are of a personal character, and peculiar to the female. This was in consequence of her dependent position. The man's punishment, on the contrary, takes a wider range, and is not merely personal and peculiar to himself or to the male portion of his posterity ; for, sustaining as he did a public character, his acts and their consequences affected the whole race, woman as well as man.

In man's sentence there are two elements of bitterness : he is subjected to a life of toilsome and exhausting labour, and made liable to the corruption of death.

Labour, which from the beginning had been assigned to man as sweet and salutary for a state of innocence, has now, by Divine appointment, been made an absolute necessity in a state of sin. It is now the stern law of man's existence on earth ; he needs food, and the ground, cursed for his sin, refuses to yield it. In this may be seen how man's punishment corresponds to his crime. In the midst of plenty, he coveted and ate that which was forbidden, and now the Righteous Judge declares, " Because thou hast eaten . . . cursed is the ground for thy sake : in sorrow (or with *hard labour*, see on verse 16) *shalt thou eat it*," (תֹּאכֲלֶנָּה) *i.e.*, its fruit or produce, as in Isa. i. 7 ; xxxvi. 16 ; compare xxxvii. 30. It is in reference to this curse that the Psalmist speaks of " the bread of trouble," (Ps. cxxvii. 2,) that is, bread procured and eaten amidst hard labour. The toil thus appointed to man shall be one ceaseless round—a life-long labour—" all the days of thy life."

As the blessing of God on the creation imparted fertility to the soil, so his curse shuts up its powers and arrests its productiveness. Thus in the case of Cain, Gen. iv. 12, " When thou tillest the ground it shall not henceforth yield to thee its strength :" and so Isaiah speaks of " the curse devouring the earth," (Isa. xxiv. 6.) But not only shall the productive powers of the soil be diminished, even its free and spontaneous products shall greatly add to man's labour, as if the blessing itself had been converted into a curse. Verse 18, " Thorns also and thistles shall it bring forth to thee,"—noxious, unprofitable weeds, the great pest of the husbandman and the scourge of the soil, and which, from their powers of multiplication and facility of growth, call for constant care and labour for their extirpation. וְדַרְדַּר קוֹץ, as in Hos. x. 8, where they are said to spring up on the deserted altars, are in sense similar to שָׁמִיר וָשַׁיִת, thorns and briars which fill a desolate and neglected land, Isa. v. 6 ; vii. 23-25. " Thou shalt eat the herb of the field :" this is usually understood as intimating that man's food was changed to the worse. The idea seems rather to be that henceforward he must procure it for himself ; the contrast being between the rich and bountiful provision made for him in the garden which God himself planted, and the comparative sterility of the open field whither he is about to be driven. God had hitherto provided for man ; in his now altered circumstances he must in a manner provide for himself.

The severity of the labour to which man must submit in order to force a livelihood from the reluctant soil, is farther declared by the circumstance of its being an exhausting toil—consuming the very body for whose support it is resorted to. Verse 19, " In the sweat of thy face shalt thou eat bread." The sweat is ascribed to the face, as it is there it is most observable, or has as it were its source. And yet with all this wearying and wearing toil, all that man can promise to himself is to eat bread, or obtain a subsistence. But notwithstanding this, with our present constitution, physical and moral, labour, and toil, and sweat, are not unmixed evils : they are part of a merciful dispensation. In regard to perspiration it is remarked, —" We may estimate the discharge from the body by sensible and insensible perspiration at from half-an-ounce to four ounces an hour. This is a most wonderful part of the animal economy, and is absolutely necessary to our health, and even to our very existence. When partially obstructed, colds, rheumatisms, fevers, and other inflammatory disorders are produced ; and were it completely obstructed, the vital functions would be clogged and impeded in their movements, and death would inevitably ensue."[1]

As a farther chastisement of his sin, man is subjected to the corruption of death and the dissolution of the body. Verse

[1] Dick, Christian Philosopher, vol. ii. p. 166.

19, " Till thou return to the ground." This is the result and the termination of man's cares and toils. His labours, and the sweat of his face, produce no true or permanent fruit ; the bread laboriously procured is " bread that perisheth," (John vi. 27,) and man himself perishes in the using and procuring of it. His labour may sustain life for a while ; but at length the life, and with it the labour, must terminate. Indeed the termination of life is partly accelerated by the exhausting toils designed and required to sustain it. Such is the lot of man, that without labour he must die ; and, on the other hand, this very labour is hurrying him on to dissolution. Surely, it may be asked, " What profit hath a man of all his labour which he taketh under the sun ?" (Eccles. i. 3.) In the woman's allotment there is painful labour as well as in that of the man, but with this difference, hers conduces to life, but his leads to death, and terminates in a return to the ground.

The clause, " for out of it wast thou taken," is sometimes regarded as assigning the reason of man's return to the dust : and hence it is inferred that this was in no respect the consequence of his sin, but of his original constitution. Elsewhere, in Scripture, death is always referred to sin, and it may be of importance to show that there is nothing contradictory of this in the present passage. The words which in the English, and many other versions, are rendered as above, may be also, and perhaps more correctly, translated, " *out of which* thou wast taken :" and thus have no reference to the reason or necessity of man's decay or dissolution, but only to the elements into which he shall be dissolved—as those of his original constitution, or as more fully described in the succeeding clause, " Dust thou art, and to dust shalt thou return." That this is no forced translation of כִּי מִמֶּנָּה לֻקָּחְתָּ, will appear from the following considerations. It is that of many ancient and modern versions, *e.g.*, the LXX, ἐξ ἧς ἐλήφθης ; Vulg., " de qua sumptus es ;" so also Onkelos, the Syriac, Saadias : of modern versions, Luther, " davon du genommen bist," and so Patrick and Geddes. Noldius[1] also has " *qua* ex ea ; *i.e.*, ex *qua*." And Gesenius[2] renders the whole clause, " donec redibis in terram de qua sumptus es." This use of the particle as a relative pronoun appears also in other passages. Of such Noldius and

---

[1] Concord., p. 372.　　　　[2] Thesaurus, p. 676.

Gesenius adduce Gen. iv. 25, "God hath appointed me another seed instead of Abel, כִּי הֲרָגוֹ קַיִן, *whom* Cain slew :" LXX, ὃν ἀπέκτεινε Κάϊν ; and so also the Vulgate, Onkelos, and the Syriac. Other instances in which the old interpreters viewed it as a relative are Isa. liv. 6, lvii. 20, but in these passages it may with equal propriety be taken in its usual signification. Enough, however, has been advanced to show that in the present case it does not introduce the *cause* of man's return to the ground, in the sentence passed upon him for sin : and thus, besides more important objections, is explained away the *tautology* which, as Gesenius remarks, the words present on the other view, and which mars the " membrorum concinnitas."

With the return of the body to the dust out of which it was taken, we might expect the announcement of the spirit returning to God who gave it, (Eccles. xii. 7,) for according to chap. ii. 7, man comprised a higher and nobler element than " the dust of the ground," and it was only in a limited sense it could be said of him, " dust thou art, and to dust shalt thou return." That no mention is made of the spiritual principle cannot be explained, from the reserve observed in the early Scriptures regarding the unseen world and the state of the dead. It is explicable only on the assumption that this sentence of condemnation had respect only to temporal and material things. While, for reasons already stated, it cannot be regarded as identical with the penalty threatened in the event of transgression, and is rather to be viewed as part of a beneficent and remedial dispensation, still it contains marked tokens of God's displeasure against sin. This is particularly seen in God's *cursing* the ground from which man was to derive nourishment: and with the intimation, "*for thy sake.*" It was not consistent with a purpose of mercy to curse man himself; but God showed his displeasure by cursing that with which man is most intimately connected; so that the curse shall be made indirectly burdensome to himself. Another indication of God's displeasure with man's conduct is the way in which death is characterized as a *return* or retrogression. As the noblest of God's works, he was designed for progress and perfection ; he was appointed to rise above and rule over nature, but now he must submit to the laws and ordinances which control all organized life.

Thus far the sentence pronounced on man, considered in itself, is exceedingly grievous: but its true character will more fully appear when contrasted with that passed upon the serpent.

The sentences passed on the serpent and on man have this in common, that in both the grounds of condemnation are announced. To the serpent it is said, " Because thou hast done this," and to man, " Because thou hast hearkened," &c., and in this respect the two sentences are distinguished from that of the woman: and in this is doubtless intimated the directly responsible and representative character of the serpent as well as of the man. In all other particulars, however, there is the greatest dissimilarity in the two sentences, and in the lot apportioned to the two parties. This is seen not merely in the more marked and noticeable fact, that in the one case the curse falls directly on the serpent, and in the other only indirectly on man through the ground, but is apparent in all the details.

Taking the language, as already explained, to be symbolical of spiritual truths, it is to be observed, first, the serpent must go upon its belly—a condition implying the very lowest degradation. There is nothing corresponding to this in the lot of man. Though bowed down to the ground by toilsome labour, he can still *consider* and contemplate God's heavens and starry firmament, (Ps. viii. 3.) The contrast is strikingly expressed in the promise of the woman's seed bruising the *head* of the serpent, whereas the latter can raise itself no higher than *his heel.*

Secondly, the serpent must eat dust, the most unsavoury and unsatisfactory food. Man's provision, though procurable only through hard toil, is nevertheless the herb of the field, which can bear no comparison with *dust* as an article of food.

Thirdly, the serpent has no prospect of alleviation or release, " Dust shalt thou eat all the days of thy life." In the case of man it is also said, " In sorrow shalt thou eat it (the produce of the ground) *all the days of thy life ;*" but to this labour and sorrow there is a limit, for it is added, " till thou return to the ground." In man's case there is *comfort* in the midst of the work and toil of the hands, as Lamech with pious and hopeful feelings expressed when he named his son Noah, (Gen. v. 29 ;)

and there is at length a release from these labours, as the afflicted patriarch of Uz felt when he asked, " Is there not an appointed time to man upon earth ? are not his days also like the days of a hireling ?" (Job vii. 1,) and when he spoke of the clods of the valley being sweet to him who is released from troubles and toils. But, more particularly :—" I heard a voice from heaven saying unto me, Write, Blessed are the dead which die in the Lord from henceforth : yea, saith the Spirit, that they may rest from their labours, and their works do follow them," (Rev. xiv. 13.)

§ 21. *The First Fruits of Faith*, Gen. iii. 20.

Since the acknowledgment of guilt, " I did eat," was drawn from our first parents after their vain attempts to conceal or deny their true condition, and the equally vain but more criminal conduct of excusing themselves by charging their sins on external circumstances, or by recriminating one another, and even the Creator himself, no information is given of their feelings or disposition. But the very silence under the condemnation indicates an altered frame of mind ; there was no murmur or complaint—none of the spirit of defiance or sullenness which was so apparent in the case of Cain, when unhumbled and impenitent he reproached his Judge with the severity of the sentence, in the words, " My punishment is greater than I can bear," (Gen. iv. 13.) We are not left, however, to the necessity of drawing conclusions as to the altered disposition of the condemned transgressors from the absence of any statements to the contrary ; the next incident recorded in the history furnishes most conclusive evidence of a bettered state of mind—evidence not merely of true penitence, but also of strong faith. Verse 20, *And the man called his wife's name Eve ; because she was the mother of all living.*

This is a most instructive incident, whether we consider the mere fact of conferring a new name, with the reason assigned for this peculiar designation, or the extraordinary circumstances in which it was bestowed.

When at her creation the female human being was conducted to the man, he, in virtue of the authority delegated to him,

conferred on her a name, calling her woman, (*Isha.*) But the
order expressed by this symbolic act had been completely
subverted in the transgression, until reinstituted and restored
by God after the Fall in the sentence on the woman, " Thy
desire shall be to thy husband, and he shall rule over thee."
Recognising the Divine order thus announced, or rather renewed in the relation of husband and wife, and probably also
recognising his own past failure in this respect, the man again
exercises the authority committed to him, and names anew the
woman united to him as wife—his partner in sin, and now in
sorrow and suffering.

The name bestowed expresses a relation entirely new. This
was to be expected from their completely altered condition,
but the relation which it exhibits is not one that could antecedently be inferred from the great facts of their previous
history. The first name was very characteristic, and displayed
an accurate acquaintance with the character and origin of the
second human being: "She shall be called woman, because
she was taken out of man." The new name is no less characteristic, but at first sight it may appear to harmonize better
with the past state of things than with the present. The
name Eve, or Chavvah, (חַוָּה, *i.q.*, חָיָה, from the root חָוָה, the old
form of חָיָה, *to live,*) *Life*, was given to the first woman, " because she was *the mother of all living,*" כִּי הִוא הָיְתָה אֵם כָּל־חָי ; LXX,
μήτηρ πάντων τῶν ζώντων. The idea of *life* had been expressed
generally in the creation by the נֶפֶשׁ חַיָּה, *the breath of life* of the
animated world, (chap. i. 20, 21,) in the waters and on the
earth, (verses 24, 30,) and particularly in man, (chap. ii. 7.)
In providence the same idea was expressed by עֵץ הַחַיִּים, *the tree
of life* in the midst of the garden, (chap. ii. 9.) The idea is, however, altogether new and peculiar as predicated of the woman.
The universal terms, כָּל־חָי, *all living*, show that *life* is here to
be considered as something peculiar and appropriate to the
case. It could not simply mean that the first woman was
destined to be the mother of the human race ; for, in this
sense, the designation had been as appropriate from the beginning as at any after period, and indeed more suitable, as it
would have been suggested by the primeval blessing, (chap. i.
28.) If, on this view of its meaning, the name were not suggested then, it is probable it would not be given until after

the birth of Cain. Accordingly Dr. Geddes, with his usual rashness, does not hesitate to transpose this and the following verse to the end of the chapter, in order to connect the name more closely with the birth of Cain. But farther, regarded merely as the mother of living or animated beings, there is in the life of man thus considered nothing so pre-eminent or distinguishing as to warrant the designation, " the mother of all living." Besides, on this view, Adam himself might have been as fitly named, the *father of all living*, while in the case neither of the woman nor the man was there anything so striking as to suggest the name, and to call for the explanation given of it.

Our first parents had heard the sentence of condemnation passed upon the serpent and upon themselves. The serpent was cursed, and also the ground upon which man trod, and from which he was to derive his sustenance. They had, moreover, heard the Lawgiver and Judge whose commandment they had transgressed and whose threatening they had disregarded, declaring that they should return to the dust out of which they had been taken ; and this declaration they heard after having learned by painful experience that all His words were true and righteous. And yet, immediately after hearing the sentence which assigned them to *death*, Adam calls his wife's name LIFE. Can this be from doubt of the threatening, or in defiance of the Judge ? This were a hard conclusion, and yet one which might be forced upon us were there no other Divine communications with which the new name can be more satisfactorily connected. Such there are, however, in the curse pronounced upon the serpent, and instead, therefore, of viewing this expression of Adam as betokening doubt or defiance, it is unquestionably to be regarded as the first fruits of faith. He recognised the judgment of God to death which had come upon him through transgression—he heard the curse which was pronounced upon the earth, and the sorrow, suffering, and death which were to constitute his portion on it. But from amidst this general ruin, disorder, and death, he is raised by the word of promise regarding the seed of the *woman*, and the triumph to be thereby obtained over the author of all his evils. Accordingly, Adam expects new life not from himself but from the woman, and in this new life he sees the power of victory over sin and death. He names his wife LIFE ; inasmuch as, in his

view, all else is in itself dead, and only living in the woman
through the Divine promise.

In these first fruits of faith, or of the operation of Divine
grace, may be recognised not merely a correct apprehension of
the word of promise, but also an altered disposition on the part
of the sinner. He justifies God ; and condemns himself, his
hard thoughts of God, his ungenerous conduct to, and accusations of, God's best gift—the companion of his life, and now
also of his sorrows, but nevertheless the source of his joys.
" Eve, the mother of all living," is a recognition which differs
widely from that exhibited in the unloving words, " the woman
whom thou gavest to be with me, she gave me of the tree."

§ 22. *The first Work of Divine Grace*, Gen. iii. 21.

In the first intimation of grace, whereby God laid a foundation for faith and hope, provision was made for stilling man's
disquieting fears, and for satisfying his anxious apprehensions
of the future. Additional provision is now made for the sinner
by a gracious act of the Divine Being, covering his nakedness
and removing the feelings of shame or guilt—*To man also and
to his wife did the Lord God make coats of skin and clothed
them.*

God himself recognised their wants and provided for their
necessities. When it is said that *God clothed* our first parents,
a contrast is intended between this complete and suitable
covering and their own vain endeavours to conceal their nakedness with fig leaves. There is no occasion for denying, with
the generality of expositors, that the coats of skin were made immediately or directly by God. If he only ordered, or prompted,
or directed our fallen progenitors to provide this covering for
themselves, it is reasonable to suppose that the fact would have
been so stated. The garments were God's gifts, God's contrivance ; and is it strange that He who clothes the lilies of the
field, that neither toil nor spin, in robes more glorious than
Solomon's, (Matt. vi. 28-30,) should, on this first and important
occasion, clothe His children, when He designed thereby to
make known to them a great spiritual truth ?

A very prominent place is given in Scripture to ideas associated with clothing. In the Old Testament how express and particular are the directions about the priest's garments, which were made for glory and for beauty, and which, it is universally admitted, were symbolical of spiritual things. What these were plainly appears from such language as this, " Let thy priests be clothed with righteousness;" " I will also clothe her priests with salvation," (Ps. cxxxii. 9, 16.) And, more generally, as descriptive of the state of all God's people, " I will greatly rejoice in the Lord, my soul shall be joyful in my God ; for he hath clothed me with the garments of salvation, he hath covered me with the robe of righteousness," (Isa. lxi. 10,) with similar expressions in the Psalms and in the Prophets. But still more striking is the language of the New Testament on this subject. Thus the repeated mention of *putting on* the new man, and *putting on* the Lord Jesus Christ, (Eph. iv. 24 ; Col. iii. 10 ; Rom. xiii. 14;) and the Apocalyptic exhortation, " I counsel thee to buy of me gold tried in the fire, that thou mayest be rich ; and white raiment, that thou mayest be clothed, and that the shame of thy nakedness do not appear," (Rev. iii. 18.) The same figure is used in reference to the glorified body of the resurrection, and is used in such a way as shews that this was the end towards which all the other spiritual investitures tended, and for which they were required : " If so be that being clothed we shall not be found naked," (1 Cor. xv. 53, 54 ; 2 Cor. v. 2-4.) It is unnecessary, however, to multiply examples of the symbolical use of the terms *naked* and *clothed ;* enough has been said to show that the whole tenor and language of Scripture on this point warrants the inference, that the clothing of our first parents in Eden by the hand of God had respect to more than the investiture of the body—that it typically pointed to the investiture of the soul— the end of all the ways, ordinances, and arrangements of Divine grace.

There was something, however, to which this act more immediately referred—some present necessity which called for it, or want which it was meant to supply. That this was not anything pertaining to the physical wants of the transgressors, or the circumstances in which they were soon to find themselves as exiles from Eden, is plain, from the fact that God himself provides the clothing, and does not leave it to their own labours

2

and resources, as he had declared his determination to do with regard to their food. But it is more particularly seen in the materials out of which the garments were prepared—בָּתְנוֹת עוֹר, *coats of skin.* Were it merely to supply a physical want, there was no reason why any of the vegetable productions, readily available for clothing materials, should not be selected in preference to the skins of animals, which necessitated the taking away of life, when animal food was not required or recognised as an article of human diet. From these considerations, and others connected with the early practice of sacrifice, what so probable as the supposition, that the animals which provided the first clothing for fallen man had been offered in sacrifice on God's altar? If this conclusion be correct, then the important truth was taught that, in order to provide clothing for sinners, which should be typical of guilt covered and atoned, *life* must be offered up. Man, in consequence of transgression, was naked, and, conscious of his nakedness, he vainly attempted some contrivance of his own to remedy this defect ; but no hand save God's could do it. When effected, it was by an act which shewed how God would accept another life in room of the life forfeited by sin. The previous promise was thus confirmed and still farther illustrated. The ideas of suffering and of substitution, and of a righteousness thus acquired to cover human guilt, were embodied in the act of God clothing the first transgressors in the skins of victims offered in sacrifice upon the altar.

With the incident here recorded some writers connect the arrangement afterwards embodied in the Levitical law, whereby the skin of the sacrifice became the property, and was at the disposal of the officiating priest. Lev. vii. 8, " And the priest that offereth any man's burnt-offering, even the priest shall have to himself the skin of the burnt-offering which he hath offered." " Here we see ' *the skin*' given to the priest, irresistibly reminding us of the *skins* that clothed Adam and Eve. If Jesus, at the gate of Eden, acting as our priest, appointed sacrifice to be offered there, then he had a right to the *skins*, as priest ; and the use to which he appropriated them was *clothing Adam and Eve.*" [1]

[1] Bonar, Commentary on Leviticus, p. 117. Lond. 1846.

§ 23. *Man's Expulsion from Paradise*, Gen. iii. 22, 23.

One other arrangement remained to be effected in order to bring the external condition of fallen man into correspondence with his internal state, or his altered spiritual and moral disposition. He must be expelled from Paradise, and made to encounter the difficulties of the world without. *And the Lord God said, Behold, the man is become as one of us, to know good and evil; and now, lest he put forth his hand, and take also of the tree of life, and eat, and live for ever; therefore the Lord God sent him forth from the garden of Eden, to till the ground from whence he was taken.*

The reasons which required the man's exclusion from the garden are stated in the determination, the result of Divine counsel, which, in the way of preface, introduces this act. The only thing in the whole preceding history which can be compared to the language of the present passage, " Behold, the man is become as one of us," is the Divine deliberation which preceded the creation of man, " And God said, Let us make man." But contrasting man's character when created " in the image and after the likeness of God," with what it became in consequence of transgression, how could it now be said that he became like God? Whence this similarity, and wherein did it consist?

These questions, from an early period, greatly occupied the attention of interpreters of Scripture, especially the Rabbinical writers, many of whose notions on the subject were, it may be readily imagined, exceedingly vague. But it is even more astonishing to observe how superficial and unsatisfactory are the expositions which have been offered of this declaration of God by a better class of expositors. Very many writers on this subject, particularly the more recent, seem to have recognised no difficulty whatever in the language; and even in cases where the difficulty was felt, an easy escape from it was found by Augustin and others of the Fathers, and by Piscator and others of the Reformation period, by viewing the declaration as irony and sarcasm. Even the judicious Calvin satisfies himself with the remark, " ironica exprobratio." That there is nothing akin to irony or reproach in the words of God on this occasion, it needs not many arguments to show. The subject and the context utterly preclude such an idea.[1] All the characteristics of the scene and the transaction are of a most solemn kind; and throughout the disposition of the Creator is one of pity and benevolence. To preclude all ideas of irony, it is enough to notice that the language is not addressed to man; in fact there is nothing to show that it was even spoken in his hearing. It is only the historical expression of the deliberative counsels of the Godhead.

Another proposed solution of the difficulty is to take the words as implying what the man *aimed at*, and *attempted* to become, rather than what he actually *did* become. This interpretation has not obtained so much currency as the preceding. But indeed it has nothing to commend it. The expression, הָיָה כְּ, is *to become as*, or *like*, and cannot be otherwise rendered. The words can be taken only in their obvious meaning, as a true description of man's character at the time in which they were uttered. Words nearly similar were spoken by the serpent, in the prospects which he held out to disobedience: "Ye shall be as God, knowing good and evil:" but, in that case, there need be no hesitation in setting them down as the deceiver's lie. The matter assumes an entirely different aspect when it is presented as a declaration of God. The difficulty is not removed, or even diminished, by regarding the likeness between God and man as only relative or partial, confined to the knowledge of good and evil; for the question still recurs, how can it in any sense be said that a creature made in the image of God became by transgression like God, and not like the devil, whose counsel he followed, and whose conduct he imitated? Dr. Candlish, when recently considering this matter, asks, How in respect of the knowledge of good and evil

---

[1] Alting—Nexus cum antecedentibus et consequentibus sarcasmo neutiquam favet. Speciem iste habuisset, siquidem hoc dixisset Deus, vel ante pronunciatam sententiam, quum ex homine quæreret, quis tibi indicavit te nudum esse? vel mox post eam recitato duro carmine, pulvis es et in pulverem reverteris. Sed quid commune habet, vel cum antegresso beneficio amictionis? vel cum subjuncta remotione ab Arbore Vitæ? Profecto non conveniebat recentissimo gratiæ operi acerba oratio insultantis: neque exprobrata ista similitudo ulla consequentiæ necessitate pone se trahebat usurpationem Arboris Vitæ, ut propterea ab hac removendus homo esset. Quæ omnia in diversum ire non tam jubent quam cogunt.—*De Sabbatho*, lib. iii. cap. 7. Opera, vol. v. Amst. 1687.

should he be as God? and in replying to his own question, that able and acute writer has succeeded only in showing a dissimilarity, and not a likeness, as he intended.[1] The whole difficulty connected with this description of man's state, arises from considering it as the result of man's sin, and not of God's redemption of the sinner: and this error again arises from want of duly considering the place which the declaration occupies in the narrative, and in the scheme of grace announced to man. This will appear from the following observations:—

1. This Divine declaration regarding man's character was not uttered immediately after the Fall and the sentence of condemnation, or the announcement of mercy on the part of God. Between the announcement of mercy and the statement under consideration, two very significant incidents intervened —the naming of the woman, and the Divine provision made for covering man's nakedness. The former of these incidents we considered as evidence of man's faith, of his submission to God, and of his acceptance of God's proffered gift : the other as symbolizing that his guilt was covered by the righteousness of the Lamb slain. The two incidents taken together showed man *clothed and in his right mind,* (Mark v. 15.)

2. The circumstances now adverted to, while manifesting the gracious purposes of God, no less clearly show an altered disposition in man. His faith in the Divine promise removed his fears, and God's righteousness covered his guilt. He might now, in the language of the New Testament, be called " a new creature," old things having passed away and all things become new. In these circumstances, what so probable as the supposition that the state of man here described was the result of redemption, and not of transgression? By transgression made like the devil, *the man*—the reference, be it observed, is only to the individual—by redemption became like God, for he was renewed in the spirit of his mind.

3. Thus considered, the language before us is the Divine approval or satisfaction with the effects of the plan of redemption as manifested in the case of the first human transgressor. It is thus parallel with God's satisfaction at creation : " God saw everything that he had made, and, behold, very good."

[1] Contributions towards the Exposition of Genesis, pp. 77, 78. Edin. 1844.

The two declarations are introduced by the same expressions, הֵן or הִנֵּה, here of admiration and delight. Man's likeness to God has been attained notwithstanding the transgression: in a manner it is the fruit or consequence of it. The tempter had assured the objects of his attack that they should be as God, and should attain to the knowledge of good and evil. This is accomplished, but in a way to disappoint the enemy— accomplished, however, not through works of righteousness, but through faith in Christ, and thus man is made really godlike, because bearing the image of the only begotten Son.

4. The fruits of redemption described are such as presented themselves in the first man :—" Behold, *the man* is become as one of us by the knowledge of good and evil ;" and not in the human race collectively, nor in Adam as its representative, but only in Adam individually. But the character thus ascribed to the first man, who passed through a fiery ordeal which illustrated and glorified Divine grace, may equally belong to his descendants through faith in the same word of promise. They also, as he, may be restored to favour and fellowship with God. Indeed, it is expressly said in terms which confirm the preceding conclusions : " Beloved, now are we the sons of God ; and it doth not yet appear what we shall be ; but we know that when he shall appear, we *shall be like him ;* for we shall see him as he is," (1 John iii. 2.)[1]

In consideration of man's altered condition, and of the new economy under which he was placed, he must be excluded from Paradise, and care must be taken to prevent his access to the tree of life. But the act of exclusion bears more the impress of a merciful necessity than of a punitive infliction. There had been a deliberation of the Godhead before the decree was put into execution or even announced. It was found to be just and expedient in man's circumstances, and in accordance with God's purposes concerning him. It was designed to prevent farther evil, and such as might have a tendency to defeat God's purposes of mercy : " And now, lest

[1] James Alting (died 1679) had a glimpse of the true exposition :—Deus in concilio trinitatis collaudavit Adami fidem, per quam uni ex tribus personis deitatis Filio Dei designato Mediatori similem esse dixit, experimentali cognitione tam summæ infelicitatis, in Christo per fidem morituri peccato quod in typo viderat, quam summæ felicitatis, in eodem per fidem viventis Deo et victuri in æternum.— *Analysis Exegetica in Gen.* Opera, vol. i.

he put forth his hand, and take also of the tree of life, and
eat, and live for ever." This sentence is defective, and the
clause omitted is to be inferentially supplied from the commencement of the next verse, which describes the means
adapted to prevent the feared contingency : verse 23, " Therefore the Lord God sent him forth from the garden of Eden."
The terms in which the tree of life is here spoken of, would
seem to imply that it was possessed of some intrinsic virtue for
preserving life ; and that, if man partook of it after the Fall,
he would become immortal. But this is to misapprehend the
text. In the first place, an absolute sentence of death had
been passed on man : "Dust thou art, and unto dust shalt
thou return." From this sentence, it may safely be affirmed,
no device or act of his own could deliver him. But secondly,
man might nevertheless cherish the expectation of deliverance
by the tree of *life*, and so be induced to take of it. He had
heard himself doomed to death and dissolution—he knew also
of the tree of life ; but, in disregard of the true object of that
tree and his own altered circumstances, he might hope to counteract or defeat the sentence passed upon him. The language
determines nothing as to the possibility or impossibility of such
a result, it only expresses a purpose which might be aimed at.[1]
From the nature of the case, there is nothing exactly like it in
any other passage of Scripture. That which comes nearest to the
language and construction, is Pharaoh's purpose and apprehensions in respect to Israel. Ex. i. 10, " Let us deal wisely with
them, lest they multiply (פֶּן־יִרְבֶּה), and it come to pass, that
when there falleth out any war, they join (וְנוֹסַף) also to our
enemies and fight (וְנִלְחַם) against us, and get them up (וְעָלָה) out
of the land." Here the purpose of the junction with the enemies of the Egyptians, and of fighting in that relation, is
expressed in the getting up out of the land. In that case,
although the contingency was not impossible, yet the language
points rather to the attempt. So in the present passage,
"Lest he put forth (פֶּן־יִשְׁלַח) his hand and take, (or *for the
purpose of taking*, וְלָקַח,) also of the tree of life, and eat, and
live (וָחָי וְאָכַל), *i.e.*, for the purpose, or with the design of *eating*,
and this with the ultimate design of *living*) for ever." One
distinction between Ex. i. 10 and this passage is, that רָבָה ex-

---

[1] Tremellius :—Hæc ad consilium hominis peccatoris respiciunt, non ad eventum rei.

presses a *state* or *condition*, while רבש describes an act ; only in the latter case does a purpose lie in all the succeeding verbs.

Were the attempt here intimated made by man, it would no doubt prove a failure ; he would be disappointed in the end. The tree of life was intended merely as a sacramental pledge that life would be continued to man, if obedient to the law under which he was placed in Eden ; but it was not endowed with the power of prolonging or restoring it when forfeited through transgression. It would have been equivalent to the endeavours after justification by works—by the deeds of the law and not by the grace of the gospel—if Adam sought life in this way. "It was, therefore, a most gracious and merciful procedure on the part of God to drive our first parents from the garden of Eden—to place them beyond the reach, and even the sight of the tree of life—that they might therefore feel how hopeless and how helpless their condition was, except for the promise of the Saviour—that they might be shut up to a simple reliance on Him as the only way of recovering the life which they had forfeited ; and from the sad experience of the bitter fruits of their transgression, they might feel how precious was the promise, 'The seed of the woman shall bruise the head of the serpent.'"[1]

Verse 23, "Therefore the Lord God sent him forth from the garden of Eden, to till the ground from whence he was taken." The *Piel* form (רבש) denotes a complete and final expulsion, which precludes all hope of a return. The term is often used in the sense of repudiating or divorcing a wife, (Deut. xxi. 14; xxii. 19, 29 ; Isa. l. 1 ; Jer. iii. 8.) It here denotes that for this world Paradise was utterly lost.

Man had been put into the garden for a twofold object— to cultivate and to guard it. To the latter part of his trust he proved unfaithful, and he is accordingly deprived of it. The labours of tillage, on the contrary, are greatly augmented and even made the condition of his existence, and are to be transferred to a less generous soil than that of Paradise. He is now sent forth into the world to encounter not only its labours but its *tribulations*, that by these he may be prepared for the rest that remaineth for the people of God, by fixing his heart and hopes on a better and more blessed state of existence, and be

[1] Gordon, Christ as made known to the Ancient Church, vol. i. p. 54. Edin. 1854.

the more resigned to quit this scene of care and toil when summoned away.   And, in the meantime, the place of his transgression and the office to which he proved unfaithful shall be committed to others.

§ 24. *The Cherubim and the Flaming Sword*, Gen. iii. 24.

But although lost for the present, and as far as regards this world, Paradise is not lost for ever.   The tree of life is permitted to grow, access to it is afforded to others, and the guardianship of it is committed to a more vigilant keeper. Verse 24, *So he drove out the man ; and he placed at the east of the garden of Eden the cherubim, and a flaming sword which turned every way, to keep the way of the tree of life.*—The residence of our first parents, though no longer within, was still in the neighbourhood of the garden.   Cain was the first who removed from this locality, which was still distinguished as the place of " the presence of the Lord," (Gen. iv. 16.)   From this place the cherubim in the garden must have been ever in sight of the fallen pair—a sight, no doubt, painfully reminding them of blessings lost, but also greatly fitted to influence their faith and expectations.   The truths symbolized by the cherubic figures require to be fully considered.

The cherubim, introduced here for the first time in the sacred history, are afterwards frequently mentioned, particularly in connexion with the sacred furniture of the Hebrew tabernacle. These mysterious figures appear also in some of the most glorious visions presented to the Old Testament seers, and were remarkably associated with the religious hopes and joys of psalmists and saints.   Yet, though frequently referred to, but little information is furnished as to their form or character.   In Genesis they are spoken of as *the* cherubim.   But not even in the detailed specifications of the furnishings of the tabernacle, where these figures occupied a very prominent place, is there any mention of their form and appearance, farther than that they were furnished with *wings*.   This silence would imply that the cherubic form was so familiar to the Hebrews—to Bezaleel and the other artificers employed upon the tabernacle —as to render any description superfluous.   It is also probable that the figures introduced into the tabernacle bore a substantial resemblance to those placed at the east of the garden of Eden. When the tabernacle was superseded by the temple, cherubic figures were engraved on the walls of the latter structure ; and, as if to identify them with the cherubim of Eden, they were surrounded by palms and flowers, (1 Kings vi. 29-35.)

The absence of direct information as to the cherubic form and character cannot be supplied by any etymological examination of the name. Formerly much labour was wasted in attempts to establish the derivation of the word *cherub*, (כְּרוּב,) of which cherubim is the Hebrew plural ; but as this led to no satisfactory results, the investigation is now wisely abandoned. Neither in Hebrew nor in any of the cognate dialects is there a *root* to which the word can with any certainty be traced.

The first description of the appearance of the cherubim is in Ezekiel's visions ; from which it appears that they were compound figures, made up of the parts of a man, a lion, an ox, and an eagle, but how the parts were united into one creature, and what parts of each were most prominently in view, cannot with certainty be learned from the description. It would, indeed, seem that the form was not fixed but variable. The cherubim first seen by Ezekiel had each four faces and four wings, (chap. i. 6.) Those described by him as sculptured on the temple walls had only two faces, (chap. xli. 18, 19,) and in another passage one of the four faces is described as *the face of a cherub*, (chap. x. 14.) That this is not to be accounted for from the difference of position and from the laws of perspective, or, in other words, because in the one case they were independent figures, and in the other sculptured on a plain surface,[1] appears from a statement regarding their position on the ark of the covenant. — " Their faces shall look to one another ; toward the mercy-seat shall the faces of the cherubim be," (Exod. xxv. 20,) which had been impossible if each had four faces. Yet with this variable form the predominating appearance was that of a man. Ezekiel expressly states, " This was their appearance ; they had the likeness of a man," (chap. i. 5.)

But a more important question is, What the cherubim were meant to signify ? Various considerations tend to show that they were not intended, as is frequently maintained, to repre-

[1] Winer, Real-Wörterbuch, *Art.* Cherubim, vol. i. p. 225, *note* 6.

sent the angelic host—a view which, in a modified form, is still advanced by Hofmann, Delitzsch, and Kurtz.[1] It may suffice to remark that, if designed to represent angels, their construction and introduction into the tabernacle were in strange opposition both to the letter and spirit of the Mosaic legislation, as expressed in the command, " Thou shalt not make unto thee any graven image, or any likeness of anything that is in heaven above," (Exod. xx. 4.)

A still more extravagant theory, which some time ago found much acceptance, but is now very much abandoned, was that which viewed the cherubim as emblems of the Trinity, with man incorporated into the Divine essence. But to this, and many other wild and conflicting opinions on the subject, it is unnecessary farther to refer, as the attention recently given to the study of the Biblical symbols has, in a great measure, dissipated the vague and confused notions which once prevailed. Acquaintance with the hieroglyphics and symbols of a religious character used in heathenism, especially in the systems of the Egyptians, Persians, and Assyrians, has been of service in this respect.

It is now established that composite animal forms, such as the cherubim of Scripture, and what was probably traditional imitations of them, the winged human-headed lions and bulls of Nineveh and the sphinxes of Egypt, were intended to represent beings, or a state of being, in which were concentrated all the peculiar qualities and excellencies which distinguished the creatures which entered into the combination. The creatures which entered into the composition of the cherub were man, the lion, the ox, and the eagle—the highest forms of life with which we are acquainted. There was thus concentrated in it all that was most strongly characteristic of *life*. This is confirmed by the peculiar designation, חיה, *living creatures*, or *living ones*, given to the cherubim in Ezekiel, (chap. i. 5, 13, &c. ; x. 15, 17,) and which is uniformly rendered by the LXX. ζῶα. The same peculiar designation is given in the Apocalypse to creatures which bear so striking a resemblance to those described by Ezekiel, that their identity

[1] Hofmann, Der Schriftbeweis, vol. i. pp. 179, 317. Delitzsch, Genesis, p. 189. 2te Ausg. Leip. 1853. Kurtz in Herzog's Real-Encyk., *Art*. Cherubim, vol. ii. p. 650.

cannot be questioned. " In the midst of the throne, and round about the throne, *four living creatures* (ζῶα) full of eyes before and behind. And the first *living creature* like a lion, and the second *living creature* like a calf, and the third *living creature* had a face as a man, and the fourth *living creature* like a flying eagle. And the four living beings had each of them six wings about him ; and they were full of eyes within, and they rest not day and night, saying," &c., (Rev. iv. 6-8.) With some unimportant differences, the same number and kind of animal forms appear in the mysterious creatures seen in the visions of Chebar and of Patmos. The names are identical—the idea of life is farther exhibited in the two cases by incessant activity, and the place is the closest proximity to the throne of God.

If from these considerations it may be concluded that *life* is the fundamental idea embodied in the cherubim, the next question will be, what *life*—*creative* or *created*, and if the latter, whether it respected all that is living on the earth, or only life in one peculiar aspect ?

Not a few writers, following Bähr,[1] who has ably examined this subject, are of opinion that the life represented by the cherubim was the fulness of life in the Divine Being, the properties of the animals combined in these forms being symbolical of the attributes, acts, and government of God. This view is not of the gross character of some of the older theories, nor is it open to the same objections. It may, with certain explanations, be received as a true exposition of the subject; for all life is an efflux, and so a reflection of the divine life ; and so also all the powers and properties in the creature as such, are only images of the same in an infinitely higher degree in the Creator. Thus considered, this view may be safely admitted, but not if it means to affirm that the representations of God's attributes was the direct or only object of the cherubim. Others, as Hengstenberg, regard the cherubim as expressive of all that was living on the earth.[2]

That the life represented by these mysterious forms was *created* life as distinct from the creative, is evident from the following considerations :—

First, the component parts of the cherub were not merely

[1] Symbolik des Mosaischen Cultus, vol. i. pp. 340-360. Heidelberg, 1837.
[2] Commentary on the Revelation, vol. i. p. 212.

creatures, but were such as existed in this lower world, thus evidently pointing to an earthly origin, or state of existence. Should it be objected to the conclusiveness of this argument, that the manifestations of God to the creature must be through the medium of nature, its laws and operations, it may be replied, this is confounding the pure, spiritual religion of the Bible with the nature-worship of heathenism, for in the former there are manifestations of God higher than any which nature can furnish.

Secondly, if the cherubim were representations of God's attributes, what reason can be given for the place which they occupied in the sanctuary? The symbolic figures standing on the mercy-seat were shrouded in thick darkness, and carefully concealed from the view of all, save the high-priest, on the annual day of atonement. Such a situation is wholly inconceivable, on the supposition that it was God's attributes that these forms represented ; for there they were *concealed* rather than revealed.

Thirdly, the acts in which the cherubim or living creatures of the Apocalypse participate are incompatible with this view. They not only join in the general song of praise to God and in the song of redemption, but they also distinctly state that they are " *redeemed* unto God by the blood of the Lamb," (Rev. v. 9.) Admitting that all God's works may be said to praise their Creator, and also that his various attributes in their manifestations combine to glorify him, and may figuratively be said to join in his praise in creation and redemption, how can it be said that God's attributes bow down to worship Him, or by what propriety of language can it be said that they were redeemed ?

From these and other considerations, it must be apparent that the view which regards the cherubim as representing divine attributes, or *creative* life, cannot be maintained. If then they are to be considered as symbols of *created* life, in what particular aspect is this life regarded ?

Although the cherub, as already noticed, was a combination of four animal forms, yet the human appearance preponderated. This has been held as " implying that it was man whom the representation chiefly respected, and that to this the others were but subsidiary and additional. Man, however, not as he now is, for then the human figure alone had been sufficient; but man raised to a new sphere of life and being, endowed with properties which he did not possess even in Paradise—man as redeemed and glorified."[1]

If any difficulties attach to this view of the meaning of the cherubic symbols, it is at least not open to the insuperable objections which have proved fatal to some of the other theories propounded on this subject. It has the merit of being simple, and if not *the* Scriptural view, it yet does not conflict with any other clearly revealed truth. But, above all, it gives a consistent explanation of all the circumstances of the case—the various relations which the cherubim occupy, and the exercises in which they take a part from the beginning to the close of the dispensation. This will be shown by an examination of the several passages of Scripture in which the cherubic forms appear, beginning with the last in order, " their manifestation in the glorious pattern which John saw of the Redeemer's triumphal court and throne."

From an examination of the passages in the Apocalypse referring to this subject, the following information is obtained relative to the place, employment, and character of the cherubim or living creatures.

1. They are represented as in the immediate neighbourhood of God's throne : they stand nearer the throne than the elders and the angels. God appears enthroned, as it were, above them, and they are always associated with his presence, (Rev. iv. 6 ; v. 6 ; vii. 11.)

2. The throne in heaven around which the cherubim have their place is closely related to the covenant of grace and the atonement. It may be called the throne of grace, or the mercy-seat in heaven. This appears, 1st, From the rainbow which encircled it :—" There was a rainbow round about the throne, in sight like unto an emerald," (Rev. iv. 3.) " Since Gen. ix. the rainbow," as Hengstenberg remarks, "has been unalterably consecrated as a symbol of grace returning after wrath." 2dly, From the occupant of the throne :—" In the midst of the throne and of the four living creatures, and in the midst of the elders, stood *a Lamb as it had been slain*," (Rev. v. 6 ;) his appearance imaged atonement and reconciliation through suffering.

[1] Fairbairn, Typology, vol. i. p. 314.

3. The cherubim take the lead in the acts of adoration and praise.   Vitringa remarks :—" In chap. v., the whole heavenly assembly before the throne is divided into two choruses or classes—the living creatures and the elders formed the one chorus, (verse 8,) and the angels the other, (verse 11.)" And Hengstenberg, on chapter iv. 9-11 : " The adorations of the cherubim turn on God's almighty power as manifested in creation ; and so does that also of the elders.   That the doxology of the elders has respect to the same great fact as that of the cherubim, is indicated by the article, *the* glory, &c., showing that *they simply respond to the doxology of the cherubim."*

4. It is expressly affirmed that they were *redeemed,* (Rev. v. 8, 9.)   This has occasioned considerable difficulty to expositors, who consider the cherubim as symbolic of the Divine attributes or government, or of the powers of nature.   Thus Barnes : *" Perhaps* the language in chap. v. 9, 'And they sung a new song,' &c., though apparently connected with the 'four beasts' in verse 8, is not designed to be so connected.   John *may intend* there merely to advert to the fact that a new song was sung, without meaning to say that the four living beings *united* in that song."   And Hengstenberg : " A celebration of the deeds of Christ so copious is nowhere else found in the mouths of the cherubim, and *does not appear to suit them,* rather indeed *opposes their nature and significations, (i e.,* on the author's theory that they are the representatives of all that is living on the earth,) and their own peculiar song of praise is addressed only to God as the almighty Creator, (iv. 8 ;) finally, all doubt is taken away by the words in verse 9, 'Thou hast redeemed us,' &c., which are *not suitable* in the mouths of the beasts." This is surely squaring the text by the theory, and not the theory by the text, especially when the author is obliged to add :—" On the other hand, we must not exclude the four beasts from any participation in what follows, after their being said to fall down, along with the elders, before the Lamb. Though the falling down does not justify us in supposing, with many expositors, that the cherubim had a full participation with the elders, yet a sort of counterpoise might have been given in what follows, by its being expressly remarked that the elders alone had part in it.   Farther, *a merely dumb prostration, where all besides, not excepting the angels, sing praise,*

appears unsatisfactory. The natural supposition is, that the elders came forth as the speakers of the chorus, which was formed of them and the four beasts. Both are connected together by an internal bond."

Should any difficulty be felt in regarding the cherubim as the redeemed from among men, seeing that these are otherwise represented by the elders, it may be enough to remark that we are not in possession of full and explicit information on this subject, and that, in the absence of such, difficulties may be expected ; and yet the fact that the redeemed are represented in one aspect by the elders does not necessarily preclude the supposition that, in another aspect, they may be represented by the living creatures, between whom and the elders there is, as Hengstenberg remarks, an internal bond of union. It has been suggested, and with great probability, that while the elders represent the whole Church—the *persons* of the redeemed, in their prospective dignity of a royal priesthood—the living creatures may represent the *nature* of the redeemed, not only rescued from the power of evil, but raised to a position wherein it is endowed with powers not originally its own.[1]

The representations of the cherubim in the visions of Ezekiel, although not so full and precise as in the visions of John, embody the same important truths. There, also, they appear in close connexion with the throne of God and the Divine glory. The visions of Chebar, although directly manifestations of oming judgments, had nevertheless an aspect of grace.[2] Accordingly, with reference to the first of these it is said, " Upon the likeness of the throne was the likeness as the appearance of a man above upon it ;" and, " as the appearance of the bow[3] that is in the cloud in the day of rain, so was the appearance of the brightness round about. This was the appearance of the likeness of the glory of the Lord," (Ezek. i. 26, 28.) It is also to be noted that, although these living creatures with their living wheels are seen to be animated in the highest degree, yet all their acts and motions are influenced and directed by one pervading spirit, (verses 12, 20, 21.)

[1] Fairbairn, Typology, vol. i. p. 316.
[2] Hävernick, Commentar über Ezechiel, p. 30. Erlangen, 1843.
[3] Hävernick quotes a remark of J. H. Michaelis on this passage :—" Iris est symbolum fœderis et gratiæ."

The next vision of this kind seen by Ezekiel related to the departure of the Divine presence from the temple, which had been polluted and profaned.   In the two visions, but particularly in the second, the main figures in the imagery were derived from the patterns of heavenly things in the most holy place of the temple, and with which Ezekiel as a priest must have been familiar ; therefore it is that he says, " I *knew* that they were *the cherubim*," (chap. x. 20.)   In this vision the Divine glory in the first instance withdrew from the inner sanctuary to the threshold of the temple ; it next departed thence, and took its place above the cherubim who moved on to the *east* or principal gate of the temple.   At length they passed from thence—paused for a time over the city—proceeded to the Mount of Olives on the east of the city, and finally disappeared from the prophet's view, (chap. x. 4, 18 ; xi. 23, 24.)

The *gracious* aspect which, through impending judgments, these visions exhibited, besides furnishing assurance of deliverance to the men that sighed for the abominations done in Jerusalem, (Ezek. ix. 4,) was designed to show that God's covenant of redemption was not so inseparably connected with, or dependent on the existence of Israel as a nation or a church, as that the overthrow of the one could in any way endanger the stability of the other.   It was shown, that though the glory of the Lord might forsake the temple and pass away from the city, it would still retain its place among the cherubim, as of old.   This union, not dependent on place or circumstances, was a token of the stability of the covenant, and as such it must have greatly encouraged God's people in prospect of the overthrow which was then announced.

To the representations of the cherubim already considered, those of the tabernacle and temple fully correspond.   The tabernacle, with its furnishings, was made according to the pattern which God showed to Moses in the Mount ; it was a pattern of heavenly things, (Heb. ix. 23.)   In the innermost compartment of the sacred tent, or the holy of holies, which was the peculiar residence of the covenant God of Israel, there was the ark of the covenant covered by the mercy-seat, or *propitiatory*, upon the ends of which stood the cherubim. They looked down upon the mercy-seat ; they *grew* out of it, as it were, being formed of the same material, and, as some

2 H

think, of the same solid piece of gold, (Exod. xxv. 19 ;) while over them, or between them, Jehovah, in the *shekinah* or cloud of glory, was enthroned.   The position thus occupied by the cherubic figures, where everything spoke of grace and redemption, and pointed to atoning blood, is highly significant.   Their place was one to which there was access only through atoning blood, of the efficacy of which their admission and continued occupancy were a type and a pledge.

But to return to the passage in Genesis which has given rise to this discussion, how far do the subsequent representations of the cherubim—the places they occupy, and the offices they discharge—harmonize with and illustrate what is said of those which were placed in Eden after the expulsion of man?

As already remarked, the manner in which these mysterious figures are here spoken of, implies that the ideas which they embodied were familiar to the Israelitish reader, an inference fully corroborated by the subsequent references made to them. This may, in fact, be correctly deemed the account of the original institution of the prototype which constituted the centre of the religious polity of the Jewish people, as it had done previously, there is every reason to conclude both from Scripture and the traditions current among the early nations of the earth, in the simpler form of Patriarchal worship, for the same symbols, variously modified, appear in all ancient religions.[1]

The idea, as above explained, which in various forms found expression in this way, was closely associated with expectations of a better and more advanced state of existence for man than the present, and in its purer scriptural form, with redemption and God's dwelling among a people delivered from sin and its consequences.   But the fact most prominently brought to view in this passage relative to the cherubim, is, that they were put into possession of the place designed and prepared for unfallen man.   Paradise was the type not merely of all that was lovely in creation, but, with its tree of life and happy human inhabitants, of life also—a life which consisted in union and communion with God.   Sin changed the scene, as far as man was concerned—but not the character of Eden as the abode of life, nor the purpose of God concerning it.   On the contrary, in the symbolic creatures constituting its inhabitants after the

[1] See Gosse, Assyria, p. 110.   London, 1852.

Fall, life, in fact, appears in a far higher form than before. As the human form was the most prominent in these ideal figures, there was thus an intimation that they held some essential relation to the beings that had been expelled on account of sin. This, taken in connexion with the promise of victory through the woman's seed, could not fail to be construed into a type of man restored to Paradise, and from the ruin of the Fall raised to a higher platform of life.

The place of the cherubim was at " the east of the garden," where it is evident its entrance must also have been. The entrance to the tabernacle, and the principal entrance to the temple, were likewise to the east; and from the eastern gate it was that the cherubim seen by Ezekiel took their departure. These coincidences in themselves may be of little importance; and so, too, it may be with the word שָׁכַן, *placed*, or *made to dwell*, used in reference to the location of the cherubim in the garden, but which is the root of *shekinah*, or the visible Divine glory *dwelling* or *tabernacling* between the cherubim in the Levitical dispensation; but they are worthy of consideration when viewed in connexion with other facts gathered from the primeval history; such as that there was a place where the Lord manifested himself as still dwelling with men on the earth, and towards which he was to be worshipped. This appears from the terms used in reference to offerings; " they brought them to the Lord," (Gen. iv. 3, 4,) that is, to some appointed place; and from the manner in which Cain's exile is described—" he went out from the presence of the Lord," (verse 16.) What can be more probable than that this primeval holy place, towards which the exiles from Eden worshipped, was just the place of the cherubim, and, as such, substantially identical with the Levitical sanctuary, which was itself a " pattern" of heaven as prepared from the foundation of the world for man redeemed, as the earthly paradise had been for man unfallen?

Viewed thus, the cherubim occupy an identical position in the successive forms of the one dispensation of grace, at the beginning of which they make their first appearance, and bear evidence to the same important truths—the same disposition on the part of God and purpose concerning man. But it is a misapprehension to suppose, that besides occupying man's original ground, the cherubim of paradise entered into his office in connexion with the tree of life[1]—a supposition which violently dissociates this passage from all the subsequent accounts of the cherubic functions. Man's office had been " to keep" the garden, and this of course included the charge of the tree of life, but having failed in his duty, he is deprived of this office now and for ever. It is God's design, however, to preserve *life*, and its symbol the tree of life, but henceforth He takes its keeping into His own hands, or commits it to the Mediator.

This truth, so plainly taught in the New Testament, found also its representation in the symbols of Paradise, not, however, in the cherubim, but in the " flaming sword" introduced in the same connexion. The ground of the misconception just adverted to consists in confounding two distinct emblems. The flaming sword, whatever it may be conceived to mean, though mentioned in connexion with, and evidently closely related to the cherubim, was yet distinct from them, and must not be regarded, as is very generally the case, although not by the author last referred to, as borne or brandished by the cherubim. Of these figures—for the term is plural—there were at least two, but the sword is spoken of in the singular; and is it to be supposed that the historian would be guilty of the incongruity of arming two cherubim with one sword ? " They were not *so* connected as to be visibly united with it, brandishing the sword, as has sometimes been supposed, in their hands, nor could the first worshippers have any reason to regard them as ministers of vengeance ;" and, accordingly, so much the less is there reason for holding them as " instituted guardians of the way to the tree of life."[2] Besides, it is not certain that there was anything which could properly be designated a sword in this representation, more than in any of the subsequent appearances of the same symbols. All that can be inferred from the terms, לַהַט הַחֶרֶב הַמִּתְהַפֶּכֶת, *the flame of a sword turning itself*, is, that there was some igneous appearance, in shape like a sword, darting out from among the cherubim with a constant flickering motion, thus answering to the description of the motion of that fire which accompanied the cherubim seen by the prophet on the banks of the Chebar. " A whirl-

---

[1] Fairbairn, Typology, vol. i. p. 314.   [2] Ibid. vol. i. p. 320.

wind came out of the north, a great cloud, and *a fire infolding itself*, and a brightness was about it, and out of the midst thereof as the colour of amber, out of the midst of the fire," (Ezek. i. 4.) The expression, מִתְלַקַּחַת, which Hävernick takes to mean " rolled together," may have some relation to the term used in Genesis, and both are very expressive of the motion of fire. Nothing then so probable as that this igneous appearance was the Divine glory manifested along with the cherubim, as on other occasions, and particularly as it was related to the salvation of man, a truth recognised by the Psalmist in his prayer, " Give ear, O Shepherd of Israel, thou that leadest Joseph like a flock ; thou that dwellest between the cherubim, *shine forth*," (Ps. lxxx. 1.)

Although not of much importance in itself, yet as evidence of an early traditionary belief, it may be interesting to notice, that the view here sought to be established, is countenanced by some of the Jewish writers themselves. Thus in the Jerusalem Targum, the passage is rendered : " And he thrust out the man, and caused the glory of his presence to dwell of old at the east of the garden of Eden above the two cherubim." So also the Targum of Jonathan Ben Uziel : " And he drove and thrust out the man ; from which time he caused the glory of his presence to dwell of old between the two cherubim."

Thus understood, the symbol is plain and consistent, and while forcibly expressing the New Testament doctrine, " Our God is a consuming fire," (Heb. xii. 29,) and " dwelling in the light" that is inaccessible, (1 Tim. vi. 16,) it also and particularly illustrated, in connexion with the cherubim and the tree of life, this other truth, " Ye are dead, and your life is hid with Christ in God," (Col. iii. 3,) which Olshausen thus expounds, " God is conceived of as the element into whose essence the faithful, like Christ himself, are taken up, and in which they are concealed, so that no one can penetrate into this element of life."

This, however, will more fully appear from the function assigned to the flaming sword, " to keep the way of the tree of life." " To keep" here doubtless signifies "to keep watch over," or " guard," for it is the same word, in precisely the same form, that occurred in chap. ii. 15, and which was expounded in this sense, and the connexion of which passage with the present is at once obvious. But now the idea expressed is more definite, the guardianship being concentrated on one specific object, "the tree of life;" with the addition, moreover, of another idea, "*the way* of the tree of life." To keep the tree of life might imply that all access to it was to be precluded; but "to keep *the way*" signifies to keep the way *open* as well as to keep it shut. The very fact that there is such a way, implies that there is access to the privileged; and so the flaming sword kept open a way for the cherubim—the representations of the redeemed from among men—while it excluded all who by force or fraud would approach in order to snatch at life, or to destroy the tree in which it typically centred. Man, indeed, had been driven out of Paradise; he had passed from a dispensation in which life was the portion of the innocent, but not to one from which life was excluded, but rather heightened and confirmed, as a free gift of God to the pardoned and renewed. So long as he himself was the keeper of the garden, there is no reference to a way to the tree of life, for he had life in his own hand, though without the certainty of retaining it; but now that this charge is committed to another, and he shut out, there must be a way, if ever he shall be restored to the forfeited blessings.

It is therefore because of man's position outside the gate of Paradise, as contrasted with his former residence within it, that mention is made of a *way* to the tree of *life*, which will remind the reader of such declarations as these, "I am the way, and the truth, and the life : no man cometh unto the Father, but by me," (John xiv. 6.) "Blessed are they that do his commandments, that they may have right to the tree of life, and may enter in through the gates into the city," (Rev. xxii. 14.) The deeply significant allusions to the *path* or *way of life*, a *way* for the *ransomed* of the Lord, and others of similar import which occur also in the Old Testament, are doubtless founded on this provision typically made at the Fall. Thus, to quote only one instance, Isa. xxxv. 8-10, a passage which borrows much of its other imagery from the history of that transaction, and the promised restoration :—" And an highway shall be there, and a way, and it shall be called the way of holiness ; the unclean shall not pass over it ; but it shall be for those : the wayfaring men, though fools, shall not err therein. No lion shall be there, nor any ravenous beast shall go up thereon, it shall not be found there ; but the redeemed shall walk there : and the ransomed of the Lord shall return, and come to Zion with songs and everlasting joy upon their heads : they shall obtain joy and gladness, and sorrow and sighing shall flee away."

It was thus that the whole symbolism of Paradise after the Fall, while in the highest degree declarative of holiness and righteousness in God, was fitted, in accordance with its character as a dispensation of grace, to attract rather than to terrify, to invite man rather than drive him away. How much this was the case, may, in a manner, be gathered even from the feelings and anxieties of Cain at the thought of being driven from the neighbourhood of the hallowed spot, and from within sight of the visions of Eden :—" Behold, thou hast driven me out this day from the face of the earth, *and from thy face shall I be hid,*" (Gen. iv. 14.) If such were the feelings of this repro-bate—this seed of the wicked one, (1 John iii. 12,) what must have been the aspirations and hopes of those who like Abel brought their offerings in faith unto the Lord, and to whom, and to whose sacrifices, He had respect ! Although " the way into the holiest of all was not yet made manifest, while as the first tabernacle was yet standing," (Heb. ix. 8,) such, neverthe-less, most undoubtedly, had " boldness to enter into the holiest by the blood of Jesus, by a new and living way," (Heb. x. 19, 20.) And thus in the arrangements contrived by Infinite wisdom, and adopted by Infinite love, to remedy the disasters of the Fall, Paradise lost was made to appear to the eyes of those who in faith worshipped at its gates, as more than Paradise restored, as its mysterious symbolic figures proclaimed, " Glory to God in the highest, and on earth peace, good-will toward men."

In drawing these observations to a close, amid the variety of lessons that may be gathered from the preceding narrative, it may be remarked that if there be any truth more than another illustrated by God's dealings with fallen man in the transactions of Eden, it is that to which the Divine Being him-self gives all the solemnity and sanction of an oath, " As I live, saith the Lord God, I have no pleasure in the death of the wicked ; but that the wicked turn from his way and live," (Ezek. xxxiii. 3.) And, in considering the schemes of creation and redemption, as unfolded and applied in these chapters of Genesis, the one perfecting what the other began, the declarations of the Apostle Paul obtain new emphasis :—" O the depth of the riches, both of the wisdom and knowledge of God ! how unsearchable are his judgments, and his ways past finding out !   For who hath known the mind of the Lord ? or who hath been his counsellor ?   Or who hath first given to him, and it shall be recompensed unto him again ?   For of him, and through him, and to him are all things : to whom be glory for ever.   Amen."

INDEX.

I.—PRINCIPAL MATTERS.

ADAM, generic name of human race, 289; not used as a proper name in Genesis i.-iii., 455; etymology of the term, 289; his naming the animals, objection to the account of, 361; purpose of this act, *ib.;* a figure of him that was to come, 174; his representative character, 455; more culpable than Eve, 404; evidence of his faith, 463; his expulsion from paradise, reason of, 137, 470.

Alford, on Matt. xix. 4-6, 194; on New Testament application of paradise, 199.

Allegorical mode of interpretation unsatisfactory, 224.

Alting, his view of Gen. iii. 22, 470, *note.*

Analogy of nature with representation of history of Fall, 161: value to be attached to this, 171.

Annihilation, not included in primal threatening, 423.

Antichrist, his claims a development of the tempter's promise, "Ye shall be as God," 185.

Apollo, the averter of evil, 155; slays the dragon Python, 156.

Atonement, prevalence of the idea of, 384.

Augustin, his remarks on the days of creation, 99; on the seventh day, 313; on the subtilty ascribed to the tempter-serpent, 407, *note.*

BALFOUR, Professor, on the indications of degeneracy in thorns and thistles, 169.

Bara, import of this Hebrew term, 63.

Barnes, on Job xxxi. 33, 200.

Beginning of matter or motion, requires an adequate cause, 74; the Bible teaches that this cause is God, 81.

"Beginning, in the," meaning of this expression, 82, 244.

Bengel, on the analogy between the temptation of Adam and of Christ, 176, *note.*

Blessing, on creation, secured the continuance and increase of the living tribes, 279; on man, 292.

Body, the animal, constituents of, 327.

Bonar on Leviticus, quoted, 466.

Buttmann, on the situation of Eden, 342.

CALVIN on Eph. iv. 24, 304; on Gen. ii. 7, 328, *note;* on situation of Eden, 337.

Candlish on Genesis, referred to, 469.

Centres of Creation, theory of, not affecting the Biblical narrative, 265.

Chalmers, Dr., his opinion that the antiquity of the globe is not fixed by Moses, 82; on the authority assigned to the husband, 453.

Cherubim, nothing known regarding the etymology of the term, 474; not representative of the angelic host, 475; nor of the Trinity, *ib.;* representatives of life, not creative, but created, 476; represented man redeemed, 477; their place in Eden, that of the primeval worship, 483; import of their location in paradise, 482.

Christ, his temptation analogous to that of Adam, 175; how the image of God, 301.

Clerc, Le, on the situation of Eden, 339.

Clothing, Biblical ideas connected with, 465; of our first parents, indicated suffering and substitution, 466.

Contradictions, the alleged, of Gen. i. and ii., 43; that the creation of man preceded that of plants, 44; that the creation of man preceded that of the lower animals, Kurtz's explanation of, 45; as to the origin of the winged tribes, explained, 46.

all animals were herbivorous before the Fall, 390.
Fourth day of creation, 266.
Fruit, the forbidden, attractions of, for the woman, 401.

GENESIS, why so called, 2 ; Luther's estimate of, *ib.* ; first three chapters of, particularly important, 3 ; and inseparably connected with the history in the Bible, 206 ; with its doctrine, 208 ; and with its prophecy, 214.
Genesis iii. 22, inadequacy of usual expositions of, 467 ; not to be understood ironically, 468 ; reasons of the common misconception regarding, 469.
Geology, modes of reconciling Genesis with, 86 ; its evidence in favour of miracles, 128 ; suggestive towards the interpretation of Scripture, 242.
" God said," import of the expression, 250.
God's first interview with fallen man intended to beget in him self-condemnation, 428.
Gordon, (Dr.,) quoted, 472.
Gregory, (Prof.,) on the balance of the atmosphere through animal and vegetable life, 275.

HEAD, bruising of, what it implies, 442.
" Heavens and earth," meaning of the phrase, 81, *note.*
Heel, bruising of, what it refers to, 450.
Henderson, (Dr. E.,) on the expression, " one day," 100.
Hengstenberg on Psalm civ., 188 ; on the tree of life in Ezekiel, 191.
Hercules, legend of, and the gardens of the Hesperides, 155.
Herder, his views of the narrative of creation, 16.
Hesiod, his account of the golden age, 147.
Holden, his definition of " literal and historical," 9.
Humboldt, on the origin of the week, 316.
Hunt, on our ignorance of the nature of light, 271.
Hutchinsonians, their views of the first chapters of Genesis, 16.

IDELER, on the origin of the week, 317.
Image of God in first man, how related to the New Testament representations of same in *new* man, 302 ; how affected by the fall, 305.
Interpretations of Genesis i.-iii. ; Jewish

interpretations, 11; early Christian, 12 ; Middle Age, 13 ; Reformation period, 14 ; recent, 15.
Introduction to work of the six days, 243.

JEHOVAH, etymology and import of, 31 ; how related to Elohim, 33 ; name apparently not known before the fall, *ib.*
Jones, (Sir William,) on unity of human race, 385.
Josephus, on the expression, " one day," Genesis i. 5, 99.

KIDDER, on interpretation of first chapters of Genesis, 15, *note.*
Kitto, on the gardens of the Hesperides, 155.
Kurtz, his explanation of Genesis ii. 19, 45.

LANGUAGE, common and peculiar to man, 380 ; one primeval, 381.
Leland, on the curse upon the serpent, 139, *note.*
Life, maintained without interruption, 77 ; this taught in Scripture, 84.
Light, Creation of, 250 ; priority of, to the heavenly orbs, no objection to the narrative, 252.
Luminaries, heavenly, purposes to be served by, 266.
Lyell on the beginning of present order of things, 74, *note ;* on the recent creation of man, 78.

MAGEE, on the prevalence of animal sacrifice, 384.
Man, creation of, a recent event, 78 ; traditions regarding his original condition, physical and moral, 147 ; his creation distinguished by the Divine counsel which preceded it, 288 ; the image of God in, 296.
Mankind, unity of, Scriptural account of, 372 ; scientific conclusions regarding this, 373 ; diffusion of, promoted by diversity of races, 377.
Marriage, institution of, 365 ; essential bond of union in, 368 ; typical of union of Christ and his Church, *ib.*
Miller, H., on recent creation of man, 78 ; on abundance of vegetable productions of the earlier eras, 264.
Miracles, not impossible, or improbable, 128.
Müller, Julius, his mistake regarding narrative of the fall, 113 ; on the cor-

Sleep, the deep, of Adam, what it was, 363.

Species, criterion of, 374 ; unity of human, consistent with differences of colour, &c., 375 ; philological considerations confirmatory of unity of human, 379 ; historical considerations favourable to same, 382.

Stier, Rudolf, on the marriage union, 368.

Sweat of the face, 457.

Sword, the flaming, what it represented, 484; its connexion with the tree of life, *ib.*

Temptation, a necessity of humanity, 177 ; of Adam and of Christ strikingly analogous, 176.

Tempter, the, described, 395 ; in appearance a serpent, 405, yet not simply the reptile of that name, but an intellectual and moral agent, 409 ; his question to the woman, 397 ; he denies the truthfulness of God's declaration, 399 ; the promise he holds out to the woman, 400.

Third day of creation, 259 ; the two works of, closely connected, 265.

Thorns and thistles indicate degeneracy, 169.

Transgression, the penalty of, not arbitrarily imposed, 349.

Tree of knowledge interdicted, 348 ; meaning of the name, 354.

Tree of life, whether a single plant, or a species, 352 ; meaning of the name, 353 ; typical character of, 357 ; traditional acquaintance with, 149.

Trees of knowledge and of life, supposed mysterious properties of, not countenanced by Scripture, 136, 355 ; whether one or two distinct productions, 352 ; purposes of, 356.

Trench, on analogy between parable of prodigal son and narrative of the Fall, 184.

Unity of mankind, objection to, considered, 139.

Universe, material, related in all its parts, 73 ; shewn by science not to be eternal, *ib. ;* as presently constituted, existed for untold ages, 75 ; the Bible assigns no date to its origin, 82.

Veda, Rig, cosmological hymn of, 51, *note.*

Vegetables, prior to animal life, 76, *note ;* not the only food of animals previous to the Fall, 137.

Wax, to keep the, of tree of life, what it implied, 485.

Whately, his misapprehension regarding the tree of life, 137.

Whewell, Professor, his reply to Laplace's objection to the purpose assigned to the moon, 273.

Wilkinson, Sir G., his remarks on serpent destroyer in Egyptian mythology, 156.

Woman, objection to the mode of her formation considered, 129 ; connexion with the Fall assigned to her by tradition, 152 ; mode of her formation described, 363 ; origin of her designation in Hebrew, 366.

II.—PASSAGES OF SCRIPTURE ILLUSTRATED.

1983-84 TITLES

TITLES CURRENTLY AVAILABLE